THE COLONATE IN THE ROMAN EMPIRE

The fourth and fifth centuries AD gave rise to a particular phenomenon in the Roman Empire: the colonate. The colonate involved the fiscal regulation of a relationship of surety between landowners and farmers in the later Roman Empire and played a major role in agrarian and social relations, with implications for these farmers' freedom of movement and transmission of status. This study provides a clear and comprehensive reassessment of the legal aspects of the phenomenon, embedding them as far as possible in their legal, social and economic contexts. As well as taking the innovative approach of working retrogradely, or backwards through time, the volume provides a thorough assessment of two critical sources, the Theodosian and Justinian Codes, and will therefore be an invaluable resource for students and scholars of Roman law and the agricultural and social history of late antiquity.

BOUDEWIJN SIRKS is Emeritus Regius Professor of Civil Law at the University of Oxford and an Emeritus Fellow of All Souls College. He was formerly Professor of Private Law and Legal History at the J.W. Goethe-Universität Frankfurt and is currently Member of the Consiglio Direttivo of the Associazione Storico-Giuridica Costantiniana.

THE COLONATE IN THE ROMAN EMPIRE

BOUDEWIJN SIRKS
University of Oxford

CAMBRIDGE
UNIVERSITY PRESS

CAMBRIDGE
UNIVERSITY PRESS

Shaftesbury Road, Cambridge CB2 8EA, United Kingdom

One Liberty Plaza, 20th Floor, New York, NY 10006, USA

477 Williamstown Road, Port Melbourne, VIC 3207, Australia

314–321, 3rd Floor, Plot 3, Splendor Forum, Jasola District Centre, New Delhi – 110025, India

103 Penang Road, #05–06/07, Visioncrest Commercial, Singapore 238467

Cambridge University Press is part of Cambridge University Press & Assessment, a department of the University of Cambridge.

We share the University's mission to contribute to society through the pursuit of education, learning and research at the highest international levels of excellence.

www.cambridge.org
Information on this title: www.cambridge.org/9781009172608

DOI: 10.1017/9781009172585

First published 2024

A catalogue record for this publication is available from the British Library.

Library of Congress Cataloging-in-Publication Data
NAMES: Sirks, Adriaan Johan Boudewijn, author.
TITLE: The Colonate in the Roman Empire / Boudewijn Sirks, University of Oxford.
DESCRIPTION: Cambridge, United Kingdom ; New York, NY : Cambridge University Press, 2023. | Includes bibliographical references and index.
IDENTIFIERS: LCCN 2023026047 | ISBN 9781009172608 (hardback) | ISBN 9781009172592 (paperback) | ISBN 9781009172585 (ebook)
SUBJECTS: LCSH: Colonate. | Colonate – Social aspects. | Colonate – Economic aspects. | Colonatus (Roman law) | Land tenure (Roman law) | Farm tenancy (Roman law) | Peasants – Rome. | Agricultural laws and legislation (Roman law) | Serfdom (Roman law)
CLASSIFICATION: LCC KJA2202 .S57 2023 | DDC 340.5/4–dc23/eng/20230609
LC record available at https://lccn.loc.gov/2023026047

ISBN 978-1-009-17260-8 Hardback

Contents

Introduction *page* 1

1 The *Status Quaestionis*: General Approaches 3

2 Sources and Working Method 12

2.1 Sources 13

2.2 Justification of the Retrograde Research Method Applied Here 17

2.3 Terminology 24

1 The Colonate in the East under Justinian, 527/534–565/642 30

3 Introduction and Background to Justinian's Code 30

4 The *Coloni* in Book 11 of Justinian's Code 32

5 CJ 11.48.20–24: The Central Texts on the Colonate 35

6 Entering or Imposing the *Condicio Coloniaria* 36

7 Effects of the Colonate: *Potestas* and *Peculium* 42

7.1 Coloni Are in the *Potestas* of the Estate Owner 42

7.2 Their Assets Are Considered *Peculium* 45

7.3 The Reality of the *Potestas* and *Peculium* 49

8 Paying Taxes 52

8.1 Taxes and Taxation 52

8.2 The *Colonus* as Taxpayer 55

8.3 The Landowner Is Factually and Administratively Surety of the *Capitatio Humana* 58

9 Occupations of *Coloni* 61

10 Transmission of the *Condicio* and the Effect of the Abolition of the *Senatusconsultum Claudianum* 67

10.1 Transmission of the *Condicio* 67

10.2 The Abolition of the *Senatusconsultum Claudianum* and the *Condicio Coloniaria* 69

10.3 The *Coniugium Non Aequale* 74

10.4 Unions between *Adscripticii* and Slaves 78

10.5 Other Cases of the *Coniugium Non Aequale* 79

10.6 Developments after the Abolition of the *Senatusconsultum Claudianum* 81

11 Moving *Coloni* to Other Places 85
12 *Coloni* Who Migrate and Recalling Them 89
12.1 Reasons for Migrating 89
12.2 Recalling *Coloni* 91
12.3 Limitation of Prescription against Recall 96
12.4 Immunities against a Recall 97
12.5 Another Way of Losing Labour: Exposition 98
13 Release from the Colonate and the 'Free' Colonate 99
13.1 Incidental Private Release 99
13.2 Institutional Release: Anastasius' Constitution 100
13.3 Institutional Release: Justinian's Constitutions 104
13.4 Other Interpretations of CJ 11.48.19 105
13.5 Anastasius' Motives 107
14 Public and Procedural Aspects of the Colonate 109
14.1 Social Mobility 109
14.2 Procedural Privileges 110
14.3 Criminal Law and Abuse of Power 111
15 The *Coloni* on State and Imperial Lands: CJ 11.63–64, 68–69 112
15.1 General 112
15.2 *Coloni* on Patrimonial Land (*Fundi Patrimoniales*), Emphyteuticarian Land (*Fundi Emphyteuticarii*), and Combined Estates (*Saltus*) 122
15.3 *Coloni* on Land of the *Res Privata* (*Fundi Rei Privatae*) 123
15.4 *Coloni* on Land of the Imperial House (*Fundi Divinae Domus* or *Domus Augustae*) 126
15.5 *Coloni* on Land of the Fisc (ταμιεῖον) 127
15.6 A Reason for the Privileges? 128
16 The 'Free' Colonate 129
17 The 'Free' Colonate: A Byzantine Serfdom? 133
18 Farmers Not Subjected to the Colonate 135
19 Conclusions 138
19.1 The Colonate under Justinian 138
19.2 Open Questions 144
19.3 Different Interpretations 144

2 The Colonate in the Year 438 in Theodosius' Code 147
20 Introduction 147
20.1 General 147
20.2 The Structure of the Theodosian Code 149
20.3 The Place of the *Coloni* in the Code 150
21 The Background to the Law in the Theodosian Code 152
22 The Term *Colonus* 156
23 Entering the *Condicio Coloniaria* 157
23.1 *Condicio* and *Condicionalis* 157
23.2 Origin of the Colonate 160

23.3 Origin of the Colonate in the East 161
23.4 Origin of the Colonate in the West 167
24 Effects of the Colonate: *Potestas* and *Peculium* 167
24.1 Effects of the Colonate in the East 169
24.2 Effects of the Colonate in the West 173
24.3 Summary 180
25 Taxation and Complying with Taxes 181
25.1 Taxes and the *Coloni* in the East 183
25.2 Taxes and the *Coloni* in the West 186
26 Transmission of the *Condicio* and the Effect of the *Senatusconsultum Claudianum* 190
26.1 In the East 190
26.2 In the West 191
26.3 The *Coniugium Non Aequale* 194
26.4 The *Coniugium Non Aequale* and the Various Categories of *Condicionales* 198
27 Moving *Coloni* to Other Places 199
27.1 Moving *Coloni* in the East 201
27.2 Moving *Coloni* in the West 202
28 *Coloni* Who Migrate and Recalling Them 205
28.1 Flight in the East 206
28.2 Flight in the West 206
28.3 Problems with Reclaiming *Coloni*: Death, Marriage, Offspring 211
29 Public and Procedural Aspects of the Colonate 215
29.1 In the East 215
29.2 In the West 215
30 *Coloni Originales* on State and Imperial Lands 216
31 *Coloni* on Patrimonial Land (*Fundi Patrimoniales*) and Emphyteuticarian Land (*Fundi Emphyteuticarii*) 217
31.1 In the East 218
31.2 In the West 220
32 *Coloni* on Land of the *Res Privata* (*Fundi Rei Privatae*) and of the Imperial House (*Fundi Divinae Domus* or *Domus Augusta*) 220
32.1 The *Res Privata* 220
32.2 *Coloni Dominici* on Land of the Imperial House 222
33 The *Patrocinium Vicorum*, *Vicani*, *Coloni Homologi*, and *Rusticani* 223
34 The 'Free' Colonate 232
35 Farmers Not Subjected to the Colonate 233
36 Texts Not Necessarily Connected with the Colonate 234
37 Conclusions 234
37.1 Beginning of the *Condicio* 235
37.2 Taxation and Taxes 236
37.3 Transfer of Land 237
37.4 Features of the Colonate 237
37.5 Recalling 238

3 The Colonate in the East, 438–527 240
38 Enactments by the Emperors in 438–527 240
38.1 Theodosius II (402–455) 240
38.2 No Constitutions on *Coloni* by Marcianus (455–457) Have Been Transmitted 241
38.3 Leo (457–473) 241
38.4 Zeno (474–491) 243
38.5 Anastasius (491–518) 245
38.6 Constitutions Not Included 247
39 Comparing the Situation in 534 and 438 247

4 The Colonate in the West, 438–ca. 506 249
40 The Situation in the West, 438–ca. 506 249
40.1 Sources 249
40.2 Background 251
41 The Posttheodosian Novels in the Roman West, 438–post 506 254
41.1 General 254
41.2 Valentinian III 256
41.3 Majorian 262
41.4 Severus 263
42 The Council of Orange of 441, Sidonius Apollinaris *ep.* 5.19, and Remigius of Reims 264
43 The Colonate in Vandal Africa 268
44 Farmers Not Subjected to the Colonate 269
45 The Colonate in the Breviarium Alaricianum Alias the Lex Romana Visigothorum of 506 (Southern Gaul, Septimania, and Visigothic Spain): Status 269
46 The Colonate in the Breviarium Alaricianum: Obligations and Restrictions 280
47 The Colonate in Legal Writings 282
48 The *Coloni* in the Summaria Antiqua, 535–554 286
49 Nachleben and Conclusions 287

5 The Colonate between Theodosius' Code and Diocletian and the Third Century, 438–293/268/249 292
50 The Period 438–293/268/249 292
50.1 Development in the East in 438–364 292
50.2 Development in the West in 438–364 293
50.3 Development before 364 293
51 A Connection with Diocletian's Tax Reforms? 294
52 Farmers in the Middle of the Third Century: The Heroninos Archive, AD 249–268 295
53 *Oiketai* and *Metrèmatiaioi*: A Pre-colonate? 301
54 Moulding the *Paramonè* into the Roman Law 306
55 Was There a Colonate? 308

56 Reconstruction of a Chronology of the Colonate 309
56.1 Development in the West between 364 and 438 316
56.2 Development in the East between 364 and 438 318
56.3 Development after the Theodosian Code 320

Bibliography 321
Sources and Abbreviations 321
Secondary Literature 322
Index Locorum 338
General Index 347

Introduction

The purpose of this book is twofold. On the one hand it intends to provide a survey and analysis of the colonate in the Roman Empire from the legal point of view, embedded as much as necessary in the social and economic context of Roman society. On the other hand, it is meant to show how to approach the sources in a case like this and, in general, how to work with the codes of Theodosius and Justinian, in a way that does justice to the place of the texts in the whole of these codifications, that is, taking account of their function within a codification. The individual texts have their value as historical sources, yet one must be aware how they have come to us, in which context and to which purpose they were selected and edited, or else their historical value might diminish or even disappear.

This is in the first place a legal-historical work. It means that its first aim is to look for legal rules. Legal rules are meant to arrange life and are imposed if not followed. In order to get a sound notion of a legal phenomenon, here the colonate, it is necessary to collect all rules and to check them against each other until a systematic survey is achieved. This may seem a bit overdone to non-jurists, but the old Byzantine scholia to Justinian's compilation prove that systematisation was all-important to the Byzantine jurists and Justinian's compilation is a product of this drive for systematisation. These jurists did not invent this. They were pupils and successors to a line of jurists, teaching in Constantinople, Beyrouth, and other places the same systematisation. We know only two of their names: Domninos and Patroklos, called the *heroes*. And they in their turn were continuing the same drive which existed in the classical period of Roman law, as the surviving remnants in Justinian's compilation prove. Also, the imposition of rules required consistency. It is thus helpful, if not necessary, to have a good grasp of Roman law and of the exegesis of legal texts. It seems exaggerated, yet it is the warning that counts: search for the system behind it, because those who formulated the law worked in that system. For these reasons it is necessary to check all possible sources and see whether such a consistency is present and makes it possible to speak of a rule. Moreover, the codes are embedded in a broader body of law which one should also keep in mind.[1] My research may be boring because of this at some moments, but it is absolutely necessary. I have relegated to footnotes what should be present but was not directly necessary for the main argument. Texts can be found through the index.

Still, since law is meant to register the rules followed and to impose these if not followed, it is connected with the way humans interact and society functions. In one way, it follows what people do and what things they think should be done; in another way, it regulates behaviour, both when that behaviour is deviant and has to be corrected, and when behaviour or circumstances arise which were not yet foreseen. In that case new rules are issued to address such problems. Law is embedded in society and there is no society without law.[2] And although in general society was rather conservative and legislation consequently more reactive and conservative, innovations happened too. Ancient man was not afraid of or averse to new things (like accepting debt acknowledgements in the form of chirographs as negotiable papers). Still, those structures set up to continue for a long time were not changed rashly. For example, the administrative structures of the overseas transportation of grain from Africa and Egypt to Rome and Constantinople remained basically unchanged for two or three centuries, only to be adapted in the east in 409. The same goes for taxation, which under Diocletian was probably more straightened and homogenised than set on a completely new footing and remained so until the Justinianic reforms.

We shall see the same with the colonate: not fallen from the sky, it was incorporated in public law to continue with the necessary adaptations for more than three centuries. Its predecessor was an answer to particular economic needs, it required certain economic conditions, it may have competed with other solutions to the same or similar problems, it evolved under the pressure of changing circumstances, and it was adapted to counter undesirable uses.

Wherever possible, the cause of changes or introduction of new rules will be discussed, but apart from that a final chapter is destined to put the entire history of the colonate in a more historical perspective. It will not

[1] See for an example the table in Sirks 2007, § 24.

[2] I do not refer to the Natural Lawyers like Grotius, but put merely the question whether we can speak of a society if there is no minimum of law, and second, more empirically, I refer to Kramer 1956, *From the tablets of Sumer, Twenty-five firsts in man's recorded history*. As Hesiod said, law distinguishes man from animal.

always be possible to make quantitative statements about the field of application, for example whether the colonate covered the entire farming population of the Empire (by the way, far from likely). Rules are made or issued when something is simply necessary, such as organising care for insane people, or when something turns up which is sizeable or important enough that it requires regulation. Nobody will assume from the extent of the regulations about the *cura furiosi* that a large part of the population is insane. With theft, it is the same: it is considered such an outrage to property that it cannot be tolerated, regardless of the frequency. However, in the punishment we can also see the value a society (through its courts) attaches to this: the death penalty in archaic times, the death penalty for grand larceny in the Bloody Code in the UK of the late eighteenth century, a few years of imprisonment nowadays. The same applies when we research other ancient laws. The *lex Pompeia de parricidis* expresses the societal horror over parricide by its special punishment (death), but we do not find any application of this.

1 The *Status Quaestionis*: General Approaches

The colonate is part of the antique agricultural exploitation. Perhaps in the archaic Mediterranean world all farmers were working on their own individual plots of land without any assistance (although it seems that, considering the dominant role of the community, anybody would have relied on the community and the community on him); but as early as there existed some division between more and less rich members of a community, there existed also some relation determined by dependency between these richer and poorer members. For Roman society the phenomenon of the *clientela* is known. We can leave aside the questions of when in Republican Rome the large estates came into existence and when and to what extent there existed farmers who no longer tilled their own land but rented land and tilled it in exchange for rent in money or sharecropping.[3] It suffices for the present to state that around AD 200 agriculture in the Roman Empire was done according to various legal and economic models. There existed the farmer who worked his own land, be it alone (with, undoubtedly, the assistance of his family) or with some farm hands (slaves or free persons). There existed the lessee, who paid rent in money (and who might be assisted by a remission in years of dearth) or in kind. If the measure of the rent was expressed as a fraction of the harvest,

[3] See, for example, Scheidel et al. 2007; more specialised is De Neeve 1985.

it was share-cropping. There were the large estates (*latifundia*) which were tilled by slaves of the estate owner if not issued in plots on lease, sometimes under the supervision of a head slave (*vilicus*). These could be attached to the land as *instrumentum* and live quasi as a family with wife and children. As we know from the Heroninos archive, large landownership did not necessarily mean an extended estate such as a Communist kolkhoz or an East German *Kombinat*: it will rather have consisted of all kinds of plots of land, which were individually administered within a centralised accounting and management system. The guiding economic and managerial principle was to reduce loss as much as possible by reducing costs and using what was available.[4] Investments were made, for example, in improving land and setting up irrigation,[5] but whether this was possible will have depended on the availability of time and capital. Richer people will have been in a better position here, but a dependency relation may have been advantageous in this respect. As somebody who was a freedman of a rich family will have had easier access to investment capital through his dependence on his patron, so a farmer who was a *cliens* of a rich patron will have had easier access to resources too. In both cases they paid a price as well, namely in independence, but the balance may have been advantageous for both sides.

Cities and temples possessed agricultural land and issued this in the form of long leases against a fixed rent (*vectigal*). These lessees enjoyed a right of lease which resembled that of an owner, it being hereditary and they being protected against disturbances by a possessory interdict.[6] The emperor possessed land which he issued in diverse forms. It could be as a normal lease to an individual lessee, or to a head lessee (*conductor*) who would sublet parcels to (under)lessees. It could be done on a more permanent basis through an imperial *conductor* with lease conditions fixed for all, as the *lex Manciana* of Africa shows. In the Later Empire we find another form of land issue, where these lands are called *fundi patrimoniales*. Here the emperor donated Treasury land to somebody under certain conditions, usually that a yearly rent (*canon*) had to be paid. The donee could not dispose of the land by sale or gift, but his right was hereditary. Failure to pay the *canon* resulted in withdrawal of the gift. As such, it resembled the long lease for a *vectigal*, which was also a hereditary tenure. But it could happen that the issue was done *sine canone*, or *iure privato*. In the first case, the donee did not have to pay a *canon*; in the latter case, the donee could

[4] Rathbone 1991, 396. His reflection on the response to his book is in Rathbone 2005.

[5] Cf. CJ 3.34.7, 11.43.4, 11.63.1 for legal evidence.

[6] Kaser 1975, 374, 388.

freely dispose of the land. Often the latter was done *salvo canone* and in that case it must have been almost indistinguishable from private property, albeit that a yearly canon had to be paid – which may have looked like a servitude on the land.[7] Another form of issue was that Treasury land was issued in *emphyteusis* under conditions like a canon. In this case the donee had to ameliorate the land or keep it in good condition; non-compliance could, like non-payment of the *canon*, lead to a recall of the gift. Here also it was possible to alienate land, even manumit the slaves attached to it. As with the *fundi patrimoniales privato iure* it must have been almost like private property, except for the canon. In all these cases the donee had to exploit the land and needed, consequently, farmers. He could use one or more of the forms of exploitations as described above. The emperor Leo (468–484) extended in the east the application of the legal construction of *emphyteusis* to land in private property (CJ 4.66.1). In the west the form of a *locatio conductio in perpetuum* was used.

In all these exploitation forms the basic assumption is that we are dealing with contracts between legally independent persons who may enter and end the contractual relationship, even unilaterally if they see a reason for this and as long as they comply with the legal rules governing this. In practice, many persons, both landlords and lessees, will of course rather have wanted to continue the contract, being both dependent on the returns of the land for their income and life subsistence. But this did not change their personal free status and did not infringe on their legal autonomy as such.

It is therefore rather surprising to see emerge in legal and other texts of the fourth and later centuries the phenomenon of people legally bound to an estate, apparently in an agricultural context. From the fourth century onwards we dispose of imperial constitutions which were issued with the purpose of tying agricultural workers (*coloni*) to the land. Precisely when this began, we do not know, neither do we know precisely why, but it clearly had to do with guaranteeing the cultivation of land and payment of taxes. This system of binding those people to an estate or plot of land is called the (Roman) colonate.

Ancient historians look at this from the perspective of the ancient economy and the agrarian exploitation which is of course an indispensable aspect of the colonate, since it functions in this context, as the texts demonstrate. It is only later, the colonate being a status, that *coloni* are

7 One wonders whether there remained a distinction: perhaps the gift could be revoked? The texts do not give a clue to this.

found in other occupations (and can be recalled). Thus the connection with the agrarian setting must be taken into account.

The colonate has generated much literature and many theories, already by Gothofredus and later by Savigny, whose essay 'Über dem römischen Kolonat' includes a reaction to Gothofredus' views, and by other authors.[8] Due to the need to take as many factors as possible into account, the theories are not sharply separated from each other. We can distinguish several approaches.

One view is connected with a shift in the mode of agrarian exploitation. The colonate is seen within the context of agricultural exploitation, as the successor to the tenancy of the Late Republic (when a *colonus* would have been a lessee). The cause of this development would have been an increasing impoverishment of the lessees, making them increasingly dependent on the landowners.[9] The Republican way of many individual lessees and individual farmers-owners made way for a slave-based exploitation on larger estates. By the end of the second century AD, the supply of slaves dwindled and landlords were forced to find new supplies of workers. These they found by subletting their great estates and fixing the sublessees to their land. The fact that the great imperial estates in North Africa (and elsewhere?) were administered by *conductores*, who in their turn sublet parcels, under a general regulation for all (the *Decretum Commodi de saltu Burunitano*, found in 1879, and the *lex colonis fundi Villae Magnae datae ad exemplum legis Mancianae*, found in 1896) seemed only to sustain this view. It led to a change in production method. The farmers/lessees on these gradually came into a state of dependency which needed little to become

[8] Already in the Middle Ages the texts on the *coloni* attracted interest: see Conte 2000; Savigny 1825–50, 1–16. One should be aware that serfdom was abolished in Prussia in 1811, in Mecklenburg in 1822 and in Saxonia in 1832: the colonate was an actual question. For a survey of other nineteenth-century authors, see Heisterbergk 1876, 7–21 and Marcone 1988; further Marcone 1997b on the Italian literature in the nineteenth century on the colonate. A previous summary of the *status quaestionis* is provided by Jones 1974; Cracco Ruggini 1990; Sirks 1993a, n. 1; Whittaker & Garnsey 1998, 287–294; Ward-Perkins 2000, 343–344; Demandt 2007, 398–401 (Seeck 1901 is rather old). Scheidel et al. 2007 does not enter into the subject of the colonate. Johnson 2012 has a chapter by J. Harries, 'Roman law and legal culture' (789–807), which hardly deals with the (private) law as such and has nothing about the colonate, as the entire 'handbook' does not pay special attention to the phenomenon. Banaji thinks *coloni* were bound tenants (2001, 615), Mathisen thinks they were tenant farmers (2012, 752); see also Liebs 2005, 1957–1960. For further literature in addition to what is cited here, see the following: Sirks 1993a, 331 n. 1 and the bibliography in Terre 1997. See, more recently Amarelli 2017 and further Carrié 2017 in the context of a survey on the problems connected with land in Late Antiquity.

[9] An example of this view is Johne 1993. Earlier contributions by Johne in this respect are Johne et al. 1983; Johne 1985, 1986 and 1987.

the colonate in the following centuries.[10] This view was first put forward by Fustel de Coulanges in 1885.[11] Clausing, following Fustel de Coulanges, thought the farmers got gradually indebted. Together with a tendency to continue tenancies, a diminishing fertility of the land and, with it, diminishing tax revenues led to a legal attachment to the land.[12] Saumagne, in a rather complicated analysis, saw the colonate as a *quasi-servilité juridique*, originating in the fiscality because the *tributum* made him subjected to the landowner. There is an echo of Fustel de Coulanges here, and Saumagne extends it by attributing to the landowner the right to levy the tax owed by his *censibus adscripti*.[13] But these suggestions are not well based, as shall become clear later. Pallasse discerned in the *lex Manciana* and the contracts in the Tablettes Albertini traces of emphyteusis and thus of lease in perpetuity.[14] Weßel assumes that these *conductores* of imperial land of the second century had in Late Antiquity become *emhyteuticarii* and, as the parallel to this, the lease of their lessee-*coloni* had turned into a property right which allowed them to sell it. However, as he himself admits, it has no relation to property.[15] Kolendo has resumed the question of continuity of the colonate in Africa, albeit with some reservation.[16] Santilli thought the same and combined this with a shortage in slave labour.[17] Mirković rejects an introduction through Diocletian's fiscal reforms because the colonate existed before: landowners could already force their *coloni* to remain on the land. She assumes indebtedness forced the *coloni* by way of their lease contract to the land.[18]

10 *CIL* VIII 10570, 11–13: *non amplius annuas quam binas aratorias binas satorias binas messorias operas debe[a]mus*; *CIL* VIII 25902, IV.24–27: *quodannis in hominibus singulis in arationes operas n(umero) ii et in messem n(umero). et in sarritiones cuiusque generis singulas operas binas*. But that could still be part of the tenancy agreement. So also Lenski 2017, 121.

11 Fustel de Coulanges 1885. Several publications followed: Wiart 1894; His 1896; Schulten 1896; Beaudouin 1897–98, and the authors mentioned by them.

12 Clausing 1925, 262–280, 284–296. Clausing mentions antique views that Italy's soil was exhausted (271–272). It would be interesting to check this against modern data.

13 Saumagne 1937.

14 Courtois et al. 1952; Pallasse 1955.

15 Weßel 2003, 109–116 on the legal position of landowner and *colonus*, who is for him a 'Kleinpächter'; here 112–113, *dominium* means more than ownership, cf. Augustine *De civitate Dei* 10.1.2, where *coloni* are *sub dominio possessorum*. There it concerns certainly *coloni originales*.

16 Kolendo 1991, 1997, 158–161.

17 Santilli 1975; repeated in Santilli 1999.

18 Mirković 1997, 15–26. See the critical review by Kränzlein 1999. Also Mirković 1986 and Mirković 1994. The arguments put forward are hard to follow. The assumption that under Verres landowners, liable for the land tax, devolved this burden by transferring this to their tenants by the lease contracts but remained liable in case the tenant fled (Mirković 1997, 20) is perhaps meant to explain why landowners got the authority to keep them on the land, but it is not confirmed by contemporary sources. The link with Ulpian (D. 50.15.4.8) is dubious (the text is much later and it does not follow from this that tenants and land tax were connected), while other texts are from the later Empire. Mirković 1997 cites on 24 P.Oxy. XLVII 3364 (in *J. D. Thomas, A petition to the Prefect of Egypt, JEA 61 (1975) 102–221*) as proof that under Caracalla the person who had sheltered a fugitive *tributarius*

Another view is that the colonate originated in the fiscal reorganisations which Diocletian (r. 285–305) carried out. At a rather early moment in his reign, Diocletian began to reform the taxation system because, due to the doubling of the number of provinces[19] and increasing the troops,[20] he needed more revenues.[21] This reform built on the previous systems; probably it was more a uniformisation which extended over the Empire. All land was taxed according to its potential yield, resulting in a potential total revenue, after which the expected expenditure was repartitioned proportionally over these assessments. In this process Diocletian would have made landowners responsible for the collection of the taxes their lessees owed, which would alleviate the task of the authorities considerably and, since the landowners were more able to carry the fiscal burden, would give the emperor more stable revenues. In compensation Diocletian introduced the bond to the estate for their farmers so that the landowner could rely on having enough labour.[22] These lessees, the *coloni*, declined by this subjugation and fixation to the land, which resulted in the colonate of the late fourth and fifth century.[23] Under Justinian, a category of *coloni*

was penalised. Unfortunately, she cites Serenus as petitioner, whereas it was Herakleides, Serenus being the lawbreaker, and the editor warns against equalising ὑπόφορος with *tributarius* and taking the term as technical. Also, although the text confirms that taxpayers should reside in their *idia*, either their village or *nomē*, it does not say that landowners had the authority to recall their tenants. And, as a matter of fact, regarding the land tax the edicts pertained to landowners, not tenants. There are more occasions where it is difficult to follow Mirković's arguments.

19 *CAH* XII, 179–181, introduction of the dioceses presumably in 297.

20 *CAH* XII, 120–124.

21 *CAH* XII, 172–176. Bott 1928 is an interesting publication, but now outdated.

22 Giliberti 1999, 86: to prevent migration and thereby a shortage in farmers. Giliberti opposes the idea of a 'genealogy' of the colonate, namely that it evolved out of a class of half-free farmers, or barbarians settled on the land, or of slaves freed with the obligation to remain on the land, or of slave-farmers, or out of hellenistic practice. Farmers, who were lessees, were or gradually became subjected to their landowners. He rejects the idea that the colonate was instituted by the imperial government in its own, and not the landowners' interest. Under Diocletian, lessees underwent the same fate as other groups like the curials and the *navicularii*, whose function was considered essential for life in the Empire: their function became hereditary and they became *obnoxii*. To that came his tax reform. But is there evidence for such a tying to the land and work? Lactantius (ca. 250–ca. 320) *De mortibus persecutorum* 23.1–2 is usually cited for this, but the word *homo*, used here (2 *Agri glebatim metiebantur, vites et arbores numerabantur, animalia omnis generis scribebantur, hominum capita notabantur* . . .), usually means slaves, and slaves were indeed put on the census. It cannot be proof that it concerned free farmers. Also adhering to this fiscalist view: Schipp 2009, 40.

23 For example, Faure 1961, 127–133, mentioning 305 and 306 as the moments of introduction. Also Marcone 1993, 825–826. I refer further for an overview with literature to Carrié 1993, 292–301 for his fiscal reforms. Fikhman rejects Carrié's fiscal cause of the colonate and stresses that great landlords had an interest in tying labour to their lands: Fikhman 1990, 171, 172, 175 = Fikhman 2006, 270, 271, 274. Harper 2011, 153–155, seems to adhere to the fiscal cause, subjecting long-term tenants, and assumes a different development in the west and east (but his subject is slavery, not the colonate). Similarly Vera 2012 = Vera 2019, 369 does not exclude such a development, assuming that it concerned private landowners/farmers. The proposition of Panitschek 1990, to explain the origin by assuming that the half-free status in peregrine legal systems by the beginning of the fourth

(the *adscripticii*) is even compared to slaves. Their number would have been considerable but there is no information about their actual size. There is certainly evidence of free labour also in this time.[24] This view differs from the previous ones in that it supposes an active legal change, initiated by the emperor.

To some extent connected with this is the idea that a hereditary tying to their profession led to the situation that the landlords treated their tenants de facto as their property, which led to their being considered *personae alieni iuris*. It is based on the view according to which all functions and professions became from Diocletian onwards hereditary in order to ensure the functioning of the administration and state. The *coloni* made no exception. In that context they were tied to their land by way of the tax registration. As such the colonate would be but one illustration of the decline of the Roman Empire from this emperor onwards by its social petrification and bureaucracy. This theory lacks the proof of a legal transition, which, however, is desirable, since in Antiquity one was very keen on the difference between freedom and slavery.[25] Connected with this is the supposed emergence in Late Antiquity of the great domains as semi-public institutions, which had the right of *autopragia*, that is, to collect taxes themselves.[26]

Another question is whether the colonate was the precursor of medieval servage, villeinage and *Hörigkeit*. I shall deal briefly with this question in Sections 17 and 49, but it requires further research. We are here only concerned with the colonate as established in the Roman Empire.

Finally, there is the stimulating opinion of Carrié that the colonate is nothing more than a nineteenth-century construct.[27] It has encountered criticism.[28] Yet, the question, is there something like 'the colonate'?, is a good question. All too quickly an interpretation becomes absolute, and

century were romanised in the form of the colonate, in the course of his fiscal reforms, is very speculative. There were indeed situations which looked like the half-free status which he mentions (*dominus–libertus*, *patronus–cliens*), but still these people were legally free – and Roman. Did similar dependencies exist elsewhere? What do we know of peregrine half-free statuses? Panitschek does not name one. I could unfortunately not consult Perelman Fajardo 2019.

24 So CJ 11.48.21.1; Whittaker & Garnsey 1998.

25 Munzinger 1998. See my review, Sirks 2003. See Sirks 1993b for a refutation.

26 The idea of the great domains as semi-public institutions, an idea set out before by Gascou 1985, is regarded with scepticism by Banaji 2001, 94–100 (on the rents paid), and by Sarris 2006, 150–154, and n. 85.

27 Carrié 1982. See below.

28 Marcone 1993, in his survey *Il lavoro nelle campagne*. As to the question whether in Africa already in the third century emphyteusis existed and was fundamental for the development of the colonate (Marcone 1993, 828–830), on which Vera 1987, I must refrain from entering into this, since it would require a study different from the present one.

the danger of projecting one's own views is always around the corner, as the work of Waltzing shows. Similar questions were posed by Scheidel: Might the apparent rise of the 'colonate' be a function of the change in evidence rather than of changes in rural labour relations? And if coercion and dependence were the norm in these relations, what is then so extraordinary about the 'colonate'?[29]

What is striking is that in the above views a general shift is assumed, that is, that the supposed changes affected the entire Empire and all farmers. Such a view has found favour with Marxists. Yet it has recently met resistance from some ancient historians specialised in agrarian history. Marcone emphasises that there were regional differences which make it difficult to speak of general developments or a uniform colonate.[30] He leaves the question open, yet in any case is not convinced that there was a continuum as Fustel de Coulanges first proposed, namely that the lease turned slowly into a bondage.[31] Similarly, Giardina has raised the question of continuity.[32] Vera has put forward that various modes of exploitation co-existed during the entire Empire, which reduces the colonate to a phenomenon amongst other exploitation modes. According to him the relation between land and work should be the focus: landowners want their lands cultivated and need farmers, who, in their turn, are because of this not so helpless as it seems. All during the Empire the contractual relationship of lease existed, while the form was predominantly that of métayage (share-cropping). Next to this, other forms of exploitation existed.[33] Such an approach is very useful because the economic foundation not only of the colonate but of antique society in general was agrarian exploitation. Rathbone's research on the Appianus estate has shown how a plurality of small estates could be unified by clever management of the available man- and animal-power and instruments. Useful in this context was the continued presence of manpower, available on demand. To have lessees indebted was a better method than force to keep them on the land. Finally, Banaji has drawn attention to evidence which indicates that there was a very varied supply of labour forces, which does not allow for monolithic descriptions.[34]

None of the above views has been adhered to completely monolithically; it is more a question of where to put the emphasis. The background of the

[29] Scheidel 2000.
[30] A broad survey by Marcone 1988. Also Marcone 1993: an excellent and balanced survey.
[31] Marcone 1997a, 233. [32] Giardina 1997. [33] Vera 2010, 15–16.
[34] Banaji 2001, also in 2009, 76: 'a mixed servile labour force'. See also Grey 2007b, 363–367 on the variety in exploitation of the land; further Grey 2012 for a survey.

theories of Fustel de Coulanges, Clausing, Saumagne, and Pallasse, partly also Santilli, is a combination of economic developments with legal constraints, before all based on the great imperial estates in North Africa, where, for example, the *lex Manciana* testifies to a system of subletting and continuation of the lease. Difficulties with finding new lessees led to the introduction of coercion. In the same line we find De Martino,[35] Santilli and Giliberti,[36] Heather,[37] and Rosafio[38] with a more or less a rather economistic view, whereas Giardina holds an intermediate position.[39] On the other hand Carrié and Vera adhere to a fiscalist view, namely that Diocletian introduced the colonate by his fiscal reforms.[40]

All positions are very valuable in drawing our attention to the way agriculture was done in Antiquity and how a shift in size of possessions demanded a different management (or vice versa? that a new way of management allowed for a shift in exploitation?). The colonate is a phenomenon embedded in a rural society, based on agriculture and the various modes of exploiting labour and exploiting land. Marcone, Vera, and Banaji are right that this should be our focus. They underline that we cannot assume general lines but must concentrate on the particularities of regions, small and large, and distinguish also periods. In that kaleidoscope

[35] De Martino 1985, 445–460, rejecting the Marxist explanation and underlining the interest the landowners had in labour being available (455); De Martino 1993, 798–822, gives a balanced survey and pays much attention to economic aspects, such as a comparison of the rentability of *coloni* and tenants.

[36] Giliberti 1998.

[37] Heather 2000, 465 refers to them as formerly free tenants who did not own the land they worked, but Heather also points to the rise of the landlord class.

[38] Rosafio 2002, a collection of papers with worked-out themes of his Cambridge PhD thesis of 1991 (previously also Rosafio 1991); he presents a history of the colonate on imperial lands. Rosafio 1991a, 157, 177–178 concurs with Harmand's opinion (Harmand 1957) that the colonate was not a legal construction in one piece, but a factual result of imperial statutes and fiscal advantages during a long evolution; and besides that it was not a uniform result. The colonate on private land was different, exclusively introduced for fiscal reasons because on these *coloni* pressed the *capitatio*, which Rosafio seems to interpret as the land tax. Under Valentinian and Valens things changed, both for the *coloni* on imperial land and on private land, and the difference between them diminished considerably. They became hereditarily bound to their function.

[39] See Giardina 2007. Giardina points out that the repetition of a law indicates a continuing interest of the lawgiver. He sees the colonate in the context of the central government's intention to influence the economy and relations of production. The colonate was based on an unequal relationship between individuals (landlord–tenant). As a consequence the *coloni* were legally reduced to a state of dependency. How many there were cannot be established. But *coloni* and slaves together were according to Giardina the dominant mode of production. How the transition to this mode took place is largely obscure.

[40] Carrié 2017, 28–31; Vera 2005 = Vera 2019, 319, and Vera 2010, 19, where he defines the *colonus* as, 'metaforicamente, "schiavo" della tassazione del stato'. Segrè 1947 also combined increasing indebtedness with fiscal reforms, and with a distribution of *ager publicus*; his views are hardly tenable. See the criticism of Banaji 1999, 204–205.

the rural individual stands, with his family, and they have to scratch their living together, as Sarris so vividly sketches for the sixth century.[41] It will not have been much different for the peasant of the previous centuries. Out of the various possibilities the colonate was one lifeline.

Apart from these theories and explanations, from the perspective of the colonate there are two essential requirements: the estate owner must dispose of sufficient capital to sustain his financial guarantee (for the poll tax) and of sufficient land nearby to make the presence of labour cost-effective. The *coloni* do not have to work every day of the year; they have to be present when needed. These two requirements imply that the single farmer will not easily have had a *colonus*. Indeed, estate complexes like that of the Apiones as described by Sarris will have been the ones where the colonate could be remunerative. Where such complexes lay is open. We should lend an ear to what the emperor himself said in CTh 11.1.26: *earum scilicet provinciarum, . . . in quibus haec retinendae plebis ratio adscriptioque servatur*, 'of those provinces . . . where this system of binding and registering of the common people is in use'.

2 Sources and Working Method

The present work is above all a reconstruction of the legal side of the colonate. This means that the legal rules as known are charted and interpreted. These rules set the boundaries of the colonate. It does not imply that this is a social or economic history of the colonate, although the legal texts will as much as possible be set in their societal context. There has always been a relation of dependency between owners of land who did or could not till it themselves and farmers who needed land to feed themselves and their families. Such dependency may have been organised in archaic days along lines of status, as Maine maintained, but in the late Republic and Empire it was done by contract. Theoretically this was a consensual contract, engaged by free will, but it will have depended on supply and demand how free parties were. Cato and Pliny were concerned to find the few good farmers. But a bad harvest could put the farmer in distress and at the mercy of his creditors and landlord, who might need to remit the lease sum. Law's function is not to regulate every aspect and detail of life, but to set standards of and limits to behaviour. It does not mean that people followed these rules. If they did (sociologically: had internalised them), there would be no need for law. But law enforces what should be done.

[41] Sarris 2006, 29–70.

Hence social and economic reality was and is always much wider than legal reality. On the other hand, the colonate presents to a certain extent a reversal, from contract to status in as far as entering the colonate in the later period implied a shift in status, which was seen as the ground for the required services.

2.1 Sources

The sources on the colonate are diverse. Many are legal texts, preserved in either Theodosius' or Justinian's Code. Some of these texts feature in both codifications. There are papyri from the fifth and sixth century referring directly to the colonate, but some third-century papyri may also refer to the colonate or a precursor of it. A few literary sources contain references to the colonate. There are further texts with reference to the inquilinate, a status which must have been quite close to the colonate. But, as usual, we do not have as many data as we would like.

The legal sources in Theodosius' and Justinian's Code consist of fragments of imperial constitutions, usually entered into the Code with addressee, date and issuing emperor. It is very tempting to consider them as fragments per se, as unrelated historical facts which are often but feeble images of the original. Yet that would disregard that they are part of a legal system the Romans developed over centuries.[42] The order of the praetorian edict may have been merely historically grown; it nevertheless served for centuries as a structure for commentaries, and the Gregorian and Hermogenian Codes, as well as the two above-mentioned Codes, partly followed its structure. But with each code also an effort was made to organise the material systematically. Moreover, two other structures were used in legal writings: that of Sabinus' treatment of the civil law, and the institutional system, of which Gaius' version gained great popularity (there were more). The commentaries on the edict and Sabinus' treatise, as well as the institutional works, are evidence of the fact that Roman law was an intellectual system. This is all the more true with the compilations of Roman law we have and which for that reason are called codifications: the Codex Justinianus and the Codex Theodosianus. As Justinian himself

[42] Even for a law collection as early as Hammurabi's Code it has been argued that it is to some extent structured and that caution is necessary: see Westbrook 1988, 74ff., who strongly argues that various sanctions in Hammurabi's Code must be read as theoretical discursions. But a lot of European medieval town statutes are indeed mere compilations of enforceable social rules without much or any coherence.

said for the Digest, *sit una concordia una consequentia adversario nemine constituto* (CJ 1.17.1.8).[43]

2.1.1 *Justinian's Code*

Both codifications[44] were built around a structure. For Justinian's Code, the structure of Theodosius' Code[45] first served as an example, but if not already changed, it was certainly overhauled for the second edition of AD 534. His compilers put the texts they considered relevant at the place in the structure they considered appropriate. This had important consequences.

First of all, the fact that at a certain moment in time all data considered particular to a subject are collected is already a statement about what people at that moment considered relevant to that subject. These data may vary in age and they may certainly also be judged upon their value at their date of issue, but they have an independent and perhaps different value for the moment they were collected and selected. Within that latter context they may *and* should be considered. It depends on the design of the codification what value may be attached to this context. Justinian was very explicit about his Code: all constitutions collected in the Gregorian, Hermogenian and Theodosian Codes and all constitutions issued after AD 438 should be collected in one code, but not simply as they were found. They had to be examined; what was superfluous should be removed, as should whatever was similar or contradictory or had become obsolete, and the same went for the preambles to the Novels. Texts could be combined, shortened and adapted (interpolated). The constitutions should be put under an appropriate title and there should be no doubt about their general validity.[46] It follows from this that the texts of Justinian's Code present in the first place valid rules of general force and that in any case within a title rules on the same subject (indicated by the title's rubric) have been gathered together. This is not to say that such a title

43 This was certainly not meant as a mere aspiration. Between AD 529 and 534 Justinian took the so-called 'Quinquaginta Decisiones' to resolve long-standing questions. In the Digest there are indeed still differences of opinion, but these served to deepen legal discussion and doctrine; the Code was primarily meant for practice. As regards the similarities and contrarieties mentioned in c. Cordi), see Sirks 1986, 299–300, and 1996, 257–259, 267. Throughout this book, unless otherwise explicitly specified, all translations of the Theodosian Code and the Post-Theodosian Novels are taken from or based on Pharr 1952; those of Justinian's Code are taken from or based on Codex of Justinian 2016; and those of Justinian's Novels are taken from or based on Miller & Sarris 2018

44 As said, I use the word codification in the wide sense of a compilation of rules, brought into a more or less systematic structure, and not in the far more restricted modern sense of a code.

45 On the Theodosian Code, see Matthews 2000; Millar 2006; Sirks 2007, 2008.

46 C. Haec 2; c. Cordi 3.

contains all the rules on that subject, because it contains them only in so far as there had been constitutions issued about it.

Roman legislation was usually reactive. The legislator was in the first place an *homme bricoleur*, not an *homme ingénieur*.[47] When a problem arose and was reported, the emperors reacted with a constitution. Or, if a case appeared before the emperor in highest appeal, the emperor might issue after his judgment also a constitution to rule future cases in the same way. CJ 1.14.2 and 3, both deriving from the *lex citandi* of 426, describe this in detail. The consequence is that the codes as we have them contain mainly such reactive legislation. Where there was no problem, we do not see direct references to practice. In short, what we have in the codes is arbitrary in the sense that it concerns mainly reactive legislation. But it does not mean that there was not, for example, a law on the colonate which was coherent. It is only through occasional mention in other legislation, or because of the connection with a problem, that we become aware of other law. In short, there are gaps in the legislation on a specific subject which were inherent in the codes.

It is thus in the nature of Roman legislation that problems were often only dealt with in a general way when they required a general remedy, that perhaps some potential problems were included too, but not that the administration tried in a perfectionist way to think up all theoretical problems in advance and deal with them in a general way in the constitution. Such approaches date from the days of the Natural Law scholars. But it is possible, and in the private law indeed very often the case, that other rules are contained in the writings of jurists, in this case collected in Justinian's Digest. Furthermore, Justinian's Institutes also gained the force of law. Thus to find the law on a specific subject as valid in the years AD 530–534, one has to check all these three works, as Justinian himself indicates (CJ 1.17.1.11, 2.11).[48]

Also, the style of these codes is not the modern codificatory style. There, the structure is from general propositions to more specific propositions;[49] here, a statement on a specific case will contain in some way a general proposition, or else it would not have been included in the code. But it is not always easy for the modern reader, who does not have the knowledge of the context which the compiler had, to detach the general rule.

[47] After Claude Lévy-Strauss' *La pensée sauvage*.

[48] For an example of this method, see Sirks 2007, Nr. 34.

[49] Pothier 1748–1752 arranged the Roman law into such a straitjacket: *The Pandectae Justinianeae in novum ordinem digestae.*

It is consequently possible that there are some points which were governed by customary, unwritten or unrecorded law, or, for example, by edicts of the Praetorian Prefects.[50] As we shall see, there are gaps. But taking this into account, normally we may in this way expect to find all the law as it was valid and recorded at that moment in constitutions (*ius novum*) and only then – and no obsolete rules. That was Justinian's intention, and that was indeed accomplished. Of course, this must be accompanied by a knowledge of the intellectual structure of the law (the doctrine of law) as prevalent at that time – after all, Justinian's entire codification had to serve legal education – or else words and concepts might be misunderstood. Only then does one get a picture of the law at that particular point or period in time. Whatever the original reason for issuing a constitution had been no longer mattered in the codification process: the texts do not present unrelated fragments of previously issued constitutions but have become (if they were not already) pieces of a system. That picture can and should of course be put into the context of the society and culture of the moment.

2.1.2 *Theodosius' Code*

With the Theodosian Code, which contains imperial constitutions over the period 312–437, the situation is less transparent. We do not have the entire Code. Much of Books 1 to 5 is missing. As to the constitutions, we know that the emperor ordered the removal of the superfluous text, leaving only the rule or prescription. But contrary to Justinian, there is doubt whether the original plan to remove the obsolete was applied to this Code. Opinions differ, but the balance is now in favour of removal the obsolete in the Books 1 to 15.[51] It implies that here also the Code presented the law, in as far as laid down in constitutions, as it was valid in 438.

Next to the codes, law is found in the legal writings (*ius vetus*). To know, for example, the law of sale in the third century, it would give a distorted view to consult merely Justinian's Code, and the same goes for the law of sale of the fourth century if only based on the Theodosian Code. One cannot do without the texts of the Digest, which were also valid at that time. Many texts, both in the codes and the Digest, testify that the lawyers of those days saw and applied a system of internal coherence: not as strict as later the Glossators or the Pandectists enforced upon these works, but still

[50] On the role of these edicts, which were often more than just edicts executing the orders of the emperor, see Schiavo 2018.

[51] See Sirks 2021b.

the coherence which they learned from their institutional books. One must of course realise that the Digest is a Byzantine selection of the classic texts which are often adapted, representing the Byzantine jurists' views on the state of the law.

Sometimes it is said that the legislation of the late antique emperors was inefficacious. For that, people refer to the Theodosian Code where, as they sustain, often a prescription is repeated. That would imply that the previous law was not followed. It is a precarious argument. First, the emperor of one part could not legislate for the other part. If the other emperor wanted to legislate the same he could issue his own rule or reissue that of his colleague. Theodosius himself refers to this in Nov. Theod. 1.5. Consequently, we find the same exemption of *angariae*, *parangariae*, and *paraveredi* granted to the *silentiarii* in CTh 6.23.3 and 4. But it is not a repetition of the same: c. 3 is issued for the west and c. 4 for the east. Also, when we see a prescription repeated it does not automatically mean that it was not enforced or could not be enforced. It may be that for a number of people it had effect but that the repetition was meant to catch the remaining number by imposing a harsher sanction. Thus yes, it was not completely effective, but no, it was not only in a number of cases effective. To say that it was altogether ineffective is impossible: we do not know enough about the efficacy of laws. Also, repetition may have served other purposes, like emphasising the authority of the emperor.

2.2 *Justification of the Retrograde Research Method Applied Here*

The legal texts of the codes can certainly be regarded and treated as historical sources and be used as they were issued in their own time, conveniently collected in chronological order in the codifications. Within that context it is also sensible to try to join fragments of the same original constitution. It is quite usual to see a treatise on the colonate start with the earliest known text on this, either CTh 11.7.2 of 319 or CTh 5.17.1, of 332, to be followed by others in chronological order. That happens usually with the awareness that they may have been edited, but often without regard for the fact that they were *later* selected and collected. The result is always a distorted representation, even if slightly. One has to realise that all this happened with regard to their later use, in any case the texts in Justinian's Code,[52] and be aware of the context within which these

[52] With Theodosius' Code, the debate is still ongoing whether the texts preserved include obsolete ones; but see Sirks 2021b and Bassanelli Sommariva 2013.

texts are transmitted. A survey of a principally philological or historical nature[53] will not be of any help, however interesting it may be, since it mixes up legal and non-legal sources and might use the legal sources as supplementary texts to philological or historical analysis. The contents of these texts, whose primary purpose was not to be literary products (although they very well may have been put into that form) or historical statements but to embody legal decisions and rules, will not be rendered justice. Further, the context in which they have been transmitted and which is as important as the single text, is often disregarded and neglected.

If we were strict, research on single legal texts in the two Codes should always be done in a retrograde way: first, the meaning as part of the code, then seeing whether that could also be the meaning at the moment of issue, and in both cases taking the wider legal context into consideration (i.e., the composition of the titles). That is the palingenetic method of the Romanists, used with the Digest, which especially the late Alan Rodger always applied. This method had lost nothing of its importance and should not be neglected. With this comes the fact that one must reckon with possible textual changes or the combining of two texts into one new text (as is proven to have been done in Justinian's Code): the interpolation check. Only after that one should turn to the meaning the text had when written, usually in the classical period. Nothing has diminished or voided the value of this working method.

Regarding the texts from the Theodosian Code, it seems to me that here the idea that the compilers did not change the actual rule and included also obsolete constitutions allows for an uninhibited use. If that were the case, it would be right. But it is precisely the question. Where there are few texts and the subject is rather special, such as the two constitutions on *maiuma*, CTh 15.6.1 (= CJ 11.46.1) and 2, it is very unlikely that a retrograde treatment will render more than a purely historical approach. The lack of other related texts will prevent a deeper treatment. It will be the same in other similar cases. Theoretically, the moment of compilation should be considered also, but as to contents it may yield little. With the colonate it is very different. Here there are many texts in Justinian's Code which allow for a thorough treatment; similarly, in Theodosius' Code many texts sustain a reconstruction for this moment in time. Both reconstructions can be compared to provide a sound basis. It is for these reasons that I chose the retrograde method. It has its disadvantages too, but at least it allows for a proper analysis at the moments of compilation.

[53] As Carrié 1982 or Grey 2007, who start from an analysis of the word *colonatus*.

2.2.1 The Retrograde Method

In order to make conclusions on as firm a ground as possible, I have chosen the retrograde method, beginning with the latest period of the colonate in the east, namely the Justinianic and post-Justinianic period (527–642). For this period our legal sources are almost complete as regards their transmission and the text is fairly secure, and we have also papyrological material available which gives us a chance to see what actual situation these legal rules envisaged. The great advantage we have is that Justinian's codification contained only valid rules (due to Justinian's orders) and that it covers a rather short time span, with the bulk of it codified in a mere five years (529–534). This means that these texts must have an identical terminology and consistency, which again allows for comparison and combination. Although older texts were also used in this codification, we may assume all texts, including these, were consistently interpreted in this period as to their actual use.[54] It is supplemented as regards the colonate with a good number of papyri from mostly the sixth century AD. This means that for Justinian's reign (527–565) we can derive from these texts a complete picture as regards the legal situation, of course in as far as this situation was laid down in legal and documentary texts. As said before, the Romans usually did not design a complete legal regulation and then issue it. Their method was rather to enact something or refine existing customary or statutory practice if the need for this came up. It is therefore not impossible that next to Justinian's codification unwritten customary rules concerning the colonate existed, while some aspects of it are merely indicated. Still, the picture we shall get will be the best and most complete picture possible.

After that, we can turn to the preceding period covered by the Theodosian Code. We have to distinguish two situations in the legal evidence presented. First are the constitutions as they are presented to us within the context of the Theodosian Code as promulgated in the year 438 (and certainly shortened, sometimes divided and probably edited), supplemented by constitutions of the Code only transmitted in Justinian's Code, by constitutions issued before 438 (mostly from the Gregorian and Hermogenian Codes), and by legal writings from before 438. Second, the constitutions in themselves and the other pre-438 texts may be considered as testimonies of the situation in the year they were issued. The dates provided by Krüger in his Codex Justinianus edition (Krüger 1877) and by

[54] Wenger 1954, 569–651 on Justinian's codification. The older texts are from the Gregorian, Hermogenian, and Theodosian Code, the eastern Posttheodosian Novels, and the legal writings as selected in the Digest. Of the Digest only D. 50.15 is of importance.

Mommsen in his Theodosian Code edition (Mommsen 1905) are used, with recourse to Seeck's *Regesten* only when no date is provided in the two editions; exceptionally, the dating is discussed.[55]

Regarding the first situation, contrary to Justinian's codification the material in the Theodosian Code is fairly incomplete. Part of this Code, Books 1 to 5, have been transmitted only fragmentarily, or indirectly. There are remainders of copies of the Code, there is the Breviarium Alaricianum with a selection of constitutions from the Code, and there are constitutions which survived because they were included in Justinian's Code. And it was precisely in these fragmentary books that texts on the colonate must have been included in the Code. We know this because texts on the colonate figure in Justinian's Code which were taken from Theodosius' Code but which are not found in the almost completely transmitted Books 6 to 16. So they must derive from the fragmentarily transmitted Books 1 to 5. And it is possible that Justinian's compilers adapted these texts, or even that they inserted texts into other texts or combined texts. We can use them as if still in Theodosius' Code, but we must be wary of potential changes. Comparison of texts where this is possible shows that in about half of the cases the texts remained unchanged. Further, we do not know in which title they originally figured; we even do not know precisely which titles figured in those five books. Yet the place where a text is inserted in a systematic compilation bears, of course, also on its purport.[56] We may therefore draw up a picture of the regulations on the colonate in 438, but it can never be as certain as that for Justinian's reign. If one adheres to the idea that this code also contained no longer valid rules (in my opinion unwarranted),[57] the coherence would even be more difficult to find.

The constitutions are further allocated to the east or the west as regards their origin and application, on the basis that any imperial constitution could only effectively have force if directed to be promulgated by the administrators under the authority of the issuing emperor. This means that, following the allocation in Seeck's *Regesten*, such a geographical division has been mentioned for the periods 337–350, August 364–July 390, and May 395–476. In other cases the addressee might seem to

[55] Since I focus on the short periods of the two codifications and treat these as synthetic representations, the individual dates are immaterial in these chapters. It is only in Chapter 4 that the date becomes important. Yet in many cases Seeck differed only a few years from the transmitted dates and thus the effect is negligible. Also, Seeck's *Regesten* (Seeck 1919), although a fine work, needs an update in light of the contributions by Pergami 1993, Cuneo 1997, and Schmidt-Hofner 2008b.

[56] See Sirks 2013.

[57] See Sirks 2007, 147–150; Sirks 2021a: unwarranted, but see Bassanelli Sommariva 2013 for a justified correction.

indicate a geographical application, but unless this is explicitly indicated in the text, one must reckon with one of many copies sent out as was usual.[58] Thus the only reliable criterion is the administrative division of the Empire with its separation of authority. I have taken as dividing moment the year 364; the period 390–395 seems to have been an interim period and it is not certain whether the administrative division was really lifted, while the period 337–350 has left insufficient traces.

Assuming that there was continuity in the law (which I think is beyond doubt, since the emperors themselves often refer to previous legislation), we can then compare the two reconstructions. Eventual gaps in one may then be reconstructed with the help of the other reconstruction. Then, it is true that a rule, of which the purpose is that it is imposed on occasion of new cases, provides continuity (of course, only inasmuch as it is indeed followed or applied). For that reason we may interpolate and fill gaps.

What will appear from the situation in 438 is that there were differences between the east and the west regarding the colonate. For that reason the period after 438 in the east and west has been dealt with in separate parts. Sources for the east are basically some eastern posttheodosian Novels (transmitted either in western collections or in Justinian's Code); for the west there are the western posttheodosian Novels, which we possess in full text, the legislations in the Germanic kingdoms and literary and documentary sources of the fifth and sixth century. In the case of the east a comparison is now possible between the colonate of 438 and under Justinian. For the west the situation is more complicated because there were several kingdoms successor to the imperial administration, each with its own rules.

Having in this way chartered the colonate from 438 onwards in time, the texts of the Theodosian and Justinian's Code as to their original moment and context of issue may be examined. Since it is better to begin from solid ground, it means examining the period 438–293/294 retrospectively; this of course only if there are no signs of a drastic change or innovation. The texts of the Theodosian Code have been edited and shortened as well. Further, it is possible that a constitution was issued but left no trace in one of the two Codes or another collection.[59] Thus, although the reconstructed colonate of 438 serves as point of departure, this reconstruction may be stripped of one or more parts, and the closer we get to the beginning of the fourth century, the thinner the reconstruction becomes. That we must take into account. Yet, if we find an indication like CTh 5.17.1 of 332 which confirms

[58] See Sirks 2010a. [59] I give an example of this (the emancipation) in Sirks 2019b and 2020b.

an essential element of the colonate, it makes that part of the reconstruction solid again and gives more probability to the rest of it. Depending on the outcome of these examinations, we shall see whether there was a colonate already previous to 293/294 or, if not, whether it had predecessors.

2.2.2 *Why the Retrograde Method Is More Rewarding*

Is this a better method than beginning with CTh 5.17.1 of 332, as usual, where it is said that the *coloni* are *alieni iuris*? Yes, it is in any case for the colonate, where we have to deal with much law in a certain time frame. That text, the earliest one on the colonate on private land, gives a few indications but nothing more. It is natural to consider connections with earlier references. As an example, in the line of Fustel de Coulanges' hypothesis of continuity, an author focuses first on the *coloni* on imperial lands, who are for him *conductores* who are privileged,[60] based on CJ 11.68.1 of 325, and others follow. The incorrectness of this interpretation makes itself felt in the following. In CTh 11.7.2 of 319 it is said *unusquisque decurio pro ea portione conveniatur, in qua vel ipse vel colonus vel tributarius eius convenitur* (each decurion must be charged for this portion in which he himself or his *colonus* or his *tributarius* is charged), which means that decurions are, according to him, liable for the tax due by their *coloni* and *tributarii* (hence the *tributum*). Then CTh 5.17.1 of 332, dealing with fugitive *coloni*, concerns only *coloni originales* because of the term *alieni iuris*. But it does not refer to *potestas*, since only in the *interpretatio* does the word *dominus* occur. Again, it concerns the land tax, as the term *capitatio* proves. This tax was introduced by Diocletian and is attested in CJ 4.49.9 of 293. The author's observations are certainly valuable, but this method makes them dependent on his assumptions in the beginning, namely that the *coloni* of CJ 11.68.1 were *conductores* and that it concerns the land tax. In the end a development of the colonate may be constructed, ending in the situation of 438. Whether it is correct must first be proven through a comparison with the situation, based on a reconstruction with only the texts of the Theodosian Code. That means one examines in the end the presumptions imported into earlier texts. What does that mean for the text of 332? For the situation in 319? Will not any statement for that text be based on either a supposition which finds its confirmation in a later constitution or in a retroprojection of a later constitution, which amounts to the same? Is there room for the colonate as a voluntary agreement as

[60] There is no need to mention a name, because the approach is shared by more than one author.

under Justinian? Is that methodologically a sound way to proceed? Although scholars of course seriously want to avoid to introduce preferences, still it is impossible.

If one wants to be sure, it is necessary to check whether that was the case in the moment these texts were codified, that is, in 534 and 438. In other words: one should begin with the texts when issued. That is 534, and the fact that CJ 11.68.1 was promulgated in 325 means that we must see it as a source for the Justinian compilers, taken from the Theodosian Code, for whose compilers it was a source too. But that version is lost. It went, so to speak, through two layers of interpretation and editing. Hence we may use it only with caution for the year 325. The same goes for texts taken from the Theodosian Code. If one does use them without taking this history of transmission into account, one might import later interpretations and uses unconsciously. In this case it appears that in 534 and 438 *coloni* were not charged for *tributum* unless they *owned* land, but were always charged for the poll tax (*tributum capitis*, *capitatio*).[61] Further, they might be lessees, but equally be farmhands or exercise another profession. Since we do not see in the period 332–438/534 a change, we may assume it was already so in 332 and 319.

With this method the full picture in as far as can be reconstructed for 529–534 is the point of departure. Assuming that changes which occurred closely before are documented, the focus can be moved first to 438 and then to the beginning of the fourth century. From there on it is more difficult. Earlier constitutions have to fit in or the reconstruction must be adapted. For example, the introduction of a new rule at a moment in the fourth century implies that the situation before was different; the reconstruction of 438 must take account of that. Metaphorically speaking, in such a case we peel off a layer. But those earlier constitutions are at least read in the meaning they had for the reconstruction. Of course, there may have been constitutions which are lost and elements may miss, but that goes also for any other method. Here other sources may help. A complicating factor is that when we need the description of the contemporary context of constitutions, this description may have been partly based on the same constitution. Perhaps we must adapt the reconstruction. In the end the reconstruction for the beginning of the fifth century is applied to the beginning of the fourth century, including eventually the removal of changes (the peeling off). Compared with what we have in evidence for that time, the reconstruction may look hypothetical. Yet the truth is

[61] For receipts for the poll tax in the second century AD, see Shelton 1990, nos. 1, 2, 5, 6, and 7.

different. What remains is the core and essence of the colonate. As long as there were no signs that essential elements were added, we may assume that. I agree that this is also an assumption. But I think it is a better founded assumption. Texts which otherwise would not yield much now, if they fit in with the reconstruction, will be evidence that the reconstruction is correct. CTh 5.17.1 of 332, for example, is no longer the point of departure for guesses, but is the confirmation that the reconstruction is correct for 332. Thus this method provides (more) solid information on the colonate for the period 294–438.

Did this method yield new results? Yes, it did. The Justinian body of texts allowed for an analysis of the function of the *senatusconsultum Claudianum*, which in its turn made the exact legal nature of the colonate in that period clear. From this it led to the nature and significance of the *coniugium non aequale*. It further allowed us to see the clear difference between the normal and the 'free' colonate, and that the colonate was originally an individual voluntary agreement. By going back in time it was possible to establish that the senatusconsultum and the *coniugium non aequale* were simultaneously applied in 438 and long before, probably directly from the beginning of the colonate as created by the census registration onwards. That result would have been impossible to achieve by starting chronologically from the earliest constitution onwards, because the few references to these two would not be sufficient, and other references would be based on assumptions which were actually based on anticipations.[62]

2.3 *Terminology*

2.3.1 *The Terms Colonate and* Colonus

For the person subjected to the status we call colonate, several designations exist. Whether these indeed indicate different legal statuses or just different legal (or social) aspects of one or a few statuses, we shall see. As regards the present study and its set-up, in which I start with the law in Justinian's reign, there is no need to distinguish more than two statuses in this period. Accordingly, I shall use the word colonate for what in the sources is called the *condicio coloniaria*. This comprises two forms of colonate: the *condicio*

[62] It does not come as a surprise that the core texts CJ 7.24.1.1 and CJ 11.48.21 and with these the application of the *senatusconsultum Claudianum* and *coniugium non aequale* have not been dealt with by ancient and other historians (e.g., in the contributions of Rosafio 2002, in themselves more profound than other studies, there is not a word on this; similarly Koptev 2009 in his otherwise valuable contribution). Then this can only be dealt with in an adequately retrograde way. CJ 11.48.21.1 is only cited in the literature for the phrase on the similarity between *coloni* and slaves.

adscripticia (the adscripticiate with the *adscripticii*, ἐναπόγραφοι, of a subjected status) and the *condicio* of the *coloni liberi* (ἐλεύθεροι, the 'free' colonate). The difference indicated by *liberi* is that the latter were not *alieni iuris*. The two *condiciones* have in common that they tie a person to a plot and that he (or she) has to perform services. The legal texts use different designations for the *coloni*: *coloni*, *originales*, *originarii*, *censibus adscripti*, *censiti*, *tributarii*. With merely *coloni* one cannot be sure whether it concerns a true lessee or a person subjected to the colonate: the context must decide that. In all the other cases it is clear that it concerns a person subjected to the colonate, and here it depends on the context whether it is the one or the other colonate. Both were registered in the *census*, hence were *censiti*, and tied to their *origo*, hence *originales* or *originarii*. But only *adscripticii* (*censiti*, *censibus adscripti*) were *tributarii* and only with the other *coloni* do we find the adjective *liberi*.

2.3.2 *Origo*

The term *origo* surfaced in the early Empire. According to Nörr it indicated the *Ortszugehörigkeit*, the bond with one's place of origin (*Ort*) and not one's domicile. That bond was established by the paternal descendance. It also determined with most or all cities citizenship. Once Rome had settled its political domination over the peregrine cities, there remained for the latter not much more than an administrative self-governance, with eventually their own private law. For that self-governance with the implicit honorific functions and duties (*honores et munera*), the *origo* became the decisive criterion of selection. Here it still applied to cities, but once the Roman state imposed and levied its taxes directly, the city became also the *idia* (ἰδία), the place originally in the countryside where one was censused. In Egypt the introduction of the municipal structure must have led to its disappearance.[63] Conversely, it must have led to the conclusion that where one is censused was once one's *idia* but is now one's *origo*.[64] Later, the domicile is also used to impose duties.[65] Nörr discusses the duality of *patria naturae* and *patria iuris*, where the first is the

[63] Nörr 1963, 545 and 548 points to the parallel between ἰδία and *origo* in that both terms are used in the context of public finances. The *idia* (ἰδία) is the place in the countryside where one is censused for taxes (Nörr 1963, 546). But Nörr does not draw the consequence that the state taxes also were levied in towns. Towns thereby became the *idia* for town citizens and fused, so to speak, with *origo*.

[64] See Section 10.3.

[65] Nörr 1965, 464–466 on the consequences of the *origo* and the bond it established. Unfortunately Nörr did not research the later use of *origo* as profoundly as he did for the earlier period, nor did he in Nörr 1963. Besson 2020, 295–299 merely deals with the consequences of the Constitutio Antoniniana. Thomas 1996 treats only of the Republic.

domicile and the second the *origo*. The expression *patria communis* for Rome which we find with jurists of the late second and early third century recalls a double citizenship, yet Nörr decidedly rejects this idea.[66] We do not have to enter into this question, but the expression may at least refer to the reality after AD 212 that with the universal grant of Roman citizenship to all free peregrines in AD 212 the paternal descendance not only defined the *origo* but also who was a Roman citizen. It is possible that other notions of citizenship crept in.[67] In short, it defined his status (*condicio*) and as such it was no empty or philosophical word.[68] A duality arises: on the one hand, one is by descendance citizen of a city (one's *origo*) with its administrative consequences; on the other hand, one is a Roman citizen (a status, *condicio*) and 'natural' citizen of Rome.[69] In the fourth century we see a shift in the application of the term *origo*. The criterion used to determine the bond is applied to units within city territories, as an estate, because in the colonate it designated a particular estate. One could say that the *Ort* has dwindled here to a piece of land with the *Ort* and, as I hope to demonstrate, the census was instrumental in this change. This is discussed in Section 55. But simultaneously the other citizenship (the Roman citizenship) with the same determining criterion of paternal descendance is applied as well to the colonate with the analogous application of the *senatusconsultum Claudianum* (see Section 10). It now determines also a *condicio*, and we find the term *condicio coloniaria*.[70] In this sense it further becomes used for the transmission of other bonds, of *metallarii*, *conchyloleguli*, *collegiate*, and others. These groups were registered in a *census publicus*, probably connected with a mine, a place where snails were dived for, or a town.[71] In the census registration both elements of the colonate come together: it registers the *origo* and the subjected status. Thus *origo* may be used in the fourth and

[66] Nörr 1963, 585. See now also Besson 2020, 291–299. [67] See Mathisen 2012.

[68] Besson 2020, 295–299 thinks the expression *Roma communis nostra patria est* is rather philosophical. But as the Latin charters of Spain show, the applicable law was that in Rome, and if somebody was exiled, he was exiled from his home town and Rome (Coll. 1.11.2: from Italica and Rome). As long as the home town had not adopted Roman law as a *municipium* or colony would, the applicability of Roman law must have been based on Rome as *origo* next to one's home town, albeit without other consequences.

[69] Nörr 1963, 587–588 also speaks of a duality, and I borrow the expression from him, but he uses it in a different way, namely that it did not designate so much citizenship as *Standeszugehörigkeit*. Where Gaius speaks in Gai 1.67, 78, 80, 87, it is about the *status civitatis*, but as soon as there is question of a union with a slave, the outcome may be that there is no *civitas* and the question has become one of the *status libertatis*.

[70] Nörr 1963, 529, citing Gai 1.67ff.: *condicio* as status. For this, see the previous note.

[71] CTh. 10.19.15.1 = CJ 11.7.7 part. with *census privatus*, meaning the census of a private person. The counterpart is in CJ 11.48.22pr, *ex publici census adscriptione*. Here *publicus* refers to the official aspect, but it could concern a private census. With the mentioned groups there is no possible

later centuries in a double meaning: either as the place where one has to fulfil one's administrative duties or as the civil status determined by the descendance (as in CTh 6.35.14.1), and sometimes both at the same time, as with *coloni* and *decuriones*.

2.3.3 *Colonus*

The term *colonus* basically refers to the person who tills land (*colere*), a cultivator,[72] and De Neeve has underlined this meaning for the Republic.[73] Is there any reason to assume that it acquired another meaning in the Empire and that by the first or second century AD *colonus* referred *exclusively* to a lessee and not, for example, also to a mere agricultural worker? I shall assume that the primary concept of 'cultivator of land' (*georgos*) was still retained. Again, it depends on the context what the legal connotation was (*conductor*, i.e., lessee, or holding *in precario*; or *locator*, a farmhand). However, I want to underline here that this does not bear upon the important discussion on the question of which pattern of agricultural exploitation became dominant by that time (namely, in terms of possibilities, small-scale landownership, or large-scale landownership with the use of slave labour or the letting out again to lessees), unless one assumes that small landowners or lessees never used labourers or hired hands.[74] But this seems unwarranted, certainly when we take into account the Heroninos archive (see Section 52). Large-scale landowners may well have used also hired hands. Also we see in CJ 11.48.8 (of 371) that when *coloni* flee, they become either lessees on a contract of métayage or hired hands. Similarly in CJ 11.48.19, the term used for farmer is μισθωτός, 'hired hand', 'hireling', whereas μισθωτής means 'lessee'.

2.3.4 *Tenant*

In English literature the term 'tenant' is always used. Literally it means 'a person who holds, occupies, or possesses land or property by any kind of right or title, especially from a landlord under a lease'. In the medieval world with its many different forms of possession, the term is very appropriate to comprise all these forms. But in Roman law and thus in the Roman Empire there is not such a wide array of modes of possession.

connection with private censuses, hence there we must assume a register maintained by the administration.

72 See in general Brósz 1959 for its meaning, but now obsolete. Cf. Giliberti 1993, 81 on the *coloni* in CTh 11.24.1.

73 See De Neeve 1985, 60–61.

74 For a survey of this discussion and the abundant literature on it, see Lo Cascio 1991 and Marcone 1993.

Somebody is owner (*dominus*) and possessor (*possessor*). Both modes have legal standing. Another rents land: he is a lessee (*conductor*) and holder (*detentor*), not possessor, and has as such no legal standing as regards the land. The lease (*locatio conductio*) had the variant of a long lease (*locatio conductio in perpetuum*), but its legal nature did not change. Or a farmer was given land *in precario*, that is, he held it as *detentor* until it would be reclaimed. He too was neither a possessor nor a lessee, since the basis of his having the land was not a lease. Being *possessor* entitled one to the protection of the interdict *uti possidetis* for land. If a lessee or precarist was disturbed in his holding of the property, he had to ask his landlord (*locator* or *dominus*, as the case may be), who was in law the possessor, to invoke an interdict from the magistrate against this disturbance, or he had to ask for a mandate from him to be able to act himself. With the imperial (and later private land) issued as patrimonial land or in emphyteusis, the basis was neither a lease nor *precarium*. It was a gift which could be revoked if, in the case a canon was imposed, this was not paid. Here the beneficiary was *possessor*. The term *colonus* means basically 'the one who cultivates the land', hence 'farmer'. It depends on the context in which legal quality he farmed. Therefore I shall avoid the term tenant and use the term lessee when the *colonus* is a *conductor* of land.

2.3.5 *'Free* Coloni*'*

I shall use the term *colonus* and the later term *adscripticius* for the person who was subjected to the colonate, later also called the adscripticiate. For the later-created 'free' *coloni* (*coloni liberi*) I shall in conformity with the texts use the term 'free' *colonus* and for this variant of the colonate the term 'free' colonate. Sometimes texts are ambiguous as to which colonate or which *coloni* are meant, and sometimes they speak of *coloni cuiusque condicionis*. Both categories were identical in as far as both were bound to an estate or plot of land.

2.3.6 Dominium *and* Possessio

In this context it may also be useful to dispel an apparently still existing myth, namely that in Late Antiquity the legal difference between *dominium* and *possessio* had become obscured or even lifted.[75] The ground for this misunderstanding, now convincingly disproved,[76] is that provincial land could only be held in *possessio*, because the *dominium* was with the Roman people or the emperor. One could have possession and this possession was

[75] So Carrié 2017, 26–28. [76] See Vandendriessche 2005; further Sirks 2019a, 99–105.

after a period protected by the *praescriptio longissimi temporis*, but it remained formally possession, which also showed itself in the fact that it was relative 'ownership', contrary to *dominium* of Italic land, which was after two years 'absolute'.[77] Justinian removed this division by declaring that one had now *dominium* also of provincial land, which now could also be absolute. On the other hand, the term *dominium* is wider than just 'ownership'. In fact, it is in Roman legal literature used in the sense of 'exclusive entitlement' and it depends on the object whether it is ownership (the usual application) or something else, like *dominium ususfructus*. Thus it is possible to speak of *dominium* of a *possessio* when indicating one's exclusive entitlement to provincial land, without it meaning that Roman legal doctrine had lost the feeling for the differences. The same can be said of *proprietas*, where we meet the expression *dominium proprietatis*. It is also used to indicate an exclusive right.[78] And it is in this sense that we see in the fourth and fifth century both *dominium* and *proprietas* being used, indicating the exclusive right of possession of provincial land; and in that case simply *possessio* too. I shall use the words owner and ownership to refer to such exclusive rights or entitlements. As to the person who owned the estate on which a *colonus* was registered, I shall use the terms estate owner or landowner.

2.3.7 *Chronological Recapitulation*

One might say that such a treatment is necessary to attain conclusions, but that after that a more conventional chronological exposition should be presented, perhaps even relegating the preceding research to a locker in the study. I do not think that I would render the reader a service by that. It would constantly force us to refer to the facts of a later period, and the danger of anachronistic statements would be present. Also it is, for those readers not familiar with a legal-historical approach, instructive to see such a method applied which is based on the nature of the sources themselves. Too often it is not done, leading to premature or wrong conclusions. Not that I pretend to give the final conclusions in this debate, but I hope to have attempted, at least, to interpret the texts in their full proper context. Since each chapter may be read separately, as if an independent article on a particular period, with a chronological summary at the end, this approach will not put too much of a strain on the reader.

[77] See Vacca 1993/94.

[78] The term indicates that an entitlement exists which is stronger than other (similar or identical) entitlements.

CHAPTER I

The Colonate in the East under Justinian, 527/534–565/642

3 Introduction and Background to Justinian's Code

For this period Justinian's Code, issued in 534, and his Novels, issued in 534–565, are the primary sources on the colonate.[1] Regarding these, some caveats are necessary. Contrary to Justinian's Digest, the earliest manuscripts of his Code date from the tenth century, which leaves a gap of about 300 years in transmission. Worse, copiers left out the Greek constitutions (which could not be read or were not read in the Middle Ages) and often the in- and subscriptions of the Latin constitutions. Not until the sixteenth century were attempts made to reconstruct the Code. Many reconstructions of the in- and subscriptions depend on Haloander, who used a manuscript which, if it existed, is now lost, so that we cannot check his readings unless there is a parallel transmission in the Theodosian Code or elsewhere. Lost constitutions have been restored on the basis of the Basilica, a ninth-century codification which drew on early Greek translations, summaries or paraphrases of the original texts of Justinian's codification.[2] In these cases there is the possibility that we are dealing with a summary or paraphrase and not with a literal translation. For example, we cannot say whether the text of CJ 11.48.19, a constitution of Anastasius, is the original Greek text, or its summary, or a Greek paraphrasis or summary of the Latin original. However, it is quite likely it will still have been an accurate rendering of the contents of the original. But the Basilica generally does not contain in- and subscriptions. The *editio maior* of Justinian's Code, Paul Krüger's *Codex Justinianus*, published in 1877, was based for these matters on Heimbach's edition of the Basilica. Meanwhile a new and better Basilica edition has been published. Further, we now possess a complete survey of all manuscripts of the Code,[3]

[1] The text of Section 3 is based on Sirks 2008, 122ff., but with changes, additions, and additional sections.
[2] Wenger 1954, 638–651; on the Basilica, see Van der Wal & Lokin 1985, 81–86. On the way to use the Basilica, see De Jong 2016.
[3] See Dolezalek 1985.

and while Krüger of course used those manuscripts which were to his knowledge the best, and which may still be the best, a check-up on this would be possible now.[4] It is therefore not impossible that a new edition of the Code would be worthwhile. Meanwhile we have to use the *editio maior* and the *editio stereotypa*, based on the former but with later additions or corrections by Krüger.[5]

Since Justinian codified the existing law on the colonate, which included some recent constitutions by him, and updated older laws, and since many of the Novels were issued shortly after the Code, the whole of the law covers the time span of 534–558, but the main part was issued in 534–540, a rather short time span. Hence we may assume that they present a consistent picture of the legal side of the colonate in as far as it is incorporated in legislation, including the Digest.

Justinian's codification marked the beginning of his reign. Justinian wanted to homogenise and harmonise the law of his time and reorder the legal study, providing the students, but also the courts, with comprehensive editions of legal writings, imperial constitutions and an institutional book.[6] As to the eastern Roman Empire, it had, since Zeno succeeded in 488 in getting rid of the Ostrogoths, enjoyed a period of peace, even with the Persians. Under Anastasius (491–518) the state finances were restored, and Anastasius supported agriculture by curtailing, inter alia, the effects of credit (the lex Anastasiana prohibited claiming more on debt papers than they were bought for). He was succeeded by Justinus I, Justinian's uncle, whom Justinian succeeded in his turn in 527. Already in 529 he published a Code, in 530 his Digest (published in 533) and in 533 his Institutes, after which a new edition of the Code was ordered, published in 534. In the same year 533 Justinian sent an army to Africa to defeat the Vandals, which was successful, and in 535 the battlefield shifted to Sicily, Italy, and Rome. It is suggested that the distribution of land in the east had meanwhile undergone a great change. Great estates would have been formed, and the question is whether their owners were responsible for collecting the taxes due from the people living on their estates (the so-called *autopragia*). A documented case of such a great estate is that of the Apiones in Egypt,

[4] As Dillon 2015 has done. It has no consequences for this study on the colonate.

[5] See Wenger 1954, 651.

[6] Current research is no longer assuming that Justinian had grand designs at the beginning of his reign, like restoring the Roman Empire in its old extension. See for this Meier 2004, 2011 and Maas 2005, particularly the contribution of Noethlichs. He suggests that Justinian followed practical goals and adapted where necessary. The suggestion of Humfress in the same volume that Justinian christianised the law by referring to God and Christ, a variation on what already Biondi 1952–1954 maintained, is, like Biondi's theory (rejected by all Romanists), not borne out by the evidence.

who themselves lived in Constantinople and fulfilled high offices.[7] In Section 9 a short survey is given of the pluriform structure of such a large estate, as analysed by Sarris; and in Section 18 the pluriformity of the agricultural labour. Around 540, disasters came to strike the Empire, first the plague which arrived in 541/542. Since the bulk of the law on the colonate is from before this moment, the history of the Empire after this moment is not treated of here.

4 The *Coloni* in Book 11 of Justinian's Code

The titles on the *coloni* are placed in the eleventh book of Justinian's Code, which in general deals with public law. Placed after titles on groups of persons obliged to perform certain services of public interest (CJ 11.2–18), titles on the organisation of the three main cities of the Empire (CJ 11.19–28), and on the organisation of towns (CJ 11.29–37), CJ 11.48–53 is about *agricolae censiti vel coloni*, the *capitatio*, *coloni censiti* and *coloni* of particular provinces. After that follow CJ 11.54–57 on *rusticani* and their villages,[8] CJ 11.58–59 on correction of the taxation rate and distribution of unexploited lands over exploited lands (*peraequatio*, *impositio agrorum desertorum*), CJ 11.60–61 on border- and pasture lands, CJ 11.62–65 on patrimonial and other lands, CJ 11.66 on land of the *res privata*, CJ 11.67–68 on land of the *res dominica* and CJ 11.69 on land of the treasure. In these last four titles there is also mention of *coloni* on these lands.[9] Book 11 finishes with some titles on the lease of public and imperial lands (CJ 11.70–74) and some titles on particular subjects not relevant here (CJ 11.75–78).

This survey already makes clear that there will have been a connection between the general title (CJ 11.48), CJ 11.49 with a single constitution on the abolition of the *capitatio humana*, the poll tax, for the urban *plebs* in the east, CJ 11.50 with the subject of litigation by *coloni censiti* against their masters (this is the consequence of the rules as collected in CJ 11.48) and finally three titles each with a single constitution, on the *coloni* in Palestine, Thrace and Illyricum (which concern the *agricolae censiti* of these

[7] See for the economic and social aspects, for example, Hardie 1931; Gascou 1985; Kaplan 1992; Banaji 2001, 2009; Sarris 2006 for a detailed exposition of the household of the Apiones.

[8] The term *rusticanus* underlines the aspect of living on the land (and not in the city), but is not used for the wealthy landowner. Its equivalent is thus *agricola*. Is it used here as translation of *georgos*? Or rather of *chorikos* (χωρικός)? Is it the term for those who live in a *vicus*? The reason for its use may precisely be the root: all those who live on and off the land, *rus*, *chora* (χώρα), without regard for status such as the colonate. The contents of CJ 11.55 confirm this. The connection with the *vicus* may lie in the subject matter, the imposition of duties which may have been organised according to *vici*.

[9] Their position did not substantially differ from the *coloni originales*.

provinces). The placement of CJ 11.49 in the middle of the constitutions on *coloni* is a sign that this tax was relevant to the group of *agricolae censiti*, a connection confirmed by CJ 11.48.10, in which the rates of the *capitatio humana* are rendered. These rates are calculation units, as the constitution proves: *per singulos viros . . . capitis norma sit censa.*[10]

Though the rubric of CJ 11.48 speaks of *agricolae censiti* vel *coloni*, we meet in its texts various designations besides *colonus*: *coloni originales* (c.4), *rustici* (c.5), *adscripticii (coloni)* (c. 6, 21, 22, 23, 24), *originarii* (c. 7, 11, 16), *tributarii* (c.12), *adscripticiae condicionis* (c. 22, 23, 24), *censibus adscripti* (c.18 and CJ 11.50.2), *colonariae condicionis* (c. 23), and the Greek *enapographos* (ἐναπόγραφος) (c.19).[11] In papyri we encounter *tychè enapographè* (τύχη ἐναπογραφή) or *tychè georgikès* (τύχη γεωργικῆς) for the *condicio adscripticia* or *coloniaria.*[12] There were also *coloni censiti* who were considered *eleutheroi* (ἐλεύθεροι), 'free' and different from the *coloni adscripticii* (c. 19). I shall use, in accordance with the title's rubric, the term *colonus* for both kinds of *coloni censiti* and differentiate whenever necessary or desirable.

The term *enapographos* and its equivalent *adscripticius* turns up in the second half of the fourth century AD (CJ 11.48.6 of 366) and certainly from the middle of the fifth century. The Greek word seems to refer to a copy or transcript (*apographos* (ἀπογρᾶφος), 'copied') which has been inserted somewhere. The Latin *adscripticius* is an adjective and means 'entered into a register'; we encounter also *adscriptus* in the expression *censibus adscriptus*, 'entered into the tax register'. We meet both expressions also used as nouns. The question of which register they were entered into will be dealt with below. Both terms seem to have emerged in order to point out the difference with the *coloni liberi*, the *georgoi eleutheroi* (γεωργόι ἐλεύθεροι), a category existing from the middle of the fourth century.

Apart from these titles, placed together in the eleventh book, there are a number of other texts in the Code and Novels in which *coloni* or *adscripticii* (*enapographoi*) are mentioned. There is further the *allotrios georgos* (ἀλλότριος γεωργός), the *kolonos* (κολωνός), and the term (*ius*)

[10] See Karayannopoulos 1958, 28–43. Both units, *capitatio* and *iugatio*, served to establish a repartition system where the expected expenditures formed the real basis for the imposition of the effective taxes on, in the end, the individuals and individual landowners. It is possible that this repartition system was exchanged from the middle of the fifth century for a quotisation system. But the texts do not allow for a decisive choice; see Karayannopoulos 1958, 84–92.

[11] But this text (see Wenger 1954, 195) is a restitution from the Basilica and the word may be a later Hellenism, or the *antecessor* used in his Greek summary or translation the current Greek equivalent, in both of which cases the original text most likely had *adscripticius*.

[12] For example, in P. Merton II 98.

colonatus.[13] In some cases this concerns *coloni* in the sense of independent lessees. They figure in CJ 4.44.65 and other places, and if and in as far as *coloni adscripticii* or *coloni liberi* were lessees, those texts also apply to them.[14] In some cases the adscripticiate has been interpolated, which shows how texts were adapted for contemporary use.[15] Furthermore, we meet *paroikoi* (πάροικοι), meaning according to Zepos *coloni*, tied to land; but it is possible that we are dealing here with *inquilini* or *casarii* (who could also be tied to an estate).[16] Finally, we encounter in the Digest several

[13] Apart from the rubrics: *colonus* and *colonarius* in D. 50.15.4.8; CJ 1.2.14, 1.3.36, 1.4.24, 1.12.6.9, 2.7.22., 2.7.24, 3.26.7, 3.26.8, 3.26.11, 3.38.11, 4.10.3, 4.10.11, 4.21.19, 4.26.13, 4.65.5, 4.65.9, 4.65.27, 4.65.35, 5.34.13, 5.62.8, 6.4.2, 7.30.1, 7.32.5, 7.32.12, 7.38.1, 7.38.2, 8.5.1, 8.15.8, 8.51.3, 9.24.1.5, 9.27.4, 9.27.5, 9.49.7.1, 10.71.3, 11.8.7, 11.26.1, 11.48.2, 11.48.4, 11.48.6, 11.48.11, 11.48.13, 11.48.14, 11.48.15, 11.48.17, 11.48.19, 11.48.20, 11.48.22, 11.48.23, 11.50.1, 11.50.2, 11.51.1, 11.52.1, 11.53.1, 11.58.3, 11.61.3, 11.62.5, 11.63.1, 11.63.3, 11.64.1, 11.64.2, 11.66.6, 11.68.1,11.68.2, 11.68.3, 11.68.4, 11.68.5, 11.68.6, 11.69.1,11.75.1, 12.10.2, 12.19.12, 12.21.8, 12.33.3, App. 1, 6, 7.16, 9; *adscripticius* in CJ 1.3.20, 1.3.36, 1.4.24, 1.12.6.9, 2.4.43, 3.38.11, 7.24.1.1, 8.51.1, 8.51.3, 12.19.12, 12.54.3, App. 1; *tributarius* in CJ 1.27.1.16, 1.27.2.11, 10.72.9pr, 11.48.12pr; *censibus obnoxius* in CJ 12.43.1(but this may include other *condicionales*); κολωνός in Nov. 123.35, 162.2 pr, 3, 4, 5, 162.2.1; ἐναπόγραφος in Nov. 22.17 pr, 54 pr–1, 123.4, 123.17.1, 123.35, 128.14.3, 156.1, 162.2–3; *colonatus* in 11.26.1, 11.66.6, App. 6, 9; ἀλλότριος γεωργός in Ed.Praef. 25. Perhaps in Nov. 167 the γεωργοί are *adscripticii* because they have to acknowledge the possession and *dominium* of the person to whom *immissio in possessionem* is given.

[14] CJ 4.10.3, 11; CJ 4.21.19pr; CJ 4.65.5, 9, 27, 35pr (here the *conductores* have taken it upon themselves to find farmers to till the rented lands as subtenants, which may therefore concern free tenants, but perhaps also *coloni adscripticii* or *liberi*); CJ 5.62.8 (where *coloni* is explained by the interpolation *id est conductores*; otherwise confusion might be created with CJ 5.34.13 where the *coloni patrimoniales* enjoy immunity from the guardianship); CJ 7.30.1 (where *colono vel* may be interpolated); CJ 9.24.1.5 (assistance with counterfeiting); CJ 11.58.3 (the owner resists a fiscal re-evaluation of his lands by retracting his procurator or by dismissing his *colonus*: it would not help to dismiss an *adscripticius*, so it must concern a tenant; further, if it concerned tied farmers, the text would rather have read *colonos*); CJ 11.61.3.1 (which concerns tenants (*conductores*) of provincial and *res privata* meadows, since meadows are not cultivated); CJ 11.62.5 (which concerns a reassignment of lands, deserted by previous *coloni* or *emphyteuticarii*). For *coloni censiti* who rented, see Section 9 and P.Oxy. LXVII 4615.

[15] For example, CJ 3.38.11 and CJ 7.30.1.

[16] CJ 1.2.24, 1.34.1 (where they are mentioned next to γεωργοί and ἐμφυτευταί, which suggests they were different from these two categories), Nov. 7 pr, Nov. 120. In CJ 1.2.24: παροικικός (see Sarris 2006, 151). See Polara 1969; Zepos 1980, 421, 424; Rosafio 1984. Zepos 1980, 427 assumes the πάροικοι later on absorbed the *coloni* and *adscripticii*. But of such a third category of farmers nothing is known for Justinian's reign in any other way, and also *inquilini* had an obligation to remain on the land. CJ 9.49.7.1 has *casarii* next to *coloni*. *OLD* has merely *casaria* and a reference to Paul. Fest. p. 48M: *-a, quae custodit casam*. Georges 1918 adds to this CTh 9.42.7, explaining the term by 'der Kolone od. Knecht auf einem Hofe, etwas Kossäte'. Yet, in view of the word *inquilinus* (inmate of the same house, tenant, from *in-quil*, *quil* being a form of *colo*, to live, cultivate), and the fact that these people were put on the same status level as the *coloni originarii* (see CJ 11.48.13.1–2 of 400), it is more likely that *casarii* will have referred to *inquilini*. See the *colonica*, a farm with attached *coloni*, what also may have been meant by *casarii*: Brown 1984, 113 (*casa coloniaria*), and Wickham 2005, 270–272 for management of land in the fifth century. I therefore doubt Sarris' interpretation of Apphous as *adscripticius* avant la lettre (Sarris 2006, 151–152). The term also occurs in the Peira, but this period is not covered in the present research: see Oikonomides 1992, XIII and Bartusis 2012, chapter 3. The term is also mentioned by Harper 2008, 100 and 101 (as free dependents) and Thonemann 2007 in some of the fourth-century Greek census inscriptions they discuss. According to Cerati 1975, for Lesbos, γεωργοί are mentioned (246), and for Thera, πάροικοι (248); for

times a *colonus*. It concerns farmers in the private law sense and of the Republic or early Empire, who, depending on the context, usually have rented a farm or land, hence are lessees.[17] Only in D. 50.15.4.8, a text of Ulpian, are the *inquilinus* and *colonus* registered people. The text must be a post-classical or Justinianic interpolation, because the *coloni originales* did not yet exist in Ulpian's times. Also the place in the fragment indicates this.[18]

In order to facilitate a synthesis, I have arranged the texts according to themes. First I treat of themes which are fundamental to the analysis of the colonate: the beginning of the adscripticiate (the *condicio coloniaria*) and the *adscriptio censu* (Section 6), the submission as evidenced by the *potestas* of the landowner and the *peculium* (Section 7), the liability for taxes (Section 8), occupations and arrangements with the landowner (Section 9), the transmission of the *condicio* and the role of the *senatusconsultum Claudianum* (Section 10), the moving and recalling of *coloni* (Sections 11 and 12), release from the colonate and the 'free' *coloni* (Section 13), and public and procedural aspects of the colonate (Section 14). After that follow sections on the *coloni* on imperial lands (Section 15), the 'free' colonate (Sections 16 and 17), and other farmers (Section 18).

5 CJ 11.48.20–24: The Central Texts on the Colonate

Within CJ 11.48 four texts date from the years 529–534, all issued by Justinian and codified in 534: CJ 11.48.20–24. Consequently we may assume that they are coherent and accurately represent the situation of 534 in contemporary idiom. They deal with the following questions: When can the owner of an estate (*dominus terrae*) claim somebody as his *colonus*?

Chios, Cerati mentions 'colons' (249) but these were πάροικοι. For Thralles, he does not mention 'colons', whereas Harper 2008, 17, assumes, in line with Jones, that the term *capita* stood for *paroikoi*. This is strange, since that might as well refer to slaves or slaves and animals.

17 For CJ 11.48 the translation of 'tenant' is too indistinct and irrelevant; it concerns, as the title indicates, *coloni adscripticii* and *coloni liberi*. See also Section 2.3.4.

18 The text is at the end of the description of the declaration, whereas one would have expected it directly before or after the slaves. Now different kinds of land use are separating them. Perhaps the statement on children, born after the declaration, was the reason to put it there. Rosafio 1991b, 263–264, on the other hand, assumes it concerned lessees whom the lessor had to declare; if he did not, he had to pay their taxes. One wonders which taxes. The landowner had to pay the *tributum solis*. If the lessee owned land himself, he had to fill out his own *professio censualis*. The tax remaining would be the *tributum capitis*. Rosafio thinks this was not the case. I agree. In Ulpian's days, what would have been the sense of registering lessees for this tax and non-lessees elsewhere? For the *tributum capitis* heads of households will have been registered in their town or village of residence. The phrase only makes sense in connection with the colonate because then people are registered in the census of an estate owner.

What if *coloni* contest that somebody is owner of their land or has a right to them? And connected with this: When is somebody considered a *colonus*? What can an estate owner claim from his *colonus*? Does the status of *colonus* pass on to his offspring? And there are collateral problems imaginable. If *coloni* are attached to an estate, what if the estate is divided? If somebody has two estates, may he transfer *coloni* from one to the other? What if a *colonus* runs away and enters the colonate with another estate owner, or works as an independent lessee or day labourer? Or runs to a town, or seeks immunity in the imperial services or the Church? What about the payment of his tax in case of flight? What if a *colonus* or *colona* (we have to think of the daughter of a *colonus*) marries another's *colona* or *colonus*? Can *coloni* litigate against their estate owners? Are there rules for this?

I take these four texts as the point of departure, but will use other texts of the Code and Justinian's Novels where appropriate in order to consolidate the examination and then deal with the remaining texts on *coloni*. The other texts in CJ 11.48 relating to *coloni* were all issued before Justinian. Theoretically it is possible that their original meaning and setting differed from their meaning and setting in Justinian's times. Because Justinian ordered his compilers to leave out the obsolete and allowed them to change and interpolate if necessary the texts, we may, as far as their republication and continuous application in 534 is concerned, leave any different original meaning aside and interpret them in accordance with what we know from CJ 11.48.20–24 and other Justinianic texts.

6 Entering or Imposing the *Condicio Coloniaria*

The word *condicio* means, next to 'requirement', 'condition',[19] the destiny of a person, his status, like *condicio humana*, the human condition, or *condicio servitutis*, the status of slavery. In CJ 11.48.22 Justinian treats the *condicio coloniaria* (or *adscripticia*)[20] as a status, namely of *coloni*. In itself it is not a felicitous word to describe a status. Cicero speaks of the *servitus condicio*, and in Late Antiquity it meant (next, of course, to condition in the sense of 'shape', 'state') slavery and the adjective or noun *condicionalis* 'belonging to slavery'.[21] Slavery the *colonatus* was not, but as we shall see,

[19] It indeed occurs in the Theodosian Code as 'condition' – as in CTh 5.6.3 – but that is not applicable here.

[20] It would be more natural to enter first the question of whether the *condicio* meant status and what status if so. That happens later on, but that it was a status is proven 'im Rückschluß'. Besides, Justinian refers to it in terms of status.

[21] Souter 1949, s.vv. *condicio, condicionalis*.

the status was one of subjection and Justinian calls it a *deterior fortuna*. App. 1 even refers to it as a *natura*, but that may be influenced by its transmission via birth. I shall deal in detail with this later (Section 10).

The question here is how did somebody enter this status? Was it voluntary or compulsory? Was it made hereditary under Diocletian? CJ 11.48.22 provides a clue:

> Cum scimus nostro iure nullum praeiudicium generari cuidam circa condicionem neque ex confessionibus neque ex scriptura, nisi etiam ex aliis argumentis aliquid accesserit incrementum, sancimus solam {conductionem} <confessionem> vel aliam quamcumque scripturam ad hoc minime sufficere nec adscripticiam condicionem cuidam inferre, sed debere huiusmodi scripturae aliquid advenire adiutorium, quatenus vel ex publici census adscriptione vel ex aliis legitimis modis talis scriptura adiuvetur. 1. Melius etenim est in huiusmodi difficultatibus ex pluribus capitulis condiciones ostendi et non solis confessionibus neque scripturis homines forte liberos ad deteriorem detrahi fortunam. 2. Sin autem et scriptura et post scripturam confessio seu depositio, sine vi et necessitate tamen, intervenerit (quid enim, si etiam {conductionale} <conditionale> instrumentum vel alium chartulam, in qua subscripsit, intimavit et inter acta deposuit sese colonum fuisse adscripticium), tunc ex utroque genere obligationis, id est tam scripturae quam confessionis vel depositionis, talem eum esse credendum, qualem et scripsit et inter acta deposuit. . . . D. x k. Constantinopoli post consulatum Lampadii et Orestis vv. cc. [a. 531]
>
> Since We know that by Our law no prejudice is created concerning status from acknowledgements (*confessionibus*) or from a writing, unless something additional has been added from other evidence, We ordain that an acknowledgement (*confessio*)[22] alone or any other writing does not suffice for this at all and does not impose the *adscripticia condicio* on anyone, but some support should be added to such a writing, to the extent that such a writing is supported by an entry (*adscriptio*) in the public census, or by other lawful means. 1. For it is better in such difficulties that *condiciones* are demonstrated from multiple sources (*capitulae*) and that people who are perhaps free not be dragged into a worse fortune by acknowledgements (*confessiones*) or writings alone. 2. If, however, a writing intervenes and after the writing an acknowledgement (*confessio*) or a deposition, but without force and compulsion – and indeed the more so if he has produced a *conditionale instrumentum* or some other record (*chartula*) in which he has written his signature and in the records has set down that he has been a *colonus*

[22] The translation with 'confession' I would avoid in view of the later meaning. It will refer to the document in which a *colonus* acknowledged that he was a *colonus*, for example, after having been summoned (back) to the estate, similar to the acknowledgements citizens gave when summoned for public duties (*agnoscere*).

adscripticius – then on the basis of each type of obligation, that is both of the writing as well as the acknowledgement (*confessio*) or deposition, he is to be believed to be of the status that he has written and set down in the records.[23]

The fragment deals with the claim by a *dominus* for an *adscripticius*. It had to be proved. Justinian says that a mere acknowledgement (*confessio*) was not sufficient. It had to be confirmed by another document such as the entry in the census (*publici census adscriptio*) or by the voluntary deposition of his acknowledgement by the *colonus* in the public record office. Documents, particularly authenticated ones, were valued more highly than oral testimonies.[24] Other combinations of documents were also allowed. It means that just one document was not enough.[25]

At this point the text needs scrutiny, because Krüger has in his edition of the Codex introduced emendations. It has instead of *confessionem* the word *conductionem* and instead of *conditionale* the word *conductionale*, implying that we are dealing here with references to a labour contract, which then would, if confirmed by another document or act, lead automatically to the *condicio coloniaria*.[26] This requires some exegesis.

Krüger chose the variants *conductionem* and *conductionale* against the manuscripts U, K, and I, which have *conditionem* and *conditionale*, while manuscript X has, respectively, nothing and *condictionale*.[27] The Vulgate has *confessionem* and *conditionale instrumentum*. Krüger made his decision on basis of Cuiacius.[28] Cuiacius cited for the emendation of *confessionem* into *conductionem*: κἂν ἐμισθώσατο ὡς ἐναπόγραφος – 'even if he was hired as *enapographos*' – and for the emendation *conductionale*: ἐι δέ τὴν μίσθωσιν ἐβεβαίωσεν ἑκὼν δὶα καταθέσεως ἢ ἐμφανείας, λοιπὸν πιστευέσθω τοιοῦτος

[23] The translation of Codex of Justinian 2016 with corrections. A *confessio* does not need to be oral. Also the 'for what is it' for *quid enim* does not seem to make sense. The point is that two documents suffice yet have to be checked for voluntariness, but with the two specified documents there is no need to. Unless otherwise explicitly specified, all translations of the Theodosian Code and the Post-Theodosian Novels are taken from or based on Pharr 1952; those of Justinian's Code are taken from or based on Codex of Justinian 2016; and those of Justinian's Novels are taken from or based on Miller & Sarris 2018.

[24] Kaser & Hackl 1996, 600–602.

[25] Carrié 1997, 946 sees in P. Ross.-Georg. III 8 (fourth century AD) such a document. This reading of the text is, however, very difficult (see Van Minnen 1997, 70ff.) and conclusions are actually not possible.

[26] Krüger 1877. CJ 11.48.22.2 equals the *conditionale instrumentum* with a *chartula in qua subscripsit intimavit et inter acta deposuit in qua sese colonum fuisse intimatur*. Until now we possess only one lease contract by an *adscripticius* (P.Oxy. LXVII 4615 of 505), but he probably was already *adscripticius* by birth through his *origo*.

[27] The Codex of Justinian translates this as 'lease', mentioning in a note that some translate it as 'a contract of employment alone'. The latter is also correct but only if based on this emendation.

[28] Cuiacius 1758, c. 844 ad CJ 11.48.22.

εἶναι – 'he has confirmed the lease by depositing or exhibiting, henceforward such a person must be believed to be'. According to the editors of the Groningen Basilica edition, Cuiacius used a now lost ms. which contained probably the books 46–60 but in any case 54–57.[29] The Vulgate has no gloss to *confessionem* but it has one to *conditionale* [*instrumentum*]: *id est adscripticiae conditionis, uel dic, id est notarii ut supra dixi. Accursius.* The *supra* refers to the gloss *conditionem* (to *adscripticiam condicionem*), which says: *alias conductionem, quia solum ut adscripticius conduxit ad quod supra de lib. cau. l. ad probationem* [CJ 7.16.18] *alias conditionem . . .. uel dic, conditionem, idest instrumentum per conditionalem, idest notarium factum: ut supra* etc. Thus there is a good tradition of *confessionem* and *conditionale* and an instance in which the Vulgate is better.

CJ 7.16.18 is a text in the title on the Cases for freedom (*De liberali causa*).[30] Zoticus sues the heir of those who leased him land for his freedom. Apparently the heir argued that the lease proved he was subjected to him. The emperors say that a *locatio conductio* is not sufficient proof for that, but neither for ingenuity. If we read this strictly within the private law, the reasoning may have been that a slave could not conclude a contract without his master's confirmation in some way. In this case the master would have leased to his own slave. That does not make sense. Conversely, the lease would have been an argument to assume that Zoticus was a free man.[31] The text nevertheless makes sense if we interpret *ingenuitas* as 'free from the colonate' and *servitutis vinculum* as referring to the colonate. The glossator would have assumed that a lease alone might lead to the adscripticiate, as the heir also argued. Thus *conductionem* is just an inference. But the glossator could equally have referred to CJ 7.16.22, which says that the single admittance to be a slave does not suffice to have servitude as consequence.

Cuiacius' citations are probably correct (why should he otherwise cite?) but it does not mean they give a correct interpretation. They are evidently scholia, old or perhaps even new scholia, made on the Basilica. *Sancimus solam confessionem vel aliam quamcumque scripturam ad hic minime sufficere*: How to place 'even if he was hired as *enapographos*'? If the person admitted he was an *enapographos* and hired as such by his master, would the admittance not have been enough? Would there have to be another proof

29 BT, Volume VI, p. xviii.

30 CJ 7.16.18: *Diocl. et Maxim. AA. et CC. Zotico. Ad probationem ingenuitatis ab eo, contra cuius successores postulas, facta tibi locatio non sufficit, nec tamen hoc solum ad servitutis vinculum argumentum est idoneum. S. id. Iul. Philippopoli AA. conss.* [a. 293].

31 We can refine the case by assuming that a manumission had been performed in an imperfect way. Yet Zoticus would still have been free and able to contract, albeit as Junian Latin.

from an independent source? The only remaining reason to emendate *confessionem* is the following emendation of *conditionale*. Here the text says that a document containing a confession, signed by the *colonus*, afterwards without force or pressure deposited by him, namely in the public record office, suffices as proof.[32] The scholion interprets this document as a contract in which the *colonus* let himself be hired and states, correctly, that the deposition confirms the trustworthiness of the document. But does it mean that any mere labour contract, if deposited, would lead to the *condicio adscripticia*? And why should people want to deposit labour contracts in the public record office? But it is different if it concerned a contract by which an *enapographos* entered his status, in the line of the preceding scholion, because in that case it confirmed not the contract but the status of the *enapographos*.

Justinian underlines the voluntariness of the adscripticiate. No force or pressure is allowed, which, unfortunately, suggests that in practice landowners used unfair means to claim people. In a lawsuit about the colonate (likely the application of the *liberalis causa*) written documents were preferable – in accordance with the law of evidence of those times – and the best proof for the landowner was then the undersigned *conditionale instrumentum* (the agreement to enter the colonate), approved in court, or any other undersigned document combined with the deposition of this document in the public records. The *conditionale instrumentum* effectuated that the *condicio* of the *colonus* changed into that of the colonate, and that would explain the adjective. Necessary after that, as we shall see, was the entering into the *census*. It follows that at the basis of the adscripticiate lay an agreement to enter this status and that the entry was voluntary.[33] Further, the agreement concerned the entry into the adscripticiate and not a lease or labour contract. I shall return to this point in Section 13.2 when discussing CJ 11.48.19, interpreted by some authors as proof that after thirty years a lease turned into the adscripticiate. That interpretation conflicts already with CJ 11.48.22, which requires a second document: a single lease does not suffice (so also CJ 7.16.18).

[32] If otherwise, the mere *adscriptio* would have sufficed and the *colonus* would have been tied against his will, which the emperor apparently – see CJ 11.48.22pr–2 – wants to prevent. In Late Antiquity, written documents prevailed over oral testimony; see Kaser & Hackl 1996, 600–602.

[33] Thus, although the colonate was a *condicio*, at its origin lay an agreement of private law nature, contrary to what Carrié maintains in Vera 2019, 11 n. 24. In Sirks 2008, 124 n. 16 I discussed the reading *conductio* and interpreted it as a labour contract, rejecting the interpretation as lease. Vera 2012 = 2019, 366 n. 24 chooses the meaning of lease. In view of my later research I opt for the readings *confessio* and *conditionale*, the latter comprising both the agreement to work and to subject oneself to the authority of the estate owner. As such the interpretation as employment contract is close to the truth; but lease is wrong.

It might be that during a claim procedure regarding the adscripticiate a settlement was reached which was valid unless it could be challenged legally (CJ 2.4.43).[34] Thus a settlement could also bring the adscripticiate. Further, the reference to a voluntary agreement implies that by Justinian's time the status of *adscripticius* did not always derive from descent, but that it could (still) be entered *ex novo* and may not necessarily have been for life. The origin of all cases of the adscripticiate (and thus often of the 'free' colonate, see below, Section 16) must consequently have been a separate agreement whose conditions could not be changed later (CJ 11.48.23.3). There is one papyrus with reference to such an agreement (it at least suggests it: P.Oxy. XVII 2479 with Pieous; see note 144).

The other cause of being an *adscripticius* was by descent, which will be discussed in Section 10.1.

Further, the colonate (*colonatus*) could be imposed directly on able-bodied beggars, obviously those of Constantinople, but perhaps also on beggars in other towns (CJ 11.26.1). It is not clear whether this was the adscripticiate or 'free' colonate (on this, see Section 16). Since these beggars were city people, they will have lacked the competence to farm unless they had fled from the harsh conditions on land. At best they could be used as farm hands. The colonate could therefore imply farming, whether or not on a lease, but did not have to.

Justinian mentions as a good document the *publici census adscriptio*. It meant that the *colonus* was entered as being in this *condicio* in a tax register. It may have been a copy of, extract from, or reference to the *conditionale instrumentum*: that would fit the term *apographos* (ἀπογρᾶφος). Every rural person was already included in the village or town census for the *capitatio humana* and, if he possessed land, in the census of that land (see Section 8.2). D. 50.15.4 with in section 5 the registration of slaves and in section 8 the registration of *coloni* and *inquilini* provides the general procedure: after the example of the slaves on an estate, under a special *titulus*, since the *coloni* are mentioned after these in the exposition of the census declaration, *coloni* were entered and so were *adscripti censibus*, cf. CJ 11.7.7.[35] Examples we find in inscriptions of towns in Asia Minor.[36] D. 50.15.4.8 is

[34] A constitution, issued in 500 by Anastasius, together with the fragments CJ 2.7.21 (protecting the advocates at the praetorian court of Illyricum from claims for the cohortalate or worse *condiciones*) and 7.39.5 (forbidding use of the forty-year limitation of prescription for warding off claims for the decurionate). All three texts deal in one way or the other with summons for public obligations.

[35] This text deals with fugitive *metallarii*, state miners, whose *condicio* was similar to that of the *adscripticii* and who were harboured by private persons who enrolled them on their census. Unfortunately, I could not consult Chechi 2017.

[36] Thonemann 2007, 441–448; Harper 2008, 1 n. 1.

likely a post-classical or Justinianic interpolation (see Section 4), but that does not matter here, since we are dealing with the Justinianic period.

7 Effects of the Colonate: *Potestas* and *Peculium*

Potestas and *peculium* are two aspects of the power of the landowner over his *colonus*, or, seeing it from the other side, of the subjection of the *colonus* to his landowner.

7.1 Coloni Are in the Potestas *of the Estate Owner*

The estate owner is said to be a *despotès* (δεσπότης), a *dominus*, of the *colonus*, as in CJ 11.48.19, CJ 11.52.1.1, 11.53.1.1 and several constitutions of CJ 11.48. He exercises power over him (CJ 11.52.1.1: *domini potestate*). The *colonus* has to perform tasks on the estate (*ruralia obsequia*, CJ 1.3.16), till the land or perform the work of a *colonus*, he had to remain on the estate (CJ 11.48.15), and he and his children stand under the *potestas* of his estate owner (CJ 11.48.21.1), who may have him recalled forcibly (CJ 11.48.6, 11, 12). The *colonus* is restricted in his faculty to sue his estate owner (CJ 11.50.1, 2), which is also an attribute of the relation between children *in potestate* and their *pater familias* and between freedmen and their patrons. He has to provide services to the estate owner, according to what had been agreed (CJ 11.48.1, 5, CJ 11.50.1). Yet it is also underlined that they are not slaves and can marry freely, albeit that their subjected condition is transmittable (CJ 11.48.21, also 13; see Sections 10.3 and 10.6).

CJ 11.48.1 does not allow any extraordinary public performances when the *coloni* are planting or harvesting, since that could also be done at a more opportune moment – a privilege which would support them in their duties, but profit far more their estate owners, since these were now certain their supplementary workforce would stay on the spot – and CJ 11.48.5 reminds the estate owners that they may not demand money payments from the farmers but must accept payments in kind, unless this is the custom of the estate (this could happen if a new owner took over). Both texts speak of farmers in general (*agricolae*, *rustici*), but, first, *coloni* who cultivated land formed part of this category and second, the inclusion of these texts in CJ 11.48 implies their application to *coloni originales*.

Their situation is one of being freeborn citizens, but also of subjection to somebody (the estate owner), comparable to that of a child *in potestate* and a slave. This *potestas* is a feature also implied in CJ 4.65.35pr, which forbids *militia* (officials) to rent land and reminds them not to oppress people, such as the *coloni* on land they had rented and whom they had taken into their charge and were their agent (*adversus miseros colonos quos procurandos susceperunt*). Since normally no charge is exercised over lessees, it must concern *adscripticii* and indicate a patronal relation. In the case of a lease, the lessee exercised the position of the estate owner/ lessor. He took it upon him to be their patron, but we may assume he also required their services.

In what relation did this power stand to the *patria potestas* of the *colonus*? What if a *colonus* had contracted out his son to work elsewhere: Could his estate owner claim his son's services? Several constitutions on the recall of *coloni* order the return of his children too. In CJ 11.48.23.1 the question is: May children of those *adscripticii* who have worked for thirty years and thereby become 'free' *coloni*, if they have not yet worked for thirty years, claim the same status, or do they have to complete their thirty years too? They did not but became 'free' *coloni* too. This implies that normally they too were obliged to work and were *adscripticii*, and thus in this respect were in the *potestas* of the estate owner. This being so, the *potestas* of the father was in any case restricted where it concerned his children's faculty to engage on their own work. All depends on how much work was requested. As is set out in Section 9, *coloni* will have done several jobs.[37] For the rest, their own *potestas* will have been that of any *pater familias*.[38]

CJ 11.50.2pr–1 couples *potestas* and *peculium* in the context of whether *coloni* could litigate against their estate owners. The text first describes the difference between the two categories of *coloni* in a very elliptic way:

> Coloni censibus dumtaxat adscripti, sicuti ab his liberi sunt, quibus eos tributa subiectos non faciunt, ita his, quibus annuis functionibus et debito condicionis obnoxii sunt, paene est ut quadam servitute dediti videantur. 1. Quo minus est ferendum, ut eos audeant lite pulsare, a quibus ipsos utpote a dominis una cum possessionibus distrahi posse dubium non est.

> Just as the *coloni* who are merely registered in the census are free from those, to whom the taxes do not make them subjected, so ought they to be seen as almost given over in some kind of servitude to them, to whom they are subjected by the annual taxes/payments and the debt of their status. 1. It is all the less to be tolerated that they dare to batter with a lawsuit those

[37] CJ 11.48.23.3: *agros colere, aliquid colonarii operis celebrare, agriculturam peragere* for the *adscripticii*, *terram colere* for the 'free' *coloni*; *adscripticii* have *peculium* (CJ 11.48.23.5, 11.50.2), 'free' *coloni* do not (CJ 11.48.19); both groups have a duty to remain on the land and consequently can be recalled (CJ 11.48.22 and 23).

[38] Augustine posed the same and other related questions at the beginning of the fourth century; see Section 24.2.1; unfortunately, we do not have the answers.

> persons by whom as owners there is no doubt that they can be sold along with estates (*possessiones*).[39]

Although the text is a brilliant example of 'celestial' correspondence, its contents is as regards the law clear. It comes down to this. The *coloni censibus dumtaxat adscripti* ('merely registered in the census') are the 'free' *coloni* who are not subjected to their estate owners through the taxes (for them, see Section 16).[40] In other words, they were registered in the estate census *nomine et titulo colonorum* which made the estate their domicile, but there was no relation between this registration and the taxes, and consequently also not between them and the estate owner regarding the taxes in the sense that the latter paid or guaranteed these. In that case he had no *potestas* over them.

That is different from the other category, of the *adscripticii*. They are subjected (*obnoxii*)[41] to their estate owners because of the yearly taxes and the obligations of their status. This subjection is illustrated by the reference that they can be sold with the estate, which does not mean they themselves are sold (they are free Romans) but that, being linked to the estate, they increase its value and are included in the sale. That puts them almost on the level of slaves, who can be sold without more. This fits CJ 11.48.21, where the similarity between adscripticiate and slavery is emphasised, yet on the other hand explains why their positions are so close. It will have been small consolation for the *coloni* to know that the difference was legally sharp, yet in practice so small.[42] These *coloni* are bound to an estate, hence are *adscripticii*. Both categories are prohibited from suing their estate owners (*domini* refers to *adscripticii*, *patroni* to 'free' *coloni*) with the exception of imposed *superexactiones* and criminal cases (CJ 11.50.2.4). The *adscripticii* are in a kind of servitude, that is, in the *potestas* of their estate owner. This relation makes it in itself impossible to litigate. For the 'free' *coloni*, it is imposed by this law. It was the same with *filii in potestate* and with

[39] This *sicuti . . . sic* construction here is also applied in CJ 9.41.4 and, for example, in the Vulgate in 1 Cor. 15:22. The analogon is in the absoluteness of both states, the free in the first part and the unfree in the second part. The translation of the Codex of Justinian does not distinguish between the two categories and even leaves open that *coloni* in CJ 11.50.1 refers to not bound *coloni*. Leaving aside that this should be checked for the original constitution, it is not correct here because the text is placed in the title *In quibus causis coloni censiti dominos accusare possunt*, hence dealing now in any case with bound *coloni*.

[40] Carrié 1997, 145 interprets the text differently. The *coloni censibus dumtaxat* are according to him the *coloni* of CTh 11.1.14 who possess their own land, and not *coloni liberi*.

[41] The word *obnoxius* can mean 'subjected to another's power', 'liable' or 'obliged'. In the latter sense it is often used in the context of public obligations (*munera*); see Sirks 1993b, 164, 1993c.

[42] It resembles the *servitutem servire* of Quintilian in *Institutio oratoria* 5.10.60.

freedmen; they were also restricted in suing their *pater* or patron.[43] It also fits the reference to the taxes. The 'free' *coloni* had, like everyone, also to render yearly taxes (liturgies, the poll tax if it had not been abolished in their province), but it did not tie them to the estate owner. It is the *potestas* over the *adscripticii* which makes the faculty to sue their estate owners very limited for them: then, as the constitution says, such a thing is unbearable where their masters have the power to alienate them together with the estate they are on (CJ 11.50.2.1). It amounts to a disrespect which is intolerable. The exceptions in CJ 11.50.2 are precisely those cases where the patron disrespects his part of the deal and is unworthy of respect. The text of CJ 11.50.2 goes on with a passage on *peculium*, discussed below.

Estate owners possessed through their *coloni*, namely *adscripticii* (CJ 7.32.12pr–1),[44] which is something normally attributed to a state of dependency such as with slaves and children in power (e.g., D. 41.2.1.5: their *peculium* is their *pater*'s property). That tallies with the *peculium* of the *coloni*, which is a similar indication of dependency by *potestas*.

7.2 *Their Assets Are Considered* Peculium

Connected with the *potestas* is the *peculium*, because *peculium* usually implies that somebody else has power over the possessions of another. The *colonus*' assets were called *peculium* (e.g., CJ 11.48.21.1), and he could not dispose of this without his estate owner's consent (CJ 11.50.2.3):

> Cum enim saepissime decretum sit, ne quid de peculio suo cuiquam colonorum ignorante domino praedii aut vendere aut alio modo alienare liceret, quemadmodum contra eius personam aequo poterit consistere iure,

43 For the capacity to sue, see Kaser & Hackl 1996, 205–208 (formula procedure) and 483 (*cognitio* procedure). Slaves and *filii familias* could only litigate in some cases. Kaser and Hackl only consider who could litigate, not against whom one could not litigate, nor do they mention CJ 11.50.1. Further, they do not treat of freedmen. A freedman was limited in suing his patron; he could not sue him without permission of the praetor (D. 2.4.4.1; Kaser 1975, 298–299). He could not initiate a lawsuit against his patron which involved infamy (thus all the *bonae fide* actions, to start with) (CJ 6.6.1), nor was he allowed in court against his patron or his patron's children (CJ 6.7.3). These prohibitions were based on the *obsequium* that freedmen had to show their patrons. If this was the case for those who were no longer in the *potestas* of their patron, how much more will this have been valid for the *coloni*.

44 The text has merely *colonus*, but it must have included the *adscripticius* because of the parallel with other persons *alieni iuris*, through whom and even through whose *peculium* the *dominus* could acquire but also lose possession (D. 41.2.1.5), and with the procurator (D. 41.2.1.9, 20). With a free lessee there was not such a relationship; the only thing the owner possessed through his lessee was the leased land (cf. CJ 7.30.1).

> quem nec propria quidem leges sui iuris habere voluerunt et adquirendi tantum, non etiam transferendi potestate permissa, domino et adquirere et habere voluerunt?

> Since it has very often indeed been decreed that it is not anyone of the *coloni* allowed to sell or alienate in any other way something of his *peculium* when the estate owner does not know of it, how will he be able to set up proceedings against his person on an equal footing, whom the laws in fact did not want to have their own property in full administration (*sui iuris*) and allowed only the faculty to acquire, not also to transfer, so to acquire and hold for the master? (tr. Sirks)

What precisely is meant by *peculium*? The word is normally used for the assets slaves or *filii familias* had received from the *dominus*, that is, the *pater familias*. These remained owner. The same with the *peculium castrense* and *quasi castrense*: this was created for acquisitions a soldier, imperial official or cleric, who was *in potestate*, had to prevent from becoming automatically of his *pater familias*. With the slave and *filius* the *peculium* functioned in practice as a separate trust within the assets of the master, that is, the *pater*. A slave could get a *libera administratio* and then deal with it as he thought best. At his death, his assets returned to his master; if he was freed, he might retain all or part of them. With *filii familias* it was a bit different: if their *pater* died and they became *sui iuris*, they became owner. So much for the classic *peculium*.

However, with *filii* who were in the *militia* it was different with respect to their *peculium castrense*. Ulpian says, *cum filii familias in castrensi peculio vice patrum familiarum fungantur*, 'since *filii familias* are considered regarding their *peculium castrense* as *patres familias*', and Papinian wrote, *filius duplex ius sustinet patris et filii familias*, 'a son upholds a double legal position, that of a *pater* and a *filius familias*'.[45] Thus the idea that somebody *in potestate* could, where it concerned patrimonial assets and rights (in other aspects these *filii* were equal to any *pater*; see D. 14.6 1.3), be subjected at the same time to two different legal regimes was accepted in Roman law. Are we to apply these particulars also to the *peculium* of the *coloni*? Their situation is the mirror of the *filii familias* in the *militia*, but for the rest it is the same. It is therefore in line with the law to assume that they too were subjected to a double patrimonial regime. Since acquisition is mentioned, it will in any case have included property which legally was the *colonus*' own. *Peculium* comprised the assets, savings and personal belongings of an *adscripticius*, further the land he might own and till and for which he was assessed himself

[45] D. 14.6.2, D. 49.17.15.3. On this aspect, see Vial-Dumas 2021, 26–27.

individually (as in CJ 11.48.4.1).[46] Are we to assume that here it was not the patron who provided the *colonus* with assets, but conversely, the *colonus* provided him these? But the fact that a *colonus* could be assessed individually proves that some assets in any case were his own. It is therefore likely that the origin of the use of the word *peculium* was not the property itself but the *potestas* the estate owner exercised. He controlled the alienation, but nothing more. *Peculium* thus means not that the estate owner owns, but that he controls. Since he controls the alienation, it is clear that his interest lay in keeping as much property with his *colonus* as possible, which again would only be sensible if he had an interest in that property. Such an interest exists if he had a claim on the *colonus* and wanted to seize and sell his property in case of non-payment. It is different from a hypothec: with that there is no need to curtail the *colonus*' faculties because the hypothec follows the goods. It has sense when there is a changing size of the estate owner's claim and connected with that a continuous credit (a floating charge, known in Roman law).

These assets could be claimed after his death by the estate owner as *peculium*, as appears from CJ 1.3.20.1, which deals with the inheritances of clerics, left to the monastery or church. If somebody has a claim, as the patron has a claim to a part of his freedman's estate, it has to be honoured. In this context the estate of a *censibus adscriptus* is mentioned: *bona seu peculia, quae aut patrono legibus debentur aut domino possessionis, cui quis eorum fuerat adscriptus* – 'the properties or *peculia*, which either are owed according to the law to the patrons or to the estate owner, with whom somebody of them was registered'. The claim of the patron competed with children of the deceased, but since all was left here to the church or monastery, that will not have been the case. The same with the *colonus*. It is not impossible that his estate owner still had a claim and in that case his estate, the *peculium*, had to go to him (presumably to the extent of his claim). It is a constraint on the *colonus*' power of disposal and based on the authority of his estate owner.

This authority is also mentioned in CJ 11.48.19. This text, which will be discussed in detail in Section 13.2, differentiates between the two forms of colonate which were evidently important to the Byzantines with reference to the *potestas* and the *peculium*. In the adscripticiate, the *colonus*' assets were, as *peculium*, subjected or engaged to the estate owner: 'their *peculia* belong to

[46] Pace Koptev 2009, 273–278, who includes the land on basis of CTh 5.19.1, we may in any case exclude land given to a *colonus* as *precarium* because that could be claimed anyway by the giver and could not be considered his.

the landowners' (τὰ τούτων πεκούλια τοῖς δεσπόταις ἀνήκει). In the 'free' colonate, the *colonus* was 'free' and with him his assets (i.e., what otherwise would have been a *peculium*): 'remaining free with their property' (ἐλεύθεροι μένοντες μετὰ τῶν πραγμάτων αὐτων). The meaning of τὰ τούτων πεκούλια τοῖς δεσπόταις ἀνήκει is clear: no independent faculty of disposition. The 'free' *coloni* were free from the *potestas*, and their property was not *peculium*; they could freely dispose of it. With the *adscripticii* it was different; their property was reserved for their estate owners (whatever may have been understood by that, it implies in any case the restriction on alienating it), and they were registered in the census of the estate.

The *adscripticius*' property was under the control of his master. He could acquire property but could not alienate it without the estate owner's permission. To what purpose? Apparently it was in the master's interest that he could keep that property in the ownership of his *adscripticius*, and that interest cannot but have been that it was reserved so that it could serve as a security for debts of the *adscripticius*. These debts were in the first place the tax which the estate owner paid for him. Next to that it may have been credit provided, for taxation or a loan (see Section 8.3). CJ 11.48.8 refers to debts *coloni* had with the estate owner. Apparently 'free' *coloni* were as regards taxes out of that system (certainly in the provinces where the poll tax was abolished). In private law an estate owner would always have been able to recover debts of his lessees and other debtors by seizing through the *interdictum Salvianum* their private assets and sell these after having obtained a judgment against them. Perhaps with the *adscripticii* it was done in this way; perhaps the estate owner took a short cut, as in the case of Pieous (see note 144). The restriction on alienation safeguarded these assets for him.

The dependency is also visible in the case of a loan. If the *colonus* borrowed money from a third party, the creditor could not recover this from the estate owner unless the latter had given an order (*iussum*), in which case he could proceed against the estate owner with the *quod iussu* variant (CJ 4.26.13pr).[47] Normally a creditor would have been able to recover a loan from the *colonus* himself. An *actio quod iussu* was not available to him unless there was a dependency relation between his debtor and somebody else.[48] Hence if the

[47] This would mean that he could recover the amount as comprised in the order. Normally we see the *quod iussu* applied to slaves and sons *in potestate*, but ratification (*ratishabitio*) was possible anyway. By this the represented *dominus* would become liable for the dealings of his procurator. This would also work for a *colonus* who functioned as *actor*. The variation of action *quod iussu* – which restricted the *dominus*' liability to the range of the *iussum* – would make sense if this was done. For the *ratihabitio* and *iussum*, see Kacprzak 2002, 91–113.

[48] Kaser 1975, 608.

text allows for this action, there must have been such a relation between *colonus* and estate owner.[49] This is, again, a parallel to the case of a slave or *filius familias* wanting to borrow money. For that they would need the authorisation of their *pater familias*, or else the *pater* would not be liable. That is here possible if the *colonus* or *actor* has no debts versus the landowner in his account books, in which case the creditor has an *actio utilis de peculio* (CJ 4.26.13.4). This is a remarkable action because the *action de peculio* is directed against the master, here, however, against the *colonus*, which indicates that his property was called *peculium*. Why did they take up loans? Apparently for exploitation or else the estate owner would not have been called upon. Was this to fulfil their duties? To buy seed or to feed the family, or to buy new utensils? Or to pay off a debt he had in his account with the estate owner? CJ 4.26.13.4 and CJ 11.48.8.2 refer to such financial practices with a periodical settlement of accounts.[50] May the restriction on alienation not also have been a control on loans an *adscripticius* wanted to enter? The property of the *colonus* was not *peculium* in the strict sense; unlike in the case of true *peculium*, the estate owner would have no prior right to it. If the estate owner had given the authority to act independently, he forfeited his right of priority and the creditor could act against his debtor for the latter's personal property. In the same line and context, CJ 8.15.8 = CJ 11.48.17 says that the presence of slaves, *coloni*, procurators, lessees, or representatives (*actores*) cannot be used as a *praeiudicium* to seize land of their masters against the will or without knowledge of these. Then they cannot pledge what is not theirs.[51]

7.3 *The Reality of the* Potestas *and* Peculium

What could an *adscripticius* do with his property apart from the restriction on alienation? The question is reflected in a case in which an *adscripticius* is pledging his possessions. In P.Oxy. LXIII 4398 (a. 553) the *enapographos georgos* (ἐναπόγραφος γεωργός) Victor gives his possessions in surety (κινδύ(ῳ) τῶν ἐμοὶ ὑπαρχόντων, 'at the risk of my properties') to his estate owner Dioscorus for a loan of wheat for sowing on the estate fields in his charge (ὑπ' ἐμὲ). He promises to return the loan together with the

49 See now Jurewicz 2020, who interprets this and other texts in the context of the economic exploitation of land.

50 They cannot oblige the estate owner by taking up a loan if the latter has not issued a *iussum* to this effect (CJ 4.26.13). For such accounts: P.Oxy. LXX 4788 (a. 586) and 4797 (a. 583).

51 CJ 8.15.8: *Nexum non facit praediorum nisi persona, quae iure potuit obligare.* CJ 11.48.17: *Per servum aut procuratorem colonum vel actorem seu conductorem praeiudicium possessioni invito vel inscio domino imponi non posse et iure et legum auctoritatibus decantatur.*

payment of the *phoros* (φόρος: μετὰ καὶ τοῦ φορικοῦ μου φόρου) in kind of the same quality. By *phoros* is meant the compensation in specie or kind the *adscripticius* himself had to pay, likely what Dioscorus had stipulated for the use of his land; why should Victor be liable for debts on somebody else's land? If his possessions were *peculium* in the strict sense (i.e., property of Dioscorus, in the charge of Victor), he could not do this, because Dioscorus would have accepted his own property. If they were *peculium* in the wider sense (i.e., his own property and savings but with restricted disposal), a pledge to his estate owner would first not be an alienation (yet, potentially, in case of default, it would), and second it implied the consent of Dioscorus. Victor was free to pledge Dioscorus his personal property. It is not likely that he could pledge a potential claim to the remainder of *peculium* in the wider sense as discussed above if Dioscorus did not agree.

It is the same in P.Oxy. LXVI 4535 (a. 600), where the *enapographos georgos* (ἐναπόγραφος γεωργός) Elias acknowledges a debt to his estate owner, for which he gives a security on his property, mortgaged to this purpose (κινδ<ύν>ῳ τῶν ἐμοὶ ὑπαρχόντω[ν ὑ]ποκειμένων εἰς τοῦτο, 'at the risk of my properties mortgaged for that').[52] Again consent is implied. That this was possible means that the right of the estate owner to satisfy himself on the property of a *colonus* was restricted: to debts out of taxation and, the case occurring, out of the estate credit system (cf. CJ 11.48.8). Another case: in a deed of surety Zacharias guarantees that the *adscripticius* of the Apiones will pay this and the *phoros* on the estate orchard he has to work on (τὸν ὑπερ αὐτοῦ φόρον; P.Oxy. XXVII 2478 of a. 595/596). Here *phoros* (φόρος), as Hickey and Benaïssa have rightly underlined,[53] refers to a compensation for use and not to a tax as the editors have it: Victor cannot have been liable for the land tax or for an anonymous other person's poll tax (see CJ 11.48.15), but what he had to turn over could be the equivalent of the land tax.[54] *Coloni* could collect all public taxes (πάντα τὰ δημόσια τῆς δεκάτης ἐπινεμήσεως, 'all the taxes of the tenth

[52] Both formulations are almost in perfect accordance with what Justinian in CJ 8.16.9 wrote as necessary to establish a hypothec: *fide et periculo rerum ad me pertinentium*. In P.Oxy. LXX 4794 (a. 580) also a hypothec of all belongings. It may look strange that in a case of *peculium* there could be a debt of the *adscripticius* to his estate owner, but the *peculium* functioned as a separate entity and was usually left with the dependent person after the dependency ended, after a final settlement to establish its net value.

[53] Hickey 2012, 68 n. 35; Benaïssa 2020, 49 and 60; my wrong interpretation in Sirks 2008, 135. Hickey uses the word 'rent', which is possible if a lease had been agreed.

[54] Other cases where an *adscripticius* is surety: P.Oxy. LXXXIII 5375 (a. 557, surety for two brothers *adscripticii*), 5380 (a. 578, surety for somebody's lease of land), 5382 (a. 582, surety for two brothers that these will pay the rent (παρ'αὐτῶν ἐκφόρια), who are presently in the prison of the Apiones), 5383 (a. 583, for the half share of a leased irrigator and its rent).

indiction') under surety of their properties (P.Oxy. LXII 4350). In P.Oxy. LXXVII 5123 (a. 555) two *adscripticii* acknowledge that they owe a quantity of wine and other things to the estate, on the security of their property. The editor suggests that there remained enough for them to trade after paying the rent, either to the estate or to third parties. In P. Oxy. LXVII 4615 an *adscripticius* X of the hamlet Monimu leases from his master Flavius Strategius land which lies in another possession of the master. Similar cases we find in P.Oxy. LXXXII 5331 (a. 474)[55] and 5332 (a. 480).[56] In P.Oxy. LXXXII 5331 two *adscripticii*, brothers, lease land from somebody other than their landlord, the halfpart of an irrigator with associated land and the halfpart of a vineyard, from their master, with a secured rent to be paid on basis of the landowner's estate roll, regardless of the level of inundation. Here we are dealing with a standard lease, which shows that *adscripticii* could act as free farmer-entrepreneurs, albeit of course that they could not leave their estate definitively and that they paid rent.[57]

Since *coloni* who had moved out of their domicile could be recalled and had to acknowledge their obligations, it seems correct to assume that if somebody was liable to the adscripticiate by *origo*, he would have had unrestricted ownership of his assets until he was summoned and had acknowledged this obligation (and be registered in the census), in the same way as was done with *munera* on account of the registration in the census. At that moment his assets must have become subjected to the *potestas* of his master.

The *adscripticii* were under the *potestas* of their estate owners and had to perform the services that had been agreed if the owner ordered so. Such a dependency was in social life considered a servitude and it put somebody on the level of slaves. This dependency may have led to the restrictions on their assets which led to it being called a *peculium*. It served to maintain his ability to pay off his debt, in as far as that was possible. In this way an estate owner had a high degree of control over a free Roman citizen. But the documents show that *coloni* contracted, owned assets and pledged these; that within these restrictions they could wheel and deal as they liked.[58] This fits the picture of the life in the country as described by Sarris and Banaji of people occupied in a diversity of activities.

55 Here the leased land is situated in their own hamlet.

56 Here three sons lease with the consent of their father, evidence of his *patria potestas*.

57 Benaïssa 2020 has dealt intensively with the *adscripticii* as lessees on the Apion estate.

58 This is not a surprise. We know of slaves and (of course) freedmen who were tenant-lessees; see Scheidel 1993. Hence there would have been no obstacle for *coloni* to lease as farmers.

8 Paying Taxes

8.1 Taxes and Taxation

The colonate was, as the texts show, in some way connected with the taxation, and some authors assume it was introduced with a reorganisation of the taxes. In the early Byzantine empire everybody was, in principle, subjected to taxes of the kind we usually associate the word tax with nowadays, like the *capitatio* and the *tributum* or the *collatio lustralis* and next to that to public duties, *leitourgiai* or, in the legal sources, *honores* and *munera*.[59] The tax system consisted of a valuation of all the land according to categories of productivity and of all the people, alongside some special taxes. The land tax was undoubtedly the largest source of state income, next to the imperial estates. The assessment was expressed in *capita*, a unit of accounting, and by adding all the individual assessments by a graduated calculation the government got a redistribution scheme. This was applied to the expected expenditures, and by graduating regressively the actual real individual tax liability was set. It was a system which required much assessing and accounting, so that it is no wonder that in practice new assessments were avoided and adjustments were made through the books.[60] Further, everybody was also subjected to public obligations which required personal activity or exertion, or doing something which nowadays is done by public services. The membership of a town council, or the collection of taxes, or being night-watch, or maintaining roads were all such duties.

The *coloni* paid taxes themselves or their estate owners paid it for them (CJ 11.48.20pr). It concerned the *capitatio humana* (CJ 11.52.1), the tax levied per head of the population (the poll tax) and not the land tax they might have to pay.[61] It was levied on individuals according to a ratio (CJ 11.48.10), but the people in towns (*plebs urbana*) in the east were exempted

[59] Karayannopoulos 1958, 94–112 on the *annona* (the *tributum* on land), 178ff. on the *honores* and *munera*. Remarkably enough, Karayannopoulos mentions the *capitatio humana* in the context of the taxation systems of Diocletian (39, 40), mentions also the immunity of this tax for Thrace in CJ 11.52.1 (194), but does not spend a section on it. It seems he only considered it in the context of the census declaration of the estate. Hildesheim 1988 confirms the existence of the poll tax.

[60] See in general Karayannopoulos 1958. See CTh 13.10.7 and Thonemann 2007.

[61] Bagnall 1993, 154 mentions the *epikephalaion*, attested only at Oxyrhynchus, which perhaps was identical with this. The land tax they had to pay themselves: CJ 11.48.4. Bott 1928 distinguished between the *capitatio humana* and the *capitatio plebeian*. The latter cannot be the poll tax on urban people because this tax taxes labour. Hence it is only levied outside towns. The real distinction is that the first concerned the slaves and *coloni* on the land, the second the lower rank of society, the *humiliores*: Bott 1928, 48–68. Bott's distinction is of no consequence here.

from this (CJ 11.49.1); in the provinces of Illyricum, Thrace, and Palaestina it had been abolished altogether for the rural population (CJ 11.51.1, 11.52.1 and 11.53.1). Individuals had to furnish a declaration for themselves, which was registered.[62] We do not know whether these declarations were checked, but it could have been done, because Roman citizens had to register their newborns since Augustus and there were birth registers in all provincial centres.[63] Registers for the poll tax will have been maintained in the basic tax units, namely in *vici* and towns. A *vicus* (κώμη, also a *metrocomia*) was a block of houses or streets in a town,[64] or a village or hamlet, an unfortified country town, or even a large farm.[65] It had its specific boundary (CJ 6.25.9.1). It belonged administratively to a town, as the territory of the town did and as any possession in the territory did (CJ 1.3.28.4; 1.5.8.6; 5.27.3.1 and 4; 8.16.7.1; 10.19.8). The children of an *adscripticius* had to acknowledge their obligation in the *vicus* or on the estate of their father (CJ 11.48.23.1). They should reside on the estates (*fundi*) or in the *vicus*, evidently where the estate of their father lay to which they were attached (CJ 11.48.23.1). The *vicus* apparently served as a subdivision of the registration for taxes and the levy of this in a town.[66] Thus, regarding the taxation, rural people would have been entered as everybody else everywhere with wife and children in the census at so many *capita* per head (cfr. CJ 11.48.10) for the *capitatio humana*, which was assessed, and after a while mutated by repartition into a real tax and collected per unit, namely the *vicus*.

Registered *coloni* were entered next to this into the census (*professio censualis*) of a property, an estate (*fundus*, *praedium*), as, for example, said in CJ 11.48.4pr: *in locis isdem censitos*; with an extract (*apographos* (ἀπογρᾶφος), *adscriptio*) of what? Probably of their *conditionale instrumentum*, as an extract of the tax register does not seem to make sense. Since they were 'inserted' into the estate census by an 'extract' (*en-apographos*), we may assume that their assessments were primarily included in the village total. If the total assessment of a town consisted of the entirety of the individual assessments, it would merge in the end anyway into the single redistribution quote. Thus a *colonus* who entered the colonate will have remained registered in the poll tax register of his village, but was also registered in the census of

[62] For example, see Karayannopoulos 1958, 33 (on P. Kairo Boak 12, a. 309 and P. Straßb. Preisigke 42, a. 310). Unfortunately, he does not deal with the registration for the poll tax, nor do other authors.

[63] Marquardt 1886, Vol. 1, 86–87. Besson 2020, 174–179.

[64] Only in CJ 1.12.5.

[65] See Berger 1954, s.v. *vicus*.

[66] For the taxation in this context, see Sirks 2010b. On the legal aspects of the *vicus* in general, see Laquerrière-Lacroix 2009.

the estate.[67] He remained liable for the *capitatio humana*. The amount established on him and his family was entered in the estate census (CJ 11.48.10), but it remained a personal tax, as he also remained personally liable for liturgies. Some *coloni adscripticii* paid the poll tax themselves – in the village, entered into the village register – and if customarily, there was not a presumption that if they did not pay, the landowners were liable (CJ 11.48.20.3: *nullo praeiudicio dominis*). Others did not pay their *capitatio* themselves but their estate owner paid or guaranteed the payment (as said in CJ 11.48.20.3a). Apparently it depended on the agreement made which mode was chosen, but the second mode did not release the *colonus* from his liability. This is confirmed by CJ 11.48.20.3a and by P.Oxy. XXVII 2478 and LXIII 4398, where the *enapographoi* promise to render the tax to their estate owner. Did the estate owner pay it directly or through his census? Probably the latter, because the *adscripticius* was on his census. Absence was no reason to strike him off the list: he could be recalled. Also, by fleeing, the *adscripticius* no longer performed his part of the deal. That may have released the estate owner from his duty to advance the tax.[68] It follows that those who were fugitives and worked as independent labourers or lessees (CJ 11.48.8) had to pay the *capitatio* themselves, or the estate owner they had stayed with had to pay (CJ 11.48.8pr).

CJ 11.48.23.5 mentions *publicae functiones terrenae sive animales* which the person who *bona fide* harboured a fugitive *adscripticius* or 'free' *colonus* (the text distinguishes with *domino ipsius adscripticii vel terrae*) and refused to return him with his possessions (he may have needed his work force), had to pay these *functiones* for the time he was with him. The prefect or governor had to enforce this. What were these *publicae functiones*? They seem to be the taxes on land and animals.[69] In CJ 11.52.1pr the *iugatio* is *terrena*, meaning the assessment on land. It might be the land tax the *colonus* would have to pay if he had land. With the 'free' *coloni* the landowner could recall his *colonus*, and if he owned land and draught animals, taxes on these had to be paid.

[67] The references are always to being tied to a piece of land, which often must have been the registration of the land, which had to be done in the town in whose territory the land lay. In P. Oxy. XXVII 2479 (sixth c.) Pieous asks to be accepted again, with his children (see notes 81, 144). Such an enrolment would not have had the same personal law consequences as under the Republic the census had, namely slavery. But it implied a *deterior condicio*.

[68] See CJ 11.48.8pr–1 as interpreted below, Sections 12.2.2 and 25.2.2 for both statements.

[69] Cf. CJ 10.36.1 with *census humani vel animali*, that is, the tax on slaves and *coloni* or animals. CJ 11.48.23.5 is not dealt with by Karayannopoulos 1958.

8.2 *The* Colonus *as Taxpayer*

If a *colonus* owned land himself, it had to be registered in his own name in the census (CJ 11.48.4). In this case his estate owner was not liable for the payment of the tax on that land (the *tributum*, due by the owner of land): the *colonus* had to fill out his own *professio censualis*, be registered by the public recorders (*tabellarii*) in the *libri censuales* and acknowledge this duty himself (CJ 11.48.4.1).[70]

In CJ 11.48.20 of 529 Justinian regulates the case of a dispute in which *coloni* contest that someone is the owner of the land they live and work on.[71] Proceedings could take much time, and an *ad hoc* arrangement was necessary for the payment of rent and taxes during that time. This arrangement gives us a good view of the tax arrangements and who was liable for them. First Justinian deals with rents. For these a surety shall be given, or they shall be deposited in a church; or, if the *colonus* is a share-cropper, the governor shall sell the crops and deposit the money as prescribed.[72] After that Justinian deals with the taxes (*publicae functiones*) in CJ 11.48.20.3:

> Haec de reditibus definientes ad publicas transeamus functiones. Et si quidem coloni more solito eas dependant, ipsi maneant in pristina consuetudine, nullo praeiudicio dominis generando, qui et quiescentibus colonis et non contradicentibus ad publicum tributarias functiones minime inferebant.

[70] Grey 2007, 172 n. 94 reads this text as if the *coloni* (for him: tenants) became responsible for the estate's taxes by their registration as *originales*. It is the reverse: the registration as *originales* makes their estate owner liable for the taxes of the *coloni*. But if the *coloni* possessed land of themselves, they were responsible – as owners, not as lessees or land labourers – for the taxes on that land regardless of their being *originales*. He cites me on 172 n. 98 for his assertion that 'registration though a landowner's tax declaration on a particular *origo* made tenants visible in the municipal or imperial tax rolls, so that they could be held responsible for the *munera* of that land', but *tenants* would not become liable in this way, nor did I state that (see Sirks 1993b, 165). The text he cites in n. 98, CJ 11.48.11, does not say anything on this point. For the meaning of *recepta* in the text, see Section 23.3 on its Theodosian version.

[71] Could the *coloni* have pretended to be owner? In that case they should have declared their land in a *professio censualis*. Perhaps, although we do not know whether the *tabellarii* would have accepted such a presumption without proof. It is not impossible but improbable. Since the emperor is only concerned about rent and taxes, this question is not dealt with.

[72] The *coloni* would, of course, not be willing to pay anything as long as their claim had not been decided, during which time the defending owner would not dispose of the revenues. Therefore Justinian ruled that the *coloni* had to give surety for a period of three years for the entire sum which they owed (i.e., the revenues, *reditus*) if they lost their case; which surety should be renewed if necessary. If the *coloni* were unwilling to do this, the bureau of the governor would annually collect the revenues and deposit these in the treasury of the city in whose territory the estate lay, or in a local church if suitable and otherwise in the metropolitan church, in anticipation of the outcome of the lawsuit. Were the revenues not in specie but in kind, the bureau should sell it and deposit the money received.

3a. Sin autem moris erat dominos totam summam accipere et ex ea partem quidem in publicas vertere functiones, partem autem in suos reditus habere, tunc, si quidem fideiussor a colonis detur, eundem fideiussorem dominis sine praeiudicio litis tantam summam inferre, quantam tributa publica faciunt, ut a dominis publicis rationibus persolvatur: nullo ex hoc colonis praeiudicio generando. Super reditibus enim domini fideiussore fiant contenti.

3. After setting these rules concerning rents, let Us go over to public payments (*functiones*). And if indeed *coloni* should pay them in the customary manner, they are to remain in their former condition, with no prejudice to be created for the landowners, who, with the acquiescence of the *coloni* and without their contradicting this, were not making payments to the public treasury.

3a. But if it was the custom for the landowners to receive the whole sum and to turn over part of that for public payments and to have part for their own rents, then, if indeed a surety should be given by the *coloni*, then the surety shall pay the landowners the same sum as the public taxes represent, without generating any prejudice from this for the *coloni*. For concerning the rents the landowners should be content with the surety.

Justinian distinguishes two possibilities: either *coloni* pay tax directly to the tax collectors or their landowners do this as intermediaries, if the *coloni* are their lessees and pay a lump sum. The first way is customary (*more solito*), which means that the *coloni* had to pay themselves their tax, namely their poll tax. This is because only if the *coloni* owned land, they had to pay the land tax themselves where the land lay, so that, apart from the tax on trading if they traded, only the poll tax remains. Since the pretending owner never paid this, there is no prejudice that he is in any way liable for this.

The text shows that there were several ways in which the *coloni* were engaged on the estate. They could be farm hands or lessees, and if lessees, paying a sum, or part of, or the whole crop to the lessor-landowner. In the latter case, the whole crop, it is probable that after deduction of the rent, they received some money or got a credit in the estate accounts. This fits the picture Sarris has drawn for the Apion estates (see Section 9). Next to that there were two ways for them to pay their poll tax. One way, the normal way, was that they paid it directly to the tax collector. The other way was that they let the estate owner pay it. This was apparently usual if they were lessees and turned over a lump sum or part of the revenues which included their poll tax. The landowner kept the rent for himself and turned over the tax to the collector.

This finishes the idea that the landowners were appointed as tax collectors by Diocletian or that it had become the custom that the 'grand domains' had usurped this function. The landowner functions, as the text makes clear, as intermediary and that only if it was customary or, as we may assume, was agreed. If the *coloni* paid directly, the landowner had no role in the process.

The text deals with *coloni* who were bound to the estate, thus *adscripticii* or *coloni liberi* (*cuiuscumque conditionis*), since it is in the context of litigation about whether the landowner is indeed legally owner of the land.[73] If it merely concerned leases, there would be no reason to say that the fact that the *coloni* pay the poll tax themselves creates no prejudice towards the landowner. Such a prejudice could only concern his pretended ownership. If there was no question of the colonate, payment of the poll tax would not matter at all. But with the colonate it is different, since the *coloni* are in this case entered in his census and the owner is entitled to their presence and services.

In that case, if the *coloni* pay it themselves, it might create the impression that they are not registered and therefore not subjected to the landowner and that the landowner is not legally owner. Then, the tax register was used as property register if the possessor of the land could not bring up a limitation of prescription (the *praescriptio longissimi temporis*) or that revenues had been received for time immemorial (*inveterata redituum susceptione*).[74] Against such evidence the *coloni* stood no chance. It is to this latter aspect that CJ 4.21.19 (529), enacted a month before CJ 11.48.20, refers, when the constitution mentions *coloni* who deny that they have receipts of the revenues delivered (*apochae redituum*) and by that hope to undermine the claim of the landowner as *dominus terrae*. To avoid that, the constitution prescribes from now onwards *antapochae* (contrareceipts), so that the estate owner has proof that he has given receipts. If the landowner had to rely on the tax registers, it became important that he had paid the land tax. If he maintained that he had a right to the people on the land as his *coloni originales*, he had also to prove that he paid or was surety for their poll tax. Justinian is lenient to the landowner by saying that if the *coloni* customarily paid it themselves, it still does not prejudice against the landowner. That makes the burden of proof heavier for the resisting *coloni*, but it accommodates his case against *coloni liberi* who do not pay the poll tax.

So why did the *coloni* contest the ownership? Were they not pleased with the present possessor? Or had they not been burdened with colonate claims until a new owner appeared and did they not want to be subjected to this? But in that case it would suffice to deny merely the colonate status, not the ownership of the land as such. Since there is no evidence of a limitation of

[73] *Coloni liberi* were not immune from the poll tax unless they lived in a province where this was abolished (see Section 16), and the general rule of CJ 11.48.19 (see Section 13.2) did not release them from it.

[74] The first possibility is according to the law of property, the second merely proves that he was authorised to grant the use. That could comprise emphyteusis or a *locatio in perpetuum*.

prescription, it must concern land that had been long without a possessor. On the land were farmers who claimed to be lessees (but will not have paid rent). Apparently somebody now claimed it and lacking legal documents the tax registers were used. In that context the colonate turns up.

The question now is: What kind of tax did the *adscripticii* pay? On this, the next section.

8.3 The Landowner Is Factually and Administratively Surety of the Capitatio Humana

We have seen that the *adscripticius* could pay his own tax, but that it happened that the estate owner did this. Was this done by a private agreement? In itself there was no objection to guaranteeing somebody else's debts or taxes. Roman law sources abound with personal sureties. They required a *cautio*, a verbal or, preferably, written promise to pay if the debtor could not pay. Justinian granted the surety the right to demand that the creditor first sue the debtor before approaching him (the *beneficium excussionis*, Nov. 4.1 of 535). But this was in private law.[75]

In administrative law things were different, as CJ 11.48.4 shows:

> Ii, penes quos fundorum dominia sunt, pro his colonis originalibus, quos in locis isdem censitos esse constabit, vel per se vel per actores proprios recepta conpulsionis sollicitudine implenda munia functionis agnoscant. 1. Sane quibus terrarum erit quantulacumque possessio, qui in suis conscripti locis proprio nomine libris censualibus detinentur, ab huius praecepti communione discernimus: eos enim convenit propriae commissos mediocritati annonarias functiones sub solito exactore cognoscere.

> Those with whom the ownership of estates resides, have to acknowledge for those *coloni originales*, of whom it is established that they are registered in the same places, either by themselves or through their own agents the fulfilment of the obligations of the tax, after the responsibility for the urging was accepted. 1. Certainly we exclude from this order those who have land, however small and who, registered in their own places, are included in their own name in the tax registers. For it is appropriate for these, leaning on their own modest resources, to acknowledge the land tax with the customary tax collector. (tr. Sirks)

This is a key text for the relation between *colonus* and estate owner. The first part deals with the *capitatio humana*, because in the second part the land tax is mentioned. The *coloni* are registered on the estates, that is, in the census for these estates. That registration implied or was the

[75] Kaser 1971, 457–461, 1975, 660–666.

consequence of an agreement to give surety for payment of the poll tax.[76] The estate owners have to acknowledge, either by themselves in person or through their stewards (*procuratores*; which will often have been the case with absentee landowners), that the obligations of the tax (*functio*) of their *coloni originales* (i.e., *adscripticii*) will be fulfilled. This is a guarantee for the obligations of the *coloni*. But apparently they had also to guarantee that they would urge them to pay the tax. This means that it was in the first place the *coloni* who had to pay.

This description of the guarantee, laid down in the registration of the *colonus*, matches with D. 50.15.4.8, where the registration of *coloni* in the estate census is prescribed. The penalty for not mentioning them in the census declaration was that the estate owner was liable for their tax notwithstanding that they were not declared in the census (D. 50.15.4.8: *vinculis censualibus tenetur*). If the owner did not have to pay tax for them at all, the penalty would be incomprehensible. It follows that the registration established the duty of the estate owner to pay or guarantee the taxes of his *adscripticii*, that is, to the tax collectors[77]

Other arguments that it concerned the *capitatio humana* are: (a) the tariff for this being placed in the middle of CJ 11.48, in CJ 11.48.10, (b) the positioning of CJ 11.49.1 with the exemption of the urban *plebs* in the east and some provinces in Asia Minor in the middle of the titles on *coloni*, (c) CJ 11.52–53 (see for these texts Section 16), and (d) Nov. 128.14 (see below). Further, the *adscripticius* who became a cleric would have to acknowledge again the *capitatio* when released by his function from the adscripticiate (and set a substitute for his service) (CJ 1.3.16). Immunities in the public registers and tax records of cities and provinces given with regard

[76] Hickey 2012, 82 mentions that some authors think the poll tax was abolished in Byzantine Egypt. He, however, opines that the principal tax the landowner guaranteed may well have been the *capitatio humana*, that is, the *synteleia kephales* in the accounts of the *pronoetai* in Oxyrhynchus. To his factual argument I would add that in view of CJ 11.48.10 and 11.49.1, which expressly mention the poll tax, it is absurd to assume that it was not levied under Justinian. It cannot be, as Vera 1997 = Vera 2019, 265 opines, that the landowners had taken upon them to collect the tax. For Justinian's times this does not agree with CJ 11.48.20.3 as set out above in Section 8.2, where there is no such duty discernible and *coloni* pay directly. Pharr 1952 translates the crucial passages as: 'he shall accept the responsibility for compulsion [n. 33: tax collection], and he shall assume the fulfilment of the duties of this compulsory service for . . .'.

[77] It would mean (see CJ 11.48.4pr) that he would be liable anyway. He could recover the tax from them. If a registered *colonus* was exempted, as were the *coloni liberi*, his liability had no consequences. The phrase D. 50.15.4.8 must have been interpolated (see Section 4). Rosafio 1991b, 264 thinks it concerns tenants and the *tributum soli*, since it would be absurd to pay the *capitatio* for an unregistered *colonus*. Yet that is precisely the point: not registered means that the estate owner profited from them, but that the state would lose the tax. It is a situation also counteracted by CJ 11.48.8pr. Further, paying the tax for somebody else is not the same as collecting his tax.

to the *capitatio* and *iugatio* on an estate, which could include *coloni censiti* and so deprive the fisc of income, were unacceptable if they could not be proven (i.e., they were most likely acquired by bribery; CJ 11.48.9). Documents of the sixth century point in the same direction.[78]

As regards the land tax, Nov. 128.14 of 545 states that no one should be bothered for land he does not possess, likewise not for farmers who are subjected to somebody else, nor for *adscripticii* who have their own plot of land (these have to pay the land tax themselves): unless he has obliged himself (as surety) for that tax: 'unless perhaps he made himself of his own will liable for such tax' (εἰ μὴ ὡς εἰκὸς αὐτὸς ἰδίᾳ προαιρέσει τῇ τοιαύτῃ συντελείᾳ ἑαυτὸν ἐποίησεν ἔνοχον – *katapodas*: *nisi forte propria voluntate tali functioni se fecit obnoxius*). Here the prescription of CJ 11.48.4.1 is continued.

Whatever the origin of the agreement between estate owner and *adscripticius* in spe may have been, as long as it amounted to a surety, the registration in the census functioned as a factual surety because the estate owner inserted in his declaration the *adscripticius* as his *colonus* and so for his *capitatio humana*. Thus a formal surety (*cautio*) was not required. But as CJ 11.48.20 and 22 demonstrate, the contents of the original agreement specified the legal situation, and the fact that the *colonus adscripticius* remained a free person made him remain the original tax payer.

What apparently happened was that tax collectors tried to make other people pay, perhaps to cover deficits elsewhere. It was not uncommon to equalise differences in the books by combining posts. But the tax collector (*exactor*) was not allowed to summon *coloni originales* for the fiscal debts of anybody (to create a post with an excess to make it compensate a deficient post). These farmers had to remain all the time on their land (CJ 11.48.15), nor could anything be taken from them which pertained to farming, because that would hinder farming (CJ 8.16.8).[79] That, however, also restricted the capacity to seize their goods for other debts.

It is evident from these and other texts that continuous and good farming was the reason for the colonate. As regards the *capitatio*, perhaps there was in some places a collective fiscal responsibility (see Section 33).[80] The consequence of the colonate arrangement was (a) that the *adscripticius*

[78] Hickey 2012, 81; Bransbourg 2016, 331–333.

[79] Codex of Justinian 2016 translates *fiscalium nomine debitorum* as 'on account of debts owed to the Treasury'; OSS has 'Namens fiscalischer Schuldner'. *Debitorum* may derive from *debitum* but also from *debitor*. Since the estate owner was primarily liable for the poll tax of his *adscripticii*, it must refer to the fiscal debts of other people.

[80] Hence perhaps a collective liability for those living in the same *vicus*, if the entire *vicus* was part of an estate: CTh 11.24.6, evidently abolished by Zeno (CJ 11.57.1, 474–491).

did not have to worry about state tax collectors if he could not pay, but (b) that if the estate owner had paid, the *adscripticius* now owed him this amount and the estate owner could recover this, or, with the same result, that the estate owner advanced the money.[81] It will likely have led to a permanent indebtedness of the *colonus*.

It has been suggested that the origin of the colonate lay in the attribution to estate owners to levy the tax from their lessees (see Section 1). As may appear from the above, it is correct that the *coloni*, who were in their adscripticiate relation in any case not lessees in the private law sense, were the tax payers. But it may also be clear that where the estate owner paid the tax directly, it was done by private arrangement and that in other cases it remained the *colonus* who paid it himself. The titles on the taxes and their collection in Justinian's Code do not give any reason to assume that in this period estate owners functioned as official tax collectors. CJ 10.16–30, which deal with the tax levy, do not mention them as such. Taxes are levied by persons who, in view of their designation, like *ducenarii*, *opinatores*, and *canonicarii*, cannot but have been officials in the exercise of their function. They may have been private landowners but did not act in that capacity (CJ 10.19.1, 6, 7, 9).

On the other hand, this arrangement meant that landowners with little or no financial reserves were not suitable guarantors. Further, the use of *adscripticii* was limited. Since they exercised various occupations (see Section 9), they will not have been required to provide yearlong continuous labour. If they paid off the credit for the tax by working, their contribution will have been more of a supplementary nature, unless they also leased land. Consequently their use will have been efficient for large estates, not for small estates. We may expect the adscripticiate where large estates existed, with sufficient capital. In Egypt the estates of the Apiones, a wealthy family, indeed used *adscripticii*.

9 Occupations of *Coloni*

The colonate was a relationship in which, as we saw, three elements were essential: the obligation of the *colonus* to perform services for the estate owner and to stay on or close to the estate, and the obligation of the estate owner to

[81] See P.Oxy. XXVII 2479 (sixth century). The farmer Pieous, a fugitive *enapographos*, cannot pay the taxes out of what he sows, thus he asks to be registered again, with his family, as *enapographoi*. This implies that his landlord will take over the tax duty. Triantaphyllopoulos 1967 has suggested that the fled *colonus* asked for remission of three years taxes and not rent, and that it was the procurator of the taxes who had seized his possessions, assuming that the landlord had paid the taxes (in this sense also Carrié 1984, 944). Yet this leads to the impossible result that the fisc who is satisfied nevertheless tries to seize the goods of someone who is no longer debtor. It should be the procurator of the landlord, then, who tries to recover the costs and the tax paid for him and his family. See further note 144.

secure payment of the *colonus*' poll tax. Their obligations would have been those connected to the *condicio adscripticia* (or, as it is said in the papyri, the *tychè enapographè* or *tychè georgikès*) but left them time for other occupations. As it happens, we see indeed in the papyri *adscripticii* with various occupations; when they are named *enapographoi georgoi*, it merely denotes their status, while *georgos* (γεωργός) does not necessarily mean they are actually farmers.[82] Likewise, we see that they own assets which they pledge.[83]

These elements could be varied in the way they were performed and combined with other arrangements. It appears that the colonate was a method by which a landowner could secure for himself labour, available at the time he needed, at a low cost (he only had to pay for the time worked) or without pay. In agriculture, where the change of seasons brings a fluctuation in work (CJ 11.48.1 mentions these periods), that is an advantage. It was better than having slaves whom he had to feed all year around. That this was indeed seen as a profitable way follows from the fact that the emperors supported it, if only out of self-interest (continuous and abundant taxes, better revenues from their own lands). Continuity in agricultural exploitation was important.

That the colonate provided labour on demand had a consequence: these labourers had to find an income if they did not want to live on the credit of the estate owner. Some were lessees, paying a rent, which presumes that they traded in the crop of their land, others were share-croppers, as CJ 11.48.20pr shows. Vera has pointed out the different concepts of agricultural exploitation behind this dichotomy.[84] The idea that in Late Antiquity large landholdings dominated the countryside is being nuanced; reality must have been more varied, and on those landholdings reality must also have been varied.

One of these was the household of the Apiones in Oxyrhynchus in the sixth century. Sarris has analysed its economic structure.[85] Their property

[82] It is therefore correct that in the latest editions of the P.Oxy. the designation *enapographos* (ἐναπόγραφος) is removed from the general list of words; it should be under statuses or liturgies.

[83] Apart from the mention in legal texts of their *peculium* and the prohibition on selling without consent, a striking example of this is P.Oxy. LXX 4794, where Ieremias, former headman and *enapographos georgos* (ἐναπόγραφος γεωργός), gives surety and pledge, and pledges all his belongings present and for the future, in particular and in general, by way of security and by right of mortgage. Another text in which *adscripticii* pledge for the contract of tax collection: P.Oxy. LXII 4350 (a. 576). See Section 7 on *peculium*.

[84] Vera 1986 = Vera 2019, 61.

[85] Sarris 2006. Further on great estates and the patronage exercised: Fikhman 1974 = 2006, 42–47; Sarris 2009; Puliatti 2017. On the leasing by slaves and freedmen, Scheidel 1999.

consisted of directly managed estates (*autourgiai*), leased property (*ktèmata*, village properties) and leased urban properties. The management of these was done by overseers (*pronoètai*). These issued the employed people credit notes (*pittakia*) as payment for their work which could be exchanged for small denomination money. Thus it was a highly monetarised economy. Amongst the *ktèmata* there were *epoikia*, each run by a *phrontistès*. These *epoikia* functioned as a kind of labour settlements from which the workforce necessary to cultivate the *autourgiai* was recruited. *Ktèmata* were also leased to these people and the revenues were in part used to support the *autourgiai*. Next to the people from the *ktèmata* there were *paidaria*, slaves, working on the *autorgiai*. It appears that the people in the *epoikia* were not workless paupers but on the contrary engaged in all kinds of economic and commercial activities. Yet they, or part of them, were also regularly summoned to work on the *autourgiai*. It is with these that we may look for *adscripticii*, if the summons were based on their duty. They too will have been paid something.[86] Hickey found that there were relatively not many *adscripticii* amongst the labour force on the Apiones estate.[87]

Papyri of the sixth century provide ample proof that the reality on such an estate could be varied and that different kinds of work were pursued, also by *coloni*. In a number of papyri mention is made of *enapographoi georgoi* (ἐναπόγραφοι γεωργοί, i.e., *coloni adscripticii*). Fikhman has thoroughly analysed them.[88] They cover the period from 441 (or, in any case, 469) till AD 616,[89] thus including the period covered by Justinian's codification and legislation. Fikhman indeed makes comparisons with laws of Justinian's reign. He observes that the term ἐναπόγραφος is found not only with farmers (γεωργός), but also with other professions or occupations like guard, gardener, and sailor.[90] Many of these papyri come from the Apion estate. *Coloni adscripticii* could combine their duties with diverse occupations. They could be a steward on their own estate or on another estate

[86] Sarris 2006, 29–70. [87] Hickey 2012, 83. Further Benaïssa 2020.

[88] Fikhman 1984. This article was originally published in 1984 in Russian, but is now accessible in German in his *Kleine Schriften* (Fikhman 2006, 190–250). The article is important not only because of Fikhman's observations, but also for the Russian articles he refers to and discusses, which enables the reader who is not capable of reading Russian to form an opinion of Russian scholarship. Other important articles by this author are Fikhman 1978, 1981, 1990, all reprinted in Fikhman 2006. Further, Sarris 2006, 60–66.

[89] Fikhman 1984 = 2006, 194–195.

[90] Fikhman 1984 = 2006, 194: P. London III 778 (ἀγροφύλαξ, guard), P.Oxy. XXVII 2478 (πωμαρίτης, fruit-grower). Now also P.Oxy. LXXXIII 5384 (a. 584) with a ναύτης. This tallies with our observation that a *colonus* might be tied through his *origo* and not be a farmer.

(P.Oxy. XVI 1985; 1896; P. Amherst II 149, P. Erlangen 37); be a guard (P. Oxy. XVI 1979); or be a fruit-grower (P.Oxy. XXVII 2478 and P.Oxy. LXIX 4789, a fruit-grower 'of the glorious house', but here we do not know whether it concerns a *colonus*). One sold wine (P.Oxy. XLIX 3512). They could collect all public taxes (πάντα τὰ δημόσια τῆς δεκάτης ἐπινεμήσεως) under surety of their properties (P.Oxy. LXII 4350, a. 576):

> ... To Flavius Apion, the all-honoured and most magnificent former *consul ordinarius* and patrician, landowner here also in the New City of Justinus, through his servant Menas, who asks the formal question and assumes the management and responsibility for his own master,[91] the same all-honoured man, Aurelius Anup manager, son of Jeremias, and Aurelius Pamouthius son of Anup, and another Aurelius Pamouthius, scribe, son of Praus, all from the farmstead [*epoikion*] Sasos Cato which belongs to your magnificence, registered cultivators [*enapographoi georgoi*] of yours, greetings. By our present written bond we acknowledge that we are free from deceit [*dolus*], fear, violence, guile or compulsion, prepared to collect all the public dues for the tenth indiction at our own risk and that of the property of each of us, and to pay these to the glorious household and to leave no part of them in arrears; but if some of the said public dues for the tenth indiction should chance to remain uncollected we agree under mutual responsibility for each other to give these to your magnificence without delay at the risk of our property ... (after Shelton et al. 1995)[92]

In this case Aurelius Anup, Aurelius Pamuthius, and another Aurelius Pamuthius (a scribe!) acknowledged that they would collect the taxes to Flavius Apion, their estate owner, at the risk of their own property and giving at the same time a mutual security. A similar acknowledgement we see in P.Oxy. LXII 4351. Presumably it concerns the taxes in the village or district. So what we have here is an arrangement for the collection, likely set up by a manager of Apion and confirmed in this way by those who have to undertake it. In short: Apion arranged the performance of liturgies in the village. Then, *coloni* would also have to perform liturgies in their village and, as these texts show, this could also be arranged by the estate owner.

91 It seems to me that this means Menas is authorised to stipulate and contract for Apion.

92 P.Oxy. LXII 4350: Φλ(αουΐῳ) Ἀπίωνι τῷ πανευφήμῳ καὶ ὑπερφυεστάτῳ ἀπὸ ὑπάτων ὀρδιναρίων καὶ πατρικίῳ, γεουχοῦντι/ καὶ ἐνταῦθα τῇ Νέᾳ Ἰουστίνου πόλει, διὰ Μηνᾶ οἰκέτου τοῦ ἐπερωτῶντος καὶ προσπορίζοντος τῷ ἰδίῳ/ δεσπότῃ τῷ αὐτῷ πανευφήμῳ ἀνδρὶ τὴν ἀγωγὴν καὶ ἐνοχήν, Αὐρήλιοι Ἀνοῦπ φροντιστής, υἱὸς/ Ἰερημίου, καὶ Παμούθιος υἱὸς Ἀνοῦπ καὶ Παμούθιος ἕτερος, γραμμ(ατεύς), υἱὸς Πραοῦτος, οἱ πάντες ὁρμώμενοι ἀπὸ ἐποικίου Σάσου Κάτω διαφέροντος τῇ ὑμῶν ὑπερφυείᾳ, ἐναπόγραφοι αὐτῆς γεωργοί, χαίρειν./ ὁμολογοῦμεν διὰ τῆς παρούσης ἡμῶν ἐγγράφου ἀσφαλείας ἐκτὸς δόλου καὶ φόβου καὶ βίας καὶ/ ιοἀπάτης κα[ὶ] ἀνάγκης ἑτοίμως ἔχειν πάντα τὰ δημόσια τῆς δεκάτης ἐπινεμήσεως εἰσπρᾶξαι κινδύνῳ ἡμῶν καὶ τῆς ἑκάστου ἡμῶν ὑποστάσεως καὶ καταβαλεῖν εἰς τὸν ἔνδοξον οἶκον καὶ μηδὲν τὸ σύνολον ἐξ αὐτῶν ἐᾶσαι ἐν λοιπάδι./ etc.

In P.Oxy. LXVII 4615 an *adscripticius* X of the hamlet Monimu leases from his master Flavius Strategius land which lies in another possession of the master. Similar cases we find in P.Oxy. 5331 (a. 474)[93] and 5332 (a. 480).[94] In these cases there was evidently no conflict with their colonate obligations, presumably because it was not a field they were ordered to work on. Receipts provide us with much information.[95] Apollos and Pecysis were charged with the estate irrigator (P.Oxy. LXVII 4697). The same charge was executed by Apollos and Victor (P.Oxy. LXIX 4755), Anup (P.Oxy. LXX 4781), Y (P.Oxy. LXIX 4782), Epimachus (P. Oxy. LXIX 4784), Pamuthius and Menas (P.Oxy. LXIX 4785), Psan (P. Oxy. LXIX 4793), and Apaor (P.Oxy. LXIX 4788). In the latter case the price of a new axle, provided by the estate owner, is credited to Apaor. It implies that Apaor has to pay for it. The same happens to an *adscripticia*, Aurelia Tarilla, who was also in charge of an estate irrigator and needed to replace an axle, the price of which was put down to her account (P.Oxy. LXIX 4797, a. 593):

> ... to the masters, the same all-renowned men, the conduct of and responsibility for (the transaction), I, Aurelia Tarilla, daughter of Andreas, mother Nonna, originating from the hamlet (*epoikion*) of Tryne, as holding of your excellence, of the Oxyrhynchite nome, your *enapographos georgos*, greetings, etc. (after Gonis et al. 2005)[96]

It is interesting that Tarilla calls herself an *enapographos georgos*, in the male form. The adjective might also refer to a female, but with *georgos* it is unlikely. It would seem that she described herself as being of a status and not being particularly a farmer. It would correspond to the *adscripticia* as generic reference we find in the legal texts. There are also *adscripticiae* in P.Oxy. LXIX 4800 and 4801, PSI 52, P. Washington University I 25.[97] Whether or how these expenditures were compensated we do not know. They may also have been paid by credits in the

[93] Here the leased land is situated in their own hamlet.

[94] Here three sons lease with the consent of their father, evidence of his *patria potestas*.

[95] Receipts by *adscripticii* for machine parts: P.Oxy. I 137, LXVII 4616, LXVIII 4697, LXIX 4755 (?), LXX 4781, 4782, 4784, 4788, 4793, 4796, 4797 (*adscripticia*), 4798, 4799, 4801 (*adscripticia*). Further cases where an *adscripticius* acknowledges a receipt: LXXXIII 5385 (584, receipt for a cogwheel), 5398 (588, receipt for a cogwheel), 5393 (591, receipt for an axle, the *adscripticius* is in charge of an estate irrigator), 5394 (592, receipt for replacement part of an irrigator). On this aspect of the adscripticiate see now Hickey 2012, 85–86.

[96] P.Oxy. LXIX 4797: – – – – – – – – – – – –/ 1 [δεσπόταις τοῖς αὐτοῖς πανευφήμοις ἀνδρά]σ̣[ιν τὴν ἀγωγὴν καὶ]/ ἐνοχήν, Αὐρηλ[ί]α [Τα]ρ̣ίλλα θυγάτηρ Ἀνδρέου μητρὸς/ Νόννας ὁρμωμένη ἀπὸ ἐποικίου Τρυνε κτήματος/ τῆς ὑ(*)μῶν ὑ(*)περφυείας τοῦ Ὀξυρυγχίτου νομοῦ ἐναπόγραφος/ αὐτῆς γεωργός, χαίρειν. etc.

[97] On women in agriculture, see Rowlandson 1996, 263–264.

estate bookkeeping.[98] An Apollos needed a cogwheel for the irrigation machine (P.Oxy. LXIX 4798), likewise Phoebammon (P.Oxy. LXIX 4799).

In P.Oxy. LXIX 4794 there is Ieremias, a former headman of the village (ἀπὸ μειζόνων). There is no reason why *adscripticii* should not have been able to perform such tasks. In P. Amherst II 149 we meet Aur. Anoup, a superintendent in charge of a garden (φροντιστὴς κηπουρὸς) who is registered. He gives a *cautio* for a loan from the owner of the garden. It appears that being a *colonus* did not always mean you had to till the land, but we have of course to take account of the transmission of documents. In the above cases a document would be drawn up, in the case of a farmer only if he borrowed seed or money (and of these we have also documents). But all these occupations are part of agriculture, the exploitation of the land where the colonate fits in. Could it be in the case of the irrigation works that the estate owner used the adscripticiate to charge capable individuals with the management of this important agricultural machinery? Since two managers are women, it is not likely that they would do heavy work, but they could have been good managers. The advantage for the estate owner would be that these subordinates could never quit their job, would always be on the spot and thus be more under his control, as would be their assets.

Hickey thinks that the *enapographoi* of Oxyrhynchus were drawn from the same labour pool as the individuals who worked on a labour contract. Although the latter seem to have been preferred for viticulture and the former for irrigation work, we should consider wage labour as the starting point for research into the adscripticiate.[99] Hickey's observations fit almost seamlessly my conclusions, that the colonate was merely a special credit/labour agreement with particular consequences, but that it left the overall capacity of the *colonus* to work or undertake unimpaired, that it provided a labour supply on demand and that many *coloni* will have been farm hands.

[98] By this is meant the system we know from the Heroninos archive, that on an estate account books were kept in which entries were made for things bought by the labourers from the estate and for salaries earned: Rathbone 1991, 166ff.; for the system in the sixth century, see P.Oxy. LXX 4788, 4797 and P. Oxy. LXXVII 5123 referring to such accounts; cf. also CJ 11.48.8.2 and Sirks 1993a, 362–364. See further Hickey 2012, 85–86. He rightly remarks that my estimate of an *adscripticius*' reward as 'some food and some pocket money' is too meagre. It will have depended on the service he performed. CJ 11.48.20 speaks of the *reditus* contributed by *adscripticii*, but we do not know how much that was; likely it varied, as CJ 11.50.1 indicates.

[99] Hickey 2012, 83.

Nothing is said in CJ 11.48 about lessees and agricultural workers not tied to an estate, but that is not what the title is about and thus not to be expected. They figure in CJ 4.44.65 and other texts.[100] If *coloni adscripticii* or *liberi* were lessees (see above and Section 16 for the possibility), those texts would also apply to them, because we do not see in CJ 11.48.20 that for *adscripticii* and 'free' *coloni* a particular regime regarding the contract of lease (*locatio conductio*) existed. They would have to pay a rent or be share-cropper, as CJ 11.48.20pr says (cfr. also P.Oxy. LXVII 4615).[101] If their duties left them enough time, there is no reason why they could not have rented land and worked on it, or done something else. Or their landlord may merely have wanted them to stay in the village and lease a plot. After all, the main advantage of the colonate was that the *coloni* were resident and available.

10 Transmission of the *Condicio* and the Effect of the Abolition of the *Senatusconsultum Claudianum*

10.1 Transmission of the Condicio

The home town (*origo*) was of great importance in Late Antiquity because of the obligations attached to the citizenship of a town, namely the liturgies (*munera*) and taxes (CJ 10.39.1, 3, 5).[102] The taxation structure of the Empire was based on this, the towns and their territories being the basic tax units. It derived from the time when the Mediterranean world was a patchwork of independent and autonomous cities that could summon their citizens for public duties. It determined one's home town (*patria*) and, notwithstanding Rome's political dominance, consequently one's public and eventually private law system (except of course Roman *municipia*, which followed Rome and *coloniae*). After AD 212 almost all peregrines in the Empire became Romans. Both Roman citizenship, one's *condicio*, and the citizenship of a town, now called *origo*, were determined primarily by paternal descendance from a citizen.[103] *Condicio* and *origo* passed on in the same way

[100] See Section 4, note 14.

[101] One may think of somebody who is *adscripticius* or 'free' *colonus* by birth but not obliged by his estate owner to work on his original estate (e.g., because there is sufficient labour force). He could rent land somewhere else and work on it.

[102] See Nörr 1963 and Section 2.3.1.

[103] CJ 10.40.7 enumerates *origo manumissio adlectio adoptio* as determining citizenship. Of course next to that there was the grant of citizenship by the emperor.

they had done previously: in legitimate marriages from a father onto his children (CJ 8.47.7, 10.39.3), otherwise from mother onto her children.[104] Freedmen took their manumitter's *origo* (cf. CJ 7.14.1, 10.39.2), which explains the application of the 'free' colonate in Illyricum to freedmen of *coloni* (CJ 11.53.1.3). A wife kept her own *origo*.[105]

Someone could not remove or change his *origo* by himself (CJ 10.39.4), and if he tried to change his *origo* by becoming a resident (*incola*) in another town, he would be subjected to the public duties of both towns (CJ 10.39.1 and 5). Living somewhere else did not have to imply such a change. These constitutions are in Justinian's Code in the title *De municipiis et originariis*. Four of the five constitutions deal with the *origo* as basis for the imposition of *munera*. One, CJ 10.39.4 (a constitution originally issued in 293/294), is a general statement that nobody can change his *origo*. It of course applies to *municipes*. But since Justinian's compilers will not have designed rubrics without a purpose, it seems very likely that *originarii* in the rubric particularly refers to this constitution, while the *municipii* point to the other constitutions. For Justinian's times this would be perfectly correct. *Coloni originarii* could not escape their estate on their own. But the term *originarii* in the addition also indicates that their status had changed into something more than being the inhabitant of a village or town. Otherwise, these might be called *originarii* also.

These rules also applied to the *coloni*, whether registered or not. Since most or all of them will have lived in villages and hamlets (*vici*), these were their *origines*.

[104] Kaser 1975, 279. After 212 Rome became *communis patria*, which implies that it was the *patria* next to one's own *patria*. But a change in domicile could imply additional eligibility for *munera* of one's residence, cf. D. 50.1.20. On this, see further Sirks 1993b, 165–166, where the significance of the *origo* for public duties is set out next to other criteria important in this respect, and Sirks 1993a, 347, where the link is made as well. Also Sirks 2005, 138, where it is set out how this *senatusconsultum* effected a deviation from the intergentile private law rule on status as regarded unions between free women and slaves. The inequity Gai 1.84 refers to in this context is the case that the owner of the slave agrees not to enslave the woman, but that, due to the *senatusconsultum*, she will bear slaves. Hadrian corrected this: in such a case she would bear free children. Unfortunately this has not been taken into account by Grey 2007, 156 and 170–171. Saumagne 1937, 506 sees the land as the *dominus* and the *colonus* as its *servus*. Legally this does not make sense, nor does Saumagne's assertion that the land is the subject of a right to the *colonus*. Vera 1992–1993, 317 states that the *colonus* was not tied to the estate owner, but to the taxation, and that the *origo* was a fiscal category. But he does not specify this and it is not clear what such a tie to the taxation meant.

[105] See Section 10 for the senatusconsultum. Further CJ 10.32.36, where the request to be transferred to the maternal *origo* is rejected, which implies that the mother of the applicant had retained hers. In Sirks 1993a, 367 it was mistakenly assumed that a wife took the *origo* of her husband: she took his domicile.

10.2 *The Abolition of the* Senatusconsultum Claudianum *and the* Condicio Coloniaria

It appears from CJ 7.24.1 that a *senatusconsultum Claudianum* was connected with the adscripticiate. It is the senatusconsultum introduced under Claudius (AD 41–54) which made the children, born of a free woman who cohabitated with a slave, slaves of the owner of that slave, and herself too, if she refused to leave her man. The reason for the introduction of this *senatusconsultum Claudianum* was that in the case of a union between a freeborn woman (*ingenua*) and a slave, children would be freeborn citizens since there was no legitimate marriage between them possible, which might make the slave less manageable, having now freeborn children and so threatening the authority of the owner.[106] It will also have been felt unfitting for a free woman to cohabit with a slave. Thus the rule was that if the woman did not leave the slave after a formal warning, she and her children would follow the status of the father and be slaves too.[107] It is a remarkable rule. First, it is likely that it concerned free women who were *sui iuris*, or else one would expect a warning to her *pater* (if he had allowed the cohabitation).[108] Second, normally an official act would be required to establish status, like the verdict of the magistrate in a liberty procedure (*causa liberalis*). Here a formal announcement by a private person sufficed.[109] The reverse case, a free Roman cohabiting with somebody else's slave woman, was not sanctioned. Children would be slaves of the owner anyway. This difference also reflects the position of women *sui iuris* in society: they were not as free as men. In only two cases the senatusconsultum was mitigated. In CTh 4.12.3 *ingenuae* who cohabitate with fiscal slaves will bear not slaves but *Latins* without a father, free but with the patronal privilege (that of the fisc over Junian Latins).[110] In CTh 12.1.178 the children of a woman of decurional descent and a slave are free and

106 See Sirks 2005 and 2011. The *potestas* of the owner might diminish, hence bringing both woman and children into his *potestas* would set the balance right again.

107 See Sirks 2008 for this.

108 For such a case, see D. 16.3.27 Paul. 7: *Lucius Titius cum haberet filiam in potestate Seiam, Pamphilo servo alieno in matrimonium collocavit, cui etiam dotem dedit, quam sub titulo depositi in cautionem contulit, et postea nulla denuntiatione a domino facta pater decessit, mox et Pamphilus servus: quaero, qua actione Seia pecuniam petere possit, cum ipsa patri heres extiterit. Paulus respondit, quoniam dos constitui non potuit, ex causa depositi actione de peculio pecuniam repetendam.* See also D. 24.3.22.13 for a case of a free woman believing her husband is free.

109 It is of no consequence whether the effect entered at once or after the third warning. As formality we may expect the delivery of the warning, either orally or written, by a special messenger. See Kaser & Hackl 1996, § 71.I.1.

110 Which implied that at their death the fisc could claim their property as if *peculium*.

eligible for the decurionate, a western measure of 415 motivated by the shortage of eligible candidates.

Justinian abolished the *senatusconsultum Claudianum* in 531–534 because he thought it did not fit his times (CJ 7.24.1pr). But it had apparently not been applied to unions with slaves only. The first section of CJ 7.24.1.1 is repeated in CJ 11.48.24:

> Si qui adscripticiae condicionis constituti mulieres liberas quacumque mente aut quacumque machinatione sive scientibus dominis sive ignorantibus sibi uxores coniunxerunt vel postea coniunxerint, in sua libertate permanere tam eas quam prolem quae ex eis cognoscitur procreata sancimus: illo procul dubio observando, ut, si ex libero marito et adscripticia uxore partus fuerit editus, is maternae condicionis maculam, non paternam sequatur libertatem. 1. Sed ne servi vel adscripticii putent sibi impunitum esse tale conamen, quod maxime in adscripticios verendum est, ne liberarum mulierum nuptiis ab his excogitatis paulatim huiusmodi hominum condicio decrescat, sancimus, si quid tale fuerit vel a servo vel adscripticio perpetratum, liberam habere potestatem dominium eius sive per se sive per praesidem provinciae talem servum vel adscripticium castigatione competenti corrigere et abstrahere a tali muliere. quod si neglexerit, sciat in suum damnum huiusmodi desidiam reversuram.
>
> If any persons established in the condition of *adscripticii* have married or marry free women with whatever intention or machination, whether the owners know or are unaware, We ordain that both they (the wives) and the offspring that is known to have been procreated from them remain in their liberty; but, far from any doubt, this principle is to be observed that, if offspring is born from a free husband an *adscripticia* wife, it follows the stain of the mother's condition and not the father's liberty. 1. But in order that slaves and *adscripticii* may not think that such efforts (to join free women) will go unpunished – which is especially to be feared in the case of *adscripticii* – and in order that the number of this class of men may not gradually decrease by their marriage with free women, we ordain that if anything of that kind is done by a slave or *adscripticius*, his owner shall have the free power, either personally or through the provincial governor, to correct such a slave or *adscripticius* by proper chastisement and to take him away from such a woman. If he neglects this, he may know that such laziness will redound to his own loss.[111]

Section 1 is identical to CJ 7.24.1.1 and regulates the outcome of the abolition. The original constitution had probably as text CJ 7.24.1pr – CJ 11.48.24pr – CJ 7.24.1.1 = CJ 11.48.24.1 and been split in 534 according to

[111] The translation of the Codex of Justinian is used with some adaptations (inter alia, because *adscripticius* is not consistently translated the same way).

subject. The last phrase of the principium refers to the rule of CJ 11.48.21.1 (see Section 10.3). We see that the senatusconsultum was applied not only to slaves (the original purpose) but also to *adscripticii*. The effect of its abolition was that the children of a slave and a free woman would be Roman citizens and the children of an *adscripticius* and a 'free' woman (*ingenua*) from a marriage would now be free from the adscripticiate (colonate) or else their numbers could not dwindle. Since these children were and remained free Roman citizens, it means that the senatusconsultum applied here not to the *status libertatis* as such but to the status of the colonate. We also see that the status of *adscripticius (colonus)* was transmitted to descendants or else the application of the senatusconsultum had no sense.

The term *ingenuus* originally meant a person born free, but in Late Antiquity we see another meaning appear: a person not subjected to the colonate and thereby to the *potestas* of the landowner, nor to any other public *potestas* (as observed by Giliberti).[112] This text also is evidence of this meaning.[113]

That the senatusconsultum applied and was applicable to the adscripticiate/*condicio coloniaria* must ground on a common feature. This is in my opinion the *potestas* of the landowner. The senatusconsultum protected the *potestas* of the slave owner and brought woman and children under his *potestas* (who would otherwise have been *liberi*); in the adscripticiate the estate owner's *potestas* was also protected and extended over the children of the *adscripticius* (who would in other respects be citizens). The state of being *in potestate* which allowed for this must consequently already have existed before. That follows also from CJ 11.48.21 (see Section 10.3). The senatusconsultum was in this time also applied to groups of people similarly *in potestate* (see Section 10.5; already since the middle of the fourth century, see Sections 26.3 and 26.4), but for the origin of the *condicio* we have to go further back: see Section 53. What we do not know is whether it required a warning by the master of the *colonus*, as still prescribed for *gynaeciarii* and *monetarii* (CJ 11.8.3 and 7, see Section 10.5). It would imply that the senatusconsultum applied the colonate apparently automatically.

112 Giliberti 1999, 81. Carrié 1997, 94 mentions this but sees it as an extreme confusion in the legal language.

113 Why was this meaning used? Elsewhere I have put forward the hypothesis that the *patria potestas* was for many new Romans after 212 a 'Fremkörper' in as far as it extended beyond juvenility. Emancipation might have become customary. Recently Vial-Dumas has put forward that the family structure moved from a patrimonial to a matrimonial system. Babusiaux has pointed out that already in the second century the position of the *pater* weakened. See Sirks 2019b, 2020b; Vial-Dumas 2020; Babusiaux 2014.

Justinian fears that the number of this class of men may gradually decrease (*hominum condicio decrescat*). This must refer to the adscripticiate and implies that the children were *adscripticii* too (and probably the woman). That these would be free from the colonate was not what Justinian wanted, and he authorised the master of the *adscripticius* to recall forcibly his *colonus* from such marriages (a necessary authorisation since otherwise a divorce had to be imposed, which was not what the Church liked). Before they would have followed their father's status. Now they follow that of their mother. It seems as if the marriage is illegitimate, which is strange because both are free Romans, their marriage is legitimate and their children are legitimate. One would expect the paternal status to be decisive. The transmission of the coloniary status was evidently a different matter.

The senatusconsultum of Claudius changed the *status* of being *sui iuris* and thereby, implicitly, because the woman became a slave (the worst case of *capitis deminutio*), both the *status libertatis* and *civitatis* of the children of the free woman. What was its effect here? Would it only have effect if the woman did not leave after a formal warning? Assuming such a warning was still required (or else children would be *ingenui*), the consequence of refusing was that she and the children became *adscripticii*, not slaves; or else this class of people could not decrease as Justinian fears. We are dealing here with their status as Roman citizen (their *condicio*) and not as citizen of a town or inhabitant of an estate (their *origo*), but we see the two become entwined in common parlance. Gai 1.124–126 distinguishes a category of *alieno iure subiecti*, which comprises both slaves and those *in potestate parentis*. In both cases the criterion is the *potestas*. Further Gai 1.10 distinguishes within the category of the free Roman citizens between freeborn (*ingenui*) and manumitted citizens (*libertini*). The latter were free citizens but nevertheless subjected in some way to their manumitters (*operae*, *obsequium*) and restricted in public life.[114] The reason for this was that the stain of slavery, hence of subjection, still clung to them. Similarly we would have to rank here those put *in mancipio* by adjudication in order to work off their debt, albeit on a lower level on account of the *mancipium* exercised. Gaius' category of *in alieno iure esse* may be more consequential than it seems.[115]

[114] Gaius further mentions here Latins and *dediticii* (Gai 1.12): it was therefore a wide category which comprised even those who were free but not Roman citizens, yet still subjected to Romans. The *lex Visellia* of AD 24 forbade freedmen to sit as town councillor.

[115] Also in the way they could be released: Gai 1.138: *Hi qui in causa mancipii sunt quia servorum loco habentur vindicta censu testamento manumissi sui iuris fiunt*. It would mean that *coloni* would lose their tax guarantee.

It seems best to put the *coloni censibus adscripti* here as well, subjected to their estate owner, since they are considered more obliged than freedmen and similarly restricted where it concerns litigation, yet still free people (CJ 11.50.2pr–2, 4). Their restrictions would be, as with the people mentioned, of private and public nature. To this came the restriction of their movement through their census registration, fixing their *origo* to the estate. They thus represented regarding the *status libertatis* a category of Roman citizens, free but less free than *libertini*, thus of a lesser status (*deterior condicio*) than the ordinary citizens.[116] In the context of *alieno iure esse* the term *ingenuus* apparently acquired the meaning of not being subjected to another Roman in public law (and perhaps also in private law; see above), because they are called *ingenui* in the sources, that is, they are free of someone else's *potestas* (see Section 6 and note 112; cf. also CJ 11.48.21pr: *liberi homines*, and the expression *coloni liberi*, Section 16). Another possibility is that where those subjected to somebody else's *potestas* which was not their *pater*'s were designated as *alieni iuris*, the term *ingenui* may have come up as indication that somebody was *sui iuris*, that is, not subjected, his own master. In the end, the meaning of *ingenuus* in this context is beyond doubt. Because of this characteristic, the expression used in this context for this union is *coniugium non aequale*, unequal marriage. It implies that it was a legitimate marriage, not a cohabitation (*contubernium*), yet still between persons unequal in status. The expression is also used in this sense in Nov. Theod. 22.1.8 = CJ 5.27.3.2 for the unions between senators and decurions with women of opprobrious fame and servile status. Justinian did not declare after the abolition of the senatusconsultum this kind of marriage illegitimate or not a *conubium*. The remedy he provided in CJ 7.24.1.1 = CJ 11.48.24.1 was that the estate owner could forcibly recall his *adscripticius*, thereby effectively ending the marriage.

Justinian says in CJ 11.48.22pr that in order to dispel any doubt about somebody's status as *colonus*, there should be proof like the *adscriptio*, the insertion into the census. We may deduce from this and the common labelling as *censibus adscriptus* or *adscripticius* that the census functioned here still as establishing a status and, at the same time, due to the prescription that nobody was allowed to change his *origo*, apparently for taxation reasons, established in this way the *origo*. Here it would be the status of a free person who was under the *potestas* of another person, not his father

[116] Hence it did not change their *status libertatis* and they were not half-free or half-slave. Cf. CJ 11.53.1, which reduces their dependency to a fixed domicile and the authority by this law of the landowner to recall them and demand services.

but the owner of the estate on the census of which the *colonus* was inserted. In that way a public status would be created which would transmit, as the *origo* would pass on from father to children.

10.3 *The* Coniugium Non Aequale

CJ 11.48.24 dealt with a union between an *ingenua* and a *colonus*. How about the converse? In 530 Justinian said that who was born from an *adscripticia*, that is, a *colona*, and an *ingenuus*, a man free from the colonate, followed 'according to previous statutes' the status of his mother, in CJ 11.48.21:

> Ne diutius dubitetur, si quis ex adscripticia et servo vel adscripticio et ancilla fuisset editus, cuius status sit, vel quae peior fortuna sit, utrumne adscripticia an servilis, sancimus ea quidem, quae in anterioribus legibus cauta sunt pro tali progenie, quae ex mulieribus adscripticiis et viris liberis progenita sit, in suo statu relinqui, et sit adscripticia proles ex tali copulatione procreata. 1. Si quis autem vel ex servo et adscripticia, vel ancilla et adscripticio fuerit editus, matris suae ventrem sequatur et talis sit condicionis, qualis et genetrix fuit, sive ancilla sive adscripticia: quod hactenus in liberis tantum et servis observabatur. quae etenim differentia inter servos et adscripticios intellegetur, cum uterque in domini sui positus est potestate, et possit servum cum peculio manumittere et adscripticium cum terra suo dominio expellere?
>
> So that it is not to be doubted any longer, if anyone has been born from an *adscripticia* and a male slave, or from an *adscripticius* and a female slave, as to what status he or she should be, or which fortune is worse, whether *adscripticius* or slave, we ordain those things that were provided for in earlier laws for such offspring as was born from *adscripticiae* and free males, that it [the issue] be left in its own status, and that from such copulation offspring of *adscripticiae* be created. 1. If someone though has been born either from a male slave and an *adscripticia*, or from a female slave and an *adscripticius*, he or she shall follow the womb of the mother and be of such condition as she was, whether she was a slave woman or an *adscripticia*: this was observed up to now in slaves alone and free persons. Then, indeed, which difference would there be between slaves and *adscripticii*, when both are in the power of their masters? And he can manumit a slave with his *peculium* and expel from his ownership an *adscripticius* with his land.[117]

The question put forward to Justinian was: What is the status of children, born of a union between slaves and *adscripticii*? Which *condicio* is worse? The answer is given by way of a detour with recourse to former

[117] The translation of *The Codex of Justinian* is used with some adaptations (inter alia, because *adscripticius* is not consistently translated the same way).

legislation. Children out of a union between *adscripticiae* and free men (*viri liberi*, cf. the use of *liberi* with *coloni* for not being subjected) follow the status of the mother. It looks like this was the effect of the *ius gentium* and thus as if there was no *conubium* between the two, but it is different: it was prescribed by ancient laws. If the *adscripticiae* had been slaves, the laws would have been superfluous because in such unions the *ius gentium* applied anyway.[118] It follows (1) that the *adscripticiae* were not and are not slaves but Roman citizens, (2) that the marriage was legitimate, and (3) that the effect remained limited to *adscripticiae* marrying *ingenui*. A law was necessary to prescribe the application of a rule, similar to the *ius gentium* rule, for *adscripticiae* women making children follow their mother's status although there is *conubium*. Justinian says applying this law solves the problem; children will follow the status of their mother: *adscripticii* with an *adscripticia*, slaves with a slave mother. The problem will have been that in the case of a union of an *adscripticia* with a slave, the master of the slave could claim both the mother and her children as slaves on basis of the *senatusconsultum Claudianum*, whereas the master of the *adscripticia* could have replied that, although free, she nevertheless was *alieni iuris* and not what the senatusconsultum required, really free. Further, it would rob him of her children as adscriptiate labour force: and was it not the purpose of applying the senatusconsultum analogously to *adscripticii* marrying *ingenuae* to provide him with *adscripticii* children? The first hypothesis is in any case legally possible and probable. It shows why the emperor had to give a decision. Justinian also applies the rule to *adscripticii* cohabitating with slave women. But in that case the law was not necessary; the *ius gentium* decided here the outcome. Justinian implicitly gives a division of children as labour force. The effect is that it looks like there is no difference in status between *adscripticii* and slaves; children of unions between them always 'belong' to the master of the mother, and Justinian bolsters this with a reference to the power of manumission, ending the subjection. Yet that was the only similarity. It is the reason for the ancient law and now for its extended application.

Returning to Justinian's example: Did these ancient statutes turn the marriages of *adscripticiae* with free persons into *coniugia non aequalia* or were these marriages already *non aequalia* and the laws merely defined the effect regarding the *condicio*? What would have been the reason to treat such marriages as *coniugia non aequalia*? Justinian says it in the following: both slaves and *coloni*

[118] That rule was that in the case of an illegitimate union the status of the mother was decisive for the status of the children. To dispel this misunderstanding, Justinian emphasises that in unions between *adscripticii* and slaves the *ius gentium* rule applies, hence the *adscripticii* are free citizens. But he also explains why the misunderstanding could arise.

are in the *potestas* (*dominium*) of somebody else. *Coloni* can like a slave be released from their status through manumission by their estate owner.[119] They have thus both a *deterior condicio.* Hence the question in the beginning: Are *adscripticii* not another kind of slave? And the answer is implicitly that they are formally not, because a law was required to have the effect as if there is no *conubium* between *adscripticiae* and free men with regard to status.

The normal private law consequences applied, but in public law its consequence of transmission of the status did not; here the rule of the *ius gentium* regarding status applied. In order to 'remedy' this, or rather to maintain the supply of *adscripticii*, as Justinian bluntly says in CJ 11.48.24.1 (*ne liberarum mulierum nuptiis ab his excogitatis paulatim huiusmodi hominum condicio decrescat*), the senatusconsultum was introduced to apply here.

Such an application of the senatusconsultum implies that there was *already* a legally sanctioned difference in status between the spouses, that is, already a legal *condicio coloniaria.* The statutes merely arranged the outcome of marriages which were before *aequalia.* If the senatusconsultum was applied analogously to marriages between *adscripticii* and free women, it implies that there was a similar distance between them as between *ingenui* and slaves. The reason to put *adscripticii* on the same level as slaves is given in CJ 11.48.21.1. Both are under the *potestas* of somebody else and can only be freed from this by manumission. But there remains of course also the difference: slaves cannot own property or contract, nor marry and have children, nor pay tax. Children are in the *potestas* of their *pater familias* and *adscripticii* will also have been *patres familias*, but the *potestas* of their estate owner did not end with the latter's death. All three groups can be categorised as being *alieno iure subiecti* (Gai 1.124–126). But those of the slaves and *coloni* was a *condicio*: it passed over to children and it did not end with the death of the master.

From CJ 11.48.21pr we know that this differentiation was accomplished by a law:

> . . . sancimus ea quidem, quae in anterioribus legibus cauta sunt pro tali progenie, quae ex mulieribus adscripticiis et viris liberis progenita sit, in suo statu relinqui, et sit adscripticia proles ex tali copulatione procreata.

> . . . we ordain those things that were provided for in earlier laws for such offspring as was born from *adscripticiae* and free males, that it [the issue] be left in its own status, and that offspring of *adscripticiae* be created from such copulation.

119 CJ 11.48.21.1: . . . *et possit servum cum peculio manumittere et adscripticium cum terra suo dominio expellere.*

This measure was for the marriages between *adscripticiae* and free men, where normally the children would follow the status of their father. The law turned this around by the assumption of a *coniugium non aequale*, which made the *ius gentium* rule apply. Since the same happened with marriages between *adscripticii* and free women, the law must have covered both situations. That constitution dates from 530, thus before the abolition of the senatusconsultum in 531–534. The result of these two rules was that in both cases, if one partner was of the *condicio adscripticia*, all children would be *adscripticii*. It safeguarded the supply of labour force on the land.[120]

It is indeed the express motive behind Justinian's correction of the abolition of the senatusconsultum. As to the children, they could wander away but in the end they could be summoned by the estate owner to return and to perform services, to know the services connected with the colonate.[121]

The social standing of *coloni censibus adscripti* may have made marriages with free people already seen as socially not equal, but it was in any case with *adscripticiae* that by legislative intervention these marriages were turned into *coniugia non aequalia*. Because the analogue application of the *senatusconsultum Claudianum* was meant to correct an unwanted consequence of the *coniugium non aequale*, it is, considering the introduction of this for *adscripticiae*, probable that it was also introduced by law for *adscripticii*. In other words, the *coniugium non aequale* was the effect of legislation. Before that, their marriages were *aequalia*. It will have corresponded with a social distinction (being *alieni iuris*), but the purpose of the statutes regarded only the transmission of the *condicio*. However, with this we already enter into the question of the origin of this rule, which is dealt with in Sections 26.3 and 26.4.

Before, the term *coniugium non aequale* was used. What is meant by this term, which occurs in CJ 5.27.3.2 (ex Nov. Theod. 22.1.8) as *coniugium inaequale* and before in CTh 14.7.1?[122] In CJ 5.27.3.2 it signifies the union

120 CTh 14.7.1 of 397 does not mention the difference regarding a *coniugium non aequale*. It says that children always follow the status of the mother, but we saw that it was the senatusconsultum that made children of a free women follow the status of the *adscripticius* father. The *interpretatio*, again, seems to refer to CJ 11.48.21, but does not say who the partner is. As to the union between a free woman and a *collegiatus*, it seems to give the outcome of the application of the senatusconsultum. That was possible because it was only abolished in the east and had no validity in the west until 554. That might indicate that the *interpretationes*, at least this one, were made before 554. CTh 14.7.1 was not included in Justinian's Code.

121 So said in CJ 11.48.22.3.

122 The *Thesaurus Linguae Latinae* also does not mention the phrase under v. *coniugium*. But s.v. *aequalis* also a difference in status amongst people is recorded.

between a decurion and his concubine, which brings forth natural children. The emphasis is not on the illegitimacy of the union but on the difference in status. In CTh 14.7.1 it is said about the status of children 'that where there is a *coniugium non aequale*, the offspring follows the mother, where on the other hand the *coniugium* is just, the free offspring follows the father' (*ut, ubi non est aequale coniugium, matrem sequatur agnatio, ubi vero iustum erit, patri cedat ingenua successio*).[123] The expression again underlines the status difference and it describes precisely what we see with the *coloni*. Normally we would expect that in the case of a marriage between a man subjected to the adscripticiate and a woman not subjected to this or another *condicio*, the children would follow the *origo* and status (*condicio*) of the father. This was the *ius gentium* rule for legal marriages, and *coloni* were Roman citizens who could own property, conclude contracts, have legitimate children, and so on. Apparently such a marriage did not carry all the consequences of a legitimate marriage between Roman citizens (a *coniugium* or *matrimonium iustum*). Hence I use the term for these unions. They were not restricted to *coloni*.

10.4 Unions between Adscripticii *and Slaves*

CJ 11.48.21 discusses also another problem: unions between *adscripticii* and slave women. There was doubt about the status of the children and which *condicio* was worse ('So that it is not to be doubted any longer, if anyone has been born from an *adscripticia* and a male slave, or from an *adscripticius* and a female slave, as to what status he or she should be, or which fortune is worse, whether *adscripticius* or slave'). Justinian's solution is that in all cases the *ius gentium* rule applies, namely *ventrem matris sequi*, children follow the status of their mother. What doubt may have been raised? In my opinion the fact that, notwithstanding their low position, *adscripticii* were still free Roman citizens, which would lead to a cohabitation and natural children. One could say: if the mother is an *adscripticia*, the children would be *adscripticii*; if she is a slave, they should be slaves. But if one considers the status of an *adscripticius* as an unfree one, equal to a slave, did the *ius gentium* rule still apply? Or, as we will see for the west in that case, should children be

[123] CTh. 14.7.1: *Impp. Arcadius et Honorius AA. Gracchо consulari Campaniae. De retrahendis collegiis vel collegiatis iudices competentes dabunt operam, ut ad proprias civitates eos, qui longius abierunt, retrahi iubeant cum omnibus, quae eorum erunt, ne desiderio rerum suarum loco originario non valeant adtineri. De quorum agnatione haec forma servabitur, ut, ubi non est aequale coniugium, matrem sequatur agnatio, ubi vero iustum erit, patri cedat ingenua successio. Dat. viiii kalend. Iun. Mediolano Caesario et Attico conss.* (a.397).

divided between the *domini*?[124] Justinian settles the question by considering the *adscripticii* for what they are, essentially free, but like slaves in the *potestas*. The statutory rule provides here also the solution: children follow their mother's status. Thus in both cases all children now were available as labour force but with different statuses. What also may have been instrumental in seeing things this way and using the senatusconsultum is the debt of the *colonus* with the estate owner. It would be unpleasant if through marriage children would not be bound to render services to pay off the debt.[125]

In the course of the fourth century, unions between slaves and free Romans were in the Church acknowledged as full marriages (if, of course, done according to Christian rite), but in law they remained without effect.[126] On the other hand, the social division between *honestiores* and *humiliores* increased. The lowering of the status of *adscripticii* fits this shift, although I assume that it was effected by a legal measure, as I hope to argue later on.

10.5 Other Cases of the Coniugium Non Aequale

How the *coloni* got into this situation and how it could become a feature of a property, will be discussed later, in Section 53; for Justinian's times we can reason only on the basis of the abolition of the senatusconsultum. The other aspects will be discussed amply in due course. The *condicio coloniaria* was transmitted as status to descendants, male or female. It was not hereditary but the outcome of rules determining the civil and civic status of offspring. The *condicio* had become a status; see also that women call themselves *enapographos georgos* (ἐναπόγραφος γεωργός) without feminising this noun.[127] As such the *condicio* was nothing particular in itself in that it transmitted to the descendance. That happened also with, for example, decurions or senators.

There were more cases of a low status which entailed *coniugia non aequalia*. CJ 5.27.3.2 was mentioned above. But with marriages between

124 As in CTh 5.18.1.3. See Sections 23.4 and 26.2.

125 In previous publications I was still uncertain about the role of the *origo* in this context and the function of the application of the *senatusconsultum Claudianum*, and only recently (see Sirks 2008) did I come to this interpretation. I have to withdraw any previous explanation I may have made. Murga 1982 merely accepts the application without explanation. It is furthermore an argument against the theoretical possibility that the estate owner exercised his rights as representative of the town as *origo* and as such in a public or semi-public function. Further Voss 1985, 143ff., 166ff.

126 Kaser 1971, 126.

127 If that were possible. *Adscripticiae* in P. Washington University I 25 (a. 530), P.Oxy. LXX 4797 (a. 593), 4801 (a. 617). They call themselves *enapographos georgos* (ἐναπόγραφος γεωργός)(sic), which suggests that this was a status and not an occupation.

free women and *monetarii*, minters, we see it with status consequences. They led to the status change of the woman and her children from free to subjected to the *condicio* of *monetarii* in CJ 11.8.7, where the compilers struck the reference to the *senatusconsultum Claudianum* in its example, CTh 10.20.10, necessary because it had just been abolished; but just as with the *adscripticii* the regulation remained:

> ... ea [secundum auctoritatem senatus consulti Claudiani] vel legitima admonita conventione discedat vel, si complexui monetarii putaverit inhaerendum, non ambigat se et liberis praeiudicaturam et eius condicioni esse nectendam.

> ... she shall [in accordance with the authority of the *senatusconsultum Claudianum*] after she has been warned by the statutory notification, either withdraw from this union, or, if she should suppose that she should cling to the embrace of the imperial minter (*monetarius*), she shall not doubt that she will prejudice the rights of her children and that she must be bound to the *condicio* of the minter.

We see that the status of the *monetarii* was also a *condicio*, similar to that of the *coloni*. It existed already in 317 (CJ 11.8.1). The mention of the senatusconsultum, present in CTh 10.20.10, has been left out here because it was abolished in 534, but its effect was present. If the free woman (*ingenua*) is warned but does not leave, she and her children become associated with the *monetarii*. This effect should have disappeared with the abolition of the senatusconsultum (as in CJ 11.48.24) but is retained. The legal basis is now this edited constitution. Similarly the *murileguli* (fishers of purple snails) were subjected to this low *condicio* (CJ 11.8.1, 11 and 12, 15), as well as the *gynaecarii* (workers in the textile factories; CJ 11.8.3). In CJ 11.8.12 the same regime for the *murilegulae* as for the *adscripticiae* in CJ 11.48.21.1 is laid down, while in CJ 11.8.15 the regime is summarised: whoever descends from a father or mother *conchylegulus/a* is bound. CJ 11.8.3 says that *ingenuae* who live with *gynaeciarii* and do not leave after a warning will be bound to the *condicio* of their husbands. These texts show that the effect in these cases of the senatusconsultum was not that the woman and children became slaves as was the original sanction, but that they were reduced to the *condicio* of their husbands. That confirms the suggestion for CJ 11.48.24.1 that the effect was to create *adscripticii*. The fact that the compilers struck the reference to the senatusconsultum in CJ 11.8.7 proves that this senatusconsultum formed the legal basis of the rules on unions between *ingenuae* and *condicionales* (the term used in CJ 8.17.11) existing in 531–534.[128]

[128] I shall return more in detail to the *coniugium non aequale* in Sections 26.3 and 26.4.

10.6 *Developments after the Abolition of the* Senatusconsultum Claudianum

As mentioned before, after abolishing the senatusconsultum, Justinian, in acknowledgement of its consequences, at once introduced the rule that the estate owner of the *adscripticius* could forcibly take his *adscripticius* away from a 'free' woman. If he did nothing, he had himself to blame for the loss of manpower (CJ 11.48.24.1 = 7.24.1.1; Nov. 22.17 pr of 535).[129] Some used the constitution to claim freedom for children previously born, but Justinian curbed this in 537, stating that only children born of free women after the enactment would profit (Nov. 54.praef., 1). For an *adscripticia* such a measure was, of course, unnecessary.

Very soon afterwards, before 539, Justinian changed the arrangement and decided that children born out of a marriage between an *adscripticius* and a woman free from the colonate would become free persons (ἐλεύθεροι) too. By that he meant 'free' *coloni* (see below, Section 16), so that they would have to stay on the estate or in the domicile (χωρίον) of their father. They could be recalled and would have to cultivate the land: the meaning of *kolonos* (κολωνός), according to Justinian. What they acquire is their own property and does not become *peculium* (πεκούλιον) of their masters as was the case with *adscripticii*. They remain liable for the poll tax and other taxes and the liturgies. Otherwise, they would have been free to leave. In short, he imposed the 'free' colonate on them. Justinian confirms this otherwise unrecorded constitution in Nov. 162.2.1 of 539.[130] Yet, if such a son, now a 'free' *colonus*, acquired as owner a piece of land large enough to sustain him to cultivate without having time to work elsewhere (namely, on the land of his birth), he was allowed to migrate thereto and stay there; that is, his *origo* was transferred to the village of his own plot where, I assume, he was registered in the census as such (Nov. 162.2.1, *in fine*).[131]

129 CJ 7.24.1 was probably issued together with 1.3.53 (533), 5.17.11 (533) and 9.13.1 (533), but these fragments do not inform us on the colonate. It is remarkable, because the Church did not like to break up marriages. Yet here it could only result from this, unless the women voluntarily accepted the adscripticiate.

130 He confirmed this in response to controversies in Illyricum on this and other subjects (Nov. 162 praef.). See Bianchini 1984, 83–91. Bianchini does not enter deeply into the question how precisely the adscripticiate was imposed, nor does she make the connection with the *origo*. Further Schmitz 1986, 384.

131 Whittaker 1987, 101 speaks of 'to sustain themselves without the need to cultivate someone else's property' and of breaking his bond. I would rather translate the Greek with 'unless they become owner of some own property, suited to occupy them with it and not joined to farm another [property], to stay on that'. One may interpret 'need' in various ways, but since it is the property that is joined and not the farmer, in my opinion it means to exclude the case that a 'free' *colonus* acquires land which he can till but remains also tied to his plot (the case of CTh 11.1.14). In that case

Until then status and *origo* posed no problem with marriages between *coloni* of different estates:[132] they were, so to speak, on the same level and here the paternal *origo* and his *condicio* were decisive for the offspring (CJ 11.48.13pr).[133] Here also Justinian introduced a change in Nov. 162.3 of 539 by introducing a division. The children were equally divided between the masters of the parents, that is, they were divided over the two *origines*. But if there was only one child, or an odd number of children, the mother got the single child or the odd one extra.

Whether it was CJ 7.24.1.1 or a constitution with the same contents as CJ 7.24.1.1, like CJ 11.48.24.1, or the constitution to which Justinian refers in Nov. 162.2.1 of 539, in Illyricum it led to problems. In Illyricum there were no *adscripticii* in the old sense but *coloni liberi*, who were, apart from their bond to the land, free from *potestas* and thus *ingenui*. Apparently they used the law to get rid of that bond. They must have argued thus: The constitution confirmed in Nov. 162.2.1 cannot refer to us, since we are *coloni liberi*. But we are still connected to the census, hence we are *adscripticii* and consequently a marriage with an *ingenua*, a free woman, is a *coniugium non aequale*. In that case our children are *ingenui*, free from the bond to the land and free to migrate. That happened indeed, because landowners from Lugdunum complained about a loss of labour.[134] That again led to reduced agrarian revenues and less tax revenue. Justinian gave assistance in 540 (App. 1) in that he restored the former rule on *adscripticii* and 'settled' *coloni* (= 'free' *coloni*) (*vetera lex de adscripticiis et colonis constitutis agricolis*) for the whole of Illyricum (*in omnibus Illyricanis partibus*, App. 1.1).[135] He probably referred

a complete shift of *origo* is not possible. Likewise, Whittaker's breaking the bond is ambiguous. In my opinion the bond with the previous plot is broken, but a new bond is created.

132 And *inquilini*, by whom probably dwellers on estates are meant, who had to perform services as well: CJ 11.48.13pr states that substantially there is no difference between *coloni* and *inquilini*.

133 There was no *coniugium inaequale* (Nov. Theod. 22.1.8) or a *coniugium non aequale* (CTh 14.7.1) here.

134 There is no Lugdunum known in Illyricum (see Cramer 1927). If Lyon was meant, we would have to assume that Illyricum was extended to reconquered parts of Gaul, which is not confirmed. But in the provinces of Illyricum the 'free' colonate was the rule. Schmitz 1986, 383 suggests on the basis of textual variations that instead of Lugdunum, Singidinum, present-day Belgrade, was meant. He suggests the invasions of the Huns had made *adscripticii* and *coloni* flee from their land and claim freedom on basis of CJ 11.48.24.

135 Schmitz 1986, 385–386 does not take this possibility into account, although he agrees that it concerned the difficult situation in Illyricum. He assumes a general return to the old situation, which makes an explanation necessary, why already ten months after Nov. 162 the new rule was revoked. Since Nov. Justini 6 of 570 and Nov. Tib. 13 of 582 both contain the rule of CJ 11.48.24, App. 1 must have been abolished in the meantime (between 540 and 570), of which, however, we know nothing. Hence Schmitz rejects the idea of a return to the old situation and proposes that the abolition of the *senatusconsultum Claudianum* in 537 by Nov. 54 did not pertain to children born before 531/534: they should remain *adscripticii*. For this he changes the interpunction of App. 1.1 and

to the constitution, confirmed in Nov. 162.2.1. That is, if a *colonus* married an *ingenua*, on ground of this law the children of an *adscripticius agricola* or a *colonus constitutus agricola* (by which he means a *colonus liber*) follow their fathers' status (again). On the other hand, if the mother is a *colona constituta*, that is, a 'free' *colona*, and not married to an *adscripticius* or free *colonus*, the *coniugium non aequale* rule will not apply and they follow here also their father's status of *ingenuitas* instead of following their mother's status. That is what Justinian means when he says *in hoc tantummodo casu obtinente lege* – 'in that case only [the first case] the law applies'. With this Justinian made the gate to freedom to migrate smaller but did not close it completely.

The rule of CJ 11.48.24.1 (531–534) was introduced everywhere in the Empire. Also in Africa after it was conquered in 533? We do not know whether Justinian's codification was introduced there; in all appearance it was not, otherwise Justinus' novel would have been unnecessary (see below). Were there still *coloni*? Geiseric had burned the tax registers, and theoretically this should have made it impossible to detect *coloni originales*.[136] Since census registers were used as property records, Geiseric may have burned only those of the lands he wanted to distribute or take himself, so that on other land *coloni* might still have been registered. How else would it have been possible to continue collecting taxes? Meier suspects the Vandals maintained the existing forms of agricultural exploitation and in that case the colonate too.[137] Even if land was distributed, the *coloni* would have gone over with them to the new owners. Hunderic condemned bishops to the colonate: Were they registered as such? And where? In municipal registers? We do not know. If, however, the status had already acquired a personal aspect, as we may see in the Visigothic kingdom, other means of proving this (municipal records) might have been used. Anyway, there was roughly a hundred years between Geiseric's destruction of the tax registers and Justinian's order to reestablish them. Absence during this period would undoubtedly have made migrated *coloni* free.

In 552 Justinian ordered for Africa that those *coloni* who had absconded and been free during the Vandal occupation should remain so and not return to the *condicio colonatus*. We may see in this an acknowledgement

proposes an emendation of *quod nascitur* into *quod natum est*, and reads *sed si* as 'aber auch wenn'. Given that the two later novels were dealing with Africa, and assuming that Nov. 162 could well be restricted to Illyricum, I do not see a reason to follow this view.

136 Meier 2019, 674. In 452 Valentinian had granted to those, conducting lawsuits over the acts of the Vandals, a deduction from the period of thirty years for the time they spent under the Vandals (Nov. Val. 35.12). Where it concerned property claims, burning the registers would have made such lawsuits difficult if not impossible.

137 Meier 2019, 672–673.

that it was impossible to recall them after a hundred years. It does not mean that the registration had been deleted: the limitation of prescription was thirty years. Further Justinian ordered that the others should return to their plot (App. 6). These others, who may have fled for the Byzantine tax levy, may have been *coloni* who had not absconded under the Vandals, or who had been entered for the first time in the new tax registers. Since only eighteen years had elapsed after the reconquest of Africa, the first category would have been reclaimed on evidence from before 534, be it with old registers or being entered in new registers on basis of old registers. In any case, there was continuity in the colonate and its registration, and consequently sufficient ground to assume that the colonate did continue under the Vandals. That must have been done either by registration in municipal records or by affidavits, or in the documents attesting ownership, or in tax registers if Geiseric had not destroyed all.

Since there were still people not obeying Justinian's order and continuing to claim *coloni*, the decision was repeated in 558 (App. 9). Further, Justinus II introduced in 570 for Africa, referring to the same rule as had been introduced in Illyricum by Justinian (Nov. 162.2pr of 539), that children of an *adscripticius* and an *ingenua* would be free but subjected to the 'free' colonate in the village of their birth (thus: *origo*) and had to work there. They had to reside in their *vici* (Nov. Justini 6, confirmed later by Tiberius: Nov. Tib. 13 of 582).[138] What Justinus did was reducing the effect of CJ 11.48.24: originally the children as *ingenui* would have been free to migrate; now as *coloni liberi* they were equal to *ingenui* but tied to their land. In all these cases the motive behind the measures is to keep sufficient labour available on the land. It seems that the landowners suffered in the second half of the sixth century from migration of farmers and farm hands. Perhaps unrest caused by Berber tribes made them flee, perhaps the oppressing tax collectors made them need more labour force than otherwise.[139]

The application of the *senatusconsultum Claudianum* had not purported to change the personal law status of the *adscripticii*, but remarkably enough the measure taken after its abolition in 531/534 did. It implied a potential marriage restriction, which was remedied in 539 by Justinian's Novel 162.2. That Novel restored the personal law status of the *adscripticii*.

In Italy the Theodosian Code was in force until Justinian, after Italy had been reconquered in 535, introduced in 554 his compilation and later

[138] In these years, constitutions for Africa were drawn up in Latin.

[139] It seems that in that period Africa suffered from unrest; see Moorhead 2005, 136; A. D. Lee, 'The empire at war', in Maas 2005, 127.

legislation there as well (App. 6.11, the Constitutio Pragmatica). But soon, in 568, the Longobards conquered large parts of Italy. How far Justinianic law was really established is a question to which the letters of Pope Gregory the Great provide some answer.[140]

This application of the *origo* meant that, as stated above, the designation *colonus* (*adscripticius*) no longer necessarily meant that this person was a farmer, and we do indeed find a variety of occupations – steward, scribe, guard, sailor; in the legal texts: functions in the imperial service, in the Church (see Sections 9 and 15).[141] His duties, however, could involve work on an estate, but it is not impossible that an *adscripticius* with funds could have contracted somebody else to perform this duty for him (cf. CJ 1.3.16).

11 Moving *Coloni* to Other Places

The purpose of the colonate was to have labour force on demand. That made it necessary to have the labour on or around the estate. Any migration was of course undesirable and contrary to the purpose of the colonate. Flight was combated. But it was another thing to deal in this kind of labour. What if somebody owned several estates and had sufficient people on one, but a shortage of workers on the other estate? Sending workers there would be one solution, as we see in the papyri that *adscripticii* work in other villages. But that was merely a temporary solution if the shortage was permanent. Or what if a landowner wanted to sell his estate but keep the attached *coloni* and apply them elsewhere? We see that devices were employed to such ends, since constitutions forbid them.

For example, one device was to agree in case of a sale or donation with the buyer or donee that the attached *coloni* would be separated by private agreement (*privata pactione*) before transfer and be attached to another estate. It would serve private interest: it might be, as the text suggests, that the owner did not think the land could be successfully exploited, or he might want the *coloni* on another land. But the emperor had not the private but the general interest in mind, namely continuous exploitation of land and, although not expressed, continuous tax revenues. His argument for prohibiting such a practice was that if the seller had thought them once useful on that estate, they would be useful for succeeding owners too and he should keep them attached to it to the benefit of his successors (CJ 11.48.2). The text

140 See Sirks 2019d. It appears that the Justinianic law was well known to and applied by Gregory.

141 Such as: P.Oxy. LXII 4350 (a. 576: steward, scribe: contracting the collection of a tax); P.Oxy. XVI 1979 (a. 613: guard); P.Oxy. LXXXIII 5385 (a. 584, an *adscripticius* of Apion who is a ναύτης is surety for another ναύτης; see also Sarris 2006, 59.

suggests that otherwise such a transfer was possible. Theoretically, a transfer could have been done by releasing the *coloni* from their bond and entering a new agreement with registration in the other estate's census. Yet it is not probable that it was done in this way because the seller would be dependent on the cooperation of the *coloni*. If the agreement was with the new owner, the *coloni* would be struck by the new owner in his census while the old owner would register them in another census. In the end it would make no difference for the fisc. By the prohibition, the first agreement with its census registration thus had an irreversible effect, in the interest of agriculture and, indirectly, fiscal revenues. It reinforced the function the census had as *origo* registration of the *coloni*.

Another constitution, CJ 11.48.7pr–2, gives an idea of the devices employed to effect a transfer of labourers:

> Quemadmodum originarios absque terra, ita rusticos censitosque servos vendi omnifariam non licet. 1. Neque vero commento fraudis id usurpet legis illusio, quod in originariis saepe actitatum est, ut parva portione terrae emptori tradita omnis integri fundi cultura adimatur. 2. Sed cum soliditas fundorum vel certa portio ad unumquemque perveniat, tanti quoque servi et originarii transeant, quanti apud superiores dominos et possessores vel in soliditate vel in parte manserunt: et emptor pretium quod dederit amissum existimet, nihilo minus venditori ad repetendos servos cum agnatione eorum vindicatione concessa. 3. Et si aliqua denique ex causa dissimulaverit legis usurpare beneficium atque iste sub hac taciturnitate decesserit, et heredibus eius et contra heredes emptoris vindicationem damus longi temporis praescriptione submota: mala fide namque possessorem esse nullus ambiget, qui aliquid contra legum interdicta mercatur.

> Just as it is not allowed to sell *originarii* from the land, in the same way it is not allowed in any way with farmers (*rustici*) and slaves entered in the census. 1. And not at all should a legal fabrication by an invention of fraud use this, what often and usually is done with *originarii*, that by the transfer of a small portion of the land to the buyer the cultivation of the bulk of the estate is taken away. 2. But when the bulk of an estate or a certain part goes to somebody, so much also of the slaves and *originarii* go over as were with the previous masters and owners either in the entirety or in the part. And the buyer may consider the price lost which he paid, notwithstanding that the seller is granted to claim back the slaves with their offspring. 3. And if in the end for any reason he shall have feigned that he took advantage of the law and this person has died, not disclosing this, we grant his heirs and against the heirs of the buyer a vindication, while the long limitation of prescription is removed. Then nobody should doubt that he is a possessor in bad faith, who buys something against the prohibitions of the law. (tr. Sirks)

The beginning is rather crude and shines a light on the *privata pactio* of the previous text, CJ 11.48.2: it is a sale. But such a sale is also not allowed with farmers and slaves who are entered in the census. Sometimes slaves were made into *instrumentum* of a land.[142] In that case they could not be separated from it, evidently to provide the cultivation of it. Such slaves should also be entered in the estate census. As to the farmers, since they are not *originarii*, they may have been lessees and of course they too could not be sold.

More interesting is the trick which apparently was commonly used to circumvent this prohibition: division of an estate. It is logical to assume that in that case the census had to be adjusted for the original estate and a new census had to be drawn up for the newly created part. In that procedure the *coloni originarii* were to be attributed to one or the other part. The trick would have been to attribute all *coloni* to a very small part. This part was bought, certainly for a good price, and the buyer could use the *coloni* on other land of him that adjoined the part, or elsewhere (see CJ 11.48.13.1, below). The remaining bulk was now devoid of labourers. This again shows that there was a great need for labour. The emperor disapproved of this, because in this way major parts of land were now in danger of not being cultivated. Thus he introduced a proportional distribution of the *coloni* over the land, so that the cultivation remained unimpaired. The buyer may have paid for more labour, but this surplus is lost and the seller may reclaim the surplus slaves with offspring, and we may assume that the same went for *coloni*. It was naturally not in the interest of the seller to disclose his dealings, but if his heirs discovered this, they too could reclaim the surplus of slaves transferred in this way, even if normally the limitation of prescription applied, that is, after a period of thirty or forty years. The reason that the limitation did not apply was that the buyer was in bad faith, which barred it. Again, this will have applied to *originarii* too. Agricultural labour consisted, as the text shows, of a mix of slaves and *coloni originarii*, next to lessee farmers.

Another possibility of transferring *coloni* was also blocked. A soldier could get permission to let his family and even the slaves in his *peculium* come over to his place of stationing, but he could not let his *coloni originales* (*adscribti censibus*) come over (CJ 12.35.10), evidently on land bought with his *peculium castrense*. The permission thus did not lift the ban on transfer of *coloni* (*adscripticii* or *liberi*) from their estate.

[142] Kaser 1971, 383.

Such prohibitions did not take away the need for labour. A landowner could order his *coloni* to do some work on another of his estates, but he might want to attach them permanently to that estate. In principle it is the same problem as above: Is it allowed to transfer *coloni* from one estate to another? The difference is that both estates belong to the same owner and that such a distribution of labour is likely to improve the yield of one estate without the other estate necessarily suffering. Such a situation might also arise in the case of an *epibolè*, when deserted land was adjudicated to a landowner. The response of the emperor (in CJ 11.48.13.1) is favourable. It is allowed if shortage of labour (*laborabat tenuitate*) requires this, but if the two estates pass into different hands, the transfer remains firm, but the owner of the estate from which *coloni* were taken could reclaim the offspring of the transferred *coloni*. This tallies with the concept behind CJ 11.48.2.1, which says that whoever thinks that *coloni* are useful on a parcel of land should keep them there; it is in accordance with the wish for permanent cultivation by tied workers. The claim for the offspring may be seen as a concession to the loss the transferring estate suffered. The transfer implied a change in *origo* and therefore this claim had to be granted specially.

The division which CJ 11.48.7 dealt with was a fraudulent one, but there were also bona fide divisions, usually in the case of an inheritance where co-ownership was ended. Here the prescription of CJ 11.48.7 will have also applied, but in the distribution of people over the parts, the families of slaves, *adscripticii* and *inquilini* had to stay together (CJ 3.38.11).[143]

Whatever somebody left by testament to the church in Constantinople was to remain property of the church and could not, under what pretext ever, by what functionary ever, be alienated (CJ 1.2.14pr, 1). Only a usufruct could be granted, be it that upon expiration the goods had to be returned to the church (CJ 1.2.14.9; it was not unthinkable that such a usufruct might be turned into property). Amongst these goods were estates with *coloni* and their *peculia* attached to it; hence it concerned *adscripticii*.

[143] The original text, CTh 2.25.1 of 29 April 325 according to Seeck 1919, dealt only with the division of inheritances of patrimonial or emphyteuticarian lands and of the slaves thereon. Apparently in line with CJ 11.48.2 and 7, which deal with the division of *adscripticii* in case of sale, it was interpolated so as to make it apply to these as well: after *servorum* was added *vel colonorum adscripticiae condicionis seu inquilinorum proxima agnatio vel adfinitas*. Further, the restriction to those particular lands was dropped.

12 *Coloni* Who Migrate and Recalling Them

12.1 Reasons for Migrating

The purpose of the colonate was to have labour at hand on the estate so that the management could proceed as efficiently as possible, as the Heroninos archive shows for the third century. It was the answer to farmers-lessees and farm hands who were free to go after their tenancy or employment had finished. With *coloni* the advantage for them was that these did not have this freedom and so provided a permanent supply of labour. Nevertheless, we see also here migration and flight.

A famous case is Pieous, an *enapographos* in the sixth century, in P.Oxy. XXVII 2479:[144]

> To my good benefactor and lord, petition and supplication from Pieous your slave from the village of Kinea. Your all-glorious lordship's love of the poor and of Christ, going out over the land, has caused many of its people to have recourse to your lordship and they come forward and receive justice and all pity. (Therefore ? . . .) I too come forward and weeping and saying of myself that I am your all-glorious lordship's registered farmer [*enapographos georgos*] and that these three years ago my beasts died and I ran away from my farm, as I have said, three years ago, and stayed away from home. And having remained away from home for that same space of three years that I might find . . . food? and to be registered along with my children . . . of the farm . . . I beg and supplicate your all-glorious lordship [lordship, if it

[144] P.Oxy. XXVII 2479 (sixth c.): (hand 1?) τῷ ἐμῷ ἀγαθῷ εὐεργ(έτῃ) (καὶ) δεσπ(ότῃ) δέησις (καὶ) ἱκεσία/ (hand 2?) π(αρὰ) Πιηοῦτ[ο]σ ὑμετέρ(ου) δούλου ἀπὸ ἐποικ(ίου) Κινέας./ (hand 3?) τὸ φιλόπτωχο[ν] καὶ φιλόχριστον τῆς ὑμετέρας πανευκλεοῦς δεσποτείας/ παρὰ πᾶσαν τὴν γῆν ἐξελθὸν πολλοὺς ταύτης προσφεύγειν αὐτῇ παρεσκευάσαν,/ 5οἵτινες προσερχ[ό]μενοι τοῦ δικαίου καὶ πάσης ἐλεη[μοσύ]ṇης τυγχ[ά]νουṣị./ [ὅ]θ̣ẹṇ(*) κἀγὼ ὁ ἐλεειṇ[ὸς](*) [π]ροσέρχομαι κ̣α̣τ̣α̣δακρύω[ν καὶ δι]δάσκων [κα]τὰ ἐμαυτὸν/ [ὡς γεω]ρ̣γὸς ἐναπό̣γραφος τυγχάνω τῆς ὑμ̣ετέρας π[α]νευκλ̣ε̣οῦ̣ς δεσποτείας/ [καὶ ὡς πρ(?)]ὸ τριῶν τούτων ἐνιαυτῶν ἐτελεύτησαν τὰ ἐ[μὰ] κτήνη καὶ ἀπέστην(*)/ [τῆς](*) [ἐμ]ῆ̣ς γεωργίας, ὡς εἴρηται, πρὸ τριῶν ἐνιαυτῶν καὶ ἔμεινα ἐπὶ ξένης./ 10[καὶ ἐπὶ(?)] τὸν α̣ὐ̣τ̣ὸν τριέτη χρόνον παραμένων ἐπὶ ξένης ὅπως εὕρω/ [-ca.?-] [-ca.?-] ἀ̣π̣ο̣[τ]ρ̣οφὰς(?)(*) καὶ ἀποτραφῆναί(*) \με/ μετὰ τῶν ἐμῶν τέκνων/ [-ca.?-] η τοῦ κτήματος/ [-ca.?-] /––––––––––/ 15[1 line missing]/ 16––––––––––/ 14[παρακα]λῶ καὶ ἱκετεύω τὴν ὑμετέραν π̣[ανευκ]λ̣[εῆ δεσποτείαν](*)/ 15[ἵνα](*) προστάξῃ(*) εἰσελθεῖν με ἐν τῷ κτήματι καὶ μὴ ἀπαι[τ]ηθῆναί με/ [ὑπὲρ ο]ὗ̣ οὐ̣κ(*) ἔσπειρα ὅπως ἐφεξῆς δυνηθῶ ἐργ[ά]σασθαι/ [ἐν τῷ] α̣ὐ̣τ̣ῷ κτήματι καὶ ἀποθρέψαι(*) τὰ ἐμὰ ἄθλια τέκνα. καὶ ἀναπέμψω/ τῷ δεσπότῃ Χριστῷ \τὰς εὐχάς μου/ ὑπὲρ τῆς ζωῆς τῆς ὑμετέρας πανευκλεοῦς/ δεσποτείας. ἀδυνάτως γὰρ ἔχω, δέσποτα, συντελέσαι ὑπὲρ οὗ/ 20οὐ̣ σπείρω. εἰσὶν γὰρ οἱ σπείροντες(*) καὶ δυνάμενοι συντελέσαι./ καὶ τοῦτο δὲ διδάσκω ὡς ὅτι ἐλθὼν ἐν τῷ κτήματι ὁ προνοητὴς/ διήρπαξεν πάντα τὰ εὐτελῆ μου πράγματα χάριν τῆς τοιαύτης/ αἰτίας. καὶ παρακαλῶ τοῦ ὑμετέρου ἐλέους τυχεῖν. μάρτυρα̣ γὰρ/ ἐπικαλοῦμαι τὸν δεσπότην θεὸν ὡς ὅτι τὸ κλάσα̣ι̣(*) ἤτοι τὸ ξηρὸν/ 25ψω̣μὶν(*) οὐκ ἔχω φαγεῖν μετὰ τῶν ἐμῶν τέκνων προκειμένης/ τ[αύ]τη̣ς [ἕνε]κα τῆς εὐθενίας(*). καὶ τούτου χάριν κατέφυγα αὐτῇ/ ὅπ[ω]σ ἐναριθμηθῆναί με μετὰ πάντων τῶν εὐεργετηθέντων/ παρὰ α̣ὐ̣τῆς, πανευκλεέστ(ατε) εὐεργέτα, δέσποτα, κύριε. On this papyrus, Keenan 1980.

> pleases your lordship] to give orders that I return to the farm and not be asked for . . . I sowed that I might labour on the same farm and bring up my unhappy children. And I shall send up to the Lord Christ my prayers for the life of your all-glorious lordship. For I cannot, lord, pay on what I do not sow. Those who sow are the ones that can pay. And this too I say: that the steward came on the farm and plundered all my poor possessions for this cause. And I beg to receive your pity. For I call the Lord God to witness that, inundation or drought, I have not a morsel to eat, nor my children, because of this helplessness (?) that I have mentioned. And on this account I have recourse to your lordship, so that I may be counted among those benefited by your lordship, most all-glorious benefactor, lord, master. (Turner 1962)

Pieous addresses an unknown landowner, probably Flavius Apion II from Oxyrhynchus, lamenting his misfortune: he left his farm, he roamed for three years in total misery. He cannot pay his debts,[145] because who does not sow cannot reap: in other words, he has not had any income in those years and the procurator has seized his possessions.[146] Now he begs his lordship to accept him again as *enapographos georgos* with his family and reinstate him on his farm.

Why did Pieous leave the estate? Why did *coloni* flee in general? One way to find out is looking at the functions and occupations from which they are ousted: the imperial service, mostly, but also being employees elsewhere. These apparently offered better lives, particularly the service. They also testify to the social mobility in those days. But Pieous does not mention these. It will have been a debt to his landowner, because he refers to the steward who seized his belongings. Perhaps he had hoped to find elsewhere a better living, a better employment. But being away did not annul his debt, and for this he implores a release from his landowner. Becoming an *enapographos* again protects him against the taxes, but also puts him into the bond with the estate. Perhaps it was precisely this which brought him to flee. We have sureties which are made expressly to keep *enapographoi* on the estate.[147] Apparently there were people who had by necessity to enter the colonate but found the bond hard to comply with. Harsh conditions of the farming life on the one side and the available possibilities of an easier

[145] The editor of the papyrus thinks of rents on the land.

[146] Triantaphyllopoulos 1967, 356–357 prefers that Pieous could not pay the taxes and not the tenancy fee as the editor thinks, and in that case the procurator may have been an official and not an employee of the landowner. But in that case Pieous owned his farm and to reclaim this from the landowner is strange, because the landowner was in no formal relation with the official. Unofficially a mighty landowner could, of course, exercise sufficient influence on an official to return the farm.

[147] See Fikhman 1981 = Fikhman 2016, 169–177, § 12.2 *in fine*; Palme unpubl. on *Burgstellungen*.

life (administration, clergy) on the other side may have had their effect. But debts may also have been a motive.

Then, unless he had his *dominus*' permission, a *colonus* was not free to move away or migrate from the estate or his *origo* (CJ 11.48.6, 7, 8, 11, 15). *Coloni* could deny the right of ownership to the estate and by that the *dominus*' entitlement over them. If they succeeded, they were at least not bound to the estate and could migrate. This case is dealt with in CJ 11.48.20pr, which has already been discussed *in extenso* in Section 8.1.

Much easier, however, was to simply go away, openly or secretly: flight. They could be recalled by their estate owner. Flight was a permanent concern for the estate owners and emperors, as constitutions testify. It would seem that *adscripticii* were prone to it, if we believe the constitutions and papyri. But we of course lack figures and we can only guess the size of their flight. The words used in this context, *fuga*, *fugitivus*, imply a subtraction from a duty, just as in the army, hence they represent the view of the estate owner and the authorities. The other view we can only deduce indirectly as above: those dwelling in the dark are invisible ('die im Dunkeln sieht man nicht'). Flight must be distinguished from absence as such, which, as long as a person liable for the colonate by status and *origo* had not been formally summoned by his estate owner to perform his duties, was possible (CJ 11.48.22.3). Also 'free' *coloni* could flee since although 'free' they were bound to an estate. CJ 11.48.23.5 deals particularly with the flight of 'free' *coloni*, about which below (see Sections 16 and 17).

Migration, but not flight, was also done by children of *coloni*. They had more freedom to go away if the landowner was satisfied with their parents performing the required obligations. Yet, in the end, they too were subjected to the colonate and could be recalled; see under Section 12.2.

12.2 *Recalling* Coloni

The *adscripticius* and the 'free' *colonus* could be recalled because they had acted contrary to their obligation to stay. It was a private person, the estate owner, who claimed not just the *colonus* but also his family and usually his possessions. The legal tools the estate owner had at his disposal were those of the administrative and private law. Procedurally there was not much difference between these two branches of law. They differed only in as much as there were special provisions for private law, criminal or administrative cases.[148] In the case of the 'free' colonate it certainly was a public

[148] See Litewski 1965–1968.

obligation since it was imposed by law, while the law entrusted the authority to recall to the estate owner (CJ 11.51.1, *possessionis domino revocandi eius plena tribuatur auctoritas*, also CJ 11.48.23.5: *admonente domino ... terrae*, which suggests that he denounced to an official, who then took measures; for the 'free' colonate, see Section 16). If liturgies were to be fulfilled, a recall by the public authorities was possible. Towns or *vici* could claim people for liturgies, like the decurionate or cleaning up canals or helping with state transports. The characterisation of their position as a *condicio* put the *coloni* on a par with those in towns who, *condicionales* too, performed public duties there, and with those *condicionales* in imperial industries like the mints.[149]

In Justinian's times, the procedure to recall no longer consisted of the actions and interdicts of the classical period. These had been incorporated into the now used *libellus* procedure. In the *libellus* the claimant submitted his petition. Substantially, the petition referred to the former actions and interdicts. Thus a father could claim a child in his power by a *reivindicatio filii* (D. 6.1.1.2)[150] and could demand that the defendant brought forward before the judge the children claimed (the *interdictum de liberis exhibendis* or *ducendis*, D. 43.30.1 pr, 1–2). Similarly, a mother could claim her child (D. 43.30.3.5). In a similar way the estate owner must have been able to claim *coloni originales*, since, as the sources state, they were under his power. This must have applied in the same way to 'free' *coloni* and the claim will have been framed similarly. If the emphasis lay on the *potestas* of the landowner, it was probably as with children *nomine potestatis*;[151] if not, the ground may have been something like *nomine coloniariae condicionis*, for both *adscripticii* and 'free' *coloni*.[152] It implies that the right to claim was based on the *condicio coloniaria*, thus based on the subjection of the *adscripticii* to the *potestas* of the landowner and comparable to that of a *pater familias* over his children and slaves. After filing a claim, his estate owner could coerce him to return, with the assistance of the provincial

149 See 'Αι Ροπαι 10, where these duties are undoubtedly categorised as public obligations.

150 D. 6.1.1.2 Ulp. 16 ed: *Per hanc autem actionem liberae personae, quae sunt iuris nostri, ut puta liberi qui sunt in potestate, non petuntur: petuntur igitur aut praeiudiciis aut interdictis aut cognitione praetoria, et ita Pomponius libro trigensimo septimo: nisi forte, inquit, adiecta causa quis vindicet: si quis ita petit 'filium suum' vel 'in potestate ex iure romano', videtur mihi et Pomponius consentire recte eum egisse: ait enim adiecta causa ex lege Quiritium vindicare posse.* The restriction Ulpian makes in the beginning is of course to exclude that one claims his children as if mere property.

151 *Ex iure Romanorum* also, as with children? We do not know. The *libellus* procedure was applied.

152 The expression is used by Justinian in the context of foundlings (CJ 1.4.24 = CJ 8.51.3pr): such children may not be claimed (*vindicare*) by anyone *nomine dominii sive adscripticiae sive coloniariae condicionis*, namely, from those who found them. This was the normal way to claim, as is also apparent from D. 6.1.1.2, above note 150.

administration (CJ 11.48.6, on *adscripticii*). Four months after the verdict it could be executed on request of the claimant: an *exsecutor* (a servant of the court) could take the *coloni* into custody and hand them over to the estate owner.[153]

A *colona* might flee to a town or another place and marry an *ingenuus* (i.e., someone not subjected to the *condicio adscripticia* or another demeaning subjected status). If she was found, she could be recalled with her offspring (CJ 11.48.16). That her offspring could be claimed as well was due to the unequal marriage rule as regards the *origo* of town and estate (see Section 10.3). Normally the children would have followed the status and *origo* of their father and not have been subjected to the *condicio coloniaria.* The case of an *adscripticius* marrying an *ingenua* was already dealt with above (Section 10.2).

Where the authorities provided means of recall, they also made flight more difficult at the other end of the spectrum, namely the receiving landowners who needed labour. It was forbidden to harbour fugitive *coloni* (CJ 11.48.23.4–5). The estate owner who had accepted such a fugitive was also punished with a fine of 12 pounds of silver to the fisc and another person of the same value to the master of the fugitive,[154] besides having to return the fugitive with his property (CJ 11.48.12; Ed. Praef. 25, of presumably 512; see Section 13.2).[155] Likewise, Justinian ordered in his mandate to provincial governors that they had to compel estate owners to return fugitive *coloni* they had taken up, whether these *coloni* came from the same or another province. If they refused, the governors had to impose on them the deserted land in their province (Nov. 17.14, 535). As a result they were in one way or another employed in the cultivation of land. After the reconquest of Africa, Justinian ordered that all *coloni* who had left their lands under the Vandal rule (429/439–533) had to be left in peace and remain as under the Vandals; but those who absconded after that (i.e., after 533 when Gelimer was finally beaten) had to be restored (App. 6, of 552).

[153] Kaser & Hackl 1996, 624, 626.

[154] *Eiusdem aestimationis*: it cannot be the purchasing price of the *colonus*. Since the fugitive could be taken and handed over, a claim may have mentioned a *litis aestimatio*, which would be the valuation of the *colonus*, but it would not have led to a condemnation to pay this sum. I assume it represented the sum needed to replace the fugitive by free labour or a slave.

[155] Zachariae 1843 (Anekdota), 275. The text resembles CJ 11.48.12, where a fine of 12 pounds of silver is set, plus the obligation to render another person of the same value to the master of the fugitive. That constitution was originally issued for the west, whereas CTh 5.17.2, with only a fine of six or 12 ounces of gold, was issued in the east. Either CJ 11.48.12 was apparently taken over in the east or it came into force in the east through Justinian's Code. The διπλάσια in the edict should therefore not be read as *duplio*, 'the double', that is, of the fine.

He decreed for Italy in 554 that all slaves and *coloni* should be returned to their masters, adding that the children begotten during the absence should also return (App. 7.16). However, the order for Africa was not well obeyed: there were estate owners who reclaimed *coloni* who had absconded before the Byzantine reconquest, even if they were clerics. This practice was once again forbidden, and particularly the recall of *coloni* turned clerics was to be suppressed firmly (App. 9 of 558).

There must have been a need for labour everywhere on the land, since it appears that *coloni* who had fled were usually found working on the land of other people, which suggests they fled because conditions were unfavourable or because of debts. The relevant constitution, CJ 11.48.8, mentions two situations. One is that estate owners knew they were dealing with *coloni* and used them to their profit. They would accomplish this by having them till land and turning over its products to them, or by having them perform other labour and not paying them any wages. The text implies that they used their knowledge to blackmail them with their fugitive status. In that case they had to pay the taxes which were otherwise lost (*tributa quae publicis perierunt functionibus exigantur*, CJ 11.48.8pr).[156] The other situation is that the estate owners did not know of the flight and that the *coloni* deceivingly offered their services as men free of the colonate bond (*ingenui*), as farm labourers, or as share-croppers. In that case the taxes should be claimed directly from the *coloni* themselves, since, as the texts state, it concerns a *contractus privatus*.[157] This means that this contract had no public law element (as the colonate agreement had) and the *coloni* were not only tax-liable but had to pay the tax themselves. Thus, as the constitution says, all fugitives will be recalled together with the *emolumenta tributaria* ('fiscal benefits', i.e., what they had to pay as tax – in any case the *capitatio humana* – and which was a benefit to the state; CJ 11.48.8 pr). In all cases, any debts (including those resulting from accounts in the giro system of the estate, where payments in money or kind were recorded next to what the employees

156 The poll tax. Where the fugitives were registered, they and not their masters paid this, and where they now dwelt they were not registered at all and thus did not pay there either. But being exploited, they had had no earnings, whereas the estate owner had fraudulently profited from them, and so it was justified that he should pay what otherwise the fugitives would have had to pay.

157 The term *contractus publicus* is used in this period in our sources for contracting out taxes (custom duties). But apparently we may here, *a contrario*, assume that the colonate agreement was also considered a *contractus publicus* by virtue of the census registration. Yet *a contrario* reasonings are not decisive. Vera 1997 = Vera 2019, 255 n.12 sees in the text a difference between manifest fugitive *coloni* and *coloni* who keep their status secret. The latter could conclude normal contracts; the former could not and had to accept disadvantageous conditions. According to Vera, I differentiated in Sirks 1993a, 362 between *adscripticii* and free *coloni*, but I wrote: 'the problem dealt with is the flight of *coloni originales*', which is precisely the same as what he says.

got on credit – a practice already recorded for the third century)[158] should be settled before the return (CJ 11.48.8.2).[159] It follows that in case of flight the obligation of the estate owner to pay for his *adscripticii* stopped (as regarded future taxes). Thus if *adscripticii* fled and were employed by another estate owner who did not pay them wages, neither from the original estate owner nor from the *adscripticii* (or *coloni*) themselves could the poll tax be reclaimed. Hence the imposition of the liability for this on the *mala fide* estate owner. In the case of the 'private contract' there was no reason why it should not be claimed from the fugitives themselves.

Did these measures make the harbouring and use of *coloni* who had fled less attractive?[160] It may have deterred the *mala fide* estate owner, but he disposed on the other hand of labour, while the original estate owner had first to track down his fugitives. Flight was evidently a problem, as these constitutions and the number of sureties for good behaviour prove.

If an estate owner possessed in good faith *coloni* who were claimed by somebody else (as in the second situation mentioned before) and the *coloni* fled to avoid the outcome of the litigation, it was this estate owner who could claim them back and not the other person; having been returned to him, the actual procedure could start (CJ 11.48.14), which is in accordance with the use of possessory interdicts in the private law.

It would be naive to suppose that estate owners always walked the path of the righteous and used official ways to recall fugitives, or that they were so naive as to assume that after return all was well. They will have chased and captured fugitives themselves and wanted certainty after their return. A number of papyri are about guarantees given for a fugitive *enapographos*, usually imprisoned.[161] The surety must guarantee that the fugitive

[158] See Rathbone 1991, 160ff. For earlier times, see Preisigke 1910.

[159] See previous note and note 98 on the accounting system in the third century which would enable a giro system. The settlement would have made clear the amount of the *peculium* of the *coloni*; see below.

[160] The harbouring estate owner would pay the taxes upon discovery which he had not otherwise, but he would have saved them otherwise; and in the second case he only had to pay their wages.

[161] There were private prisons, whether in a town house or on estates, although it was forbidden by CTh 9.5.1 of 388, E, to put people in them (forbidden for Alexandria, the diocese of Egypt and other provinces, so the main cause seems to have been the situation in Egypt). The penalty was accusation of *crimen maiestatis*. The papyri date from later, so evidently neither the constitution nor its later repetition by Justinian, CJ 9.5.2 of 429, served as a deterrent. See on this kind of surety Palme unpubl. Cautions were required not only by estate owners but also by officials. Cautions that an *adscripticius* will abide: P.Oxy. I 135, 200 (by adscr.), P.Oxy. VI 996 (by adscr.), XVI 1979, XXVI 2478, XVII 2203 (?), XLIV 3204, LXX 4756, 4757, 4758 (?), 4787, 4790, 4791, 4794, 4802(?); P. Heidelberg III 248, P. London III 778, PSI 52 (*adscripticia*), 59 (?), 62, P. Merton II 98, *SB* XVI 12484, XVIII 14006. Sarris 2006, 61–65 assumes that these sureties were given for *adscripticii* who entered employment (with the Apiones). It is not inconceivable that this might have happened, and *cautiones* abounded in Antiquity, but several cases undeniably concern imprisoned *adscripticii*. See

enapographos will answer for all that pertains to his person or rather his status as *enapographos* (ἀποκρινόμενον εἰς ἅπαντα τὰ ὁρῶντα τὸ αὐτοῦ πρό[σ]ωπον ἤτοι τὴν τοῦ ἐναπογράφου τύχην),[162] that is, as formulated extensively in P.Oxy. I 135, that he will remain continuously on the estate (μηδαμῶς αὐτον καταλεῖψαι τὸ αὐτὸ κτῆμα μήτε μὴν μεθ[[ε]]ίστασθαι εἰς ἕτερον τύπον) with his children and wife, cattle and utensils, that he will be answerable for all that pertains to his person or his status as *enapographos*, that he will not go to another place; often also,[163] that he will pay his *phoros* (φόρος) himself, that is, his poll tax;[164] that in the case of a second flight the surety will deliver him; or else the surety will pay a fine or will do his duties.[165]

12.3 Limitation of Prescription against Recall

The flight of *coloni* from the estate is compared to the flight of slaves who steal themselves: *secundum exemplum servi fugitivi sese diutinis insidiis furari intellegatur*, 'after the example of the fugitive slave he is considered to steal himself by plots of long duration' (CJ 11.48.23pr).[166] This is a peculiar characterisation. A slave was property and as such could only be stolen by somebody else. The construction of a 'self-stealing' in case of fleeing was merely to avoid usucapion by somebody else, or loss of the vindication by limitation of prescription, because a stolen thing could not be usucapted.

on this also Fikhman 1981 = Fikhman 2016, 169–177 on the guarantees, and further Fikhman 1984 = 2006, 204.

162 Fikhman 1984 = 2006, 195.

163 See also Hickey 2012, 81–89 on the ἐναπόγραφοι γεουργοι.

164 In P.Oxy. LXIII 4398: μετὰ καὶ τοῦ φορικοῦ μου φόρου (see Section 7), in P.Oxy. I 133 (a loan) μετὰ καὶ τοῦ φορικοῦ ἡμῶν φόρου (translated by the editor as 'tax payable by us'), P.Oxy. XXVII 2478 (a deed of surety) τὸν ὑπερ αὐτοῦ φόρον, translated by the editor as 'the tax due on it' (the land). The tax will have been the poll tax. If not, it must have been a rent and he would have leased a plot, unless he held land in his charge, which suggests a *precarium* as in P.Oxy. LXIII 4398. Banaji 2001, 97 considers this in P.Oxy. XXVII 2478 to refer to the rent. Similarly Hickey 2012, 68 n. 35, who draws attention to my wrong interpretation in Sirks 2008, 135. As in other texts, the orchard must have been put in his charge. Banaji interprets δημοσία in PSI I 62 as taxes and not as rent, but in my opinion Petrus had to perform liturgies: τὰ αὐτῶν δημοσία. In P.Oxy. LV 3804 (a. 566, an account of an estate), there is explicit mention of the poll tax being received (τοῦ κοιν(οῦ) τῶν γεωρ(γῶν) ὑπὲρ συντελ(είας) κεφ(αλῆς)) but this does not conflict with the above. The *adscripticius* may have been obliged to promise in a general way to perform all payments he had to make, whereas the steward had to make a precise account of what he collected.

165 Fikhman 1984 = 2006, 202–206. In P.Oxy. XVI 1979 (a. 614) the surety, an ἐναπόγραφος himself, even guarantees that he himself will perform all that is required from the still imprisoned ἐναπόγραφος. Apparently the duties were in this case not so burdensome that he could not take somebody else's upon him.

166 See Sirks 1993a, 348–351, 366.

That is the reason here too: to avoid liberty being claimed after thirty years. But it also implies that the *colonus* was put on a par with property.

This general limitation of prescription applied both in private and public law (e.g., CJ 7.39.41), with the exception in public law regarding the summons of people for public duties on basis of their birth status (*condicio*) as here and elsewhere.[167] An exception is CJ 11.66.6, which states that those *coloni* or *inquilini* of the imperial *res privata* or *domus* who have served for thirty years on a town council, in a municipal *corpus* or any other *corpus* or *burgus*,[168] cannot be recalled by the *res privata* or the *res dominica*, that is, that the managers raise the *quaestio colonatus vel inquilinatus.* They remain, however, tied to the function and place where they serve, that is, they have a new *condicio* (CJ 11.66.6). This exchangeability demonstrates that the *condicio* and the duties of the *coloni* were or had become of a different nature. They became exchangeable with *condiciones* which were public (as the obligation for the town council).[169]

Children of *coloni* (namely, *adscripticii*) could be claimed as well. If they raised the exception of limitation of thirty or forty years against the claim,[170] it would be of no avail (CJ 11.48.22.3–5). It could indeed be argued that since their father had fulfilled the demands of the estate owner, who had not required next to that their presence, the estate owner had lost his rights. They might have been away from the estate for a long time and could have pursued occupations other than farming, as CJ 11.48.22.3 says. The emperor solves this problem by the fiction that part of their body had stayed on the estate, namely in the form of their father or relatives. Thus they had never really been away in freedom (CJ 11.48.22.4). It is an argument for the occasion and further evidence that the emperor went a long way to assist landowners in their need for labour force.

12.4 *Immunities against a Recall*

It might turn out that a *colonus* had availed himself of a position which provided immunity from obligations, based on his *condicio.* Clerics enjoyed a general immunity, but if a *colonus* became cleric in the *vicus* of his master,

167 Rejected, for example, in CJ 7.39.5 by Anastasius for curials and their children when summoned for municipal duties, with confirmation of previous rulings. The other exceptions are unimportant here.

168 A *burgus* was a castle or fort. There too people were tied to serve in these: CTh 7.14.1 (398 W), as were *muliones publici* at the *mutationes*: CTh 8.5.58 (398 W) = CJ 12.50.17.

169 A good question: How was the liability (*obnoxietas*) for these other functions established? The census register might help if wife and children were nominally mentioned in it. Otherwise it should be established on the basis of birth registers or common knowledge and witnesses.

170 The general limitation of prescription, introduced by Theodosius in 424 in the east (CJ 7.3.9) and Valentinian III in 449 in the west (Nov. Val. 27).

he had to give a substitute who would acknowledge the *capitatio* and the tasks on the land (CJ 1.3.16; see Sections 8.3 and 14.1). The acknowledgement of the *capitatio* was because churches and thus clerics were exempted from this tax. Recall was also possible if *adscripticii* had been chosen as clerics or as monks without the approval of their masters (CJ 1.3.36pr).

The imperial services offered such enviable positions of immunity, and in order not to harm the estate owners, it was forbidden to accept *coloni* without their estate owners' consent (CJ 11.48.18 for lower *militia* posts and as *apparitores* of the *magistri militum*) or at all where it concerned recruitment for the army (*tirones*): CJ 12.43.1 forbids the acceptance of *censibus obnoxii*. That certainly includes *coloni*, but it may have included also other groups of registered workers like the *monetarii* or *collegiati*. Further, the function of *apparitor* in the office of the *magister militum* was off-limits for them (CJ 12.54.3). If it nevertheless happened, the immunity was ineffective, as was the *auctoritas census* (CJ 11.48.11, mentioning *originarii*, i.e., persons bound to an estate on account of the census as *origo*, here of course including *coloni*). By *auctoritas census* must have been meant the effect of a (fraudulent) enrolment elsewhere.

12.5 Another Way of Losing Labour: Exposition

Next to flight, exposition could be a way to lose hands. Exposing children was a feature of antique life. The parents may have hoped that their child would get a better life – be it because their resources were insufficient, be it that they hoped the child would be free of the *condicio coloniaria* (but it was not impossible that foundlings were raised to be slaves, a worse condition). In any case, if it concerned *coloni originales*, their estate owners might thereby lose potential labour. If a child of one's slave woman or *adscripticia* was abandoned without the estate owner's knowledge or approval, he could in virtue of his power claim such a child from its foster parents under compensation of the costs he had incurred in nourishing it or having it learn a trade (CJ 8.51.1 – in this text *vel adscripticiae* has been interpolated due to CJ 8.51.3 of 529). If they had stolen the child, he did not have to compensate. But if it had happened with his knowledge or according to his wishes, he would have lost his right to reclaim it.

In line with the rule existing in his time that parents lost their rights if they exposed their children, Justinian forbade any reclaiming by people of foundlings (it would have been attractive for an estate owner to claim a foundling as his *colonus*; the rule partially conflicts with CJ 8.51.1), but at the same time he forbade the foster parents to impose a lower status upon the child and thus that a foundling would be drawn into, for example, the adscripticiate on account of its foster parents (CJ 1.4.24 = 8.51.3).[171] He ruled that foundlings would always be free people with full rights, regardless of their original birth status (which might even have been servile) (CJ 8.51.3.1–2).

13 Release from the Colonate and the 'Free' Colonate

13.1 Incidental Private Release

Could an *adscripticius* be released from the colonate? One reference to release from the colonate we find in CJ 11.48.21.1. The estate owner was a private person and had the *adscripticius* in his *potestas*, as CJ 11.48.21.1 says. Justinian goes on to say that the master can free a slave together with his *peculium* and eject an *adscripticius* with his land from his *dominium* (*et possit servum cum peculio manumittere et adscripticium cum terra suo dominio expellere*). *Expellere* is rather crude, but since it is the release from the *potestas* of the master for both, it must mean that the *adscripticius* too could be released with his own land. It is possible that this was a plot which his master had previously allocated to him *in precario* and now donated to him, but also that it was his own plot (*arva*) which now was released from being treated as if *peculium* (see Section 7.2). It is a fitting comparison, as slaves and *filii familias* could have a *peculium* which they often were allowed to keep after release. Justinian's remark is meant to show the similarity in practice between the two, because in the preceding lines he has implied the fundamental legal difference between slaves and *adscripticii*, the latter being free people. How this release was done is not said, but Justinian's Institutes 1.5.1 say that next to the traditional ways there were many other modes to release, without specifying this (*sed et aliis multis modis libertas servo competere potest, qui tam ex veteribus quam nostris constitutionibus introducti sunt*), for example manumission in a church before the bishop. Release must here be interpreted in that the estate owner had the *colonus* struck from his property census (as CJ 11.52.1pr implies by the abolition of the *capitatio humana*). The *colonus* would thereby have become free from his authority. He might now get permission to migrate (one needed official permission to change one's *origo*). The duty

[171] There is no reason to suspect the reference to the *adscripticia sive coloniaria condicio* in this constitution as an interpolation, as Fikhman 1984 = 2006, 193 does. The text, issued by Justinian, fits the other Justinianic texts, and the claim was not as property but for the services on basis of the *origo*.

to pay poll tax was independent from this, and the now former *adscripticius* remained liable for it.

An implicit and *de facto* release of the adscripticiate was possible if an *adscripticius* wanted to become a priest or monk in his own *vicus*. His estate owner had to approve of this, and the *adscripticius* had to provide a substitute who had to acknowledge the poll tax (*capitatio*) of the *adscripticius* (CJ 1.3.16). Ordination was in general forbidden unless the estate owner approved (CJ 1.3.16, repeated in 1.3.36.pr). Whether this led to full release in cases other than CJ 1.3.16 is not clear. The clerical post may have granted a temporary immunity, as other functions might do in the imperial services, for example, or as in CJ 2.7.21, where the prohibition for certain advocates to be of a *deterior condicio* seems to imply an immunity. Nov. 123.35 (546) says that if a *colonus* wants to become monk and he is accepted in ignorance of his condition, he can be recalled within three years by his master as fugitive and returned with his assets. Implicitly, this means he would be immune after these three years; also, that if his condition is known he may not be admitted. In general a *colonus* was not free to use a privilege which provided an immunity from the colonate (CJ 11.48.11, 18); see Section 12.4 for some immunities.

13.2 Institutional Release: Anastasius' Constitution

These releases were all dependent on the master's consent. Releases independent of this were (a) if the poll tax was abolished (it took the basis for the colonate away), yet it was replaced in three provinces by the 'free' colonate; and (b) by a transformation of the colonate: if an *adscripticius* had performed his duties for thirty years, he would be released from this, but he could not migrate from the estate, as CJ 11.48.23.1 states. The freedom was thus a freedom from the *potestas* of the estate owner over him, particularly as regards property (see Sections 7.1 and 7.2), in short: the adscripticiate was replaced by the 'free' colonate. CJ 11.48.23.1 attributes this status change to a constitution of Anastasius (491–518). The only text which qualifies for this is CJ 11.48.19. It is a reconstruction of the Code by way of the Basilica, where CJ 11.48 has been included. Theoretically this particular text, which probably was a résumé by a Byzantine professor in the first years after the Justinianic codification,[172] could have been issued by another emperor than Anastasius. Yet since Justinian himself, who

[172] But, being transmitted in the Synopsis, could have been reduced again by the author of this tenth-century work; see Van der Wal & Lokin 1985, 92.

otherwise is the only emperor after Anastasius to be a possible candidate for this, refers to Anastasius himself, and because of its phrasing it is impossible for it to have been a résumé of CJ 11.48.23.1. The attribution is therefore well founded.[173] CJ 11.48.19 grants the 'free' colonate to those *adscripticii* who have served thirty years, a period which equals the limitation of prescription of thirty years:

> [Αὐτοκράτωρ Ἀναστάσιος Α.] Τῶν γεωγῶν οἱ μὲν ἐναπόγαφοί εἴσιν καὶ τὰ τούτων πεκούλια τοῖς δεσπόταις ἀνήκει, οἱ δὲ χρόνῳ τῆς τριακονταετίας μισθωτοὶ γίνονται ἐλεύθεροι μένοντες μετὰ τῶν πραγμάτων αὕτων· καὶ οὗτοι δὲ ἀναγκάζονται καὶ τὴν γῆν γεωργεῖν καὶ τὸ τέλος παρέχειν. τοῦτο δὲ καὶ τοῖς δεσπόταις καὶ τοῖς γεωργοῖς λυσιτελεῖ:
>
> [Emperor Anastasios Augustos] Of the farmers some are *enapographoi* (ἐναπόγραφοι = *adscripticii*) and the *peculia* of these belong to the masters, others become by thirty years free labourers, although remaining with their property; and these are obliged to till the land and provide the tax. This profits the masters as well as the farmers. (tr. Sirks)[174]

That we probably do not have the original text is no problem: if it were a résumé by a Byzantine professor of the sixth century, he would have rendered its essential meaning, while the relatively short time lapse would not have allowed for a change in interpretation. What confirms this is the fact that Justinian repeats the disposition in CJ 11.48.23.1. Apart from this repetition, any possible further doubt is removed by the confirmation by an in origin probably contemporary Byzantine work, Αἱ Ῥοπαί, which in section 10 states: Οἱ λ' ἔτη γεωργήσαντες συντελείτωσαν, κἂν μὴ ὦσιν ἐναπόγραφοι – 'Those who have worked on the land for thirty years have fulfilled their obligations and so they are not *enapographoi* (*adscripticii*).'[175]

CJ 11.48.19 defines the differences which were evidently important for the Byzantines. In the adscripticiate the *colonus* was under the authority of his estate owner and the estate owner guaranteed his poll tax. In the 'free' colonate, the *colonus* was free from this authority and with him his assets, that is, what otherwise would have been considered as if *peculium* (ἐλεύθεροι μένοντες μετὰ τῶν πραγμάτων αὕτων). This implies that

[173] The doubts of Carrié 1983, 221–222 as to its authorship are unfounded.

[174] Based on B 55.1.19 = BT 2533.1–5. Krüger gives as last phrase in his *editio maior* of the Codex Justinianus (Krüger 1877): τοῦτο δὲ καὶ τῷ δεσπότῃ καὶ τοῖς γεωργοῖς λυσιτελές, but there is no manuscriptal evidence for this. On the contrary, the plural of *masters* as it is now in the end corresponds to the previous plural and there is no reason why it should not.

[175] Public obligations, since the verb indicates a public burden, and some mss. have λειτουργήσαντες. The work is considered to have been composed essentially in the sixth century and expanded by successive persons in the tenth century; see Burgmann 1984, 21–22.

there was no longer any reason for these to serve as security, which again implies that the landowner had functioned before as security. 'In exchange' he was tied to his *origo* and had to work as farmer. The *editio stereotypa* translates *to telos* (τὸ τέλος) with *tributum.*[176] If these 'free' *coloni* tilled their own land they were liable for the land tax. The text has already that they have to render services, so what remains to pay in all cases is the *capitatio humana*, unless they lived in a province where this was abolished. Nov. 162.2.1 of 539 defines the duties of a 'free' *colonus*: 'that those inhabitants stay in their district and be cultivators of the land, since they are born there' (ὡς βούλεται τοὺς τοιούτους οἰκήτορας τῶν χωρίων διαμένειν καὶ τῶν ἀγρῶν ἐργάτας, οἷα ἐκεῖσε γεννηθέτας). Like other people they are bound to their home stead, here also an estate.

We should not assume there were two kinds of 'free' colonate, one in which the *colonus* paid poll tax and one in which he did not. There is no sign of such a double 'free' colonate. The essential matter was that the 'free' *colonus*, despite having his *origo* fixed and to farm (CJ 11.48.23.1 *in fine*), was free from subjection, was *sui iuris* and what he had or acquired did not become treated as *peculium* (καὶ τὰ παρ'αὐτῶν κτηθέντα ὑπ'αὐτοῖς ἔσται καὶ οὐ πεκούλιον τῶν δεσποτῶν). Whether he was free from the *capitatio humana* depended on the province or an immunity. It was not permitted to the estate owner to introduce something new or apply violence against him (CJ 11.48.23.2 – which suggests that against *adscripticii* the latter was not uncommon). The advantage for the farmer was that he was released from the *potestas* of the estate owner: he was free from the *condicio adscripticia* with its restrictions.[177] Rosafio acutely points out that his

[176] Τὸ τέλος can mean tax, but its general meaning is indeed wider, namely (Liddell and Scott): coming to pass, performance, consummation; but also outcome, power, office, decision, something (ordered to be) done, task. In CJ 11.51–53 the situation was reversed: because of the abolition of the *capitatio humana*, the ground for the adscripticiate fell away. For that reason the *adscripticii* were turned into 'free' *coloni*. Since the *capitatio* had been abolished in these provinces, they did not have to pay this tax.

[177] The text may suggest that it actually concerned labourers or that these were prevalent at the time of the final version of the Greek, although it should not be ruled out that the word in question was differently accented. However, the prescription applied to the *censibus adscripti* and in this respect the private law difference with tenants is irrelevant. See Popescou 1978, 99–106 for the use of the term μισθωτός, which replaced, in the process of exhellenisation, the earlier term κολῶνος, the usual term in the sixth century for the *colonus liber*. It gives the impression that there were three species of *coloni*: *adscripticii*, 'free' *coloni*, and *coloni* in the private law sense who were not subjected to a public obligation to cultivate land; and that the latter were subjected after thirty years to the coloniary state known as the 'free' colonate. Thus the text is often interpreted. For example, Jones 1974; Bianchini 1984, 63, 63 n. 7; Zepos 1980, 421–424, who adopts the identical views of Zachariae 1892, 218ff. Panitschek 1990, 146, however, points out the illogicality of this. Puliatti 1984, 179ff. thinks similarly, concluding (in n. 39) that this conflicts with Justinian's *favor libertatis*. Yet Puliatti's analysis does not apply, since it is based on the assumption that the colonate was

peculium has become *bona*; that is, he was free now to alienate his goods, and the consent of his estate owner was no longer needed.[178] The *colonus* was now an *ingenuus* (CJ 11.52.1.1), which means that he could fulfil offices. He might have slaves to do the work and occupy himself with something else (CJ 11.53.1.3, mentioning freedmen). His position definitively improved. On the other hand, the estate owner was now released from providing, either as guarantee or as creditor, the sum of the poll tax, but could still dispose of a reservoir of farmers, available either as farm hand or as lessee, without obligations resulting from the subjection. This was indeed profitable for landowners.

The Praetorian Prefect Zoticus issued an edict (Ed. Praef. 25) regarding the taking on of fugitive *coloni*. Who took one on had to return him to his land with his *peculium* and restitute all gains and damages. The request (for return? for a move to another plot of land? for release?) had to be handed over to the provincial governor, either by the receiving estate owner or by the *colonus*. He had to pay a fine of 25 pounds of silver to the fisc and double that amount to the estate owner. Botta assumes that Zoticus was prefect under Anastasius in 511 and 512, when there was a PPO Orientis of that name.[179] In that case the edict would have been the actualisation of an otherwise unknown constitution of Anastasius, of which CJ 11.4.8.19 could have formed part, or the lex Anastasia, which is cited in CJ 11.48.23.1 (8–9); or we have the same constitution before us. Much is in favour of the latter interpretation, since the prescriptions of CJ 11.48.23.4–5 cover those of the Edict of Zoticus.[180] Botta thinks the edict shows resemblances with the way the crime of kidnapping (*plagium*) was dealt with. The texts do not unequivocally confirm this, but it is clear from D. 48.15.5 that the taking on of a fugitive slave was in any case made equal to *plagium*.[181] And to connect this with the flight of slaves and view this kind of migration in the wider context of agricultural exploitation as Botta does is of course very useful.

CJ 11.48.19 was likely part of a larger constitution or of a convolute of related constitutions.[182] In a constitution of 500 addressed to Thomas,

a status between the *status libertatis* and the *condicio servilis* (189) whereas it is a species of the *status libertatis*.

[178] Rosafio 2009, 298. [179] Botta 2017, here 6.

[180] Zachariae 1843, 275; Botta 2017 with a new transcription. See also Schiavo 2018, 114 n. 89: she too assumes the edict to have worked out Anastasius' law as cited in CJ 11.48.23. She also links the measure to the asylum of Nov. 123.35 of 546.

[181] Botta 2017, 6, 11–12. The rest of his article is dedicated to the question of the difference or non-difference between *coloni* and slaves and the economic exploitation of the land.

[182] Haarer 2006, 285–287 provides a survey of Anastasius' legislation but unfortunately arranged according to subject, not to original issue, and thus the connection between the various parts of

Praetorian Prefect of Illyricum, of which we have the fragments CJ 2.7.21, 2.4.43 and 7.39.5, Anastasius dealt with claims based on a *condicio* and with advocates. He ruled that in the case of curials being cited to perform, no prescription was of any avail; with other *condiciones* the limitation of prescription of forty years, as confirmed by him in 491 (CJ 11.62.14),[183] remained in force (CJ 7.39.5, referring to CJ 7.39.4.2 of 491, which was on purpose misinterpreted by curials).[184] Although it seems a generous measure, such a period was quite long, as was the thirty years for the *coloni adscripticii*. In CJ 2.4.43 he ruled that transactions in lawsuits about the *condicio* of slaves and *adscripticii* (with of course a claim to return to the owner, in this case the estate), made or to be made in the past, present or future, were not invalid merely because they concerned the *condicio servilis* or *adscripticia*. Consequently these transactions remained valid and in force. In another constitution, CJ 2.7.21, he prescribed that no advocate at the praetorian prefecture of Illyricum, or his children, should be liable for the duty of *cohortalis* or a worse status (*deterior condicio*).[185] In view of the fact that all deal with the summons for the duties of a *condicio*, it is plausible that CJ 11.48.19 was also part of the original constitution or convolute of constitutions and that it therefore dates from 500.

13.3 Institutional Release: Justinian's Constitutions

As already said, we have to read CJ 11.48.19 in the light of CJ 11.48.22 and 23 and these two constitutions define the colonate and 'free' colonate extensively. CJ 11.48.23 starts by stating that the *adscripticii* cannot hope to escape their duty towards their landlord (the colonate) because of a prescription of thirty years after being absent for that period. Section 1 says that those who are retained in the coloniary state (*coloniaria condicione detenti*) for thirty years remain free but do not have the *libertas migrandi*,

one constitution is missed, also with the fragments CJ 2.7.21, 2.4.43, 7.39.5, and 11.48.19. The famous *lex Anastasiana* (CJ 4.35.22) on the purchase of debts is missed altogether.

183 The general acquisitive prescription of forty years for patrimonial and other public land would have enabled *adscripticii* to acquire ownership, but it would still have been quite a long period (CJ 11.62.14, 491).

184 The constitution issued previously (CJ 7.39.4.2, of 491) concerned other statuses and hence could not abrogate the earlier statute on curials. In it Anastasius introduced a prescription of forty years for the other actions and exceptions, so that after forty years all cases would be extinct. This included cases about *condiciones* (CJ 7.39.4.2). In another part of this constitution, CJ 11.62.14, he regulated the prescription of forty years in regard to *fundi patrimoniales*.

185 This privilege had already been granted to the advocates enrolled at the prefecture of Oriens.

that is, to leave their estate or *origo* (*in fundis vel vicis*). The text says 'he wanted them to remain free' (*voluit liberos quidem permanere*) but that is, though legally correct, in practice something of a euphemism. If this section did not treat of the *adscripticii* it would be senseless. It would do nothing for the 'free' *coloni*. Of the *coloni* in the mere private law sense, not subjected to any obligation to cultivate land, one cannot say that they were *detenti in coloniaria condicione*. In civil law all *coloni* were free persons, whereas the *adscripticii* were subjected to an inferior legal status (they were not free lessees, as some authors think; see below).

13.4 Other Interpretations of CJ 11.48.19

Zepos and later Mirković and Carrié interpret CJ 11.48.19 in a precisely contrary way: they assume that free, unindebted *coloni* who had spent thirty years on an estate were made *liberi adscripticii*, namely on account of CJ 11.48.19.[186] Mirković applies the word *adscripticius* for both kinds of *coloni*, and she means that such *coloni* became 'free' *coloni*. The other kind of *coloni* (for whom I reserved the name of *adscripticii*) came into existence either because they fell into rental arrears or because they, as *originarii*, were born on the estate and had inherited debt and dependence.[187] In this view all farmers became *coloni censiti* of one or another kind and the colonate would have been a universal phenomenon. Against the fundamental and decisive arguments of CJ 11.48.23.1, Nov. 162.2.1 and Aἱ Ῥοπαί 10, these views do not hold at all. We saw that the adscripticiate was established by a voluntary agreement. Further, such an acquisitive prescription for free labour would be the exact opposite of the general extinctive prescription of thirty or forty years applicable to *adscripticii* on private lands. We know of acquisitive prescription of people, but it always

[186] Zepos 1980, 422; Mirković 1997, 65, 69–70; Carrié 1997, 113. The same error with Kaplan 1992, IV, II, 2, b (*Les colons*) (assuming all *coloni* in CJ 11.48 were lessees; Kaplan, however, does not pretend to give a legal analysis), Whittaker & Garnsey 1998, 292, and Haarer 2006, 212 and 212 n. 150, who even mentions an obvious counterargument by Lemerle that in that case *coloni* would simply move out shortly before the thirty years elapsed. Haarer's argument that sufficient people would remain to justify legislation does not convince. Schipp 2009, 226–229 argues in the same sense. According to him the second group consisted of lessees who, after thirty years, attained the status of free μισθωτοί ('Pächter') and who were tied to the land and obliged to dues. If they became free lessees after thirty years, what would they have been before? Unfree lessees? Also I cannot follow his argument of a parallel between 'Adskriptizität – freies Kolonat' and 'kaiserlicher Dienst – grundherrlicher Dienst'.

[187] Mirković 1997, 70. There is no reason for them to have inherited debts: they could have renounced the inheritance, with debts and all. Her suggestion would only work if the inheritance consisted of enough assets to live on and pay off debts incurred by the *de cuius*.

concerns people already subjected to the *condicio coloniaria* and the acquisition is by a new owner. But even considered in themselves these views already suffer from considerable objections. In Justinian's law there is no question of rental arrears as a legal cause of the colonate. And if a lease of thirty years led to the adscripticiate, why did farmers-lessees not migrate after, for example, twenty-five years to escape this consequence? The text says that it is advantageous for a farmer to become a 'free' *colonus* and to render service, that is, to till the land (see Nov. 162.2.1). How could this be if one was a free lessee-farmer not subjected to any public obligation to cultivate land, already paying the poll tax and eventually other taxes or fulfilling public obligations and free to dispose of one's possessions? These objections have been mentioned before by Eibach.[188] The change of the adscripticiate into the 'free' colonate after thirty years of steady performance would on the other hand encourage fulfilment of the duties and make flight less attractive (which would be advantageous for the landlord). Compared to the western rule of 451, which reimposed, in general, the adscripticiate on the barely discharged (Nov. Val. 31.1; see Section 41), it would be far less harsh to the *colonus*.

It is clear that under Justinian adscripticiate and lease were two not commutative concepts. To describe *adscripticii* as 'registered lessees' is consequently wrong for Justinian's reign.[189] CJ 11.48.23.1 does not speak of free lessees on an estate, but of men 'held in the *condicio coloniaria* for thirty years' (*homines qui per triginta annos coloniaria detenti sunt condicione*). Since Anastasius and Justinian wanted to release them from a *condicio deterior*, this could only concern a transition from the adscripticiate to the 'free' colonate, and so it is understood in the text (*sancimus liberos colonorum esse quidem in perpetuum secundum praefatam legem liberos et nulla deteriore condicione praegravari*). The legal question dealt with in the text is whether such a grant also applied to children who had not (yet) spent thirty years of service; they would not have raised the question if it had not meant better

[188] See Eibach 1980, 158–162 with a survey.

[189] As in, for example, Grey 2007, passim, particularly 173, where he cites me in n. 104 for this characterisation of *adscripticii* as 'indebted, landless tenants'. Yet I expressed in Sirks 1993a, 334–335, at n. 9, grave doubts about *adscripticii* as being in general tenants and pleaded for an interpretation as hirelings, which he apparently did not see. That Grey does not find debt mentioned in the sources is only possible if he interprets it as private law debts, but that is missing the point. The adscripticiate is always connected with the taxes, and taxes are a debt the *adscripticii* had to pay and which their estate owners guaranteed or took over. As to being landless, the fact that the *adscripticii* were not prohibited from owning land does not necessarily imply that they regularly owned land. CJ 11.48.4.1 suggests that it was an exception. Grey further, in the wake of this, states that there were not two different *condiciones*, referring in n. 105 to a critique by Carrié 1997, 113 which apparently is convincing to him; but see my comments in Sirks 2008, 129 n. 44 and 130 n. 45.

conditions for them. This point is not seen or dealt with by the aforementioned authors, nor by Carrié, who uses CJ 11.48.19 to interpret the term *condicio coloniaria* in CJ 11.48.23.1, which is, in view of the reliability of these two texts, the reverse of what is methodologically correct.[190]

Regarding Mirković's interpretation of *adscripticius* for both kinds of *coloni*, the term *adscripticius*/ἐναπόγραφος is not attested before perhaps 366, certainly 474, and only in the east. It is not impossible that it was created to distinguish these original *coloni* from the *coloni liberi*, created from at least 371 onwards.[191] The moment of its occurrence might hint at that.

13.5 Anastasius' Motives

What may have moved Anastasius to introduce his institutional release? First of all it would make flight less attractive. In order to escape the *potestas* a fugitive had to live for thirty years out of the reach of his master. Perhaps his master did not care to look for him and claim him, but would he know this? And it might be easy to find a new occupation, but it might also be difficult. As fugitive he would live permanently under the threat of being recalled as *adscripticius*. The new rule replaced the effect of the thirty-year limitation of prescription, and in that sense Anastasius did landowners a favour. A potential loss of labour force was stopped. But he did the *colonus* a favour too: now he could be sure that after thirty years, although he remained tied to the land, he would quit the control and authority (*potestas*) of the estate owner and the restrictions of his *condicio* and his children would

[190] I cannot enter here into a complete discussion with Carrié 1997, but his approach suffers from not taking the entire legal dossier in a proper way into account. Thus he does not analyse CJ 11.48.22: not on 113, nor on 99 (on 119 he neglects the contractual part of the adscripticiate and only mentions the *adscriptio*); neither does he consider D. 50.15.4 for the census declaration as I do. It becomes understandable then that he reproaches me for speaking of the census as a 'lista' and suggests I took over a misunderstood reading of CTh 11.1.26 by Goffart 1980 (113), when I did not do this at all. It is understandable too that he denies any contractual origin of the adscripticiate and the difference from the 'free' colonate, adhering to the mentioned interpretation of CJ 11.48.19, which I consider absolutely incompatible with CJ 11.48.23.1, a text which neither he nor Mirković analyses. He merely mentions this text on 122: but instead of accepting the meaning of (*condicio*) *coloniaria* as *adscripticia* on the basis that the Latin text is in any case reliable, he attributes another meaning to *coloniaria*, on the basis of the less reliable Greek text of CJ 11.48.19 (which is a Greek summary of the Latin constitution), which saves this interpretation. Apart from that, this is a circular argument (the wrong interpretation of one text is proved by applying it to another text); this seems to me a methodologically rather questionable approach. The legal content of the text is not discussed at all. This is precisely the approach it is necessary to avoid.

[191] In Justinian's Code the mention of the term in CJ 3.37.11 of 334 and 8.51.1 of 224 is certainly interpolated, in CJ 11.48.6 of 366 it is likely but not certain. All other texts in the Code mentioning the term date from 474 or 484 and later. In papyri it does not occur before the sixth century. See also Section 4 on the term ἐναπόγραφος.

be free from this also. He was no longer a second-rate citizen. He could fulfil offices. If his children were away for thirty years, they would not benefit from a limitation of prescription, but if their father became 'free' in this way they too would follow his new status (CJ 11.48.23.1). We must be realistic: not many will have profited from this unless they were enrolled or summoned at an early age. Thirty years was a long time in Antiquity.

In this way the constitution would fit the words of Priscianus in his Panegyric of Anastasius, that he alleviated the burdens of the farmers.[192] But it would also fit his aim to improve public finances by a higher tax revenue, since it would have promoted agriculture. In this he succeeded grandiosely: the treasury was full at his death.[193]

In this line would also lie Anastasius' constitution on the assignment of debts, CJ 4.35.22 of 506. The problem was the transfer of debts (*cessio*), presumably by way of transfer of an acknowledgement of debt (*chirograph*),[194] used by some to accumulate by purchase such acknowledgements by the same person, as we may assume with a discount, and then to press the debtor with a number of these debt papers. Such an accumulation might be too much and consequently, presumably by a forced sale or by *cessio bonorum*, there was an opportunity for the creditor to enrich himself in this way. This later so-called *lex Anastasia* introduced that when an acknowledgement of debt was bought, the purchaser could claim no more than his purchase price. In this way this evil would have been curbed. Since such practices will have been more successful with small owners than with rich magnates, and considering that taking up credit happens more often with the less affluent and certainly more often with farmers who are subjected to vicissitudes (see CJ 4.26.13 on debts claimed from people engaged in agriculture), it is not unlikely that Anastasius would have helped the small independent farmer by this. The effect would have been that such farmers would have been relieved and better capable of rendering their taxes. If so, it would be a measure which can be related to that of CJ 11.48.19, issued probably six years before.

[192] Priscian *De laude imperatoris Anastasii* 193–194. On Anastasius, see Oehler 1899 and Haarer 2006; Ostrogorsky 1963, 54–57ff., considers Anastasius' successful financial policy as very hard to the population on the land. But that concerned those who had to pay the land tax, that is, the landowners. On the other hand, a continuous good exploitation of the land was also in the interest of the emperor and from that perspective an alleviation of the life of the farm hands and land labourers made sense, particularly since it did not cost the emperor anything. To call CJ 11.48.19 a relief (and similarly CJ 4.35.22) does not, therefore, contradict Ostrogorsky's remark.

[193] See in general on this Haarer 2006, 193–206, 216–222.

[194] See Sirks 2016.

14 Public and Procedural Aspects of the Colonate

14.1 *Social Mobility*

Social mobility in Antiquity was not as low as sometimes was assumed. There are enough examples of people leaving their birth status and moving into different occupations, rising in their profession or society. The emperor Diocletian is a good example of the opportunities the army offered. His parents were of low status, yet he rose in the army to the post of commander of the *protectores domestici* in 282, to be proclaimed emperor in 284. Restrictions in this respect were therefore a real disadvantage. Being a *colonus originalis* was such a disadvantage.

The disadvantage was that functions in the imperial army or bureaucracy (*militia*) were forbidden to them. *Coloni* (*censibus adscripti*) were unacceptable for the function of *apparitor* in the office of the *magister militum* (CJ 12.54.3). The prohibition included also curials and cohortals. It will have been the immunity the office gave from all *munera* which made entrance so attractive (CJ 11.54.1: *ab omni nominationis iniuria excusentur*), whereas these groups were needed for the duties of their respective *condiciones*. The immunity was certainly a financial benefit for the curials and cohortals, while for the *coloni* who will not have had much property the function would have offered the possibility of escaping their duties and of gaining a better life. In all cases a further motive was of course to retain them all for their duties. With the *coloni*, their subjection to the *potestas* of the master will also have been a reason. We see this in the case that a slave or *colonus* had been appointed as *tabularius* (town clerk). If this was done with the knowledge of his master, he could perhaps remain in office, but his master was in any case liable for eventual damages occurring in the keeping of the public records (CJ 10.71.3.1).[195] Such a liability is a parallel to the liability of owners for their slaves for damages and is based on the power of the owner.

Further, it was not easy for an *adscripticius* (*censibus notatus*) to become a cleric. Against the will of his estate owner it was impossible. Even if an *adscripticius* became a priest in his own hamlet (*vicus*), his estate owner could compel him to acknowledge his liability for the *capitatio* and that he has his estate duties (*ruralia obsequia*) performed

[195] A slave was also to be flogged. The reason for the prohibition is clear: they might commit fraud in the (tax) records in favour of their master.

by a substitute of his own choice. If his church was exempted from the *capitatio*, he would be exempted as well (CJ 1.3.16). The implication is that he remains an *adscripticius*, but without the duty to remain on the estate or in the village. As stated before, an *adscripticius* could pay his tax directly or let his estate owner do this for him. CJ 1.3.16 raises the question whether *coloni* could in other cases also give substitutes for the work they had to do. Apart from this text there are no indications of such a possibility.

14.2 *Procedural Privileges*

On the other hand, their position might bring with it that they could profit from the privileges of their masters. *Coloni* were treated as part of the household in several constitutions granting privileges to certain civil servants. The heads (*principes*) of the *agentes in rebus* enjoyed the privilege after their retirement that, once retired, they did not have to pay more than one solidus in fees (*sportulae*) in litigation, whether they or their families or their slaves or *coloni* were summoned, in their own person or through their procurators (CJ 12.21.8pr). In view of the relationship, this will have concerned *adscripticii*, since *coloni liberi* and lessees will have been summoned in their own person. *Comites* of the consistory, their families and dependents, including *coloni* (*adscripticii*), enjoyed in court the same privileges as plaintiffs and defendants as the principals of the *agentes in rebus* did (CJ 12.10.2 and CJ 12.21.8 pr). Those who worked in the *sacra scrinia*, as their families and their slaves and *coloni seu adscripticii* (*coloni ad eum pertinentes*) if these stayed in Constantinople, could not be summoned criminally or civilly without leave of the *magister officiorum* (CJ 12.19.12pr, 3). Those persons who had fulfilled the office of *patronus fisci* (i.e., attorney for the fisc) also had the right to represent as advocate themselves, their families, and their slaves and *coloni ad se pertinentes*. The term *pertinentes ad se* is rather wide ('to concern', 'to belong') and it might theoretically concern free lessees, but it is more probable, in view of the context of families and slaves, that it concerns *coloni* who belong to them, that is, are subjected to them, thus *adscripticii*. (CJ 2.7.22.1, 3 = 2.7.24.1, 3; see Section 13.2 on CJ 11.48.19).[196]

In their relation with their masters, *coloni* suffered the restrictions usual for people who were in the *potestas* of another or obliged to respect their master or former master, like freedmen. Yet their particular situation made

[196] Why this is added is unclear. Why should the charges have been made higher in this case?

allowances possible, namely where more was demanded from them than usual or on account of *superindictiones* (CJ 11.50.1 and 2, see Sections 7.1 and 7.2).

Some procedural protection existed for them also. According to CJ 8.5.1, if they were driven out of the estate while their master was absent, assistance should be given so that they could return.[197] It implies that normally the estate owner should protect them. Why they would be driven away we do not know. They could file a request for reinstatement in their possession (an interdict). Somebody could represent the absentee owner in court; it could be the *detentor* too, hence also the *colonus*. This is expressly said in CJ 8.5.1.1. It is evidently a concession due to the importance of a continuous exploitation of the land: normally a *colonus* would have had to wait till the owner had returned and started proceedings. Working on their master's land, they were at best holder, *detentor*. As such they had no recourse to possessory interdicts which would restore the land to them. It would be the same if they were lessees.[198]

14.3 Criminal Law and Abuse of Power

Disadvantages existed also in the criminal law. If counterfeiting was committed on an estate (*fundus*) and its owner was, in consequence of absence over a long distance, unaware of this, his representative and the slaves, residents (*incolae*) or *coloni* who had provided assistance were punishable with death (CJ 9.24.1.5).[199] By these *incolae* and *coloni* must have been meant *inquilini* and *coloni originarii* or *adscripticii*, since they are connected to the estate.

Slaves and *adscripticii* were not allowed to seek asylum in a sacred place after having destroyed or stolen things, or having fled from their masters' authority. Either they should be punished or, if pardoned by their masters, be returned to them so that they would not miss any of their services (*obsequia iusta*) nor the Church be encumbered by having to feed them (CJ 1.12.6.9). Another fragment of this constitution is directed against public unrest and seditious behaviour (CJ 9.30.2).[200]

197 The text has *colonus vel libertus* interpolated as an extension of *servulus*, which is a sufficient indication that it concerns also *coloni originales*; furthermore, the following *quolibet titulo retinebat* covers also their legal relation.

198 If they held the land *in precario*, they would have such a recourse, but this will not have been the case normally; see Section 2.3.3.

199 The death penalty as set by the lex Cornelia *de falsis*.

200 A third part is CJ 1.3.7.

On the other hand, *adscripticii* had the power to raise complaints according to the *lex Julia repetundarum* over extortion and concussion, both regarding administration and judgments in general (CJ 9.27.4)[201] and regarding administration by the *comes Domorum* for a year after he left his office (CJ 9.27.5).[202] The latter was analogue to the rule with municipal officers. If the year passed without a claim, sums paid were considered as debts due.

Two constitutions offer *coloni* relief against abuse of power by judges and state officials. CJ 9.27.4 grants, inter alia, *coloni* the faculty to indict judges who abuse their position or sell their judgment. Further, CJ 9.27.5 granted, inter alia, *coloni* who had been forced to pay bribes to a *comes domorum*, the faculty to reclaim within a year after the end of the office term of this official the money paid. The texts can refer to all *coloni*, both *originales* and 'free' *coloni*. The mention of this *comes* might perhaps imply that it particularly concerned *coloni* of the *patrimonium* and *domus divina*. The fact that they enjoyed these privileges implies that the rejected practice did occur, and often enough to justify this measure.

'Free' *coloni* did not suffer disadvantages.

15 The *Coloni* on State and Imperial Lands: CJ 11.63–64, 68–69

15.1 General

The distribution of land in the Roman Empire was, certainly with the beginning of the Principate, far from even. Some private persons had much land, most likely consisting of small tracts which were managed as a whole, as we know from the Heroninos archive. Probably the largest landowner of all was the emperor. The story that Nero by confiscating six senators owned one-sixth of Africa testifies, even if it is exaggerated, both to the largeness of private landholdings and to the size of the imperial lands. From an economic point of view much literature exists about these large imperial landholdings, fired by the inscriptions found in Tunisia: of Henchir-Mettich of 116–117 (the *lex Manciana*), Aïn-el-Djemala of 117–138, and Aïn-Ouassel of 198–212 (the *lex Hadriana*). These *leges* regulated the lease of land to cultivators. There was uncertainty whether these regulations were continued during the following centuries. But the so-called Tablettes

[201] The text puts the *coloni* on the level of an *ordo*, thus attributing it a *condicio*.

[202] Since it concerns a *comes domorum*, it is likely that the *colonus* mentioned is a *colonus dominicus*. On these, see § 20C.

Albertini, depositions of land sales from the period 493–496, found in Tunisia in 1928, show that the *lex Manciana* was apparently still in use, suggesting a continuity of those lease regulations over centuries in the province of Africa.[203] As for other parts of the Empire, we have indications of large landholdings elsewhere, but only sufficient reliable data for Egypt with, next to Rathbone's work on the estate of Appianos in the middle of the third century, for the early Byzantine period Gascou's publication on the landholdings of the Apiones in Oxyrhynchus and Sarris' more general work on the economy of Egypt, with also the Apiones.[204] They focus on private landholdings. In how far this made a difference economically with the imperial estates we can only guess, because we do not know how free the managers of these estates were in their management. As it is, in this section we restrict ourselves to the imperial domains.

For some information about the exploitation of the imperial estates, we have to look at the Tunisian inscriptions, next to the texts of the Codes which make it clear that not only in Tunisia there existed estates. The inscriptions present a putting of the domains into a prolonged lease under the supervision of procurators to individual farmers. Such an exploitation is to be expected. If an acquisition was not at once liquidated, the emperors were interested in a long-term income from the land.

There is not much literature on the imperial estates. We have the publications of Schulten, His, Wiart,[205] which three works have been discussed by Beaudouin in a critical and extensive review article,[206] and more recently Delmaire. All these works deal in detail with the various imperial officials involved with the management and with the modes of exploitation, which are of course important. However, in the context of the colonate we have to consider other aspects. The *coloni* have to pay the poll tax, they get exemptions from *munera* and privileges of jurisdiction. Therefore, what is of interest to us is whether the imperial domains were part of the municipal territories or formed separate entities, eventually with its own *munera*, and whether the people on them paid taxes, particularly the poll tax. These two aspects are of interest for the colonate.

203 The edition of the Tablettes Albertini: Courtois et al. 1952. For the most recent analysis, see Weßel 2003.

204 Gascou 1985; Sarris 2011. Of particular interest are Hickey 2012, 82–83, and Bransbourg 2016, because he deals with the link between taxation and management on the estates of the Apiones and Dioskoros.

205 Wiart 1894; Schulten 1896; His 1896.

206 Beaudouin 1897–1898.

From the titles in Justinian's Code the following scala of state and imperial domains appears. There were estates which stood in a certain relationship to the emperor: *fundi patrimoniales*, *fundi emphyteuticarii*, and *fundi saltuenses*, *fundi rei privatae* and *saltus divinae domus*, and *fundi et saltus rei dominicae*, and further *praedia tamiaca*. There were on these lands also *coloni* who were in a *condicio*.

The imperial lands were divided into several categories: patrimonial lands (*fundi patrimoniales*), emphyteuticarian lands (*fundi emphyteuticarii*), lands of the *res privata* (*fundi rei privatae*) and of the Imperial House (*fundi divinae domus* or *domus augustae*), and the *fundi saltuenses*. The precise differences between these cannot be the subject of investigation here.[207] Delmaire separates the *fundi patrimoniales* from the *patrimonium*, the *res privata*, and the *domus*, which are synonymous before the function of *comes patrimonium* was created. The *fundi patrimoniales* were once part of the *patrimonium* but leased in perpetuity.[208] The *patrimonium* may probably best be compared with Crown estate,[209] the *res privata* was the private property of the emperor,[210] and the *domus augusta* was the House of the emperor with their properties. *Fundi patrimoniales* passed over to the next emperor. The emperor could issue them to private persons. Imperial land could be sold or donated with the imposition of a rent (*ius privatum salvo canone*). It is evident that such sold land was no longer part of the *res privata* or the *patrimonium*.[211] The *fundi emphyteuticarii* were patrimonial lands issued to private persons under the regime of the emphyteusis.[212] Both categories remained Crown property of the emperor as follows from CJ 11.63.2.[213] *Saltus* were tracts of land in Africa which were cultivated

[207] The adjectives refer to proprietary and functional differences. This is not the place to enter into the question of how precisely these categories differed from each other; it is quite possible that we are dealing here with historically grown designations for various lands, acquired in the course of time by confiscations and inheritances, which had their individual regimes but did not differ so much as to allow for loose categorisations, with the exception of the *emphyteusis*. Important here is that altogether they formed a category clearly apart from private lands and lands, belonging to a temple or town (*praedia urbana et rustica templorum et civitatium, praedia civilia, praedia templorum*, on which CJ 11.70 and 71). See Burdeau 1972, 1973 for a differentiation and literature. Unfortunately, I could not consult Pergami 2019.

[208] Delmaire 1989, 675–676 and Ch. XX.

[209] See Berger 1954, s.v. *Fundus patrimonialis* and s.v. *Patrimonium Caesaris. PW.*

[210] See Berger 1954, s.v. *Res privata Caesaris. PW.*

[211] Wiart 1894, 41–44.

[212] The mode of issuing in emphyteusis was first designed for the Crown lands, but later the emperor Zeno introduced this kind of long lease in private law with CJ 4.66.1 in 476–484.

[213] The constitution denies validity of manumission of slaves attached to these lands, on the ground that their possessors are not owners. CJ 11.59.17 allowed people to take and cultivate deserted emphyteuticarian land and keep this as long as they paid the canon. The same applied to limitrophic lands (CJ 11.60.3).

(e.g., *saltus Burunitanus*), and Delmaire assumes the term designated a group of domains, also in the east.[214] On the other hand the *saltus divinae domus* and *rei dominicae* will have been part of the private property of the emperor and the imperial family (CJ 11.66). *Tamiacus* (from ταμιακός, fisc, treasury) was the Greek term for *fiscalis*, but the contemporary *katapodas* as in Nov. 38.6 translates the term with *aerarii*.[215] It would concern therefore Crown property, but the addition in Nov. 38.6 of *sacer* indicates a closer connection with the emperor. The fact that in CJ 11.69 R and constitution 1 children of *coloni tamiaci* are considered *coloni dominici* supports this and suggests that the *fundi tamiaci*, though fiscal land, were especially reserved for the emperor as regards their revenues. CJ 11.69.2 refers to *fundi tamiaci* set up in provinces, in any case situated in Cappadocia and Pontica. Whether their revenues served the imperial kitchen as Cuiacius and Perezius suggest is a question which cannot be dealt with here.[216] Nov. 38.6, of 536, on the *condicio tamiaca*, will be dealt with below. The size of these lands is unknown, but whether scattered or not they must have been large.[217] Their direct exploitation was not a matter for the emperor; they were either leased short term or long term, directly or, more likely, through *conductores* who subleased again.[218] Long-term exploitation could

[214] See Schulten 1896, 28–41; Jones 1964, 416, 713; Delmaire 1989, 216. But Schulten's opinion (17–25) that *saltus* was the technical term for a territorial autonomous imperial domain has no support in the sources, although Jones 1964, 416 and 713 mentions *saltus* and *tractus* in Cappadocia as being extraterritorial blocks (I assume, outside of city territories). But the evidence he adduces does not show this. What the proconsul gets is the authority to collect the taxes which otherwise would have been collected by the praetorian prefect, and of course the rents of the imperial domains. Berger 1954, s.v. *Saltus*, assumes it concerned mountain forests or woodland pasture and the *fundi saltuenses* would therefore have consisted of woodlands and woodland pasture.

[215] See Delmaire 1989, 13–15.

[216] Cuiacius 1758, c. 931: . . . *& ad praedia tamiaca, id est, quae erant proprie deputata cubiculo, & cellario, & penui principis, & erant in Cappadocia, ut ostendit l. 3 infr. de palat. sacrar. larg. [= CJ 12.23.3] & Graeci recte explicant infra ad l. 1 ff ad leg. Juliam repentund. [= D. 48.11] et interpres Juliani antecessoris in Nov. 30 quae praedia erant sub cura comitis domorum, & potissimum sub cura praepositi sacri cubiculi. Et inde in notitia Romani imperii sub dispositioni viris illustris praepositi sacri cubiculi ponitur domus divina per Cappadociam.* Yet Nov. 30.1.1 also mentions ταμειακὰ χωρία (*praedia aerarii*) in Pontica, further in Cappadocia in 1.1 the ταμειακοὶ ἄνθρωποι (*homines aerarii*) and ταμειακὰ πράγματα (*res* and *causae aerarii*); in 5 pr the ταμειακὴ ἐξουσία and the ταμειακὴ κτῆσις (*aerarii potestas* and *possessio*; the latter also in 5.1 and 7 pr, where the *katapodas* has *aerarium possessionum*); in 5.1 the διοίκησις ταμειακῶν πραγμάτων; in 6 pr the ταμειακοὶ πόροι (*aerarii quaestus*; also in 7.1); in 7 pr γῆ ταμειακή (*terra aerarii*); in 7.1 the ταμειακὴ ζῶνη (*aerarii cingulum*); in 8 pr the ταμειακά (*quae aerarii sunt*); Nov. 32.3 ταμειακά (*aerarii*). In all these cases *tamiacus* is in the contemporary *katapodas* rendered with *aerarii*. Accordingly it is clear that it concerns Crown land. Further, Perezius 1661, 339–340, in the same sense.

[217] Jones 1964, 415–416 estimates it for 422 at 18.5 per cent of Africa Proconsularis and 15 per cent for Byzacena.

[218] See CJ 11.73.1, where it is forbidden to functionaries of the *res privata* to act as *conductor*, evidently to prevent collusion and fraud.

also take the form of issuing in perpetuity (*ius perpetuum*) or as patrimonial land under imposition of a *canon*; or as emphyteuticarian land with the obligation of *melioratio* and also a rent. Sometimes patrimonial land was issued in *ius privatum* with a *canon*, sometimes even without a *canon*.[219]

Whatever the precise proprietary position of these lands may have been, from Justinian's Code it appears that in any case under this emperor the patrimonial and emphyteuticarian lands were treated together as one category and the lands of the *res privata* and the Imperial House together as another category. The same applied for the *coloni originales* on these lands. The difference most striking is, however, that the first two land categories were granted to private persons under various conditions, not to be discussed here, although they remained Crown land, whereas the last two categories remained with the emperor or his family. There were *coloni* on these lands who were tied to these as to an *origo*, which justifies the qualification of *originales/originarii*. This is terminologically confirmed by CJ 11.68.1 (*colonus originalis*).

15.1.1 Status and Taxation

Returning to the two questions of interest here, the status of the imperial domains with regard to the municipal territories and their fiscal status, the literature has shown different views.

As to the status, it was Schulten who, after the acute remark that a 'Großgrundbesitz' either consists of large landholdings (*latifundia*) or of the combination of many small landholdings near each other (as now evidenced by modern research),[220] put forward the thesis that the large domains, imperial, senatorial or, later, ecclesiastical, formed territorial units which were not part of the territories of the cities. The imperial domains also formed separate jurisdictions because the *procurator saltus* exercised the *coercitio* and *cognitio* granted him by the emperor. The private domains remained under the jurisdiction of the governor. As to *munera*, only senatorial domains were exempted from these, since senators were exempted. Private domains of curials were not exempted. They formed quasi-municipal territories.[221] Also Jones has maintained that the *saltus*

[219] There is no need to enter into the distinctions between these various forms. It suffices to retain that in almost all cases the imperial treasure received income and could reclaim the land. See further Jones 1964, 417–420 on the exploitation.

[220] We see with Appianus and the Apiones indeed large estates of the second category.

[221] Schulten 1896, 107–115, part. 108–110. Schulten 1896, 1 refers to the landholdings east of the Elbe, uses the term 'gutsherrlich' and seems inspired by the Prussian situation.

were 'extraterritorial', referring to Nov. 30,[222] which reference, however, fails: the proconsul is merely authorised to collect the taxes instead of the prefecture. There is no indication of extra-territoriality. Further, the fact that *coloni* were granted the privilege of freedom of municipal charges in CJ 11.75.1 for lands of the *res privata*, and that the possessors of patrimonial lands were exempted from maintaining roads in CJ 11.65.1, proves that these lands were part of municipal territories. Whatever privileges existed on these lands, they implied that normally they were treated as any other land, thus subjected to the rules and jurisdiction of cities and the governor.

As to taxation, the situation for Justinian's reign is equally clear. Possessors of *fundi patrimoniales* had to fulfil all obligations burdening their lands, hence all taxes and *munera* (CJ 11.65.3). What goes for these *fundi* will have been the same for the *patrimonium* itself. Regarding the *res privata*, the exemption from *munera sordida* and *extraordinaria* granted in CJ 11.75.1 for its lessees implies that these lands were subjected to municipal claims and the usual taxes, including the land tax.[223] However, there is a text which mentions an immunity for the *res privata*.

CJ 10.19.4, addressed to the praetorian prefect, says:

> Actores ceterique rei privatae nostrae ad solutionem specierum sollemnium debiti vigoris auctoritate cogantur, ne provinciales rei privatae nostrae fatiget immunitas.
>
> The overseers (*actores*) and other managers of our *res privata* must be coerced by the authority of owed effort to pay the standard dues in kind (*solutio specierum sollemnium*), so that an immunity of our *res privata* does not wear out the provincials (*ne provinciales rei privatae nostrae fatiget immunitas*).[224]

The translations speak of 'the' immunity, but the text does not compel to this.[225] The immunity may have been the result of not having to pay the established tax. Moreover, the overseers are already bound to pay or else there is no need to speak of due effort, namely effort owed on account of their appointment. Besides, the constitution addresses the praetorian

[222] Jones 1964, 416, 713, referring to Nov. Just. 30.

[223] Jones 1964, 454 deals with the finances of the Empire and says that imperial property was assessed. But he does not specify this here. Delmaire restricts himself to the *tituli largitionales*, namely what the *comes sacrarum largitionum* levied. Karayannopoulos 1958, 96: the *annona* was too important to exempt even the lands of the *res privata*.

[224] Or else the provincials had to make up for this. The lands of the *res privata* were thus subjected to the land tax. This makes it at the same time unlikely that they were not included in city territories.

[225] Codex of Justinian 2016 has 'lest the immunity of Our Privy Purse wear out the provincials'; OSS has 'damit nicht die Steuerfreiheit Unseres Privatschatzes den übrigen Provinzialbewohnern zur Last falle'.

prefect who was responsible for the levy of land tax. Other special taxes were levied by the *comes sacrarum largitionum*. Further, such an interpretation would not fit other texts like CJ 11.74.1–3 which show that the land of the *res privata*, of the fisc and of the *domus augusta* had to yield *debita fiscalia, debitae pensiones, species annonariae*, and *cursitationes debitae*. Thus these lands were not free from the normal *tributum*. The conclusion must be that land tax and poll tax were levied by the praetorian prefects and their bureaux on these lands.[226]

It follows for Justinian's times that the domains of the *res privata* and the *patrimonium* were not autonomous territories but land, forming part of a municipal territory, subjected to the land tax and *munera* and to the jurisdiction of the towns and the provincial governor. They rendered revenues to the state through the taxes, imposed on land (the *tributum solis* or *annona* in the first place) and next to that either through the rent the lessees had to pay or through the *canones* imposed on patrimonial or emphyteuticarian lands; the former being levied by the praetorian prefects, the latter by the *comes rei privatae*.

15.1.2 Coloni *on Imperial Land*

It is in this context we encounter *coloni* on imperial land. All the legal texts on them date from before Justinian and are therefore rules which applied. Only CJ 11.62.14 (a. 491), 11.69.1 and 2 (Zeno) are 'relatively' recent, yet still more than forty years old, but the titles on the various subjects were considered appropriate in 534 and the rules still useful, so there existed under Justinian such *coloni* and they formed categories of the *coloni originales*, attached to these particular categories of land and with particular rules. Both categories were subjected to, or enjoyed, the *forum privilegiatum* of the *rationalis summae rei*, and other courts were

[226] A question is whether imperial domains were censused and had to pay *tributum*. Burdeau 1973, 13 refers to Karayannopoulos 1958 and in n. 59 to older literature according to which these were subjected to all public charges, including taxes. However, this led to contradictions. As a solution, authors assume that taxes and rents fused (Burdeau 1973, 13 n. 60). Still, it is undeniable that the *res privata* was subjected to taxation (Burdeau 1973, 15–18). For the *fundi patrimoniales*, Burdeau is, contrary to other authors, of a different opinion (Burdeau 1973, 18ff.). Considering that confiscations, *bona vacantia* and inheritances were separately administrated and consequently were liable for the *tributum*, I assume that there was no difference and that all land was censused. Another argument is that if imperial lands were not censused and taxed, there would constantly be a shift from taxed to untaxed and back again, as, for example, with the distribution of *bona vacantia*. That again would seriously affect the imperial budget planning. Further, how would the *coloni* on these estates be registered otherwise than in the *professiones* of these, and recalled? The circumstances being the same, it is therefore possible that also on imperial estates *paramonai* were concluded. As to Burdeau's distinction, even if patrimonial lands were not taxed, the people on them would have been taxed.

not allowed to take cases by or against them on (CJ 3.26.7). The *rationalis* was competent in all fiscal cases (CJ 3.26.5). It was but a step further to decide that wherever a *colonus* connected with the fisc came up, he was competent too. It started with the *conductor* of fiscal estates (CJ 3.26.6) and extended to *coloni fisci*.

But it is not always clear whether a text deals with a *colonus originalis* or a private *colonus* who is a free lessee of imperial land. And it is also possible that a *colonus originalis* leased. The difference may lie in the use of a genitive, as in CJ 3.26.11, or, more substantially, in the use of an adjective. But decisive is the mention of an element of the colonate, like the duty to remain. Such a text is CJ 11.68.2, which orders the recall of imperial *coloni* (*dominici, fiscales sive rei privatae*), who are now on private land and fit to manage (*ratiocinia gerere*) or to farm. Apparently there was concern to use the talents of *coloni*.

Other texts which are less explicit but which are indeed dealing with *coloni originales*, because Justinian's compilers put them under the title *Quod cum eo qui est in aliena est potestate negotium gestum esse dicitur, vel de peculio seu quod iussu aut de in rem verso* which deals with actions over transactions with persons in the power of another, are CJ 3.26.7, 8 and 11.

In the case of civil or criminal lawsuits concerning a *colonus domorum nostrarum*, the *praepositus sacri cubiculi*, or the *comes domorum* was competent as *forum privilegiatum* (CJ 3.26.11).[227] It was a refinement of the general rule, since for cases regarding *coloni dominici* and *patrimoniales* the existing rules remained applicable (i.e., the *rationalis summmae rei*, CJ 3.26.7, as competent and exclusive judge), as for the *coloni rei privatae* (the provincial governor, CJ 3.26.8).[228]

If *coloni dominici* and *coloni patrimoniales* were subject of a legal claim, competence lay as said with the *rationalis summae rei* and not with functionaries as *duces* and provincial governors (CJ 3.26.7).[229] Regarding crimes committed by *coloni rei privatae*, the provincial governor was competent, but the *rationalis* or *procurator domus nostrae* had to

227 Was it necessarily an advantage for the *coloni* in these two instances? It might be in the first case, since the *rationalis* and *procurator* could counter the governor, but in the second case it might be a disadvantage, since the *coloni* would not have that kind of advantage. In both cases, however, the interests of the *res privata* and *domus augusta* will have been taken care of before all.

228 Jones 1964, 412–413.

229 The title of CJ 3.26 indicates that it concerns the summoning of these categories of *coloni* (*ubi causae . . . hominumque eius agantur*), which must consequently have existed already in 349, as also follows from the following text, CJ 3.26.8 of 358. There is no reason to presume an interpolation here. See Delmaire 1989, 201–204 on his jurisdiction.

be present at the proceedings (CJ 3.26.8). It is likely that this was to protect the interests of the emperor, perhaps also as a guarantee for the *colonus*. Delmaire defines this *rationalis* as the *rationalis rei privatae*, formerly called the *magister rei privatae* and responsible for, inter alia, the fiscal domains.[230]

The fact that these privileges were granted implies that normally *coloni* were subjected to the traditional civil and criminal jurisdiction of towns or governors. The privilege was restricted for *coloni rei privatae* to civil cases. The presence of the imperial functionary may have served as guarantee for a fair trial. But what about those on the imperial lands who were not tied *coloni* but free lessees or independent farmers? And further, what precisely made the imperial functionary (*comes domorum*, *rationalis*, *procurator*) competent in jurisdiction? Thirdly, did the privileges comprise all kinds of lawsuits? As to the first point, we must assume that it was the special position of the *coloni* which was the reason for the privilege. It did not apply to others. Why this privilege? And was it an advantage for the *coloni*? Assuming that it was in the interest of the imperial management to maintain a qualified working force on its lands, the privilege may have implied a fairer treatment and more protection of their interests. It will certainly have been the case in criminal matters. The presence of the *rationalis* as imperial functionary will have functioned as a restraint on the ordinary judge. In this way the privilege may have been advantageous to the *coloni* but also have functioned as a check on them. As to the last question, the *rationalis* was already competent in fiscal matters. To extend this competence is not so singular, in view of the fact that governors exercised both civil and criminal jurisdiction and that we see, as Peachin has shown, that on the lower level people like centurions also functioned as judges in practice.[231] But what about complaints about the duties requested? We saw that ordinary *coloni* could not litigate against their masters except for unreasonable demands on account of their colonate. Here the privilege would rob the *coloni* of this possibility, since it would be the same *rationalis* who requested; if they ever had the possibility, then to sue the emperor, who was supreme judge, was an

230 Delmaire 1989, 175–176. From the fourth century onwards the interventions of the *rationalis summarum* ceased and the *rationalis rei privatae* was solely responsible, albeit that certain *fundi patrimoniales* and *emphyteuticarii* in the west remained under the *rationalis summarum*; Delmaire 1989, 200.

231 See Peachin 1996. Although he treats of low military people like centurions, his study demonstrates for the countryside both the need for fast and effective justice and the nature of the conflicts, which apparently often just required a fair and reasonable decision and not complicated legal reasoning. That may also have been the case with the *coloni*.

impossibility. The only solution would be an appeal, which we must assume also in CJ 9.27.5, below. This must have been also the answer to the question of what *coloni* could do if the verdict was not to their liking. To whom could they appeal? According to Delmaire, to the *comes rei privatae*, or the proconsul in Africa, or the Urban Prefect, depending on the circumstances.[232] In the case of *fundi patrimoniales* and *emphyteuticarii*, it will have been the praetorian prefect or his *vicarius*.

Next to these general rules, the situation of both categories, those *coloni originales* on private lands and those *coloni originales* on imperial lands, differed in other aspects, on which see Sections 15.2–15.5. But the underlying questions are: Why did the management of the imperial lands agree to the colonate and how extensive was this colonate? Did it concern those people who were directly engaged by the imperial management per estate as lessees or workers, or those engaged by the general contractors (*conductores*) as sublessees, or people engaged by these sublessees, per estate? The colonate applied to the poll tax; the guarantee to pay this was recorded in the census of each estate and in this way the census defined their *origo*. The fact that the imperial management gave that guarantee can be explained: the poll tax was levied by the bureaux of the praetorian prefects and thus by another administrative branch. The way taxes were administered barred any administrative short cut. As with private estate owners, the guarantee prevented unwelcome attachments by the prefectural tax officers, that is, the appointed decurions and the workforce tied to the estate. It was good agricultural management. The privileges concerned jurisdiction. It was in the emperor's power to grant this privilege. He thereby withdrew his *coloni censibus adscripti* from the normal jurisdiction which was exercised by the governors and kept any conflict within the administrative, fiscal sphere. Thus any litigation over the poll tax, if generated by the levying decurions, would be drawn at once into the sphere of the managing imperial administration. Once imperial lands were issued to private persons as *fundi patrimoniales* or *emphyteuticarii*, the fiscal situation would be set right with that of other private possessors; the difference would still lie in the separate jurisdiction. The question remains of how many *coloni* fell within this colonate and privileges. The answer is: we do not know. If we may apply what we know or assume about the situation with private estates, it will have been a way of employment amongst an array of agricultural exploitation modes.

[232] Delmaire 1989, 203–204.

15.2 Coloni *on Patrimonial Land* (Fundi Patrimoniales), *Emphyteuticarian Land* (Fundi Emphyteuticarii), *and Combined Estates* (Saltus)

The *coloni originales patrimoniales* were bound to an *origo* on *fundi patrimoniales* and, when gone away but needed for the recultivation of lands, could be recalled, regardless of where they were or of their being in the *militia*, to their *condicio* and their own laws. Those who had already become *emeriti* of the *militia* were, however, excused. There was no requirement that their father should have been registered. It sufficed that a forebear (here: grandfather) was registered; the level of evidence was lowered. Also their children and further descendants could be reclaimed, notwithstanding whatever imperial service they had entered (CJ 11.63.4pr–1, 11.64.1).[233] There is no clear indication whether the registration was to a *massa* of patrimonial lands in general or to a particular parcel. CJ 11.63.4 suggests, by its reference to *fundi* which were once cultivated by the gone *coloni* and now needed recultivation by their descendants, that the latter was the case. CJ 11.64.1 repeats the authority to recall children and grandchildren of *coloni* of patrimonial lands, not as a resource of labour within the context of improvement (*emphyteusis*) of land, but within the context of flight (thus: also from land well cultivated). Flight into the *militia* (both military and civil) was of no avail. They had to return to work the land (*agrorum cultus*). The persons to pursue and enforce this were the superior administrative ranks (*duces*, *tribune*, and *praepositi*). Also CJ 11.64.3 serves as a reminder that service in the *militia* does not exempt from the *condicio*, even if buttressed before or afterwards by an imperial *adnotatio* or rescript (which, not surprisingly, could be obtained fraudulently).[234] Fugitive *coloni patrimoniales* were not to be admitted or hidden. Their hosts had to surrender them and would be fined one pound of gold (CJ 11.64.2).

The obligation to stay on the land had a reverse side. *Coloni originales patrimoniales* had a right to stay on their plot and could not be dispossessed by private possessors of their lands to whom these had been granted, and who wanted to people these lands with slaves of their own or *coloni* from another land.[235] If this happened, the grant would be voided (CJ 11.63.3). The land would thereby revert to the emperor and he could readmit the *coloni* to their

[233] CJ 11.64.1 mentions also *municipes* and *coloni saltuenses*. The former were citizens of a towns and likely in this context those who had to implement the *munera sordida* (the *collegiati*); the latter were *coloni* on the *fundi saltuenses*.

[234] These rules may apply to *coloni* both of the adscriptician kind and of the 'free' kind; we cannot tell.

[235] The mss. have *alios* and *alienos*, but important here is that the *coloni* were not attached to this land.

plots. CJ 11.63.1–3 speak merely of *coloni*, and one might interpret these also as applying to free lessee farmers. Yet CJ 11.63.4 and 11.64.1–3 deal with tied *coloni* and thus CJ 11.64.1–3 applied to these and not to free lessees.

Further, the *coloni originales patrimoniales* enjoyed the privilege that they could not be burdened with guardianships (*tutela*, CJ 5.34.13). This privilege, considering the mortality in those days, will not have been of little importance.

Whether emphyteuticarian lands were subjected to a duty of improving uncultivated land, or to a permanent cultivation duty, we have to leave aside here. However, it seems that cultivation or recultivation of unused land was policy here, because *coloni originales* on these lands could keep usurped parts which they had put into cultivation if this had been done with olive trees or as vineyard. If not, for example if they cultivated vegetables or grain, they could not keep these parcels (CJ 11.63.1pr). Since such cultures were considered more valuable, it may have been intended to stimulate *coloni* to invest their own property in the upgrading of the land. In addition they were, where there was irrigation, entitled to as much water as they needed for the plots they cultivated (those assigned to them by the *emphyteuticarii*, the possessors of these lands; but now also for the usurped lands). They could not take more water. For those usurped lands they were allowed to keep, they had to ask for admission to the irrigation system and to pay for what they needed from this (CJ 11.63.1.1–2).

There were also *coloni* attached to *saltus*, presumably *saltus patrimoniales* or *divae domus*, mentioned in CJ 11.61.3, 11.64 R, 11.64.1, and 11.66 R. In CJ 11.61.3 the military is forbidden to disturb or molest the *coloni pratorum*. These will have been the *coloni saltuenses*. If *saltus* refers to meadows or forests, it will have been sheep- or swineherders.[236]

15.3 Coloni *on Land of the* Res Privata (Fundi Rei Privatae)

On the lands of the *domus*, *fiscus* and *res privata* there were *coloni* who were tied to these as their *origo*. They could not be summoned to perform service to the towns or be appointed in the councils, CJ 11.68.1:

> Nullus omnino originalis colonus rei privatae nostrae ad aliquos honores vel quaelibet alia civitatis munera devocetur. Nec enim civitatum ordinibus et ceteris, ex quibus pro multitudine fieri nominationes oportet, per omnia florentibus ad haec suprema praesidia iniuriosa nominatione descendendum est.

[236] Where they herded swine or sheep of the emperor we do not know. In the South of Italy, herds of swine were kept from which Rome was approvisioned with meat for the public distributions.

> A *colonus originalis* of our *res privata* may not be summoned for any magistracies or whatever other duties of a town. Nor should the city councils and other bodies, from which nominations must be made because of their numbers, when they are flourishing in all respects, lower themselves by an unlawful nomination to these vanguard positions (*praesidia*).

First, this text demonstrates that these lands formed administratively part of city territories. Cuiacius suggests that this text implied that these lands did not fall under the territory of towns.[237] But in that case there would have been no ground to summon them nor to exempt them.[238] The text demonstrates something else as well: these *coloni* seem to have been eligible for the decurionate. Although they were tied to the imperial estate by census and could be recalled, their status of *alieni iuris* apparently did not block an appointment in the curial council or as magistrate, whereas the *militia* was closed to them (CJ 11.68.3). Or is this an implied prohibition to serve? But the prohibition to perform *munera* would have been seen as a desirable privilege. Are we to suppose that within the subcategory of *alieni iuris* there was a differentiation between the *coloni* of private persons and the *fundi patrimoniales* and the *coloni* of the *res privata* who, like *filii familias* could notwithstanding their being *in potestate* perform public functions? Were they because of their connection with the emperor on a par with the 'free' *coloni*? The question remains open.

If they were *privati* and if they were able to keep accounts (*ad ratocinia gerenda idonei*), that is, to manage, or able to till the land (*ad colendos agros*), they had to be recalled. Their offspring should be checked as well. This was evidently to prevent them taking up private business of somebody else as, for example, manager or farmer (CJ 11.68.2). By *privati* is meant that they have not yet been formally summoned to acknowledge their obligations and may have been living somewhere else (such as in the town, or else they would not be summoned for the council, as in CJ 11.68.1).[239] We see here again that *coloni originales* did not always work as farm hands or till their own plot of land, but could also function as manager (*actor*, *procurator*) or overseer. Wherever they

[237] Cuiacius 1758, c. 931.

[238] Cuiacius turns the argument around: because they were exempted, the imperial estates were outside the jurisdiction of the towns. But the colonate itself, the special jurisdiction, and this exemption all presume that the estates were under the administrative control of towns. The effect may have been that in the end they were practically completely out of that control, but still for a formal independence a law would be required, which does not exist. Besides, as soon as imperial land was issued to private persons, the estates would have to be censused by towns and therefore brought into their control again, if they had been outside of it. We do not see any act to this end.

[239] It is not the same as *ingenuus*, which refers to somebody who cannot be summoned for any *munus* entailing subserviency, contrary to the translations of OSS and Codex of Justinian 2016, which interpret it as referring to the *res privata*. But that would be an awkward construction.

were, they could be recalled and no excuse was of avail; if they were found in the *militia* and even in the palace guard (*protectores*), their immunity did not help (CJ 11.68.3). Also no limitation of prescription was valid in this matter regarding *coloni rei privatae*, and thus they and all their descendants could always be summoned, even if they were enrolled in the *militia* (CJ 7.38.1). On the other hand, CJ 11.66.6 states that those who have served for thirty years on a town council, in a municipal corpus or any other corpus or border fortress (*burgus*) cannot be recalled by a private person or the *res dominica.* They remain, however, tied to the position in which they serve (CJ 11.66.6). In this case they will have entered the council fraudulently.

An interesting constitution, CJ 11.68.4, states:

> Ex ingenuo et colonis ancillisque nostris natos natasve origini, ex qua matres eorum sunt, facies deputari.

> You make that those men and women born from an *ingenuus* and our *colonae* or slave women be assigned to the *origo* from which their mothers are.

The primary object of this constitution is that the children of such unions (between not subjected men (*ingenui*) and *colonae originariae* of lands of the *res privata*)[240] shall follow their mothers' *origo*, thus be registered in the census of that estate which thereby becomes their *origo*. It is the same rule as in CJ 11.48.21.1. But implicitly we see here the application of the *senatusconsultum Claudianum* with regard to the *condicio* (not to the state of freedom; these children do not become slaves) which means that they also took the *condicio* of their mother. With these *coloni*, too, evidently the analogous application of the *senatusconsultum Claudianum* prevailed, namely that in case of a marriage between an *ingenuus*, that is, between a man not subjected to a *condicio* like the adscripticiate, and a *colona*, the offspring would follow the *condicio* of the mother – the consequence of a *coniugium non aequale*, as in the case of such unions with slave women, but there the children became slaves. The senatusconsultum was abolished but CJ 11.48.24pr continued here the rule of the *coniugium non aequale*. The rule of the *coniugium non aequale* had got now a life of its own. CJ 6.4.2 adds for freedmen that if these with the consent of the patrons entered unions with *colonae* or slave women of the *res privata*, their patrons would lose all their patronage rights.[241] That loss implied more assets for the adscripticiate children of the freedman upon succession and so more assets for agriculture.

240 The text has *nostris*, but since the constitutions is directed to the *comes rei privatae* and not the *comes domorum*, it must be restricted to the *coloni rei privatae*.

241 See Kaser 1975, 298–301 thus: *operae* and the share in the inheritance of the freedman.

15.4 Coloni *on Land of the Imperial House* (Fundi Divinae Domus *or* Domus Augustae)

The same rule regarding offspring as set out above in CJ 11.68.4 for the *coloni rei privatae* applied to unions between decurions and *inquilinae dominicae* (CJ 10.32.29), and it is likely that this applied as well to *colonae originales dominicae*, since the difference between these kinds of *coloni* was not essential in this respect.[242] Further, sales by *coloni dominici* of land or of towns or temples (apparently, this concerns land incorporated by the *res privata* or Imperial House) were invalid and their possession could not be validated through any *praescriptio longi temporis*. (The parallel to the towns and temples implies that it concerned in the first instance land, assigned to the *coloni* and not their own property.) The land could always be reclaimed and the buyers could not reclaim the price, evidently as sanction (CJ 7.38.2, cf. CJ 7.32.12).[243]

CJ 11.66.6 states that those *coloni* or *inquilini* of the imperial *res privata* or *domus* who have served for thirty years on a town council, in a municipal *corpus* or any other *corpus* or *burgus* cannot be recalled by the *res privata* or the *res dominica* if these instances raise the *quaestio colonatus vel inquilinatus*.[244] They remain, however, tied to the function and place where they serve, that is, they have a new *condicio* (CJ 11.66.6; see also Section 15.3).

These *coloni* enjoyed privileges as well. They were free from sordid *munera*, extraordinary *munera* and *superindictiones* (CJ 11.75.1). Next to this they were free from a special tax (*descriptio*)[245] and from extraordinary taxes (*extraordinariae functiones*) (CJ 11.68.5).[246] As already related above (Section 15.1), if they had offended public order (*disciplina publica*), they were to be tried before the provincial governor but the *rationalis* or procurator of the Imperial House had to be present as well. If the crime was proven, justice had to be done fully (CJ 3.26.8). As with the *coloni saltuenses*, it was forbidden for the military (*milites*) to bother or burden the *coloni* of the meadows of the *res privata*, presumably by letting their horses graze or claiming hay (CJ 11.61.3).

If land of the *res privata* was sold to a *colonus*, it had to be sold to him together with two or more from the same village (*origo*) and of the same

[242] On the administrative reorganisation by Anastasius, see Svoronos 1976–1977.

[243] Normally they could have because the sale would be invalid: the *colonus originalis* had not been entitled or empowered to sell. Thus it was a punishment.

[244] A *burgus* was a castle or fort. There too people were tied to serve in these: CTh 7.14.1 (398 W), as were *muliones publici* at the *mutationes*: CTh 8.5.58 (398 W) = CJ 12.50.17.

[245] *Descriptio* is used for the assessment of land (see CJ 9.49.7.1), but also for taxes (see CJ 1.55.4, 11.28.1.1). In Nov. Theod. 22 a *descriptio* is levied on profitable land.

[246] What seemed to happen, according to the constitution.

status (*ius*) as co-buyers, to avoid him becoming a burden on his fellow *coloni* (CJ 11.68.6). Why was this prescribed? A possibility is that fellow villagers were personal surety for the purchase: if the buyer overextended his finances, they would be liable. With co-buyers, this risk was spread.[247] Here we see that these *coloni*, like the *coloni* on private lands, could own their own plot and they were directly liable for the taxes on these.[248] Otherwise they were, apparently, not liable for taxes (except for, eventually, the poll tax) but had to cultivate or manage imperial estates and render part of the revenues.

15.5 Coloni *on Land of the Fisc* (ταμιεῖον)

As related above, in Section 15.1, the lands of the *ταμιεῖον* must have formed part of the *fundi dominici*. Their exact purpose is unknown. CJ 11.69.1.pr deals with this particular category of *coloni*. Both in marriages between a 'free' *colonus* and a *colona tamiaca* and between a 'free' *colona* and a *colonus tamiacus* (*tamiacus* referring to the separate fund for the expenses of the imperial household)[249] the children will follow the status of the imperial lands and become *dominici*. Since this concerned free citizens, this was a deviation from the rule on status (*condicio*) in the first case: normally the child would follow its father's status. We therefore see here the application of the *coniugium non aequale* rule as already applied with private *coloni originales*. But this deviation applied, apparently, only to those *coloni dominici* who were posited on *fundi tamiaci* and did not apply to *coloni dominici* on other estates. In the case of marriages between male or female *adscripticii* or slaves on one side and male or female *coloni dominici* or *servi dominici* on the other side, the rules of the previous laws were maintained (CJ 11.69.1.1). This must mean that the *condicio* with the analogous

247 This suggestion is based on the preceding part, only retained in the Theodosian Code, where *fideiussores* are mentioned.

248 The question is what *qui forte consortibus suis gravis ac molestus existat* means. Perezius 1661, 339–340, thinks it refers to somebody who is dominant and difficult for his neighbours. But since the buyer has to assume the tax burden on the plot bought, it is more likely that the emperor feared he might not be able to pay this, as a consequence of which his fellows in the *sors* would have to make up the deficit.

249 They were called *coloni dominici* or *tamiaci*. On *tamieion*, see Schmitz 2002, according to whom it represents the *aerarium populi Romani* or the fiscus of the emperor; see further the next section. Kaplan 1992 has nothing on the subject. It follows from these names and the rubric of CJ 11.48 that this referred to lands of the *res privata*, at least in 534, according to Cuiacius ad h.l. situated in Cappadocia and administered by the *comes domorum* and the *praepositus sacri cubiculi*. *The coloni* on them were from that point of view both *dominici* and *tamiaci*, depending on whether one considered the soil or the administrator of the land. It follows from this that the *tamiaci* were apparently a category of the *coloni dominici*. See also Nov. 20 and 30.

application of the *senatusconsultum Claudianum* applied undiminished as a new rule and indeed, in three of the four combinations in which the child was freeborn, it thereby became a *colonus dominicus*; while in the fourth case, an *adscripticia* cohabitating with a *servus dominicus*, it became an *adscripticius*. Application of the senatusconsultum would have led here to the status of slave. Apparently the emperor favoured here himself and his slave.

Offspring of a *colonus liber* or *colona libera* and, as the case may be, a *tamiaca* or *tamiacus* was always incorporated (*adnectentur*) into the group of *coloni dominici* (CJ 11.69.1pr). It follows from this that the *tamiaci* were apparently a special category of the *coloni dominici* (we saw above that the *katapodas* translates the adjective by *sacer*, which suggests a fiscal category reserved for the emperor). Normally the offspring would follow the *condicio* of the father, but that was apparently only the case with the father being a *tamiacus*. With a *tamiaca* as mother they followed the status of the mother, so *adnectentur* should be read as a subjection *de novo* to this status. Thus here the rule as applied to *adscripticii* was followed (see Section 10). A later exception was made by Nov. 38.6 of 536 to favour the towns. Sons of a union between a curial and, inter alia, a *tamiaca*, were subjected to the decurionate (town councillorship). The reason was the paucity of candidates for this burden. With unions between male *adscripticii* or slaves of another person and *colonae* or slave women of the *domus and* unions between *adscripticiae* or slave women with a slave or *colonus* of the *domus*, the offspring would follow the *condicio* as was ordained in the existing laws (CJ 11.69.1.1). They became slaves or *coloni* on the estates of their fathers or mothers, depending on the nature of the union.

15.6 A Reason for the Privileges?

The *coloni* on imperial lands, even if these were issued as patrimonial or emphyteuticarian lands, enjoyed privileges the *coloni* on private lands did not enjoy. Why did such a difference exist? One reason might be that the presence of the emperor put the *coloni* on a higher level, just as in CTh 4.12.3 of 320 (?) the children of a union of a fiscal slave and a free woman (*ingenua*) did not become slaves as the *senatusconsultum Claudianum* would have it but Latins, not subjected to servile duties, only under the patronage of the emperor. Similarly, freedmen of the emperor had, socially, a better position than ordinary freedmen.[250] Another reason might be that these privileges made the imperial *coloni* less burdened and so more available for

[250] See Weaver 1972.

their duties towards the emperor. A third reason might be that these privileges made it more attractive to enter the colonate on imperial domains and kept them from migrating. But was there much migrating? For example, CJ 11.48.8 contains in its Justinianic context rules for solving the problem of a migrated *colonus* who has worked elsewhere, either as *colonus* or as a free farmer or farm hand. As rule it was certainly useful in 534, but it does not say whether the situation occurred often or not. The historical occasion to issue it, in 371 in Gaul, testified to such cases, but that was some 160 years earlier, in another region; likewise the many other rules on fugitive *coloni*. Only the contemporary Justinian constitutions may testify. What those in the Code concern, they primarily deal with the proof of colonate, only CJ 11.48.22.3–4 and 11.48.23 demonstrate that in the years 531–534 children of *coloni* might indeed have been away for a long time. In that period they may have tried their luck elsewhere and worked on another estate or done something else.

16 The 'Free' Colonate

We saw in Section 13.2, which discussed CJ 11.48.19, that next to the common form of the colonate a different colonate existed, which the sources call the *coloni liberi*, the 'free' *coloni*.[251] Totally free they were not, bound as they were to an estate and subjected to the poll tax if their province was not exempted from this. Apart from CJ 11.48.19, which provided an incidental source of 'free' *coloni* and which must have caused a random distribution of 'free' *coloni* over those provinces where the adscripticiate existed, there were some provinces in which the 'free' colonate had been imposed by statute generally at an earlier moment on former *adscripticii*: Illyricum in 371, Palestine in 386, and Thrace in 393 (CJ 11.53.1 11.52.1, and 11.51.1). Those subjected to the 'free' *condicio* were in these provinces *censibus dumtaxat adscripti*, that is, *tributa subiectos non faciunt* (CJ 11.50.2pr): they were only registered in the estate census and not (on account of the taxes) subjected to their estate owner, hence *liberi*.[252] The inclusion of these texts in Justinian's Code implies that the situation in those provinces was still legally the same.

[251] Assuming that CJ 11.51 *De colonis Palaestinis* also concerns *coloni liberi*. However, if it did not, it would be a strange constitution, confirming for Palaestina what is amply stated in CJ 11.48.

[252] Wickham 2005, 523 assumes a 'village registration' for 'free' *coloni* which would have been a more complex business in those parts of the west where village identity was weak or non-existent. Yet there were in all probability no 'free' *coloni* in the west, and the registration was by census, which system continued for a long time in the west.

Of these three constitutions, the one on Thrace gives the most information. It deals with a situation in 383, but its details were apparently in 534 still actual enough to be included in the Code, just as those of CJ 11.51.1 and CJ 11.53.1. The abolition of the *capitatio humana* in Thrace in 383 would release the *coloni tributariae sortis* of their bonds (*nexus*). *Tributaria sors* may be coupled with the *coloni* or with the *nexus*. *Sors* means literally 'lot' ('Losstäbchen'), hence 'that which is attributed', 'destiny'. But *sors* may also refer to a (measure of) land, or to capital. Thus it could mean *coloni* subjected to the 'destiny of the tax', and the phrase might be an equivalent of *condicio adscripticia*. But since the *tributum* was levied on land by ways of registration, *sors* may also refer to the registered estate where a *colonus* was entered on the census. In that case it means '*coloni* of a land, registered for the *tributum*'. This seems to be the better interpretation. Hence it must refer to the *adscripticii*, and it demonstrates that the designation *tributarii*, used elsewhere, must also refer to these *coloni*. It implies that the abolition was done by a striking in the census of the *colonus*, releasing the estate owner from guaranteeing the poll tax but also taking away his *potestas* over the *colonus*. What it also implied was that the *coloni* now had the faculty to migrate elsewhere (CJ 11.48.23.1: *facultatem terra derelicta in alia loca migrare*, CJ 11.52.1: *vagandi et quo libuerit recedendi facultas*; *nec recedendi quo velint aut permutandi loca habeant facultatem*), evidently not only within their village or district, but also to other districts as long as they did not change their *origo* (but they could ask for permission).[253] In this case there would be no reason to stop them, and in any case there would be no private person authorised to pursue them. In order to prevent a massive migration, these *coloni* (it does not say that it concerned all *coloni* or farmers of Thrace!) are turned into *coloni liberi*. They are retained *originario iure*, which shows that this designation comprises the two kinds of *coloni* (CJ 11.52.1.1) and they were not allowed to migrate (CJ 11.48.19, 11.48.23.1,11.51.1, 11.52.1.1, 11.53.1.1). The only exception to the prohibition to migrate was if a 'free' *colonus* acquired land elsewhere, sufficient for self-sustenance; then he could move thereto (Nov. 162.2.1).

How was this accomplished and enforced? If the *capitatio humana* was abolished, the need to keep the registers for this tax fell away. Likewise, the

[253] That would be contrary to CJ 10.39.4, unless we interpret this as a prohibition to migrate without official allowance. Carrié 1997, 102–103 denies this liberty. According to him, both the duty of the *capitatio* and the duty to stay were co-existent from the beginning, and the emperors merely reminded the *coloni* that they could not migrate: the *ius colonatus* was reduced to an *originarium ius*. This, however, goes against the tenor of the text. It also goes against the idea that the *autopragia* of the landlord necessitated the duty to stay.

adscriptio (the extract of the agreement which placed them in the *potestas* of the estate owner) in the estate census could be struck, no longer being necessary and valid: the debt based on the *capitatio* had ceased. Hence it is ordained that they remain on the estate census *nomine et titulo colonorum*. As to the enforcement, it was now the constitution which granted the estate owner in case of absence full authority to recall him (*plena auctoritas revocandi*, CJ 11.48.23.4–5, 11.51.1, 11.52.1, 11.53.1). Apart from that authority, the estate owner had no rights over the 'free' *colonus*. Whoever took up a fugitive 'free' *colonus* had to return him with his assets and family and pay a fine of two pounds of silver (CJ 11.52.1.2).

Nothing is specifically said here about what a 'free' *colonus* was expected to do, but they were expected to farm (CJ 11.52.1.1: *possessor eorum iure utatur*; in CJ 11.53.1.2: *operae*), perhaps as lessee, perhaps on a plot allotted to them, perhaps as farm hand. Similarly, those who after thirty years became 'free' *coloni* (ex CJ 11.48.19) had to till their plot (CJ 11.48.23.1 *in fine*: *terram colere*), perhaps as a compensation to the landowners for the loss of their *potestas*. The system provided the estate owners with a pool of available workers. Since the *colonus* could not migrate, he will have been obliged to accept whatever work was available, or as owner of a plot work on this. The last will not have been often the case; *coloni* were not the richest of people. But being now treated as *ingenui* (CJ 11.52.1.1), they were free to contract and to fulfil functions which before they had been barred from on account of their inferior status.

Previously the same had been done in Illyricum in 371 (CJ 11.53.1, with reference to the *tributarius nexus*) and in 386 in Palestine (CJ 11.51.1). In Illyricum apparently the *capitatio humana* was abolished but the *coloni*, though no longer bound *tributario nexu* to land, were to serve it *nomine et titulo colonorum*, that is, through the estate census. Here it seems to be the governor who recalls them, because he also collects the fine from those who take up fugitives (CJ 11.53.1.2: *in auctoritate iudicis*). These persons also have to compensate the owner for the loss (in not having this labour force) and pay for the work done (CJ 11.53.1.2: *in redhibitione operarum et damni quod locis quae deseruerant factum est*). Here, as we shall also see in the Lex Romana Burgundionum 14.6, there is no loss of tax which must be compensated but the loss of labour force.

The constitution for Palestine underlines the faculty of the estate owner to recall them (CJ 11.51.1: *exemplo aliarum provinciarum ita domino teneatur ut sine poena suscipientis non possit abscondere, additio eo, ut possessionis domino revocandi eius plena tribuatur auctoritas*). Although the text suggests that this colonate was introduced for *all coloni*, the phrasing suggests that it concerned those *adscripticii* who were released: reference is made to the estate they once took upon them to till and *nullus omnino colonorum suo iure velut vagus ac liber exsultet*: it cannot be that every farmer rejoiced at this (the independent farmers will not have liked it), but only those who were released from a more oppressive bond.

These three constitutions functioned in their Justinianic inclusion as the legal basis for defining the position of these *coloni*. Those who admit fugitives are, as we saw before in CJ 11.48, fined (CJ 11.52.1.2, 53.1.2). They functioned further as the legal basis for recalling these *coloni* if they had fled from their land and defined the conditions of the 'free' colonate for each region. The constitutions established a colonate which was without a private agreement. It was now completely a public law institution with an *origo* and the inherent duty comparable to a *munus*, with the landowner authorised to enforce it. It is not known whether their estate owner could release the *colonus* from this as he could an *adscripticius*. It is not probable because (a) the estate owner had no *potestas* over him and he was not *alieni iuris*, and (b) the basis of his obligation was a statutory regulation, not a private agreement. And with the *adscripticii* who ex CJ 11.48.19 became 'free' *coloni*? Lacking any differentiation in the sources we must assume that they now shared the same fate, without possibility of release.

Interesting is that in Illyricum the rules for children of 'free' *coloni* also applied to their freedmen (CJ 11.53.1.3).[254] What applied to their children? It is nowhere specified. I assume that it concerned the transmission of the *condicio*, then, if the *condicio* did not pass on, in one generation the land might suffer under migration. So I assume that in the same way as with *adscripticii*, the *condicio* passed on. Applying to freedmen of the 'free' *coloni* it means that they in the first place upon manumission got the same *origo* as their manumitters, thus the estate where he was censused, but that the *condicio* passed also on to them, as if they were children. This may have been exceptional but necessary in consideration of the shortage of manpower in 371 and retained afterwards.

By turning into 'free' *coloni*, *adscripticii* became *ingenui* again (CJ 11.52.1.1). This implies that they could fulfil public functions, otherwise inaccessible to them, for example become a cleric or *tabularius* without

[254] Normally freedmen had the *origo* of their manumitters (see above, Section 4) and on the basis of this rule theirs would have been the estate of their manumitters. But could *adscripticii* have slaves and set them free? Not if these would have been part of their *peculium*. It would be different, probably, if they had possessed land with slaves attached to it. With 'free' *coloni* it was different. They were not subjected to the *peculium*. Freedmen would take the *origo* of their manumitter.

needing the consent of their estate owner (see Section 14.1). They could own slaves, which might have left them free to pursue such interests. Since *adscripticii* could own plots of land and could become 'free' *coloni*, there could have been *coloni liberi* (CJ 11.53.1.3) who may have owned land or leased it and were not subjected to their landlords (no *peculium*; the word in CTh 11.52.1.2 will have meant 'assets', because they could dispose freely of it). If his estate owner requested more than was usual, they could litigate (CJ 11.50.1). It was forbidden to reduce their status, that is, to make them *adscripticii* (CJ 11.48.23.1). They had to pay the tax and they could freely dispose of their possessions (CJ 11.48.19, 11.52.1pr). Since a 'free' *colonus* was free versus his estate owner, we may assume that there was no bar for him to litigate in general against other landowners. Further, CJ 9.27.4 and CJ 9.27.5 might well apply to them too (see above, Section 15). We see that when in 535 farmers in Illyricum and Thrace appear to have lost their land to creditors, no mention is made of a mandatory consent of landlords.[255] When in 535 Justinian forbade moneylenders to seize, apparently by force, the land from their farmers-debtors, it could concern independent farmers, or 'free' *coloni*, or *adscripticii* with their own land.[256]

After 539 a third source of the 'free' colonate were the marriages between *adscripticii* and *ingenuae*, which were discussed above, in Section 10.2. It may have led to the existence of the 'free' colonate in Africa after 570. In Italy the *Constitutio Pragmatica* of 554 prescribed that slaves and *coloni* held elsewhere had to be returned with their offspring to their masters (App. 7.16). This might concern *coloni originarii* or 'free' *coloni*, or both categories.

17 The 'Free' Colonate: A Byzantine Serfdom?

With the 'free' *coloni*, the *condicio* was different from that of *adscripticii*. According to CJ 11.53.1.1 they remained registered *nomine et titulo colonorum* in the *census* of the estate, they could be recalled by the estate owner but they were not under his *potestas*. Their property was *bona*, not *peculium*. It is evident that the need for workers caused the emperors to impose

[255] Nov. 32, 33, 34, and 35, of 535. No distinction is made between *adscripticii* and other kinds of *coloni*. Although it may be argued that for *adscripticii* the laws were not needed, in view of the extensive legislation this absence is remarkable.

[256] Nov. 32–34 (535) forbid this and order the return of the seized lands in the provinces of Thrace, Illyricum, and Moesia Secunda. See Kaiser & Chronopoulos 2012, with on 476 n. 8 a bibliography to the Novels. On 478 n. 16 they cite Velkov, who opines it were *coloni liberi*. But since *adscripticii*, 'free' *coloni*, and independent farmers all could own land, there is no clue to the status of these farmers.

on them the obligation to remain on their estate and continue to work as agricultural labourers, under the now statutory authority of their estate owners. Their obligation was solely based on a statute and was thereby a public obligation, not based on a private contract. If they exploited the land with capital from the estate owner, it must have been organised and settled according to the usual private law rules on loan. The yearly settling of accounts would have made them owner of their credit balance. Being obliged to stay there, what else could they do but farm? The same fate will have befallen those *coloni* who had become free ex CJ 11.48.19. In their case they remained also registered in the estate's census (or else they would not be bound to the land) but now with the *adscriptio* struck, while they had to pay the *capitatio* themselves and had the duty to till the land. The need for a loan from the estate owner might still be there.

The break with the private contract and the imposition of a public obligation which made them, although *ingenui*, yet *servi terrae* (CJ 11.52.1), poses the question whether we may call the 'free' *coloni*, certainly those who did not pay the poll tax, serfs in the medieval sense. To do so seems to me wrong, because serfs in the meaning usually applied for western Europe implied more, namely a personal bond of comprehensive subjection such as the need to obtain the master's assent to marry and the possibility to be manumitted.[257] Sometimes those serfs were even subjected to the jurisdiction of their lord (see further Section 40.2 on the question whether there was a transition in the west from colonate to serfdom). We do not see that here, notwithstanding the restrictions of CJ 11.50.1–2, which in my opinion were the corollary of the authority conceded to the estate owners.

The use of the term serfdom is consequently hazardous. Yet, if we use the term 'serfs' as English equivalent for the term *servi terrae* used by the Byzantines for them (CJ 11.52.1.1), that is, people who are completely free and *sui iuris*, only by public law limited in their freedom of movement, then we may speak of a Byzantine serfdom. It was a particular Byzantine serfdom, established as early as 371. It is in no way to be linked to any serfdom of early medieval western Europe, and the position of the *coloni* in the west at the end of the fifth century was definitively different (see Section 49).[258] The 'free' *coloni* were not subjected to the law on marriages of *adscripticii*, their situation was not subjected to the rules as for

[257] The subject is vast, the distinctions very varied, and the literature enormous. But for the two contentions above, see De Blécourt 1950, 107–108.

[258] See, inter alia, Goetz 1993 and recently Rio 2017, 175–214 on the different forms of dependency in the west.

adscripticii, they could take on ecclesiastical positions without needing consent of their estate owner, they could become *tabellarii* etc. In short, they were free of all the encumbrances the adscripticiate (*condicio coloniaria*) implied; they were no longer *condicionales*.

18 Farmers Not Subjected to the Colonate

As Sarris, Banaji and other authors state, labour in the countryside was pluriform and thus the modes of exploitation too. *Coloni* formed just a part of the array of labour. We dealt until now with the *vicani* (CJ 11.54–57) and *coloni*. Nothing is said in CJ 11.48 about lessees and agricultural workers not tied to an estate, but that is not what the title is about and thus not to be expected. Those farmers and farm hands who were free of the colonate figure in CJ 4.44.65 and other texts, as we have already seen.[259] If *coloni adscripticii* or *liberi* were lessees next to their duties (a case is P.Oxy. LXVII 4615, where somebody was through descent subjected to the *condicio* but apparently free to pursue other interests like leasing land or houses, as we know for other cases), those texts would also apply to them, because we do not see in CJ 11.48.20 that for *adscripticii* and 'free' *coloni* a particular regime regarding the contract of lease (*locatio conductio*) existed. This constitution only provided a special arrangement for the payment of the rent in a special case. Where *coloni adscripticii* were given by their estate owner a plot to cultivate and render services, there would be no lease contract but rather a *precarium*.

But there were farmers who were fully free and either worked their own land (which, if sizeable, would make such owners local elite) or in some or other capacity earned a living, for example as seasonal workers, as servants or as specialised workers such as vine-dressers (*ampelourgoi*). According to Banaji they formed a deeply differentiated group. In the sixth century the monasteries

[259] Some texts: CJ 4.10.3, 11; CJ 4.21.19pr; CJ 4.65.5, 9, 27, 35pr (here the *conductores* have taken upon them to find farmers to till the rented lands, which may concern free tenants, but perhaps also or just *coloni adscripticii* or *liberi*); CJ 5.62.8 (where *coloni* is explained by the interpolation *id est conductores*; otherwise confusion might be created with CJ 5.34.13, where the *coloni patrimoniales* enjoy immunity from the guardianship); CJ 7.30.1 (where *colono vel* may be interpolated); CJ 9.24.1.5 (assistance with counterfeiting); CJ 11.55.1–2 (prohibition to impose *obsequia* upon them); CJ 11.58.3 (the owner resists a fiscal re-evaluation of his lands by retracting his procurator or by dismissing his *colonus*: it would not help to dismiss an *adscripticius*, so it must concern a tenant; further, if it concerned tied farmers, the text would more likely have read *colonos*); CJ 11.61.3.1 (it concerns tenants (*conductores*) of provincial and *rei privatae* meadows, since meadows are not cultivated); CJ 11.62.5 (it concerns a reassignment of lands, deserted by previous *coloni* or *emphyteuticarii*: because *coloni adscripticii* and *liberi* may have owned lands, but not from the Crown, it must refer to free tenants (*conductores*)).

in Egypt provided a new opportunity to lease and cultivate or sublease land. As to labour, he distinguishes a variety of ways in which labour was contracted, which reflected the variety in agricultural deployment. There were different ways to make these free people economically dependent, for example by advancing wages in the form of a loan (the προχρεία (*prochreia*) agreement), or by paying them the next year when they returned.[260] Banaji assumes that the market for hired work was well organised. This makes it likely that the colonate was not the result of a shortage of labour.[261]

If the independent farmers held land for their estate owner in lease or in *precarium*, as *detentor*, licensee, they could not usucapt. CJ 7.30.1 states this for leased land, but either the reference to a *colonus* may have been interpolated here, or the words *vel conductori*, in order to make the lease clear: in both cases its purpose would have been to make clear that a *colonus originalis* too could not usucapt his master's land; it is obvious that this did not concern land they owned themselves. How many of these not subjected farmers existed we do not know. Zuckerman and Banaji have submitted that the majority of the village people in Egypt were (contractual) lessees or hired farm hands on large estates.[262] Banaji assumes that, in general, in Egypt estate owners relied structurally on a large proportion of hired work.[263] It is not impossible considering the data for the previous period. Probably we must assume that it depended on the agricultural strategy of the elite landowners.[264]

Another text seems to point to free lessees. CJ 9.27.5 reads:

> Unusquisque procurator, praepositus gynaecei, tabularius susceptor colonus vel quicumque se a comite domorum meminerit esse concussum, cum ipse cui pecuniam numeraverit administratione decesserit, intra anni spatia ad iudicium spectabilitatis tuae quidquid dederit repetiturus occurrat, ut prosit pensionibus, quidquid ille reddiderit. 1. sin vero ex tempore depositae administrationis praestituti temporis curricula transfluxerint, nulla vox advocationis emergat, sed ipsos procuratores praepositos colonos tabularios susceptores obnoxios ad solutionem volumus artari.

[260] So also Hickey 2012, 84–85 and Jördens 1997, 81–84 on the *prochreia* and the dependence.

[261] See Banaji 2001, 190–212 on wage labour and the peasantry in the Byzantine period, and in particular 197–206 on the variety in deployment. His digression on the colonate (206–212) unfortunately does not take enough account of the legal aspects.

[262] Zuckerman's calculations for Aphrodito would yield at least this (Zuckerman 2004, 221–240), and it would coincide with Banaji 1999, 193–196; see the cautious review by Palme 2007, 335 on this point.

[263] See Banaji 2001, 202, mentioning 60 per cent for the middle of the third century for the Appianus estate in the Fayum.

[264] On this, see Vera 1986.

> If any procurator, a head of a weavery (*gynaeceum*), a registrar, a tax receiver, a *colonus*, or anybody recalls having been extorted by a *comes domorum*, when he to whom the money has been paid has left his administration, he should come within the term of a year before Your Spectability to reclaim what he had given, so that it may profit the taxes, whatever he shall have returned to him. 1. But if the whirlwinds of the set time have passed from the moment the administration was laid down, no voice of a lawyer may emerge, but we wish that those very *procuratores*, heads, *coloni*, registrars, receivers, and *coloni* will be tightly held liable to payment. (tr. Sirks)[265]

This is a remarkable text. First of all, it proves that extortion was not below the dignity of a *comes domorum* or his underlings. Some persons mentioned were functionaries of the *res privatae*: the *procuratores*, the heads of the weaveries; others were municipal functionaries: the registrars, the receivers. Of the *coloni* it is not clear whether they were lessees of land of the *res privata* or merely *coloni originales*, or both. In all cases they have to render payments to the *res privata*. The nature of these depends on their function (collected rents, collected taxes, collected income, rents). They have to reclaim within a year after the *comes* left his office, which was the term set for the *lex Iulia repetundarum*. Remarkable is further that the reclaimed sum is not paid out to them but will be settled with what they owe to the *res privata*. The final sentence assumes that there were outstanding debts. That high officials extorted is not news. They may have paid to get the position (see CJ 9.27.6) and now wanted to replenish their coffers. But the extorted people apparently dallied with paying their normal dues as a kind of informal settling, perhaps hoping for a general indulgence. Where or from whom may they have reclaimed? As CJ 9.27.5 is addressed to him, it was the *comes rei privatae*: the *domus* formed part of the *res privata*.[266] The mention of this *comes* suggests that it concerned *coloni* of the *patrimonium* and *domus divina*. Yet if they were merely *coloni originales* they would only have to pay the poll tax to the praetorian tax collectors, not to the *res privata*.

[265] CJ 9.27.5: *Valentin. Theodos. et Arcad. AAA. Severino com. rer. privat. Unusquisque procurator, praepositus gynaecei, tabularius susceptor colonus vel quicumque se a comite domorum meminerit esse concussum, cum ipse cui pecuniam numeraverit administratione decesserit, intra anni spatia ad iudicium spectabilitatis tuae quidquid dederit repetiturus occurrat, ut prosit pensionibus, quidquid ille reddiderit. 1. Sin vero ex tempore depositae administrationis praestituti temporis curricula transfluxerint, nulla vox advocationis emergat, sed ipsos procuratores praepositos colonos tabularios susceptores obnoxios ad solutionem volumus artari. [a 390] d. prid. non. iun. Mediolani Valentiniano A. iiii et Neoterio conss.*

[266] Cf. Delmaire 1989, 222.

19 Conclusions

19.1 The Colonate under Justinian

The law under Justinian consists of many laws, issued in previous times and which were included as rules. The titles under which they were placed indicate the situation as it was and prove that the included texts were considered useful and actual rules in this setting. It implies that the covered situations were either actual or could occur. Next to that there are some contemporaneous constitutions which refer to existing situations. They together present a colonate which knows three variants, of which one is a species of another. One is the colonate of old, called later in the east the adscripticiate. The other is a variant of this: the colonate on the lands of the *patrimonium*, the *tamieion*, the *domus augusta* or *divina*, on the emphyteuticarian lands, and on the *saltus*, in short: on imperial land. The third variant is the 'free' colonate. They distinguish themselves by different consequences, but all are a *condicio coloniaria* and all are *coloni originales*, which means that all are free citizens but have a particular *status* (*condicio*) and that all are registered in the census of a village or estate and bound to remain there and in the first two cases to provide services, usually of an agricultural nature.

In the foregoing, several specifics of the colonate were established.

Becoming a *Colonus* and Transmission

- The colonate was entered voluntarily by an agreement (CJ 11.48.22pr–1) or it was transmitted by descent (CJ 7.24.1.1) or imposed on beggars (CJ 11.26.1).
- For proof of the colonate in proceedings, at least two documents were required (CJ 11.48.22pr–1).
- The colonate was formalised through the registration of the *colonus* in the census of the estate owner.
- It thereby became formally a status of subjection to the estate owner.
- A *coniugium non aequale* made the transmission of the colonate different (CJ 7.24.1.1, 11.48.21).

Colonate and Tax

- Colonate and poll tax were linked by the guarantee of the estate owner for this (CJ 11.48.22pr, CJ 11.48.4pr; CJ 1.3.16 *a contrario*).

- Abolition of the poll tax finished the colonate (CJ 11.51.1) and in some provinces it was turned into the 'free' colonate.
- The estate became the *origo* of the *colonus* (CJ 11.48.15, P. Merton II 98).

The Power of the Estate Owner over the *Colonus* and Its Effects

- A *colonus* was in the *potestas* of his estate owner (CJ 11.50.2pr, 11.52.1.1, 11.48.6, 1.3.16).
- The *potestas* of the estate owner derived from his ownership of the land and was of a public nature (CJ 11.48.8.1 *a contrario*).
- Transfer of the estate brought the *colonus* a new *dominus*; it was not possible to change this by private agreement (CJ 11.48.2.1).
- A *colonus* had to stay on or near the estate (P.Oxy. I 135 and other papyri).
- The estate owner could recall his *colonus* (CJ 11.48.6).
- The *colonus* had to render services to the estate owner (CJ 1.3.16).
- A *colonus* could own property, but for alienation the knowledge and consent of his estate owner was required, hence it was considered as if a *peculium* (CJ 11.48.19; 11.52.2.3).
- A *colonus* was limited in his power to sue his *dominus* (CJ 11.50.1 and 2).
- A *colonus* was not a slave but a free man, yet on account of the *potestas* considered to be on the same level as a slave (CJ 11.48.21.1).
- The position of a *colonus* was in respect to a *filius familias* with a *peculium castrense* a reversed one. The *filius* was considered to be *in potestate* regarding his *pater* but *sui iuris* regarding his *peculium* (D. 14.6.2, D. 49.17.15.3.). Contrariwise, the *colonus* was as freeborn Roman citizen *sui iuris* in many respects (family law, contract and patrimonial law, law of succession), but considered *in potestate* regarding his estate owner and his property. Apparently the Romans could live well with such a dual approach.
- Being in the *potestas* made marriages with people not in public *potestas* into *coniugia non aequalia* (CJ 7.24.1, 11.48.21).
- Conversely, an estate owner will have needed financial reserves to function as guarantor and to sustain the adscripticiate, and this form of labour must have been economically attractive and useful for his estate. These probable conditions will have restricted the application of the adscripticiate.

- Fulfilling one's duties over thirty years turned a *colonus adscripticius* into a 'free' *colonus* (CJ 11.48.19).

The 'Free' Colonate

- In the 'free' colonate the *colonus* was not subjected to the *potestas* of the landowner but still registered in the estate census; he could consequently be recalled by the landowner and had to till the land.
- Abolition of the poll tax entailed in the provinces of Illyricum and Thrace the establishment of the 'free' colonate.

Coloni in Public Law

- If a *colonus* owned land, he would as owner be registered there (CJ 11.48.4.1).
- The colonate was a subcategory of the category *in alieno iure esse.*

In P. Merton II 98, a surety for an *adscripticius* (a 'Gestellungsbürgschaft') of the sixth century, the colonate is well defined:

> that they should continually remain and live in the same village (κώμη), with their families and property and cattle and all their belongings, maintaining peace and proper conduct and be accountable for all that regards their person, namely, the fate or destiny of one who has been enrolled as a cultivator (ἐναπογράφη τύχη). (tr. by the editors)

There are several such 'Gestellungsbürgschaften' for *adscripticii.*[267] Fikhman is right in observing that the surety reflects the duties of the *adscripticius*, but the question is: Are these the duties of an *adscripticius* who entered an adscripticiate agreement and was registered in the census, or of one who had this status on the ground of his *origo*? Many sureties we have are for *adscripticii* who are in prison because they fled. We see that in these cases the enumerated duties reflect the legal description of the status: to do what pertains to their status, which included work on the land or to perform other agricultural services (CJ 11.48.22.3: *neque agrum coluit neque aliquid colonarii operis celebravit*). It seems thus better to assume that the surety reflects the previous or simultaneous acknowledgement (*confessio*, comparable with the *agnoscere* in administrative law of *munera*) by the *adscripticius* of his obligations. Furthermore, the obligation to keep his goods on the estate fitted the prohibition against alienation from his *peculium* without the

[267] Fikhman 1981 = Fikhman 2016, 169–177, Section 12.2 *in fine*; Palme unpubl. on *Burgstellungen.*

consent of the estate owner.[268] At the moment of entering the adscripticiate, it may have been different. The agreement between estate owner and prospective *adscripticius* must have consisted of several elements. For the farmer these would have been to provide labour, to remain on the estate with all and everything (which resembles the *paramonè* agreement, about which see below, Section 53),[269] to render his 'rent' to the estate owner – perhaps these were simply comprised in the phrase: the duties of an *adscripticius*. There may have been special clauses, or it may have been left to custom (cf. CJ 11.48.5). On the other side stood the obligations of the estate owner towards the *adscripticius* and the fisc (as guarantor).

The colonate as the surety makes clear that it comprised two elements. The first was the bond to the estate which was his *origo*. It was the enrolment in the census which had this effect. The other element was the subjection to the estate owner which resulted in being *alieni iuris*. The census registration fixed this.

The status (*condicio*) of an *adscriptius* resembled very much that of a *filius familias*: a free person, able to marry and be father himself, yet under the power of another person, who could command him and recall him. Similarly their powers to sue their *dominus* were limited.[270] A difference, albeit slight, was that he could own assets by himself (contrary to a *filius* who could do so only with *peculium castrense*, but, as said above, he was considered as a *pater familias* in this respect), but this advantage was taken away because his assets were treated as if *peculium*, which gave the *dominus* discretion over alienation. But an *adscriptius* was of course not a son or *loco filii*. In classical times there existed the person *in mancipio*, namely a debtor who was assigned by the praetor to pay off his debt in the service of his creditor; he was *alieni iuris*, that is, in the *potestas* of his creditor. We do not know whether this construction still existed in Justinian's time: it does not figure in his Institutes. But it resembles that of the *adscripticius*. A freedman was also limited in suing his patron: he could not sue him without permission of the praetor (D. 2.4.4.1).[271] The position of an *adscripticius* may have lain in between, better than one *in*

268 CJ 11.50.2.3: . . . *ne quid de peculio sui cuiquam colonorum ignorante domino praedii vendere aut alio modo alienare licet.*

269 See Sirks 1997, 183–184; Sarris 2006, 65. Waldstein 1986, 143–146 compares *paramonè* clauses in Hellenistic Greek enfranchisement documents with *operae libertorum*. He sees fundamental differences. Further, he does not discuss *paramonè* agreements in the later imperial period.

270 Kaser 1975, 343–344.

271 Kaser 1975, 298–299.

mancipio, worse than that of a freedman. The way he might have been released is similar to that of a slave: dismissal from the *potestas*.[272]

The adscripticiate was in origin based on the duty to pay the *capitatio humana* (poll tax) which the estate owner paid or credited or guaranteed, creating a debt for the taxable person, for which, in return, this person promised to stay on the estate and do what the estate owner ordered him to do, as antichresis for the debt. He subjected himself so to the *potestas* of the estate owner and became *alieni iuris* (his family too). This was set out in a document. An extract (*apographos*) was entered into the census of the estate (*adscriptio*). By the entry into the census the bond with the estate owner as contract partner became impersonal: the now *adscripticius* was obliged to any successive owner of the estate. Further, by the census the estate became his *origo*. As a consequence of the transmission of the *origo* to his descendants and probably also because they were his heirs and inherited his debt, they too were tied to this estate. Thus the colonate as birth status came into being. With the 'free' colonate it was different. Here the *colonus*, though bound to the estate by the census *nomine et titulo colonorum*, was not in the *potestas* of somebody with all accompanying restrictions, but an *ingenuus*, a person not *alieni* but *sui iuris*. Either the adscripticiate turned into the 'free' colonate after thirty years of service, or the adscripticiate was turned by statute into a 'free' colonate if the poll tax was abolished in a province.

The adscripticiate had following consequences. In the domain of personal law, the *condicio adscripticia* led for the *adscripticius*, being *alieni iuris*, to consequences for marriage with a woman not subjected to this or another *condicio* (see below). In the domain of property law, it implied a grave restriction regarding his assets (his moveables, and probably for most of the *adscripticii* their only capital), notwithstanding that it was their own property. It was called *peculium* and considered as if *peculium* without *libera administratio*. This implied the prohibition against alienating anything without the permission of the estate owner, including the faculty to dispose by testament of his *peculium*. Regarding procedural law, in this *condicio* the possibility for the *colonus* to sue the estate owner was reduced to the position of a freedman against his manumitter, that is, it was almost nil.

In administrative law, the consequences of the adscripticiate and the 'free' colonate were the same: both *coloni* could be summoned or, in case

[272] Gai 1.138: *Hi qui in causa mancipii sunt quia servorum loco habentur vindicta censu testamento manumissi sui iuris fiunt.*

of absence, be recalled, together with their family and *peculium*. Both could be ordered to perform services within the exploitation of the estate that was their *origo*. Regarding procedures, it was the same: they could sue their estate owners for unjust claims regarding their *condicio*. With the *coloni* on imperial lands the latter is not known, but they had a *forum privilegiatum* in case of public disorder. They had also other privileges: the emphyteuticarian *coloni* could occupy abandoned land, the patrimonial *coloni* were exempt from guardianship, and those on land of the *res privata* could not be recalled after thirty years of service on a town council or another *corpus*.

In the adscripticiate and the 'free' colonate, the poll tax (*capitatio humana*) had to be paid, unless it was abolished. If the landowner paid this, it was on the basis of an agreement, not because he functioned as tax collector. If they possessed land, they had to make a *professio* in the census of the territory where it lay and pay the tax on it themselves. We may assume this was the same for the *coloni* on imperial land.

Regarding the marriages of these three variants, the normal rules on *conubium* applied, but with an adaptation modelled on the *senatusconsultum Claudianum* if a union was considered *non aequale*. Normally the *origo* of the father prevailed in an equal marriage. But if the father was an *ingenuus*, that is, not subjected to such duties, and the mother *adscripticia*, thus a *coniugium non aequale*, the children would follow by law the lesser status of the mother. However, with an *adscripticius* and *ingenua* the senatusconsultum effected that the children followed the status of their father instead of that of their mother. When the senatusconsultum was repealed in 531–534, the estate owner got the authority to take his *adscripticius* away from an *ingenua*, to prevent loss of future workforce, that is, the children who would now follow the *ingenuus* status of their mother. From these consequences of the repeal we can conclude the effect the senatusconsultum had on the adscripticiate. From 539 onwards, if a male *adscripticius* entered a marriage with a woman not subjected to the *condicio adscripticia*, the children out of such a marriage would be 'free' *coloni* and could even transfer their *origo* to their own estate if they acquired one large enough for them to be fully occupied with it. There was no division of offspring in the case of unions between *coloni* of different estates.

As a result of the voluntary entering of a colonate agreement, we may not assume that agrarian exploitation shifted massively from exploitation by farmers-landowners or by farmers-lessees to exploitation by *coloni*. These various forms will have existed next to each other, supplemented by occasional workforce. Further, within the colonate there existed differentiations: the adscripticiate, colonate on the imperial lands, 'free' colonate. Besides, it would probably only exist where there was sufficient capital with the estate owner and a need for this form of labour supply. Also, the colonate will have become for some people simply an inherited *condicio*, while they pursued other professions or offices.

19.2 Open Questions

Some points remain open. Although Justinian refers in CJ 11.48.21.1 to a release of *coloni originales* from their *condicio*, it is nowhere made clear in the texts transmitted how it was done, what it implied and what consequences it had. Did the *colonus originalis* become completely free and thus an *ingenuus*? Or did he become a 'free' *colonus*? The comparison with the state of 438 (Chapters 2 and 3) does not answer this; we have to look at the period after 438 in the west (Chapter 4) to find examples.

These questions are basically the effect of the nature of our sources: legislation was usually the result of a problem which had to be solved, and Justinian's compilation is the collection of many such ad hoc solutions. It did not aim at a complete review of all existing rules on a subject.

19.3 Different Interpretations

There are regarding the colonate under Justinian seven main issues on which interpretations differ. The first is the question whether there are one or more kinds of colonates. Grey denies the existence of two colonates.[273] In view of the above, that cannot be correct.

Second, is there a slow deterioration of the condition of farmers? Although the *adscripticii* were apparently in a deplorable position and the comparison with slaves not excessive, it is certainly not right to consider this period as their nadir.[274]

Third, the interpretation of the key text of CJ 11.48.19. Zepos and Mirković are of the opinion that free unindebted *coloni* who as lessees

[273] He does not analyse CJ 11.48.23.pr and 1 (he only mentions CJ 11.48.19). According to him, the adscripticiate has been constructed by some modern authors: Grey 2007, 173 and 173 n. 4. Mirković, whom Grey criticises, is precisely interpreting CJ 11.48.4 correctly in assuming it concerns *adscripticii*.

[274] Already Eibach 1980, 170 resisted the idea of a deterioration under Justinian, followed by Gascou 1985, 21.

had spent thirty years on an estate were made *liberi adscripticii*, namely on account of CJ 11.48.19.[275] Mirković uses the word *adscripticius* for both kinds of *coloni* and she means that such *coloni* became 'free' *coloni*. The other kind of *coloni* came into existence either because they fell into rental arrears or because they, as *originales*, were born on the estate and had inherited debt and dependence.[276] As set out in Section 13.4, this interpretation does not hold. The text must be read in combination with CJ 11.48.23, which repeats Anastasius' measure (as already Cuiacius did).

The fourth issue is the connection between colonate and taxes in the sense that this caused the colonate because it was in the interest of the authorities.[277] Yet CJ 11.48.20 demonstrates that people entered the colonate by agreement, although likely forced by economic circumstances; but the initiative lay with them (Section 6).

The fifth issue links the existence of large estates (usually combinations of several estates) with the taxation of the *coloni*. This is the view of Gascou. He points out that in the sixth century such large estates existed, particularly that of the Apiones. Here *coloni* paid the *phoros*, which Gascou sees as 'rentes-impôts'. Since the estate owner collected from the *adscripticii* a lump sum which served as both rent and tax, the *coloni* saw now in him a tax collector and administrator rather than the estate owner. Hence the landowners stood in a public law relation to their *coloni*, collecting their tax.[278] Yet CJ 11.48.20 shows that *coloni* also could pay their taxes themselves, which implies that no such public relation existed (Sections 8.2–8.3). In order for Gascou's thesis to be valid, it has to be proved that *all* persons on a big estate paid their taxes to the estate owner, that is, those who were *adscripticii* and those who were not, and that this was the case on all great estates.[279] That has not been done. Further, Justinian's legislation argues against it. It is said that paying the estate owner a lump sum is a *mos* (CJ 11.48.20.3), which does not square with a tax levy. And even assuming that all labourers on a big estate were

[275] See note 186 on, inter alia, Zepos 1980, 422, Mirković 1997, 65, 69–70, and Whittaker & Garnsey 1998, 292.

[276] Mirković 1997, 70. [277] Carrié 1997, 99–100, 101–102.

[278] Gascou 1985, 22–23. As Gascou: Kaplan 1992, 162, but Kaplan then assumes that in 545 all *coloni* became *liberi* on account of Nov. 128.14. This is not correct. Gascou's thesis has been doubted by Bagnall 1993, 115, who does not see a gradual submission of free farmers to rich landowners nor a pre-feudalism. Kaplan 1986, 198–199ff. also assumes the existence and continuation of the small farm exploitation.

[279] Or else we would have the figure of an estate owner who is partly responsible, partly not responsible, which, however, is not enough to make him a semi-public institution.

adscripticii, those who would fulfil their obligations for thirty years would be 'free' *coloni*, their children too, and would have to pay their taxes themselves, bypassing the estate owner (cf. CJ 11.48.20.3). In this context the *autopragia*, the right to levy taxes oneself and deliver these straight to the officials, turns up. It is connected with cities like Aphrodito. This town claimed that it was granted fiscal independence from Antaiopolis by the emperor Leo (P. Cairo Maspero I 67019) and could thus, being autopract and autonomous, pay its taxes straight to the provincial authorities. It is possible that Aphrodito was a *metrocomia*. According to Poethke, *autopragia* (αὐτοπραγία, free, independent action) arose and expanded in the fifth century; this fits in any case the period of the measures of Leo of 468.[280] But we do not see it with individuals.[281]

The sixth issue is the *patrocinium vicorum*, the bad patronage because it was used to evade paying taxes. But in Justinian's times there is no connection visible with the colonate (contrary to the situation in 438, as we shall see in Chapter 2), and therefore the question is open whether amongst these *vicani* also *coloni* resided.

Lastly, there is the issue whether we may see in the large estates the beginning of a feudalism. Carrié opposes this idea,[282] Goetz supports it.[283] It depends of course on what we understand by feudalism. If it is an administration with a structure based on or implying personal bond (vassalry), hereditary or not, it is not the case. For one thing, the Apiones did not have such a local authority. Percival has researched seigneurial aspects of the landowning classes, but only for the west.[284] As to the position of the 'free' *coloni*, there is no connection whatsoever with serfdoms of the early Middle Ages in western Europe. If we keep to the Byzantine expression *servi terrae* as the definition of a Byzantine serfdom, implying merely a limitation of the freedom of movement and the duty to farm, then the 'free' *coloni* might be called Byzantine serfs.

280 Poethke 1984, 41–43.

281 See Mirković 1996 on *autopragia*; since it could only have been an exception, there is no need to deal with this further. CJ 11.48.20 gives no ground to assume that it was mandatory for *adscripticii*, nor for other peasants. The basic rule was that each was responsible for his own taxes.

282 Already in Carrié 1982; see Carrié 1997 with literature; on 86–87 his argument.

283 See Goetz 1993.

284 Percival 1969. He seems to think of jurisdictional authority as well, but in the period covered here there is no sign of this.

CHAPTER 2

The Colonate in the Year 438 in Theodosius' Code

20 Introduction

20.1 General

This part deals with the colonate as we can trace it in the texts transmitted in the Theodosian Code, which present the situation as it was in 437 when the Code was handed over to the emperor. The Code was confirmed in the east and west in 438, hence this year is usually linked to the Code. I shall also use this year for convenience's sake. We are evidently handicapped by the fragmentary state of the first five books of the Code, whose subjects also covered the colonate. The compilers collected imperial constitutions issued since 312. In 364 the administration of the Empire was divided, and we must reckon with diverging legislation from that moment on, or perhaps even before that date. Next to that there are texts from the Gregorian and Hermogenian Code which still had validity in 438, but these have almost all been transmitted through Justinian's Code. It is the same with legal writings, including imperial constitutions, which were valid in 438 but also transmitted through Byzantine hands in the form of the Digest. As to those texts of the Theodosian Code which we only possess through means of Justinian's Code, that is, which would have been in the first five books, they may have been changed or abbreviated and are therefore dealt with in as much as this does not conflict with what we know from the Theodosian Code itself.[1] However, where we can compare both versions (for which Mommsen's edition is very helpful), it appears that the changes are often immaterial. Even if it seems not to be the case, still they are theoretically less reliable, since conflicting, supplementary or other material may have been removed and not included in the version in Justinian's Code. Further, I take account in so far as possible of an eastern or western origin of a constitution

[1] See Sirks 2013, 132.

after the division in 364. It would in any case be wrong to leave out in detailed research the possibility that there were differences in legislation between the two parts of the Empire. Although the Theodosian compilers had to insert the constitutions chronologically, it may be sensible not to distinguish between older and younger rules, but between rules and refinements or additions to these rules: what was outdated, the compilers had to remove.[2] Inevitably a chronologically older rule will thereby turn into a more general rule (except, of course, if a new rule was not a refinement or adjustment but arranged a new situation). Due to the habit of changing law by reacting to a new situation rather than setting up completely new systems, newer rules are usually a partial change to an older rule, and due to the setup of the Code (chronological arrangement under one title) a *lex prior* may become a *lex generalis* and a *lex posterior* may become a *lex specialis*, and so an historical order turns into a systematic one.[3]

The purpose of this chapter is to reconstruct the colonate for the year 438. It is inevitable that there will be parts which look like a copy of what we found for Justinian's reign in Chapter 1. But there is a difference: the reconstruction for this year must be based on sources valid in 438. Only then is a comparison between the two reconstructions possible, meaningful, and worthwhile. Only then can we say whether there are indeed things similar or identical. To make the difference better visible, for every constitution in the Theodosian Code which has been included in Justinian's Code, whether adapted or not, the corresponding place in that Code is given. It might seem as if the Byzantines took that rule over, but again, the context might have been different. Also, for all constitutions in this chapter, the year of issue has been added and sometimes something is said about its history. This is done primarily to establish the rule as valid in

[2] See Sirks 2007, 147–154. This has been criticised on account of the grammar of the phrase in CTh 1.1.1. and there is indeed a point. The emperor orders the text which does not relate to the *vis sanctionis* to be cut. This *vis* is the force of the rule: if the conditions are fulfilled, the result will follow through the judge who has to apply. Outdated law no longer has *vis*, it is forceless. It is at best a conditional sentence with a hypothetical outcome. To assume that *vis sanctionis* concerned also obsolete law is to misunderstand the antique philosophical concept behind *vis*. Although the emperor does not say that obsolete laws should not be included (but this might have been said in a part struck by the compilers), the order has only living law in mind. Further, when Anicius Achillius Glabrio Fausus presented the Code on 25 May 438 in the Roman Senate, he said: *ut in unum collectis legum praeceptionibus sequenda*. It would be strange to say that of obsolete laws, all the more since one might argue that the constitutions included were thereby confirmed once more, which we do not expect for obsolete laws.

[3] The rule *lex posterior derogat legi priori* is of course a valid rule, but for the Theodosian Code it would only have sense if obsolete rules were included, which is not necessarily the case; see Sirks 2007, 86–91, 2021b.

438, but also with a view to Chapter 5, where constitutions are discussed in a retrospective chronology.

20.2 *The Structure of the Theodosian Code*

The constitutions included in the Code were issued in the period 312–437. They are interpreted here in the sense they had in 438 in the context of the Code and according to what the Theodosian compilers thought of them. Their meaning or purport may have been different originally, notwithstanding that the compilers should retain the rule. The Code contains constitutions or fragments of these, valid in 437 and stripped of the superfluous. Obsolete constitutions, that is, rules, were not included.[4] Further, the inclusion of constitutions did not mean that they became now valid in the entire Empire. They kept their original territorial validity; that is, in principle, if issued from 364 onwards, they were valid either in the west or in the east. This explains why we have constitutions regulating the same matter: they do not repeat a rule but deal with the different parts of the Empire.[5] This is evident from Theodosius' Novel 1.5, dealing with the regional validity of imperial constitutions. Lastly, the compilers retained only the actual rule or rules of the constitutions and adapted the text if necessary to fit it in, and they arranged them under titles according to subject matter (*negotium*). Thus the Code presents a homogeneous picture, at least intended as such, of the law valid in 438, which should be supplemented with the *ius vetus* (supplied through the Digest), and the Gregorian and the Hermogenian Codes in as far as these contained still valid law.

The Theodosian Code was to be structured after the Gregorian and Hermogenian Codes, of which we have hardly anything. Justinian's Code is of little help, since in any case its second edition of 534 (the only one we possess) differs considerably from Theodosius' Code. It is a pity, since in this case the structure is very important: the Theodosian Code has only been transmitted in part. Of the first five books, about two-thirds is missing, both of the titles and texts, leaving us with 75 to 80 per cent of the entire original Code.[6] There are a number of texts, transmitted only through Justinian's Code, which most likely had their place in these

[4] See Sirks 2007, 147–154 and 2021b. But see the refinement by Bassanalli Sommariva 2013.

[5] In view of the plans of 429 it has been maintained that the Code contained all constitutions issued since 311, obsolete and valid ones. Yet this must be rejected. If it had been the case, the code would have been much bigger, whereas the number of cases where a law is referred to but not present in the Code is minimal. See Sirks 2007, 86–91.

[6] See Sirks 1993d, 65, 2007, 83–84.

lacunae. Because Books 6 to 16 have been transmitted almost completely, the constitutions from the years 312–437 on the colonate (and inquilinate) which we only find in Justinian's Code must derive from these five deficient books and many of these again presumably from Book 5. But we do not know where precisely they were included, we do not know whether they were edited, we do not know whether there were more texts not transmitted in the manuscripts of the Codex Theodosianus or in Justinian's Code, and we do not know all the titles the first five books contained. Thus we can collect all texts included in the Code as transmitted but, contrary to Justinian's Code, we cannot assume that we dispose of all the texts relating to the colonate and included in 438 in the original Code.[7]

20.3 *The Place of the* Coloni *in the Code*

If the *coloni* were defined as being tied to land, as in Justinian's time, then a connection with the titles on the various categories of land is logical, particularly if this tie was in these times restricted to these or some of these categories of land. In Justinian's Code the same connection is also made, albeit that these categories follow in this case after the titles on the colonate. But the titles on census and revision and reassignment of taxes, which found their place in Justinian's Code as CJ 11.49 amidst the colonate and as CJ 11.68, between colonate and these categories, are in the Theodosian Code placed at the very end of Book 13, as titles 10 and 11, after titles on several corporations charged with duties for the *annona*. In both cases it makes less sense than a placement in the book on taxes (CJ 10 and CTh 11.1–29). CJ 11.69 deals with allocation of deserted land in order to make these productive again; as such this forms a logical sequel to CJ 11.68, the repartition of taxes. In the Theodosian Code it was presumably CTh 5.15 and as such the sequel to the categories of land, whereas the reassignment of taxes stands, as said, in CTh 13.10–11. It is impossible to say whether these differences derive from a conscious structuring and hence a different view on the function of these elements, or whether we see here still a provisory joining of the structures of the Gregorian and Hermogenian Codes, or whether Justinian's compilers were simply more up to the job with their second design than Theodosius', or whether the latter were as able as the former but simply did not have enough time to do it properly. Or, as

[7] See Sirks 2007, 109–141 on the question of the sources and the collection, 147–150 on the question whether the constitutions no longer valid were left out, and 2013 on the possibility of a reconstruction.

is also a possibility, we are faced with a structure set up initially to be able to assign the constitutions found in the archives, occasionally extended with a title to accommodate provisionally constitutions otherwise not fitting, and which structure has not been revised after the collecting was done, due to a lack of time or opportunity. Probably Justinian's first Code, of 429, may have been structured much more like Theodosius', but since there is almost nothing left of this, it is of little avail.

It starts already with the question whether there were special titles on the colonate in the Theodosian Code as there are in Justinian's Code. As it is, the only titles we can be certain of are CTh 5.17–19 in Mommsen's edition, since these have been preserved in the Breviarium Alaricianum as Brev. 5.9–11:[8] *De fugitivis colonis inquilinis et servis*; *De inquilinis et colonis*; *Ne colonus inscio domino suum alienet peculium vel litem inferat civilem*. We know that the Breviarium was a mere extract of the Theodosian Code, without adaptations. The rubrics of the titles CTh 5.12–16 are simply suggestions, based on titles in Justinian's Code: in itself an argument with merit, but not decisive. The fragments, on the other hand, are not suggestions: they derive from the Breviarium, and some figure in a few folia of a manuscript of the Theodosianus Code that were lost in a fire in 1904 in the Turin Library where they were kept. Fortunately, Krüger had made an apographum previously. The numbers of some fragments were legible and thus we know that there are great lacunae (such as in CTh 5.16, where Mommsen had to attribute the number 29 to the first preserved constitution). Another manuscript, the Ambrosiana, has also transmitted parts of the beginning of the Code. There are further constitutions on or relating to the colonate in other books of the Code, but these books have been transmitted quite well and there are as such no problems as we find in Book 5, apart of course from the question of how reliable even a manuscript as early as the one in the Vatican Library (*Reginensi Latini* 886), dating from the sixth century and containing Books 9 to 16, is.[9] Errors could occur quickly during copying.

Keeping to the three titles transmitted and the fragments which preceded them, their place in the remainders of Books 4 and 5 is not as logical as it was in Justinian's Code Book 11. Book 4 dealt with, broadly, inheritances, manumissions, actions and interdicts. Book 5 starts with inheritances in general, of decurions, of clerics, then it has a gap of perhaps two titles, after which follows a title on the inheritances of soldiers. Next come the *ius postliminii*, the status of those who have lost their original free birth

[8] Edited by Haenel 1848. [9] See on this now Sirks 2020a.

status under tyrants, exposed children, and children given away to be reared. A lacuna of perhaps two titles follows, after which there would have been at least twenty titles. The first six probably dealt with various categories of land (including the reallocation of deserted lands), analogously to CJ 11.59–71. CTh 5.17–19 dealt with *coloni* and *inquilini*, and CTh 5.20 was about the *longa consuetudo*, a subject one would rather expect amidst procedural law (Book 4). It is a rather mixed bag, but we have to keep in mind that the Theodosian Code was not a perfect code and most likely not finished in an orderly way. Thus CTh 5.19 (*Ne colonus inscio domino suum alienet peculium vel litem inferat civilem*) may well have been a provisional title, since its rubric is rather specific, inserted at a later moment, to allocate temporarily a constitution which was hard to place elsewhere.[10] But in any case the end of Book 5 was meant to mark a shift, because Book 6 deals with senators and other dignitaries of the Empire. The clean break is between Book 5 and Book 6, not, as far as we can see from the remains, between Book 4 and Book 5. Krüger has tried to reconstruct the first five books and even published his results.[11] However attractive this may be, one has to keep in mind that at the most 50 per cent of the constitutions can be recovered in a book, although it is not certain that they are all in the right title, whereas it is certain that the Justinianic constitutions have been shortened or changed in about half of the cases. The picture Krüger's reconstruction offers is, in the end, deceptive and scholarly unusable.[12]

21 The Background to the Law in the Theodosian Code

Many laws in the compilation of 438 reflect the circumstances under which they were made and which led to the situation in 438. Some elucidation of the political and economic events and changes is therefore useful. A major event was the invasion of the Goths in Thrace and their victory over Valens in the battle of Adrianople of 378, in which the emperor died. They plundered those areas, causing distress and worsening the already existing agricultural problems (see CJ 11.48.53 of 371). In 401/402 part of the Goths, the Visigoths, wandered to the west, and invaded Italy from the North to retreat into Illyricum. But in 408 they invaded Italy again, and this time in 410 they plundered Rome, a feat which had great resonance in the experience of their contemporaries. After that they went to the south of Gaul and

[10] An observation by Bassanelli Sommariva; see Sirks 2007, 82, 174–175. [11] Krüger 1923–1926.
[12] See Sirks 2013, 126–131.

settled there, finally, in 418. Of course Italy had to recover economically from their ravaging visit. Next they extended their kingdom to Spain. About the same time, in 406, a tribe crossed the Rhine and invaded Gaul, defeating the army there: the Vandals, joined by Suebes and Alans. They moved in 409 to Spain and settled there in the south. That was not enough for them. In 429 they crossed the Straits of Gibraltar and conquered the greater part of North Africa: both the provinces of Mauretania and the province of Numidia were ceded to them in 434. In 439 they conquered the province of Africa and took Carthago.[13] In the west the general Aetius beat the invading Burgundians in 436. It is against this background of increasing barbarian influence, diminishing imperial central power and economic hardship that the laws of the forty years previous to the code must be understood.

The taxation system plays an important role in understanding the rules on the colonate. Under Diocletian the taxation had undergone a major change, of which the details are still not clear. Likely many features of the previous system were included and continued to be applied. Certain is that the land was registered according to its rentability, which then was expressed in *iuga*, where a *iugum* was a fiscal unit of value. These units might differ in value for different provinces. The population living on the land was registered and also their number was expressed in a fiscal unit of value, the *caput*. It was a poll tax. Again, this unit might differ in value for different provinces. Land tax and poll tax might be mixed, but in Egypt, Africa, and Gaul they were separate. Each land parcel was to be declared in a *professio censualis* by its owner. The declaration included land, slaves and animals, but as we shall see also *coloni* (*originales*, *originarii*). Registrars in the town in whose territory the land lay, the *tabularii*, drew up the *census* register on the basis of these declarations. Peasants were registered in their villages for the poll tax, perhaps grouped as such. In the end every town formed a tax unit with a total of *iuga* and *capita*, according to various registers. Combining towns, provinces, dioceses, and prefectures resulted in a fiscal value for the entire Empire. At the imperial level the praetorian prefects estimated the fiscal needs for the upcoming year, which then were distributed proportionally according to the fiscal resources as numerically established. This *indictio* was communicated by letters all the way down the administrative pyramid. If necessary a supplementary levy was imposed, the *superindictio*. To that extent, it was a *système de répartition*.

[13] See Vössing 2014, 2018 on the Vandals and their kingdom; Meier 2019, 191–223 and 562–573. For their legislation, see Aiello 2005.

At the level of the towns the taxes were by way of division turned into the quantitative tax assessment per registered landowner, attributed to the various different taxes like the *canon vestium* or *canon equorum*, still according to the *répartition*. The most important tax was the *annona*, the main land tax. The poll tax fell on individuals. It is an open question whether villages were collectively liable for this.[14] Per town the various taxes were specified and then divided over the estate owners or groups of people (as with the *homologi*; see Section 33). Imperial officials (*ducenarii*, *centenarii*, and *sexagenarii*) or decurions had to collect these *portiones*, usually from their fellow decurions and others.[15] Theoretically the census registers had to be checked and revised every fifteen years (the period of an *indictio*). This should be done by inspecting the land and population, but in practice this did not happen often. Rather it seems changes were taken into account in the registration system by corrections and interchanges in the assessments.[16]

What were the *realia* of agriculture exploitation in 438 (and, of course, the centuries before and after)?[17] In the sources, we no longer find the typical *conductor idoneus* of Pliny. Farmers are met with under various names like *ecclesiae colonus* or *rusticus*. Their legal position is often unclear. But the private contract of *locatio conductio* had certainly not disappeared (see the references in the legal sources and in agrarian authors). The question is rather how often and where did such exploitation occur? Next to this there were the large estates (as that of Appianus in the third century and of the Apiones in the sixth, or of Melania in the fifth century), which were dispersed over provinces and may have consisted of large estates, but will often have been a conglomeration of small estates (grouped, as we see later, in *massae*). The view of Fustel de Coulanges, so influential still (Clausing, Finley), that there was a decline in the *locatio conductio* and the social position of the farmers, resulting in the Late Empire in the colonate, is no longer viable. We should avoid schematism. The reality was that next to the classic lease there were other forms of land exploitation: métayage, rent in nature, working as day labourer; and naturally also the small independent farmer who owned his land. Slaves might be used. The legal sources are in these respects to be read with

[14] See Jones 1964, 448–456; Karayannopoulos 1958, 28–53, 84–91; Carrié 1994.
[15] For a short description of the system in the fourth century, see Jones 1974, 65. CTh 11.7.1 mentions the imperial officials as collectors, CTh 11.7.12 the decurions to collect from decurions.
[16] See Thonemann 2007, 438–440 on the permanence of the census, CTh 13.10.7 on the adjustments in the accounting.
[17] See also Jaillette 2012.

caution, since they present the point of view of the authorities, which was often fisc-orientated. A link between estate owner and farmer is understood, but that is all. As to practice, the question was, of course, also how agricultural exploitation could be maintained when droughts or enemy incursions (like the invasion of the Visigoths of Italy in the early fifth century, causing a migration of *coloni*) disrupted it, or when manpower dwindled due to diseases or migration. But it also appears that the farmers were not so miserable as is sometimes assumed. Libanios experienced how his tenants knew how to defend themselves. Again, we have to avoid stereotypes. What is really remarkable is that the *peculium* (the moveable assets of a farmer) were under a lien, but it is comparable to the lien on the *invecta et illata*. Also the authorities tried to counteract excessive demands by estate owners. The latter's dues were, as we may see from letters like those of Symmachus, exactly defined. Also, we see appear the *colonicae* (or *coloniae*) and *villulae*, or *casae*, which seem to supplement or replace the classic *fundus* as local unit of exploitation.[18] In short, reality was much more diffuse and varied than appears from sources.[19] It is in that context that the colonate and inquilinate must be placed.

In the same period, plans for ordering the law and even a compilation of the law sprung up in Constantinople. Theodosius II, emperor since 408, had in 421 married Eudocia, a well-educated woman. She may have been the inspiration to order in 425 the establishing of chairs in Constantinople for Greek, Latin, rhetoric, and law. In the same year his nephew Valentinian III, born in 419, was made emperor. In 426 a constitution was issued in the west regulating the citation of legal writings in court, probably conceived in the east. In 429 Theodosius ordered an ambitious plan: all imperial law should be collected and merged and then merged with the writings of the jurists (the *ius vetus*). The project stalled, perhaps because the theological disputes over Nestorianism required Theodosius' attention, but then, in 435, it took flight again with a new commission. The Code, notwithstanding that the original program now merely consisted of imperial constitutions issued between 311 and 437, was offered in the autumn of 437 on the occasion of the marriage of Eudoxia, Theodosius' and Eudocia's daughter, to Valentinian III. Its purpose was, according to Theodosius in his Novel 1, to unite the Empire again. The Code was

[18] In LRB 38.8, the *colonus in agro regio vel colonica* (a *colonica* being a farm) who refuses hospitality to someone is to be flogged. For *colonica*, see Brown 1984, 113: *casa coloniaria*. Also in P. Ital. 3, II, 1, l. 11–13 a *colonia* and in P. Ital. 13, l. 8 a *colonica*.

[19] For surveys and details on agriculture and agricultural exploitation, see Vera 1986, 1992–1993 (particularly on rural slavery), 1997, 2007 and Marcone 1993 with profound analyses.

promulgated in the east on 15 February 438 and in the west on 25 May 438.[20] These factors define the character of the Code and the whole of its contents.

22 The Term *Colonus*

The designation of a tied *colonus* is not consistent in the Theodosian Code.[21] We find in the Theodosian Code circumscriptions like *censibus adscribti* (CTh 5.3.1, 5.6.3), *origini cohercentes* (CTh 4.12.3),[22] *originalis* (CTh 5.18.1, 11.1.14), *originarius* (CTh 5.18.1, 10.20.10), *servili condicione pollutus* (CTh 4.12.5), *coloni iuris alieni* (CTh 5.17.1 and 2), *obnoxii servituti* (CTh 8.2.5 = CJ 10.71.3), *adfixi censibus* (CTh 7.13.6), *censibus insertus* (CTh 7.13.6), even *homines iuri proprio subditi* (CTh 16.6.4), but mostly simply *colonus* while the context makes clear that it concerns a bound *colonus.*[23] We also find *tributarius* (CTh 10.12.2; 11.7.2). This refers to the connection with the *tributum* through the census registration and means here a *colonus originalis*. This *tributum* was the *capitatio plebeia*, that is, *humana* (CTh 11.23.2, 362).[24]

20 See Sirks 2015 for the entire episode and 2010a, 422–425 for the promulgation in the west. See Atzeri 2008 for the date of 25 May.

21 Leaving out the constitutions only transmitted through Justinian's Code, since these may have been changed.

22 The ms. has *origini cohercentes*, which could be read as an intransitive (see Feltenius 1977, 21 and 23, according to whom Late Latin knows of many cases of verbs of movement and, oppositely, of staying, becoming intransitive), thus as *origini coercentes*, 'being forced to the *origo*', but perhaps it is a mutilation of *cohaerentes* ('sticking', that is, to the *origo*). Mommsen's emendation into *originarii* goes in any case too far, since he does not provide a reason why or how the text would have been mutilated in this way (he leaves out the *cohercentes*) and it does not fit the rhythmical clauses (see on this Sirks 2013, 133–134). Wisely, Krüger 1923–1926 keeps to the text as transmitted and merely suggests a change into *cohaerentibus* to accommodate the sentence, but the original may well have had *qui* ... *origini coherentes* in view of the following *qui*. However, it is also possible to read the words as connected to the preceding *fiscalibus servis*, in which case we have to add *servis* here. In that case the *colonus originalis* would only enter the ambit of the senatusconsultum in CTh 4.12.5.

23 Likely not in: CTh 11.7.11, 11.16.5, 11.17.1; unknown: CTh 4.22.1, 13.1.8, 13.1.10.

24 *Tributarius* refers to a connection with the *tributum* and often means a person or land subjected to taxes. Here one might think of a person registered in the census for the *tributum* in the sense of the *tributum capitis* (poll tax), perhaps in some cases also with the *tributum solis* (tax on private land of a *colonus*). Yet there is another context in which the term is used. In CTh 11.7.2 a decurion is liable for the levy of his *portio* in the taxes, which includes both his own taxes and the taxes of his lessees (*colonus*) and his *coloni originales* (*tributarius*); thus he does not have to collect the taxes of a *portio* where he is not taxed. In CTh 10.12.2.2, on an equal footing with fugitive slaves, those free persons are treated who have absconded from their fixed residence: *tributarii* and *inquilini*. With the first *coloni originales* must be meant, and the designation therefore merely refers to their registration in the tax register; the *inquilini* were not, likely, obliged to work a plot of land. This connotation of being registered in the census and thus tied to this we find in CJ 11.52.1.1 (*coloni tributariae sortis nexibus absoluti*) and CJ 11.53.1.1 (*inservire tributario nexu*), where they are freed from these ties. The two constitutions were in the Theodosian Code but are not transmitted in the manuscripts. The term *tributarius* further figures in CJ 11.48.12 in the same meaning of *colonus originalis*.

Inquilini (e.g., CTh 10.12.2) and *casarii* (CTh 9.42.7, 369 W) were treated the same. Carrié has published extensively on these terms, but whether they denote different qualities as he maintained is to be seen.[25]

In this chapter I shall use (in accordance with Chapter 1) the term *colonus* for the *colonus originalis* (also *colonus originarius* in the west, *adscripticius* in the east), that is, for anyone tied by *origo* to an estate or plot of land.[26] If somebody was tied by *origo* to an estate or plot of land of which the owner was not liable for his poll tax (e.g., because it was abolished for him), being only subjected to the power of the estate owner to recall him, I shall use the term 'free' *colonus* and 'free' colonate for this status. Since with the 'free' *coloni* the status was also transmitted through *origo*, we might call these also *originales* or *originarii*, but in the texts this is not the case. In the east the term *adscripticius* might have been just the way to solve this potential confusion, whereas in the west we do not find 'free' *coloni* existing. In both cases the tie to the estate was made by registration in the census. This tie is also called the *ius colonatus* or *ius census*. It could be imposed and would thereby establish the *origo*. Of course, analysis of the texts must prove these interpretations correct for the year 438.

23 Entering the *Condicio Coloniaria*

23.1 Condicio *and* Condicionalis

The Theodosian Code has a number of texts in which *condicio* means a status with legal consequences, as *servilis condicio* in CTh 5.17.1 (slavery), *curialis condicio* in CTh 5.3.1 (434 E), the status of a decurion, with the public obligations involved), *materna condicio* in CTh 4.8.4–5 and 7 (322, 322, 331), the maternal status, here slavery, and *condicio ingenua* in CTh 7.1.10 (367 W), dealing with soldiers. With the term *ingenuus* another problem arises. In principle it denotes the status of being freeborn, which it certainly was and still is in this period. But since people subjected to the patronage of another, like the *coloni*, were not admitted to the army or the civil service because they were not *ingenui*, *ingenuus* also means not subjected to the *potestas* of somebody.[27] This subjection and its legal and

[25] Carrié 1982, 1983, 1984; a reaction by Marcone 1993; Carrié 1997 resuming his thesis with responses to criticism; scepticism with Sarris 2006, 150–154, and n. 85 regarding the idea of the great domains as semi-public institutions.

[26] As we shall see, of which the owner was liable for his poll tax, and being under the *potestas* of the estate owner and his assets considered *peculium*.

[27] The term *ingenuus* was already discussed for Justinian's times, but it has to be established for 438 on the sources for this year: see also Chapter 1, note 112.

social consequence is well set out in CTh 6.35.14.1 (423 E), a constitution on those who work in the imperial services. It provides an immunity from the claim for the *condicio originalis* for those who have entered imperial service illicitly. In the case of decurions, they are immune from the decurionate after fifteen years. In the case of *cohortales*, people who work on the staff of governors, the term longer is because they are persons *inferioris sortis*, that is, below the status of decurion. If they have been there for twenty-five years without being reclaimed, they are free from the *macula prioris condicionis*. Their children, however, have to follow their *condicio originalis*. If already between decurion and *cohortalis* the emperor distinguished between *condiciones*, calling the latter an *inferior sors*, how much more was this for those lower on the social scale. We see here also that not just with *coloni* but also with decurions and *cohortales* a *condicio originalis* existed.

The term *condicio* even led to the word *condicionalis*,[28] which refers in texts to certain low fiscal officials (*annonarii*, *actuarii*, and *numerarii*) who were reduced since Julian to a low legal status of subjection (the *vilior condicio*): CTh 8.1.3, 5, 7, 8 and 11 (333, 357, 362, 363 and 365 W). After seven years *numerarii* are, if they have served well, dismissed with a raise in rank, by which the *vilitas* was taken away from them (CTh 8.1.7; further 8.1.3 and 8.1.5, both for the entire Empire). Although CTh 8.1.3 and 5 were issued before him, Julian bore the brunt of these measures, witness CTh 8.1.11 365 W (= CJ 12.49.3): 'he [Julian] ordered the *numerarii*, the cincture taken away, conscious of their low status, to assist the public service' (*numerarios omisso cingulo, condicionis conscios vilioris necessitati publicae obsecundare praecepit*), but Valentinian restored the *numerarii* to their former dignity. In practice the demotion was temporary. Likewise, in CTh 8.1.3 the *actuarii* and *numerarii* (the accountants) were made *condicionales* in the public interest. If they were *censiti*, they were now released from the *capitatio*.[29] The demotion meant that they were immutably assigned to their task and could be tortured. The reason for this temporary demotion is that they are involved in the assessment for the taxation. Fraud has to be prevented, and if an investigation is necessary it should be possible to torture them as if they were slaves (CTh 8.1.4, 6, 8). Similarly decurions, when they entered the

[28] Remarkably, Georges 1918 does not discuss the noun, nor does Souter 1949, nor the OLD. Heumann & Seckel 1907, on the other hand, have: 'c. servus, einer der persönlich und für immer zu einem gewissen Amt verpflichtet ist', with references from the CJ and CTh.

[29] CTh 8.1.8 (363) released the *numerarii* from their military oath (they were in the service of the *militia civica*, the civil service) and made them into *condicionales*. The purpose of this was that the dignity of the civil service not be blemished by their frauds. From that moment onwards they were for five years subjected to their task as a public duty.

census registration office to work there, lost the dignity of their status and got the *condicio* they chose, that is, a lower status (CTh 8.2.4, 384 E). This aspect of the low *condicio* we may see also with some other groups but not with the *coloni*. With them the important matter was that they did not leave their place and duties. We do not see that they could be tortured. So there were differences and gradations in the state of *condicionalis*.

Condicionales are also mentioned in CTh 10.1.5 (326) (as *servi condicionales*)[30] and 14.9.2 (372 E). In the latter case they probably were *collegiati*. The Code even has a separate title *De his qui condicionem propriam relinquerunt*, 'On those who have deserted their own status', CTh 12.19, which deals with *collegiati*, *coloni*, and *inquilini* who have fled their residence and duties. They are to be recalled unless a limitation of prescription applies. Thus *condicio*, next to meaning condition in the sense of requirement, may have the meaning of a public law status. It may apply to decurions as to *coloni* and *collegiati*, but the latter's status is *vilior* because they are considered subjected (about which more later). The noun *condicionalis* always refers to a person of *vilior condicio*. It refers to somebody subjected to the *potestas* of somebody else, becoming thereby almost as if a slave, yet still free. In that sense a *colonus originalis* was a *condicionalis* too, as were, for example, the *conchyleguli*.

We also find the term *iuris alieni* used in connection with *coloni* to indicate their low status (e.g., CTh 5.17.1). Koptev has made an analysis of the meaning in public law of this expression. It does not denote private property, that is, of an estate owner, but 'of the estate of another landlord', hence of another *origo*.[31] But after 400 he sees a shift from *origo* to *dominium*, although we find the old meaning still in texts.[32] It would, if I interpret this well, mean that the bond with the estate owner had become one of property law, no longer of a public nature. Yet Koptev also says that *suo iure* in CJ 11.51.1 means 'free to go' and thus *alieni iuris* in CTh 5.17.1 means 'not free to go', that is, subjected to somebody's will, not being able to change the *origo*.[33] In my view, as I shall set out later on, *alieni iuris* implies something else, namely being subjected to the *potestas* of somebody else.[34] But the connection with the estate is correct, as is the consequence that one is not free to go.

[30] It concerns people who have to check the accounts for the fisc and therefore are comparable to the *numerarii* of later constitutions, who were also of *vilior condicio*. Either this is an asyndeton or it concerns slaves who were especially assigned to this job. The term here would be an adjective, implying a special status for these slaves, just as slaves could be attached to an estate as *instrumentum*.

[31] Koptev 2012, 307–309. [32] Koptev 2012, 312, nn. 30 and 31. [33] Koptev 2012, 313.

[34] And as set out for Justinian's time in Section 7.

23.2 *Origin of the Colonate*

In the Code we find only two unequivocal causes of the colonate: *origo* and imposition. Imposition is rare. It occurred in the east with captives of war (CTh 5.6.3, 409 E), and in the west with able-bodied beggars (CTh 14.18.1, 382 W). For both east and west we see that the *origo* brings this *condicio* to descendants. As to an agreement as source of the colonate, perhaps in CTh 11.1.14 (366 E) we may read a reference to it.

The *origo* is the most important cause in the Code. The *origo* is identical with home town. It was not possible to remove one's *origo*, that is, to relinquish it or to change it on one's own (CJ 10.39.4, 293/294). We may assume that it was possible if the authorities allowed it, but it will not easily have happened, since it formed the basis of the taxation system. It determined where one must perform liturgies (CJ 10.39.3, 244–249). One could settle in another town but then one had to perform liturgies in both cities (CJ 10.39.1, 211–217). It means that the bond with the *origo*, in the case of *coloni* a village, was already present. The colonate would narrow this bond down to an estate. Villagers could always be recalled to perform their liturgies.

It is connected with the birth status, here the *condicio coloniaria*, both in east and west. The normal way was that in a legitimate marriage children followed their father's status. Originally this saw to the *status civitatis*, but it extended to the differentiation in the civic status. Thus between a man who was *colonus originalis* and a woman who might or might not be a *colona originalis*, the children followed the status of their father. The census registration (*adscribtio*) for the estate settled this *condicio*, but since the personal census was also performed in the *origo*, through the census both elements were connected. There is no constitution which states this explicitly for the entire Empire, but it follows from CTh 10.20.17 (427 E), which implicitly formulates the normal census registration and CTh 5.6.3 (409, E) (for these two, see below, Section 23.3), which connects this with the census registration, as well as from the special rules, both in the east and the west, which are based on this same principle.

For the entire Empire, CTh 5.17.1, issued by Constantine in 332 to the provincials and thus valid everywhere, provides several attributes of the colonate, which constitutions for east and west complete:[35]

[35] CTh 5.17.1 [a. 332] *Const. A. ad provinciales. Apud quemcumque colonus iuris alieni fuerit inventus, is non solum eundem origini suae restituat, verum super eodem capitationem temporis agnoscat. 1. Ipsos etiam colonos, qui fugam meditantur, in servilem condicionem ferro ligari conveniet, ut officia, quae liberis congruunt, merito servilis condemnationis compellantur implere. Dat. III. kal. Nov. Pacatiano et Hilariano conss.*

Apud quemcumque colonus iuris alieni fuerit inventus, is non solum eundem origini suae restituat, verum super eodem capitationem temporis agnoscat. Ipsos etiam colonos, qui fugam meditantur, in servilem condicionem ferro ligari conveniet, ut officia, quae liberis congruunt, merito servilis condemnationis compellantur inplere.

Any person in whose possession a *colonus* who belongs to another is found not only shall restore the aforesaid *colonus* to his birth status but also shall assume the capitation tax for this man for the time that he was with him. 1. *Coloni* also who meditate flight must be bound with chains and reduced to a servile condition, so that by virtue of their condemnation to slavery, they shall be compelled to fulfil the duties that befit freemen.

It deals with the recall of a *colonus iuris alieni*. The designation makes it clear it is not the private law lessee-farmer, who was *sui iuris* anyway, but somebody who is subjected to somebody else, that is, is in his *potestas*. If he is residing somewhere else (on another estate), the estate owner must restitute him to his *origo* and acknowledge the *capitatio* for him during his absence. This is the poll tax, because that was the only tax which could concern people who flee. It implies that normally the estate owner acknowledged the poll tax for a *colonus* in his *potestas* and paid (even during absence? likely, since even senators had to; see CTh 11.1.7). Why should the fugitive profit from his flight by not having to pay his tax? These *coloni* were free people (or else they could not be condemned to slavery; but Koptev argues that it means the *colonus* will be shackled only and work then as a free man)[36] but had to perform services (*officia*). It is not said whether the services performed compensated the tax. Further details we have to extract from constitutions for each part of the Empire. But what is certain is that it concerns *coloni originales* (they must return to their *origo*) and that they are free but subjected to somebody else, for whom they have to perform services and who guarantees their poll tax. This, as we shall see, fits CTh 11.1.4 (366 E) well.

23.3 *Origin of the Colonate in the East*

An eastern constitution gives essential information about the colonate. It is CTh 11.1.14 (366 E = CJ 11.48.4):

Penes quos fundorum dominia sunt, pro his colonis originalibus, quos in locis isdem censos esse constabit, vel per se vel per actores proprios recepta conpulsionis sollicitudine implenda munia functionis agnoscant.

[36] Koptev 2009, 264–270.

> Sane quibus terrarum erit quantulacumque possessio, qui in suis conscribti locis proprio nomine libris censualibus detinentur, ab huius praecepti communione discernimus; eos enim convenit propriae commissos mediocritati annonarias functiones sub solito exactore cognoscere.

> Those with whom the ownership of estates resides have to acknowledge for those *coloni originales*, of whom it is established that they are registered in the same places, either by themselves or through their own agents the fulfilment of the obligations of the tax, after the responsibility for the urging was accepted. 1. Certainly we exclude from this order those who have land, however small, and who, registered in their own places, are included in their own name in the tax registers. For it is appropriate for these, leaning on their own modest resources, to acknowledge the land tax with the customary tax collector. (tr. Sirks)

The text states that those who own estates have to acknowledge (*agnoscant*) for their *coloni originales*, of whom it is established that they are registered (*censos*, *censitos*) in these places, the obligations of the tax (*munia functionis*).[37] Because the text is included in CTh 11.1 (*De annona et tributis*) and because in the second part the land tax (*annonariae functiones*) is mentioned, the *functio* will have been a tax too. The owners have taken upon them, that is, guaranteed (*recepta*), either by themselves or through their agents, that the *coloni* will pay the tax and further to urge the *coloni* to pay this. The *coloni* remain in the first place obliged to pay the tax, and the landowners are not to collect the tax, only to take care that their *coloni* will pay it to the tax collector. In other words, the performance of the tax was guaranteed by the owners. It concerns a tax which was levied from those not possessing land. The only tax that remains for these is the *capitatio humana*, the poll tax (CTh 13.11.2, 386 E = CJ 11.48.10 set a new calculus for the poll tax). Apart from this they had to fulfil liturgies, but the text does not deal with these.

Theories on the creation of the colonate stumble on the phrase *pro his colonis originalibus, quos in locis isdem censos esse constabit, vel per se vel per actores proprios recepta compulsionis sollicitudine implenda munia functionis agnoscant*. Thus Pharr 1952 translates

> Penes quos fundorum dominia sunt, pro his colonis originalibus quos in locis isdem censos esse constabit, vel per se vel per actores proprios recepta conpulsionis sollicitudine implenda munia functionis agnoscant

[37] Apart from the version *censitos* for *censos* (which may indeed have been the original wording), the text is identical with CJ 11.48.4, but for the interpretation we cannot rely on the presence of CJ 11.48.20–2 as in Section 8.3.

as

> If any person should have the ownership of any field, either through himself or his own overseers, he shall accept the responsibility for compulsion [Pharr in n. 33: tax collection], and he shall assume the fulfillment of the duties of this compulsory service for those coloni who were born to their condition and who are proved to have been enrolled on the tax lists on such lands.

Pharr evidently assumes that the estate owner agrees to collect taxes which are imposed on his *coloni*.[38] In that case the estate owners would have become tax collectors on their estates regarding their *coloni*. Likewise Jones, who assumes it concerned free *coloni* who did not possess land: 'If on the other hand a colonus owned even the smallest plot of land he was registered independently ("proprio nomine") in the census and his capitation tax was (after as before 371) collected by a public official.'[39] Hence, *a contrario*, in the other case it was the estate owner.[40]

It is understandable to contrast the first and second parts and focus on the collection. Thus Harper assumes that as soon as a *colonus* owned land, he had to pay both the poll tax and the land tax himself; the landowner guaranteed in this view only the landless registered *coloni*.[41] That is not cogent, because the text says that the landowning *coloni* pay the *annonariae functiones* themselves, thus the taxes on land. For these their landowner should not guarantee. It leaves open that the poll tax was still guaranteed by the landowner.

The text can also been read differently, namely from the point of view of a guarantee. The *colonus*/small landowner is excepted from the order and has to pay from his own capital, however small it may be. That, *a contrario*, suggests that in the first part somebody else may pay the tax if the *colonus* cannot pay it. Further, opposing both parts of the constitution, in the first part it concerns *coloni* who do not own land. The only tax which can burden them in that case is the poll tax. Further, the landowner must acknowledge the fulfilment of the tax which the *coloni* must pay. To read this as if they

[38] In CJ 3.12.6(7).6, of 389 *compulsio* indeed means collection. Likewise Vera (see preceding note).

[39] Jones 1953, 51 and n. 19. For a refutation of his interpretation, see below, at CTh 11.1.14.

[40] Vera 1997 = 2019, 265 links *recepta* to *sollicitudine* and interprets it as 'siccome i proprietari hanno ricevuto l'incarico (*sollicitudo*) di esigere (*compulsio*)', as Pharr 1952 does. His argument is CJ 11.48.20pr, where *coloni* have to guarantee the yield and public taxes instead of the landowners. But the difference is that in that text the *coloni* contest that the owner is really (still) the owner, because a *longi temporis praescriptio* set them free. However, in that case they have to render the land tax. Here it is different: it concerns the poll tax. *Recipere* can mean both 'to receive' and 'to guarantee', but the landowners do not acknowledge the tax for themselves but for their *coloni*, and they guarantee to press them, not to collect it. *Sollicitudo* does not mean 'charge'. Also Carrié's theory, in Carrié 1997, 100–101, on which the necessary has been said in Section 1 and Chapter 1 note 90.

[41] Harper 2008, 85. He assumes that the landowning *coloni* leased extra land.

have to collect the tax is forcing the meaning of the phrase, because it does not necessarily follow that the tax is not paid to another person, for example the levying official. The only thing one may deduce is that the landowner acknowledges that the tax of somebody else will be paid: that is a guarantee. Hence the interpretation of Jones and Pharr cannot be followed.

This duty of a formal guarantee was only imposed for *coloni* registered in the census of an estate. Why would this be restricted to these? It is an advantage for these *coloni* because those who are not registered lack such a security. And why would a landowner accept the registration of *coloni* in his estate census if it implied an additional burden for him? Considering that such *coloni* had to render services, it would be a *quid pro quo*. The question remains as to what the underlying cause for this was.

The estate owners do not acknowledge to collect taxes, they acknowledge that they will exert pressure on others to pay them and that those taxes will be paid. This is an act of guarantee. The acknowledgement is imposed upon them, but the ground for that lies in the census registration of the *coloni*. I consider the effect of the census registration below. Here, the question is: What caused this registration? CTh 11.1.14 speaks of *coloni* who are registered, which implies that there were also *coloni* who were not registered, yet were in some relation with a landowner, for example as lessee. This tallies with CTh 11.1.26, which also shows that there were registered and not registered *coloni*. It was the registered *coloni* who were subjected and through the census *originales*. In view of the fact that there was a *quid pro quo*, namely a guarantee for the poll tax versus the duty to perform services and remain on the estate, it could be either a general imposition by the authorities or an individual agreement. Since in the first case it would be very likely that it was imposed on all *coloni*, which is not the case, an origin as private agreement is a more likely ground. Unfortunately, there is no unequivocal text for 438 to bolster this hypothesis.

What was the role and effect of the census registration? As Giglio and others assume, the bond to the estate as *origo* was registered and effected through the fiscal registration.[42] An argument for this is the imposition by law of the colonate, which happened to the Scyri in CTh 5.6.3, 409 E.[43] They were barbarians who were captives of war and therefore booty.[44]

[42] So Giglio 1995, 50–51, citing De Martino and other authors.

[43] The Scyri were a tribe which had itself associated with the Huns (Chuni in CTh 5.6.3). The Huns showed up around 375 at the Lower Danube. In 408 they made Thracia unsafe (*PW*, Bd. 2, s.v. Hunni). It will have been in this period that the Scyri were made prisoners of war by the East-Romans. The prohibition against settling them in Thracia or Illyricum may refer to this.

[44] CTh 5.6.3 is included in the title on assets of soldiers, thus it deals with booty. On barbarians: Scyri in CTh 5.6.3 (409, E). The Alamanni in Northern Italy who became *tributarii* (Ammianus Marcellinus 28.5.15) and the Visigoths, established in 382 to pay tax and to render military service

It concerned a great number of them, and therefore everybody – presumably soldiers; the text is under the rubric *De bonis militum* – was permitted to receive or take as many captives as he wished. The Scyri were to remain with him according to the *ius colonatus* and not be taken out of the law of the *census* (*a iure census*), hence not made slaves or released from the bond. They might not be transferred under the cover of a *peraequatio* or *census*, that is, through a new census of land, joined with another estate (see Section 29). It was not allowed for others to abduct them fraudulently or receive fugitive Scyri. The penalty was the same as for those who received people registered on the *census* (*censibus adscriptos*) of another (CTh 5.17.1; see above). This implies that the Scyri were assigned to this person and enrolled in his land census. Their masters were entitled to their services, namely working on the land. It was forbidden to detract them from the colonate and enslave them or assign them to the works of towns (*urbana obsequia*). They were not to be brought to Thrace or Illyricum (where they were presumably too close to their home lands and might flee). The only exception was that they might be transferred within two years to overseas provinces if there was a dearth of labour for the *res frumentaria* and after that to a permanent place. Further, during five years a transfer was possible within a province. Lastly, there would be no recruiting for twenty years. The reason is not clear. Was the emperor afraid that Scyri would be supplied as recruits or as auxiliaries? Landowners were obliged to provide recruits, and the Scyri may have been good warriors. Or is this a passage which was left in the text by accident (*praedictos* refers to a lost part in the original text)? The constitution kept its use as basis for future disputes over these *coloni* and theoretically for future dealings with captives.

In any case, the use of the words *ius colonatus* and *ius census* as equivalent shows that the colonate was an institution in itself. Here, the bond with the land is established by the census and not by agreement or descent, that is, by *origo*. Hence the words *ius census*. These captives will have been single men, so we may not expect rules about women and children. Where for slaves, animals, and *plebs rustica* the *capitatio* was levied (CTh 11.23.2, 362), we may assume that their estate owners had to pay *capitatio* for these people too. It did not matter that they were not Romans; slaves were not Romans either, nevertheless they could be attached to land as *instrumentum* and

(see Ausbüttel 1988), did not become Roman citizens nor became *coloni* unless they too were settled *iure colonatus*; but nothing is known on this. They must have been *laeti* or *dediti*. The Goths defeated under Claudius Gothicus were made slave-farmers (Scriptores Historiae Augustae Cl.9.4). Kaser 1971, 148 suggests that also the *laeti* became *coloni*, whether *adscripticii* or 'free', but this does not follow from CTh 13.11.10; perhaps he was thinking of CTh 5.6.3?

capitatio was due for them. Unfortunately the text does not say what the census registration held in store for the Scyri beyond just an *origo*.

On the way the *condicio* was transmitted, CTh 10.20.17 (427 E) gives not just information about the way conflicting attributions were solved, but implicitly also about this point:

> Placet, si conchyliolegulorum filiae condicionis alienae nubserint viris, qui ex ipsis fuerint procreati ab eo tempore nexum maternae adscribtionis gnoscant, ex quo promulgatum super hoc cognoverint legem. De his vero, quos ante eam natos esse constiterit, huiusmodi forma servetur, ut sive conchyliolegulorum seu adscribtorum progenies fuerit colonorum, paternam tantum condicionem sequantur. Si qui vero post legem aut patre conchyliolegulo geniti probabuntur aut matre, memoratae adscribtioni obnoxios se esse non ambigant.

> We decide that if daughters of purple dye fish collectors should marry men of another status, those who are born of them shall acknowledge from that moment the bond of the maternal registration, when they learn of this law that was promulgated with reference to this matter.[45] But about those, who were born before, this rule shall be observed, namely, that whether the children are born of purple dye fish collectors or of registered *coloni*, they shall follow only their father's status. But if after this law children are proved to have been born from either a father or a mother of the guild of purple dye fish collectors, they shall not doubt that they will be obligated to the aforesaid registration.

The law introduces a new arrangement for marriages between different *condiciones*. The basic rule is that the paternal *condicio* is followed, and here both the purple dye fishers and the *coloni* are mentioned as fathers. But the new arrangement is that if the mother is of the *condicio* of the purple dye fish collectors, it changes: in that cases her *condicio* prevails. Where it concerns unions with *ingenui*, the law introduces or confirms the *coniugium non aequale*; where it concerns unions with other *condicionales*, like the *adscripticii*, it is a special arrangement as in CJ 11.48.21pr, which refers to ancient statutes, setting aside the ordinary rule of *coniugia aequalia*, which the marriages between *condicionales* are. The text also refers for the *condicio* to the registration (*adscribtio*) in the census, and this registration must be acknowledged, that is, the obligations connected with it must be recognised. Thus the census served to register the duty to pay tax (the poll tax), the *origo* and the *condicio* with its obligations. What was the purpose of the new arrangement? The result was that in both kinds of marriage all

[45] Normally a constitution acquired immediately force of law upon the emperor's confirmation, but there were exceptions, as here. See further Sirks 2021a.

children would be *conchyleguli*. Apparently there was a need to attach offspring to this occupation.

23.4 *Origin of the Colonate in the West*

The nature of the colonate is not expressly defined in western constitutions. It was a *condicio* (CTh 5.18.1.3, 419 W) and it implied that the *colonus originalis* or *originarius* was tied to an estate (*possessio*) which was his *origo* (CTh 5.18.1 pr–1). He may be recalled to this by his *dominus* (the estate owner)(CTh 5.18.1). *Originarius* insinuates a bond with an *origo* in the sense of a home and with duties connected to it. It is shown by CTh 8.4.22 (412 W), where soldiers after their dismissal lose their privileges and are once more liable for the *obsequia status* in their *originarium sol*, that is, their attachment to their *origo* with its liturgies is revived. Thus both the adjectives *originalis* and *originarius* denote the bond with an *origo*, and this *origo* is here a piece of land. There is no text for the west linking the *capitatio* to the colonate, although this tax was levied (see below).

As regards imposition, able-bodied beggars in Rome could get arrested and assigned as *coloni* to specific lands (CTh 14.18.1, 382 W = CJ 11.26.1), which is an instance of the colonate being imposed *ex novo*. They will have become *originales*. And what about their status? They were condemned to an eternal colonate to the favour of their informer; they will have been put under his authority. That implies the *condicio coloniaria*, and consequently legally their status was lowered (socially it will not have made any difference).

Regarding the way the colonate was initiated, CTh 11.1.4 might indicate an agreement, CTh 5.6.3 and CTh 14.18.1 an imposition. Further, the transmission through *origo* was the regular way of transmission, be it that east and west had for some cases their own rules; but this point will be discussed in more detail in Section 26. It appears that the colonate was a legal institution on its own (*ius colonatus*, *ius census*). In both parts imposition was possible and applied, but only to special groups and as a punitive measure.[46]

24 Effects of the Colonate: *Potestas* and *Peculium*

The already mentioned constitution CTh 5.17.1, issued in 332 to the provincials and thus valid everywhere, makes it clear that a *colonus* was *iuris alieni*, which means that he was subjected to somebody else, in this case the estate owner. The term designates the being in the *potestas* of another person.

[46] Punitive is not quite the word for what happened with the Scyri, but it was certainly not a reward.

The constitution says also that he had to perform services: *officia quae liberis congruunt*. The word *officia* indicates that these were services done because of duty towards a person set over him, that is, somebody who had in a way power over him, just as a patron had power over his freedman and could request *operae* and *obsequia*; here it is the estate owner. Farmers had occasionally to perform *munera extraordinaria* (CTh 11.16.4, 328 = CJ 11.48.1; i.e., next to their usual liturgies).[47] But this was not allowed during the sowing or harvesting season, since other moments were more suitable for this (CTh 11.16.4, 328; section 1 = CJ 11.48.1). CTh 11.16.4 deals in general with extraordinary charges (*munera*) imposed on farmers (*agricolae*). *Coloni* are not specifically mentioned but are also farmers. Yet these services were not of the kind just related, not *munera*, but services at the wish of the estate owner.

Their status was low, since, as CTh 5.17.1.1 says, they could be forced to work in chains, if they contemplated flight, and perform their services in a *servilis condicio*. This is of course bad, but important is that such a thing was allowed, which proves their low position. It will have been a consequence of their being in the *potestas* of their estate owners.

They were free people and could therefore own assets. Nevertheless, they were not free to dispose of these. According to a constitution in the Hermogenian Code and to a constitution in the Theodosian Code, this being presumably CJ 11.50.2 (see below), referred to in the Lex Romana Burgundionum 14.6, slaves and *coloni* may not sell their *peculium* and, on top of that, the buyers are held for *furtum*, theft.

> LRB 14.6: Nec servum vel colonum peculium suum posse distrahere, insuper et ementes furti actione tenendus, secundum constitutionem Hermogeniani sub titulo: De eorum contractibus, qui alieno iuri subiecti sunt, vel Theudosiani legem libro v, sub titulo: nec colonus inscio domino suo alienet peculium vel litem inferat ei civilem, ad Nebridium vicarium Asie.

> Neither a slave nor a *colonus* can sell his *peculium* and next to that the purchasers are held liable with an action on theft, according to a constitution of Hermogenian in the title: On the contracts of those who are subjected to the right of somebody else, or to the law of Theodosius book 5 in the title: That no *colonus* in ignorance of his master alienate *peculium* or raise a civil law against him, to the vicar of Asia Nebridius. (tr. Sirks)[48]

Such a title and the text may indeed have figured in the Hermogenian Code, because we have the title CJ 4.26 *Quod cum eo qui in aliena est potestate*

[47] Also in CTh 5.3.1 (434 E = CJ 1.3.20) and CJ 1.3.16 (409 E): *ruralia obsequia*.

[48] This title is CTh 5.19 in Mommsen's edition. As the text referred to in LRB 14.6 Mommsen inserts CJ 11.50.2.

negotium gestum esse dicitur, vel de peculio seu quod iussu aut de in rem verso, which seems to be a composite of several titles and which contains rescripts from the Hermogenian Code. The Hermogenian constitution will have dated from the years 293–294, unless it was a later addition to this collection. It is therefore probable that this constitution was valid for the entire Empire. If the compilers of the Lex Romana Burgundionum made an error and had meant the Codex Gregorianus, it might have been CJ 4.26.10 of 294 where the action for theft in case of a not allowed sale is mentioned. In this case, too, the rule would be valid for the entire Empire. The subjection does not allow for a *libera administratio*. It was a control mechanism for the estate owner, as the rubric of CTh 5.19.1 proves.

There are no texts transmitted for 438 about the release from the colonate, that is, from the *potestas*, but the possibility must have existed. This I deduce from the fact that it is mentioned for Justinian's time and for the west in the sixth century (see Section 42). It is unlikely that it was introduced in both parts without any reference to this in the remaining texts, at least more unlikely than assuming that it was possible in the common basis of laws, the Theodosian Code.

24.1 *Effects of the Colonate in the East*

24.1.1 *The* Coloni *Are in the* Potestas *of the Estate Owner*

CJ 11.50.2pr (396 E) describes *adscripticii* as being obliged (*obnoxii*) because of the yearly taxes and the obligations of their *condicio*, which make them subjected as dependents. The word *obnoxius* can mean subjected to another's power, liable or obliged, and here it clearly means the first.[49] CTh 5.17.1, which allows unwilling *coloni* to be put to work in chains is also valid, but if an estate owner contemplates putting them in a private prison, this is not allowed, since the use of private prisons was in general forbidden (CTh 9.11.1, 388 E).

24.1.2 *Their Assets Are Considered* Peculium

Their assets were treated as *peculium*. CTh 5.19.1 (365 E) states that without doubt *coloni originales* have not the right to alienate the plots of land they tilled (*arva*) – which is evident – nor is it allowed for them to alienate land they own (*propria*), if they have any, without the knowledge and consent of their estate owners. The *arva* was not land they owned but merely land that

[49] Carrié 1997, 145 interprets the text differently. The *coloni censibus dumtaxat* are according to him the *coloni* of CTh 11.1.14 who possess their own land.

they tilled.[50] The rubric of CTh 5.19 has that without the knowledge of their master they may not alienate their *peculium* or start a civil lawsuit. So apparently land they own privately is considered *peculium* and their power to dispose of it is restricted. As Koptev observes, this rubric was taken from the Breviarium and does not mention the word *peculium*.[51] It was the Alarician compilers who made the connection. But we can link it to another eastern text which confirms the idea that the *propria* concern *peculium*. This other text connects litigation, alienation and *peculium*: CJ 11.50.2.3 (396 E, perhaps once in title CTh 5.19 too, since LRB 14.6 refers to it as placed in Book 5 of the Theodosian Code).

> CJ 11.50.2.3: [Arcad. et Honor. AA. Nebridio com. Asiae.] Cum enim saepissime decretum sit, ne quid de peculio suo cuiquam colonorum ignorante domino praedii aut vendere aut alio modo alienare liceret, quemadmodum contra eius personam aequo poterit consistere iure, quem nec propria quidem leges sui iuris habere voluerunt et adquirendi tantum, non etiam transferendi potestate permissa, domino et adquirere et habere voluerunt?
>
> Very often it has been decreed that it is not allowed to anybody of the *coloni* to sell or in any other way alienate anything from his *peculium* without his master knowing. In what way will he be able to stand up against his person on an equal legal footing, he whom the laws did not want to have his own possessions under his own authority and who is granted only the power to acquire, nor also to transfer, (but) to acquire and hold for his master? (tr. Sirks)

CJ 11.50.2.3 rhetorically puts the question of how such a *colonus* may alienate anything he has in his *peculium* without his master's knowledge, when the law did not want him to have an independent faculty to do so and allows him only to acquire for his master. Indeed, it has been *saepissime decretum* that they may not alienate anything without the knowledge (read: consent) of their estate owner; they may only acquire and hold for him. This defines the *peculium*. It is property of the *colonus* and not of his estate owner, but the *colonus* is restricted in his faculty of disposing. Because as a result his property is called *peculium*, it is obvious that it is resulting from the *potestas*. At the same time the text says that he cannot litigate against his master, which is also the consequence of the latter's *potestas*. A *decretum* was issued in a legal proceeding. Hence it would confirm a claim; the claim itself may have been founded upon an agreement between parties or an imperial constitution. If based on an agreement, it must have been settled as part of the *ius colonatus* by the census registration. But CTh 5.19.1 (365 E)

[50] So too Koptev 2009, 271–272. [51] Koptev 2009, 272.

suggests an introduction by constitution and, because of the *non dubium est*, apparently before 365.

That they could own land themselves, which means that they were free men and could theoretically alienate it at will, demonstrates next to CTh 11.1.14 (366 E) the constitution CTh 5.16.34 (425 E = CJ 11.68.6) which allows the sale of land to them. If a *colonus* wanted to purchase land from the *res privata*, he had to find co-buyers of his own *origo* and *ius*, because the emperor did not want to sell to only one person; he might prove too much of a burden for his fellow *coloni*. The reason behind this is unclear. Was it that fellow villagers were usually personal surety for the purchase, and if the buyer overextended his finances they would be liable? Or did the emperor fear that the care for his own plot might make him less available for the liturgic duties of his hamlet (which CTh 11.24.6 pr mentions for the *coloni homologi*; see below, Section 33)? With co-buyers these risks were spread.[52] Or are we dealing here with the sale of land whose owners no longer paid the land tax? CTh 13.11.13 says that the purchasers may be *vicini* or *peregrini* but that they have to be solvent. In that case, and that argues for this interpretation, having co-buyers would be a better guarantee that the tax would be paid.[53] In any case, *coloni* could own private property but it was under a restriction: they needed their landlord's permission to alienate it.

The nature of this lien on the *peculium* is not made clear in these texts but can be deduced. First, the designation *peculium* returns in another text and is connected with a claim of the *colonus*' master. If a *colonus originalis* had become a cleric or monk,[54] his estate went, if he had died intestate and without relatives, to his church or monastery. However, the claim of his estate owner (*patronus*, where he had been *censibus adscriptus*) for his *peculium* was excepted from this (CTh 5.3.1, 434 E = CJ 1.3.20).[55]

[52] The first part of the text also treats of a sale of something belonging to the *res dominica*, but more cannot be deduced. In it *fideiussores* are mentioned, hence the suggestion.

[53] On this application of CTh 13.11.13, see Laquerrière-Lacroix 2009, 253–254.

[54] It is not impossible that such a cleric could have contracted somebody else to perform his colonate duties for him (cf. CJ 1.3.16, 409 E).

[55] CTh 5.3.1: … *exceptis his facultatibus, quas forte censibus adscripti vel iuri patronatus subiecti vel curiali condicioni obnoxii clerici monachive cuiuscumque sexus relinquunt. Nec enim iustum est bona seu peculia, quae aut patrono legibus debentur aut domino possessionis, cui quis eorum fuerat adscriptus, aut ad curias pro tenore dudum latae constitutionis sub certa forma pertinere noscuntur, ab ecclesiis detineri* … 'Excepted from this rule shall be those properties left by clerics or monks of either sex who are, perchance, registered in the tax rolls, or persons subject to the rights of a patron or obligated to the status of decurion. For it is not just that the churches should retain estates or *peculia* that are due by law to the patron or to the owner of a landholding on whose tax list one of the aforesaid men had been enrolled, or that they should keep property known to belong to the municipal councils,

This means that the master had a preferred or secured claim, a lien, on the estate in as far as this was considered *peculium*. It was not a formal security like a general hypothec or a special pledge, since that would have been formulated differently. Such a preference (*ius deductionis*)[56] is known from the *peculium* slaves and *filii familias* had. Formally it was property of their owner, or *pater familias*; factually they could dispose of it as they wanted if they had a *libera administratio*. But if the *actio de peculio* was raised against their owner, or *pater*, the latter had the right to cash in first his own private claims on the *peculium* and clear the accounts of his slave, or *filius*, as debts and claims on both sides. The remnant served the external creditors.[57] Here the private property of the *colonus* was not property of his master, but treated in the same way: the master's claim on him was preferred in the sense that, as with a real *peculium*, it had priority and what remained was for other creditors.

Peculium is a word denoting a *Sondergut* or the *Sparpfennig*, the saved money. It depended on the legal situation what its legal status was. Was this *peculium* in the classic sense of the word, that is, socially of the *colonus* but legally of his estate owner/patron? Rosafio has worked along this line, taking into account the titles CTh 2.31 and 2.32. He considers these *peculia* as a third, new kind of *peculium* (next to the classic *profecticium* and *castrense* or *quasi-castrense*)[58] which was reserved for the obligations of the *colonus*, just as the fortunes of the *curiales*, the *pistores*, and the *navicularii* were reserved for the collective capital of the *corpus* and could not be disposed of at will.[59] The parallel with the two known *peculia* is a good one, taking into account the *potestas* exercised over the *coloni* by the landowner. In practice it will have been a *Sparpfennig*, given the scant means of the farmers, which then were nevertheless the security for their debts, private and public (as in CJ 11.48.8.2). Rosafio underlines that the claim of the landowner is of a public nature, to guarantee him the *capitatio* of the *colonus* for which he was responsible.[60] Thus in as far as with a *peculium* first accounts were settled with claims of the *pater familias* or

subject to the fixed general rule and in accordance with the tenor of a constitution formerly issued . . .' (tr. Pharr 1952).

56 See below, CTh 2.31.1 and Section 24.2.2; Kaser 1975, 609 sub 6; Gamauf forthcoming.

57 Kaser 1975, 287–288, 606–607 on the *actio de peculio*.

58 The *peculium adventicium* from *bona materna* should also be mentioned, but that is not important here.

59 Rosafio 2009, 299–300. The *obnoxiae corpori suario boario pecuario personae* in Nov. Val. 26.8 I think were not the patrons but lesser people, where the word *peculium* would be suitable for their assets.

60 Rosafio 2009, 295, citing also Krause 1987, 96. But if Rosafio means by *capitatio* the land tax, as he seems to do in Rosafio 2002, chapter 3, this part is incorrect.

patron before external creditors were served, the parallel is all right. However, the latter comparison with the corporations is difficult to follow. There the obligations were tied to the assets: renunciation of these liberated from the duties, here the *colonus*' assets are tied to the obligations and these remain, even if the assets are gone. However attractive this explanation is, the term seems to me to be the consequence of the *potestas* (in view of the *vilior condicio* it brings) rather than conversely. It indicates merely the preferential claim of the estate owner: If it were real *peculium*, how would his claim otherwise be paid? And if it were *quasi peculium*, it was the property of the *colonus* (see also Section 24.2.2). The fact that the *colonus* was subjected to the estate owner will have facilitated the application of the *peculium* construction.

The use of the word *peculium* does therefore not refer to a proprietary claim, that is, that the possessions of the *colonus* are in reality owned by his estate owner, but implies that the estate owner has a preferred claim over the possessions of his *colonus*, which, just as in a real *peculium* relation, must be satisfied first before the claims of other creditors. That is proven by the fact that in such cases in the west not an *actio de peculio* is granted, but an *actio utilis de peculio* (CTh 2.32.1, 422 W): the action is not against the landowner but against the person who borrowed (thus also the *colonus*) but after the landowner has been satisfied. The adjective *utilis* indicates an analogous application, but remarkable here is that the *peculium* is not a real *peculium*.

24.2 *Effects of the Colonate in the West*

24.2.1 *The* Coloni *are in the* Potestas *of the Estate Owner*

From the period 396–430 we have letters by Augustinus, written in Africa: *ep.* 247, *ep.* 10*, *ep.* 20*, *ep.* 24*. In these letters there is question of *coloni*.[61] In *ep.* 10* a *colonus* has sold his wife to slave traders. In *ep.* 20* *coloni* threaten their estate owner that they will migrate. In *ep.* 247 an actor (manager of an estate) vexes his *coloni*. These are without doubt invaluable testimonies of the reality of the colonate. But legally *ep.* 24* is more interesting. In this letter Augustine asks Eustochius for legal advice. He has six questions: (1) What status have children born from a free woman and a slave? (2) What about the children sold by their fathers for a number

[61] In *Ennarratio in psalmem* 93. Augustine also refers to somebody who is *colonus, inquilinus, cliens*, who dwells in the house of his patron. There are other places with Augustine which may refer to *coloni* but they are not of assistance to the present research.

of years? (3) What if those who bought them died: can their fathers force their children to complete the number of years, or are they, being *sui iuris*, freed by this? (4) Can fathers sell their children in perpetual slavery or can their mothers sell them to work? (5) If a *colonus* sells his son, just as he can sell him, will the buyer have more entitlement to the sold person than the owner of the estate from where the colonate originates? (6) May an estate owner turn his *coloni* or their children into slaves?[62] (7) If a free person (*ingenuus*) agrees to become *actor* for an estate owner, will he lose his *ingenuitas*? Humbert has written on the first four questions, so we do not have to deal with them.[63] Our interest is in the last three questions.

Regarding question (5), as Humbert has set out, the buyer of a child has a restricted entitlement, namely, to demand his workforce. The child can at any time reclaim his freedom. But the estate owner has also a claim to the child, namely for his workforce, to work on the land where its *origo* is. Augustine's question is very relevant and acute: How do these two claims relate, one being purely private law, the other rather public law in character? If the latter's claim is stronger, it would be a way to liberate the sold children quickly. They would be *coloni*, but that would be better than being a slave, not knowing that they are free. The answer to (6) is: according to CTh 5.17.1 they may, if they refuse to work, be forced to comply, in chains, as if slaves. But they may not become slaves. The *terminus ante quem* of the letter is AD 430, so it is very unlikely that the opinion of the *interpretatio* to CTh 5.17.1, namely, that they are turned into slaves, was already current in Africa or elsewhere. As with (7),[64] here Lepelley has not seen that *ingenuus* does not mean 'freeborn' but 'free from *potestas*' and that becoming *actor* implied that the *ingenuus* entered a status of dependency, similar to that of the *colonus*, so losing his *ingenuitas*. The phrase runs: *nam ut sint actores saepe ingenui homines postulantur et beneficium se praestare existimant, si faciant quod petuntur*, 'because *ingenui* people are often asked that they be *actores* and they consider this a benefit,

[62] Augustine *ep.* 24*: *item quaero utrum, si colonus vendiderit filium, quemadmodum licet ut vendatur a patre, plus in illo qui venditur iuris habeat emptor quam possessionis dominus, unde colonatus originem trahit, et utrum liceat possessori servos facere colonos vel filios colonorum suorum*, 'Likewise I ask you whether, if a *colonus* would sell his son, inasfar as it is allowed that he is sold by his father, the buyer more entitled is in regard to him who is sold than the owner of the estate from where the colonate traces its *origo*, and whether it is the owner allowed to make his *coloni* into slaves, or the sons of his *coloni*.' Mentioned by McLynn 2012, 318 and Koptev 2012, 315–316.

[63] Humbert 1983.

[64] Lepelley 1983. The subject is primarily the episcopal faculty to arbitrate, but also the colonate and the *actor*. Lepelley obscures the legal question by an impossible so-called 'reconstruction' of the letter; see below.

that they do what is asked [from them]'. What could the benefit be they think they enjoy? Becoming *actor* and having a regular income? How would they become a slave by this? True, such functions implied a kind of subjection. But what if part of the benefits was that the estate owner now paid their poll tax? In short, did the agreement also imply subjection to the *potestas* of the estate owner and consequently entrance into the colonate? If so, it suggests that entrance could be based on a voluntary agreement.

Also in his commentary to Psalm 93, Augustine places the *colonus* amongst persons subjected to somebody else.[65] As to his questions, unfortunately we do not have the answers. It is anyway clear that the *potestas* of the *colonus-pater* clashed with the *potestas* of the estate owner. From a constitution of Justinian we can conclude that the claim of the estate owner had priority, but depending on the size of services requested would leave time for other enterprises (see Section 7). But for the fourth century there are no indications. What is certain is that after a *colonus* died, his children were in any case subjected to the *condicio*, and if they had contracted elsewhere they should first of all provide the requested service, considering CJ 11.48.8 (371 W).

If the Lex Romana Burgundionum 14.6 mentioned above refers to a Valentinian constitution (since the author of the Consultatio mentions Valentinian constitutions as being in the Hermogenian Code, hence this might have been one) and therefore dates from after 364, it is still possible that this was a western constitution.[66] Of course parties could agree that the *peculium* would be reserved for debts to the estate owner. But CTh 5.19.1 (365 E) says, *non dubium est* that they may not alienate without knowledge and consent, which makes it very likely that already before 365 a constitution regulated this restriction for the entire Empire.

Although *coloni* have to render services and maybe cultivate a plot assigned to them, they are not completely at the mercy of their estate owners. These have to accept from the *coloni originales* what the land produces, thus not other products (CJ 11.48.5, 366 W: for *rustici*, farmers, but these include *coloni originales*; again, why an exception only for *rustici* and not for all farmers?). It must refer to what the *coloni* had to produce as compensation for the use (otherwise they would be rewarded with money or checks). It will have depended on the nature of the land and its cultivation, but will mostly have been grain. This must have been the

[65] Augustine, *Enarratio in Psalmem* 93.7: ... *nisi patronum suum, in cuius forte domo manet, cuius inquilinus est, cuius colonus est, cuius cliens est.*

[66] The Valentinian constitutions are all or almost all issued by Valentinian and not by Valens.

general rule, since the text forbids the owners of the land (which implies, again, that we are not dealing with the plots the *coloni originales* had as their own) from demanding money instead, nor may the *coloni originales* want to do this. It means that share-cropping was the standard. But if it was a custom on an estate that money payments were required,[67] parties could continue with this. Customs may of course come into existence by long use, but such an arrangement had started once by way of an agreement. The obligation to stay on the land they were born on and to till it corresponds to the almost contemporary reference to this by Augustine in his *De civitate dei*, written between 413 and 426.[68]

The nature of the *potestas* is also connected with the *peculium* in another text, but this also mentions wages (*mercedes*). It concerns migrated *coloni* who apparently worked elsewhere for wages.

> CTh 5.18.1.2 (419 W): Quod si forte ipse, de cuius proprietate certatur, fatali sorte consumptus est, eius posteritatem agrorum iuri cum omni peculio atque mercedibus, velut eo superstite qui decessit, celeri iubemus executione revocari.
>
> But if perchance the man whose ownership is contested should be destroyed by the lot of fate, We command that, with swift execution of the order, his offspring shall be recalled to the legal claims of the fields, along with all the *peculium* and wages, just as though the man who had died were surviving.

In CTh 5.18.1 (419 W) there is question of *proprietas* of *coloni* and *inquilini* who are vindicated (*de cuius proprietate certatur*). What was meant by the *proprietas* of a *colonus*? *Proprietas* is derived from *proprietas* (quality) and this from *proprius*, which in its turn is derived from, according to Georges, the primitive form *pro-p(a)trios, that is, 'belonging to/stemming from the προπάτωρ (= forefather)'.[69] As such it refers to

[67] The phrase *quam rustici optare non audent* is somewhat strange; but considering the *nisi consuetudo praedii hoc exigat*, there cannot have been any choice for both farmers and landowners in mode of payment.

[68] Augustine *De civitate Dei* 10.1.1: *dicimur enim colere etiam homines, quos honorifica uel recordatione uel praesentia frequentamus. nec solum ea, quibus nos religiosa humilitate subicimus, sed quaedam etiam, quae subiecta sunt nobis, perhibentur coli. nam ex hoc uerbo et agricolae et coloni et incolae uocantur, et ipsos deos non ob aliud appellant caelicolas, nisi quod caelum colant, non utique uenerando, sed inhabitando, tamquam caeli quosdam colonos; non sicut appellantur coloni, qui condicionem debent genitali solo, propter agriculturam sub dominio possessorum, sed, sicut ait quidam Latini eloquii magnus auctor: urbs antiqua fuit, Tyrii tenuere coloni. ab incolendo enim colonos uocauit, non ab agricultura. hinc et ciuitates a maioribus ciuitatibus uelut populorum examinibus conditae coloniae nuncupantur.* See also Giliberti 1999, 80 n. 15.

[69] Georges 1918. Walde & Hofmann 1982, s.v. *proprius*, also mention this explanation, but are of the opinion that its etymology is too uncertain.

a certain quality, and its primary meaning is 'belonging to somebody exclusively', in opposition to communal; and from there also 'particular'. In other words: the litigation was about who was entitled to the *colonus*. That is also clear from the entire constitution which deals with limitation of prescription. It is without any implication of owning him literally as one would own a slave.[70] In various texts reference is made to this state of subjection of the *colonus originalis*. Two texts speak of possessing a *colonus originalis* (CTh 4.23.1, 400 W = CJ 11.48.14: *quos . . . possedit*; 5.18.1, 419 W: *a quo forte possidetur*). Again, we may not interpret it literally: free people could not be possessed as if chattel. But procedurally they were treated as if they were possessed, so that the *reivindicatio* could be applied to claim them.

From several constitutions it appears that in the west *coloni* were subjected too, in a way reminiscent of *filii familias* and slaves. One manifestation of this is the case that a *colonus originalis* has been appointed *tabularius* to record tax declarations and so on in the *tabularium*, the fiscal records, a post which should only be performed by free people (*liberi homines*), that is, not subjected to low services (*obnoxius servituti*). Had the estate owner (*dominus*) known this, he would be liable for mistakes in the administration (CTh 8.2.5, 401 W = CJ 10.71.3). The unspoken suggestion is that he had the power to prevent this, hence he had *potestas* and that, because of this, he was liable for the administration done (*obnoxius pro ratiociniis*), just as a *pater familias* was liable himself for wrongful damage by his *filius* or slave of which he had known.

24.2.2 *Their Assets Are Considered* Peculium

Another instance of subjection shows when a *colonus* takes up a credit. A *colonus originalis* (and likewise a slave, *actor*, or *procurator* of the estate owner) may take up a loan if his estate owner has agreed to that and his creditor may claim it again from the estate owner with the action *quod iussu*. Had the latter not agreed, he would not be obliged. Nor is it accepted that credit is given on the basis of a letter of recommendation. If the estate owner has not consented specifically or if personal surety has not been given, the creditor is fined with the loss of the credit, that is, he cannot sue the *colonus* individually (CTh 2.31.1, 422 W = CJ 4.26.13; part of a convolute constitution).[71] The application of the *quod iussu* indicates

[70] The context excludes that it concerns the ownership of the estate to which the *colonus originalis* was said to belong, although that had to be proved too; see above, Section 28.

[71] CTh 2.13.1, 2.28.1, 2.30.2, 2.31.1, 2.32.1, 8.8.10; on this, Fusco 1980.

the subjected position of the *colonus* as similar to that of a *filius familias* or slave. It also implies that he had no or a limited *libera administratio*. A similar rule we find in CJ 4.10.11 of 294, where the *creditrix* who lent money to a *colonus* for private purposes cannot reclaim it from the owner of the land, even if his representative was present at that moment. It might have concerned a lessee. Yet, why would the *creditrix* in that case have approached the lessor, and why the mention of his representative, if not for the idea that she could use the *quod iussu*? And why would the compilers have included it, if not for its similarity with CJ 4.26.13?

LRB 14.6 with the reference to a constitution in the Hermogenian Code was mentioned above, which may have been issued for the entire Empire, but may also have been issued for the west after 364 if it were a Valentinian addition. It forbids *coloni* to alienate anything from their assets without their master's consent. Hence their assets were called *peculium*. This is confirmed by CTh 5.18.2 (419 W) insofar as it prescribes the return of fugitive *coloni* with their *peculium* and by CJ 11.48.8.1 (371 W) where fugitive *coloni* reserve part of their revenues for their *proprium peculium*. But basically it was their own assets. Two constitutions against Donatists threaten them with flogging if they do not return to orthodoxy (CTh 16.5.52, 412 W), while the second adds to this confiscation of one-third of their *peculium* (CTh 16.5.54, 414 W). This shows that the *peculium* consisted of their own property, otherwise it would be their estate owner who would be punished. In this case eventual claims of the estate owner evidently did not matter, or he could settle them beforehand.[72]

In a part of a convolute constitution of 422, which clearly was the sequence of CTh 2.31.1, the question of credit is further worked out.

> CTh. 2.32.1: Impp. Honorius et Theodosius AA. Iohanni praefecto praetorio. post alia: Hoc quoque creditoribus non negamus, ut, si liber a rationibus fuerit quas regebat inventus actor servus procuratorve praediorum, utilis actio pateat de peculio. et cetera. dat. v id. iul Ravenna dd. nn. Honorio xiii et Theodosio x AA. conss.
>
> (After other matters.) This (remedy) also We do not deny to creditors, namely, that if an overseer, slave, or procurator of landed estates should be found to be not obligated in the accounts which he manages, an adapted action for payment from his *peculium* shall be available. (Etc.)

[72] Riedlberger 2020, 583 ad CTh 16.5.54 sees *peculium* as a metaphor, caused by the weak, slave-like position of the *colonus*. He underlines that it was property of the *colonus* and that he did not need his landowner's consent to alienate it. It is a fine suggestion, but the legal context tells another, not so metaphorical story.

In classic law the *actio de peculio* was the action of the creditor of a slave or *filius familias* out of a contractual debt against the master or *pater*. It was to the amount of the *peculium* granted. The master or *pater* could first settle his own claims (*ius deductionis*). Here a creditor could in the case of slaves and representatives of the estate owner sue for a loan, granted to them without consent, if these people were found in the account books to be not indebted to the owner (likely, after settling all claims). This action is called the *actio utilis de peculio* (CTh 2.32.1, 422 W = CJ 4.26.13).[73] But against whom may the creditor proceed? Against the master or the underling? The text is clear: against the representative if he is found free of claims of his master, which has only sense if it is his property. Second, he and not the estate owner was the beneficiary of the loan. Accordingly, his assets are now available for payment. In that case the term *utilis* means that the action is not directed against the master but the contract partner and for his own goods. That proves that the term *peculium* was used for personal property with these free people. The term *peculium* is normally reserved for the factual property of slaves and *filii familias*. Here it is used to designate personal property of free persons under the same state of subjection.[74] On the other hand, the constitution speaks also of slaves, and here the classic categories apply. In that case the term *actio utilis de peculio* must mean that, notwithstanding that the master had not ordered the taking up of a loan, an action for the loan is granted. But in that case too we expect the action to be directed against the master, that is, an action against the landowner, to the amount of the assets of his underling. It is difficult to decide which one of the alternatives is valid. What argues for the first is that the master's claims had been paid. That would leave the loan, or whatever remains of it, with the underling. If we follow the *interpretatio*, it is the first too.

These constitutions are part of a large constitution which dealt with credit and repossession for debts. CTh 8.8.10 (422 W = CJ 12.60.4) forbade the fisc to sue people for the public or private debts of other persons. Annex to this, CTh 2.30.2 (422 W = CJ 8.15.8 and 11.48.17) says that the presence of slaves, *coloni*, procurators, lessees or representatives (*actores*) cannot be used as a *praeiudicium* to seize land against the will or without the knowledge of their owners. Thus, though CTh 2.32.1 does not mention *coloni*, it is likely that it concerned them as well because the other parts of the original constitution put them on the same level as the slaves and

73 See now Jurewicz 2020 on this, restricting it to those representatives who disposed of working capital. With the claim of the landowner on his assets, even if a *colonus* did not have working capital assigned, his own assets would as a result function as working capital.

74 Partly already dealt with in Section 7.2.

actores, and because their property was considered *peculium* with a preference or lien in favour of the estate owner – or else this prohibition would not be issued.[75]

24.3 Summary

In CTh 5.17.1 *coloni originales* appear to be in the *potestas* of their estate owner, a position in which they have to obey him and perform services for him. They can own things, even land, but they were restricted in their power of disposal: their estate owner had to consent. They could take up loans, but when it came to repaying these, their estate owner could preferentially settle his claims; only after that could creditors claim and execute. These rules were valid in 438 in the entire Empire, with modifications in each half, depending on the apparent need to regulate.

The term *peculium* is used for their property. It is clear that this was not the *peculium* of old, namely the *peculium profecticium*, *castrense*, or *quasi castrense*. There it concerned property that was either given by the *pater familias* or should become his property, and the *peculium* served to separate it from the *pater*'s assets.[76] Here it concerns property which is without doubt the *colonus*'s own, and *peculium* is used as term to create or design a hold over it by the estate owner, both in the east and in the west (and combined with the *potestas* already before 364). What do they have in common? It is the *potestas* over the slave, son or daughter, and *colonus*. In the former case it makes it that only the *pater* can own; in the latter case it makes it that the *colonus* cannot completely exercise his ownership rights but has to ask permission for alienation (a permission a slave or son with *peculium* did not have to ask).[77] The reason for this is not stated in CTh 5.19.1 (365) nor in CJ 11.50.2 (396), but CTh 2.32.1 and CTh 5.3.1 suggest that it was meant to safeguard claims of the estate owner on his *colonus* over other claims. The effect is that a *colonus* experienced a double personal law regime: both *alieni iuris* and *sui iuris*.

75 See also Rosafio 2009, 288–295 on these constitutions.

76 See Kaser 1971, 287–288; the same with the *peculium quasi castrense*, Kaser 1975, 216.

77 Rosafio 2009, 301 sees acutely the difference between these two kinds of *peculium* and the role of the *potestas*. But I cannot follow him on 300 where he argues that with the *pistores*, *suarii* and *navicularii* their property, as incorporated in the *corpus*, was also considered, by the *corporati* themselves, gradually as *peculium*. It would help here to consult Sirks 1996. Nor do I see a reverse gradual development with the *coloni* to a private dimension in as far as it would have become a guarantee for the estate owners. The problem is that we nowhere find a guarantee expressed; we have to deduce it.

25 Taxation and Complying with Taxes

The tax that burdened *coloni* before all was the poll tax, then liturgies and, if they owned land, the land taxes. This follows from CTh 8.1.3 (333):

> Utilitate suadente annonarios et actuarios condicionales esse praecipimus, annonis etiam adiuvari et capitationem eorum qui censiti sunt haberi immunem. Ideoque tua sollertia competentia monebit officia, ut actuariis binas annonas, annonariis vero singulas protinus subministrent, capitationem quoque ipsorum tantum, qui ex his censiti sunt, faciat haberi immunem, quoad in actu fuerint constituti, nam postea vel laus eos et dignitas honorabit vel, si in culpa fuerint deprehensi, poena comitabitur.

> In the interests of the public welfare We command that assistant military accountants and military accountants shall be *condicionales*, that they shall also be sustained by subsistence allowances, and that those of them who are enrolled on the tax registers (*censuses*) shall be exempt from the capitation tax. 1. Therefore Your Wisdom shall admonish the competent officers to pay forthwith two subsistence allowances to each military accountant and one allowance to each assistant military accountant. Of the aforesaid persons, you shall provide that only those who are enrolled on the tax registers shall be exempt from the capitation tax as long as they are engaged in actual service; for afterward they shall either be honored by glory and dignity, or else attended with punishment if they should be apprehended in wrongdoing.

The constitution prescribes that the *annonarii* and *actuarii* (assistants in the tax collection) are for the time of their appointment *condicionales*. This implies that they are fixed to their posts, they are unfit for honourable functions (and therefore cannot claim exemptions or immunities from these), and may be tortured if frauds occur (e.g., CTh 8.1.7). Being *condicionalis* places them consequently on the level of slaves who could be tortured. But they will receive food allowances (as officials) and be free from the *capitatio* if they are *censiti*. The word *censiti* is rather wide; it indicates anybody who is registered in the census (tax register), like the *collegiati* of towns (the probable sources of supply here), but, consequently, also the *censibus adscripti*. If they owned land they would therefore have registered it and be independently liable for the tax on it, as prescribed in CTh 11.1.14, because the land would be *censitus*, not they. The *capitatio* may theoretically comprise any tax levied by way of *capita*, but in this case, applied to individual *censiti*, it means the poll tax. Diocletian released in 313 the *plebs urbana* in the east from the poll tax (CTh 13.10.2, 313 = CJ 11.49.1). It implies that the *plebs rustica* remained subjected, which is proved by CTh 13.11.2 (386 E = CJ 11.48.10; see below). This matches CTh 5.17.1 of

332, which prescribes that a *colonus iuris alieni*, that is, subjected to somebody's *potestas*, must be returned to his *origo*; who harboured him on his flight must acknowledge his *capitatio*, hence must pay it for the time he spent with him. Contrariwise, it will have been the estate owner who normally paid the *capitatio* for his *colonus*. According to CTh 11.1.7 (361), senators do not have to pay taxes for an absconded *colonus originalis* if the lands he tilled were never part of their lands, which corroborates the existence of land held privately by *coloni*. As to the land tax and other *munera patrimoniorum* (and *mixta*), he as owner is liable himself.[78]

A complicated constitution is in this respect CTh 11.7.2 in the title *De exactionibus*.

> CTh 11.7.2 (319): Unusquisque decurio pro ea portione conveniatur, in qua vel ipse vel colonus vel tributarius eius convenitur et colligit; neque omnino pro alio decurione vel territorio conveniatur. Id enim prohibitum esse manifestum est et observandum deinceps, quo iuxta hanc nostram provisionem nullus pro alio patiatur iniuriam.
>
> Every decurion shall be sued for only that portion of land in respect to which either he or his *colonus* or his taxable dependent is sued and from which they collect the fruits, and no decurion shall be sued at all on account of another decurion or for the territory of another. For this is manifestly prohibited, and henceforth it must be observed that in accordance with Our provision no person shall suffer wrong on account of another.

CTh 11.7.2 says that a decurion has to be convoked for the *portio* in which either he himself or his *colonus* or his *tributarius* is assessed and he deploys these people (or includes them in the census).[79] He may not be assessed for another decurion or *territorium*, as is also formulated in CTh 12.1.186.[80] The constitution is about levying taxes and assessing the right persons. *Portio* is used in the Code in its general sense of 'portion', but in this context it rather refers to the part in the tax levy which must be paid, here by a decurion (see also CTh 7.6.5). Apparently a decurion had to pay for himself, for his land, and for certain *coloni* and *tributarii*. Since he was not liable for another *territorium*, we may assume that these two groups resided in his *territorium*, that is, in the territory of his home town, thus

[78] See, for example, CTh 11.3.3.

[79] Pharr 1952 on this passage interprets *portio* as part of land and reads *colligit* as 'collect the fruits' (of that land), applying *colligit* to all three named persons. *Colligere* may mean to collect, but also to arrange.

[80] The Summaria Antiqua on this passage refers to CTh 12.1.186, where the same prohibition is formulated; yet that dates from 535 or later and corresponds to CJ 11.59.16.

in his tax district. Further, since he is also not liable for the tax of another decurion, that is, in his home town, those two groups were linked to him and not other decurions. The *eius* confirms this. These must have been *censiti* on his estate census or he was guarantee for them. They were in the first place themselves liable for the poll tax and therefore assessed, but if they were registered on the estate census, it was the estate owner who paid their tax (the poll tax) and credited them for it, or, alternatively, he may have provided a credit so that they paid it themselves. In both cases it must have been recorded in the tax registers.

These specifics of the colonate for the entire Empire are corroborated and specified by the rules for the two parts of the Empire.

25.1 *Taxes and the* Coloni *in the East*

25.1.1 *Taxation*

The *coloni* were registered for the poll tax in their home village. The adjustment of the taxation assessment is prescribed in CTh 13.10.7 (371 E), in the context of a *peraequatio*. The beginning and essential (to us) part of the text is difficult to understand. Gothofredus, Haenel, Mommsen, Seeck, and Jones have suggested emendations.[81] It runs thus:

> Sicubi subscribtorum modo sorte fatali morientibus de scribto aliquid fuerit imminutum contraque in vicina vel contermina eius vel in eodem vel ubilibet simili substantia ratione nascendi ultra conscribtorum numeris adcreverit, modus censuum intraque servetur, ut ex eo, qui superest, ille, qui defuerit, suppleatur.

A possible translation is:

> As where from the entered number (*modo describto*) of subscribed people something was taken away by those dying naturally, and on the other hand in its neighbouring or adjacent total (*substantia*), or in the same [*territorium*] or wherever the total (*substantia*) by the similar principle of birth has increased over the numbers of inscribed people, the amount (*modus*) of the censuses

[81] Gothofredus: *integre* instead of *intraque*. Haenel: *utrimque* instead of *intraque*. Mommsen: *sicubi <censuali in possessione cuiusdam hominibus quibusdam de> subscribtorum* etc.; *conscribtum numerus* instead of *conscribtorum numerus*; *in utraque* instead of *intraque*. Jones 1964, 1191 n. 108 emendates the text thus: *Sicubi <in aliqua metrocomia de> subscribtorum modo sorte fatali morientibus de scribto aliquid fuerit inminutum contraque in vicina vel contermina eius vel in eodem <territorio> vel ubilibet simili substantia ratione nascendi ultra conscribtorum numeris adcreverit, modus censuum int<er u>tra<m>que servetur, ut ex eo, qui superest, ille, qui defuerit, suppleatur*. He accidentally inserts an extra *t* but his suggestions are sensible. The insertion of *metrocomia* is due to the mentioning of *defensores*. His results are the same as mine.

> among each other must be maintained, namely that from that [*numerus, modus*] which is higher that [*numerus*] which lacks is supplemented.[82]

What induces me to take this line of interpretation is an inscription from Kos which deals with the same matter.[83] The inscription speaks of complaints about groups being taxed too high due to deaths, whereas neighbouring groups, despite having more people through birth, are taxed less. The first require their number (*arithmos*) in the census to be lowered and thus a lesser tax while the others be censused higher and thus taxed higher. In the end there will be a balance. The same here too. There are complaints of *defensores* or *plebeii* about disparities, and the solution is to change the accounting: *eos tantum qui mortui videbuntur ex adcrescentibus repleturi* and the census will be stabilised.

It is not said what the *substantiae* are with which we are dealing here. Jones assumes it concerns villages of peasant proprietors which were corporately liable for their registered population, and this law allows for transfers of liability from one village to another, where one had grown and the other shrunk.[84] It might indeed be villages with the census for the poll tax. The amount was once set and, as we know from the inscriptions from Asia Minor, not changed for a long time. In that case disparities would creep in and lead to injustices. A *peraequatio* would redress this, and the editor Feissel has laid indeed this connection. This requires the interpretation of *modus* as 'number' and *substantia* as 'stock', but that is possible. The words *vicina* and *contermina*, and *eodem* and *ille* would fit, since in this way the compensation in the returns would take place on the lowest level. But perhaps the text also covered *coloni* entered on an estate census, because these also will not have been updated often; the Asia Minor inscriptions are about estate assessments. The *peraequatio* has to balance these. As Grey emphasises, the government reacted in this way to diminishing tax revenues, generally caused by so-called *agri deserti*.[85] The *modus censuum* – by which is meant the total number of people in a tax district – must be adjusted. Per unit a new tax total must be set so that individually everybody pays the same, and the differences between the actual and the

[82] The *Interpretatio* says that in Sicily *peraequationes* were adjusted in this way (*e dinumeratis moriatur . . . debere eius nomine reputari*). It adds that fugitives must be recalled to their *cultura*. The fact that it concerns an eastern constitution, as the use of *substantia* also confirms, proves that the first word, *sicubi*, cannot have been a corruption of *siculorum*. See on this now my Summaria Antiqua (Sirks 2020a) with the suggestion that this was added after 535 by a Byzantine working in Rome.

[83] Feissel 2009, the reference to and comparison with CTh 13.10.7 on 302–305.

[84] Jones 1964, 455.

[85] Grey 2007b, 368–273.

registered number (which evidently remain, or else the equalisation would not be necessary) are to be evened out. That is done in the accounts, and in the end the total remains the same without the need to re-census everything. It was a fairly simple method to maintain the system which was, as Thonemann suggests, only sporadically adjusted, so that the first assessments could be used over centuries.[86] Hence this text is included in the title on *peraequatio*. There is no need to assume with Jones that liability was transferred, that is, that the censuses themselves were adjusted, if that is what Jones means. Not only did such adjustments not happen often, as Jones says himself,[87] the balance might sway after some time the other way. If the tax levy was individually fixed, all this would make no sense. The problem as described only arises if a fixed taxation is set, based on a once set number of people, after which the total tax sum is divided over all. In that case a decrease in people leads to a heavier individual tax burden.[88] This is not a collective tax liability in the strict sense. All assessments are on an individual basis. The aggregate makes a quote in the end, and this quote is used to establish finally the sum expected from the tax unit. In theory this should be distributed proportionally according to the individual assessments. Adjustments were preferably made, at certain moments, in the bookkeeping: one entity had to equalise another entity. In the meantime,

[86] Jones 1964, 454–455; Thoneman 2007, 439. [87] Jones 1964, 454.

[88] It could certainly happen that on an estate the number of registered *coloni* decreased (by death or flight) or increased (by birth). In the first case the owner was liable for the missing persons (see CTh 5.17.1). Those fled he had to recall, but what about the dead, for whom he still had to pay? What if CTh 13.10.7 (371 E) addressed this problem? There are *subscribti* (i.e., *coloni originales* registered in the census) and their numbers are fixed – that is, until the next assessment – but some of these numbers are depleted by death. The stability of the census (*stabilitas census*) is thereby threatened: one estate owner has to pay more than he should, and another, where there was an increase, less than he should. The constitution mentions complaints of *defensores* (of the city) or *plebei*, probably because of the burden upon the remaining *coloni*, who had to compensate their dead fellows (but we do not see any reference to this for estates) or, more likely, on the estate owners who had guaranteed the dead. The solution would in that case have been that if there was on a neighbouring estate or on an estate of the same property owner or of the same kind (*similis substantia*) (although *substantia* is generally used for the whole of one's assets, we would have to interpret it here as either 'of the same kind' or as the Latin word, used by the drafters of his eastern constitution for κτῆμα, usual to designate an estate) a surplus in *coloni* over the censused number, as many from that surplus as were needed to fill the difference were now in the accounting attributed to the depleted assessment and the supplying estate owner had to pay for this difference. Or (the text is not clear) the deficits were filled by surplus *coloni* by transferring them. As a result, the sum assessed on the tax unit for the poll tax could be levied and the *modus censuum* maintained for the current indiction for the entire district. This solution is, however, only allowed if there are complaints, and it may not be used to make up the number of fugitives (these, as we see, should be reclaimed by their masters, or the persons who hide them should pay). If it did not imply a real transfer of *coloni*, the solution would have been a temporary solution and would imply that at the next census the number of people would be adjusted to the actual numbers. Since the constitution is placed in the title on *peraequationes*, hence permanent solutions, this hypothetical reading cannot hold.

the imposed sum had to be paid, regardless of the changes in the basis. That gives the impression of a collective tax liability, and de facto it was at that moment. But fundamentally it was not so.

25.1.2 Complying with the Tax

A *colonus* has to pay his poll tax, but it follows from CTh 11.1.14 that his estate owner gave a guarantee for its payment but had also to urge the *colonus* to pay himself. In the end he paid if the *colonus* did not pay. Fiscally the farmer would be registered in his homestead, a *vicus* or town. In private law a guarantee of the estate owner could be done by way of a *cautio*. In that case the fisc would have to sue the owner in case of default, a rather cumbersome way. An alternative was that the estate owner acknowledged the tax, as it was usual to acknowledge public obligations like *munera*. Such an acknowledgement one could do by way of the tax declaration (*professio censualis*). He would have to include the *colonus* in it and thereby warrant payment. He could do this in his own declaration for the poll tax, or include the *colonus* in the census declaration of an estate. We see in CTh 11.1.14 that this was the regular way: the *coloni* are *censibus adscripti*, they are inserted (*adscripti*) into the estate census and thereby linked to an estate. In a way it is understandable: the registration of slaves and livestock on his census settled his *capitatio* liability for these, so why not the same for the *coloni* included? Since the farmer was obliged to provide services (labour), registration on the census of the estate where he would work would be logical. As to the level of the poll tax, CTh 13.11.2 (386 E) set a new and lower level (*caput*) for the inhabitants of several provinces.

Next to the poll tax, *coloni* had in any case to perform liturgies as mentioned in CTh 11.24.6pr (415 E).

25.2 Taxes and the Coloni *in the West*

25.2.1 Taxation

In CJ 11.48.13.1 there is a question of the discomfort of an unequal *partitio*, which should not burden the landowners. This must refer to the attribution of a tax according to a division over the individual lands, since in the continuation of the text a transfer of land is mentioned.[89] CTh 11.1.26 (399 W), addressed to the Praetorian Prefect of Gaul, is not specific in this respect:

> Omni amoto privilegio beneficiorum possessores sublimitas tua praecipiet universos muneribus adstringi, earum scilicet provinciarum, ex quibus orta

[89] See Section 11.

querimonia est aut in quibus haec retinendae plebis ratio adscribtioque servatur. Nullum gratia relevet, nullum iniquae partitionis vexet incommodum, sed pari omnes sorte teneantur; ita tamen, ut, si ad alterius personam transferatur praedium, cui certus plebis numerus fuerit adscribtus, venditi onera novellus possessor compellatur agnoscere, cum plebem constet non tam in omnibus praediis adscribendam neque auferendum ab eo, cui semel posthac deputata fuerit. Et cetera.

Every privilege of special grants is removed and Your Sublimity shall order that all landowners be constrained to the public obligations, viz. of those provinces from which a complaint has arisen or in those this method and assessment of holding the plebs is observed. No person shall be relieved by favoritism, no person shall be vexed by the disadvantage of an unfair assessment but all shall be held by the same fortune; provided, however, that if a landed estate should be transferred to another person upon which a certain number of plebeians has been assessed, the new possessor shall be compelled to acknowledge the charges, since it is established that the plebs must not be thus assessed upon all estates nor be taken away from that [land] upon which they hereafter have been assigned. (Etc.)

It seems that in Gaul a reassessment of land had been ordered to correct the situation where special grants (likely obtained by bribery or favouritism) had distorted the original tax assessment. This included the assessment of *coloni* on estates. The correction implied also that *coloni* might be ascribed to estates where there had not been *coloni* before. If the constitution was the prelude to a *peraequatio*, it means that in a *peraequatio* not only land was assigned to solvent landowners but also *coloni* assigned to such land (from other plots). Not everybody liked such a reassignment of *agri deserti* because of the costs involved in bringing land into culture again. One argument used to avoid this was, apparently, that *coloni* should be distributed over all lands (thus also other their land) or transferred elsewhere; another trick was to use the old assessment without *coloni*. The constitution, now used for future cases, prescribes that if somebody acquires such land (*praedium*) to which a *plebis numerus* has been ascribed, that is, *coloni originales*, he has to acknowledge the burden (*onera*) of his new acquisition. The *plebs* may not be removed from the plot of land (*praedium*) they were now ascribed to. In other words, he has to take upon him the obligations for the registered number of *coloni* on the acquired land (*adscribtioque servatur*). The phrase *cum plebem . . . fuerit* indicates that purchasers tried to remove *coloni* and so reduce their number. Theoretically, one might say that because all *coloni* were added, their total could not, if the censured acts remained with one territory, lead to a drop in taxes. Yet the purchasers may not register them elsewhere or shift them to land outside the territory.

The new owner must acknowledge the charges (*onera*) of his property. What are these? If it were *agri deserti*, first of all the investment in recultivation; but since it concerns land to which a definite number of *plebs* has been registered (*praedium cui certus plebis numerus fuerit adscribtus*), also their tax. If it had been the charge of the land tax, there would have been no reason to mention this detail, as other texts sufficiently state the duty of an owner to pay this tax. So it must concern the taxes due over or by this *plebis numerus*: it must have been at least their poll tax. But it may also have concerned *munera publica* of another nature, namely *munera sordida* which the *plebs* had to perform, as in CJ 11.48.1 (328). That the poll tax (*capitatio plebeia, exactio plebis*) was levied follows from the exemptions granted. Widows beyond marrying age, women living in perpetual abstinence (e.g., nuns), male *pupilli* until the age of 20, and female *pupilli* until married were exempted from this tax (CTh 13.10.4 of 368/370), rephrased in CTh 13.10.6 of 370.

CTh 11.1.26 also annuls any privilege granted to landowners regarding *munera*. This was already indicated by another not transmitted constitution. Any specially accorded immunity of *iugatio* or *capitatio* and registered in the public books (i.e., the tax accounts) is, if not proven, declared invalid by CTh 13.10.8 (383 W = CJ 11.48.9).

There were not *coloni originales* and *inquilini originales* present on every estate, nor in every province, as CTh 11.1.26 (399 W) implies (*earum scilicet provinciarum, ex quibus orta quaerimonia est ... non tam in omnibus praediis adscribendam nec auferendam*). The colonate was thus, in any case around 400 and later, and in the west, an isolated phenomenon (theoretically it might have changed after that, but we do not see any indication of this in the Theodosian Code). It fits Fikhman's observation that a great part, if not the majority, of the land in the nome of Oxyrhynchus was in the hands of free farmers.[90]

25.2.2 Complying with the Tax

For the west, CTh 5.17.1 is corroborated by CJ 11.48.8 (371 W)[91] with regard to both the commitment to return fugitive *coloni originales* and the duty to acknowledge the tax due from them. Fugitive *coloni originales*

[90] Fikhman 1990, 174 = Fikhman 2006, 273. Cfr. also CJ 11.51.1, 52.1 and 53.1, which demonstrate that the colonate was not a universal phenomenon.

[91] This text may of course have been changed, but since it conforms with CTh 5.17.1 in these respects, there is no reason to suspect the remainder. CJ 11.48.8 was issued to the praetorian prefect of the Gauls, but it apparently was valid for the entire west wherever there were *coloni originales*. The constitution has already been discussed before, in Section 13, for Justinian's time.

work on another estate, whose owner knows of their status and apparently treats them accordingly without registering them in his census (this possibility is not mentioned in the text and otherwise he would have had to pay the poll tax for them, by which his profit would diminish even more – the text assumes that he let them work on the land or do other work without paying them). The fugitives must be returned and the harbouring estate owner has to pay the taxes which have been lost for the treasury (*ab illis tributa quae publicis perierunt functionibus exigantur*). This is the same liability as in CTh 5.17.1. If they were lost, it means that the rightful estate owner did not have to pay taxes for his fugitive *coloni*, while the second estate owner had not enrolled them on his census. Otherwise this makes no sense. The other possibility the constitution addresses is that fugitive *coloni originales* pretend to be free of the colonate, rent land as share-croppers and keep part of the proceeds as savings (*partem fructuum pro solo debitam dominis praestiterunt cetera proprio peculio reservantes*), or get an earning as farm hands (CJ 11.48.8pr). In that case only the fugitives were liable and they could and had to pay their own taxes (as any other lessee), that is, in any case the poll tax; they had not concluded a contract of colonate (evidently a *contractus publicus*) but a mere private law *locatio conductio* (CJ 11.48.8.1: *ab ipsis profugis quaecumque debentur exigantur: nam manifestum est privatum iam esse contractum*).

It is thus certain that an estate owner might in the end have to pay the taxes of his *coloni*, but also that these had to pay in the first place. It was a guarantee. CJ 11.48.8 speaks of *tributa* and *functiones publicae* and is therefore not precise regarding the taxes the fugitives were subject to. In any case the estate owner's liability covered the poll tax on his *plebs rustica*. It is not evident what other tax was relevant for them, in view of their economic situation. The plural may simply correspond to the plural *coloni*.

CTh 11.1.26 (399 W) reminds estate owners in certain provinces of the *munera* they have to fulfil (including taxes). In one group of these provinces, 'this method and assessment of holding the plebs is observed' (*haec retinendae plebis ratio adscribtioque servatur*). The preceding, not transmitted part of this constitution must have said something about the rule, but in view of what follows, combined with the other texts, it is clear that it concerns in any case *coloni originales* and, since there the general term *plebs* is used, also *inquilini* who could, as we see in CJ 11.48.13pr (400 W), similarly be tied to an *origo*. Further, the constitution makes clear that the colonate existed in some but not all provinces.

From the constitutions we have for both parts of the Empire it appears that the *coloni* were in the first place liable for their poll tax, just as other people were who did not have a guarantee. Estate owners were obliged to guarantee payment of this, relieving the *coloni* from the stress taxes may cause. One might say they functioned as bank guarantee. They also took care of the liturgies of the *coloni*. The *coloni* were included in the census registration of the estate of their guarantor. The registration in the estate census turned the estate into the *origo* of the *colonus* (and his family). The colonate was, in any case in the west, not present in every province, and, where it was, not in every place.

26 Transmission of the *Condicio* and the Effect of the *Senatusconsultum Claudianum*

For the entire Empire there are no texts on this subject, perhaps due to the defects in Book Five or due to newer legislation which set older legislation aside. CTh 4.12, on the senatusconsultum, is only transmitted in a twelfth-century copy and does not seem to have contained a constitution on *coloni* or other groups.

26.1 In the East

In the east the transmission of the *condicio* in case of marriage is only recorded in one constitution; perhaps other constitutions were in the lost parts of the Code. The basic rule is that in case of a marriage of a *colonus adscriptus* and a woman not subjected to this or another *munus*, the children follow the paternal *condicio*. This follows from the exception phrased in CTh 10.20.17, 427 E (= CJ 11.8.15; see above, Section 23.3). It introduces a new rule for the case that somebody marries a daughter of *conchylioleguli* (fishers of purple snails, an industry concentrated on the coast of the province of Syria). If these men are of another *condicio*, children will follow the *condicio* of their mother. Thus from now on all children will be subjected to the registration (*adscribtio*)[92] as *conchylioleguli*, whether their father or their mother is *conchyliolegulus* or *conchyliolegula*.[93] It is a deviation from the normal rule that children follow the status of their

[92] The ubiquitous use of *adscribtio* and *adscriptus* are evidence of an extensive system of registration, in this case the census registers.

[93] Apparently there was a scarcity of *conchylioleguli*. In the case of *monetarii* a different solution was chosen; see below. The *senatusconsultum Claudianum* would not apply, since any union here was *aequalis*.

father unless there is no *conubium* between the two spouses, for example if the mother is a freeborn (*ingenua*) and the father a slave. Children out of such unions, born before this law was promulgated, would follow the status of their father, whether these were *conchylioleguli* or *coloni adscribti*. That would be the normal succession of status. The different new rule is the same as that for *adcripticiae* and free men, introduced by ancient statutes (CJ 11.48.21pr; see Section 10.3). It is possible that the ancient statute of CJ 11.48.21pr already existed in 438 or before. CTh 5.18.1.4 of 419 also refers to *vetera constituta* which may have been the same.

26.2 *In the West*

In the west more legislation on the transmission of the *condicio* exists, due to the turbulence in the countryside caused by the barbarian invasions in the early fifth century. One way by which the bond is established was descent from a *colonus*. CTh 5.18.1.1–2 (419 W) orders the return of any fugitive *originalis* with all his offspring (*posteritas*) according to the *ius agrorum*. There should be no doubt about his *condicio*. It follows that his *condicio* passed over to his offspring. We see the same with *colonae*, as it appears from CTh 5.18.1.3 and 4 (4 = CJ 11.48.16). CTh 5.18.1.3–4 (419 W) issues rules for women who are subjected to the colonate and who have absconded from their estate. They are called *originariae*, and the constitution decides when and how they are to return. Here it is important that if they are to return (i.e., the prescription period of twenty years has not yet elapsed), a substitute woman (a *colona*?[94] a slave woman?) may be given together with one-third of their offspring (*agnatio*) if they married a *colonus* of another estate. If she married a man not subjected in this way and living in a town or elsewhere, she and her entire offspring must return. Evidently in the latter case the *origo* of the mother prevailed, whereas in the former case both *origines* competed with a division into one- and two-thirds, the latter for the paternal *origo*. Thus attachment to the *origo* by descendance was in 419, and since the constitution reaches backwards thirty years, in 379 in any case, the rule, both for *coloni* and *colonae*.[95] Koptev assumes that *consortium* in CTh 5.18.1.4 means cohabitation and that there was no lawful marriage in the second case. However, then the parallel with the first case, which does not say anything on the legality of the union, disappears.

[94] In that case the census register would have to be adjusted in two places. However, that would likely be done anyway if all returned.

[95] For a more detailed discussion of CTh 5.18.1, see below, Section 28.2.1.

It rather hints at the applicability of the *senatusconsultum Claudianum* and the treatment of such unions as between persons of unequal status (see below). Further, he draws the attention to the division of the children and assumes it was considered fair that the new landlord received more children who had been born anyway on his estate.[96] Perhaps it was a compensation for the loss of the substitute.

These are the rules for unions between *coloni* and *colonae* and for *colonae* who married *ingenui*. Another rule regulates unions between an imperial minter (*monetarius*) and *colonae* of an imperial or private estate. This text, CTh 10.20.10, 380/379 W = CJ 11.8.7, declares unequivocally that its rule is an application of the *senatusconsultum Claudianum*. The minters worked in one of the imperial mints and were bound to their *condicio*. The reasons for this are unknown, but it is obvious that, as with the divers for the purple snail (*conchyloleguli*) and the (silk) weavers (*gynaecarii*), the necessity to have people available to provide these indispensable services, and to survey the minting or collecting of these precious goods better, required that they be bound to their task by way of a public college. Another aspect is that these groups dealt with expensive goods: gold, silver, purple dye, silk. The texts do not mention it, but as with the *numerarii* and *actuarii* (the tax officials), it may perhaps have been possible to apply torture in case theft were to be investigated.

> CTh 10.20.10: Edicimus, ne qua mulier splendidioris gradus monetarii adhaerens consortio decus nativae libertatis amittat. Quod si quam ab hac praeceptione statutum nostrae perennitatis abduxerit, ea secundum auctoritatem senatus consulti Claudiani vel legitima admonita conventione discedat vel, si complexui monetarii putaverit inhaerendum, non ambigat se et liberis praeiudicaturam et eius condicioni esse nectendam. Nihilo minus autem et eas, quae ante legem nostram monetariis videntur esse coniunctae placuit praedicto titulo conveniri scientes, nisi interdicta coniunctione discesserint, mutasse se statum. 1. Si qua vero originaria seu colona possessionis alienae, ignaro domino seu sciente, monetario adsociabitur, ii conventi mox iuri agrorum debitas personas retrahere festinent vel de cetero sciant repetendi facultatem silentii sui coniventia perdidisse. 2. Sed ut monetario nullam necti volumus, ita et monetario patre susceptas prohibemus extraneis copulari.

> We issue an edict that no woman of a more splendid degree of birth shall cast away the honor of her natal liberty by adhering to a union with an imperial minter. But if he should lead any woman away from the observance of this regulation, she shall in accordance with the authority of the

[96] Koptev 2009, 279–280.

> *senatusconsultum Claudianum*, after she has been warned by the statutory notification, either withdraw from this union, or, if she should suppose that she should cling to the embrace of the imperial minter, she shall not doubt that she will prejudice the rights of her children and that she must be bound to the *condicio* of the minter. Moreover, we decide that notification according to the aforesaid title shall be given nonetheless to those women also who appear to have been united to imperial minters before the issuance of Our law, and they shall know that unless they withdraw from the interdicted union, they will change their legal status. 1. But if indeed any *colona originaria* or a *colona* belonging to another estate, without the knowledge or even with the knowledge of her owner, should be united to an imperial minter, such owner shall be notified, and he shall immediately hasten to drag back such persons who are owed to the *ius agrorum*,[97] or he shall know that thereafter he has lost the right of recovery [of the woman] by connivance through his own silence. 2. But as we wish that no woman shall be united to an imperial minter, so also we forbid that women begotten by minters shall be united to extraneous persons.

The law regulates two sorts of union. First, if women, *splendioris gradus*, that is, *ingenuae* or of decurional status, stay in their union with *monetarii* notwithstanding a warning, they and their children are subjected to the *condicio* of the *monetarii* (CTh 10.20.10pr). This was a *condicio* in which people had to stay (CTh 10.20.1, 317 = CJ 11.8.1, the constitution which confirms their *condicio* in 317 so that this existed already in that year) and could be recalled, similar to the *condicio coloniaria*. The woman changes her *condicio*, and the paternal status of the *monetarius* will prevail. There is no division of children as above in CTh 5.18.1.3–4. As the text says, this is an application of the *senatusconsultum Claudianum*. This is remarkable because the *senatusconsultum* originally aimed at unions of free women with slaves. Now the minters are set on the same level as slaves although they are free Roman citizens, or else CTh 10.20.1 would not have been necessary. Their marriage is called *consortium*, *coniunctio*, or *adsociari*, which are not flattering descriptions. Their union should have been considered a full legitimate marriage, yet it was not, or else all offspring would have followed the father. Because they followed the mother, it was not considered so, and the senatusconsultum was used to achieve the desired result by a different analogue application. A formal warning to the woman was required, and if she did not leave, its effect was that she acquired the *condicio monetaria*, as her children did too. Accordingly, the senatusconsultum which originally brought about a change in the *status*

[97] This term also in CTh 5.18.1.2.

libertatis and as a consequence in the *status civitatis* (making her *alieno iure*, but as slave, losing Roman citizenship) now brings about a change only in the first state, making her *alieno iure* as *monetaria*, while her *status civitatis* remains Roman. It effects a change in the *condicio*, from being free of subjection to being subjected. CTh 10.20.10.1 deals with *colonae* marrying *monetarii*. Here the children would be *monetarii* anyway, hence the warning to her landowner to recall her. The last phrase is a remarkable prohibition (one was free to marry) and if effective would enlarge the supply of brides.

The same machinery applies to unions between *ingenuae* (women not subjected to a *condicio*) and workers in the imperial weaveries (*gynaecearii*): if the women do not leave, they and their children are subjected to the *condicio* of the *gynaecearii* (CTh 10.20.3, 365 W). Again they do not become slaves but are drawn into the *condicio* of the weavers. Similarly with *murileguli*: here children begotten in marriages with *ingenui* or those of another *condicio* become *murileguli* (CTh 10.20.16, 426 E). This rule is introduced as an innovation in CTh 10.20.17 (427, E) for *conchyleguli*. Further, the *collegiati*, people who were subjected to cities and had to provide services, were also subjected to the *coniugium non aequale* (CTh 14.7.1, 397 W). Of all these groups, we encounter in the Breviarium only the *coloni* and the *collegiati*. Their *condicio* was lower than that of an *ingenuus* (on account of the *potestas* exercised; see above). The usual social division in Late Antiquity is that between *honestiores* and *humiliores*. That division is visible in the criminal law texts. Here we see within the *humiliores* a new and also legally defined difference, that of the *condicionales*: free Roman citizens who are under the *potestas* of somebody else according to a public law arrangement. They cannot aspire to honourable functions. This low and subjected position caused their *matrimonium* to be called degradingly *consortium* and so on. We are here in face of the *coniugium non aequale*.

26.3 The Coniugium Non Aequale

This means that there were marriages between people which were not treated as usual legitimate marriages in which children would follow their father's status. Characteristic of these is that one partner has a *condicio* and that this *condicio* is one of subjection (see below). Such a marriage was, as CTh 14.7.1 (397 W) says, a *coniugium non aequale*; where there is a *coniugium non aequale, matrem sequatur agnatio, ubi veri iustum erit, patri cedat successio*. A union between a *colona originalis* and a *collegiatus* would seem to be one as between equals, because the children were divided equally between the respective claimants; or, more likely, this was a special solution (CTh 12.19.1, 400 W), because according to CTh 14.7.1 (397 W) all children should have become *coloni*. For that reason, CTh 10.20.10.1 warns the master to recall the *colona*. CTh 14.7.1, however, expresses the general rule.[98]

Children were registered too. According to D. 50.15.4.9, whatever is born or acquired after the declaration may (and should) be added as long as the census was not completed. Slave children will certainly have been implied by this, probably also children of *coloni originales*; after all, poll tax was also due for them. As a consequence, during each *professio censualis* where *coloni originales* were entered, the number remained fixed. This was the point of departure for the taxation, which worked with an overall registration of land and people. Separately censused land was such a basic unit, a village register for the poll tax too. With *monetarii*, *gynaecarii*, *murileguli*, *conchyloleguli*, and *collegiati* there was no estate, and here similar registrations of persons must have been kept (cf. CTh 13.10.7).

Children begotten in unions between *coloni* and *inquilini* have to acknowledge the *condicio* of their father, whether both or neither of the parents are registered in the census (CJ 11.48.13pr, 400 W).

> CJ 11.48.13pr: Definimus, ut inter inquilinos colonosve, quorum quantum ad originem pertinet vindicandam indiscreta eademque paene videtur esse condicio, licet sit discrimen in nomine, suscepti liberi vel utroque vel neutro parente censito statum paternae condicionis agnoscant.
>
> We decide that between *inquilini* and *coloni*, of whom in as far as it concerns the recall to their *origo* the *condicio* is considered to be not different and almost the same, although there is a difference in name, the begotten children should acknowledge the status of the paternal *condicio*, whether both or neither of the parents is registered in the census.

First, the *inquilini* are tied to an *origo* in the same way as *coloni* and hence may be reclaimed likewise. They seem to have been dwellers on an estate, perhaps renting a room. They too may have seen it better to register in the estate census and have in this way some guarantee for their fiscal obligations. Second, we do not know precisely what the *inquilinorum condicio* was,[99] but apparently a legal marriage between the two *condiciones*

[98] That is, by *iustum coniugium* is meant a marriage in which both partners are *ingenui*. The *interpretatio*, on the other hand, combines in its rendering the rule with the *senatusconsultum Claudianum*, as applying automatically as of 451; see Section 41.2, on Nov. Val. 31.6.

[99] For *inquilini*, see Chapter 1 note 16 and Section 26.3.

was possible and acknowledged, or else the paternal *condicio* and, because the text refers to this, his *origo* would not be determining that of the children. Because there is reference to the paternal *condicio*, it cannot be that *neutro parente censito* refers to not being registered in the sense of somebody not subjected to the *condicio* of a *colonus originalis*, such as an *ingenuus*. Otherwise there is no sense in referring to the paternal *condicio*, and *utroque* in the phrase *in utroque neutro* would make no sense. The words *in utroque neutro* must refer to the case that somebody, who has children, is subjected to this *condicio* but has not yet been registered in the census. Since children were included in their father's assessment, they had, once they became *sui iuris*, to register themselves. That may be the situation behind this text. In its turn this means (a) that being by birth subjected to the *condicio* is not sufficient for the effects to be realised, but that a registration and an acknowledgement (perhaps done at the same time, or the one implied in the other) is necessary, and (b) that *censitus* or *censibus adscriptus* might only refer to those actually registered. As such the procedure is the same as for public obligations (*munera*) and for a *condicio* like that of the decurions.[100] Thus it a good argument to assume that the *condicio coloniaria* was of a public, *in casu* administrative law nature and that its inherent obligations were of an administrative law nature.

This text implies that women could be subjected *inquilinae* and *colonae*, and this concurs with CTh 5.18.1.3–4 (4: = CJ 11.48.16) according to which women too could be subjected to the colonate. There is no text which explains this, but if children of both sexes could, as in CTh 5.18.1.3–4, be claimed by the estate owner of their father or mother, one source at least of the *condicio* was descent, passing also to daughters.[101]

Although this chapter deals with the situation as laid down in Theodosius' Code, it is the place to deal with the question when these rules were introduced and what exactly they did introduce. It is likely that the *condicio coloniaria* was already, if not from the beginning onwards, seen as a *deterior condicio* on account of the subjection to the estate owner (see CTh 5.17.1 of 332 and CJ 11.58.2 of 319). But it does not have to imply that originally it passed also on to the children, nor that it made them unfit for imperial service. First of all, the introduction of the *coniugium non aequale* implies that the transmission of the *condicio* was tied next to the *origo* also tied to the *condicio*, or else the arrangement would have had no sense. The analogue application of the *senatusconsultum Claudianum* was a correction of the outcome of this, necessary if the purport was to keep as much labour force

[100] On this, see Sirks 1993b. [101] For a more detailed discussion of this text, see Section 28.2.1.

tied to land as possible. Second, the introduction had sense only if there was already a *condicio coloniaria* which was transmitted. It is possible that the transmissibility was introduced at the same time as the *condicio*. Then, the first transmitted mention of children of *adscripticii* being also liable dates from 400 (CJ 11.48.13, W), while CTh 14.7.1 on the *collegiati* dates from 397; we have no earlier mentions of it. It is also possible that the *coniugium non aequale* was introduced at different times for different groups. In that case the earliest mention is 379 (CTh 10.20.10), but that may be due to the textual tradition or selection of the Theodosian compilers. Similarly, the prohibition on appointing *condicionales* (*qui sit obnoxius servituti*) as *tabularii* in CTh 8.2.5 dates from 401. The reason given in CJ 11.48.18 (426, E) for the prohibition on appointing *coloni* in official functions is that the emperors have to take account of public decency and the right of the masters (*quia in hac parte et dominorum iuri et publicae consulimus honestati*). The masters could not command their *coloni*, these being compelled to obey the higher functionaries; conversely, the public authorities could frustrate the rights of the masters and the subjected status of the *coloni* would blemish the service. These are arguments which would apply right from the beginning of the colonate, and I assume therefore it was indeed the case. Further, the *condicio* was already a fact in 332 and 319; that of the *monetarii* existed already in 317 (CTh 10.20.1). Consequently, at some early moment in the first half of the fourth century the *condicio* as a particular public law status of *alieni iuris* came into existence and simultaneously or shortly afterwards the transition of the *condicio* to descendants must have been introduced if the census enrolment did not already imply this, after which, in order to enlarge labour on the land and in special imperial industries, the *coniugium non aequale* was introduced with the senatusconsultum as correction. This was also introduced for some particular groups of interest for the emperor (the purple snail divers, the imperial (silk) weavers, the minters, the miners). The reasons will have been the same, namely to maintain a steady labour force in these industries. The same goes for municipal services: the *collegiati* or *corporati*. How the *condicio* for them came into existence is unknown. Being also subjected to the poll tax, it is possible that they were registered in the same way as the *coloni*, but the question then is: Who exercised the authority over them? Or it was done analogously to the corporations of the *navicularii*, *suarii*, and *pistores* which were created before to provide a long-term sustenance of public services by long-term accumulation of capital, their labour being the valuable asset? Probable candidates are here municipal officials or executive decurions. But in the absence of sources, nothing can be said on this.

26.4 *The* Coniugium Non Aequale *and the Various Categories of* Condicionales

The deviation from the normal rule on transmission of status and *condicio* is recorded in several texts:[102]

(1) *aliquis alienae condicionis* × *conchyliolegula*: children are *congyliolegguli* by this law (CTh 10.20.17, 427 E) (before: *colonus* × *conchyliolegula*: children follow paternal *origo*, CTh 10.20.17, 427 E)
(2) *ingenua* × *monetarius*: *ingenua* and children are *monetarii* (CTh 10.20.10pr, 379 W: SC)
(3) *colona* × *monetarius*: *colona* and children are *monetarii* (CTh 10.20.10.1, 379 W)
(4) *ingenua* × *gynaecearius*: *ingenua* and children are *gynaecearii* (CTh 10.20.3, 365 W: SC*)
(5) *ingenua* × *servus fiscalis*: *ingenua* and children are *Latini* (instead of *servi*; CTh 4.12.3, 320 E/W: SC)
(6) *collegiatus* × *ancilla*: children are *servi* (CTh 14.7.1, 397 W, *interpretatio*)
(7) *ingenua* × *collegiatus*: children are *collegiati* (CTh 14.7.1, 397 W, SC*, *interpretatio*)
(8) *colona* × *ingenuus*: children are *coloni* (CTh 5.18.1.4, 419 W, CJ 11.48.21pr: ancient laws)
(9) *decurio* × *inquilina Domus Augustae*: children are *inquilini D.A.* by law (CJ 10.32.29, 365 W; see Section 32.2.2)
(10) *collegiatus* × *colona*: children are divided between father and mother (CTh 12.19.1, 400 W)
(11) *ingenuus* × *colona dominica/rei privatae*: children are *coloni* by law (CJ 11.68.4, 367, W)
(12) *aliquis alienae originis* × *filia murilegulorum*: children are *murileguli* (CTh 10.20.15, 425 E)

SC*: implicit analogue application of the senatusconsultum.

In cases 1, 3, 6, 7, 8, 9, 10, 11, and 12 the shift in status happened either because the statute said so (in 1, 9, 10, 11, and 12), or because of the *coniugium non aequale*, or, if the senatusconsultum applied (7), before an eventual formal warning, because after the fugitives are recalled, the children would not have followed the maternal status. With 2, 4, and 5

[102] *Conchylioleguli*: purply dye snail collectors; *monetarii*: minters in the imperial mints; *gynaecarii*: workers in the imperial weaveries; *collegiati*: workers attached to towns for the public works; *inquilini*: people living on estates.

the change occurred after the formal warning was disregarded. What we see is that in most cases the shift in status for the offspring takes place automatically, either because a constitution imposes it or because the new variant of the senatusconsultum applies automatically. Perhaps if in the latter case a formal warning was issued and the woman did not leave, the original sanction may have applied, but the sources for 438 and the period before do not contain information on this (whereas in Nov. Val. 31.6 does: *ingenua* and children become slaves).

All categories except the *coloni* and *inquilini* have in common that they are involved in a state or imperial service, where highly valued goods are processed; or are engaged on imperial land (*coloni*). The special rules are attested from 365 onwards. The *coloni* and *inquilini* are also involved in an area important for the public good. In all cases, tying them to their task and making arrangements so that new generations of workers are amply provided is of importance and effected by those rules.

27 Moving *Coloni* to Other Places

It was the purpose of the colonate to keep *coloni* on the estate where they were censused: they were to provide labour. But landowners who have more than one plot of land and those who were able to accept *coloni originales* would likely have more than one plot of land, and might want to deploy their *coloni* elsewhere when needed. That was possible, as we know from the Heroninos archive. But what if land was alienated for lack of revenues?

> CJ 11.48.2 (357): si quis praedium vendere voluerit vel donare, retinere sibi transferendos ad alia loca colonos privata pactione non possit. Qui enim colonos utiles credunt, aut cum praediis eos tenere debent aut profuturos aliis derelinquere, si ipsi sibi praedium prodesse desperant.

> If somebody wants to sell or donate a field, he cannot retain by a private pact for himself the *coloni* in order to transfer them to other places. Those who believe that *coloni* are useful to them have to keep them together with the fields or leave them to the advantage of others, if they themselves have lost hope that the field is of profit for them.

That land was relinquished because the yield had become insufficient was a well-known phenomenon in Late Antiquity. But if *coloni* had been attached to it (through the census), it was of course a waste of labour to leave them there: they could be used elsewhere. As long as such land remained in ownership, such deployment elsewhere would be no problem, but the taxes had to be paid as well. What we see is that such land is sold or donated but without the *coloni*. Assuming that the census remained the same, the *coloni* remained also registered in it. Thus, as the text says, the way to move the *coloni* was by a private agreement. That will have included both the pledge by the new owner to order the *coloni* to go elsewhere and by the former owner to pay the taxes, bolstered on both sides with *stipulationes poenae*.[103] Such private agreements to go around legal prescriptions were not pleasing to the authorities, who forbade such and other private agreements (FV 35). In this case they decide that if land (*praedium*) is transferred in ownership on account of sale or donation, the transferor cannot not remove its attached *coloni originales* from it by way of a private *pactum adiectum* to the sale and place them somewhere else, but has to leave them together with the land to the transferee. Then, if he thought that he could use the *coloni*, he should use them on this land and not alienate it, or leave the *coloni* to other people (namely, the new owners) to be useful for them, if he did not think they were useful for his land. The economic importance of *coloni* as sector of the workforce for the sustenance of agriculture next to other forms of workforce such as slaves or lessees, and thereby for the sustenance of tax revenues and local expenditure, is evidently the reason behind this. Their tie to the land resembles the private law tie of slaves as *instrumentum*, and we see the comparison indeed made (see below, Section 27.2).

Division of land would be done by contract, by a division (e.g., in the wake of succession) or by sale of a part of it,[104] in which the new borders were set out. After that the seller would perform the *traditio*, the delivery. For this FV 35, included partly as CTh 3.1.2 (337, = CJ 4.47.3), prescribes that nobody may sell or purchase land without acknowledging the census of it. To dispel all doubt about who is owner (and thus liable), the transfer should demonstrate clearly the borders of the sold land, while the neighbours should confirm the ownership of the seller. This should also be done with the *subsellia*, literally 'banks/benches', commonly called *scamna*. These were probably the stripes of land between adjoining lands which were left uncultivated or were used as a road.[105] Regarding the taxes, CTh 11.3.1 (331, = CJ 4.47.2) forbids any dealings

[103] Was there another way? The owner was able to undo the registration unilaterally. A release from his *potestas* should have effected that the registration, which formalised the subjection, became void. The guarantee or payment of the landowner for the poll tax would fall away as well. At the same time he must have enticed the *coloni* to enter an agreement to be *coloni* on the other land and be registered there. Since the constitution assumes that the *coloni* were still registered on the land, this way was evidently not feasible. *Coloni* who were released would not easily have surrendered their freedom again, particularly if there was a shortage of labour.

[104] Other possibilities: donation, agreement to divide *condominium*.

[105] Pharr 1952 translates it with 'benches', leaving open its precise meaning. Georges 1918 also mentions 'die Erhöhung des Erdreichs, die Erdbank, auf einem gepflügten Acker, die noch hervorragende

by which the acquirer would be free from former burdens: he was liable for any remaining tax liabilities. Similarly, CTh 13.3.2 (327) and CTh 13.3.3 (363) forbid any private dealings by which parties try to evade this prescription. Even if the *professio censualis* was not yet in the name of the transferee, he would be liable. Ownership is the criterion: he who reaps the revenues has to pay the tax (CTh 13.3.4 (363)).[106]

That the retention of *coloni* on their land as a guarantee that it would be properly worked was paramount we see also in another text. A military could enjoy the favour of having his family and slaves bought with his *peculium castrense* come to join him on his station, which could be anywhere in the Roman Empire, but this did not include his *coloni* (*censibus adscripti*) (CJ 12.35.10, 349). They were of course not part of his *peculium castrense*, and one wonders why he would have wanted to take them with him. Perhaps he hoped to put them at work elsewhere and collect the reimbursement.

27.1 *Moving* Coloni *in the East*

Regarding transfer of land and *coloni* for the east, only CTh 11.3.5 (391 E) is transmitted. It prescribes in case of a transfer that the new owner has to register at once his name in the *paginae censuales* and acknowledge his liability for the *capitatio*.[107] The *paginae censuales* were the tax registers of the district. *Capitatio* is the poll tax. If it means here the complete land tax, it would include *coloni* and their poll tax.[108]

Coloni might be transferred from one land to another by way of a *peraequatio* or through the *census*. In a *peraequatio* deserted land was joined to exploited rentable land with the purpose that it would be recultivated with the help of the revenues of the other land. They were fused into one entity and thus into one tax declaration,[109] because in that

ungepflügte erde', also 'in Weinbergen, der Raum zwischen zwei Gruben, in die Weinstöcke gesetzt werden', further 'die Breite der Äcker (hingegen die Länge striga)', and finally 'ein 50 bis 80 Fuß breiter Raum, abgesteckt für die Zelte der Legaten u. Tribunen im Lager'. Notwithstanding that according to Frontinus I.4–6 *strigae* and *scamna* result in parcels which in the centuriation are assigned, the fact that the word is used here *vulgo* allows for a non-technical interpretation. It therefore seems that it concerned the area between two lands left open, five or six feet, which could be nobody's property, or joint property, or property of one of the adjoining landowners; see Hyginus, *De limitibus* 129 and 148. For the way the land registration was done in ca. AD 197, see Sijpesteijn & Worp 1993.

106 Ownership in the provinces meant generally exclusive possession; see Section 2.3.5.

107 A papyrus text suggests that this was already in the Principate the usual way: P. Pher. l. 301ff., where parts of an estate are auctioned and the new owners report to the komogrammateus.

108 The *interpretatio* explains *paginae censuales* as *libri publici* and the *capitatio* as *tributum agri*. That, however, might be a later application.

109 See Enßlin 1937, 564.

way *coloni* who were registered on one land could be transferred to another land (if the *peraequatio* was done here by adjusting merely the accounts as described above in section 25.1.1, a transfer would be impossible). Or perhaps accepted in other cases in the context of recultivating the deserted land; without labour, recultivation would be impossible. The other possibility mentioned and prohibited is doing it through the census, evidently by re-registering *coloni* from one estate to another. CTh 5.6.3 (409 E) prohibits moving *Scyri coloni* to another estate by way of a *peraequatio* or the census. This would involve adjustments in the public records, and in the process one could cook the books.

27.2 *Moving* Coloni *in the West*

In CTh 11.1.26 (399 W) the final part of the text underlines that the *plebs* must remain forever on the land they have once been adscribed to (namely, *coloni* and *inquilini*), which implies that this did not always happen.[110]

Another constitution, CJ 11.48.7 (371 W), repeats the prohibition of CJ 11.48.2 of illegal reallocation of *coloni* when it addresses a trick to circumvent it. It is issued for slaves, attached through the census as *instrumentum* to a plot of land, but its rule is an analogous application of what was the rule for *coloni originales*, where, according to the constitution, the trick was done very often. An estate had a number of *coloni* attached to it. What the owner did was to sell only a very small part of the estate while transferring with it all *coloni* of the estate. Whether this small part was joined with a neighbouring plot, or whether the *coloni* were simply moved to another plot, is not clear. What is certain is that the remaining greater part of the estate was now devoid of labour. The censuses were of course adjusted, and for the fisc the result remained the same. The evident problem was that the greater part, now devoid of labour, might become uncultivated (CJ 11.48.7pr–1). CJ 11.48.7.2 (371 W) counteracted this route. In the future, in case of a division the *coloni originales* should be allotted to each part in proportion of their size. This makes sense, since it relates the apportioning to the presumed need for labour per land or estate.

The sanction for not complying with the prescription of CJ 11.48.7pr–2 is that the buyer will lose the price he paid (i.e., the seller could keep the money) while the seller may reclaim as his property the *coloni originales* together with their offspring. If the seller for some reason did not reclaim

[110] We saw before the attempts to remove *coloni originales* from their land to other lands (or perhaps to the towns, to serve as *collegiati*).

with a *vindicatio* his *coloni*,[111] his right passed over to his heirs and against the buyer or his heirs, while the limitation of prescription was lifted since the buyer was not a bona fide possessor (CJ 11.48.7.2–3, 371 W). The constitution makes clear that agricultural labour was a coveted commodity.[112]

CJ 11.48.3 (365 W) rules that if somebody has been granted fugitive slaves from deserted estates, he will be liable for the tax on these lands (*fiscales pensitationes ad integram terrae professionem*), even if he has received permission to transfer these men to his own lands. Its inclusion in CJ 11.48 implies that this applies to fugitive *coloni originales* of deserted lands as well. It is the mirror case of CTh 5.6.3 (see Section 25.1).

As to limitation of prescription, in the east Theodosius' constitution of 424 introducing a general prescription of thirty years (CTh 4.14.1, 424 E = CJ 7.39.3) replaced all former prescriptions.[113] This constitution was not copied in the west until 449 (Nov. Val. 27, already in 451 by Nov. Val. 31 refined for *coloni originales*). Thus in 438 Constantius' constitution which introduced a limitation of prescription of forty years for anything except money claims (CTh 4.11.2, 349) was still valid in the west.[114] CJ 11.48.7.3 would in any case bar the resort to a prescription of lesser duration, but it is not clear whether it sets aside CTh 4.11.2, if the invalidity of the transfer is merely based on an *initium iniustum*, which includes buying illegally (*contra legum interdicta*). But on the other hand, CJ 11.48.7.3 expressly lifts the *praescriptio longi temporis*. The conclusion should be that CTh 4.11.2 did not apply in this case, being set aside by a *lex specialis*. As a result the seller or his heirs, who remained owners and consequently responsible for the land tax and the taxes of the *coloni*, had an interest in vindicating land and *coloni*.

> CJ 11.48.13.1 (400 W): Definimus, ut inter inquilinos colonosve, quorum quantum ad originem pertinet vindicandam indiscreta eademque paene videtur esse condicio, licet sit discrimen in nomine, suscepti liberi vel utroque vel neutro parente censito statum paternae condicionis agnoscant. 1. Illud etiam servandum est, ut, si quando utriusque fundi idem dominus de possessione referta cultoribus ad eam colonos quae laborabat tenuitate transtulerit, idemque fundi ad diversorum iura dominorum qualibet sorte transierint, maneat quidem facta translatio, sed ita, ut praedii eius dominus, a quo coloni probantur fuisse transducti, translatorum agnationem restituat.

[111] He may have felt bound to the illegal agreement.

[112] Schmidt-Hofner 2008a, 280 n. 125 mentions other cases where the owner tried to move *coloni* to other land: CTh 13.10.3 and CJ 11.48.15.

[113] Kaser 1971, 285–286. [114] See Kaser 1971, 285.

> We define that children raised among *inquilini* and *coloni*, for whom, as far as claiming their origin is concerned, there seems to be an indistinct and almost identical condition, even though there may be a difference in the name, shall acknowledge the status of their paternal condition, whether either parent or neither one has been registered in the census. 1. But this also is to be observed, if ever the same owner of two estates transfers *coloni* from a possession teeming with cultivators to the one that is struggling because of a shortage, and the same farms by any sort of chance pass to the rights of different owners, the transfer that has been done shall remain in effect, but subject to this condition, that the owner of the property from which the *coloni* are proved to have been moved restore the offspring of the ones transferred.

The constitution allows for transfer of *coloni originales* from one estate to another if both have the same owner and the latter estate is short of labour.[115] This does not imply a transfer in the census, but it means that the *coloni* cannot not refuse to work on the other estate. If, however, these estates turned into different ownership (e.g., through inheritance), the transfer now became consolidated. The 'borrowed' workers did not have to return, which had to be effected in the census register. But the offspring of the transferred *coloni*, which apparently were censused in the first estate, had to be transferred in that case; that is, in line with the rules on *origo* they were to be censused in the same place as originally their father. All in all this was supporting agriculture. One can image that, as in CJ 11.48.7, others who were in need of labour but could not afford an entire second estate tried to help themselves by merely buying a small plot with more *coloni* than required for its exploitation and then using the possibility of CJ 11.48.13.

If land was confiscated, the *adscripticii* on it had to be registered in order to prevent embezzlement (CTh 9.42.7, 369 W = CJ 9.49.7.1),[116] which could have been done by transferring them to another land.

The legislation suggests that in the west in the fourth century the need for labour on the land was greater than in the east. There were more western rules on the transfer of *coloni*. Even if the supply of captive Scyri in 409 took away the need for labour, eventual rules for the east would still have been valid. But there are not many. Hence the east estate owners may have been less pressed for labour. Anyway, in both parts the basic rule was the same: *coloni* should remain on their *origo* in order to provide labour.

115 It recalls Heroninos, who deployed his workers on whichever estate was in need; see Section 61.

116 The text has *casarii vel coloni*. By *casarii* are probably meant the same people as *inquilini*; see Chapter 1, note 16 and Section 26.3.

28 *Coloni* Who Migrate and Recalling Them

As we saw, it was the first obligation of a *colonus* to be and remain on the land he was registered on or could be registered on after having been summoned. He was as if *instrumentum* to it. This is not expressly said in any text prior to 364,[117] but it is implied, or else there would have been no question of flight and recovery in CTh 5.17.1 (332) and of transfer of *coloni originales* in CJ 11.48.2 (357). Still, *coloni*, like other rustic people, did migrate and deprived their estate owners of workforce. Legislation aimed at redressing this was issued, particularly in the west, where the barbarian invasions may have provided the opportunity to migrate finally. As follows from CTh 5.17.1pr (332; see Section 23.2), a *colonus originalis* could be recalled to his *origo*, that is, his estate, if he was absent, without permission as we may assume. There is no reason why a *colonus* could not have been away if his estate owner allowed this, but such cases did not require legislation. If he resided on another estate, its owner had the obligation to return him (*restituat*). Together with the *coloni originales*, slaves and *inquilini* (i.e., *originarii*) are mentioned. All three groups, though on a different legal basis, formed labour necessary for estate exploitation and were therefore bound to their estate.

It was the estate owner who could recall his absent *coloni*, or summon them to come and register there in the census. A revindication for *coloni* would have been possible and applicable, even in its Late Antique forms of *litis denuntiatio* and *postulatio*,[118] since the claimant had merely to state that the claimed person was *in potestate eius* and on his census, or descendant of one of his *censiti*. *Potestas* was a defining element of the colonate: the constitution speaks of him as being in somebody's right in the same way as were slaves and *filii familii* (*coloni iuris alieni*). The revindication was possible since this action was applicable for the recall of sons *in potestate* (D. 6.1.1.2).[119] CJ 11.48.7.2 (371 W, see below) indeed refers to the vindication. Such a recall will eventually have been executed by force by the governor (*manu militari*). In order to prevent flight, estate owners were authorised to chain *coloni originales* who planned to subtract themselves from their obligations, namely by absconding (CTh 5.17.1.1). The western tradition provides more details; see below.

117 It is in CJ 11.48.13 pr (400 W). 118 Kaser/Hackl 1996, 566–567.

119 Nov. Val. 31.2, INov. Val. 35. Yet this does not mean they were slaves. In D. 6.1.1.2 *filii* are vindicated as well, be it with the addition *filium suum* or *in potestate ex iure Quiritium*. This adaptation will also have been used for the *coloni originales*.

Was the vindication of *coloni* subjected to limitation of prescription? Regarding *res mancipi* and *nec mancipi*, the limitation equalled the period necessary for *usucapio*. Regarding provincial land, of which in the fifth century still only possession was possible (the Roman people or the emperor being formally owner), any recovery was limited to periods of ten or twenty, and later thirty or forty years, depending on the circumstances.[120] If a thing had been stolen, it could always be recovered. A fugitive slave was considered to have stolen himself,[121] and so with him there could be no limitation. But for *coloni originales* there are no constitutions on this matter transmitted for the entire Empire. Perhaps it was in the missing parts of Book 5. As we shall see for east and west, in any case in the fifth century a limitation of thirty years applied in both parts by way of parallel legislation.

28.1 *Flight in the East*

The wish to flee may arise autonomously with a *colonus*, but the other side of flight is that of another estate owner encouraging, receiving, hosting, and sometimes hiding a *colonus*. CTh 4.14.1 (424 E = CJ 7.39.3) contains a general prescription of thirty years, extinctive and acquisitive. This should have covered claims for *coloni originales*, but we shall see that it apparently did not cause such problems as were already manifest in the west by the early fifth century.

28.2 *Flight in the West*

CJ 11.48.6 (366 W) says that all *coloni originales* and *inquilini* (likewise bound) of either sex and regardless of their *munus* and *condicio* must be returned by the provincial governors to their *origines*, where they were born, raised and censused. It is open whether the governors have to investigate this themselves or whether it implies their duty to execute claims of owners after examination of these. *Exactores* were tempted to hold *coloni originales* liable when pursuing fiscal debts, a practice forbidden in CJ 11.48.15 (414 W). Apparently the *exactores* tried to seize *coloni*, probably to pressure their estate owners to pay the taxes by taking away their workforce. This constitution underlines that they may not be moved from the land they are to remain on. This and CJ 11.48.6 testify in any case to the imperial policy of supporting agriculture by ensuring the presence of

[120] Kaser 1975, 429–425;,1971, 71–72. [121] Kaser 1975, 618 n. 48, referring to CJ 6.1.1 (Diocl.).

colonate workforce. Absconding was for all these reasons illicit or undesirable and in any case combated.

CJ 11.48.12pr (385 W)[122] stresses that slaves, *tributarii* (i.e., *coloni*) and *inquilini* have to stay with their masters. Whoever harbours such fugitives is fined with twelve pounds of silver and must surrender on top of this another person of the same value to the master. The burden of proof is on the hosting part: only *ingenui*, that is, persons unburdened with a *condicio*, whom he knows he may accept (as *coloni*, or also as labourers or lessees?). In this way the emperors hope to deter estate owners from harbouring and to take away from *coloni* the hope that they can find a place elsewhere. The 'same value' (*eiusdem aestimationis*) may refer to the value of the fugitive *colonus* as if a slave, or to his expected productivity in connection with his bond.

A particular case of forcing a return, from which it once again appears that *originarius* connotates a bond with an *origo* as legal domicile, is CTh 8.4.22 (412 W) where *cohortales*, that is, military administrators on a provincial level, who have arisen above their status by a *maioris splendioris officium*, after their dismissal lose their privileges and are to return to their *status* and *originarium sol.* The connection with status and *originarium sol* proves that it concerned people whose low status was connected with a census registration and subjectedness. It may have concerned *coloni*,

[122] In the Lex Romana Burgundionum 6.2, a constitution from the Theodosian Code addressed to Florentius is mentioned, which Mommsen placed in his edition as CTh 5.17.3. Yet that is not so obvious. The constitution cited in LRB 6.2 has Florentius *comes sacrarum largitionum*, whereas CJ 11.48.12 is directed at Florentius. Seeck dates CJ 11.48.12 at 18 April 396, attributing it to Florentinus, PU and combining it with CTh 8.21.3, which deals with decurions and their bond. But CJ 11.48.12 deals with fugitive *coloni*, which was not the competence of the Urban Prefect. Contrariwise, the content of LRB 6.2 fits that of CJ 11.48.12 and the addressees have the same name. The placing in the CJ puts the date at between 386 and 400. A Florentius *comes sacrarum largitionum* is known for 364 and 365, which is too early. It is possible that the name, written as Florent. in the copies used, was interpreted as Florentius in Justinian's Code and in the Vatican Theodosian Code, since for Florentinus, *comes sacrarum largitionum* in 385, in the Theodosian Code variants of the name occur (Florianum and Florentium) and in the LRB too (Florento). On this basis I would attribute CJ 11.48.12 to Florentinus *comes sacrarum largitionum* and date the constitution at 385, also because the other constitutions (CTh 1.10.3, 11.30.46 and 11.36.30) deal with fiscal appeals and CJ 11.48.12 with the reclaiming of fugitives. Moreover, is the reference for the entire content of LRB 6.2 or only for the imposition of the fine? Seeck attributes this constitution to the Urban Prefect of Constantinople Florentinus and dates at 396, but the content fits that of the constitutions addressed in 385 to the *comes sacrarum largitionum Florentius*, namely CTh 1.10.3, 11.30.46, 11.36.30 and also the supposed constitution CTh 5.17.3, which is cited in LRB 6.2. The *editio maior* mentions for the *inscriptio* of CJ 11.48.12 as readings: florentio ual *U* [= Berolinensis 274, saec. XII], flo. co (= comiti?) *Bononiensis*, florentino *Paris.* 4429. The Bononiensis pleads for the combination as suggested, and why Seeck restricted himself to the *Parisiensis* is understandable (an older ms.), but older manuscripts may contain errors too.

inquilini or *collegiati* who had absconded and were hiding in the imperial administration as if free to join it.

CTh 10.12.2 (368? 370? 373? W) deals with the case that a fugitive slave is reclaimed with the procedural question, which official must be addressed and under which conditions. It also mentions *coloni*. Section 2 states that when after a denunciation a *tributarius*, that is, a *colonus originalis* (as appears from the sequence), is found or an *inquilinus* is discovered, they have to return at once to the person they declare themselves to belong to. Nevertheless, so continues section 3, the investigation must continue to see whether the denunciator denounced in order to conceal that he was hiding *coloni* in the same way. If so, he will repair the loss in taxes (*tributa*) which were not paid by the estate owner or the *coloni* during their absence (and of course the *coloni* have to return). The language is contorted, but the sense is clear.

CTh 4.23.1 (400 W = CJ 11.48.14) deals with the recovery of fugitive *coloni originales*:

> Post alia. Si coloni, quos bona fide quisque possedit, ad alios fugae vitio transeuntes necessitatem condicionis propriae declinare temptaverint, bonae fidei possessori prima oportet et celeri reformatione succurri, tunc causam originis et proprietatis agitari, non expectatis temporibus nec denuntiatione sollemni, quae locum in his negotiis non habebunt.

> (After other matters.) If *coloni* whom any person possesses in good faith should pass to another person by wrongful flight and should attempt to escape the necessity of their *condicio*, the bona fide possessor shall first be granted assistance by a swift restoration, and then the case of *condicio* and exclusive right (to the fugitive) shall be tried, without awaiting the statutory time limitations or the formal notification of suit, for these formalities have no place in suits of this kind.

The text is placed under the rubric *Utrubi*, that is, the prohibitory interdict *utrubi*: *utrubi vestrum hic homo quo de agitur apud quem maiore parte huius anni nec vi nec clam nec precario ab altero fuit quo minus is eum ducat vim fieri veto.*[123] Such interdicts prohibited the use of private force, for example when claiming something. The magistrate addressed with it both parties. The interdict restored possession to the previous possessor, after which a lawsuit could start about who could rightfully claim the object of recovery. In this case this would involve two questions: first that of the *condicio*, that is, whether the fugitive was indeed a *colonus originalis*, which is circumscribed here as the *causa originis*; and second, the result of

[123] See Kaser 1975, 398, 1971, 259.

this, namely who was entitled to him as estate owner, here circumscribed as *proprietas*. The text speaks of possessing *coloni*, but since *coloni* could not be possessed like slaves or things, this must be interpreted metaphorically. *Proprietas* means the entitlement to the *colonus*, namely to his presence and labour, which was reserved for the owner of the land. *Proprietas* may be best read as 'exclusive entitlement/right' and not as ownership as if of a moveable. An extract from the census might do as proof. In the fifth century the sharp procedural distinction between actions and interdicts had faded, the interdicts being called *actio momenti* or *momentaria* (as in the Interpretation to CTh 4.23.1), but their character of 'fast law' with a temporary character had remained.[124] We may assume that the formulation will not have differed substantially from the classic formula. Since this referred to a slave as *homo*, it would have been possible to claim here a *colonus originalis* as well. Although the interdict *utrubi* was formulated for slaves, animals and moveables, they, like real petitionary actions, could be used in adapted form to reclaim persons *in potestate*.[125]

This interdict must be applied for within a year, and this term seems to have been retained; see the references in CTh 4.23.1 to a quick help (*celeri reformatione succurri*). After that the claim for the fugitive is to be dealt with in a normal procedure (namely, a *rei vindicatio*, CJ 11.48.7.2, 371 W: *vindicatione concessa*; see Section 27.2). Possession was important, since it forced the other party to prove its right, while the possessor could wait till this was done and then begin with his rebuttal. If the claimant did not succeed in his proof, the defendant could continue possessing. If the former possessor was too late in asking for the interdict, he had to establish first that the 'new' possessor did indeed have the fugitive (necessary to summon him as defendant). If the possessing estate owner, when asked to produce the fugitive in court, refused to do this, an *actio ad exhibendum* to force him to do so was possible, as also a letter by Sulpicius Severus shows.[126] After that, litigation could start.

If a *colonus* was reclaimed, he had to take his children and all his belongings with him. This must have been included in the claim. It is not stated explicitly, but it follows from the prescription to return his offspring with all his belongings (*peculium* and *mercedes*, thus his savings and earned wages) if he had died in the meantime (CTh 5.18.1.2, 419 W). What was to be returned after his death would certainly have to be returned

124 See Kaser & Hackl 1996, 637–638.

125 Kaser & Hackl 1996, 418–420; see nn. 229 and 482 for the adaptation.

126 Kaser & Hackl 1996, 275–276; applicable with *coloni originales*; see Sirks 1982, 148 for the letter of Sulpicius Severus where *coloni* are claimed with the *actio exhibendi*.

in his lifetime. But the situation could be more complicated. The payment of outstanding taxes has already been discussed (see Section 27.2). If it appeared that fugitives still had debts, these had to be settled before they were returned (CJ 11.48.8.2, 371 W). This must refer to cases in which fugitives had borrowed from the estate owner or had acquired food or goods on credit.[127]

Privileges which otherwise would shield against a recall (such as likely in CTh 8.4.22, Section 28.2) were to be disregarded when a return was ordered, so CJ 11.48.11 (396 W). This text refers to privileges and *dignitates*, high functions which provided an immunity or excuse against *munera* and which might be acquired through bribes or influence (*gratia*).[128] Probably the excuse was based on the exemption *rei publicae causa abesse*, which relieved from public duties as long as one was away on public business (originally: on an embassy for one's home town). It would suggest that the colonate itself had public aspects. The text also mentions the *auctoritas census* as a possible defence.[129] Since it figures in the same category as the *dignitates* and *gratia*, it seems its refers to a fraudulent striking of the *adscriptio* in the census, achieved by means of a bribe. As to the functions and *dignitates* which shielded, CJ 11.48.18 (426 W) mentions two kinds, the imperial *militia* and the *apparitores* of the *magistri militum*. The constitution forbade the *coloni originales* to have any function whatever here, even the lowest in the *militia*, in order to protect the rights of their masters and the standing (*publica honestas*) of these functions. The latter would have been diminished by the 'servile condition', as with the *tabularii*. Also CJ 12.33.3 (395–402) prohibits the acceptance or forcible enlisting of *coloni originales* into the armed *milita*. The prohibition would have made any eventual enlistment void, thereby making a recall easy. But on the other hand, if a *censibus insertus* is offered as recruit (landowners had to make recruits available) and accepted, he will be excused from the poll tax and after five years of service his wife as well (CTh 7.13.6, 370 E). The same and with more excusations is said in CTh 7.13.7.3 (375 E). The constitutions may have meant people other than *coloni* who were also registered for the poll tax, but they do not expressly exclude *coloni*, unless the later version of CTh 7.13.6, CJ 12.43.1, gives a correct interpretation, namely that *coloni* and other *condicionales*

[127] See Rathbone 1991, 318ff. for the credit and debit system on large estates.

[128] See, for example, MacMullen 1988 in general on corruption.

[129] It of course cannot concern the census registration for the land *coloni originales* had in their own property, since they would have been registered in their own name in the census of the territory where their land lay (CTh 11.1.14.1).

were not envisaged.[130] Other shielding functions, or dignities like that of clerics in the east, are not known for the west in the state of the law for the year 438.[131]

28.3 Problems with Reclaiming Coloni*: Death, Marriage, Offspring*

Several problems presented themselves when recalling *coloni*: How long could one still recall them? What if they had died? What if they had married? What about their children? In the east no constitutions on these questions are transmitted, but in the west there are several extensive ones. The legislation on recall generated, as happens, new legislation. Evidently these were problems which needed addressing. Since claiming *coloni* included their children, born eventually during their absence, claiming these depended on the *condicio* these children had. This aspect is dealt with below, but also in Section 26.2.

If a fugitive *colonus* or *inquilinus* of a private person had gone to a town and served there as decurion, as *collegiatus*, in a border fortress or any *corpus*, the prescription of limitation period was thirty years within the same province, forty years for another province; and they could not be reclaimed, but they remained bound where they were (CTh 12.19.2, 400 W = CJ 11.66.6). CTh 12.19.3 (400 W) confirms this. A limitation of prescription of thirty years applied to the vindication (*de cuius proprietate certatur*) of *coloni originales* and *inquilini* (CTh 5.18.1, 419 W), evidently from another estate.[132] If the *colonus* had already died, his children together with all his *peculium* and earnings (*mercedes*) had to be returned at once, *iuri agrorum*. It is not clear whether these limitations existed already or were established in these constitutions; they were in any case a rule in 438.

For a woman who was subjected to the colonate, a *colona originaria*, the period of prescription is set at twenty years (CTh 5.18.1.3, 419 W).[133] If she had been reclaimed within this period and there was no doubt about her status (*condicio*), the claim was accepted but with a modification. If she had meanwhile married a *colonus originalis* of the estate she resided on, she was not taken away from her husband: a replacement woman was to be surrendered (if it was also a *colona*, evidently an unmarried one, her census

[130] Jones 1964, 455 assumes it concerned *coloni* only. [131] Cf. CJ 1.3.36.pr, 2 (484).

[132] The text has been abbreviated. The reclaiming is a right and, as with other rights, the question must have been posed in the preceding, now missing text, whether in this case a prescription of thirty years could apply, since there is mention of *hos triginta annos*.

[133] Such a period was known as limitation for the revindication of immoveables (*longi temporis praescriptio*, e.g., CJ 7.33.1, Sev. & Ant.). Perhaps it served as an example here.

registration had to be changed; otherwise it was a slave woman). Further, only one-third of her offspring which she had with her husband were to be surrendered to her now former estate owner. In the case of sons, replacements were to be given for them as well. It means that if in the remaining two-thirds there were still sons, replacements were to be given: the work on the land evidently required male force. In this way the estate owner would not lose, that is, would not lose useful labour force. It goes without saying that the woman was now census-registered in his estate, if she had not already been. Because both statuses were equal, theoretically the *condicio* of the father should have prevailed as regards the children but the mother should have been returned. The solution is clearly a compromise, probably inspired by the wish not to split the family too much. We do not know whether this division took place only after the children to be rendered were adults.[134]

If a *colona* or *inquilina originalis* had married somebody from a town, a so-called *collegiatus* who was subjected to presumably sordid municipal services, who had fled his obligations and was recalled within the prescription period set for these (forty years), her husband had to return and the

[134] CTh 5.18.1 is rather detailed. In section 3 the constitution establishes the period of prescription for *colonae* at twenty years. If they are reclaimed within it and there is no doubt about their status (*condicio*), the claim is retained but with this modification: that a replacement women is surrendered together with one-third of the offspring which she might have with the *colonus* of another; for sons, replacement could be given too. The underlying motive may have been that her husband, who was somebody else's *colonus*, had to stay: recall would have implied the separation of the spouses, which would have been unacceptable. With children the situation was different. If, according to section 4, the *colona* had married a man not subjected to the colonate or the like, and she was reclaimed within the said period, all of her offspring had to be surrendered, but she herself did not have to return. Again the bond of the colonate extends to the offspring. But also if a *colonus* or *colona* was not reclaimed within the time set for their respective prescription, their children could not be claimed either and they were no longer subjected. Since the time limit will, in general, not yet have run out for them, their immunity must have derived from their father's or mother's immunity. Conversely, their subjection must have lain herein as well. This leaves us with their descent as explanation. Since their parents were bound to the colonate with respect to a particular piece of land on the basis of the census and *origo*, it is reasonable to assume that it was the *origo*, which they shared with their father as regards public duties in general, which was the connecting element. If their father had married a woman not subjected to the colonate, or subjected to the same estate owner, there would be no problem regarding their *origo*. If he had married a woman subjected to the colonate with another estate owner, or if a woman married somebody not subjected to this, a problem would arise. In the latter case children would share their father's *origo* and not be subjected. In the first case the claim of the woman's estate owner would, theoretically, cede as well. This is confirmed by CTh 5.18.1.3, which implies that normally her estate owner would have no claim at all: not for the woman, since she was married and had to remain with her husband, and not for the children, since they had the *origo* of their father. Hence the solution of a replacement and of dividing the offspring. We do not know whether she thereby became her husband's estate owner's *colona*. In the latter case the woman cannot be claimed either, but since the husband is a free man there is no estate owner who can give a replacement. But neither is there somebody who may have an interest in the children as labour force, and therefore the entire offspring have to be turned over.

offspring was divided between the town and the estate owner of the woman (CTh 12.19.1, 400 W). With the division is meant that they could be summoned when necessary to acknowledge their public obligation. Thus an exception was made expressly where public interest was involved, as CTh 12.19.2 (400 W = CJ 11.66.6) says.

If a *colona originalis* had married a man not subjected to the colonate or to another *condicio* (like a *collegiatus*), that is, an *ingenuus*, and she was reclaimed within the said period, she did not have to return. Apparently there the wish not to separate spouses prevailed again. But all of her offspring had to be surrendered. Normally the *condicio* of the (free) father would prevail. It implies that the union was considered *non aequale*, the woman being subjected to a servile *condicio* and the man not; it was thereby as if there was no marriage and therefore the children followed their mother's *condicio* and *origo* (CTh 5.18.1.4, 419 W = CJ 11.48.16). In this way the bond of the colonate passed over to the offspring. Since her husband was not subjected, there was no need to require replacements (all children should be turned over),[135] nor is the question relevant whether she would thereby become *colona* of her husband's estate owner.

On the other hand, if a *colonus* or *colona* was not reclaimed within the time set for their respective prescription, neither he nor she nor their children could be claimed and were no longer subjected. Since the time limit will, in general, not yet have run out for them (since they were born after the absconding), their immunity must have derived from their father's or mother's immunity as a result of the procedural rules. About their *origo* nothing is said. In theory this would remain the village or town they had been in, the only change being that the registration as *colonus* in their estate's or village census would be struck. If they had turned to another estate owner, they could now be registered there, with their children.

This consideration for retaining families intact as much as possible finds its parallel in CTh 2.25.1 (325 = CJ 3.38.11) on division of imperial patrimonial estates (in Sardinia) with slaves attached to them. That is in itself remarkable, given that slaves were assets. Here it concerned free people who could legitimately marry.

A *colonus*' children had to return as well, since they were subjected to their father's *condicio*. The fiction in the case of the dead *colonus* was that he

[135] Perhaps this was done by giving them straightaway, even as babies, but it seems more likely that the claiming estate owner waited till the children were capable of farm work and then required their labour force.

was still alive (*velut eo superstite qui decessit*), in which case he would have had to take his children with him anyway (CTh 5.18.1.2). Normally children would fall under their father's *potestas* and thus had to follow him. After his death they could be vindicated individually, being now *sui iuris*. The rule would theoretically have been unnecessary, but then a guardian should have taken care of the orphans as long as they were under age (*pupilli*). Doing it with this fiction was easier.

For flight of *coloni* of the *res privata* (CJ 11.68.3, 364 W; CJ 7.38.1, 365 W), see Section 32.1.2. For flight of *coloni* or *inquilini* of the *res dominica* (CTh 12.19.2, 400 W), see Section 32.2.2.

The differences in legislation as included in the Code between east and west are striking. In the east we find only one constitution on the limitation of prescription and a fine for harbouring fugitive *coloni* (CTh 4.14.1 (424 E = CJ 7.39.3). In the west several constitutions on fugitive *coloni* and *inquilini* were issued and retained, with an elaborate regulation of the problems marriages between *coloni*, *collegiati*, other *condicionales* and *ingenui* could create. The limitation of prescription is mentioned as a matter of fact. The duty to stay on the estate is expressed. The procedure to reclaim *coloni* is regulated in detail, while privileges which might block the procedure are cancelled. The cause of the differences in number and regulation are undoubtedly the tribulations of the west from the late third century onwards, with the incursions of the Huns and Goths, culminating in the capture and plundering of Rome in 410.[136] The disorders in those years created the conditions for *coloni* and others to escape their bond and try an existence elsewhere, either again as *coloni* but with better conditions, or as independent farmers, or in another profession. Or they simply made it necessary for people to flee the wars and seek elsewhere a better life. On the other hand, landowners will have wanted to restore their income source, namely their estate revenues, and for that the labour which could be forced to work came in the first place in consideration: the *coloni*. There must have been considerable manhunting going on, resulting in various legal questions which the emperor had to solve by legislation. That this legislation was retained in 438 shows that those questions still required attention in 438. Perhaps some of it was, on the other hand, already outdated. To know that, one must reconstruct potential problems in connection with those incursions and see whether legislation might have existed.

[136] See Meier 2019, 205–214, 302–306.

29 Public and Procedural Aspects of the Colonate

If on an estate counterfeiting was committed while its owner was excusably unaware of this (being far away), his representative (*actor fundi*) and the slaves, residents (*incolae*) or *coloni* who had provided assistance are punishable with death (CTh 9.21.2, 318 = CJ 9.24.1.5). The context with persons unfree or in a position of dependency makes it probable that this *colonus* was not a private law lessee-farmer but a *colonus originalis*.

29.1 In the East

The status of a *colonus originalis* was low. A *colonus* is threatened, as is the *actor* (the estate owner's representative), with capital punishment if he hides a deserter without the knowledge of the estate owner (CTh 7.18.8, 383 E). In CTh 13.11.3 (386 E = CJ 11.58.3) the estate owner who arms his *coloni* to ward off *peraequatores* (the inspectors for the redistribution of taxes and land) is punished. Their status did not allow them to be recruited for the army at all as *tirones* or for the function of *apparitor* in the office of the *magister militum* (CTh 7.13.6, 370 E = CJ 12.43.1). In the first case also the wish for sufficient labour supply on the fields may have played a role.

The prohibition for *coloni* to sue their estate owners (CJ 11.50.2, 396 E) is similar to the prohibition for *filii* and freedmen to sue their *pater* or *patronus*. So *coloni* were in a similar position to these: free, but in a state of submission or dependence regarding their estate owner. The parallel to *filii familias* is close and would explain the said restrictions. The eastern texts do not give more clues. CJ 11.50.2 pr describes the *adscripticii* as being obliged (*obnoxii*) because of the yearly taxes and the obligations of their *condicio*, which make them subjected as dependents. This again made their faculty to sue their estate owners very limited: such a thing is unbearable where their masters have the power to alienate them together with the estate they are on (CJ 11.50.2.1, 396 E). Like other persons, *coloni* could raise an accusation of venality against any governor at whose hands they had suffered extortion, or whose judgment had been venal, for example (CTh 9.27.6, 386 E = CJ 9.27.4).

29.2 In the West

No special rules are found for this part of the Empire for *coloni*. This does not have to mean that there were none, merely that there was apparently no occasion to issue or retain anything; or some regulation was amongst the lost texts; or there were no such lands in the west.

30 *Coloni Originales* on State and Imperial Lands

These lands were divided into several categories: patrimonial lands (*fundi patrimoniales*), emphyteuticarian land (*fundi emphyteuticarii*), lands of the *res privata* (*fundi rei privatae*), and lands of the Imperial House (*fundi divinae domus* or *domus augusta*).[137] The precise differences between these cannot be the subject of investigation here, but from Justinian's Code it appears that in any case under this emperor the patrimonial and emphyteuticarian lands were treated together in one category and the lands of the *res privata* and Imperial House together in another category. For the Theodosian Code the situation is less clear due to the lacuneous transmission of Book Five where regulations on these lands may have been arranged. In the Code as directly transmitted there are but four constitutions referring to *coloni* from imperial lands, but in view of those included in Justinian's Code there must have been more constitutions. They will have figured particularly in Book Five, but since these lands were of little or no interest to Alaric's compilers (the emperor having disappeared and the imperial lands presumably being now the king's lands, fiscal lands, occupied or distributed land), few were included (see Section 45). Yet there is no immediate reason to assume that the above division was not already present in 438 or before. Hence to those Theodosian constitutions which were placed by the Justinian compilers in a title dealing with *coloni* on imperial estates, and assuming that if in 529–534 scholars saw it that way it likely will have been the same in 438, I have applied the same division. The same applies for the *coloni originales* on these lands and consequently I shall keep this division into three categories. The difference is that the first two categories were granted to private persons under various conditions, not to be discussed here, whereas the last two categories remained with the emperor or his family. There were *coloni* on these lands who were tied to these as to an *origo*, which justifies the qualification of *originarii*. This is terminologically confirmed by CJ 11.68.1 (of 325: *colonus originalis*). Although many texts derive from Justinian's Code, the few additional texts from the Theodosian Code mean that these sections cannot be called duplicate expositions. Of course we cannot exclude the possibility that the Justinianic versions have undergone textual changes, but for the reconstruction of the situation in 438 we have to do with

[137] I leave out here the *saltuenses*, the imperial lands used as pasture, since these did not require cultivation and thus no *coloni*.

them. Further, for taxation, these lands formed administratively part of the city territories; see Section 15.1, where this is argued for the fourth to sixth centuries.

The *coloni* of the patrimonial and emphyteuticarian land enjoyed the *forum privilegiatum* of the *rationalis summae rei.* Other courts were not allowed to take on cases by or against them (CJ 3.26.7, 349 E – probably applying also to the west in view of CJ 3.26.8). For *coloni originales* of the *res privata* there was an exception: if they had offended public order (*disciplina publica*), they were to be tried before the provincial governor but the *rationalis* or procurator of the Imperial House had to be present as well. If the crime was proven, justice had to be done severely (CJ 3.26.8, 358).

It follows from CJ 11.48.6 (366 W), which orders the return of all *coloni originales* and *inquilini* of either sex and *condicio*, that this rule also applied to *coloni originales* of imperial estates. In one aspect these different categories will not have differed from the common *coloni*: the bond to the *origo*, which was by census established on a piece of land.

31 *Coloni* on Patrimonial Land (*Fundi Patrimoniales*) and Emphyteuticarian Land (*Fundi Emphyteuticarii*)

A constitution of the early fourth century, CJ 11.63.1pr of 319, hence applicable to the entire Empire, deals with emphyteuticarian land. Whether emphyteuticarian lands were subjected to a duty of improving uncultivated land, or to a permanent cultivation duty, I have to leave aside here.[138] However, it seems that at least cultivation or recultivation of unused land is policy here, because *coloni* on these lands may keep parts which they had put into cultivation with olive trees or as vineyard (CJ 11.63.1pr, 319). In addition, they are, where there is irrigation, entitled to as much water as they need for the plots they already cultivate (having been assigned to by the *emphyteuticarii*, the possessors of these lands). For those usurped lands they may keep, they have to ask for admission to the irrigation system and to pay for what they need from this (CJ 11.63.1.1–2). It may have concerned farmers in general, who may have leased from *conductores* or *emphyteuticarii*; no connection with the colonate is establishable. But the fact that it was inserted into CJ 11.63 by Justinian's compilers is an argument for assuming that in any case by that time one saw it as also applicable to *coloni originales*.

[138] See also Grey 2007b, 371, who mentions the possibility that the emphyteutic leaseholders may often have been wealthy and powerful landowners themselves.

We cannot exclude that this was also the case when it was issued, or in 438.

31.1 *In the East*

Patrimonial lands were a special category of imperial land, but that did not exempt them from the problem of migrating *coloni* and the need to recall them. The need for recultivation (*emphyteusis*) may have exacerbated this.

Apart from CJ 11.63.1 of 319 all constitutions regarding these lands were issued for the east. Perhaps these categories of land existed only in the east, and then CJ 11.63.1 may have been restricted to the east too.[139] In regard to the recultivation of these lands, it had already been settled that those who once tilled them and had migrated or fled could be recalled, regardless of where they were or of their being taken into the *militia*, to the *condicio* and its particular law (*propria iura*) which had been those of their forebears. Those who had already become *emeriti* of the *militia* were, however, excused (CJ 11.63.4pr–1, 384–389 E). It concerned thus *coloni originales patrimoniales* who were bound to their *origo* on *fundi patrimoniales*. There is no indication of whether the registration was in a village, in a *massa* of patrimonial lands in general, or to a particular parcel.[140] CJ 11.63.4 suggests, by its reference to *fundi* which were once cultivated by the migrated *coloni* and now need recultivation by their descendants, that the latter was the case. CJ 11.64.1 (386 E) repeats the authority to recall children and grandchildren of *coloni* of patrimonial lands, now not as a resource of labour within the context of improvement of land, but within the context of flight (thus: also from cultivated land). Flight into the *militia* is of no avail: they have to return to work the land (*agrorum cultus*). The persons to pursue and enforce this are *duces*, *tribuni* and *praepositi*.

CJ 11.64.3 (408–415 E) says the same:

> Cuiuscumque adnotationis vel oraculi dudum impetrati vel postea eliciendi auctoritate submota omnes, quos patrimonialium agrorum vinculis fortuna tenet adstrictos, sub quibuslibet gradibus militantes ad provinciae moderatoris iudicium ilico sub idonea intercessione mittentur.

> While removing the authority of whatever annotation or imperial grant once obtained or hereafter to be elicited, all those who fate holds tied to the bonds of the patrimonial lands, under whatever grade they are employed in

[139] Jones 1964, 713 mentions them for the east. However, what about Africa, where in the second century the emperors possessed so much land?

[140] See Chapter 1, note 226 about the taxation. The poll tax will have been levied anyway.

> the imperial administration, must be sent at once with suitable force to the office of the provincial governor.

The constitutions reminds us that service in the *militia* did not exempt from the *condicio*, even if bolstered before or afterwards by an imperial *adnotatio* or rescript (which could be obtained fraudulently).

But the other side of the colonate was not forgotten. CJ 11.63.3 warns:

> Cognovimus a nonnullis, qui patrimoniales fundos meruerunt, colonos antiquissimos proturbari atque in eorum locum vel servos proprios vel alios colonos subrogari. Edicti itaque huius auctoritate sancimus eos, qui deinceps huiusmodi aliquid crediderint attemptandum, isdem possessionibus esse privandos.

> We have learned that some people, who earned patrimonial estates, disturb the *coloni* settled there of old and put their own slaves or other *coloni* in their place. For that reason we order by the authority of this edict that henceforth those who have thought to attempt something of this kind will be deprived of the same properties.

It appears, not only here (cf. CJ 11.48.1 and 5), that *coloni* both were to stay on their estate and had a right to stay there. That will have been particularly important if they cultivated a farm and lived on the proceeds. What the constitutions describes is a change in cultivation by owners who can afford it: substitution by their own slaves or *coloni*. If the exploitation of the patrimonial lands was done by métayage, the gain may have lain in the savings on what slaves cost, or a lower portion for their own *coloni*. The text also shows that for the agricultural exploitation landowners disposed of various labour options.

In the east, to the general rule of CTh 5.17.1 (see Section 28) was added a fine for the harbouring person, whether he took the *colonus iuris alieni* on or hid him. To discourage exhortations to abscond or assistance with flight, fines were established: six ounces of gold in the case of a *colonus originalis* of a private person, one pound of gold in the case of a *colonus originalis* of the imperial patrimonial lands (CTh 5.17.2, 386 E = CJ 11.64.2). The same fine applied if a harbourer did not exhibit the fugitives when requested by the governor. This may have concerned a *fundus patrimonialis* in the possession of a private person (as the result of an imperial grant) or in the possession of the emperor, and the host a private estate owner.

On the other hand, *coloni originales* of patrimonial lands have a right to stay there and cannot be removed by private possessors to whom these lands have been granted nor be replaced by their slaves or own *coloni*. These will have been slaves, *coloni* from another land or even lessees.[141] If this happens, the grant is voided (CJ 11.63.3, 383? E). The land will thereby revert to the emperor and he can readmit the *coloni*. What could the reason for such replacement have been? Perhaps the fact that these *coloni* enjoyed privileges like the *forum privilegiatum*, which protected them against the possessors?

Further, the *coloni originales* of patrimonial lands enjoy the privilege that they cannot not be burdened with guardianships (*tutela*; CJ 5.34.13, 409 E).

31.2 In the West

No special rules are found for this part of the Empire. This does not have to mean that there were none, merely that there was apparently no occasion to issue or retain anything; or some regulation was amongst the lost texts; or there were indeed no such lands in the west.[142]

32 *Coloni* on Land of the *Res Privata (Fundi Rei Privatae)* and of the Imperial House (*Fundi Divinae Domus* or *Domus Augusta*)

32.1 The Res Privata

As with the patrimonial and emphyteuricarian lands, the lands of the *res privata* were part of the city territories, perhaps only in the east.[143] If *coloni rei privatae* are needed and not yet subjected to a *condicio* (*privati*) or able to manage or to till the fields, they should be recalled, as should their children, and in the future they should not work or manage for somebody else (CJ 11.68.2, 319). CJ 11.68.1 (325) forbids summoning a *colonus originalis rei privatae* for the decurionate or municipal *munera*. We see that *coloni* did not always work as farm hands or till their own plot of land, but could also function as manager (*actor*, *procurator*) or overseer.[144] Regarding lawsuits involving people of the *res privata* (*actores ceterosque rei privatae*), the provincial governors were competent as judges (CTh 2.1.1, 349).

[141] The mss. have *alios* and *alienos*, but important here is that the *coloni* were not attached to this land.
[142] See Jones 1964, 713: only eastern possessions. [143] Jones 1964, 205–206.
[144] The question should be posed whether these two constitutions might not have been intended originally to plain lessees and later interpolated with, for example, in CJ 11.68.1 with the mere insertion of *originalis*. Yet that is not likely. The phrasing of CJ 11.68.2 from which the bond to the soil follows is too intricate to have been interpolated, while CTh 12.1.33 proves that in 342 the prohibition of CJ 11.68.1 enjoyed popularity as a means to escape the decurionate. In short, in 319 or 325 the colonate existed already firmly on lands of the *res privata*.

32.1.1 *In the East*

CTh 12.1.33 (342 E) deals with the escape from the decurionate: there are curials who try to do this by availing themselves of the privileges of the *coloni* of the *res privata*, namely that these cannot be summoned for the decurionate.

Neither the *conductores* nor the *coloni* of the *res privata* should be required to perform *munera sordida*, the 'dirty' public obligations, nor extraordinary *munera*, nor contribute to the superindictions (CTh 11.16.5, 343 E = CJ 11.75.1). If one interprets *colonus* as lessee, one must translate, as Pharr does, *conductores* with 'chief lessees'.[145] Yet in view of CJ 11.68.1 and 2 there is no reason to do so; the *coloni rei privatae* are privileged and here we see another privilege, that of being free from *munera sordida*.

Above (Section 24.1.2) was already mentioned CTh 5.16.34 (425 E = CJ 11.68.6) dealing with the sale of land of the *res privata* to *coloni*. They had to find co-buyers.[146]

32.1.2 *In the West*

The privileges of the *coloni rei privatae* were evidently restricted to immunity from municipal duties, unless this was changed later in the west. Wherever they are, they can be recalled and no excuse is of avail; if they are found in the *militia* and even in the palace guard (*protectores*), their immunity does not help (CJ 11.68.3, 364 W). Also, no limitation of prescription is valid in this matter regarding *coloni originales rei privatae*, and thus all descendants could always be recalled (CJ 7.38.1, 365 W).[147]

Coloni of senators, as well as their farmers (*rusticani*), should not be assessed for the *collatio lustralis*, the tax on merchants, if they merely traded their own products on their farms (CTh 11.1.33, 361). CTh 13.1.10 (374 W) grants the immunity of the *collatio lustralis*, already given by CTh 13.1.8 (370 W) to the *coloni dominici*, to the *coloni rei privatae* and extends this to other farmers (*rusticani*). Apparently they, like the *coloni dominici*, drew income out of trading with the surplus revenues of their land. It would make the payments to the fisc more secure.

As to the taxes due (*iugatio* and *capitatio*), the provincial governors should not raise litigation against the *coloni*, that is, of the *res privata*, about payment of taxes and so oppress them (CTh 11.7.11, 424 W). Another constitution (CJ 11.68.4, 367 W) states that children of unions between not subjected men (*ingenui*) and *colonae originariae* of lands of the *res privata*

[145] Pharr 1952. [146] On the sale of these and of the Imperial House, see CTh 5.13.4.
[147] Schmidt-Hofner 2008b, 578–581 joins CJ 11.68.3 and 7.38.1.

or Imperial House shall follow their mother's *origo* and are thus of their *condicio*. This confirms it was considered a *coniugium non aequale*. CJ 6.4.2 (367 W), part of CJ 11.68.4 (367 W), adds for the case of freedmen that if these with the consent of the patrons enter such unions, their patrons will lose all their patronage rights.[148]

CTh 10.4.3 (370? 373? W) prescribes that if the presence of *conductores* and *coloni* of the *res privata* in litigation is requested, they must be summoned by the *rationalis* in criminal matters, in civil matters by the *defensor domus nostrae*. The argument to interpret *coloni* here as *originales* is the connection with the already existing *forum privilegiatum* of these (CJ 3.26.7, 349 E – probably applying also to the west in view of CJ 3.26.8 – and CJ 3.26.8 (358) (see Section 15.1).

Perhaps CTh 9.27.7 (390 W = CJ 9.27.5) relates to *coloni* of the *res privata* or even to *coloni dominici*, but it may also relate to free lessees (see Section 35).

32.2 Coloni Dominici *on Land of the Imperial House*

Another category of *coloni* were the *coloni dominici*, that is, *coloni* on land of the emperor and his family, sometimes mentioned together with *coloni patrimoniales*. The difference is not clear and may merely reflect the different registration within the imperial chancery of the real estate involved.

32.2.1 In the East

In CTh 10.1.11 (367 E) = CTh 12.6.14 the emperor reduces for *coloni* the addition to the usual payment to the imperial house to 1 per cent for the tenth year of the indiction. As Pharr says, it concerns the *epimetrum*, the excess to be paid over the quantity which the *coloni* (and others) had to deliver in kind, to make up for waste, shrinkage and other loss. However, it is not clear whether the text means bound farmers who leased or plain lessees. If *coloni dominici* have sold municipal or temple land, the limitation of prescription will not run for the purchasers. These will have to return the land and cannot not reclaim the price (CJ 7.38.2, 387 E).[149] Apparently this was land which was worked on by those *coloni* and, since it was *res dominica*, it will have been confiscated land that was administered

[148] See Kaser 1975, 298–301, thus: *operae, obsequium*, and the share in the inheritance of the freedman.

[149] Normally they could have because the sale would be invalid: the *colonus originalis* had not been entitled or empowered to sell. Accordingly it was a punishment.

separately from the *res privata* (which was responsible for confiscated goods) (*terras quae . . . iuris rei publicae vel iuris templorum*).

CJ 3.26.7 (349 E) prescribes as judge for cases involving them the *rationalis summae rei*. They enjoyed the privilege of not being appointable as tutor (CJ 5.34.13, 409 E).

Coloni dominici enjoy a privilege: They are free from a special tax (*descriptio*)[150] and from extraordinary taxes (*extraordinariae functiones*) (CJ 11.68.5, 386 E).[151] This must have given them opportunity to form some financial latitude.

32.2.2 In the West

Coloni dominici could raise accusations of extortion against the *comes domorum* (CTh 9.27.7, 390 W = CJ 9.27.5).

CTh 13.1.8 (370 W) grants the *coloni dominici* (*coloni rei nostrae, in dominicis possessionibus*) an immunity of the *collatio lustralis*, the tax on merchants. The text says that they sell the yearly produce of their lands.

In unions between decurions and *inquilinae domus*, the children will follow their mother's status (CJ 10.32.29, 365 W). Apparently this was considered a *coniugium non aequale*.[152] Since the difference between *coloni* and *inquilini* was nominal, this rule may have applied to *colonae dominicae* as well.

If a fugitive *colonus* or *inquilinus* of the imperial estates (*res dominica*) has gone to a town and served there as curial, as *collegiatus*, in a border fortress or any other *corpus*, the prescription of limitation period is thirty years within the same province, forty years for another province; and they cannot be reclaimed, but they remain tied where they are (CTh 12.19.2, 400 W= CJ 11.66.6). CTh 12.19.3 (400 W) confirms this.

33 The *Patrocinium Vicorum, Vicani, Coloni Homologi,* and *Rusticani*

In the Theodosian Code a title, CTh 11.24, occurs which is placed between the first part of Book 11, which deals with taxation and the collection of taxes, and the second part, CTh 11.25–28, which deals with the administration of

150 *Descriptio* is used for the assessment of land (see CJ 9.49.7.1), but also for taxes (see CJ 1.55.4, 11.28.1.1). In Nov. Theod. 22 a *descriptio* is levied on profitable land.

151 What seemed to happen, according to the constitution.

152 Schipp 2009, 153 opines that this was new, because it had to be emphasised that the maternal and not the paternal descendance counted.

taxes and public finances, after which penal procedure begins (CTh 11.29–39). It is therefore likely that the subject has a connection with taxation and public finance.[153]

The antique world was one of cities and countryside, yet the separation between the two was not so definite as it might seem. It is perhaps better to speak of communities and of a gradual scale from hamlets via villages to cities, each with its own amenities.[154] Administratively, however, in the third century AD the land was divided into cities each with its own territory. Large farms, hamlets, and villages formed part of the town administratively, and a town itself might be divided into neighbourhoods, *vici*.[155] Conversely, the term *vicus* was also used for the first. Although the town was the centre of administration, the *vici* had administrative functions too. In Justinian's Code four titles deal with *vicani*, inhabitants of *vici*, namely those living on the land, because they are also called *rusticani*, and their *vici* will have been hamlets or communities of that size. Notwithstanding that the constitutions are not referring to the colonate, it is useful to examine them because we are dealing here with people who lived under the same conditions as *coloni*.

It concerns a specific exercise of *patrocinium*, only attested in regard to *coloni originales* for the east and in particular for Egypt; all constitutions in CTh 11.24 deal with Egypt. Yet it does not have to have been restricted to this group, nor to the east. *Patrocinium*, originally the protection offered by representing and defending a client in court (*nomina potentiorum*), then extended to protection in a wide sense, was widespread. Another form was to affix *nomina et tituli* to buildings or ships.[156] It was used to evade the taxes, in different forms. One was to have property transferred to persons who could resist taxation or had an immunity, as CTh 13.7.1 and 2 show. Another way was to put oneself under the protection of such a person, who could then defend them in court. Libanios in *or.* 47.11 mentions for Syria

[153] Previously treated of in Sirks 1997, 166–173, 174–176, but here revised. CTh 11.24 *De patrociniis vicorum* is a title, of which a part of one constitution (CTh 11.24.6.5) was included in Justinian's Code. This was probably due to the issuing of a Novel of Leo, included as CJ 11.54.1. The part is of no consequence here. On *patrocinium* in CTh 11.24, see De Zulueta 1909; on *patrocinium* in general, see Harmand 1957 (more focused on city patronage); Hahn 1968; Fikhman 1978; MacCoull 1989; Giglio 1995, 50–60 (second ed. 2008, 43–52), on its relation to the colonate; Krause 2000. Registration in the *professio censualis* was necessary to establish the status. For *vicus*, see note 53.

[154] See Grey 2011 on communities, and Dossey 2010 on the peasant life.

[155] In Rome there existed even special religious ceremonies for the *vici*: the Compitalia.

[156] *Patrocinium* in the original sense: Georges 1918, s.v.; Van Minnen 1997; Wacke 1980. Cf. CTh 2.14R and 2.14.1, its *interpretatio*, LRB 43, ETh 46 for *nomina et tituli*; for this application to ships, CTh 13.7.2. It implied a formal transfer which connected the object with an immunity or socially big hurdle to collect tax or impose *munera*.

small landowners who do this, but also people on an estate, namely *coloni* or lessees, or in villages, and he mentions a general as powerful patron. The six constitutions in CTh 11.24, on the other hand, seem to have been restricted to Egypt. Their purport was the struggle against *patrocinium* in the context of farmers (*agricolae, rustici*) who lived in a *vicus*. The patronage was exercised as it appears by high officials of the Prefecture in Alexandria and other officials, for example under the *comes Aegypti* (CTh 11.24.1, 3 and 6). Giliberti underlines here the parallel with *patrocinium* in Syria, exercised by military persons.[157] The protection consisted of shielding the farmers from paying taxes, evidently by the power the *patroni* had or by his immunity extending over land or *vici*. Individuals accepted patronage, either in respect of their person (CTh 11.24.1, 2) or of the land they possessed.[158] Fines were set for them (twenty-five pounds of gold in CTh 11.24.2, 370 368? E; forty pounds of gold in CTh 11.24.4, 399 E for accepting people as clientele – here also doubled for other people who sought protection in order to evade taxes; confiscation of property in CTh 11.24.5, 399 E); punishment for the farmers (CTh 11.24.2) or confiscation of their own property (CTh 11.24.5).[159]

How was this *patrocinium* realised? The way to do this was to transfer the land formally to the patron (keeping it actually for oneself), who would be formally owner and by his immunity or powerful position ward off the public claims (CTh 11.24.4–6).[160] It appears from CTh 11.24.6 pr that a *patronus* possessed estates (*possessiones*) in *patrocinium*. The public obligations connected with these estates could thereby no longer be exacted or liturgies imposed (CTh 11.24.6.7). This was only possible if in the public

157 Giliberti 1993, 84: CTh 11.24.3 is addressed to military who exercise *patrocinium*.

158 CTh 11.24.5 has *agricolis vel vicanis propria possidentibus*; it concerns (see Giliberti 1993, 88) *agricolae* who are member of a *vicus publicus* and thus *vicani*.

159 The remedy the emperors conceived against the *patrocinium* over individual farmers was twofold. On the one hand, those who had been seeking *patrocinium* were punished: farmers (*agricolae*) with an unspecified punishment (CTh 11.24.2), for those who offered patronage fines (twenty-five pounds of gold) and acceptance of only half of what the fisc usually accepted (CTh 11.24.2). The fine was raised for higher officials to forty pounds of gold for each single estate brought under patronage, unless they abstained still (CTh 11.24.4). For those who had sought this patronage in order to defraud the taxes, the fixed fine was doubled (CTh 11.24.4). In case *patrocinium* was given to farmers who possessed their own lands, the patron forfeited his land. If the farmers had sought the patronage and owned land, they forfeited this too (CTh 11.24.5). Since the constitution says that this is an additional punishment, we may assume that it was imposed in addition to the sanctions of CTh 11.24.2 and 4. Against *vici* resisting the execution of their public duties, a fitting coercive measure was announced (CTh 11.24.3).

160 CTh 13.7.1 describes this practice with ships whose owners wanted to escape the compulsory transportation.

registration of these estates (the census) he was registered as possessing them and if he had an immunity from these obligations; or, if not possessing them, he as *patronus* was too powerful or influential to have the obligations enforced on the *vicus*. The emperor tried to have such 'privatisations' undone,[161] or ordered that the *patroni* had to acknowledge their duties and that without permission it was not allowed to possess in this way (CTh 11.24.6.pr, 6 and 8). However, although protection meant alleviation of public burdens,[162] it had its price: the patrons levied a contribution from the farmers, as Giliberti already concluded (CTh 11.24.2 states that by way of sanction the fisc takes half of this 'contribution').[163] What Libanios particularly deplored was that the farmers became neglectful and left land uncultivated (or. 47.11–12). Apparently, they only cultivated what they needed for themselves, depriving their landlords and indirectly the fisc of the revenues of the untilled land.

Metrocomiae in publico iure and *vici publici* were the administrative entities, used for the assessing and levying of taxes (CTh 11.24.6.1 and 6).[164] The adjective *publicus* refers to the normal state, implying that those under *patrocinium* were private, which agrees with the allowance to possess in CTh 11.24.6 and 8. This was the administrative designation for the village which served as an administrative centre for itself as *vicus* and for some surrounding

161 CTh 11.24.6 pr refers to people who started to possess lands, and it orders the extinction of the *nomen patronorum*, that is, their formal ownership, presumably striking the transfer in the census registers. It will have happened that an entire *vicus* came in this way under the control of a patron. He put himself then between the subjects of the public obligations and the authorities. In that sense those townships would no longer be public. It was a situation which the emperors did not permit except by special grant (mentioned are the churches of Alexandria and Constantinople), and then only if the possessors guaranteed that the public obligations of the inhabitants would be fulfilled. Not only that: if they were allowed to 'possess' a *metrocomia*, they had to bring under their guarantee also the still public villages (*vici*) which resorted under the *metrocomia* (CTh 11.24.6.6–8).

162 Libanios *Orationes* 47.7–8 describes how the tax collectors – his fellow decurions – are chased away and then, since they are liable for the uncollected taxes, are forced to sell their own assets.

163 Cf. Giliberti 1993, 82–83 and 87. He rejects here, on good grounds, Gothofredus' interpretation of *dimidium fiscus adsumat* as referring to confiscation of the lands. Libanios *Orationes* 47.11 mentions the price, which in turn was at the cost of the estate owner, since he would receive less.

164 Between the *vicus* and the town stood the *metrocomia* (μητροκωμία), a kind of major hamlet. Regarding the administrative function of the *metrocomiae* little is known. Evidently it was an administrative unit, because inhabitants were registered there (*adscriptum eidem metrocomiae*, CJ 11.56.1). The law prescribed that if land within a *metrocomia* was for sale, only *vicani* from this *metrocomia* could purchase it and not outsiders. Thus the law established more than a right of pre-emption: it barred any sale to outsiders (CJ 11.56.1). But not all towns were wholly or partly divided into *metrocomiae*, because it was possible for outsiders to buy land outside of these (CJ 10.19.8). If a *vicus* could be a tax unit, a *metrocomia* certainly could. Where a *metrocomia* had lost much or all of its resources in the course of time, it was to be replaced by a village which flourished (CTh 11.24.6.4). Since a *metrocomia* functioned as a centre, it implies that its functions in this respect were to be borne by its inhabitants. See also Poethke 1984 on the *metrocomiae* and their function in taxation.

villages, the *vici publici*. These are attested for Egypt and Syria.[165] The inhabitants were registered for the census in the place where they lived, as everybody was. CTh 11.24.6.1 forbids to acquire estates in *metrocomiae* or the entire *metrocomia* (and consequently also in the subordinated *vici*), to prevent the introduction of *patrocinium* in these (and, likely, to prevent them becoming 'privatised' by purchases).[166] An exception was made for acquisitions, made before the year 397. *Convicani* may buy land in the *vicus*, but they must acknowledge the public duties (CTh 11.24.6.1). Who nevertheless possesses fertile land in a *vicus* must perform the public obligations (including taxes) and accept uncultivated land in a *peraequatio* (CTh 11.24.6.2). It is clear that this combated form of 'bad' *patrocinium* implied that taxes could not be levied and liturgies not executed. That meant a higher tax and liturgy burden (on account of the repartition system) for administrative entities which had remained public. At his point the question arises whether there existed a collective tax liability in Egypt or whether what one tax unit did not deliver had to be made up, through a *superindictio*, by other tax units. That is in the end also a collective liability, but the basis of distribution is different.

This can be best dealt with in connection with the question of what *homologi* in CTh 11.24.6.3 means. This constitution is the reason for this excursus. The important part here is CTh 11.24.6.3, but it must be read in its context:

> pr. ... Possessiones autem adhuc in suo statu constitutae penes priores possessores residebunt, si pro antiquitate census functiones publicas et liturgos, quos homologi coloni praestare noscuntur, pro rata sunt absque dubio cognituri. 1. Metrocomiae vero in publico iure et integro perdurabunt, nec quisquam eas vel aliquid in his possidere temptaverit, nisi qui ante consulatum praefinitum coeperit procul dubio possidere, exceptis convicanis, quibus pensitanda pro fortunae condicione negare non possunt. 2. Et quicumque in ipsis vicis terrulas contra morem fertiles possederunt, pro rata possessionis suae glebam inutilem et conlationem eius et munera recusent. 3. Ii sane, qui vicis quibus adscribti sunt derelictis, et qui homologi more gentilicio nuncupantur, ad alios seu vicos seu dominos transierunt, ad sedem desolati ruris constrictis detentatoribus redire cogantur, qui si exsequenda protraxerint, ad functiones eorum teneantur obnoxii et dominis restituant, quae pro his exsoluta constiterit. 4. Et in earum metrocomiarum

165 See Giliberti 1993, 84 and 86 for the range of application of CTh 11.24.4, comprising the territory of the Praetorian Prefect of *Oriens*. Further in *Sancti Hieronymi vita Malchi monachi captivi*, II, there is Maronias, a *viculus* thirty miles east of Antiochia, which has had many *domini* or *patroni*, and finally pope Euagrius. Malchus (before 420) was there *colonus* of a very small plot (*agellus*, *possessiuncula*), but it is clear that he was an independent farmer, owner of his land, which he later wanted to sell.

166 Reading, with Gothofredus, *ne recusent*.

locum, quas temporis labsus vel destituit vel viribus vacuavit, ex florentibus aliae subrogentur.

pr ... Moreover, the landholdings that are still established in their own status shall remain under the control of the former landholders, if in accordance with the antiquity of the tax lists they will undoubtedly assume their proportionate share of the compulsory public services and the acknowledgement of *liturgi* which the *coloni* are known to provide. 1. But the *metrocomiae* shall continue under the unchanged public law, nor shall any person attempt to obtain possession of such villages or of any property in them, unless he has undoubtedly begun such possession before the aforesaid consulship, but fellow villagers (*convicani*) shall be excepted, to whom they cannot deny the payments that must be made in accordance with the condition of their fortune. 2. If any person, contrary to custom, should obtain possession of small fertile landholdings in the villages themselves, according to the proportion of his holding he may not refuse the unproductive land and its tax and compulsory public services. 3. Of course, if any persons called in the native manner *homologi* should desert the villages to which they are assigned and should pass either to other villages or to other masters, their detainers shall be obligated, and the *homologi* shall be compelled to return to the abode of the desolated country district. If their detainers should delay the execution of this regulation, they shall be held liable to the fulfillment of the compulsory public duties of such *homologi* and they shall restore to the masters whatever the masters prove that they have paid for such *homologi*. 4. And in place of those *metrocomiae* which have either been made destitute or emptied of their resources/manpower by the lapse of time, from other flourishing villages shall be substituted.

These were *vicani*, and therefore they lived in a *vicus*. CTh 11.24.6.3 (415 E) mentions *qui vicis quibus adscribti sunt derelictis* and moved to other *vici* or *domini*. Evidently people were registered in the census of a *vicus*. That this registration led to a bond to the *vicus* follows from the following, namely that they can be forced to return and to do their duties. They are *ad sedem desolati ruris constricti*. Such *coloni* are commonly known as *homologi*.[167] In CTh 11.24.1 (360 E) *vicani* paid from their own means the taxes of those *vicani* who left the *consortium*. A *consortium* is a community and thus it comprised all the people who inhabited a *vicus* and who were all registered, or it was a group of *vicani* within all *vicani*, which group was registered. Hence these *vicani* must have formed a kind of legal community

[167] CTh 11.24.6.3: *Ii sane, qui vicis quibus adscribti sunt derelictis, et qui homologi more gentilicio nuncupantur, ad alios vel vicos seu dominos transierunt, ad sedem desolati ruris constrictis detentatoribus redire cogantur, qui si exsequenda protraxerint, ad functiones eorum teneantur obnoxii et dominis restituant, quae pro his exsoluta constiterit.*

in which members were indirectly liable for the taxes of migrated members, that is, as a tax unit it had to pay the set amount regardless of whether some debtors defaulted. On the other hand, Zeno's rule of CJ 11.57.2 (457–473 E) later prohibits one *vicanus* being held liable for the debts of another *vicanus*.[168] It might theoretically have concerned private debts, but its wording is wide and its placing in the title makes it probable that it was about public debts, thus tax debts. The difference from CTh 11.24.1 is that the latter concerns debts of migrated *vicani* and not debts of *vicani* still living in the *vicus*. Further, if we assume the second interpretation of the *consortium*, it might mean that *vicani* outside the *consortium* were not liable for debts of migrated *vicani* with the *consortium*.

Giliberti rejects the view of Johnson and West, according to whom the previous owners and the *homologi coloni* were different people, because the latter would then have been landless people, living off casual work. Similarly, he considers De Zulueta's opinion more plausible yet still unsatisfactory. De Zulueta proposed to interpret in CTh 11.24.6pr *homologi coloni* as the old possessors (*convicani*) who were protected. The new possessors have to acknowledge their duties in their stead.[169]

With Giliberti I assume these registered *vicani* were the same as the *homologi*.[170] The adjective *homologus* (clearly a Latinisation of ὁμόλογος) is not easily explained. It is translated as 'agreeing', 'confessing', 'agreed to', 'undisputed', and 'admittedly liable (to taxation etc.)'.[171] In CJ 2.55.4.6 it means also *consenseo*, or as 'mit dem Grundstücke auf jeden neuen Erwerber übergehende Ackerbürger (rein lat. *ascripticii*)',[172] which, however, does not explain the word in question but is an interpretation; or 'liable in common'.[173] As to the papyri,[174] it appears that the editor of

168 CJ 11.57.2: *Grave est et non solum legibus, verum etiam aequitati naturali contrarium, pro alienis debitis alios molestari. Idcirco huiusmodi iniquitates contra omnes vicanos perpetrari modis omnibus prohibemus.*

169 Giliberti 1993, 91–92; De Zulueta 1909, 57.

170 If not, the consequence would be that in every *vicus* the inhabitants were liable for the debts of migrated *vicani*, even if they had not been censused in the *vicus*.

171 See Liddell & Scott, which for the last meaning cites some papyri of the first to third centuries, and CTh 11.24.6; but the latter text is under discussion here. Followed by Pharr 1952 in the translation of this text.

172 Georges 1918, s.v. *homologi*.

173 Kränzlein 1999, 365 n. 2, suggests for *homologi*: being together subjected to a responsibility, or the same responsibility ('Gemeinsam einer Verantwortung unterliegen, bzw. der gleichen Verantwortung').

174 The papyri are: P. Rylands 209.40, Wilcken Chrest. 63, P. London 2.254.137, 141, al., BGU 560 and 618. In P. Rylands 209 (early third century, Arsinoite) lands are registered under the heading *abrochoi*, *epèntilèmenoi*, and *homologoi*, thus 'unwatered', 'uncultivated', and 'undisputed'. The last category has to pay the full tax, the first two can claim a reduction or even a remission. But all are, of

P. Rylands 209 rejects the meaning of *dediticius*, proposed by Wilcken for *homologos* (ὁμόλογος) and says that the *homologi* are 'simply those who tacitly or overtly agreed to something determined by the context'. That does not lead to a liability for taxes as such, because a primary liability for that, based on other factors, already existed. It could only be interpreted as an undisputed liability for the full amount. Yet in CTh 11.24.1 and 6pr it is the *possessores* who are primarily liable for the *publicae functiones* as set by the former census and for the *liturgi* (CTh 11.24.6 pr), not the *coloni homologi*; these merely provide the *liturgi*.[175]

The phrase *ii sane, qui vicis quibus adscribti sunt derelictis, et qui homologi more gentilicio nuncupantur* makes a connection between the *adscriptio* and the adjective or noun *homologus*. If we follow this line, another possibility turns up. *Homologus* means 'joint *logos*', that is, sharing the same *logos*. Such a meaning of *logos* occurs in the fiscal terms *homodoula* and *homokensa*,[176] and Avotins gives three other examples where *homo* with a noun means this.[177] *Logos* has a variety of meanings, but one is 'public accounts', 'account', 'list', and it might mean here indeed 'sharing the same account/list', namely in the fiscal register, just as in *homokensa* it would mean 'being registered in the same census district', which meaning was already mentioned by De Zulueta and Giliberti.[178] That would fit the reference that these people were registered in one village (*qui vicis quibus adscribti sunt*). It would also explain the insinuation that they were liable

course, liable to taxation. *Homologos* means here that from the fisc's viewpoint the fiscal claim for full assessment had not met any objection. The editor rejects on this basis Wilcken's interpretation of the word *homologou* in the other papyri, used as a heading for people, as *dediticii*. According to him it merely means that with those people no legal claim for a reduction on poll tax (such as age) had been raised. Thus the stress would not be on a liability for the tax, but on the fullness of this liability. As such this meaning does not conflict with Giliberti's mentioning the possibility that the term refers to 'inclusi in un eleco', 'compresi in un lista fiscale' (Giliberti 1993, 92) in reference to something, as land or a tax. On the other hand, De Zulueta's interpretation as 'liable along with the rest of the group' (De Zulueta 1909, 55–57) goes too far, since this meaning (implying, thus De Zulueta, a joint liability) cannot be read in the papyri, cited above.

175 The text has *noscuntur*, which could be used as equivalent of *ag-* or *cognoscere*, but here merely means that it is known of the *homologi coloni* that they provide *liturgi*, because it is the landowner who has to acknowledge (*cognoscere*).

176 Jones 1974, 815 on the ἐπιβολὴ ὁμοδούλων and ἐπιβολὴ ὁμοκήνσων. I cannot enter into the specifics of the *peraequatio* here, but the assumption that it did not have to imply that an estate owner became owner of the deserted land he had to pay tax for also seems to me not logical in view of the improvements and accompanying investments required. See Thonemann's article on the census registration and above, note 16, on the way the once established figures were maintained. Also the fact that in the later Byzantine empire the tax registers functioned as proof that land passed over in ownership.

177 Avotins 1992, 153–154: ὁμόδουλος, ὁμόζυγος, and ὁμόθρονος.

178 Giliberti 1993, 92, with reference to de Zulueta. Giliberti mentions BGU 618.13 with the enrolment for the *laographia*.

for each other's debts and the rule that they had to pay for the migrated people on the list. The account as such had to be paid fully in the end. In my opinion this interpretation is better, because it is in line with the situation and avoids the rather construed interpretation through 'agreeing' as set out above. This still leaves open the question whether this registration was done on a voluntary basis or imposed – if indeed the *vicani* agreed voluntarily to do this, *homologi* could also refer to this agreement, yet in that case the agreement would also have to be approved by the authorities and given fiscal effect, that is, lead to a collective joint account, and *homologus* could then also indicate this. But it does not seem probable: Why should one *vicanus* want to be liable for another *vicanus*?

In any case, being all registered in one *vicus* they were responsible for the total of the poll tax expected from their *vicus*. Those who harbour the fugitives have to pay these expenses to the remaining *convicani*. The taxes were assessed individually, but within the fiscal system of the Empire the *vicus* formed a tax unit on the lowest level, presumably next to the *possessio*.

It has been suggested that in rural Egypt a collective liability resulted from a collective nomination of candidates for the various duties. This existed in the *vici* (κώμαι) and was called *allèleggyè* (ἀλληλεγγύη).[179] Yet such a liability (whether a *Korreal-* or *Partialhaftung*) could only have existed for liturgies, not for taxes. But was a collective nomination a standard feature of the Egyptian countryside or was it a feature of specific townships? De Zulueta deals only in general terms with this question, thinking of the *epibolè* (ἐπιβολή) and *epimerismos* (ἐπιμερισμός), but here clearly liturgies are meant, or included.[180] Wollentin speaks of this in a general way. According to him the comarchs were in the first place responsible for their nominees (citing P.Oxy. X 1254 of 260), and then the inhabitants and all residents (citing P. Florence 2 of 265: the κωμῆται).[181] Κωμῆται is indeed a synonym for *vicani* (CJ 11.54.2, 370, 368? E). In itself it is not impossible that an entire village took over the responsibility of a nomination; councils did so. The result would indeed be a collective liability, although there is still the problem that the comarchs were responsible in the first place and had to execute the liturgies themselves (cf. P.Oxy. LXI 4118, third century, post ca. 245). Still, liturgies are, though public obligations, not the same as taxes, and the argument does not solve the question. In any case, the texts in CTh 11.24 cannot be an argument for such a collective liability.

[179] See Wollentin 1961, 98–103, particularly 100–101. See also Gorecki 1981, 192.

[180] De Zulueta 1909, 65–72.

[181] See Wollentin 1961, 98–103.

It happened that some of these *vici* with *homologi* came under *patrocinium*. These *homologi* will have been subjected to the poll tax, as in principle everybody was. But they also provided people to perform liturgies: *liturgi*. The effect of the protection was that these were no longer enforced. On the other hand, protection had its cost: a contribution to the patron (CTh 11.24.2). That the *homologi* had to be *liturgi* (CTh 11.24.6pr) is an aspect we did not see expressed so clearly before with the *coloni originales*. Various liturgies are enumerated in CTh 11.24.6.7: *cefalaeoti, irenarchi, logografi chromatum*: 'capitation tax collectors, municipal officers of the peace, registrars of the river levees', as rendered by Pharr.[182] It may have been a particularity of Egypt, but it does not have to be so, as CTh 11.1.14 (E) suggests. After all, the *collegiati* and *corporati* we find in the west, and whose status is so much alike to that of the *originales* that they may be taken together as *condicionales* (see Sections 10.5 and 23.1), had to perform menial tasks which would have been liturgies too (or *munera*, in Latin). It is therefore likely that the *coloni originales* elsewhere had to perform liturgies too, unless there the duties of *coloni originales* were restricted to the land they were ascribed to, while the *munera* were reserved for special groups.

The regulation in 438 was that those whose *patrocinium* was accepted (i.e., those established before 397 and that of the Churches of Constantinople and Alexandria) were obliged to organise the supply of people for the liturgies (i.e., the *coloni homologi*).[183]

34 The 'Free' Colonate

In at least three provinces there existed since 371–392 a colonate in which the *coloni originales* were not subjected to the *potestas* of their estate owner. They all lay in the eastern part of the Empire: Illyricum and surrounding regions (371), Palestine (386), and Thrace (398) (CJ 11.51–53, 386, 393, 371). But it may have existed in other places as well, for CJ 11.51.1 (386 E) refers to other provinces under the eastern rule (*per alias provincias quae subiacent nostrae serenitatis imperio*) where it already existed (by a *lex a maioribus constituta*); perhaps also in the western part, since CJ 11.48.6 (366 W), directed to the praetorian prefect of the Gauls, speaks of *coloni sine condicionis discrimine*, if we may read this as referring to *coloni* and 'free' *coloni* and not referring to *coloni* of the *res privata*. Due to the fact that there

182 Pharr 1952.

183 Cf. Giliberti 1993, 91. This situation reminds of the arrangements on Heroninos' estate in the third century, where Heroninos organised the supply of liturgists to the comarch; see Section 52.

are no constitutions in the transmitted Theodosian Code or the Breviarium Alaricianum on this colonate that might change the description and analysis of these constitutions for Justinian's period, the reader is referred for the year 438 to Sections 16 and 17.

35 Farmers Not Subjected to the Colonate

CTh 11.1.26 speaks of those provinces where the colonate is applied. That implies that there were provinces where it was not. Moreover, the constitution does not suggest that within a province the colonate was applied in all cases. So there must have been farmers who were not *coloni*. They may have been slaves, as mentioned in constitutions, or lessees, or independent farmers, tilling their own property. For the latter we have as testimonies CTh 11.1.14, CTh 11.24.6.1 and 2, *Sancti Hieronymi vita Malchi monachi captivi* II, Libanios *Orationes* 47.11, enough to conclude that the texts in the Gregorian and Hermogenian Codes on lease and labour contracts were still reality where it concerned independent farmers. Further, the tax registers of eleven eastern cities (some on Aegean islands, some in Asia Minor) show estate and smallholders who employ slaves and, in the case of Chios and Astypalaia, apparently *coloni* because they pay *anthropon kephalai*. That must refer to *coloni*, but it proves also that the landowners themselves were independent farmers and, as Harper emphasises, the registers also show that the registered labour was spread unevenly over the land. It implies that where there was no registered labour, there must have been slave or unregistered labour. Unfortunately, the date is not certain: Thonemann dates the inscriptions at AD 310, Harper prefers a later fourth-century origin.[184]

CTh 9.27.7 (390 W = CJ 9.27.5) grants, inter alia, *coloni* who had been forced to pay bribes to a *comes domorum* the faculty to reclaim within a year after the end of the office term of this official the money was paid. The texts can refer to all *coloni*: *originales*, 'free' *coloni*, and unregistered farmers.[185]

[184] Thonemann 2007, 458 n. 75 and 476–478 for the *anthropon kephalai*, 434 for the dating; Harper 2008, 86 for the dating, 99 for the spreading. He assumes as regards the Thralles inscription that the mere mention of *capita* refers to *paroikoi* is right if he means by that *coloni*. But I cannot follow Thonemann 2007, 458, who, following Jones 1953, 51, includes all *paroikoi* in the *capitationes*. That is turning the evidence around: it presupposes there were *paroikoi* everywhere and thus they would have been included; neither can CJ 11.48.7 be an argument for this. But I agree with Harper 2008, 98 that the census registers comprised only those for whom the estate owner paid the poll tax.

[185] See further Section 20, where a detailed analysis is given.

36 Texts Not Necessarily Connected with the Colonate

A number of constitutions mention *coloni* but do not add information on the colonate. CTh 4.12.3 (326?) is about the *senatusconsultum Claudianum*. It mentions next to *servi fiscales* the *patrimoniorum fundorum origini cohercentes*, emended by Mommsen into *originariis*.[186] But it is possible that it concerns *servi originarii*, that is, slaves who were linked to a piece of land as *instrumentum*.[187] If it concerned indeed *coloni originarii*, it would be an early testimony to the variant application of the senatusconsultum, but it would remain open whether the children would become *Latini* or *coloni*. CTh 5.12.3 (434 E = CJ 11.62.12) deals with the possession or emphyteuticary possession of *fundi patrimoniales*; reference is made to a *colonus*, but the term must be interpreted here as referring to the *possessor* or *emphyteuticarius* who cultivates the land; in any case it is not possible to interpret this without doubt as a *colonus originalis*. CTh 7.7.4 (415 E) mentions *possessores* next to *coloni*. It concerns the foraging by soldiers, and the text must have had in mind both landowners and lessees, who were the categories to suffer here. The same applies to CTh 7.7.5 (415 E = CJ 11.61.3). CTh 11.17.1 (367 E) mentions *coloni*, but it cannot be established whether it concerns *coloni adscripti*. The term *tributarius* was used in the west for a *colonus* registered in the census (CTh 10.12.2.2 and 3 (368? 370? 373? W); CTh 11.7.2 (319), both texts dealt with before) and for the rest to designate anybody subjected to pay the tribute (as in CTh 12.6.21, 386 E).

37 Conclusions

The Theodosian Code presents, by both its directly and its indirectly transmitted constitutions, the colonate as it was in 438. We have to take account of the differences between east and west. The Alarician *interpretationes* cannot assist here, since they must date from a moment after 451 and will have been made in the west. Further, we may not expect that the Theodosian Code provides us with a fuller picture than Justinian's Code does for its time apart from the missing texts, because the Theodosian Code was meant to contain only constitutions from the period 312–437. There may have been constitutions issued prior to 312, and rescripts, which were known to the contemporaries through the Gregorian and Hermogenian Codes and in that case should be added to the 'dossier'.

[186] On the emendation and a better reading, see Sirks 2013, 133–134.

[187] See Sirks 2011, partly a reaction to Harper 2010; on the emendation of CTh 4.12.3, see Sirks 2011, 632.

In the same way we should not exclude the *ius vetus* in the legal writings. But these do not yield much. We have almost nothing of these sources. Those constitutions transmitted only in Justinian's Code certainly add to the picture, but we have to be aware of the possibility of editing and of a different context.

As to the legal position of the *coloni*, the constitutions of east and west link up with each other and those for the entire Empire. They present a homogeneous picture for 438. As demonstrated by CTh 5.17.1, issued for the entire Empire, the colonate in both parts must have had a common origin and thus common features.

37.1 *Beginning of the* Condicio

It appeared from the texts that the colonate could be entered as an agreement for a guarantee by the estate owner for the public obligations (CTh 11.1.14 E, Augustine *ep.* 24*). Combining this with the evidence for the colonate under Justinian that it was in origin a voluntary agreement means that we may assume that in 438 it also was entered as a voluntary agreement. It could further be imposed for the first time on a person, as an independent legal institution (*ius colonatus*, *ius census*), in the case of a captive barbarian (CTh 5.6.3 E) or an able-bodied beggar in Rome (CTh 14.18.1 W = CJ 11.26.1). The *condicio* was established by registering the *colonus* in the estate census. It implied that the subjection to the estate owner was formalised as was the latter's guarantee. It was a *condicio* which became a subcategory of the category *in alieno iure esse*, other subcategories being slavery and being in the paternal power.[188] It is clear that while making the estate into the *origo* of the *colonus*, the entry also registered the status, which was transmitted to descendants. What may help to underpin the role of the census registration is the imposition of the colonate on the Scyri, where the census registration is fundamental.

Further, a person liable on the basis of his or her *origo* could be summoned by the estate owner, and would have to acknowledge the obligation and be registered in the census (CTh 10.20.7 E; 5.18.1.2 W). CJ 11.48.13pr W, must have been originally placed in CTh 5.18. It states that there is no difference between *coloni* and *inquilini* as regards their tie to their *origo* and recall. Their children will have to acknowledge the paternal *condicio* in any case. Further, in the east the 'free' colonate existed, either

[188] Gai 1.124–126 distinguishes a category of *alieno iure subiecti*, which comprises both slaves and those *in potestate parentis*. In both cases the criterion is the *potestas*.

commuted out of the colonate or imposed *de novo*, as *ius colonatus* or *ius originarium*. It did not have as the colonate the subjection of the *colonus* to the *potestas* of the estate owner as a person and his assets as if *peculium*. Several constitutions make clear that a union between an *ingenuus* and a *colona* was a *coniugium non aequale*, making all children subjected to the *condicio coloniaria*.

The colonate was not a universal phenomenon, in any case not in the west: it existed in some provinces only (CTh 11.1.26).

37.2 Taxation and Taxes

For the poll tax, provincials were registered in their village (*vicus*, *metrocomia*) census (CTh 13.10.7, E). In the case of the colonate, a registration in the *census* of an estate was required, which anchored this as his *origo* (and *condicio*), and the connection of this with the poll tax of the *colonus* is evident (CTh 11.1.14 E; 11.1.26 W). Connected with the registration in the census of a *colonus* was the guarantee the owner of the estate had to give for the poll tax the *colonus* was liable for (CTh 11.1.14 E; 11.1.26 W). It created a debt for the *colonus*, for which his assets served his landlord's preferential claim (CTh 2.32.1). It made his assets treated as *peculium*. In connection with this function it was forbidden, both in the east and the west, for *coloni* to alienate personal property without the knowledge and, as this implies, consent of their estate owners. Evidently this prevented loss of security for the estate owners to realise their preferential claim. It implies that there were financial relations between *coloni* and their masters. Imperial constitutions had introduced this restriction. The liability of the *colonus* as such for the tax remains (CTh 11.1.14 E; 11.1.26 W), but the estate owner is now liable as guarantee (CTh 5.17.1 E/W; 11.1.14 E = CJ 11.48.4; 11.1.26 W; 11.7.2 E/W). At the same time the estate owner should have been sufficiently solvent to function as guarantee towards the fisc (*ex* CTh 11.1.14). If the *colonus* was not or no longer on his premises, he did not have to pay (11.7.2 E/W). The person who solicited the *colonus* to leave his estate and stay with him, or who hid him, was liable for this tax the time the *colonus* stayed with him (CTh 5.17.1 E/W; 10.12.3 E). CJ 11.48.15 (W): *coloni* may not be harassed for fiscal debtors; they must remain on the land. Although agriculture was the basic subsistence form everywhere, the fact that the law in 438 presents more interventions in these matters in the west than in the east is likely due to the fact that the barbarian inroads in the early fifth century in the west made it necessary for the government to take measures to stabilise agriculture with accompanying financial arrangements and with, of course, an eye on the fiscal revenues. The migration of *coloni* over a long period will have been due to those turbulent times as well.

37.3 Transfer of Land

CTh 13.10.3 (357, Seeck 356 = CJ 11.48.2) prohibits the sale of land without the *coloni* attached to it, even in case of shortage elsewhere. CJ 11.48.13.1 W regulates the transfer of *coloni* from one estate to another in case of labour shortage, with compensation for the buyers of such depopulated lands in that the offspring of the transferred *coloni* will be subjected to them (i.e., they can summon them).

37.4 Features of the Colonate

The effects on the *colonus* were:

(1) He was bound to that estate or plot of land through the census registration of its owner, becoming a *censibus adscriptus* or *adscripticius*, the estate being now his *origo* (CTh 5.6.3 E; 4.23.1 W).

(2) He was now *alieni iuris*, subjected to the *potestas* of his landowner. A marriage with an *ingenua* was, because of that, his *condicio coloniaria*, a *coniugium non aequale*. The effect of this was that the *senatusconsultum Claudianum* was applied analogously to make children *coloni*. Sometimes a formal warning (*denuntiatio*) of the woman was required for this effect, but in most cases it happened at once, creating thus along this line a continuity of the colonate also. This status also prevented him from taking higher offices. On the other hand he was *sui iuris* as regards his family and his assets, except for its treatment as *peculium* (see item 4 below). The reason to apply the senatusconsultum lay in providing more bound labour force for agriculture, rather than the socially lower position of the *coloni*. The many regulations on fugitive *coloni* argue also for this explanation.

(3) He had to perform duties (CTh 5.17.1; 5.6.3; 4.23.1 W; 11.24.6.3; CJ 11.50.2pr E), and this the estate owner could even enforce this on his own (CTh 5.17.1). CJ 11.50.1 (325) contains a limitation to the duties. Estate owners may not require more from *coloni* than what has been the custom and what has been required before; if they nevertheless do, the *colonus* may approach the authorities and litigate against his estate owner. CJ 11.50.2.1 E forbids the *colonus* to sue his estate owner in

private law cases, but CJ 11.50.2.4, in line with CJ 11.50.1, makes an exception for *superexactiones*, which apparently estate owners tried to devolve upon their *coloni*. CJ 11.48.5 (W) says that estate owners may not demand money but must accept the revenue of the fields, unless the custom is different; the text merely has *rustici* and thus could apply to any farmer who has to pay a debt, for example as rent.

(4) In the east his personal assets were as if *peculium* under control of the estate owner during his life (CTh 5.19.1 E; CJ 11.50.2.3 E), and in the west as well (CTh 5.18.1.2 W)

(5) His inheritance could be claimed as *peculium* by his estate owner after his death (CTh 5.3.1 E; 5.18.1.2 W), to ensure the preferential claim of the estate owner.

(6) As to the transmission by descendance, in the east very few rules on this existed, whereas for the west an elaborate system was developed for the *coniugia non aequalia* and retained in 438 (see below, Section 37.5). It implies that in the west during a long period *coloni* had migrated and settled elsewhere. In the east either fugitive *coloni* were quickly searched for and found or estate owners did not bother much.

Since this situation of dominance might entice the estate owner to enslave his *colonus*, it was expressly forbidden to enslave him (or her) (CTh 5.6.3 E; 5.17.1 E/W).

37.5 Recalling

If a *colonus* left his land, whether to escape his duties, or solicited by another estate owner, or for another reason, he could be recalled by his estate owner, who had to petition for this with the authorities (CTh 5.17.1 E/W; 5.17.2 E = CJ 11.64.2; 4.23.1 W; 5.18.1 W; 11.24.6.3 Egypt). In the west the *colonus* could raise a limitation of prescription against this, of different duration for *colonus* and *colona* (CTh 5.18.1.3 and 4 W (4: = CJ 11.48.16), but with a *colona* a division of the offspring over claimants would take place in the west (CTh 5.18.1.3 and 4; 5.19.1 E). The person who allowed the *colonus* to stay with him or hid him would be fined (CTh 5.17.2 E = CJ 11.64.2; CJ 11.48.12 W). CJ 11.48.6 (W) states that fugitive *coloni* and *inquilini*, of both sexes, must be returned. This measure will have been supplemented by the constitution on limitation of prescription and division of offspring, CTh 5.18.1. CJ 11.48.7 (W) forbids the selling of *coloni originarii* by way of a transfer of land, presumably done thus, that only a small piece of the land they are tied to is sold, and all of them with it. *Coloni* should stay attached to their land, and if this was divided, they should be apportioned proportionally, which shows that they were primarily attached to the land and not its owner. CJ 11.48.8 (W) deals with the case that a fugitive has been working for another estate owner and is recalled. If the estate owner knew they were somebody else's *coloni*, he has to pay the taxes (in line with CTh 5.17.1). If he did not and hired him as if free, whatever he owes the *colonus* must be rendered, after settling any outstanding accounts, and this to the estate owner, in line with CTh 5.18.1.2 W, where also the earnings can be claimed together with the *peculium*. CJ 11.48.12 W, which forbids the harbouring of fugitives and defines the fine for those who harbour fugitive *coloni* and *inquilini*, I assume to be the constitution which LRB 6.2 mentions and which Mommsen inserts as CTh 5.17.3. The name would have to be corrected as Florentinus.[189]

CJ 11.48.11 W revokes all privileges by which *coloni originarii* resist a recall or summons. CJ 11.48.18 W gives an example of such privileges: it states that *coloni* (*censibus adscripti*) may not be admitted to posts in the imperial service, not even to the lowest ones, to avoid the rights of their masters being hurt (by an immunity). CJ 12.33.3, 395–402 states the same, now specified for the armed service.

[189] See note 122.

CHAPTER 3

The Colonate in the East, 438–527

38 Enactments by the Emperors in 438–527

The Theodosian Code was promulgated in the east on 15 February 438. Theodosius would reign till 455 and after him five emperors followed until Justinian ascended the throne in 627: Marcian, Leo, Zeno, Anastasius, and Justin. Of Theodosius, Marcian, Leo, Zeno, and Anastasius we possess constitutions concerning the colonate. Regarding the economic aspects of their reigns, those of Theodosius and Marcian were characterised by prudent financial administration which created a full treasury. Leo, however, by his disastrous expedition in 468 against the Vandals, depleted the treasury, while the many revolts under Zeno and the military campaigns forced this emperor to increase his income by selling offices. Under Zeno, Macedonia and Thrace were ravaged by the Goths, of whom he got rid in 488 by sending them under their leader Theoderic to Italy to defeat Odoacer. It was Anastasius who rehabilitated the Empire's finances. It seems he achieved this by preventing bribery and waste and by reducing the levy in kind, amongst other measures. He further introduced the *vindices*, who supervised the tax collection by the provincial officials and the curials and the municipal finances, which will have reduced fiscal loss as well. At the end of his reign he had reduced the *capitatio humana* in the dioceses of Asiana and Pontica by one-quarter. In other ways he also alleviated the burden of the peasantry.[1]

38.1 Theodosius II (402–455)

Under Theodosius we find two constitutions issued on *coloni*, which merely concern the effects of their status. It was absolutely forbidden to accept *coloni* (*censibus adscripti*) for the function of *apparitor* in the office of

[1] For a short overview, see Jones 1974, 204–237.

the *magister militum* (Nov. Theod. 7.4.2 of 441). It seems logical in view of their low status, but since the constitution also forbids it for curials and cohortals, status cannot have been the reason or sole reason. It will have been the immunity the office gave from all *munera* which made entrance so attractive (CJ 11.54.1: *ab omni nominationis iniuria excusentur*), whereas these groups were needed for the duties of their respective *condiciones*. The other novel granted the imperial *coloni* a *forum privilegiatum*. Constantine had decided that all cases regarding the fisc were to be dealt with in the court of the *rationalis* and would not follow the normal administrative way, that is, before the provincial governor (CJ 3.26.5). In 442, for civil or criminal lawsuits concerning a *colonus domorum nostrarum*, the *praepositus sacri cubiculi* or the *comes domorum* became competent, with exclusion of other courts (CJ 3.26.11 of 442).[2] It was a refinement of the general rule, since for cases regarding *coloni dominici* and *patrimoniales* the existing rules remained applicable (i.e., the *rationalis summmae rei*, CJ 3.26.7, was competent and exclusive judge), as for the *coloni rei privatae* (the provincial governor, CJ 3.26.8).

38.2 *No Constitutions on* Coloni *by Marcianus (455–457) Have Been Transmitted*

38.3 *Leo (457–473)*

Leo had to handle difficult political situations and enemies and did not dispose of a full treasury. After the failure of the expedition against the Vandals in 468, the treasury was depleted. It therefore does not surprise to see his engagement with bad *patrocinium*, that is, patronage by which people evaded taxes (CJ 10.19.8). In 468 he issued a constitution which dealt with several aspects of *patrocinium*. First he forbade luring people into *patrocinium* (i.e., to become *clientes*) by promises of gains, that is, transferring their land into ownership of the patron under the cover of a fake contract in order to evade taxes (*in fraudem circumscriptionemque publicae functionis*). *Vici* and estates (*possessiones*) which had been transferred would be confiscated (CJ 11.54.1pr).[3] A fine of 100 pounds of gold was set for high-

[2] Was it necessarily an advantage for the *coloni* in these two instances? It might be in the first case, since the *rationalis* and *procurator* could counter the governor, but in the second case it might be a disadvantage, since the *coloni* would not have that kind of advantage. In both cases, however, the interests of the *res privata* and *domus augusta* will have been taken care of before all.

[3] Cf. Giliberti 1993, 101.

placed prospective patrons (*nobiliores*), while lower patrons were to lose their fortune, as would those who assisted (CJ 11.54.1.1). Then he declared all *patrocinia* established since 437 in Thracia and those established since 441 in Asia, Oriens, Pontica, and Egypt (almost the entire east) invalid (CJ 11.54.1.2). Something similar had already been done by Theodosius in 415 with *patrocinium*, entered from 397 onwards, and by Marcian (451–457) as referred to in CJ 11.54.1.2, apparently without effect (CTh 11.24.6, CJ 11.54.1.2). It did not mean all *patrocinia* were now rooted out. It was the bad *patrocinia* by which people tried to evade taxes which were forbidden.[4]

Another constitution, CJ 11.54.2, was issued together or after CJ 11.54.1 by an unknown emperor. The reference to punishments suggests it is another part of CJ 11.54.1; in any case it fits with the measures of this constitution, hence Leo may have been its author. It prohibits the offer of *patrocinium* to *vicani* (κωμῆται) or the acceptance of farmers (γεωργοὶ) in *patrocinium* under the promise to these of revenues or gains (i.e., keeping what otherwise would have been paid as tax). The above-mentioned punishments are imposed and a more severe one added. If the *vicani* are slaves, they must be flogged and returned to their owners, if free people they are fined twenty pounds of gold and banished, while the leaders of the *vicus* who knowingly let them go are to be banished. If it had been *coloni originales*, they could have been recalled anyway. The punishment seems exorbitant and somewhat symbolic: How could a *vicanus* ever pay twenty pounds of gold?[5]

Further, Leo decreed that it was forbidden for outsiders to possess land in a *metrocomia*. It is a repetition of CTh 11.24.6.1 of 415. Instead it should be sold and transferred to a *habitator adscriptus eidem metrocomiae* (CJ 11.56.1),[6] a person domiciled in the same *metrocomia*. Perhaps the *habitator* was a *colonus adscripticius*. Any contract contrary to this was void. This made it impossible that an outsider could evade the tax on a plot inside the *metrocomia* by using his privilege. All three fragments, CJ 11.54.1, 2, and 56.1, may on account of their contents have been part of one constitution fighting undesirable *patrocinium*.

Other constitutions of Leo covered the relation of *adscripticii* with the Church. In 466 he issued in an extensive constitution on church asylum,

[4] So in CTh 11.24.6pr those which acknowledged the duty to pay taxes and to take care of the liturgies; and in Nov. 17.13 it is the *iniusta patrocinia* which are to be pursued.

[5] Since these texts, although important for the context of the colonate, show no reference to *coloni* in this period and consequently in the Justinianic context, they have not been dealt with in Chapter 1.

[6] Cf. Giliberti 1993, 100.

inter alia, the rule that slaves and *adscripticii* were not allowed to seek asylum in a sacred place after having destroyed or stolen things or fled their masters' authority. Either they should be punished or, if pardoned by their masters, be returned to them (with, eventually, the stolen goods), so that the masters would not miss any of their rightful services (*obsequia iusta*) nor the Church be encumbered by having to feed them (CJ 1.12.6.9). Another fragment of this constitution is directed against public unrest and seditious behaviour (CJ 9.30.2).[7] It seems there was unrest in this period, with *coloni* seeking refuge in churches.

In a constitution of 470, CJ 1.2.14, Leo ruled that whatever somebody left by testament to the church in Constantinople was to remain property of the church and could not, under what pretext ever, by what functionary ever, be alienated (CJ 1.2.14pr, 1). Only a usufruct could be granted, be it that upon its expiry the goods had to be returned to the church (CJ 1.2.14.9; it was not unthinkable that such a usufruct might turn into property). Amongst these goods were estates with *coloni* and their *peculia* attached to it, hence *adscripticii*. They could of course not be bequeathed themselves, since they were free persons; it is only as a consequence of the bequest of the land to the church of Constantinople that they will now respond to their new master.

Next to division by sale, a division could occur when an inheritance was liquidated. In case an inheritance was divided, families of *adscripticii* and *inquilini* had to stay together (CJ 3.38.11).[8] It will have concerned land with *coloni* attached to it, which then was divided with the *coloni* distributed over the new parts.

38.4 Zeno (474–491)

Under Zeno a new category of *coloni* appears in the texts: the *coloni tamiaci* (CJ 11.69.1pr; for an exposition, see Section 15.5). We do not know when this category was created or whether it was just a specific designation for a group of *coloni* on particular lands of the *res privata*. The emperor rules that both in marriages between a 'free' *colonus* and a *colona tamiaca* and

[7] A third part is CJ 1.3.7.

[8] The original text, CTh 2.25.1 of 29 April 325 according to Seeck, dealt only with the division of inheritances of patrimonial or emphyteuticarian lands and of the slaves thereon. Apparently in line with CJ 11.48.2 and 7, which deal with the division of *adscripticii* in case of sale, it was interpolated as to make it apply to these as well: after *servorum* was added *vel colonorum adscripticiae condicionis seu inquilinorum proxima agnatio vel adfinitas*. Further, the restriction to those particular lands was dropped.

between a 'free' *colona* and a *colonus tamiacus* the children will follow the status of the imperial lands and become *dominici*. Since it concerned free citizens, this was a deviation from the rule on the transmission of status (*condicio*) in the first case: normally the child would follow its father's status. We therefore see here the application of the *coniugium non aequale* rule combined with the *senatusconsultum Claudianum* as already applied to private *coloni originales*. Why was it now applied to *tamiaci*? Was there a shortage of workers on these estates? And did it imply a lowering of their status? But this divergence was, apparently, only applied to those *coloni dominici* who were posited on *fundi tamiaci* and not applied to *coloni dominici* on other estates. In the case of marriages between male or female *adscripticii* or slaves on one side and male or female *coloni dominici* or *servi dominici* on the other side, the rule of the previous laws was maintained (CJ 11.69.1.1). This must mean that the principle of a lower *condicio* applied undiminished and indeed, in three of the four combinations in which the child was freeborn, it became by this a *colonus dominicus*; while in the fourth case, an *adscripticia* cohabitating with a *servus dominicus*, it became *adscripticius*.

This household fund (*tameion*) will have been created before or under Zeno, since CJ 11.69.2, issued by him, refers to a *sanctio pragmatica* of him, ordering the sale of *fundi tamiaci* in the provinces and the possessions in the *saltus Gonaticus, salvo canone et tributariis collationibus*.

Further, Zeno abolished the practice that *vicani* were pressed for the debts of *convicani* (CJ 11.57.1).[9] Since *adscripticii* may have lived in *vici*, it may have concerned them too. The constitution is directed at a brutal way of collecting debts, either by having others pay or by applying pressure through the social network. Although it is possible that a *vicus* formed a tax unit with all inhabitants on one list for the poll tax (*homologi*), which would explain such pressure, there is no suggestion of a collective liability for debts.[10]

Several decisions related to the personal status of *adscripticii*. In 484 Zeno granted the heads (*principes*) of the *agentes in rebus* various privileges after their retirement, including that, once retired, they did not have to pay more than one solidus in fees (*sportulae*), whether they or their families or their slaves or *coloni* were summoned, in their own person or through their procurators (CJ 12.21.8pr). In view of the relationship, it will have concerned *adscripticii*. They were treated as part of the household.

[9] Cf. Giliberti 1993, 100–101.

[10] Justinian repeats this prohibition in Nov. 52.1 of 537.

In 484, *adscripticii* who were chosen as clerics or bishops, or who wanted to become monks, were only allowed to do so if their master approved of it. Without his approval, their election or ordination was invalid (CJ 1.3.36pr, 2; see Section 12.4). Clerics enjoyed a general immunity. The prohibition referred to an already established prohibition, namely CJ 1.3.16 of 409 on the admission of *coloni censibus adscripti* to the clergy (where the owner could approve; see Section 13.1). The reason will have been their subdued status. The Church was not closed for them, contrary to the west (see Section 42).

38.5 Anastasius (491–518)

Anastasius is attested as conducting an efficient administration and introducing reform laws,[11] particularly after the Isaurian rebellion was put down in 498, which measures resulted in a great surplus in the imperial treasury.[12] Next to his administrative and monetary reforms, he introduced a reform in the collection of the land tax, in the distribution of *agri deserti*, by which is meant land whose owner was lost or could no longer pay the tax, and a reform in the colonate.[13] This colonate reform is found in CJ 11.48.19. Here Anastasius introduced the 'free' colonate (introduced in 371 for Illyricum) for *adscripticii* who had remained for thirty years on their plot. They still had to remain on the estate, provide services, and pay their poll tax, but they were no longer subjected to the estate owner's *potestas* and their property was no longer under the control of the estate owner (see Section 13.2). Notwithstanding the bond to the land, it will have implied some improvement for them. When this constitution was issued is unknown, but Anastasius issued a constitution with two fragments on prescription in 491 (CJ 7.39.4, 12.62.14) and one on *coemptio* and the *munus sitoniae* (CJ 10.27.1). Two constitutions on prescriptions followed after that (CJ 7.39.5 and 6), both of unknown date. It is likely that CJ 11.48.19 dates also from 491 or later. Another advantage for farmers was that in 513 he reduced the *capitatio humana* in the dioceses of Asiana and Pontica by one-quarter.[14] A so-called *lex Anastasiana* which forbade collecting more on debt-paper than it had been bought for will also have helped indebted farmers.[15]

[11] On Anastasius: Haarer 2006; Meier 2009; *CAH* XIV, 52–62. [12] Haarer 2006, 221ff.
[13] See Haarer 2006, 211–213. I am of a different opinion than she regarding the reform of the colonate.
[14] John of Antioch *Excerpta de insidiis* 103, John Lydus, *De magistratibus reipublicae Romanae* III.47.
[15] See CJ 4.35.23.

In 507, Anastasius bought with money from the *tamieion* (ταμιεῖον) a village which belonged to the church of Amida, franchised the inhabitants (*inquilini*) and gave them land and a *domicilium*, thus an *origo*, thus establishing the town of Dara-Anastasiopolis.[16] These inhabitants were certainly not slaves; the word used in the Syriac is *gur*, which means 'dweller'. It must have concerned *inquilini originales* who otherwise would have become *inquilini tamiaci* and who were now released. They were granted land, which indicates that before they had no land, or perhaps land in charge. But was this a release by the emperor as landowner or by the emperor as public authority? How to interpret *domicilium*? It seems to me that this translation is better than 'house' in another, modern translation and that these people's *origo* was now set in a town.[17]

Other constitutions relating to *coloni* deal with privileges for high officials, such as CJ 12.10.2 (of 491–518) which grants procedural advantages to *consistoriani* and, inter alia, their *coloni*, which Zeno had already granted to the *principes scholae* (CJ 12.21.8pr). Another constitution rules that those who worked in the *sacra scrinia*, as their families and their slaves and *coloni seu adscripticii* (*coloni ad eum pertinentes*), if these stayed in Constantinople, could not be summoned criminally or civilly without leave of the *magister officiorum*. Further, these workers in the *scrinia* did not have to pay fees (*sportulae*) and enjoyed all further existing privileges (CJ 12.19.12pr, 3). This may have been a small advantage for *adscripticii*. Also it was ordained that those persons who had fulfilled the office of *patronus fisci*, that is, as attorney for the fisc, had the right to represent as advocate themselves, their families and their slaves and *coloni ad se pertinentes*. The term *pertinentes ad se* is rather wide ('to concern', 'to belong') and it might theoretically concern free lessees, but it is more probable, in view of the context families and slaves, that it concerns *coloni* who belong to them, that is, are subjected to them, thus *adscripticii*. Also, landlords usually had no reason to represent their lessees. With persons subjected to one's *potestas*, it was different. The administrative court charges (*sportulae*) should be not higher than prescribed (CJ 2.7.22.1, 3 = 2.7.24.1, 3).[18] Of all these constitutions the date is unknown.

16 Zacharias Rhetor *Historia ecclesiastica* VIII.6 [p. 24.21–24] in Brooks 1919–1924, 36: *Et rex Thomae episcopo [Amidae] aurum dedit, τιμήν pagi qui ecclesiae fuit, et ταμείῳ eum emit; et omnem inquilinum qui in eo erat liberavit et terram eius et domicilium sibi attribuit*. I thank Professor L. Van Rompay (at that time at Leiden, now at Duke University) for his help with the Syriac original.

17 If they were made *coloni* with their own land to which they were tied, they would have been masters over themselves. That is impossible. However, the text gives no cause to other interpretations.

18 Why this is added is unclear. Why should the charges have been made higher in this case?

38.6 Constitutions Not Included

Some constitutions in the Theodosian Code were not incorporated in Justinian's Code. It may imply that they were superseded by later constitutions which dealt with the same subject, or that a rule was abolished in the meantime. For example, the famous CTh 5.17.1 was not copied, nor CTh 5.17.2. But these rules on fugitives were amply covered by CJ 11.48.6 and 8 and by CJ 11.48.12.2. The rule in CTh 4.12.3 on unions between *ingenuae* and *originarii* of imperial lands was no longer applicable due to the abolition of Junian Latinity in 531 (CJ 7.6.1) and the *senatusconsultum Claudianum* in 531–534 (CJ 7.24.1). The privilege of *coloni* of the *res privata* not to serve in the town council, adjusted in CTh 12.1.33 to fight fraudulent use of this and simulated sale of property, was not included, perhaps because in the east town councils had lost much of their importance. And what we do not find at all in Justinian's Code are the various constitutions in the Theodosian Code on the division of offspring of fugitives. For the entire Empire it was prescribed that in case of an inheritance division, families of *coloni* should remain together (CJ 3.38.11). That was feasible because in the *actio communi dividundo* a compensation was possible. The western rules on recall gave the opportunity to provide substitutes. It seems, however, that the east opted for a principal application of the rule which left families always intact; perhaps we see here an influence of the Church. Also, there may have been less or no occasion for such rules to exist under Justinian, as it was probably already before and in 438. After all, the east was not so stricken by barbarian invasions as the west. These factors might have caused the exclusion of the western rules.

39 Comparing the Situation in 534 and 438

Although Justinian's Code of 534 contains western constitutions from the Theodosian Code, it is not certain that these were especially meant for the west or that Justinian had separate constitutions for the west in mind as the Theodosian Code had. There the Theodosian Code still applied. It was only upon the request of Pope Vigilius that Justinian's codification was promulgated in 554 in any case for Italy, nineteen years after Rome had been taken. During that time the Theodosian Code was still valid, also in Africa.[19] Special constitutions had been enacted which were only (CJ 1.27) or also (Nov. 14) valid in the west, and CJ 11.23 and 26 (Rome, *nautae Tiberini*)

[19] See Sirks 2020b, and 2007, 82, 174–175 with the observation by Bassanelli Sommariva 2013.

were likely meant especially for Rome. Also, the Theodosian Code had become interpreted in the east in a unificatory way, with the east–west differentiation dropped, which then was used for the Justinian Code.[20] Western laws would be confirmed for the east by their inclusion in and the confirmation of Justinian's Code.

The state of the colonate in 438 and in 534 does not differ greatly. Partly this may be caused by the number of constitutions which were transmitted only through Justinian's Code. Due to the possibility that these texts were edited, they are not the constitutions a comparison should fundamentally be built upon, but they can serve of course if there are sufficient other constitutions to support a comparison independently, which is the case.

As in Justinian's Code, the sources for the colonate in the Theodosian Code are manifold: by agreement with a guarantee for a debt; by imposition on barbarians captured in war and on beggars; by descent; by imposition of the 'free' colonate. An important later addition is Anastasius' automatic mutation of the adscripticiate into 'free' colonate after thirty years of service. Descent as source is regulated in far more detail in the Theodosian Code, with divisions of offspring, than in the Justinian Code and particularly for the west. Likewise, the limitation of prescription is more detailed in the Theodosian Code. What we do not find in the Theodosian Code (except perhaps CJ 11.48.2pr) but see mentioned in the Justinian Code is the release from the colonate. It is possible that release was formulated in a text in Book 5 or in one of Books 2–5 (later references to it in the west argue for this; see Section 42). By finding the agreement and release present both in the west in that period and in the east under Justinian, we may conclude that they must have existed also in their common source, the law as comprised in the Theodosian Code.

What we further see is that in the east *coloni* are allowed to enter the Church and monasteries. It is no surprise considering the great Byzantine interest in theology and a Christian life, nor is it a surprise that merely the master's consent was required. Yet the difference from the west is remarkable: there it was forbidden. On the other hand, refuge and immunity in the imperial services were combated. It is also remarkable that the privileges of high officials were extended to their dependents, including *coloni*. It gives the impression of a household, independent from the authorities. Perhaps there is a connection with the *patrocinium* heavily combated in the fifth century, exercised by influential or powerful persons able to resist the authorities.

20 C. Haec 2; and in the Summaria Antiqua, of course with the exception of constitutions, specifically issued for a particular region or province.

CHAPTER 4

The Colonate in the West, 438–ca. 506

40 The Situation in the West, 438–ca. 506

40.1 Sources

Our information for the situation of the colonate in the west in this period is primarily based on what the Theodosian Code provides for the year 438, supplemented with the Novels of Valentinian, a Novel of Majorian, and a Novel of Severus for the time till 476. We do not know whether Justinian's codification was introduced in Africa after its reconquest in 533, because there is no explicit reference or testimony to such an event,[1] contrary to Italy, where it was introduced in 554. There it had the opportunity to establish itself for the Northern part of Italy before the Langobard invasion of 568, as it is the applied law in the letters of Gregory the Great. Further, as a result of Nov. Val. 26 of 448, all the novels of Theodosius sent over to the west in 447 gained validity in the west, as did some Novels of Marcian and certainly one of Leo through Anthemius (Nov. Anth. 2 and 3).[2] In the novels of Theodosius, Marcian, and Anthemius we do not find any reference to *coloni*.[3] For the period after 438 we find *coloni* mentioned in the authoritative and binding selection of constitutions of the Theodosian Code in the Lex Romana Visigothorum alias the Breviarium Alaricianum, in the legal writings in the Breviarium, and in the Novels in the Breviarium; further in the Lex Romana Burgundionum, the Lex Burgundionum, the Edictum Theoderici, the Formulae of the Frankish and Visigothic kingdoms, the Council canons of Gaul, and letters of popes. Further, there are *interpretationes* to many texts in the Breviarium. They may have been made on the

[1] The very long constitutions CJ 1.27.1 and 2 deal only with establishing the administrative structure of Africa.

[2] See Sirks 2007, Nr. 60.

[3] In Nov. Marcian. 2.1 *in fine* the word *obnoxii* seems to indicate also *coloni*, but it more likely refers to those obligated to collect taxes.

occasion of the compilation of the Breviarium, but may also be taken from earlier commentaries or, taken and adapted; it is uncertain. These texts inform us about the colonate as it functioned in the end phase of the west Roman Empire and in the Germanic kingdoms. These may theoretically still have been part of the Roman Empire, but in practice they were not. I shall deal with them in the next sections. I take 438 as point of departure and proceed chronologically.

As characteristics of the colonate we found (a) the acceptance of the *potestas* of the landowner, (b) the guarantee for the poll tax and eventually other public duties, and (c) the registration of this in the census of the estate. In the Edictum Theoderici, the Lex Romana Burgundionum, the Lex Burgundionum, and the Formulae of the Frankish and Visigothic kingdoms the poll tax is no longer discernible, while it is very doubtful whether *coloni* were still registered in the census. The disappearance of the poll tax should have led to either freedom or a 'free' colonate, yet both possibilities are not evidenced. The *condicio* passes over from parents to children; they are connected with an estate but can be moved elsewhere easily. The same goes for the letters of the popes Gelasius and Gregory the Great. It appears that around 500, with the breakdown of the fiscal system and the changes in administration and perhaps social life, the colonate changed character, at least visibly, and can no longer be identified with the Diocletianic colonate. That colonate was based on the registration in the census for the poll tax, and where the liability for this fell away, the reason for the guarantee fell away too (as CJ 11.53.1 shows). Even if the census as such continued to exist, if it served to establish the colonate the basis for the colonate would have changed. Or did registration in the municipal archives serve this purpose? Such a change we see in the east with the creation of the 'free' colonate, but it is absent in the west.[4] The Novels, which go till 468, do not refer to such a measure, but perhaps it was lost. Did an edict of Odoacer effect it? We do not possess edicts of him on this matter.[5] Moreover, if *coloni* are reclaimed in the Burgundian kingdom, it is their earnings for the work done (*exacta operarum solutio*) which must be paid, not the poll tax (Lex Romana Burgundionum 6.4).[6] The same in the Edict of Theoderic c. 84: the fugitive had to be returned with his savings

[4] See on the taxes in Italy under Odoacer and Theoderic: Barnish 1986. The contribution does not deal with the *capitatio* but is focused on the grant of one-third to the barbarians.

[5] There is one edict of him known, a donation of 489: see Santifaller 1952.

[6] LRB 6.4: *Quod si actor nesciente domino fugitivum suscipere aut tenere praesumpserit, aut iudici praesentare distulerit, factum eius fustuario supplicio a iudicibus vindicetur, et fugitivi dominus servum suum cum peculio, quod habet, et exacta operarum solutione recipiat.*

(*peculium*) and earnings (*merces*) to his master. This was already the case in CTh 5.18,1.2 (*cum mercedibus*). In the Formulae of the Frankish kingdoms there is no question of earnings. The new colonate was not an application of the 'free' colonate on the basis of Justinian's Code, because that was introduced in Italy in 554, long after the Edict and Lex Romana Burgundionum.

Hence these sources are not included in the research, but if appropriate they are adduced to sustain an argument. It seems that what is called colonate or *coloni* in those texts is based merely on a *potestas* of a landowner. In any case the link with the taxation and therefore the ensuing necessity of registration in the census is gone. The Diocletianic colonate has ended with the end of the Roman Empire in the west. Perhaps the census registration now took over as status registration in itself, but that is another chapter. The precise nature of this bond and whether this is a precursor of the later medieval villeinage is another theme and falls outside the scope of the present research, which focuses on the (Diocletianic) colonate in the Roman Empire.

40.2 *Background*

As to the political and economic events and changes after 438, the situation in the west did not improve for the Roman government. In the South of Gaul and Spain the Visigothic king reigned. But in 507 the Franks, coming from the North of Gaul, defeated him at Vouillé and incorporated the South of Gaul into their kingdom, except for Septimania (kept thanks to the help of the Ostrogoths). The Visigothic kingdom continued as the Kingdom of Toledo in Spain until the invasion of the Moors around 725. The Ostrogoths fared differently. In 476 the German army commander, Odoacer, deposed the Roman emperor Romulus Augustulus and took over the government of Italy, having been promulgated by his troops as king. Although he acknowledged the emperor Zeno, the latter looked for ways to depose him. He asked the Ostrogoth king Theoderic to move to Italy, defeat Odoacer and rule as his governor (getting rid by this of the Ostrogoths at the same time). Theoderic complied, moved westwards with his tribe in 488, and defeated and killed Odoacer in 493. After that he ruled until 526, succeeded by his grandson and then by the usurper Theodahad. Italy enjoyed a period of peace and we may also assume of economic rest. Justinian reacted to Theodahad's usurpation with a war in 534–535, beginning with the conquest of Africa and Sicily, after which a long war over Italy followed between the Byzantines and the Ostrogoths, ruining Italy. The invasion of the Longobards in 568, who conquered the North and most of the middle of Italy, put an end to the

Ostrogothic rule but brought new warfare. A further invasion in Gaul brought the Burgundians on the theatre. They had crossed the Rhine in 406 (together with the Vandals and other tribes) and settled first south of Mainz. In 443 they moved southwards to the present-day regions of Burgundy and Savoye to settle again. There they reigned until finally in 532 they were beaten by the Franks, who now ruled over almost all of Gaul, which became known as Francia.[7]

Did these events imply disruptions on local level, in daily life? Or was there a continuity under the new masters? First of all, the Church remained as it was, that is, it was not cesaropapistic as the church in the east and, being a great landowner itself, it could hold its position under strong popes like Gregory the Great and local bishops like Avitus of Vienne or Remigius of Reims. Its power shows itself in the conversion of the Franks from Arianism in 500 to orthodoxy, of the Suebi in 556, and of the Visigoths in 587.[8] Bishops fulfilled locally a public function and could form a counterbalance to the Germanic rulers, whose presence created tensions.[9] But these newcomers were not eager to subvert existing structures, rather they wanted to reap in ease the fruits of their conquest. The way they were settled was apparently the military use of *hospitium*, the enjoyment of one-third of the property of their Roman host. For Roman soldiers that was the use of his house, but with the German tribes we do not know whether they received one-third of the land or one-third of the revenues of it (the state revenues, i.e., the taxation, or the entire revenues?), or, as Meier suggests, first the latter and then a gradual shift to land distributions.[10] The other public obligations, the *munera publica* such as the obligation of landowners on a road to provide replacement horses if needed (the *paraveredus*), remained in general in force.[11]

But was the way taxation was registered and levied continued too? Wood deals with the taxation in the Merovingian kingdoms. It seems that tax

7 A still useful survey with Lot 1927 [1968], 293–323 on Italy and Spain, with on p. 318 Lot's view that in the North of Italy Justinian's codification never had the time to implant itself, its Roman inhabitants still living under the previous law. Recent: Meier 2019, 546–590 on the developments in Gaul and Spain in the period 410–475.

8 See Marrou 1963, 214–216.

9 For the way Romans saw the Germans, see Demandt 2007, 382–387.

10 Meier 2019, 556–557, 568–569. See also Demandt 2007, 315 n. 108. It is likely the second possibility, since that would have been more comfortable for them. The theory of Goffart 1980 that it concerned a slice of the tax revenues is rejected by Wickham on the basis of the many recorded instances of barbarians owning land: Wickham 2005, 84–86 (but is it excluded that barbarians bought land?). Porena 2012, 188–207 sees the success of the Praetorian Prefect Liberius (493 till ca. 500) in that the land, allotted to the Ostrogoths, remained liable for the land tax. Accordingly there was no fiscal fallout. The *tertiae* were actually the part expropriated and forming the *sortes* assigned to the Goths. But the term may also indicate a fiscal quote (Porena 2012, 208ff.). Porena does not mention the *capitatio*.

11 See Esders 2009, 195ff.

registers were still present but not always updated. The king's *res privata* may have played a greater role in the public finances than before.[12] Simplification of the system is not improbable. Wickham distinguishes between two theoretical political models, one tax-based (i.e., tax levied on everyone, through a fiscal system), the other rent-based (i.e., based on the rent-paying part of the inhabitants on the land controlled by the ruler, thus based on a part of the population). In practice both types co-existed, even in the Roman Empire with its tax system, since the emperor as large-scale landowner received much income from his estates. The Ostrogothic and Visigothic kingdoms retained much of the tax-based system.[13] The system there was relatively simple: registration of land, of its owners, then census, imposition, and levy. We do not know whether the *tabularii* were officials of the king. There is no sign of a poll tax. Does the inclusion in the Breviarium of CTh 10.19 on *metallarii* mean that there was still a state-controlled mining industry in the Visigothic kingdom?[14] In Francia the change toward the land-based system happened in the seventh century. Wickham assumes that already in the sixth century not much was left of the Roman tax structure.[15] Such a change would have influenced the colonate, since that required a census registration. In a rent-based system, the census registration would have become less important or even unimportant, less likely to be kept updated and with that the registration of *coloni*. We see indeed in the Burgundian kingdom that the link with land is severed from the taxation and the colonate has become a serfdom of personal status. The continuation in the Visigothic kingdom of the taxation system would have prevented all that. Esders posits that the public obligations (*munera*) turned more and more into charges on real estate, which would fit the abolition of the poll tax.[16]

There are also changes in life visible: towns are becoming smaller. This does not mean that economically we see a decline of commerce and industry. Meier rather sees a shift in the priorities of the elite, from embellishing of and investing in cities to moving on the land and living on luxurious estates.[17] Politically, the German immigrants ruled the various kingdoms. But next to

[12] See Wood 1994, 62–63.

[13] For the Visigoths, see the copying of CTh 11.1 (on the *tributum*) into the Breviarium. The system was maintained with the inclusion of Ch 13.10.1 on the *tabularii*, that is, the registration of the census and the *exactio*. As in the Summaria Antiqua, the difference between east and west is disregarded.

[14] Edmonson 1979, 87, mentions 231 mines in northwest Spain in Roman times. He does not rule out that small mines continued to be operated in Late Antiquity (Edmonson 1979, 91).

[15] Wickham 2005, 57–59, for Spain 98–102, for Gaul 105–108. [16] Esders 2009, 242.

[17] Meier 2019, 549. On the other hand, see Ward-Perkins 2005, 87–122 on the decline in the pottery industry. Although earthenware was still made, the quality and design declined significantly.

them we see that the Church was a formidable power. Its bishops and abbots were important men; their landholdings gave them secular authority. Likewise the social structure underwent a change. Although already in the fifth century a growing division is visible between the elite of rich landowners and those depending on agriculture, whether still as independent farmers or as farm-hands, there is still the fundamental differentiation between slaves and free people, with for freed people legal obligations towards their manumitters. That differentiation remains but becomes blurred. People are called free, but nevertheless seem to be in a subjected position, often to a church or an abbey, but from the sources it appears that personal dependencies existed too. Rio has aptly summarised this in the words 'freedom and unfreedom'.[18] Slavery existed too, but there no miscue is possible about 'unfreedom'. Should we use *alieni iuris* for this unfreedom? Was this a change under the influence of the German peoples? Did they have gradations in dependency which were now framed in Roman terms? The situation in the west in the sixth century, with the domination by the German tribes, raises the question whether we may distinguish here the beginnings of what is later the feudal society and whether the colonate transformed into the villeinage, *Hörigkeit*, or whatever the forms of rural dependency were later called. Schipp has given ample attention to these phenomena.[19] But we must remember that in the late antique Roman society, as before, social relations were very important and many people depended on powerful persons. So reciprocal dependencies as in feudality were in themselves not new. The question is what precisely defined feudality (or vassalry), whether 'Treue' and 'Gefolgschaft' were specific German values or not, and what precisely defined the colonate. There is no definitive answer to these questions and they lie outside the scope of this work, but we must reckon that in the course of the fifth century in the territories governed by Odoacer, the Ostrogoths, and the Visigoths, such tendencies may have already been present.

41 The Posttheodosian Novels in the Roman West, 438–post 506

41.1 *General*

After the Theodosian Code was promulgated, new statutes were issued, both in the east and in the west.[20] We possess collections of several western emperors (Valentinian III, Majorian, Severus, and Anthemius). Several

[18] Rio 2006, 7–40, 2017. [19] Schipp 2009, Teil B and C.

[20] Nov. Val. 23, 27, 31, 35; Nov. Maior. 7; Nov. Sev. 2; with *interpretationes*. On these, see Wenger 1954, 541–542; Liebs 2005, 118–119, 148. The page numbers to the Novels and the Interpretationes refer to the standard edition by Meyer of the Posttheodosian Novels.

times, eastern collections were sent to the west where they were confirmed and so gained validity (of Theodosius and Marcian). Next to these Novels, which were preserved later in a probably cumulative collection,[21] we dispose in many cases of short summaries, the *interpretationes*, of those of the Novels that were included in the Breviarium Alaricianum of 506 (see Section 45) and so preserved.[22] They sometimes present a change or adaptation, interpreting the text in its actual application. There are also internal references, which may have been made in the Alarician compilation, or date from an earlier collection of Novels with an interpretation, or from a collection of separate interpretations.[23] Fitting argued that they were made in the second half of the fifth century, presumably in Gaul, and his arguments still hold.[24] In that case they were made under Visigothic rule (see below). Di Cintio assumes that the compilers often adapted these texts, obeying the words of Alaric's Commonitorium that the *interpretationes* were meant to clarify the constitutions and take away iniquity. Yet it is not always certain that where they present a difference with a constitution, this difference originated in 506.[25] Piquer Marí assumes the Alarician compilers used a pre-Alaric collection of commentaries and chose constitutions which fitted practical purposes.[26] The Visigoths reigned since 410 over their own state and the west Roman Empire was without an emperor since 476, so even if there seems a change in Visigothic sense in 506, such a change may have occurred much earlier (here much depends on further research). In any case they present us with the way the Novels were read and applied under the Visigoths between 476 and 506, perhaps also for the period 438–476, in which case they might be valid for Italy as well. For that reason I shall deal with them, if necessary, in as far as the authorship of the Alarician compilers cannot be established, for this period; for the *interpretationes* as part of the Breviarium, for the period from 506 onwards, see Sections 45 and 46. The latest *interpretatio* is to Nov. Sev. 1 of 463, but we cannot exclude that other *interpretationes* date from before 463 if they were made previously to individual Novels.[27] Their terminus *ante quem* is 506.

[21] See Sirks 2007, Nr. 60.
[22] References to them cite the page and line of the edition Meyer 1905.
[23] For example, INov. Val. 35.5 (p. 149.141–142) refers to Nov. Maior. 7.7. See Sirks 2007, 226.
[24] Fitting 1873, 228–237. Mommsen rejected this, assuming full authorship by the compilers, but this position was not substantiated. For the entire discussion, see Liebs, who agrees with Fitting: Liebs 2005, 148–156.
[25] Di Cintio 2013, 2018. [26] Piquer Marí 2016, 163.
[27] A thorough legal analysis of the posttheodosian Novels is evidently needed. For a start, see Sirks 2007 Nr. 60.

The texts regarding *coloni* we have for this period almost exclusively deal with the flight, or migration, of *coloni* and other persons subjected to a *condicio*, either of the same status, or of that of the decurions. The rules of the Theodosian Code (primarily CTh 5.18.1) on limitation of prescription and marriage were refined, extended, or restricted. Nov. Val. 23.3 (447) mentions *coloni* alongside slaves as a category of tomb violators who may be tortured. After them *ingenui* are mentioned and differentiated: those who are plebeians are, as slaves and *coloni*, capitally punished. They belong to the lower category of freeborn men but are not subjected to the power of somebody else.[28] Therefore *coloni* in the previous section must refer to *coloni censiti*.

41.2 Valentinian III

In 449, Valentinian introduced a general limitation of prescription for all kinds of claims of thirty years (the *praescriptio triginta annorum*: Nov. Val. 27). The reason was that officials of the imperial service (which granted them an immunity) who were originally *coloni*, were bothered in their retirement with claims for, as it is said, a most rejectable colonate and had to suffer risks (*trahi ad laquaeos vilissimi colonatus et tunc periculosius laborare*), instead of enjoying their rest (section 1). Like slaves, these *coloni* should also have the opportunity to attain a better status than their original one (*condicio*) (section 2) – in itself a remarkable motive. The law of Theodosius on the *praescriptio triginta annorum* – CTh 4.14.1, 424 E – had spurred him to enact the same (section 3; proving, by the way, that the constitutions in the Code retained their original range of application after promulgation or else this constitution of Valentinian would not have been required). In order to prevent chicanery through interpretations, the rule would simply be general with no exceptions. Every claim regarding *originarii* and *coloni*, *inquilini*, slaves, of both sexes, and claims regarding the *peculia* and offspring (*agnatio*) of the said legal status (*designati iuris*), by which are meant the children and the properties of these persons who had the status of *coloni patrimoniales*, *coloni emphyteuticarii*, and of those of the towns (which must refer to *collegiati*), would extinguish after thirty years (section 5). For claims which were already before the court, the law of his father Honorius, that is, CTh 5.18.1 (419 W), as regards the period of

[28] That *ingenui* mean in this context those who are not subjected (i.e., not *alieni iuris*) becomes clear from Nov. Val. 31.5. Here those *nulli quoliber modo obnoxius civitati* are opposed to *obnoxii*, and in 6 paralleled to *ingenui* to *servi seu coloni*.

limitation (thirty years for male, twenty for female *coloni*), as well as its section on the attribution of offspring, had to be observed. A penalty of thirty pounds of gold should deter frivolous claims. This Novel demonstrates splendidly the geographical limitation of constitutions in the Code and the continuity of western legislation.

The Novel was disadvantageous for women, because for them the time lapse was thereby increased from twenty to thirty years. The *interpretatio* (INov. Val. 27) says that a subsequent Novel deals with the subject and therefore it refers the reader to the *interpretatio* to that Novel.[29] Meant is, explicitly, Nov. Val. 35 of 452, dealing with the *episcopalis audientia* and other matters (*diversa negotia*). The subject is indeed treated there, but also, albeit less, in Nov. Val. 31 and its *interpretatio*.

Nov. Val. 31, of 451, dealt specifically with vagrant *coloni* and migrants. It remedied an unintended effect of Nov. Val. 27. The general formulation in that Novel enabled *coloni* on estates to escape their *condicio* by running away and, through moving from estate to estate (as migrant workers?), evade recall by their estate owners. If they succeeded in doing this for thirty years, they would be free of the colonate. It is an irony that they achieve a better status by dodging their obligations, so remarks the emperor sourly. Nov. Val. 27 set thus a premium on flight (Nov. Val. 31pr).

Valentinian decided therefore that the roaming *colonus* or *colona* would become subjected after thirty years *colonario iure* as *originarius* to that estate owner (i.e., be his *colonus originarius*) with whom he had spent the last period, if he had spent equal periods with different landowners; if he had spent different periods, to him with whom he had spent the greater part of those thirty years (Nov. Val. 31.1). The claim for a *colona* was denied after twenty years (in line with CTh 5.18.1.3; here the inequity of Nov. Val. 27 was remedied), but her offspring borne before should belong to her former master. In that respect the rule of CTh 5.18.1.3 was modified: now all offspring were subjected to her former estate owner. But substitutes should be rendered, because children should not be separated from their parents (Nov. Val. 31.2). Likewise, a substitute should be given for the woman (i.e., in case she should be reclaimed) so that her marriage would not be broken up (Nov. Val. 31.3, already in CTh 5.18.1.3). Substitution, previously allowed for women (CTh 5.18.1.3)

[29] INov. Val. 27, p. 125.62–126.1: *Ista lex ideo non interpretata est, quia sequens sub titulo 'de episcopali iudicio et de diversis negotiis' et de tricennio loquitur et omnia, quae hic conprehensa non sunt, evidenter habet expressa.*

was now also allowed with regard to men. Substitutes should be *coloni originales*,[30] whose *origo* had consequently be commuted. How was this done? By a transfer in the municipal records? Or a transfer in the census registers? As long as taxes were collected, the census registration would still be in order. In Nov. Val. 31.5 the registration is in the municipal records, but these may have been the ones used for the tax assessment. All personal mutations were confirmed by this law, but not those mutations by which a part of land was first spoiled of its *coloni* and then transferred to another person (Nov. Val. 31.4, a practice already reprehended in CJ 11.48.7, 371 W). The *interpretatio* to Nov. Val. 31 summarises the rules,[31] but refers for the claim to the children of the *colona* to Nov. Val. 35. According to this latter novel, these will after the twenty years be subjected to the new master, something which is not said in Nov. Val. 31. Further it refers to an apportioning of the children in accordance with CTh 5.18.1.3 (= Brev. 5.10.1), again a detail not mentioned in Nov. Val. 31. It shows that the composer of the *interpretationes* disposed both of the Novels and of the Theodosian Code and that the *interpretationes* on the Code (as transmitted through the Breviarium or made for it) were made by the same person or persons.

Next to these roaming *coloni* there were other migrants (*advenae*), who sought shelter with estate owners, pretending to want to work. As soon as they had been accepted and taken care of, they joined women, *colonae*, of the estate and then migrated again, leaving their family behind. This had to be stopped. If the migrant was somebody not subjected to the status of a *collegiatus*, that is, an *obnoxius civitati* who had to perform low-estimated duties in a town, he had to register in the municipal records that he wanted to stay there where he had chosen to be (i.e., at the estate of his wife), so that he would now be obliged to stay there and could not leave at will. Actually, he established his *origo* there and was now bound to it (CJ 10.39.4). Now the *gesta municipalia* served as register. His *ingenuitas* would remain unimpaired, that is, he would not become subjected to the estate owner as if a *colonus* (Nov. Val. 31.5). As Höbenreich points out, there are no indications that he would become a *colonus* – the Novel says, *salva ingenuitate* – and thus the views of De Martino and Voss, that the colonate was the consequence of the choice to cohabitate, are wrong.[32]

[30] Not slaves, or otherwise the confirmation of the shift would be unnecessary: with slaves the owners were free to place them where they liked.

[31] Nov. Val. 31.3, p. 131.47–132.69. Schipp 2009, 333.

[32] See Höbenreich 2007, 280–284.

The same rule was issued in Nov. Val. 31.6 for women not subjected to a *condicio* (*ingenuae*) who migrated to the countryside to live with slaves or *coloni*:

> Pari lege mulieres ingenuas iubeo detineri, a quibus coniunctio appetita est et electa servorum vel colonorum, ut his abire non liceat. Filii earum, si denuntiatio non praecessit, in eorum iure et dominio, apud quos creati sunt vel creantur, colonario nomine perseverent: post denuntiationem vero editos secundum scita divalia servos esse censemus, ut illos nexus, sicut dictum est, colonarius teneat semper obnoxios, hos condicio servitutis, Firmine, parens carissime atque amantissime.
>
> interpretatio: ingenua idemque mulier si contubernium coloni elegerit alieni, si ei denuntiatum non fuerit, coloni sint domino profuturi quoscumque eius partus ediderit; pot denuntiationem vero quoscumque ediderit, non colonos sed servos noverit esse futuros.
>
> By a like law, I order that freeborn women shall be detained if a union with slaves or *coloni* has been sought and chosen by them, in order that they may not be permitted to depart. The children of such women, if a formal notification did not precede their birth, shall remain under the title of *coloni*, in the ownership and power of those persons on whose property they have been born or may be born. But We adjudge that according to the divine imperial decrees, children born after such notification shall be slaves. Thus, as has been said, the bond of the colonate shall always hold obligated the former, the condition of slavery, the latter, O Firminus, dearest and most beloved Father.
>
> *interpretatio*: Likewise if a freeborn woman should choose the slave union of the *colonus* of another, and if she should not be formally notified, whatever offspring she bears shall profit the master of the colonus. But she shall know that whatever children she bears after formal notification shall be not *coloni*, but slaves.

The novel organised several matters. Preceding was the question of *advenae*, immigrants not subjected to duties towards a city (*nulli quolibet modo obnoxious civitati*) who came and lived with *colonae* and then wandered away, who were now forced to declare in the *gesta municipalia* that they would stay on the estate; they would not thereby lose their *ingenuitas*. The emperor orders the same for *ingenuae* who arrive on an estate to live with slaves or *coloni*: they too may not leave. Two situations are distinguished. If there was no formal warning to leave (*denuntiatio*), children will remain on the land where they were born according to the law of the colonate, under the power of the estate owner. But if there was a warning and the woman did not leave, the children (and probably the woman) will be slaves.[33] That was

[33] On this, see Höbenreich 2007, 280–284; on 281 and 281 n. 19, her position regarding De Martino and Voss.

what the *scita divalia* prescribed and the original purport of the senatusconsultum, and so we may assume this referred to the *senatusconsultum Claudianum*.

The text raises questions. If the woman lived with a slave, why in the first case should any children not be free as herself instead of being bound to the colonate? However, the measure has its parallel in CTh 4.12.3, 320, issued for the unions between *ingenuae* and fiscal slaves: their offspring were free but of Latin status.[34] But according to the original senatusconsultum they should be *ingenui* too; and indeed we saw that with CJ 7.24.1 = CJ 11.48.24 when Justinian abolished the senatusconsultum. And if she lived with a *colonus*, if she stayed after the warning would the children be slaves? But was that sanction not reserved for living with a slave?

The *interpretatio* to Nov. Val. 31 says it slightly differently from the novel:[35] the migrant will for no reason leave the home of the master of his *colona*, to whom he is married, and he has no right to migrate again and leave her (*de domo domini colonae, cui iunctus fuerit, nulla ratione discedere et ingenuitate manente nullam habeat licentiam evagandi aut cui iunctus fuerit deserendi*). Had he been a *collegiatus*, the rule of CTh 12.19.1 (400 W) or 14.7.1 (397 W) would apply, and if he had been a *colonus censitus*, the rule of Nov. Val. 31.1–4 would apply. Further, it reduces section 6 to a union between an *ingenua* and a *colonus*: if there is no warning, children become *coloni*, if there was a warning the children will be slaves. This is clearer than Nov. Val. 31.6 and apparently the way the novel was generally interpreted and applied. It confirms that the *senatusconsultum Claudianum* automatically applied in the sense that children (and probably the mother) became *coloni* if there was no warning. That in the case of a warning they all become slaves would in that context be a punishment because the woman did not heed the wish of the estate owner. The *interpretatio* speaks of *mancipia* and *contubernia*. These words are more the expression of the low status of these people than that they had become at that time formally slaves, and that it was a *coniugium non aequale*. Otherwise the distinction made would be senseless.[36] Was this automatic application of the senatusconsultum new? We saw that in the east in CJ 7.24.1 it was automatically applied before, thus it is probable that it was long before so. Moreover, the texts in the Theodosian Code do not hint at a warning.

[34] In CTh 4.12.3 their children would be *spurii Latini* and subjected to the patronage of the emperor. This might mean that they were subjected to the same restrictions as the Latini Juniani.

[35] Nov. Val. 31, p. 132.65–66. Schipp 2009, 333.

[36] In INov. Val. 35 the interpreter speaks of *mancipia originaria vel coloniaria*.

A year later, in 452, Valentinian issued more rules on *coloni* in Nov. Val. 35, of 452. He forbade *originarii*, *inquilini*, slaves and *coloni* to become a cleric or to enter a monastery in order to escape the bond of their due *condicio*. Contrary to the east (CJ 1.3.16 of 409; see Sections 13.1 and 14), the consent of the estate owner could not help and did not matter (Nov. Val. 35.3). Being a cleric or monk provided an immunity.[37] Those *originarii* or slaves who had already entered the Church should be returned to their masters (with the exception of bishops and priests) unless they had been in the same office for the full thirty years (of the limitation of prescription). But a deacon of this status could supply to his former master a substitute (*vicarius*) and render his entire *peculium*. If this was not possible, the rules regarding the *collegiati* as set out in Nov. Val. 35.5 were applicable (Nov. Val. 35.6). This means that those deacons who were ordained in the last ten years were to be returned.[38]

Nov. Val. 35.18 regulates the transfer of *coloni* by somebody from one land of his which has a surplus to another land of his. If the owner wanted this and had it so arranged, then it remained in force when the lands were later transferred to third parties in any way. It is the same situation as addressed in CJ 11.48.13.1 (400 W) – which allowed such a shifting of *coloni* – but without the last phrase in that constitution about the offspring reclaimable by the owner of the land that lost *coloni*.

The next section, Nov. Val. 35.19, refers to the rule about the children of a *colona* in Nov. Val. 31.2 and forbids challenging this rule, which prescribed a division of the offspring. As stated before, CTh 5.18.1.3 suggests the children became free too after the prescription had run, whereas this was later changed for the worse by Nov. Val. 31.2. It states (Nov. Val., p. 152.200–203) that the division of offspring as mentioned in CTh 5.18.1.3–4 should be applied. The Novel merely mentions the constitution, but the *interpretatio* renders its contents correctly.

The *interpretatio* INov. Val. 35 repeats the prohibition of Nov. Val. 35.3 (p. 148.129–131). As to Nov. Val. 35.6, it repeats this also (Nov. Val., p. 149.143–145). Nov. Val. 35.18–19 is rendered in the same way (Nov. Val., p. 151.196–204).

This succession of Novels on the recall of *coloni* and on marriages with others than *coloni* in the period of 449–452 is a testimony to the ability of the Imperial Chancery to react quickly to unwanted consequences of new legislation. It also shows that in the decades before there must have been much migration (flight) amongst the *coloni*, as we have already seen in

37 Schipp 2009, 334. 38 See also Jones 1964, 921–922.

Section 28.2. Perhaps Nov. Val. 27 initially meant to set a cap on all reclaims, both for fugitive *coloni* and properties.

41.3 Majorian

Under Valentinian's successor, Majorian, in Nov. Maior. 7 of 458, a phenomenon signalled before in CTh 12.1.6 (319) and 33 (342 E) showed up again. Curials tried to escape their liability to serve as town councillors and the taxes by moving to the countryside and join *colonae* and slave women, gaining thereby the protection of the powerful, further lowering the status of their children, perhaps in the hope that in this way these would escape the decurionate. If they were found within thirty years, they could be forced to return, together with their wives. There was no compensation for the estate owners for the loss of these women, since they deserved a punishment for allowing it (Nov. Maior. 7pr–1; punishment set in Nov. Maior. 7.4). This applied also to the imperial estates (*domus nostra*). Their offspring should be divided: sons would follow their father, daughters would remain with the estate owner of their mother. The latter's status would evidently be the colonate. If the mother was a *colona*, the sons became liable for the town council, that is, they were considered curials; if she was a slave the sons were enrolled in the *collegia* of their father's town (presumably as *servi publici*; it would be remarkable if they became free and *collegiati*, but it is not impossible: see Nov. Val. 31.6), which fitted better the low status of their mother and kept the status of the town council high (Nov. Maior. 7.2, not repeated in the *interpretatio*). The status of *collegiati* was very low and subjected. They provided services to their town and were not allowed to live outside their town's territory (Nov. Maior. 7.3).

If a curial made his daughter enter cohabitation (*contubernium*) with a slave, who was *actor* or *procurator* of an estate owner, or allowed her to cohabit with him, she should within a year be returned to her home town. She would inherit on equal par with the other children, and her offspring – *spurii* and freeborn – were liable for the council.[39] If her so-called husband was a slave, he would be condemned to a punishment fit for slaves (flogging or death); if he was an *originarius* and had married her against the prohibition (*contra interdictum legis*),[40] he would be made a *collegiatus* (Nov. Maior. 7.5). It is clear from this text that a *colonus* could be an *actor* or

[39] The *Interpretatio* lets this be children by her out of an ensuing marriage with a curial.

[40] Which prohibition? It is not known. Perhaps it was a western law in Book 5 which was not transmitted.

procurator and of course a free man, but that equally a slave could be appointed to such offices. It is also clear that the municipal councils badly needed new members.

The remainder of this constitution (Nov. Maior. 7.5–17) deals with the curials and town councils and the collection of taxes within the imperial system. It demonstrates the abysmal state the town administration in the west (Italy, Gaul) had fallen into at the middle of the fifth century. It explains the desire of curials to enter unions with women otherwise considered too low in status to be partners. A curial's daughter who does not want to marry a curial and elopes has to render one-quarter of her assets to the town and she will bear curials to that town (Nov. Maior. 7.6). Further it says that a curial or *corporatus* in ignorance of their status, wanting to become a cleric and having entered any office lower than that of deacon, will without delay be recalled to their duties. If they have been ordained as deacon or bishop, they do not have to render anything (Nov. Maior. 7.7). The *capita* 12 to 17 are not summarised, *quia haec quae continet usu carent et certo ad intelligendam non habent obscura*. In other words, they were not applied. Majorian had tried to reorganise the western administration, but in the end only Italy was under imperial control.[41] The *interpretator* will have written after these events, or we see here the text of or an adaptation by the Alarician compilers.

The *interpretatio*, INov. Maior. 7, does not deal with the marriage or *contubernium* of a curial with a *colona* or slave woman, but with the union of a curial's daughter with a *colonus* (a *contubernium*) with the master's approval (a reminder of the *senatusconsultum Claudianum*), that is, Nov. Maior. 7.5–6. She will be returned after a year and has to succeed in the inheritance so that, if she marries a curial, the council will be repaired. If she does consent to this but runs to another town, she has to surrender one-quarter of her assets to her council. If she marries a curial of another town, she will bear curials (p. 173.130–140). There is no mention of flight of curials to the countryside to marry women of subjected status.

41.4 Severus

The emperor Severus issued in 465 a constitution in which he describes how men and women, subjected to public corporations, assigned to duties of a town or of Rome (*alia corpora publica obsequiis deputata*, i.e., the corporations of the *collegiati*), move to the countryside and cohabitate with

[41] Jones 1974, 243–244.

coloni or *famuli* (*inquilini*?),[42] that is, *originales*, without the knowledge of the estate owners. Their children would be slaves or, according to the law, *coloni* or *inquilini originales*, but under reference to their *corporatio publica* they pretended their children were not *coloni*. As for now this was accepted, but in the future children would be of that status and belong to the estate owner of their father or mother (Nov. Sev. 2).[43]

42 The Council of Orange of 441, Sidonius Apollinaris *ep.* 5.19, and Remigius of Reims

The Church in Gaul, the 'eldest daughter of the church', has a long tradition of local councils. It started in 314 with the Council of Arles where the convening bishops issued twenty-two canons.[44] Such canons were regulating doctrine, pastoral and ecclesiastical matters, but since the bishops also wanted to impose morality on the lay, canons could be effective through the ecclesiastical censure on secular matters. Thus the Council of Orange of 441 threatened those who challenged a manumission *in ecclesia* or the protection of the church as commended in testaments in *caput* 7 with the *censura*:

> In ecclesia manumissos, uel per testamentum ecclesiae commendatos si quis in seruitutem uel obsequium uel ad colonariam conditionem imprimere tentauerit, animaduersione ecclesiastica coercebitur.
>
> If somebody will have tried to impose slavery or services or the *condicio coloniaria* on those who were enfranchised in the church, or who were by testament commended to the church, he will be corrected by the church through punishment. (tr. Sirks)[45]

In this way the censure had a secular effect. The canon implies, as already observed by Koptev,[46] that a release from the *condicio coloniaria* was possible by a manumission *in ecclesia* or by testament and commended to the church; although it should be researched whether the canon law had a role here, as Koptev suggests. But in law the act had effect. The *manumissio in ecclesia* conferred freedom upon slaves since 316 (CJ 1.13.1), Roman

[42] Pharr 1952 refers for this interpretation of *famuli* to Nov. Maior. 7.4–5, Nov. Val. 35.3ff, LRB 46 (*famuli*).

[43] Pharr 1952 refers here to CTh 12.19.1, Nov. Maior. 7.3.

[44] Editions of these councils: Sirmond 1629; recent: Munier 1963.

[45] Concilium Arausicanum a. 441 (CPL 1779 b), c. 7; Mansi Vol. 6, col. 434, c. 7. In Mansi Vol. 7, col. 875, a Council of Arles is mentioned, with in c. 33 a similar rule (only testamentary manumissions). There did not turn up such a rule in the Italian Councils for the period 347–536.

[46] Koptev 2004, 300.

citizenship in any case since 321 (CJ 1.13.2), and was, *vide* the canon, extended to *coloni originales* as a release from the *potestas* (also confirmed by ICTh 4.8.7). It implies that this manumission also released from the bond by the *ius census* or else reclaiming would be successful. They therefore became free from the *condicio* and became *ingenui*. We do not see the manumitted become 'free' *coloni*.[47] The canon says: by testament commended to the church. In the Formulae Andecavenses 20 and 23 we see the same phrase.[48] It was a commendation to the local church to protect the freedom of the enfranchised person. Another testimony of the manumission as release is a letter by Sidonius Apollinaris.

Sidonius Apollinaris was a Roman from Gaul, born in the early 430s, from a distinguished family, who was prefect of Rome in 468 and bishop of Clermont from 470 onwards. He died ca. 490.[49] Amongst his literary works is a collection of letters. In one of these, 5.19, he discusses a case of abduction by a *colonus originalis*. Dalton dates this letter to around 472.[50]

> *Ep.* 5.19: Sidonius Pudenti suo salutem. Nutricis meae filiam filius tuae rapuit: facinus indignum quodque nos vosque inimicasset, nisi protinus scissem te nescisse faciendum. sed conscientiae tuae purgatione praelata petere dignaris culpae calentis impunitatem. sub condicione concedo: si stupratorem pro domino iam patronus originali solvas inquilinatu. mulier autem illa iam libera est; quae tum demum videbitur non ludibrio addicta sed assumpta coniugio, si reus noster, pro quo precaris, mox cliens factus e tributario plebeiam potius incipiat habere personam quam coloniariam. nam meam haec sola seu compositio seu satisfactio vel mediocriter contumeliam emendat; qui tuis votis atque amicitiis hoc adquiesco, si laxat libertas maritum, ne constringat poena raptorem. vale.
>
> Sidonius Apollinaris to his friend Pudens. The son of your wet nurse has abducted the daughter of mine. It is a shameful crime,[51] and one which would have destroyed our friendly relations, had I not learned at once that

47 One might read the text as if people tried to impose the colonate on a freed slave, next to trying to reduce freed slaves to slavery again. However, the text is about the recognition of the *manumissio in ecclesia* and it is more logical to assume that people try to turn around an act of release than to impose something different on the manumitted person. That requires different proof, so that this interpretation is not taken into account.

48 Formulae Andecavenses 23 (a manumission): ... *nec nullum obsequium heredum hac proberedum meorum te quicquam redebere cognuscas, nisi sub defensione sancti basileci domni illius praehebeas obsequium, non requaeratur* ...

49 On Sidonius Apollinaris, see Harries 1994.

50 See Grey 2008, 292, who assumes the man was a registered resident tenant; Schipp 2009, 199–213. In the context of this book we do not have to enter into all the aspects of the case.

51 CTh 9.24.1 = Brev. 9.19.1, and IBrev. (partly repeated in EdTh 17–20); EdTh 17: *raptorem ingenuae mulieris aut virginis, cum suis complicibus vel ministris, rebus probatis iuxta legem iubemus extingui, et si consenserit rapta raptori, pariter occidatur*; EdTh 21: *si quis ancillam alienam aut originariam violenter*

> you knew nothing of the man's intention.[52] But though your conscience is thus acquitted in advance, you yet do not scruple to ask that this crying offence should be allowed to go unpunished. I can only agree on one condition: that you release the ravisher from his *inquilinatus originalis*, by changing your relation to him from that of master to that of patron. The woman is already free; but she will only be regarded as a taken into marriage[53] instead of being given over to dishonour if our criminal, whose cause you espouse, as soon as he is created client out of *originalis*, starts assuming the status of a plebeian freeman rather than that of a *colonus originalis*.[54] Nothing short of these terms or these amends will in the least condone the affront. I only yield to your request and your protestation of friendship on condition that, if liberty shall make him a free bridegroom, he as ravisher be not bound to justice.[55] Farewell. (tr. Dalton 1915)

The facts in this letter fit the information we have on the colonate.[56] The woman was either born free or freed from slavery (or perhaps from the colonate), whereas the man was a *colonus originalis* or *inquilinus originalis* (the difference being negligible).[57] If the woman remained unmarried or lived with him in concubinage, her children would be fatherless but free

cum multitudine congregata rapuerit, si ingenuus est, raptoris poena feriatur, quia violentiae crimen admittit: si servus est aut colonus et sua hoc tantum voluntate commisit, simili ratione puniatur.

[52] This makes only sense for the EdTh 22, where the master is punished too if he knew of the crime. We do not find this in the Theodosian Code or the Breviary. EdTh 22: *si vero conscio conductore aut iubente aut connivente vel non prohibente hoc fecerit, etiam conductor ipse tamquam facti reus simili poena feriatur. si autem domino sciente vel iubente hoc fecit, eandem possessionem, de qua raptor egressus est, fisco profuturam dominus incunctanter amittat.*

[53] Sidonius expects the two to stay together and marry, as custom would have it. EdTh 59 prescribed that if an *ingenuus* had violated a virgin *ingenua*, he had to marry her. The woman might have been a virgin, and an *ingenua* she was without doubt, but the man was not an *ingenuus*. Turning him into this, with some flexibility of mind one could sustain that he would be forced to marry her.

[54] The dishonour would follow from having been abducted but not married. The marriage would be an unequal one, since the woman was an *ingenua* and the man an *inquilinus originalis*. Their children would be subjected to the *condicio inquilinatus* or *coloniara*, since they would follow their father's status. Harries 1994, 212 thinks that since the man was of unfree status the marriage would not be legitimate and that there would be no real marriage but concubinage. But there would be a legitimate marriage, and Sidonius' concern is not, as Harries thinks, that the Christian concept of full marriage could not be accommodated with the inequalities of status as established by Roman law.

[55] As a free man, the man would not be *ipso iure* unpunishable, but he could marry the woman.

[56] See Demicheli 2012. Further Koptev 2004 with an extensive analysis of the case; Grey 2008.

[57] Carrié 1997, 146–161, suggests on 147 that the seducer may have been 'schiavo e colono agricolo' (thus: a slave as *instrumentum fundi*). In that case the word *inquilinatus* would have had a more metaphorical than technical meaning. It would explain why those who see in the colonate a *ius personae* may refer to this text. Schipp 2009, 201 proposes two possibilities. One is, that Pudens transfers land to a child of his slave nurse: now the child is bound to this as *originalis inquilinatus*. Because he is now subjected to the tribute, he will be entered under his master's name in the census, as *tributarius*, and so he became a *persona colonaria*. I cannot follow this argument. Such a slave would become *instrumentum*, but he would not have to pay taxes. Schipp's second possibility, that the abductor was *inquilinatus* by birth, is the correct hypothesis.

Romans. If she married him, which convention would demand (and Sidonius as bishop had to insist on this), her children would be subjected to the colonate, since they would follow their father's status. The marriage would be unequal and considered less respectable for a free woman; her children would be of lesser status than she was. Hence Sidonius' concern that the man be released. In exchange for that he will not claim justice on the man (who, as abductor and perhaps violator, was punishable with death).[58] The letter demonstrates that the son of Pudens' nurse can be released from the inquilinate or colonate and that he turns from a *tributarius* into a *plebeius*, that is, a free man of low status, perhaps paying tax. Yet, being manumitted, he would at the same time be obliged as any freedman to his manumitter, whom Sidonius calls his (future) *patronus*.[59]

Remigius (437–534), bishop of Reims, left a testament.[60] In it he bequeaths the *coloni* he has to the Church of Reims (*Tu ... colonos, quos .... habeo, possidebis ... colonas*). He does not mention land to which these might have been attached. Tennaredus, who was born of a freeborn (*ingenua*) mother, may use the status of freedom (*statu libertatis utatur*). His father was evidently a *colonus*, and Tennaredus as a consequence of the *senatusconsultum Claudianum* also, but was now released from the colonate.[61] The *colonus* Vitalis is ordered to be free; likewise Cispiciolus, the *colonus*, but this person will belong to Remigius grandson. Was Cispiciolus now bound? The text does not give a clue.[62]

Thus for the west, though the remains of the Theodosian Code do not contain any reference to the possibility of a release, it is certain that this was possible in the way slavery or the *patria potestas* could be ended.[63] The texts date from 441 and 472, early after 438, so that we may assume that in the law of the Theodosian Code this possibility existed too. We also know from CJ 11.48.20 for the east that release was possible and from the case of Dara-Anastasiopolis (see Section 38.5, Anastasius) that it happened. It follows from these texts that release in the form of manumission, with, as we may assume, a striking of the registration in the census, was common to both east and west. Perhaps it was mentioned in a lost text of Book 5 of the Theodosian Code. We find in the later Formulae texts which may have

[58] As established through the *lex Iulia de vi publica*, see D. 48.6.5.2 (*ultimum supplicium*), CJ 9.12. In extenso with Mommsen 1899, 664–665.

[59] So also Koptev 2004, 298–290. [60] See on this Jones et al. 1957.

[61] If his father had been a slave, Tennaredus would have been a freeborn anyway and therefore his father must have been of subjected status which passed on to his son.

[62] Krusch 1896, 336–339.

[63] The *manumissio vindicta* is not mentioned, but in the fifth century the *manumissio in ecclesia* in presence of the bishop may have taken over.

been modelled after the deed of such a release (Formulae Andecavenses 20 and 23). The Formula Visigothica 34 (615–620) is a deed for the release from the paternal power, which shows that such deeds were still practised.[64] Grey suggests that striking the person's name in the tax declaration would in any case have been required, which is of course true if the census still functioned as such.[65] It would have implied that this person was liable for his tax, now without the estate owner guaranteeing this – if, of course, in this period the poll tax was still levied.

The Novels issued in the west after 438 and up till 465 (after that only eleven years remained till Odoacer would depose the western emperor and take over), show a permanent concern over the supply of working force on the land, in agriculture, and in the cities for municipal services and the municipal administration. Was the situation as disastrous as this might suggest? One thing is certain: the need to make more and more refined rules about the return and division of families of *coloni* implies an increase in the reclaiming of *coloni* who migrated and a need for labour. It may have been that normally a part of the *coloni* was always on the move. In that case the legislation would indicate that the need for labour could no longer suffer this deficit in the nominal supply. It may also have been the case that after 400 there had been an increase in flight, growing bigger after 438, leading to attempts to keep the nominal number per estate on level. And perhaps the constitutions reflect the situation in Gaul, while Italy enjoyed mere stability. The political unrest will have incited *coloni* and others to take their chance, to flee seek refuge with those landowners who could provide better protection than the imperial administration of small landowners.

43 The Colonate in Vandal Africa

The Vandal king Huneric condemned bishops who did not want to convert to Arianism to banishment with the duty to cultivate land *colonatus iure*, which suggests the *condicio coloniaria* was imposed on them,[66] just as with the beggars in Rome in CTh 14.18.1. As argued in Section 10.6, the colonate continued to exist under the Vandals and after the reconquest of Africa in 533 by Justinian's general Belisarius. For the situation after 533, see Section 10.6.

64 See Sirks 2019b, 183–184, 2020b. It was, however, done in a diluted way.

65 Grey 2008, 297. He doubts whether a manumission would be required. Yet the Council of Orange makes clear that this was the normal way.

66 Victor Vitensis, *Historia persecutionis Africanae provinciae* 3.20: *relegati colonatus iure ad excolendum agros.*

44 Farmers Not Subjected to the Colonate

We do not possess references to independent farmers for the latter half of the fifth century. There will have been some, if we assume that the *coloni* who were released by manumission in the church went on to become farmers, be it on their own land, as lessees or as farmhands. Agriculture was the dominant mode of existence. But next to this possibility there will have been people who farmed independently. The case of the Christian slaves working on the land of Jews in Luni a century later shows that.[67]

45 The Colonate in the Breviarium Alaricianum Alias the Lex Romana Visigothorum of 506 (Southern Gaul, Septimania, and Visigothic Spain): Status

The Breviarium Alaricianum was compiled by order of the Visigothic king Alaric II for his Roman subjects and confirmed by him in 506.[68] It is a selection of texts from the Theodosian Code, coupled with Posttheodosian Novels, the Pauli Sententiae, the Gai Epitome, and some fragments from the Gregorian and Hermogenian Code. The collection is complete and therefore presents by way of its selection – in as far as it followed the Theodosian Code – the entire written complex of Roman law rules as currently applied in the Visigothic kingdom.[69] The constitutions

[67] Gregorius Magnus *ep.* IV.21, of May 594.

[68] The Lex influenced later legal compilations like the Lex Romana Curiensis, various Epitomae, the Frankish Capitularies, or even laws like the Lex Baiuvariorum. I do not deal with these, since they relate to a society with a different concept of *coloni*. See Schipp 2009, 310ff. with a fine survey. On the Breviarium, see Fitting 1872, 1873; Wenger 1954, 555–558; Conrat 1903; Lambertini, 1991; Liebs 2002, 109–110, 166–176 with literature; Rouche & Dumézil 2008. The article therein by Bondue 2008, 91–101, does not bring anything new. Conrat 1903 is a rearrangement of the laws in the Breviarium in a way reminiscent of the German Civil Code. It is useful as a survey of the law for the Romans as under the Visigoths, but in the context of this study on the colonate of little use because he did not use the *interpretationes* (astonishingly for a man so capable). After the Franks beat the Visigoths at Vouillé in 507, the rule of the latter in Gaul was restricted to Septimania, but the Breviary remained in force in the part of Gaul, formerly part of the Visigothic kingdom. The research of Di Cintio (see Di Cintio 2013 and 2018) is until now restricted to Books 1, 2, and 9. In as far as the texts treated by her are relevant here, they are cited. For the economic conditions, see Wickham 2005, 102: in the North under the Franks there was a breakdown of the tax system, whereas south of the Loire land tax registration remained in force for a long period.

[69] Piquer Marí 2016 speaks of a Visigothic colonate; in 118 n. 16 he assumes that the norms of the Breviary did not only concern *coloni* of Romans, contrary to what Schipp 2009, 313 thinks. He bases his research on the Breviary. But this was a collection made for the Roman subjects and not for the Visigoths. Unless we find Visigothic sources which deal with *coloni*, as we are able for the Burgundians, and unless these show differences with the Roman colonate (as we do not see with the Burgundians), it is, terminologically, not warranted to speak of a Visigothic colonate, even if we find that the Visigoths used the colonate and applied Roman law rules. But in the Code of Euric the colonate is not mentioned. What we have are testaments such as that of Victor of Huesca

from the Theodosian Code, the Novels, and the Pauli Sententiae are usually accompanied by *interpretationes*, on which see Section 41. Piquer Marí assumes the compilers chose constitutions which fitted practical purposes. Because of that, so Piquer Marí, their choice was not sufficient to cover the entire reality of the colonate: it focused on the productivity of the estates. The result was that the colonate degraded to an iron subjection, lowered in status but still a free status.[70] Whatever be of this, the texts chosen from the Theodosian Code present in any case for 506 the existing situation. The Breviarium answers the question of which law in the Visigothic territories applied to the Roman inhabitants. These texts were taken from the *leges* and *ius*; the Visigothic king did not have the authority to change them (he could only issue edicts for the Romans). But their application might be different and indeed often was; the *interpretationes* demonstrate this.[71] Thus in order to know the law on the colonate in the late fifth-century Visigothic kingdom, we have to consider in the first place the *interpretationes*. Inasmuch as they are relevant for the Posttheodosian Novels they have already been dealt with. Now those interpretations to other texts, namely of the Theodosian Code, are taken into consideration as well as testimonies to the situation in 506. In as far as they may have been made before, they may reflect the situation in the second half of the fifth century in the (Visigothic) west.

We have already dealt with the Posttheodosian Novels regarding *coloni*, and several of them figure in the Breviarium: Brev. Nov. Val. 5 (= Nov. Val. 23), *id.* 8 (= 27), *id.* 9 (= 31), *id.* 12 (= 35) and Brev. Nov. Maior. 1 (= Nov. Maior. 7) (the numeration of the Breviarium edition differs from that of the Theodosian Code). We merely have to add those constitutions from the Theodosian Code, with their *interpretationes*, which the Alarician compilers considered still applicable in the Visigothic territory and which are relevant for the colonate. They are Brev. 2.30.1 (= CTh 2.30.1), Brev. 2.30.2 (= CTh 2.30.2),[72] Brev. 2.31.1 (=CTh 2.31.1),[73] Brev. 2.32.1 (= CTh 2.32.1), Brev. 4.8.3 (= CTh 4.8.7),[74] Brev. 4.20.1 (= CTh 4.22.1),[75] Brev. 4.21.1 (= CTh 4.23.1),[76] Brev. 5.3.1 (= CTh 5.3.1), Brev. 5.9.1 (= CTh 5.17.1),[77] Brev. 5.9.2 (= CTh 5.17.2), Brev. 5.10.1 (= CTh 5.18.1),[78] Brev.

(see Section 49), a Roman. Bueno 2003, 632 cites Reccesvinth, who in 660 forbade the use of Roman law from now on (Liber 2.1.10). That indicates its application until then. How do we know whether the compilers focused on productivity? Should we not have had more constitutions like CJ 11.48.1?

70 Piquer Marí 2016, 163.
71 See Di Cintio 2013 and 2018. Her work deals with other themes.
72 Piquer Marí 2016, 131–133.
73 Piquer Marí 2016, 133–136.
74 Piquer Marí 2016, 140–144.
75 Piquer Marí 2016, 138–139.
76 Piquer Marí 2016, 151–153.
77 Piquer Marí 2016, 144–151.
78 Piquer Marí 2016, 153–160.

5.11.1 (= CTh 5.19.1),[79] and Brev. 8.1.1 (= CTh 8.2.5).[80] Since the edition of Mommsen and Meyer is nowadays standard, references to the *interpretationes* carry here the reference numbers of this edition, for example ICTh 5.17.1 instead of IBrev. 5.9.1. Likewise, references to the other parts of the Breviarium are to modern editions.[81]

The position of the *colonus* had changed considerably.[82] CTh 5.17.1 (Brev. 5.9.1) deals with the return of a fugitive *colonus*:[83]

> Apud quemcumque colonus iuris alieni fuerit inventus, is non solum eundem origini suae restituat, verum super eodem capitationem temporis agnoscat. 1. Ipsos etiam colonos, qui fugam meditantur, in servilem condicionem ferro ligari conveniet, ut officia, quae liberis congruunt, merito servilis condemnationis compellantur inplere.
>
> interpretatio: Si quis alienum colonum sciens in domo sua retinerit ipsum prius domino restituat et tributa eius quamdiu apud eum fuerit cogatur exsolvere: ipse vero qui noluit esse quod natus est in servitium redigitur.

> Any person in whose possession a *colonus* who is subjected to another is found not only shall restore the aforesaid *colonus* to his birth status but also shall assume the capitation tax for this man for the time that he was with him. 1. *Coloni* also who meditate flight must be bound with chains and reduced to a servile condition, so that by virtue of their condemnation to slavery, they shall be compelled to fulfill the duties that befit freemen.
>
> *interpretatio*: If any person should knowingly detain in his own household a *colonus* that belongs to another, he shall first restore the man himself to his owner, and he shall be compelled to pay his tribute for as long a time as the man was with him. But the *colonus* himself who was unwilling to be what he had been born shall be reduced to slavery.

Koptev convincingly argues that *in servilem conditionem ferro ligari* in CTh 5.17.1 cannot be interpreted as saying that the constitution reduced the fugitive to slavery (as the Pharr 1952 translation suggests). According to him, the fugitive will be shackled only during (or, in my view, upon) his return, and he will work as a free man; in the Breviary, on the other hand, he will be enslaved.[84] I would leave open the possibility that the text allows that those *coloni* suspected of flight might be chained already before and during work (working on the fields will have allowed for fleeing). In that way he, a free

79 Piquer Marí 2016, 136–138. 80 Piquer Marí 2016, 160–162.

81 Petot 1963, 3 interprets *servus* in LRV = Brev. 4.8.2, LRB 37.5, and Lex Ribuaria § 10 as 'serf', which of course changes everything since that would imply a free but tied person, thus a *colonus*. I do not see a reason to follow him.

82 On this, Santilli 1999, 280; Koptev 2009, 264–270; Piquer Marí 2016, 113–163.

83 Piquer Marí 2016, 144–151. 84 Santilli 1999, 280; Koptev 2009, 264–270.

person but chained as a slave, will be performing duties fit for free persons (*officia quae liberis congruunt*). In ICTh 5.17.1, he indeed is enslaved if he does not want to be what he was born to (*noluit esse quod natus est*).

We see here a shift in his personal status. The shift is from doing things to being: born into a condition which he may not deny; from being *alieni iuris* to being of somebody else, *alienus*. A way of entering the colonate the *interpretatio* does not know, which may be due to the contents of the Theodosian Code,[85] but for the *interpretatio* the colonate is a birth status and to all appearance it was the normal way by which somebody was a *colonus*. The *colonus*' condition implied that he was obliged to stay on an estate and was subjected to the owner of it: ICTh 5.17.1 says that who knowingly keeps somebody else's *colonus* in his estate exploitation (*domus*) must return him to his master and pay the taxes for the time he was with him.[86] The *colonus* is enslaved because he denied his birth, which implies that this birth obliges him to stay on the estate of his master. The *coloni* were subjected (*obnoxii*) to their master, since they were not allowed to sell land or personal property (*peculium*) without their masters knowing this (ICTh 5.19.1, cited below). Because I take the connection with the payment of tax (the poll tax) as essential for the Roman colonate, I consider the situation under the Visigoths as being still this colonate, but the situation may be more complicated; I shall return to this in Section 49.

> CTh. 5.19.1: Non dubium est colonis arva, quae subigunt, usque adeo alienandi ius non esse, ut, et si qua propria habeant, inconsultis atque ignorantibus patronis in alteros transferre non liceat. –
>
> interpretatio: In tantum dominis coloni in omnibus tenentur obnoxii ut nescientibus dominis nihil colonus neque de terra neque de peculio suo alienare praesumat.
>
> There is no doubt that *coloni* do not have the right to alienate the fields that they cultivate, to the extent that even if they have any belongings of their own, they may not transfer them to others without the advice and knowledge of their patrons.
>
> *interpretatio*: *Coloni* are held obligated to their owners in all things, to such an extent that without the knowledge of their owners they may not presume to alienate either any of the land or any of their own *peculium*.

[85] CTh 5.6.3 is not included in the Breviarium, but that may be due to the fact that is speaks of Scyri. If there was no text in the Theodosian Code on entering the colonate by agreement, there was nothing to include in the Breviarium. This, however, does not take away that for the *interpretatio* being *colonus* by birth is evidently the normal way, and if that was the dominant view, there would be no reason for the Alarician compilers to include a constitution on entering the colonate by agreement.

[86] ICTh 5.17.1 calls the *capitatio* the *tributa*, which is correct (see for CTh 10.12.2 note 390 and § 28.2 West). Schipp denies the existence of the *capitatio*. Piquer Marí 2016, 149 sees it as the *capitatio terrena* and *capitatio humana*.

The *interpretatio* turns the argument around: where the constitution merely says that *coloni* may not alienate their land or other properties unless their patrons consent, it says that *coloni* are held to be subjected in everything, which includes the alienation of their properties, which makes the assent of their master required.[87] It uses the word *obnoxius*, 'subjected'. In administrative law it means that somebody is liable for a public duty; here it will refer to the *potestas* of the landowner. In the Formulae Andecavenses of ca. 600 (Angers, Francia) we find it in the form of *obnoxietatio*, the procedure by which somebody subjects himself to the power of another person.[88] Piquer Marí notes that the *interpretatio* is much wider than the constitution; it is a social degradation and a pre-Alarician comment because already in CTh 8.2.5 of 401 the *colonus* is *obnoxius servituti*.[89] The latter is certainly correct, but whether it makes the *interpretatio* so very much pre-Alarician remains to be seen. It means that one is as if a slave and has to obey the master, a shift in view, as Koptev observes.[90] The status has become more important. Schipp remarks that similarly in ICTh 5.17.1 and ICTh 5.17.2 the expression *colonus iuris alieni* has been replaced by *colonus alienus* and he should be returned to his former master, not his *origo*. The bond with the *origo* was lifted and replaced by a bond with the master. Schipp applies here also later law collections. He is right in pointing out the shift from *iuris alieni* to *alienus* and the insertion of *sciens* in ICTh 5.17.1.[91] The first may indeed also indicate a shift in view. Yet, as long as *tributum* has to be compensated in the *interpretatio*, and lacking other evidence for the Visigothic times, we may still see this as the consequence of a fiscal arrangement.

Schipp, however, assumes on basis of the *interpretatio* to CTh 5.17.1 that the *capitatio* was no longer levied in Gaul. Instead of the *tributa*, the estate owner had to pay *mercedes* for the fugitive *colonus*. The *tributum* was now

[87] Schipp 2009, 345 on this *interpretatio*, which he also reads as a complete restriction of the faculty to dispose of personal goods and their land. Yet the goods, though not in the text, are mentioned in the rubric and may have been mentioned in another, lost constitution, like CJ 11.50.2, which also restricted their faculty to litigate with their masters (see above). Schipp 2009, 348 assumes this was still valid, but we would have expected CJ 11.50.2 to be included in the Breviarium, which is not the case.

[88] Formulae Andecavenses 19: the *obnoxietatio*, that is, the subjecting of a person to the state of *servitium*.

[89] Piquer Marí 2016, 136–138.

[90] Koptev 2009, 273–278, connects CTh 5.19.1, which does not mention the word *peculium*, with CJ 11.50.2, where it is used. Koptev assumes this constitution was not included in the Theodosian Code, but that must be a slip of the pen. It will have been included in Books 1 to 5. Originally *peculium* did not include land. That the interpretation includes it shows, so Koptev, the change in view about the status of the *coloni*.

[91] Schipp 2009, 328–332.

the 'eingefrorene Steuerquote' or the 'dem Grundherrn geschuldeten Abgaben', which leaves the reader with the question: Who owes what?[92] Schipp here, as elsewhere, combines CTh 5.17.1, ICTh 5.17.1, and the *interpretatio* of the Lex Romana Curiensis, namely 5.9, where it is said *domino suo reddat et mercedes eius.*[93] This way of using later texts to interpret the Alarician *interpretatio* is problematic and may cause confusion. First, the Lex Romana Curiensis dates from a considerably later period (eighth century), and second, is from a region a great distance from Visigothic Gaul, namely Roman Raetia (Churrätien).[94] Time and distance may well have caused a difference between them. Actually, the mention of *mercedes* fits c. 6.4 Lex Romana Burgundionum, from the region of Burgundy between Visigothic Gaul and Churrätien (and also EdTh c. 84).[95] It is therefore no argument to assume that the *capitatio*, also known as the *tributum capitis*, was no longer levied in Visigothic Gaul. After 506 it may have been different, namely when the Franks took over. Another argument for assuming that life under the Visigoths went on as before, at least in essence, is the maintenance of several constitutions on taxes by the Visigoths, including those on the tax registration (CTh 11.1.15, 17; 11.3.3, 5; 11.6.1; 11.7.4, 20; 13.10.1, 5 on the *libri exactionis*). Schipp bases his view of the colonate on the assumption that every *colonus* was a lessee ('Nur-Pächter'), without property or assets, who had to pay *capitatio*, rent, and who was liable with his property (which he did not have).[96]

ICTh 5.17.2 repeats the fine for those eliciting flight or harbouring fugitive *coloni.*[97] The long constitution CTh 5.18.1 (Brev. 5.10.1), repeated and supplemented in Nov. Val. 31, is efficiently summarised in ICTh 5.18.1.[98] Who has held back a *colonus*, whether a fugitive or somebody who migrated voluntarily (the original merely has *discessit*), for thirty years may claim (*vindicet*) him as his own (*suum*). This jargon is not found in CTh 5.18.1 but in Nov. Val. 31.1 of 451 (*eum vindicet iure coloniario serviturum*), which means that the *interpretatio* of CTh 5.18.1 was made after 451 with knowledge of Nov. Val. 31. But the addition there, that the same rule applied to *mulieres originariae*, is not mentioned here, nor in

92 Schipp 329: he cites for this the Epit. St. Gall where the earnings must be turned over. But *mercedes* earned is not the same as *tributa . . . quam diu apud eum fuerit cogatur exsolvere* (ICTh 5.17.1).

93 Schipp 2009, 328–329. Schipp combines his treatment of the *coloni* under the Visigoths with their presence under the Franks; yet even then the use of the Lex Roman Curiensis is daring.

94 See Meyer-Marthali 1975, 5–6.

95 In these two codifications the situation has definitively changed. Now the earning power of the fugitive must be compensated.

96 Schipp 2009, 256. 97 Piquer Marí 2016, 150–151.

98 Koptev 2009, 278–282. Not dealt with by Schipp 2009. Piquer Marí 2016, 153–160.

INov. Val. 31.[99] The *interpretatio* there simply states that she will likewise become after twenty years the *colona originaria* of the other estate owner, together with her offspring (*cui colonam tempus addixerit*). Here the *interpretatio* must have drawn on Nov. Val. 27 (Nov. Val., p. 125.62–126.1). If the *colonus* is reclaimed within these thirty years, he has to be returned with his offspring, which is due according to the law, and entire personal property. If he has died meanwhile, his offspring with their and their dead father's personal property must be returned. If it is a *colona*, the period after which she can no longer be claimed is twenty years. If claimed before and if she had children with a *colonus* of the other estate, she and one-third of her children must be returned, while two-thirds stay with the father-*colonus*. But in order not to split the marriage, the master must give substitutes, both for her and one-third of her children; Koptev remarks that this must have been done to protect the families in the same way as slave families were protected in the early Empire.[100] Could it have been influenced by the Church? The possibility of substitution is not mentioned in EdTh c. 67. Lastly, if a subjected woman marries an *ingenuus*, her whole offspring belongs to her master. The ICTh 4.8.7 adds to this an escape possibility (see below).

The question of reclaiming and substituting turns also up in an *interpretatio* in the context of the *causa liberalis*, the lawsuit in which somebody claimed his freedom or was claimed as slave. CTh 4.8.7 (331) states that the limitation of prescription of sixteen years does not apply to those born out of a slave woman and a free father. Nor will the redemption from slavery or the delivery of a substitute slave be of avail.[101] The constitution evidently has here freeborn children, sold as slaves by their father, in mind (see CTh 3.3.1). Very interestingly, the *interpretatio*, ICTh 4.8.7, gives a twist to the text. Like the constitution, it says that the limitation of prescription will not be of avail for those born of a free father (*ingenuus*) and a slave woman or – here an addition – a *colona*, unless (here is the twist) the father has paid to the owner of the slave woman compensation in the form of substitute slaves with *peculium* or paid for a release of status. Otherwise they cannot change the status of the mother, except by manumission which releases

99 It would lead to a conflict with the twenty-year limitation of prescription for *colonae originales*, if the period was indeed thirty years: there would be an interval of ten years in which they were unassailable in law. On this, Schipp 2009, 332–333. He underlines the question of proof: according to Gregorius Magnus *ep.* 1.53, documents were required, or witnesses may have sufficed. If the fiscal registers were still kept, these would of course have sufficed. As we saw, the Visigoths maintained constitutions on this, so that will have been the rule in their kingdom.

100 Koptev 2009, 281. 101 Piquer Marí 2016, 140–144.

them from their servile condition. We may apply the text in its entirety to *colonae*. It concerns *ingenui* who live with *colonae* of somebody else. It is the situation also addressed in CTh 5.18.1 and Nov. Val. 31. In CTh 5.18.1 all the offspring of such a union belong to the master of the woman, just as with slave women. Here it is different. The *interpretatio* allows for substitutes or a release price. We may, considering the addition, see here an application of the adaptation of CTh 5.18.1 by Nov. Val. 31.2–3. There, in order to keep the family together, Valentinian III allowed for substitutes for the woman who cannot be reclaimed after twenty years and her children. Her children were born before the lapse of time, hence reclaimed less than twenty years after their birth. Here they are reclaimed before sixteen years have lapsed. This means that between the sixteenth and twentieth year after absconding a woman could be claimed but her children no more. The *interpretatio* INov. Val. 31 says: substitutes are due for that part which should return to her former master; but where all must return, all may be substituted. Finally, if no substitute or release price is paid, only manumission can release the children. Here we find for the time of the *interpretationes* an unequivocal reference to manumission as way of release from the colonate. It concurs with the Council of Orange and Sidonius' letter (see Section 42).

This care for retaining marriages intact as much as possible finds its parallel in ICTh 2.25.1 (325 = CJ 3.38.11) on division of patrimonial estates (in Sardinia) with slaves attached, which the *interpretatio* extends to *coloni*.[102] There, however, children and spouses were kept together.

At the end the *interpretatio* says that the remainder about the offspring of a *colona* is found in new constitutions.[103] These are Nov. Val. 27 [Brev.: Nov. Val. 8] (affirming that the limitation of prescription of thirty years applied to all claims), where the *interpretatio* refers to that on 31 [Brev.: Nov. Val. 9], where all is set out, and 35 [Brev.: Nov. Val. 12]). The language used there and in the other *interpretationes* to the Novels is different from and more verbose than that in ICTh 5.18.1. Also, in ICTh 5.18.1 the *colona* is married (*coniugium*, *maritum duxerit*), whereas in the INov. Val. 31 she lives together (*contubernia*, *contubernium*). In classic Roman law the *contubernium* was for slaves and people between whom there was no *conubium*. In the Later Empire and in the Visigothic kingdom, where Christianity was the official religion in which there was no difference between free and slaves, the Church nevertheless accepted the

[102] No treatment with Piquer Marí 2016.

[103] Nov. Val., p. 240.12–13: *Quod hic minus est de colonae agnationis, in novellis legibus invenitur.*

secular rules.[104] If *coloni* were free Romans, which the fact that the constitutions treat them as such proves,[105] unions between them would be *iusta matrimonia*, albeit that some combinations were *coniugia non aequalia*. The qualification in INov. Val. 31 should therefore rather be seen as a social depreciation of the colonate too, since the *coloni* are free people in the Novels. The difference in those days (after 468, if these *interpretationes* were made on the entire collection of Novels) was apparently one between *personae alieni iuris* like *coloni* and *ingenui*, where the designation *alieni iuris* had acquired a meaning, indicating a legal status within the category of free people.

We may not consider this to be slavery, because the difference between *coloni originales* and slaves is evident everywhere. There were *coloni* of private persons and *coloni* of the fisc (the emperor no longer being present, all assets which were *patrimonialis* will have become *fiscalis*) and soliciting them to take flight was punished with a fine (ICTh 5.17.2). They had to render services.

> CTh 8.2.5: Generali lege sancimus, ut, sive solidis provinciis sive singulis civitatibus necessarii fuerint tabularii, liberi homines ordinentur neque ulli deinceps ad hoc officium patescat aditus, qui sit obnoxius servituti. Set et si quis dominorum servum suum sive colonum chartas publicae agere permiserit – consensum enim, non ignorantiam volumus obligari – ipsum quidem, in quantum interfuerit publicae utilitati, pro ratiociniis, quae servo sive colono agente tractata sunt, obnoxium adtineri, servum autem competentibus affectum verberibus fisco addici. In praeteritum quoque decernimus cura dominorum praesentari eos, qui ratiocinia tractaverint, quorum interfuit ab initio providere, ne publicis actibus privata servitia immiscerentur, ut temporis sui quisque rationem positus in quaestione depromat.
>
> By a general law We sanction that when registrars may be needed either for entire provinces or for separate municipalities, free men shall be appointed, and hereafter entrance to this office shall not lie open to any person who is subject to servitude (*obnoxius servituti*). 1. But also if any master should allow his own slave or *colonus* to undertake the administration of public records – of course, it is Our will that the master shall be bound for his consent and not his ignorance – the master himself shall be held obligated for the accounts that were managed by the slave or *colonus*, to the extent that the interest of the public welfare is involved, but the slave shall be punished with the statutory scourging and assigned to the fisc. 2. Against such actions

[104] Gaudemet 1958, 529–530.

[105] Perhaps with exception of the Scyri in CTh 5.6.3. As for the west, there are many Germanic names amongst the occupants of farms in the testaments of, for example, bishop Remigius or Abbo (see Geary 1985, 27–33 on the structure of the testament). Were these descendants of former captives? Or, if *coloni*, had they entered the colonate by *obnoxatio*?

in the past, We also decree that at his own charge a master shall deliver any person who in the past administered such accounts, for it was to the master's interest to provide from the beginning that persons subject to the servitude of private citizens (*privata servitia*) should not be involved in public administrative services. Thus each such person shall be subjected to torture that he may disclose the account for the time that he was in service.

interpretatio: Sive in solida provincia sive per singulas civitates tabularii fuerint ordinati, hoc est, qui rationes publicas tractant, ingenui a provincialibus ordinentur: coloni vel servi ad hoc officium nullatenus admittantur, quia, quibus fides publica committenda est, tales eligi debebunt, de quibus querela esse non possit. Quod si dominus colonum vel servum suum tabularium esse consenserit, pro consensu dominus hac mulcta feriatur, ut quicquid colonus ille vel servus detrimenti admiserit, hoc dominus sine mora restituat: colonus ille vel servus verberatus fisci viribus addicatur.

interpretatio: If in a whole province or for separate municipalities registrars should be appointed, that is, those persons who handle the public accounts, freeborn persons (*ingenui*) shall be appointed by the provincials. *Coloni* and slaves shall in no case be admitted to serve in this office, because such persons must be chosen that there can be no complaint about them, when the public faith must be entrusted to them. But if a master should consent that his *colonus* or slave should be a registrar, because of such consent the following penalty shall be inflicted on said master, namely, that he shall restore without delay whatever damage was caused by said *colonus* or slave. Such *colonus* or slave shall be flogged and assigned to the account of the fisc.

CTh 8.2.5 (= Brev. 8.1.1) prohibits appointing slaves or *coloni originales* as *tabularii*, that is, municipal or provincial tax registrars. In that function they would be subjected to service (*obnoxius servituti*) and would mix public administration with private servitudes (*privata servitia*). Public administration should only be done by free men. Thus both slaves and *coloni* perform private servitudes. If the master consented, he was liable for damages. The *interpretatio* (ICTh 8.2.5) repeats the prohibition, but its argumentation is different. There is no mention of *servitia*. They are not allowed since a legal dispute might arise over them (*de quibus querella esse non possit*), namely about their status. The sanction is different too; in the *interpretatio* both slave and *colonus* are flogged and forfeited to the fisc.[106] The emperor wanted only *ingenui* appointed, presumably because they were not subjected, hence men of a higher status. The mention of *tabularii*

[106] Piquer Marí 2016, 160–162.

suggests that there was in any case the intention to maintain the census system with its registers, either in the provinces or in the towns.

This low status of *coloni* we encounter with the crime of grave-robbing. Those *coloni* caught were tortured as if slaves, and if they confessed, they got the death penalty. If their masters were found to be involved, these were punished too (Nov. Val. 27.3; the *interpretatio* says this novel does not need an interpretation).

ICTh 2.1.1 states that provincial governors are competent to judge over lawsuits where slaves and *coloni* (the *ceteri* in the constitution) of the *res dominica* are involved.[107] Interdicts were part of procedure. Two constitutions supplement two interdicts, *unde vi* and *utrubi*.[108] CTh 4.22.1 (Brev. 4.20.1) orders judges in the case where someone has been forcibly dispossessed of land belonging to a landowner who was absent not to refuse this person as plaintiff, because he (*propinquus*, *amicus*, *colonus* under *quolibet titulo*) lacks a mandate (of the *dominus* or *possessor* who had legal standing, necessary for a *detentor*; see Section 2.3.3) or, if a slave, because slaves have no standing in court.[109] The *interpretatio* ICTh 4.22.1 simplifies this: those the landowner commissioned to manage his goods while he was away, namely his representatives (*actor*, *procurator*) or any slave, should be admitted in court. *Coloni* are not mentioned here, only in the constitution.[110] CTh 4.23.1 (Brev. 4.21.1) reminds us that when *coloni* have fled to another estate, the reclaiming estate owner (*quos bona fide quisque possedit*) does not have to prove ownership for the interdict. The *interpretatio* ICTh 4.23.1 merely summarises, but turns the *coloni quos bona fide quisque possedit* into *coloni rei alienae*, thereby shifting the emphasis from the person to the estate. This argues contra Schipp at ICTh 5.17.1 and 2 regarding the nature of the bond, as also remarked by Piquer Marí.[111] It was still forbidden for them to enter the Church in order to evade their birth status, and they could be recalled within thirty years unless they were bishop or presbyter, while a deacon had to render a substitute and his property (*peculium*) (Nov. Val. 35.3 and 6, the same in INov. Val. 35, Nov. Val., p. 148.129–131, Nov. Val., p. 149.142–145).[112] Further, CTh 5.3.1, an

[107] Piquer Marí 2016, 125–130.

[108] These interdicts were granted to dispossessed possessors to regain goods, taken by force, and their moveable goods, after which a regular procedure over the entitlement to it could start. See Kaser 1975, 261.

[109] Piquer Marí 2016, 138–139. [110] Piquer Marí 2016, 151–153. [111] Piquer Marí 2016, 152.

[112] Schipp 2009, 334–335. He does not see here a 'schwache Reflex der Bodenbindung' but a separate status and underpins this with the Lex Romana Curiensis 18.11. Again, this is a testimony from a much later and different region. The *condicio* of the *coloni* is tied with the land. That these texts speak of the *debita condicio* is because the entrance into the Church was to escape this *condicio*, by

eastern constitution, was included in the Breviary (Brev. 5.3.1). It regulates the case of clerics dying intestate, reserving in the case of *censibus adscripti* what legally is due to the patron. The *interpretatio* (ICTh 5.3.1) is short: if they die intestate all goes to their church or monastery if they do not owe anything to, inter alia, a patron. This is about the *censibus adscripti* of the text. But they are free to draw up a last will. This will have concerned the free part of their estate. Further, it shows that the Church allowed *coloni* to become clerics.

46 The Colonate in the Breviarium Alaricianum: Obligations and Restrictions

In 422, Honorius issued a constitution addressing malpractices in the countryside which threatened the financial stability. This constitution dealt with the various aspects of these and was divided into fragments in the Theodosian Code according to subject. It appears that there was a pressure to collect private debts (*quae civiliter poscuntur*), for which the provincial governors had appointed enforcement officers. These took as surety from the land slaves, used to plough, and plough oxen, which, in the end, threatened the collection of tax revenues. This was forbidden (CTh 2.30.1). Honorius underlined that only the owner of land was liable, not his slave, representative, *colonus* or lessee (*conductor*, hence a *colonus* was not necessarily a lessee) against the estate owner's will (CTh 2.30.2). Further, estate owners were pressed to pay for the loans taken up by their slaves, *coloni*, and representatives on their estates, although they had not ordered this. Letters of recommendation to a creditor were of no value, unless these expressly ordered borrowing (which generated the *actio quod iussu*). The fine was the amount of money lent (CTh 2.31.1). But if an account book was presented in which the representative or slave did figure and had satisfied his master, the creditor could sue with the *actio de peculio utilis* (CTh 2.32.1; see Section 24.2.2). Likely it implied a financial relation between the two and may have created a debt for the *colonus* in the accounts.[113] Here the *interpretatio* is clearer than the original constitution.

> ICTh 2.32.1: Hoc sane creditoribus volumus esse praestandum ut actor vel servus sive procurator possessionis qui pecuniam a creditore susceperit si

which they were tied to an estate. *Dominus* refers to the estate owner in his capacity as having the *potestas* to reclaim.

[113] See before all Fusco 1980, further now Jurewicz 2020.

nihil de rationibus suis domino debuerit pro pecunia quam accepit de peculio quod habet creditoribus reddat.

It is Our will, of course, that this remedy shall be afforded to creditors, namely, that if an overseer, slave, or procurator of a landholding should receive money from a creditor and should owe nothing from his accounts to his master, he shall repay the creditors out of his *peculium* the money which he received.

This leads to the question of which accounts might have to be settled. What might a *colonus originalis* owe his estate owner? CTh 5.17.1 states that the person who harboured a fugitive *colonus originalis* has to pay the *capitatio* on him for the time the fugitive stayed with him; the *interpretatio* says *tributa eius quamdiu apud eum fuerit cogatur exsolvere*. An estate owner in the Visigothic kingdom apparently had to pay tax for his *colonus originalis*. The basics of the Roman tax system were still present, it seems: CTh 3.1.2 (Brev. 3.1.2) reminds the buyer of real estate (for the *interpretatio*: a *villa*) to acknowledge the census of the asset.[114] The *interpretatio* reduces this to the duty to acknowledge, when purchasing a *villa*, the *tributum rei ipsius*. We saw before that tax registrars (*tabularii*) were still active.[115] Those constitutions from Books 11 and 13 which deal with the taxation and have been included in the Breviary (CTh 11.1.15, 17; 11.3.3, 5; 11.6.1; 11.7.4, 20; 11.11.1; 11.16.11; 13.1.13; 13.10.1, 5)[116] would have allowed for a sober but sufficient continuation of the taxation system of the Roman Empire, with tax registers, appeal against unjust imposition, imposition of extra burdens, and prevention of extortion. There is nothing on the poll tax here, but neither was that in CTh 11.1 nor is it to be expected; the title is on land tax (*annona*) and connected charges.[117] Perhaps not all real estate was taxed in those days (if the barbarians had received one-third of the land, they will not have paid tribute on this to the emperor; but perhaps to their king?),[118] but the large estates evidently were still existing and taxable, and it would have been there that *coloni originales* were needed to cultivate. Also possible is that in 506 these were all good intentions but that in the next year, when the Franks had beaten the Visigoths and conquered their

[114] That may still have been the case: see Wood 1994, 62–63.

[115] ICTh 13.10.1; see Wood 1994, 64 on the tax registers.

[116] CTh 4.12.3, although with an *interpretatio*, was certainly not retained. That constitution would otherwise have suggested that the categories of emphyteuticarian and patrimonial lands still existed in the Visigothic kingdom. But there is anyway nothing in the *interpretatio* on *coloni originales* on these or on a possible special position of these.

[117] Wickham 2005, 93–102: the tax system was upheld, right until ca. 700, when there was a breakdown.

[118] On the point of the *tertiae*, see Goffart 1980 and the ensuing discussion.

Gallic lands, the taxation changed. At the same time (see the *interpretationes*), socially the appreciation of the colonate may already have shifted towards a colonate without fiscal link. So it is probable that for slaves and *coloni originales* the estate owner had to pay a poll tax as well, although the texts retained do not mention it, apart from CTh 5.17.1 (Brev. 5.9.1), where the *interpretatio* makes the *capitatio* into *tributa eius* (which was the same). If so, he would have a right to reclaim this from them. But it is certainly possible that the debts of a *colonus originalis* could include food and clothing received, as Nov. Val. 31.5 so vividly sketches of immigrants (*advenae*) who seek shelter and help: *simulata laboris et obsequiorum patientia, accepto sumptu ac vestitu inluviem et squalorem egestatis evandant*, 'by pretending endurance of labour and services, they may receive food and clothing and thus escape the filth and squalor of want' (trans. Pharr 1952). That had a price and it would be booked in the accounts until it was paid off by working. Thus if a fugitive had worked elsewhere as if a free labourer, it is no surprise that upon returning he had to bring his savings and other assets with him; if there were outstanding debts, they could be reduced or settled.

47 The Colonate in Legal Writings

Next to the Theodosian Code, Alaric's compilers drew from Gaius' Institutes, the Gregorian and Hermogenian Codes – which texts do not contribute to the rules on the colonate – and the Pauli Sententiae (*PS*), an in origin third-century work ascribed to Iulius Paulus and authorised by Constantine (CTh 1.4.2).[119] This work contains interesting sections on the *coloni*. A very interesting text is *PS* 2.18.1:

> Homo liber, qui statum suum in potestate habet, et peiorem eum et meliorem facere potest: atque ideo operas suas diurnas nocturnasque locat.
>
> A free man, who has his status in his power, can make it both worse and better; and, as soon as he leases out his work for day and night.

Though it is presumed that the (pseudopaulinian) Sententiae originated in the third century, it is possible that this is a late addition, perhaps even a fifth-century one.[120] For the third century it would be a remarkable statement, because for that period such a change in status is unknown. This suggests that under the Visigoths a Roman could change his status, that is, perform a *capitis deminutio minima* and be in the *potestas* of

[119] See Liebs 2005, 41– 88, 1995, 1996. [120] See Sirks 2011, 623–635.

somebody else. Then, if he hires himself out full time, it will be close to slavery, but not slavery. If the lease for day and night led to a position in which the free man has to be available day and night, implying that he could not move elsewhere without the consent of his master, then this position would indeed be low and subjected to the will of the employer as if *in potestate*, yet still not slavery.[121] Perhaps that possibility was meant here, to avoid the prohibited sale of oneself into slavery or indenture. It is in any case remarkable that it figures at the beginning of the title on Lease and Hire. It fits the sixth-century Formula Andecavensis no. 38, a *cautio* of a loan:

> Domino magnifico fratri illi ego illi. Constat me aecipisse et ita acepi de vobis per hanc caucione ad pristetum beneficium hoc est in argento uncias tantas. In loco pignoris emitto vobis statum meum medietatem, ut in unaquisque septem ad dies tantis, qualecumque operem legitema mihi iuncxris [= iniunxeris], facere debiammus. Que annus tantus conpliti fuerint, res vestras redere debias, et caucionem meam recipere faciam. . . .

> To the magnificent lord brother. It is established by this deed of security that I received from you, as I did indeed receive, a loan of *n.* ounces of silver. Instead of a pledge I give to you half my [free] status, so that I will have to do whatever appropriate work you order me to do for *n.* days out of every seven. After *n.* years have elapsed, I will have to return your property, and I will recover my deed of security. . . . (after Rio 2006)

Instead of giving a security or paying interest, the debtor will work for the creditor so many days per week. He calls this *emittere statum meum medietatem*, giving half his status. Deducting the Sunday, the debtor will be available for three days per week.

If a legacy of an estate comprises all its *instrumenta*, it comprises also the *peculium* of the *actor* if this person was of the same estate and had died before the testator (*PS* 3.6.47):

> *PS* 3.6.47: Fundo legato cum mancipiis et pecoribus et omni instrumento rustico et urbano peculium actoris ante testatorem defuncti, si ex eodem fundo fuerit, magis placet ad legatarium pertinere.

> An estate was bequeathed with its slaves and cattle and all agricultural and urban utensils; the *peculium* of the testator's manager, who had died before him, is considered as included in the bequest if he was from the same estate. (tr. Sirks)

[121] It is very different from the voluntary sale of oneself into slavery, a possibility for majors attested in D. 1.5.5.1 Marcian. 1 inst. and D. 28.3.6.5 Ulp. 10 ad Sab. In that case the *status civitatis* would suffer *capitis deminutio maxima*. *PS* 2.18.1 does not suggest that at all.

If the *actor* had been a slave, not attached as *instrumentum*, his *peculium* would have fallen anyway into the assets of his owner and now of the heir. It therefore concerns a free man who as manager also represented the owner. This meant there may have been an accounting relation between them, with reciprocal claims. The *actor* died before the testator, and we may assume the accounts were after that settled. If the *actor* had heirs, these would normally be entitled to his possessions. If there was still something to settle, they would be liable. But the decisive remark is: if he came from the same estate. Either the *peculium* was working capital, but in that case it would be said, or it refers to a bond with the estate and then the *actor* would have been a *colonus*. In that case the *peculium* had functioned as guarantee for the claims of the estate owner, as we saw in Brev. 2.32.1 (= CTh 2.32.1) on the *actio utilis de peculio* and its *interpretatio*.[122] If the accounts had not yet been settled when the testator died, then it is understandable that the *peculium* had to be retained and connected with the land or estate the *actor* had been responsible for so that a settlement could follow. The text recalls Augustine's *ep*. 24*, where he poses the question whether by becoming *actor* one becomes also a *colonus* (see Section 24.2.1).

The next rule, *PS* 3.6.48, states that if an *actor* or *colonus* from another estate has been transferred to one which was bequeathed with its *instrumentum*, they are only included in the legacy if the testator had wanted that. It means that these people could be attached by will to land.

> *PS* 3.6.48: Actor vel colonus ex alio fundo in eodem constitutus, qui cum omni instrumento legatus erat, ad legatarium no pertinet, nisi eum ad ius eius fundi testator voluerit pertinere.
>
> A manager or *colonus* who has been settled from another estate into the same estate which was bequeathed with all its appurtenances is not included in the bequest unless the testator had wanted him to be connected legally with his estate. (tr. Sirks)

Was the manager or *colonus* an *instrumentum*? Slaves could be that, but their position, being linked to an estate, looked very similar. The text implies that the official link is there and so *coloni* cannot be transferred to another estate. Yet the text says that if such a legacy comprises *coloni* of another estate, they nevertheless remain attached to this estate if the testator had wanted that. Assuming that the other estate also belonged to the testator, it means that now the estate owner could transfer his *coloni* at

[122] See Jurewicz 2020.

will, disregarding what the census established. CJ 11.48.13.1 (W) allowed for that if it served the cultivation of land. It ruled that, in that case, if in any way the ownership of the two estates came into different hands, the actual *colonus* could stay but his descendants should return (see Section 11). Here it is different. *PS* 3.6.48 deals with a preliminary point: whether the estate owner really wanted to transfer the *colonus* or just temporarily outplace him. If the owner wanted to transfer him, then the transfer holds. After that, CJ 11.48.13.1 could still apply. Another rule, *PS* 2.31.30, fits with this agricultural context.[123] Both *coloni* and estate owner may sue the thief for the products he stole from the land (already in D. 47.2.83pr and 2).

All in all, the main occupation of the Alarician compilers seem to have been the absconding of *coloni originales* and the recall of them, with, as likely consequence, the recall or division of offspring – this preoccupation is in line with the legislation for the west of the early fifth century on absconded *coloni* (see Sections 28.2 and 41). Migration of labour seems to have been a persistent problem. It implies a care for the continuation of agricultural exploitation. This is not surprising, in view of the fact that they also kept the taxation system basically intact and consequently relied on revenues mainly or all from agriculture.[124] The situation of the *coloni originales* was not improved by that, but neither did it deteriorate: they were free but subjected, with their *peculium*, their personal property, as surety for their debts with their estate owner. The rule on legacies of estates with *instrumentum* and *actores* or *coloni* attached to the estate we do not find in the Theodosian Code part of the Breviarium. Perhaps such a rule was present in the fragmentary Book 5, as CJ 11.48.13 must have been. Since the Pseudopaulinian Sentences were probably in the course of time enlarged, it is not possible to fix an early date for this.

Notwithstanding all this, the link between the colonate and the poll tax to all appearances seems to have still existed, with the estate owner being its guarantee. Consequently, the position of the *colonus originalis* was still administratively determined and would disappear at once if the poll tax were abolished. Their personal status was as a consequence of the guarantee function of the estate owner that of a person of *status libertatis alieni iuris*,

[123] *PS* 2.31.30: *Frugibus ex fundo subreptis tam colonus quam dominus furti agere possunt, quia utriusque interest rem persequi.*

[124] Wood 1994, 62 for the Merovingians; these found what the Visigoths had left. Wood mentions that the Romans had to pay tribute whereas the Franks did not have to; further immunities and the duty to billet, also apparently the duty to provide *tirones*. Wood mentions the phenomenon of servility (211–213) but does not enter specifically into the colonate.

comparable with *in mancipio esse*.[125] But we cannot exclude that under the veneer of the Roman legal texts a change was occurring.

48 The *Coloni* in the Summaria Antiqua, 535–554

Coloni are mentioned in a series of comments to Books 9 to 16 of a manuscript of the Theodosian Code, the so-called summaries of the first hand (V2),[126] made probably in or shortly after 535 in Rome, where the Code remained in force until Justinian's codification was introduced and validated in 554.[127] Whether the colonate was still the same in Italy as before Odoacer or had changed (as the Edict of Theoderic suggests) is open to discussion, but in Africa it was still the same and probably in Sicily too. This occurs in SCTh 10.1.11 (*c[oloni] rei privatae*) and 14 (*c. rei privatae* under reference to CTh 10.1.11; but the constitution itself does not mention *coloni*),[128] 10.4.3 (*c. rei privatae*), 13.1.3 (*c. senatorum*), 8 (*c. domus regiae*, while the constitution has *c. rei nostrae*), and 10 (*c. rei privatae*), 13.10.3 (*c.*), 13.11.3 (*c.*), and 16.5.52 (*c.*, twice). The summarist seems to have made short summaries of the constitutions in order to be able to access the Code quickly and not, as Fitting thought, for educational purposes.[129] Sometimes a summary reveals a change in situation, for example bishops replace priests, and perhaps the situation had changed too for *coloni*. But there is insufficient evidence to make conclusions. The replacement of *res nostra* by *domus regia* may rather indicate the Byzantine imperial power than be still a reference to a situation when the administration was exercised by a barbarian king.

[125] Whittaker 1987, 101 deduces from the absence of the 'free' colonate in the west that 'by the time of the collapse of the western Empire, *coloni* had never reached that state of abject servility which later developed in the east'. It is, however, precisely the other way around. The 'free' colonate of the east preserved from abject servility and *adscripticii* would become 'free' *coloni* after thirty years of work. Since the poll tax was not abolished, there is no ground for Schipp's contention (Schipp 2009, 329) that the tie to the *origo*, that is, the land census, was exchanged for a tie to the former *dominus*. He considers the terms *possessio* and *proprietas* as used in a constitution of Honorius of 400 as proof that the *coloni* were seen as property. If so, it would only be so in the west, since in the east Justinian expressly rejected this idea in CJ 11.48.21.1. That constitution of 400, by which Schipp probably means CJ 11.48.18, speaks of *possessor* and *proprietas* (as we also see in CTh 5.18.1.2 of 419, west). But we must see this as procedural terms; it does not mean that the *coloni* were property as were slaves.

[126] For the Summaria, see Sirks forthcoming. The notation SCTh 10.1.11 refers to the principal summarium on CTh 10.1.11.

[127] See Sirks 2020b.

[128] V2 connects correctly 14 with 11 and evidently bases on this his view that 14 applied to *coloni rei privatae*.

[129] Fitting 1872.

49 Nachleben and Conclusions

The distinctive feature of the colonate of the fourth and fifth century is the fiscal link, established in the census registration. That is apparent from the fact that when a fugitive *colonus* was reclaimed, the harbouring estate owner was liable for the lost tax. Similarly, when the poll tax was abolished, the bond dissolved, as we see in the east. Thus the status of the *colonus* (subjection to his estate owner, duty to perform tasks) was determined by this fiscal arrangement or guarantee and hence one of administrative law. But when we look for the 'Nachleben' of the Roman colonate, we see that in the later period the fiscal link has disappeared.[130]

Although the Breviary was till 654 the law in Visigothic Spain, we have only one testimony for *coloni* for Spain.[131] In the donation (551) and testament of Vincent, bishop of Huesca, who died 576, a bequest is made of land with on it, as appurtenance, inter alia, *coloni vel servi*, with their *peculia* (folio 1, 35).[132] This indicates people bound to the land. However, the rest of the testament does not give any solid clue to these *coloni*. Freedom is generously given, sometimes accompanied with land. But there is no further information. García Moreno has concluded that no *coloni* in the ordinary sense are found. The only mention is in a notary form in a collection from Córdoba, used even after the Moorish invasion of 711. It is a request to have land *in precario* and to pay rent *ut colonis est consuetudo*. García Moreno opines that this cannot refer to *coloni originales*.[133] Schipp, on the other hand, mentions the second Synod of Sevilla of 619, which refers to a secular law which prescribes that *coloni* must remain on their land, and therefore rejects García Moreno's conclusion.[134] But since we cannot establish the system of taxation, this

130 Wickham 2005, 519–529 deals with the *coloni*, the patronage system and the tax assessment. His proposition to use taxation as a means to distinguish the nature of a society is very appealing. He also connects patronage and colonate, but not as specialised as I do, namely to tie colonate and *capitatio*.

131 Teja 1988, 575–580 assumes there were *coloni*, but actually only mentions a suggestion that a Moorish institution was the remnant of antique *patrocinia vicorum*. The only concrete source given is one by Orosius, who mentions an army in 408–409 consisting of *servuli* (580). But to assume that this consisted of *coloni* is a bold assumption. Perhaps there were *coloni* amongst these, perhaps not. The testament of Vincent, on the contrary, provides hard evidence.

132 Corcoran 2004; Díaz 1998; Roth 2016.

133 García Moreno 2001, 204–206. It concerns no. 36 in Gil 1972, 104. García thinks the phrase was added to distinguish this from the payment in kind, the *xenia*. But it is more likely that it was to make this a *precarium* with rent without turning it into a *locatio conductio*. The only other mention of *colonus* and *inquilinus* is in Isidore's Etymologiae.

134 Schipp 2009, 395 n. 612: *scribitur enim in lege mundiali de colonis agrorum ut ubi esse iam quisque coepit, ibi perduret*. The text is in Mansi, Vol. 10, c. 558.

'Nachleben' is left out here, and it may refer to a differently based colonate (as in Burgundy and Francia).

For the Burgundian kingdom, it is clear that there is no fiscal link. Fugitive *coloni* must be returned with the wages they earned (*exacta operarum solutio*, Lex Romana Burgundionum 6.4).[135] Here the *tributum* turned into what the fugitive could earn as farmhand.

In Francia, the Formulae show us a society in which the term *colonus* refers to a subjected personal status and *colonitium*, the duty to act accordingly, that is, obey one's master, perform services and remain on one's place. There is no link with the taxation. Their work is called *servitium*, but they were not slaves: marriage is as a matter of fact assumed to be legitimate. The status is inherited from one's parents if they were *coloni*.

This world shows great similarity with that of the Edictum Theoderici. From its texts, a status (*condicio*) presents itself which we may call a colonate and which is connected with the colonate of the Theodosian Code. But it is a different status. There is no longer any fiscal link; the colonate is a personal status. This is evidenced by EdTh c. 128. It defines a general liability of the *dominus* for delicts or crimes of *filii in potestate*, *servi* and *coloni*, which resembles the classical noxal liability, now with the addition of *aut colonus*. If he refused to defend them, he had to surrender them to the judge for punishment. Only the *filii familias* had the option to defend themselves, if they wanted (c. 128).[136] As for the surrender to the judge instead of to the harmed party, there are classic precursors of this.[137] What, however, is new is that also crimes of *coloni* – like arson, in c. 98 – led to a liability of the master.[138] There is nothing of this kind in the well-transmitted Book 9 of the Theodosian Code. As such, this liability is the logical consequence of the *potestas* of the estate owner over his *coloni*, in analogy to his liability for *filii* and slaves. Further, whoever owned legally and possessed land could transfer from this *rustica mancipia* of both sexes, even if they were *originaria*, to other land in his ownership or even assign them to the ministries (services) of a town (*ministeria urbana*, as *urbani famuli*).[139] These transfers would be valid and irreversible; no claim about

135 LRB 6.4: *Quod si actor nesciente domino fugitivum suscipere aut tenere praesumpserit, aut iudici praesentare distulerit, factum eius fustuario supplicio a iudicibus vindicetur, et fugitivi dominus servum suum cum peculio, quod habet, et exacta operarum solutione recipiat.*

136 Schipp 2009, 301. The latter is compliant with D. 9.4.32–35.

137 See Kaser 1971, 431 at n. 50.

138 For EdTh c. 98, see also Schipp 2009, 303.

139 Those labours will have been a kind of city work force for the ingratiating assignments and rather a slavish task, done by a *collegium* which is also mentioned in EdTh c. 64.

the *origo* would succeed. He could even alienate by deed persons of this condition (*supradictae condicionis*) without the land (EdTh c. 142).[140] Lafferty sees this as an indication of labour shortage.[141] It also implies that the estate owner no longer registered them (or had to register) for the poll tax, that registration only bound them to an *origo* and that their status was now a personal one.

With the loss of the fiscal link of the colonate, we have to draw the line for the Roman colonate as having come into existence under Diocletian. It is another move towards the medieval world with its serfdom and villeinage. Assuming that there is a continuation (with changes), we see the transition from *colonus originalis* on the basis of a fiscal arrangement to that of a villein. Indeed, if tied to a *villa* (as in Formulae Senonenses 5), the *colonus* becomes a villein. It is not a new remark that in this world not only did sharp status distinctions reign, but there was an array of accommodations (such as giving one's status for several days a week to another to pay off a debt), in a move from contract to status, and that this may not just the result of a long social development but also due to the presence of the Germanic immigrants. An author such as Harper, in his broad and well-documented work on slavery in Late Antiquity, has also pointed out that slavery was replaced by other forms of exploitation of human labour,[142] and Wickham has referred to the rise of the manorial system.[143] The loss of the link with the fiscal system also corresponds with Wickham's view on the differentiation between states based on tax-raising and states based on land or rent and the collapse of the western Empire as its tax system broke up.[144] It is not possible to pinpoint exact moments in which the shift happened. Schipp has concluded that the shift from Late Antiquity to Early Middle Ages regarding the colonate occurred when the *Bodenbindung* was replaced by a bond to the *Grundherr*.[145] But is it not so that where there is a *Grundherr* there is a *Boden*?

Finally, was there a transition? And if so, was it sudden? It is not clear whether the poll tax was abolished or just lost in oblivion. In the east, such abolitions in 371 and 393 made the *coloni* free from the bond and

[140] EdTh c. 142: *liceat unicuique domino ex praediis, quae corporaliter et legitimo iure possidet, rustica utriusque sexus mancipia, etiamsi originaria sint, ad iuris sui loca transferre, vel urbanis ministeriis adplicare, ita ut et illis praediis adquirantur, ad quae voluntate domini migrata fuisse constiterit, et inter urbanos famulos merito censeantur: nec de eiusmodi factis atque ordinationibus, velut sub oppositione originis, quaestio ulla nascatur. alienare etiam supradictae conditionis liceat dominis, absque terrae aliqua portione, sub scripturae adtestatione, vel cedere, vendere cui libuerit vel donare.* Schipp 2009, 284–287; Lafferty 2010, 353–354, 2013, 218, also referring to CTh 2.31.1 and 2.32.1.

[141] Lafferty 2013, 218–219. [142] Harper 2011, 499–504. [143] Wickham 2005, 288–293.

[144] Wickham 2005, 57–58. [145] Schipp 2009, 329.

subjection, but there was still a strong government at that time. That was not so in the west in the second half of the fifth century. So if the poll tax had been abolished, it would be possible that the government did not draw the consequence of it. And in those cases where an estate owner had guaranteed more than the debt for the tax, the obligation to repay of course remained, but nevertheless the registration in the census should be struck. It is also possible that the poll tax was still on the books but no longer levied. In that case, the colonate might have continued, although I would say that its basis had actually changed. It would no longer be dependent on the poll tax; it would no longer be the creation realised under Diocletian.

Assuming that there was a transition (and, e.g., Formulae Andecavenses 10 suggests this strongly), what may have worked towards such a transition? That the Council of Orange of 441 and Sidonius saw manumission as the way to be freed from the bond might indicate that the bond was already perceived as a purely personal status, but it is not necessarily so: CJ 11.48.21.1 mentions the manumission as release. The *interpretatio* to CTh 5.17.1 gives an indication that within the formal administrative structure another structure – that of the *in potestate alieni esse* – became gradually dominant. The *colonus alieni iuris* became a *colonus alienus*, the *officia* which befitted a free man became something, due to his birth. It seems that the personal status aspect, originally depending on the census, may have been considered gradually a separate feature, independent from the census. And once the link with the census registration is no longer necessary (we do not see it mentioned, while in Formulae Andecavenses 10 only witnesses are used to ascertain the status of the defendant) or replaced by municipal records, the colonate has really become a personal status. The rules on the *coniugium non aequale* and the analogue application of the *senatusconsultum Claudianum* with its automatic effect, in any case after 451, would have regulated its transmission independently of the census: regardless of which of the parents is a *colonus*, the children are always *coloni*.[146] We see with Justinian the dangers of such a reliance on descendance. He combated prejudices which were used to enforce colonate claims and required at least two independent documents. The mere registration in the census (*publici census adscriptio*) did not suffice, which implies that this was used. That was in the east, with an involved emperor and an efficient

[146] The senatusconsultum applied automatically since Nov. Val. 31.6 of 451, creating *coloni* (see Section 41.2) and was not abolished in Gaul. For the *coniugium non aequale*, the *interpretatio* to Brev. 14.1.1 (= CTh 14.7.1) summarised it for the *coloni*. See Chapter 2, note 98.

administration. In the west, the situation was different, and the *coloni* could not expect an emperor to safeguard their rights against powerful landowners who might scramble for all the labour they could get. The disappearance of the fiscal connection would have had, from that perspective, no effect. The colonate continued but in a different setting, that of the German jurisdictions, which deserves a different treatment.

CHAPTER 5

The Colonate between Theodosius' Code and Diocletian and the Third Century, 438–293/268/249

50 The Period 438–293/268/249

The legal constellation of the colonate in the year 438 has been set out in Chapter 2, supplemented by the findings in the Chapters 1, 3, and 4. The origin of the colonate in a private agreement, similar to a *paramonè*, by a private person and an estate owner was based on the situation in the east under Justinian and fitted the situation in 438, and in the west on *PS* 2.18.1, and the possibility of a release by private act, similar to a manumission, was based on later sources in the west. The question is now how the colonate developed in the period between 285 and 438. For that we have to proceed as if peeling an onion: by going retrogradely, changes can be removed and the situation before a change can be established or surmised. In the end we should arrive at what may have been the 'Ur-colonate', if that ever existed. I shall not deal with all constitutions issued in this period, but only with those which introduced a change in the status. There are not many. I leave out what refined or partly repeated a previous ruling, and what added but did not change the elements of the colonate, like being bound to the land or in the power of the estate owner.

50.1 Development in the East in 438–364

In 409 it became possible for a *colonus* to become a cleric and be relieved from the obligation to remain on the land, but that was all. An innovation was the introduction of the 'free' colonate in 371 in Illyricum and later in Thrace and Palestine (CJ 11.48.51–53). It was seen as necessary when the poll tax was abolished. That implied that the *coloni originales* were no longer bound to the land, it dissolved their *condicio*, they could migrate freely now, and so a new *condicio* was created. The *origo* of these *coloni* was now legally fixed to their land and so they had to remain on it and cultivate. They were no longer under the *potestas* of a landowner. For *coloni* in other provinces the situation did not change.

50.2 Development in the West in 438–364

In the first quarter of the fifth century, several constitutions (CTh 5.18.1, 414; 12.19.1–3, 400) introduce limitation of prescription for the recall of fugitive *coloni*, which means that after that period they were free from that bond (but they might be under another new bond). These also changed the transition of the *condicio* in introducing divisions of offspring born out of unions between *condicionales* (CTh 12.19.1–3, CJ 11.48.13, 400).

In the middle of the fourth century, the *coniugium non aequale* becomes visible together with the analogue application of the *senatusconsultum Claudianum*, first with the *gynaecearii* (CTh 10.20.3, 365), then with the *monetarii* and *coloni* (CTh 10.20.10, 379). If we include the *inquilinae*, it became also visible here at the same time for unions with decurions (CJ 10.32.29, 365).[1] The *coniugium non aequale* presumes that the *coloni* (and other groups involved) are, though free citizens, of the category *alieni iuris* and subjected to the *potestas* of somebody else who is of course *sui iuris* (called *ingenuus*). Because in CTh 5.17.1 *coloni* are *alieni iuris*, which makes marriages with *ingenui* treated as if there is no *conubium* regarding the *condicio*, it must have been already the case in 332.

50.3 Development before 364

What the period after 364 brought in changes did not afflict the existing elements of the colonate. For the period prior to 364 we do not see such changes too. The few references to the colonate indicate that the essentials were already present. So CJ 11.68.2 (319): *coloni* (of the *domus* of the emperor or of the *res privata*) who are able to manage an estate, or to work on the land, were to be recalled. This confirms that they were bound to the land and had to provide services. On private land, *coloni* were in a *condicio* (they were *alieni iuris*), they were bound to the land, they had to provide the services the landowner wanted and tax was paid for then (CTh 5.17.1, 332). In 319 the duty to pay tax for one's *coloni* (CTh 11.7.2, 319) fits this. The *condicio* as public law institution in this sense existed in 317 (CTh 10.20.1 for *monetarii*).

Thus all the essentials of the colonate which the reconstructions of the situation in 438 and under Justinian show were present in the first two decades of the fourth century. Earlier texts are mere references, but if they fit the essentials, they can serve as pickets to hang on the colonate as legal

[1] See Schmidt-Hofner 2008a, 280–284, who rightly assumes that *ingenuae* women were not analogously to the *senatusconsultum Claudianum* reduced to the colonate. That there was no system behind this I cannot agree; see above, Section 26.

institution. One reference is the rescript by Diocletian and Maximian of 293/294, related in the LRB 14.6, which says that a *colonus* may not alienate anything of his *peculium* without the knowledge and consent of his master. It implies the existence of *potestas* and with it the *condicio*. That is a thin reference, but it fits essentials of the colonate and allows the assumption that other essential elements were present as does CJ 7.16.18 of 293 (p. 39 n. 30). But CJ 10.39.4 of 293/294, which says that nobody could change his *origo* at his own will, cannot serve as such because it was a rule for everybody. It may have been part of a taxation reform, reinforcing any obligation to stay on an estate as *origo*.

The result is that we may hypothesise that the core of the adscripticiate/colonate in 293/294 consisted of a voluntary agreement,[2] entered in order to have a surety against the debt for poll tax, in which a landowner guaranteed payment of this towards the fisc, while the *colonus* was to be promised to work off the debt (thus: a kind of antichretic credit), and for this to be under the orders and power (*potestas*) of the landowner, that is, *alieni iuris*, while the landowner had a preferential right to his assets for the debt, aptly named, in connection with the subjection, *peculium*, implying a preferential right for the landowner for compensation of claims. The fact that this agreement, put down in writing, or an extract of it, was inserted in the census of the landowner's estate made the guarantee of the landowner towards the fisc easily executable, but due to the functions of the census it turned the estate also into the *colonus*' *origo* and made him now the *colonus* of any owner of the estate. There is no constitution transmitted introducing one of these elements for the period 293–438. In later constitutions they are always understood as existing.

51 A Connection with Diocletian's Tax Reforms?

Can we connect the colonate with taxation reform by Diocletian?[3] There is the theory that, since it would have made landlords liable for the taxes their lessees had to pay, he granted them the right to keep these lessees on the land rented (thereby destroying the lease as a free contract, substituting a kind of bondage for it). Is that correct? Certainly not in this sense. Some authors maintain that Diocletian started his taxation reform in 297, basing this on an edict of the Egyptian prefect Optatus. In that case the reform dates from three years after the colonate is testified. Others maintain that Optatus started already in 287

[2] It would be remarkable if the colonate had begun as imposition to turn later into a voluntary engagement. Such things usually develop the other way around.

[3] For the theories mentioned in the following I refer to the résumé in Carrié 1994, 50 and Section 1.

with reforming, and according to Carrié the mention of *kephalè* in the edict might both refer to the *tributum capitis* (the poll tax) and to the new unit, the *caput plebis rusticae*, for which Optatus defined the tariff. Yet, notwithstanding the author's references to later formulas for the *capitatio*, the fact that the edict gives a certain monetary amount per *aroura*, thus a physical measure and not an amount per unit of account, poses an unsurmountable obstacle to this view. Since it is not logical to assume that the edict gave two different standards (why should Diocletian have made such a differentiation?), the edict must also have provided the monetary amount per *head*, that is, the level of the poll tax, and not per unit of account for people.[4] Perhaps Diocletian had in 287 introduced the lustral cycles (*epigraphai*) and a reorganisation of liturgies, but had not yet at the time of the edict introduced the reform of the cadastration. Around 293 he may have tried to generate more revenues by merely making the taxation more effective, later on passing over to more drastic measures.[5] The cadastration reform began after that, in 297, by which all land was valued in a uniform way, thus providing the taxation with the basic elements (*iuga*, *capita*) used to apportion the tax burden. Consequently, a reorganisation of the taxation consisting of this *capitatio* and *iugatio* system, in which the *coloni originales* were liable and which could be incorporated into the assessments of land, did not exist as such at the time when the colonate already existed, in 293/294.

Apart from the general prohibition on changing one's *origo* without official authorisation, which concerned everybody, it is therefore not possible to see the birth or existence of the colonate as a feature of Diocletian's fiscal reforms. But it is possible that in his fiscal reforms an element was added which made existing arrangements into the colonate we know for later times. Did similar arrangements exist previous to those years or to Diocletian? We see indeed something like that for people on the properties of a landowner in the middle of the third century, namely Appianus' managers Heroninos and Eirenaios.[6]

52 Farmers in the Middle of the Third Century: The Heroninos Archive, AD 249–268

About the situation of farmers before Diocletian's reforms we are rather well informed through the many documents of Heroninos, a *phrontistès* (*procurator*) on the estates in the Arsinoite region of Egypt of a rich

[4] See Sirks 2012, 138–139, refuting Carrié's assumption that the *capitatio* in this context was a measure of taxation and not a poll tax.

[5] Bowman 2005, 76.

[6] On the Appianus estate and the *metrèmatiaioi*, see Rathbone 1991, 116–147 and Sirks 1997, 163–184.

landowner Appianus. They have been researched in an admirable way by Rathbone.[7] Appianus was an Alexandrian councillor and important citizen who as large landowner owned until his death in 260 an estate consisting of plots of land and properties in various villages, each organised as a *phrontis* with a *procurator*. His daughter Diodora succeeded him as heir. Heroninos ran the village-based property of Theadelphia, as his colleague Eirenaios the village-based property of Euhemeria, in the Arsinoite, during the years 249–268. Next to Appianus' there were other estates, combining also plots of land and properties, such as that of Posidonios, another large landowner, also Councillor of Alexandria and Appianus' father-in-law. All these properties were in private ownership until some time before 288/289 they became property of the fisc (*tamieion*). Rathbone's research provides us with an excellent survey of how estates were run. On these estates there were farmers or farmhands, *oiketai* and *metrèmatiaioi*, who were in a state of dependency which resembles that of *coloni*. Further, the documents give us an insight into the way Heroninos and other *phrontisteis* managed their finances with regard to the workers on the estates, the taxes and the liturgies.

From the documents it appears that there were two kinds of workers on the estates (apart of course from the slaves and the *phrontisteis* themselves). An *oiketès* was a free man who received *opsonia*, distributions in kind and a little money, being on the payroll of the property. It was sufficient for one person to live on subsistence level. Presumably he enjoyed also a room in barracks on the property for free. His time and labour were completely at the disposal of the estate owner, probably for life; but his wife and children were free. The term *oiketès* is usually used for a slave (belonging to the *oikos*, household) and *oiketai* were apparently considered as belonging too to the household, yet were free people.[8] *Metrèmatiaioi* were free people who for a set period were employed on the property. Essential in their agreement was the *paramonè* part, the promise to stay for a definite period on the property. They too were included in the property accounts, receiving *opsonia* and money. The *paramonè* construction is already known in the first century AD.[9]

[7] Rathbone 1991. [8] Rathbone 1991, 106–107, 111.

[9] Berneker 1949, 1213, defines it as 'ein rechtsgeschäftlich begründetes Gewaltverhältnis, auf dessen Dauer die Freizüglichkeit des Gewaltunterworfenen aufgehoben wurde'. Berneker is right in emphasising the subjection, necessary to enforce the promised services, and further distinguishes between the debt-*paramonè* and enfranchisement-*paramonè*. In the first case he connects it with 'Zins- oder Kapitalantichrese'. But Berneker's use of the term *antichresis* is confusing, because the creditor, although having power as if a *pater familias* over his debtor, may not sell him as if a pledge. *Antichresis* is in the legal doctrine either always coupled with *pignus* (Dernburg), or a separate agreement (*pactum*

However, as Hengstl in his fundamental but unfortunately not sufficiently considered study underlines, the duty to remain on the estate was secondary. The characterising element of the *paramonè* was that the *paramonarios* owed a debt, either for a sum paid out or for a credit, and that he promised to be at the service of the creditor and do what the creditor ordered him to do, instead of paying interest or repaying the whole sum. There is a similarity with *antichresis*. With the agreement of *antichresis*, the creditor could use the revenues of the pledged object as interest or pay off the debt. Instead of the debtor he had the use (*chresis*) of the pledge. Here the *colonus* – who has *not* pledged himself – and who had the use of his own time, offered to work for his creditor as replacement of the money for interest (his work being valuated) and subjected himself in this context. The similarity lies herein: in both cases it is the creditor who can dispose of potential revenues based on an existing and continuing debt relation. It implied that the *paramonarios* stayed where the creditor stayed, around or in his house, not to move away, sometimes with the express obligation to stay day and night at his disposal. He would receive a loan for his services, coupled sometimes with food or the like, and the creditor could also agree to pay taxes for him. The sum had to be paid off in order to end the *paramonè*. If that did not happen, the situation would continue forever. It could only be ended prematurely by a formal release (*dialysis*). Only the *paramonarios* could repay the debt, but others might be in the agreement as well and be liable too. The agreement may contain the word *paramonè*, but does not have to as long as the distinguishing elements are present.[10] Although Rathbone

antichreticum), yet still with proprietary consequences (see Bobbink 2021, 20–83) and never imposed on persons. His definition comes down to that of Hengstl as a separate agreement, although Hengstl emphasises that the debt is essential, to which comes the agreement of *paramonè*. Also on the *paramonè*, Adams 1964, who, however, sees it as a contract of services. Rathbone calls a debt on account of a loan an antichretic loan: Rathbone 1991, 116–117. About the private law *paramonè* nothing further is known. Although any debt passed on to the heirs (unless they rejected the inheritance), it is unlikely that the *paramonè* passed on as well, being a personal disposition of one's status. Papadatou 2008, 214–215 mentions *paramonè* when dealing with the practice of *antichresis* by labour of the debtor, forbidden by Justinian in Nov. 134.7. She remarks that this practice remained allowed if slaves were used (CJ 4.24.1) and unfree persons, without specifying the latter category and not mentioning the colonate at all.

[10] Hengstl 1972, 14–31; 14: 'Dieses Verb [*paramenein*] hat keine scharf umrissene, technische Bedeutung, sondern bezeichnet jedes Verbleiben einer Person oder Sache. Außerdem ist es eine Voraussetzung jedes Dienstverhältnisses daß der Dienstnehmende verfügbar ist; die Anwesenheitspflicht ist daher kein Charakteristikum eines bestimmten Dienstverhältnisses; 24: Der Kontext aller Paramoneverträge beginnt mit der Erklärung des Schuldners, einen bestimmten Geldbetrag – hier als Paramonalsumme bezeichnet erhalten zu haben und anstelle einer Zinszahlung oder außerdem für den ganzen Betrag bleiben und Dienst leisten zu wollen. Diese besondere Stilisierung unterscheidet die Paramoneverträge von den im folgenden Paragraphen erörterten

mentions in two examples the debt, this aspect is further neglected by him.[11] He focuses on the mention of *paramenein*, as later Sarris also does.[12] But as Hengstl has set out, the essential element in the *paramonè* is the mention of the *paramonè* sum, the debt of the *paramonarios*, and the *antichresis*. *Paramenein* cannot be the decisive element, because, as Hengstl demonstrates, to stay somewhere is an obligation inherent in several agreements, such as in a labour or nursing contract.[13] Such a financial arrangement we encounter also in a sixth- or seventh-century text from Gaul, Formulae Andecavenses no. 38.[14] Rathbone also underlines the accounting system of the estate, in which the workers were debited or credited according to the situation: in that system the *paramonè* fitted well because the estate owner could administer it in his accounting system. The position of a *metrèmatiaios* or an *oiketès* may seem deplorable, but for people without any means of subsistence it was not so bad a living, because on subsistence level they were at least secured by the *paramonè* against the fiscal claim and further needs by the credit, as Rathbone also emphasises. Hengstl underlines that the *paramonè* should be differentiated from credit in general. Credit serves primarily the debtor's need for capital. *Paramonè* serves primarily the creditor's need for labour force. Hence it is a misfeasance if the debtor abandons his work. It should not be seen as a surety for the credit. If the debtor did not pay it off and the creditor did not proceed to execute his claim, it became a permanent bondage.[15] It provided the landowner with a reservoir of labour force at low cost. Fikhman has emphasised the need of great landowners for labour and the favourable response of the lawgiver as primary cause of the colonate.[16]

Dienstverträgen auch dann, wenn in einem Dienstvertrag eine Lohnvorauszahlung erwähnt ist'. Rathbone 1991, 116 also mentions that the landowner paid the taxes for his worker.

[11] See Rathbone 1991, 117 n. 43 referring to Hengstl 1972 but not applying Hengstl's criterium. Bagnall 1993 has nothing on *paramonè*.

[12] Sarris 2006, 168, nevertheless identifies a *paramonè* in Nov. 14 proemium.

[13] Rathbone 1991, 118 mentions P. Fuad. Univ. 25 and P. Alex. inv. 281 recto, in which the order to credit the new *metrèmatiaioi*. That aspect is not further worked out. Also Rathbone 1991, 117 n. 44.

[14] Formula Andecavenses 38. *Incipit caucio de homine. Domino magnifico fratri illi ego illi. Constat me accipisse, et ita acepi de vobis per hanc caucione ad pristetum beneficium hoc est in argento uncías tantas. In loco pignoris emitto vobis statum meum medietatem, ut in unaquisque septena ad dies tantis, qualecumque operem legitema mihi iuncxris, faceré debiammus. Que annus tantus conpliti fuerint, res vestras redere debías, et caucionem meam recipere faciam. Et si exinde de ipsa opera aut de ipsas res ad ipso plácito necligens aut tardus fuero, aut volumtate vestra exinde non abuero, tunc me constat res vestras in dupplum debiam is esse rediturus, aut vobis, aut cui caucione ista dederis ad exagenda.* It shows that this arrangement, which suited those who needed credit but had only time to offer, was not restricted to Egypt or the early Empire.

[15] Hengstl 1972, 31–32.

[16] Fikhman 1990, 172 = Fikhman 2006, 271.

Both groups, as all the other villagers, had to pay taxes and perform liturgies.[17] Supervision was exercised by officials like on the lowest level the *komarch*, the head of the village, and the property *procurators* could perform such offices as well. Details are given by the accounts of Theadelphia of the *phrontis* of Euhemeria run by Eirenaios and of the estate of Sabina. In Theadelphia, Heroninos paid the taxes for the *metrèmatiaioi*. These remained responsible, and we see here nothing more than Heroninos acting for the *metrèmatiaioi* as their banker.[18] In Euhemeria, the situation seems to have been different. There Eirenaios levied the *isophorion* from the *metrèmatiaioi* and a number of independent villagers. Rathbone thinks that the *procurator* added all the personal tax dues of these people, paid the total to the authorities, arranged the discharge of the liturgies they were as a group subjected to, and then divided the entire sum over the individuals in this group, charging each a *per caput* charge, with the exception of some favoured *metrèmatiaioi*.[19] Although the *komarch* remained responsible for the nomination and thus also for the case that a nominee did not turn up to perform his duties, he would nominate the persons whose names Heroninos had given on a list. It must have been an informal arrangement.[20] For Heroninos this arrangement was also attractive. He could keep those labourers he needed on the farm, substituting somebody else for the liturgies. As to the taxes, Rathbone cites an example in which Heroninos is urged by Alypios to make some workers of the estate Sabina pay their *isophorion*, since the managers there were pestered by the tax officials for an outstanding debt in *per caput* taxes.[21] Why would the fisc have pestered those managers if not for having given some guarantee?

The same question turns up in P. Prague 108, a letter from Ischyrion to Heroninos, dealing with the nomination for the liturgies. The *komarchai* of Theadelphia had nominated people for liturgies, and at once Heroninos had sent them a letter 'π̣ẹρ̣ὶ τῶν διαφερόντων σοι ὀνομάτων', the nominees. Evidently Heroninos wanted his choice to be nominated. The crux is in the meaning of the cited phrase. Rathbone translates with 'about the individuals who are your concern'.[22] It is a cautious translation, since we may without doubt translate it also with 'about the persons who belong to your household'. In that case it would refer to *oiketai*. According to

[17] Rathbone 1991, 117, cites *PSI* VIII 902/ P. Michigan V 355, of the first century AD, where the employer will pay for the employee the poll tax, the weaver's tax, the expenses and surtax on the embankments, the bath tax, the tax on the fountains.

[18] Rathbone 1991, 118–119, 133. [19] Rathbone 1991, 121. [20] Rathbone 1991, 133–135.

[21] Rathbone 1991, 182. [22] Rathbone 1991, 133.

Rathbone it must fairly certainly include the *metrèmatiaioi* attached to the Theadelphian *phrontis*, perhaps the *oiketai* too, and maybe also some tenants of estate property there.[23] Perhaps the *metrèmatiaioi* were considered for the time of their employment as belonging to the household; the external villagers were certainly not. But that point is not as important as the arrangement itself. It shows that the estate management could make deals with the authorities (which some *procurators* were also in their turn) to the advantage of the estate, but also of the dependent people on it. If some were held free, others could earn some extra money by performing their liturgies. Those on *paramonè* could be ordered to perform those liturgies.[24]

The term *isophorion* (ἰσοφορίον) occurs twice, in P. Florence 151 (AD 266, see above), *SB* 6.9429 (AD 247)[25] and P.Oxy. XV 1684 (late fourth century).[26] In the latter it is combined with *sticharion* (στιχάριον), which means according to Rathbone 'undergarment-tunic'.[27] That would make a strange apportionment, and it is hard to believe that it concerned the *collatio vestis*. In *SB* 6.9429 a receipt is given εἰς λόγον ἰς[ο]φορίου ἀννώ/νας, 'for the account of the *isophorion* of the *annona*'. *OLD* refrains from giving a translation. Thus, apart from the grammatical interpretation as 'equal levy', we have only P. Brussels descr. of 247–249.[28] This papyrus contains individual accounts by Eirenaios of *oiketai* and *metrèmatiaioi* on the property in Euhemeria, and was for his own use. According to Rathbone it seems that for all *metrèmatiaioi* there and a number of independent villagers the property paid the personal taxes and discharged the liturgies (like on the property in Theadelphia). But here, apparently, these expenses were periodically added up and divided by the number of taxpayers, resulting in an equal apportionment, the *isophorion*.[29] This seems strange, because the poll tax would have varied per head of the

[23] Rathbone 1991, 134. [24] Rathbone 1991, 134.

[25] *SB* VI 9429: ἔτους δ τῶ(ν) κυρίω(ν) Φιλιπω(*)/ Σεβαστῶ(ν) Φα[ρ]μọ(ῦθι). διέγρα(ψεν)/ Αὐρή(λιος) Δίδυμ[ο]σ οὐετρα(νὸς)/ εἰς λόγον ἰς[ο]φορίου ἀννώ-/5 νας δραχμὰς ἕξ. APIS translation: 'The fourth year of our lords Philippi Augusti, Pharmouthi(?). Aurelius Didymos, veteran, has paid to the account of the distributed charge(?) for the annona six drachmai'. Rathbone 1991, 121 finds the interpretation of the text hampered by its uniqueness.

[26] P.Oxy. XIV 1684: κυρίῳ μου υἱῷ Τιμοθέῳ/ Ὡρίων./ ἀ̣π̣εδεξάμην τὰ δύο/ στιχάρια εἰσοφόρια(*)/ 5 καὶ βαρβαρίκια δύο/ κὰ(*) φακιάριον καὶ οὐη̣-/ράρια(*) δύο. ἀπέστε̣λά(*)/ σοι στιχάριον ἰ(*) σοφό-/ριον(*) ἓν καὶ βαρβαρίκι-/ 10 ον ἓν καὶ φακιάριο̣ν/ καὶ ο̣ὐ̣ρ̣άριον(*) ἓν/ καὶ ὕ(*)μισου(*) με-/κάλου(*) δελφακίου./ ἔγραψές(*) μοι περὶ/ 15 ἀμμας(*) Δωροθέῳ̣./ εἴπερ ἀληθές ἐστιν/ καὶ καλῆς τιμῆς,/ δήλωσόν μοι, καὶ/ περὶ τοῦ σίτου/ 20 καὶ τῶν κριθῶν./ ἀπαντᾷ πρὸς σὲ/ Φῖβις ἐν τῇ αὔ-/ριον. εἴ τι θέλις(*),/ μετάδως(*) αὐτῶ̣ι/ 25 καὶ ἀποστέλλω σοι./ ἐρρῶσθαί/ σε ε̣ὔ̣χ̣(ομαι).

[27] Rathbone 1991, 121 n. 54. [28] Bingen 1951, 378–385; Rathbone 1991, 112–114.

[29] Rathbone 1991, 121–123, 1991, 121: 'It seems that all the *mêtrematiaioi* on its payroll, together with a number of independent villagers there, were under the fiscal patronage or protection of the

household, depending on the number of people in it. The other personal taxes varied also. It would imply that some had to pay more and others less than they otherwise would have. Rathbone underlines that this system could have concerned only a minority of the population of Euhemeria.[30] Yet even then, why would people agree to this and to a tax collectivity? Until P. Brussels descr. is fully edited, a *non liquet* may be the best approach.[31]

53 *Oiketai* and *Metrèmatiaioi*: A Pre-colonate?

The arrangements on Appianus' properties in Theadelphia, Euhemeria, and Sabina show a great resemblance to the social and economic arrangements of the later colonate. There is even a request of 265, similar to that of Pieous (P.Oxy. XXVII 2479, sixth century; see Chapter 1, note 144), in which a smith from the village of Kaminoi begs the owner of the Philoxenos estate to let him return to his village and offers to do all tasks he is told to do.[32] One is inclined to think of the *coloni adscripticii* (the *metrèmatiaioi*) and *inquilini* (the *oiketai*) as known from later sources, and indeed Rathbone draws our attention to this similarity.[33] The arrangement that for some *metrèmatiaioi* Heroninos paid the taxes (booking it in their accounts) while other *metrèmatiaioi* paid them themselves resembles the system described in CJ 11.48.20pr of 529. But it is equally important to note what Rathbone on several occasions emphasises, that these arrangements did not comprise entire villages but were restricted to certain properties, while the *isophorion* was only mentioned in Euhemeria and not Theadelphia.

phrontis, which paid all the personal tax dues of this collectivity and arranged the discharge of the liturgic functions to which as a group they were subject. Periodically these expenses were totalled up and then divided by the number of taxpayers in the collectivity to produce a per caput charge known as the *isophorion* (equal levy) which all the taxpayers, except some favoured *metrèmatiaioi*, had to repay to the *phrontis*. The *isophorion*, it should be emphasised, was a private, not a public charge'.

30 Rathbone 1991, 123. 31 Rathbone 1991, 123–127.

32 P. Reinach 113 (AD 263); see Rathbone 1991, 145 with P. Reinach 113: τῷ κυρίῳ μ[ο]υ Ἀντωνίωι/ Φιλοξένωι./ παρὰ Αὐρηλίου Ἐπιμάχου/ χαλκέως ἀπὸ κώμης Κ̣α̣-/ϲμείνων. δι᾽ εὐχῆς μοί ἐστι,/ δέσποτα, παρὰ τοὺς πόδα̣ς̣ [σο]υ̣/ ὑπηρετεῖν. διὸ δέομαι [ὅπως]/ μου ἀνθρωπον(*) πρεσβυ̣τ̣η̣ν̣(*)/ καὶ σχεδὸν τοῖς ὀφθαλμοῖς ἀμ-/ιοβ[λ]υωπησαντα(*) ἐλεήσις(*), ὅπως/ συντηρήσ̣ης με ἀπὸ ἀ̣ς̣[θενεί-]/ ας, ἵνα σου τὰ ἔργα ὅσα β[ούλει τε-]/λέσω ἄνευ μισθοῦ, ἐμο[ί σου]/ σίδηρον παρέχοντος̣ [ ]/ ις̣ ἄνευ̣ π̣ρ̣α̣[- ca.10 -]/ προῄρημαι ὑπηρετή[σ]ιν(*) [ ]/ εως καί, εἰ δόξι(*), ἐπ̣[ανελ]θ̣ώ[ν]/ ἐν τῇ ἡμετέρᾳ̣ κώμῃ Κ̣α̣[μεί-]/ νων ἐκεῖσε ἐργάζεσθαι [του]σ̣(*) μ̣[α-]/20θητας(*) μου ἐν τῇ αὐτῇ [ὀ]ν̣τα̣ς̣(*)/ καὶ δεομενους(*) τῆς ἐ[μ]ῆς διατά-/ξεως· ἐπιτρεψε(*) δὲ Σ̣α̣ρ̣α̣π̣[ίω-]/νι φροντιστῇ Βέβρυχος ὅσα/ ἔχω ἐκεῖσε ἀπολῦσαι πρ[ὸ-]/25ς τὸ ὅσα βούλει ἔργα, ὡς ἔφης,/ ἀποπληρωσω(*) καὶ διᾳ̣ π̣αν-/τὸς τῇ τύχῃ σου χάριτας ὁμο-/λογεῖν.

33 Rathbone 1991 p. 404–407. Also Sarris 2006, 65 draws attention to the similarity and possible link.

Notwithstanding these similarities, some questions remain. Were the *metrèmatiaioi* indeed employees, free after their contract? Rathbone says they were, but it does not appear so from the Heroninos Archive. If the designations say anything about a characteristic of them, then it is that the *oiketai* dwelt on the property, probably as Rathbone says in a room in a barracks, while the *metrèmatiaioi* were resident in the village in their own dwelling, receiving cash *opsonia*. Rathbone assumes their designation comes from *metrèma*, a ration in kind, which they apparently also received. They had agreed to work full time for the estate, evidently to pay off their debts.[34] If this was a *paramonè* agreement, a *metrèmatiaios* had in effect become a member of the household.[35] What if the *metrèmatiaioi* had agreed for life, just as the *oiketai*, or were necessitated by poverty to do so? And what did they do? Rathbone deduces that they were mostly people without specific skills and of low economic status who entered into a long-term work contract to gain their livelihood.[36] That seems right, but the work they did on the estate will consequently have been as a farmhand, a day labourer, or a farmer on a plot of land assigned to them by the steward of the estate owner. Another possibility is that they owned or were leasing a small farm and were at the same time *metrèmatiaios* to have a minimal life subsistence, working for the property at occasional moments. Or they just worked intermittently. Bagnall points out that there were many small independent farms in Egypt where families patched a living together from many sources.[37]

Another question: How could Heroninos have recalled a fugitive *metrèmatiaios* (or *oiketès*)? He would have filed, once he had traced the fugitive, a claim for execution of the *paramonè* agreement. If the defendant had the money, he could pay the *litis aestimatio* and be off, but these people will not have had that much money. Thus the alternative, condemnation to debt-slavery, would be applied. In the post-classical period it was possible and usual to execute personally, that is, the debtor was seized in person, which would also enable him to be returned if he were a fugitive. Kaser and Hackl refer for this to texts from the fourth and later centuries, but they deal with the private procedure.[38] And how could the *komarch* have recalled a fugitive whom he had appointed to a liturgy? Here a public law claim must have been available. In public law, certainly in criminal law, the authorities had much power, and already at the beginning of the third century, if not earlier, public obligations like liturgies were forcefully

[34] Rathbone 1991, 118–119. [35] Rathbone 1991, 116–117. [36] Rathbone 1991, 119.
[37] Bagnall 1993, 115 and 123, and in general 114–130. [38] Kaser & Hackl 1996, 625–627.

imposed (see D. 50.4.3.15). From the Theodosian Code it is also evident that the authorities had the power to recall somebody for *munera* and *honores* and from, for example, CJ 10.33 that they could impose these. With *honores* it was usual to provide for a personal security (*cautio, satisdatio*): the nominator guaranteed that the nominated would perform. That was of course possible in private law too. Similarly, we see in the sixth century such guarantees for *adscripticii*. Otherwise assets would be seized and sold, which we also see happen with *coloni* (the case of Pieous mentions this). Still, how could the claim for recall based on a *paramonè* agreement turn into a revindication modelled after that for people *in potestate*, if *metrèmatiaioi* and *oiketai* were not formally brought under the estate owner's *potestas*?

Heroninos had sent a letter with the people he considered for performing the liturgies. He paid in some cases the personal taxes for his underlings, and he will have communicated this to the authorities. These kept already in the first two centuries AD registers of all villagers.[39] This will have continued after AD 212. We saw from the Ischyrion letter that the authorities in Arsinoë were well informed about the people in the village of Theadelphia. Further, birth registers were indispensable for the census and the imposition of the poll tax.

We do not know whether, when Heroninos paid the tax for an *oiketes*, it was registered simply as a payment by the *oiketès* or as a payment by Heroninos on behalf of the *oiketes*. For Heroninos the latter may have served as proof, but before all it mattered to him that in the internal accounting system it was registered. He had an interest in it that it be clear he and not the other had paid. If the *oiketès* paid himself, he will certainly have been interested in the receipt. Yet if he had received an *opsonion* for that amount, the estate owner would also book the expense in his accounts as a debt. Rathbone assumes there were tax collectivities on the estates through which the landowner paid all taxes for the members of the collectivities. This would have saved the authorities the trouble of setting these up. Diocletian merely would have reintroduced the old Roman rule that taxpayers should be hereditarily liable for payments in their local administrative unit of origin and thereby inadvertently have made hereditary pre-existing local arrangements such as the tax collectivities in the Heroninos archive. These collectivities would have been the reality of the original 'colonate'.[40] Rathbone's hypotheses do not fit the facts. Diocletian did not set up tax collectivities; people were individually

[39] Marquardt 1886, Vol. 1, 86–87; Besson 2020, 174–179. [40] Rathbone 2002, 163.

responsible for their taxes. Of an old-Roman rule that taxpayers were hereditarily liable for taxes nothing is known. The *coloni* were as all citizens as citizens individually liable for taxes and liturgies. Where they were assessed depended on their *origo*, eventually also on their domicile and estates. And that Diocletian would have caused the colonate inadvertently is an interesting suggestion, but it needs hard evidence to be considered seriously.

One point remains: the *potestas* of the estate owner over his *coloni* and *inquilini*. In the Heroninos archive the factual situation certainly was one of dependency. In a papyrus of AD 120 the *paramonarios* even promises to do a slave's services.[41] He entered by this the 'Hausgemeinschaft' of the creditor, who had the right to chastise him. Also a first-century *paramonè* Rathbone cites suggests this strongly: 'And I will not absent myself by day from Heron's establishment, but will accompany him everywhere according to the law. And for each day that I do not remain with him, I will pay to Heron two drachmas of silver, and I will do everything as aforesaid'. In return Harmusius, the *paramonarios*, asks that the other will pay for him the poll tax and several other taxes.[42] Likewise Epimachos pleads in AD 263 for sustenance, and in return he shall work ('so that I may carry out for you whatever task you wish . . . so I can discharge whatever tasks you say you wish'.[43] They show resemblance to the sureties ('Gestellungsbürgschaften') for *adscripticii* in the sixth century. Getting into the *potestas* of somebody else, later called a *capitis deminutio minima* (Justinian *Institutiones* 1.16.3),[44] is less than *capitis deminutio maxima*, the loss of freedom as by the voluntary sale of oneself into slavery, a possibility for majors in the third century.[45] If that was possible, why should the lesser deed not have been possible?

Is it possible that the *paramonè* survived into the sixth century? Nov. 14 proemium (of 535), when mentioning *syngraphai*, may refer to deeds of *paramonai* which would mean the construction was still used.[46] For us it is

41 Hengstl 1972, 13–23.

42 Rathbone 1991, 117: *PSI* VIII 902 and P. Michigan V 355 (trans. E. Mullet Husselman).

43 Rathbone 1991, 145: P. Reinach 113. Citation from Rathbone.

44 I. 1.16.3: *Minima est capitis deminutio, cum et civitas et libertas retinetur, sed status hominis commutatur. quod accidit in his, qui, cum sui iuris fuerunt, coeperunt alieno iuri subiecti esse, vel contra.*

45 Attested in D. 1.5.5.1, Aelianus Marcianus *Institutiones* 1, and D. 28.3.6.5 Ulp. 10 ad Sab.

46 See Sarris 2006, 168. Nov. 14 of 535 forbids brothels and the acquisition and use of girls for prostitution. It says in the *praefatio* that these girls are lured by food and clothes, which they have to pay for by prostituting themselves. This is formalised in *syngraphai* and the *lenones* give guarantees, presumably for the girls to the suppliers. (the *katapoda*: *promittentes calciamenta et vestimenta quaedam et his venari eas et deducere ad hanc felicissimam civitatem et habere constitutas is*

more important to see whether the colonate was a particular kind of *paramonè* with public effect through the census registration. The *adscripticius* had permanent debt with the *dominus*, namely the poll tax which the *dominus* guaranteed or paid. If the poll tax was abolished, the adscripticiate ended automatically. If the *adscriptius* paid it himself, it was the same, which means that the *dominus* must have guaranteed it towards the fisc, which also indebted the *adscripticius*. *Adscripticii* may have been indebted in other ways as well, but that was not essential here. The agreement put them into the power of the *dominus*; they had to stay with him and do the work he ordered. This work was the antichretic element in the agreement, presupposing a debt. They may have been the people who had to work on the *autourgiai* of the Apiones (see Section 9). The *paramonè* defined only their relation in as far as it was based on the debt with the *dominus*. It means that in as far as this left them free to do other things, they were free to conclude agreements like working or leasing, and it should not have been a problem if they did this also with their *dominus* as party. But in their financial relationships, that with their *dominus* will have been a preferred one. In the slave–master relation, the master had the *ius deductionis*, that is, he could before other creditors settle his own claims.[47] *Adscripticii* were not slaves, but by treating their assets as if *peculium* the same effect was achieved. This explains the prohibition of alienation. It must have been an element of the agreement.

But there are also differences from the *paramonè*. The *paramonè* was a personal agreement; the *paramonarios* was bound to the estate because it was his creditor's, and if the creditor died, the heir would continue the agreement. But if the creditor sold the estate, the *paramonarios* had to follow him to his new estate. In the adscripticiate, on the other hand, the *adscripticius* was bound to a particular estate, independently of who its owner was. Also, a new owner had to continue in the relation. This shows that this was perhaps in origin a personal agreement but that through the *adscriptio censu* it changed character, or it had from the beginning a different nature. Was it a *contractus publicus*, since in CJ 11.48.8.1 the common labour contract is called a *contractus privatus*? The analogue application of the *senatusconsultum Claudianum*, making unions with

suis habitationibus et cibum eis miserandum dare et vestem et deinceps tradere ad luxuriam eas volentibus et omnem quaestum miderabilem ex corpore earum accedentem ipsos accipere et celebrare conscriptiones quia usque ad tempus quod eis placuerit observabunt impiam et scelestam hanc functionem implentes quasdam vero earum etiam fideiussores expetere.) The *syngraphai* or *conscriptiones* (a literal translation) would fit the *paramonè*. The girls would have to remain until they had worked off their debt.

47 See below, CTh 2.31.1 and Section 24.2.2; Kaser 1975, 609 sub 6; see Gamauf 2023.

ingenui to *coniugia non aequalia*, confirms that these elements contributed to a legal status in the law of persons of being *alieni iuris* which would be transmitted: the *condicio coloniaria* or *adscripticia*.

54 Moulding the *Paramonè* into the Roman Law

The question is how these special elements could be achieved within the framework of Late Roman or Byzantine law. It is not impossible that we are in the sixth century confronted with a situation created at the end of the third century. Above, it was stated that the situation of an *adscripticius* also resembled that of somebody who, being adjudged by the magistrate to his creditor to work off his debt out of a delict, was *in mancipio*: an indenture in modern terms. He was, as Gaius says, *alieni iuris*; he had suffered a *capitis deminutio minima*. But that was a personal relation with his creditor, after a verdict, independent of an estate. Because of the requirement of the verdict, the *in mancipio esse* cannot be the model for the adscripticiate, apart from that this status no longer existed in the sixth century (it is not mentioned in Justinian's Institutes, contrary to Gaius'). More helpful is *PS* 2.18.1, which says: 'A free man, who has his status in his power, can make it/himself both worse and better; and, as soon as he leases out his work for day and night'.[48] It shows that somebody could *voluntarily* subject himself to the *potestas* of another. It does not have to mean that this happened in all respects. Roman law accepted that a *filius familius* was *in potestate* regarding his *pater* and *sui iuris* regarding his *peculium castrense*. Such a division may have been present here as well. If those were standard conditions in these *paramonè* agreements (not necessarily in those set for a specific period and task), then one can say they voluntarily subjected themselves to the *potestas* of the estate owner. He could certainly enforce it legally. But did it also carry a legal change in the status of the *paramonarios*?

The key to this must lie in the registration in the census, because here the liability for the poll tax and the bond to the estate come together. The census of the third–sixth century was first of all the basis for the assessment of the taxes one had to pay, private landowners or imperial estates.[49] In the east, individuals who lived in the countryside had to declare themselves and

[48] *PS* 2.18.1: *Homo liber, qui statum suum in potestate habet, et peiorem eum et meliorem facere potest: atque ideo operas suas diurnas nocturnasque locat.*

[49] See Chapter 1, note 226. Further, how would the *coloni* on these estates be registered otherwise than in the *professiones* of these, and recalled? The circumstances being the same, it is therefore possible that also on imperial estates *paramonai* were concluded. And if patrimonial lands would not have been taxed, the people on it would have been taxed.

their families for the *capitatio humana*, the poll tax, likely in census registers in their villages (the *census humanus*). Landowners had to declare the size and constitution of their estates, with the accessories (slaves, animals, instruments, eventually *coloni*) in the village or town where an estate lay (D. 50.15.4.8; CJ 10.36.1 with the separate entries or lists). Thus *census* could also mean one's assets, fortune (CJ 1.3.27.2, 5.70.7.6a, 6.30.22.14a), and the *officium censuale* functioned as an official archive, for example for testaments (CJ 6.23.18; of course useful for the levy of the *vicesima hereditatum*, CJ 6.23.23). The *census* also functioned as registration of ownership, and its archive was used as such (CJ 7.38.3 = 11.67.2).[50] Thus a donation of slaves could be made by letting the donee register them in his name in his census (in 290!).[51] If an estate was alienated, the *professio censualis* had to be transferred too (CJ 4.47.3: *etsi necdum translata sit professio censualis sed apud priorem dominum forte permanebit*). Because the tax was otherwise levied from somebody who did no longer possess the land, *translata* must mean that the *tabularii* who kept the census records had to register the name of the new owner in the census registration of the estate (so also in CJ 7.39.3.1: *novus census* is the entry of the new owner). That implies that in the census the estate remained continuously registered as once had been done, with at best occasionally an adjustment (as in CJ 7.41.2, inundation by the Nile). If a *colonus* was registered here as *adscripticius*, he would remain on the roll, regardless of who became the new owner. His possessions were also registered (CJ 1.3.20.1). If he was removed from the census, he was no longer bound (CJ 11.48.11). Similarly, the registration in a *census privatus*, that is, as *colonus* in the estate census of a private person, could not release

[50] Originally CTh 10.1.15 and issued in 396 in the east. Considering that in the provinces only possession was possible, which would be protected by the *longi temporis praescriptio*, yet in every lawsuit proof had to be submitted, the recourse to the census as evidence of exclusive entitlement is understandable. This may have begun with the constitution of Constantine of 313 or 337 on the transfer of land (FV 35). But the fact that proprietary transfer of land had to be accompanied by a transcription in the census implies that there must have been a previous prescription, which is likely one issued in the context of Diocletian's reforms of the taxation. For the nature of exclusive possession in the provinces, see Vacca 1993–1994; see also Bartusis 2012, 188–199, where in the period 1204–1261 paying taxes on land is used as proof of ownership. On the function of the census in the provinces from the first century onwards: Kubitschek 1897, 1918–1922, who only mentions census as property registration and assessment for taxation. The census as requirement for ranking as senator, *eques* or decurion will have been retained for the first and third categories, while the rank and title of *eques* turned into an honorary designation.

[51] CJ 8.53.7: *Diocl./Maxim. AA. Iulio. Censualis quidem professio domino praeiudicare non solet. sed si in censum velut sua mancipia deferenti privigno tuo consensisti, donationem in eum contulisse videris. [a. 290] pp. Id. Iul. ipsis AA. IIII et III conss.*, CJ 8.53.8: *Diocl./Maxim. AA. Florae. Si praeses provinciae non donandi voluntate filiorum tuorum nomine praedia in censum detulisse te manifestis probationibus cognoverit, quod fides veri suggesserit, statuet. [a. 290] pp. VIII id. Sept. ipsis AA. IIII et III conss.*

from another bond (so for *metallarii*, CJ 11.7.7) nor could the appointment to an imperial or provincial office impair the *dominus*' rights (CJ 11.48.18, 12.43.1, 12.54.3). But although the Institutes mention the *capitis deminutio minima* (I. 1.16.3), they do not give an example (except if this is implied in the arrogation). Nor is the manumission by census mentioned; only CJ 7.6.1.10 refers to the public records.

The fact that the *professio censualis* of an estate remained in principle as it was with only changes in ownership registered explains why the *adscripticius* was bound to the owner of the estate as such. An extract of the agreement between him and the *dominus* was inserted into this census. The private agreement of *paramonè* implied a subjection of the nature of being *alieni iuris* in Roman law. The entering of it in the census as *adscriptio* made it a *contractus publicus* and turned it into a *condicio*. This could only be so if the census had also a declaratory function in the law of persons. We saw that the census was declaratory regarding ownership, not just of immoveables but also of slaves, implying *potestas*. It is therefore submitted that the *professio censualis* had such a force too regarding *coloni* and that entering *coloni* as being in the *potestas* of the estate owner, that is, being *alieni iuris*, had declaratory force (cf. CJ 11.48.22.2) and imposed this as *condicio* upon them. This *condicio* then, because of the continuity of the census and because the estate was now their *origo*, was transmitted to their descendants. Next to this the village was also their *origo* and they had to perform liturgies there as well. The census registration thus had a twofold public law effect: it defined their personal status but it also lifted their duties towards the estate owner out of the private law of obligations and made it part of their status. That would explain why they were later put on a par with other *condicionales*. This is a hypothesis, but it is one that is compatible with the few clues we have in Justinianic law. For the fisc, such a registration in the census had the advantage that it could always charge the estate owner for the poll tax if the *adscripticius* had not paid it himself.

55 Was There a Colonate?

Was there a colonate? Yes, already for the reason that legal texts of the fourth to sixth century speak of a *ius colonatus* and a *condicio coloniaria*, thus of a complex of legal rules around a phenomenon called the *colonatus*. This complex of rules is linked to some specific agrarian features: being indebted to an estate owner, working on an estate. The term *ius census* indicates that it is linked to the census. It is also linked to the fisc: the poll tax is essential, and when this is abolished, the colonate is imposed in a slimmer form in some provinces. In that sense the colonate was a 'condizione tributaria'.[52] Conversely, only a particular part of agrarian life is affected by the colonate. It requires estate owners with sufficient capital amongst private persons (the imperial domains are of course sufficiently solvent), and it requires an estate of sufficient size to make the use of additional work force remunerative. It was an individual choice and thus a scattered phenomenon, present in a few provinces. With the variety of agrarian exploitation, as is nowadays assumed amongst ancient historians who occupy themselves with ancient agriculture, it means that the colonate was one of several choices of exploitation and it will have depended on the local circumstances whether this choice was made.

Was there a colonate? No, not in the sense that it was a sharply outlined legal or social status which was at a certain moment in its entirety introduced, or that it was a phase in the agrarian production mode of Antiquity, succeeding the slave economy and being a precursor of the serfs of the early Middle Ages.[53] It was a combination of factors, some existing already for a long time, others added to it at a particular moment. The result of these causes was the *ius colonatus*. It further developed in time, resulting in two strands. That it ends in the west is not due to an evolution but to the loss of a particular factor, namely the link with the poll tax which first had made the census registration necessary and effective. That loss made what remained different in nature and closer to later serfdom.

56 Reconstruction of a Chronology of the Colonate

As ancient historians have so competently set out,[54] life was not easy for many people who had little and whose sustenance was metaphorically floating on what the day might bring or on the harvest on a little plot of land, if they disposed of this.[55] The fisc levied in any case the poll tax, and

[52] But not quite as Vera 2010, 19, idem 2007, 493 = 2019, 356 opines. Vera underlines in this essay on Finley's *Ancient Slavery and Modern Ideology* that the *coloni* were completely free people. However, as argued above, they were in a position of legal submission (being *alieni iuris*) and their marriage was a *coniugium non aequale* involving free citizens.

[53] As Vera 2010 makes clear, the slave economy was particular to Italy, but remained there a long time until under Gregory the Great. As for Finley's view of the colonate as successor to the slave economy and the disappearance of the lease, see Vera 1997, 185–186.

[54] To accommodate the more conventional way of historical research, I set out at the end of this retrograde treatment of the colonate a chronology of the colonate, based on the results achieved in the foregoing and under reference to Section 1 for literature.

[55] See Dossey 2010, 55 on the living conditions of rural people in North Africa in the third century. The *coloni* he mentions are not identifiable as *coloni originales*, but his research gives a good picture of their social and economic conditions.

every year they needed sowing seed if they farmed. Crop failures happened. Debts will often have burdened their finances. It made many dependent on those who were rich, usually through possession of land, and who disposed of capital. They could lease land from them or work as labourers and participate thereby in the estate giro system, as we see in Egypt.[56] It is this giro system which made a refined economic activity and management of the estates possible. Rathbone has described on the basis of the Heroninos archive how the lands of Appianus in the third century were managed, and Sarris' description of the economy of the estate of the Apiones in the sixth century shows that it may not have functioned very differently from that. In other regions it will have been the same. Such great estates disposed of capital and needed labour force. Here credit might be available, but it should not burden the debtors so much that they perished under their debts. On the other hand, there was with the great landowners always a need for labour force. It is evident that land without labour does not yield revenues. Although the Physiocrats as the first economists valued labour as a source of riches, in Antiquity this was well known without theorisation. Anyone who wanted to have more revenues than he could accomplish by himself and his family needed extra work force. Slaves were bought as extra hands. Anyone who owned large tracts of land had to let them out to lessees-farmers (and Cato already emphasises that a good farmer is very valuable, while Pliny prescribes remission of rent to help farmers through crop failure), or needed slaves.

In this context a particular agreement, existing already in the first century AD in Egypt, fitted: the *paramonè*. Its basis was a debt of A with B. A would pay the interest by working for B, which makes the *paramonè* very much like an antichretic loan. But the *paramonè* could already be entered for a future debt, or for the commitment to pay taxes. The obligation to work implied the duty to remain on or nearby the estate and to follow orders. How much work or services should be done depended on the actual agreement and the moment at which they should be done might also be arranged by the *procurator* of the landowner. If the creditor-landowner died, the agreement would continue with his heir. As such, the *paramonè* could be the lifeline for a farmer: next to other activities, he could earn by doing some work for the estate and be shielded from the fisc. We see in the Heroninos archive examples of this and how it worked.

[56] Preisigke 1910; Rathbone 1991.

At some moment, this private law construction must have come into the reach of the imperial administration where it concerned the administration's business, namely the taxation. Where an estate owner had given a farmer the promise to pay his poll tax or provide the money for this, the fisc may have wanted to have more certainty. In private law a *cautio* was usual, in public law for nominations, for example, too. What we see here is that in the estate census an insert (*adscriptio*) is made, apparently based on or made from this agreement, because its effect was that now the owner was liable if the farmer himself did not pay. Was this first introduced on the patrimonial lands of the emperor and afterwards extended to private lands? Perhaps: such a guarantee would have favoured *coloni* on these lands, and we see later that they were favoured in other ways. What the registration in the census also effected was that the insert now was coupled with whoever owned the estate. The personal–private law link was in this respect severed. The agreement had become a *contractus publicus*. But the census had at the same time declaratory force (it served also as property register) and this appears to have its effect on the status of the *coloni* who were registered as subjected to the estate owner. A *colonus* turned, metaphorically speaking, by this from a *debitor alicuius* into a *servus terrae* (as a fifth-century text says, albeit for the 'free' colonate). He was indentured. It implied that by being on the estate's census, the farmer was in the *potestas* of the landowner, and his assets were correspondingly treated as if *peculium* because they served as security. This shift implied that he was from now on within the category of people *alieno iure subiecti*, as slaves were too. The effect of the census was to turn it into a public law *condicio*, making a marriage with an *ingenua* due to his being *alieni iuris* as if without *conubium* regarding the transmission of the *origo*. For the rest, however, contrary to slaves, he was still a free Roman citizen like *filii familias*, being both *sui iuris* and *alieni iuris*. His landowner could release him at will, which implies that the private law remained fundamental, and his duties remained private law too. For the later 'free' colonate it was different: that was fully public law.[57]

The insertion into the census had another effect: it laid down the *origo* of the farmer. The census registration had more functions than just registering the tax, and anyway the fact that the census was based either on *origo* or, where it concerned the land tax, on the place of the land, being censused somewhere suggested that one had his *origo* there as well. Hence the designations *censibus adscripti*, *coloni originales* and *coloni originarii*.

57 Thus the landowner did not exercise an administrative function nor did the *colonus*' duties become a kind of half *munus* as I suggested in Sirks 1993a, 359. That fits only the 'free' colonate, which was imposed by law and the authority of the landowner too, without any agreement.

The earliest references to this system date from 293/294, which means that the colonate as public law institution began under Diocletian. It is assumed that with the arrival of the first Tetrarchy in the spring of 293 a reform of the army (increase of troops, introduction of the *praebitio tironum*) necessitated more state revenues. First the tax collection was improved, after which the taxation system was reformed on basis of the existing system.[58] In that context a new use of the census registers may have taken place. If the first *indictio* took place in 297, on the basis of a five-year census, then the innovation may have taken place just after the census of 292 as preparation for the new system.[59] Such a change may have been introduced by edict, which would have not been included in the Gregorian or Hermogenian Codes (containing only rescripts), nor in the Theodosian Code (containing only constitutions from 312 onwards). It may also have been introduced by an edict of the Praetorian Prefects,[60] just as we know of the edict of Optatus of 297 which set a tariff for the poll tax. In that case, since Optatus refers to a correction in the assessment, it may have been introduced earlier than 297.

We may attribute the origin of the colonate as legal institution to that period and those reforms, because *in nuce* it contains the later developments, which were occasioned by later circumstances. But the colonate was not a fiscal creation in order to secure the tax levy, as some authors maintain. First, it came into being only where such an agreement was concluded; second, it did not give the landowner a duty to collect the tax, he only guaranteed voluntarily the tax; third, substantially the colonate existed already, albeit in private law terms (the *paramonè*); fourth, the landowner needed to be financially solvent. The change was its transition from private into public law, and then only if the farmer agreed to this transition. Others may have preferred to keep their *paramonè* out of public law. Consequently, the colonate could only make its appearance on an individual basis and only where its conditions, namely an estate of sufficient size and with sufficient capital, were present. It means that its presence was diffuse, as it is later said in CTh 11.1.26: *earum scilicet provinciarum, ... in quibus haec retinendae plebis ratio adscriptioque servatur*, 'of those provinces ... where this system of those provinces ... where this system of binding and registering of the common people is in use'.

58 *CAH* XII, 74–76, 173–175.

59 As Giliberti 1999, 94 assumes. Yet he does not give an analysis of how this might have been achieved, nor does he refer to the *paramonè*.

60 See Schiavo 2018 for the role of the Praetorian Prefects in calibrating the execution of general rules and correcting practice.

We cannot say that the colonate was the result of the disappearance of the lease contract or the continuation of the *leges* of the great imperial estates in North Africa, where *coloni* were supposedly getting more and more into a state of dependency. First, the lease contract was very much alive, considering the amount of space given in the Digest and in Justinian's Code. Second, there was no need: *coloni* could also lease from their landlord and others; later papyri testify to that. Nor can we say that the *coloni* became impoverished and dependent on account of that. Dossey has recently argued that the third century presents for life on the land a time of prosperity and entrepreneurship, in free tenancy.[61] That means that the idea that people on the land suffered more in general and were more in debt, and that this led to a shift in agricultural exploitation, is not probable or tenable. This of course does not alter the fact that there were (and will always be) individuals who got into debt and that crop failures may have caused many farmers distress and forced them to borrow. But such incidents do not alter the manner of exploitation. They may, however, have made the colonate appear as a lifeline.

The question has also been posed whether the colonate might have been a reaction to a diminishing slave market. The need for a permanently available workforce, which slavery provided, would have been handicapped by a drying-up of the supply during the second and third centuries.[62] The colonate with the bond to the land would have been a solution. Giliberti opposes this view: the colonate never replaced slavery. Slavery itself was not a stable way, depending as it did on external sources. Nowhere is there a sign that an abandonment of the slave-production caused problems.[63] Martini pointed out that there was a shortage of *coloni*.[64] Moreover, Lenski has recently shown first of all that tenancy (lease) and free labour remained important in North Africa on the imperial domains (and likely elsewhere), but shifted proportionally with the arrival of the colonate, while slavery was in any case not a factor on those domains.[65] There was a preference for free people as lessees over slaves.[66] It is not clear whether Lenski applies this to all lessees or just a part (as I think it is), but it is certain that they were in the early fifth century considerably more important in agriculture in North

61 Dossey 2010, 8, ch. 2. Also Ward-Perkins has, in an evaluation of Jones' *The Later Roman Empire*, observed that Jones' picture of the economic circumstances is relatively optimistic, contrary to his predecessors: Ward-Perkins 2008, 203ff. Nonetheless, Jones too believed in some decline. Ward-Perkins attributes this to his ignoring the archaeological evidence.

62 Notwithstanding the 'house-born' slavery. See, for example, Bradley 1987, who nevertheless doubts that it sufficed to sustain the slave population by itself.

63 Giliberti 1999, 1–19, an excellent overview. 64 See Martini 1986.

65 Lenski 2017, 119–120, 122. 66 Lenski 2017, 130.

Africa than slaves.[67] To this I would add another, economic argument. Slaves are present all the time but also have to be housed and fed all the time. With the colonate the landowner disposes of workers who have to house and feed themselves; he may not ask everything from them and may have to give them some loans, but he can also decide not to use them when it is convenient for him. Everything they need he can charge them for. His claim can be used permanently as with supervising irrigation work; it can be used for labour on demand. These aspects may have favoured the colonate over slavery.

The colonate has further been linked to a supposed introduction of heredity of status and professions under Diocletian. But with some groups such a heredity was not linked to the person but to inherited capital and this already in the early third century (particular groups of *navicularii*, *pistores*, and *suarii*, forming permanent aggregates of capital),[68] whereas with the decurions there was already in the second century a hereditary election of new members. The fact that the status of the *coloni* passed on to their offspring is detached from that and connected with their subjected status and census registration.

We see after the beginning under Diocletian two strands of development of the colonate, differentiated essentially by privileges granted: one on imperial lands and one on private lands. Then, everybody in the countryside had to pay poll tax, regardless of where they lived. The imperial lands, being large and having the back-up of the imperial capital, were of course well suited to provide financial backing to people. In 325, *coloni* on imperial lands enjoyed the privilege that they were exempted from *honores* and *munera* of towns (CJ 11.68.1) and, in 343, they enjoyed immunity from superindictions, extraordinary duties, and *munera sordida*, by which was probably meant charges fitting the lower ranks of society (CTh 11.16.5). They had a *forum privilegiatum* with the *rationalis* or *procurator Domus* since 349 (CJ 3.26.7, confirmed in 358 in CJ 3.26.8). But they were not allowed to enter the imperial service (*militia*), since in 365 in the west these *coloni* were recalled from offices (CJ 11.68.3 jo. CTh 7.1.8). The reason is obvious: the privileges were meant to make it attractive to bind oneself to imperial land, but the privileged should stay there and not flee to imperial offices that provided an exemption. In the east in 384–389 *coloni* of patrimonial lands had to leave the imperial service (*militia*) (CJ 11.63.4, 11.64.1), repeated in 409 (CJ 11.64.3), and it was forbidden to host a fugitive *colonus* of patrimonial lands. On the other hand, the *coloni*

[67] Lenski 2017, 141. [68] See Sirks 1991.

of the lands of the imperial House were granted immunity from extraordinary charges or superindictions (CJ 11.68.5, 386 E). In 386, *coloni* of dominical lands got the right to complain about extortion, concussion by venal judgments (CTh 9.27.6, E). In 390, this faculty was restricted to one year where a *comes domorum* was administered (CTh 9.27.1, E). These privileges remained under Justinian. It seems that being an imperial *colonus* was not such a low condition as being a *colonus* with private landowners.

The *coloni* on private lands were not so lucky. Only the *coloni* on senatorial lands enjoyed some privileges, because in 361 they were exempted from the *collatio lustralis* when trading (CTh 13.1.3). For the rest, they were considered to be of as low status as those on other private lands.

We see with *coloni* of both imperial and private lands that they abscond, which meant of course more a loss of labour than a loss of the granted credit and, for the imperial taxes, of the poll tax due. These will certainly have amounted to something but, as I assume, far more important was the need for continuous cultivation of land.

The status of the *colonus* was that of an *alieno iure subiectus*, which made him unfit for the imperial administration (the *militia*) and for public functions. This condition, the *condicio coloniaria*, was connected with his census registration and passed on to his children. That this status as such existed very early in the fourth century is shown by CTh 10.20.1 of 317, which states that *monetarii* have a *condicio* which ties them to their work (and presumably their particular mint). We know that the *condicio coloniaria* existed in 332 (CTh 5.17.1), and it will have existed before, perhaps right from the beginning; the necessary elements were all present at that moment (realised by law? see below). But it had an effect in the area of marriage. Around the middle of the fourth century, texts mention the *coniugium non aequale* (see Section 26.3 and 26.4; a particular case being CTh 4.12.3 of 320). This rule presumed that the colonate was a status *alieni iuris*, just as slaves and those who were *in mancipio* and who were considered as if slaves (*servorum loco*),[69] and that this status was legally fixed. When this was introduced is not clear. Considering the ease with which the emperor imposed the status of *condicionalis* temporarily on *actuarii* in 333, it seems it was definitively standard in the later years of Constantine. The *condicio coloniaria* put the *coloni* on the level of slaves and thereby made their legal marriage not one with all the legal consequences. In case of the

[69] Gai 1.138: *Hi qui in causa mancipii sunt quia servorum loco habentur vindicta censu testamento manumissi sui iuris fiunt.*

marriage of a *colona* with a man free from this status (*ingenuus*), the effect would be that the children were *coloni*. Since it said that this was effected by a law, the appraisal of the *condicio coloniaria* to one which made a *iustum matrimonium* partly into a *coniugium non aequale* must have been done by law. That implies too that basically it was a legitimate marriage. The effect was that, regarding the transmission of status, it looked as if the *ius gentium* applied. The status of *alieni iuris* made further the application of the *senatusconsultum Claudianum* possible. In case of a marriage of a *colonus* with a woman free from subjection (*ingenua* is the term), it made all children *coloni* instead of them following the free maternal status. It was applicable to *coloni originales* both on private and on imperial lands. The supply of *coloni* was enlarged by this: in all cases the children were *coloni*, as would, of course, be the case if *coloni* married amongst themselves.

56.1 Development in the West between 364 and 438

In the following period, we see in the west repeatedly laws issued to counteract this unwanted migration. In the first years after Valentinian's accession, several general measures were issued. In 365, fugitive *coloni* in Gaul were recalled *sine condicionis discrimine* (CJ 11.48.6), probably in the wake of the invasion of the Alemanni.[70] In 368 or later, Valentinian ordered the claims and cases of fugitive *coloni* to be examined carefully, which means that there was a search for them going on (CTh 10.12.2, W). In 371, fugitive *coloni* who have worked on another estate or as independent labourers and earned wages are mentioned; the problem of how to deal with these earnings and financial claims is dealt with (CJ 11.48.8, W). In the same year, he forbade the trick by which slaves, in the same way as *coloni*, were moved from one land to another (CJ 11.48.7). Evidently Valentinian wanted to restore labour supply on the land and ordered his administration to realise this. It will have assisted not only the landowners involved but also his treasury, through higher tax revenues. Fugitives could be recalled, unless a limitation of prescription applied, namely thirty years within the same province and forty years in another province, if they had served a town (CTh 12.19.2 of 400, W). These long periods did not really make escape easy and demonstrate the need for labour.

From the beginning of the fifth century, the west suffered from barbarian incursions and political unrest. Many *coloni* must have used the opportunity to migrate from their estates and work elsewhere, depriving

[70] See Schmidt-Hofner 2008a, 274–276.

their landowners of labour force. It will have concerned the large landowners, undoubtedly a politically important group. Legislation followed with several constitutions on *coloni*. First, in 400 a large constitution on the recall of fugitive *coloni* in the prefecture of Gaul was issued (CTh 12.19.1, 2, 3, CJ 11.48.13, CTh 4.23.1). It dealt with the question of *colonae* who had married *coloni* or other bound people from elsewhere: what to do with their children (instead of following the paternal status, divisions were introduced); what to do if a fugitive had died meanwhile; with terms for limitation of prescription and what to do if the term had passed; with marriages between *coloni* and *inquilini*. If a fugitive *colonus* or *inquilinus* had served a town in the same province for thirty years or in another province for forty years, he could not be recalled. The constitution also regulated the application of the interdict *utrubi* (temporary reinstatement of the possession of moveables) for a quick recovery. Further, it allowed for the transfer of *coloni* to another land under the condition that both lands remained in the same hands, that is, the *origo* of the *coloni* did not change. It is evident that in Gaul there was, due to flight, a great shortage of labour and that (see the limitation of prescription) this had been the case for a long time already.

Similarly, there was apparently a shortage of *tabularii*, municipal registrars or accountants, and *coloni* were accepted in 401, notwithstanding their low status (CTh 8.2.5). These functionaries were indispensable for the assessment of taxes and their realisation.

A constitution of 414 (CJ 11.48.15, CTh 7.8.11, CJ 8.16(17).8, CJ 11.59.13) dealt with fiscal debts. It says that the tax collector (*exactor*) may not summon *coloni originales* for the fiscal debts of anybody but these must remain all the time on their land (CJ 11.48.15), and that anything which pertains to farming may not be taken (CJ 8.16(17).8). For all lands the owners or representatives (thus not, e.g., *coloni originales*) are summoned, and if it appears that the debts were due to a fault of the *actores* or owners, a shift in ownership will take place, that is, the land of the latter will be transferred to somebody else (CJ 11.59.13). If we interpret this in accordance with the title in which the text was placed under Justinian, on deserted land, it would refer in the fourth century to a *peraequatio* in which land that was not cultivated, and because of that no longer yielded tax revenues, was joined with cultivated land and its ownership transferred with it. The situation in 414 was, on the basis of these texts, that plots of land no longer yielded the taxes due on them. The emphasis on the bond of the *coloni originales* to the land aligns with this aim of the government. Without labour present, cultivation is impossible and land will be devoid of revenues. Further, the *coloni originales* were not responsible for the land tax or the outstanding and uncollectable fiscal debts. The law confirms standing practice.[71]

The first quarter of the fifth century saw a firm policy in the west to keep *coloni* on the land. In 419 an extensive constitution regulated the recall of fugitive *coloni* (CTh 5.18.1). The text seems to confirm a limitation of prescription of thirty years, reduced here to twenty for *colonae*. This was not the general prescription of thirty years as introduced in the east in 424 (CTh 4.14.1), since that was not introduced in the west until 449. It further adjusted the division of offspring. The entrance to the *militia* was also forbidden in 426 for *coloni* (CJ 11.48.18), nor was this or *honores* open to any enfranchised person (CTh 4.10.3, 426), under whom we may also understand released *coloni*.[72] Neither could they become clerics (affirmed in Nov. Val. 35.2 of 451). The *coniugium non aequale* rule remained in force (Nov. Val. 31.5–6 of 451).

56.2 *Development in the East between 364 and 438*

In the east we see in the same period the same phenomena reflected in similar legislation but also an innovation. In 365, the emperor ruled that *coloni* did not have the right to alienate the plots they tilled or their own property without the consent of their masters (CTh 5.19.1). It was the logical outcome of the structure of the colonate: the *colonus* was in the *potestas* of his landowner as if a slave, and his property served as security for his debt. The constitution will have been a confirmation, not a new rule, and one which also will have been applied in the west.

The *coniugium non aequale* appears in 371 with the application of the *senatusconsultum Claudianum* to unions of *conchyloleguli* (CTh 10.20.5), these and *monetarii* (CTh 10.20.5, 380), then these and *coloni* (CTh 10.20.17, 427). The rule applied later on to all unions of *coloni*.

Around that time we see in the east the term *adscripticius* or *enapographos* used for the *colonus originalis*. This was probably done to distinguish them from the 'free' *coloni* whom we see first in 371. In that year it was introduced

[71] This regulation must be seen in the perspective of the plundering of Italy and Rome by the Visigoths in 410 and the revolt of Heraclianus in Africa, who was defeated in 413 (CTh 15.14.13, 413). In several constitutions the emperor tried to organise the taxes and to alleviate the burdens (CTh 7.13.20, 411; 11.1.31, 412; 11.1.31, 412; 8.4.23, 11.1.32, 11.7.19–21, 12.6.31, 412; 11.28.7, 412; 8.10.4, 412; 11.28.8, 414). To this came the question of the Donatists in Africa, which was settled in Carthage in 411 (CTh 16.5.52, 411; 16.5.54, 414).

[72] Because the taint of servility still clung to them.

in Illyricum, where the poll tax was abolished (CJ 11.53.1: *inserviant terris non tributario nexu sed nomine et titulo colonorum*). The region had suffered under the invasion of the Goths, just as later in Thrace, where the 'free' colonate was introduced in 393 (CJ 11.52.1), and in Palestine in 386 (CJ 11.51.1). After the treaty in 382 with the Goths, who even argued in 376 that accepting them as auxiliary recruits would leave the farmers free to farm,[73] which treaty settled them in Thrace and otherwise south of the Danube,[74] there would have been an opportunity for the emperor to reorder agrarian relations. Abolition of the poll tax, as in these provinces, or a lowering of poll tax in a number of eastern provinces in 386,[75] would alleviate the burden on farmers. But abolition implied also that the ground for the tax guarantee, and with that for the *adscriptio*, fell away.[76] Consequently the *coloni* were no longer in the *potestas* of their landowner. To prevent a migration of labour to other regions, Valens introduced a colonate which consisted merely in the bond to the land and a duty to cultivate. The landowner got by law the authority to recall them and force them to work. After his victory over the Goths in 386, Theodosius issued also a constitution which forbade accepting fugitive *coloni*, whether *privati* or *patrimoniales*. This measure was connected with the recultivation of deserted land (CTh 5.17.2). According to Schmidt-Hofner, Illyricum was just in this period harshly taxed. He therefore interprets CJ 11.53.1 as merely distinguishing the status of *coloni* from the ordinary tax payer.[77] It seems to me that this is not compatible with the text, which expressly releases the *colonus* from the *tributarius nexus*. Further, the way the prefect Probus oppressed the inhabitants, perhaps legally but more likely illegally, struck the wealthier part of society, not those who only paid the poll tax.[78]

On imperial lands, circumstances required a recall too in those years. In CJ 11.63.4 of 384/389, *coloni* of patrimonial lands must return from the *militia* or other places or occupations. CJ 11.50.2.3 of 393 says that alienation by *coloni* without the knowledge and consent of their masters is forbidden. It is a repetition of the previous prohibition. The emperors underlined in 396 that the *condicio coloniaria* did not allow the estate owner to be sued, except for excessive demands, contrary to the *coloni liberi* (CJ 11.50.1 and 2). This restriction shows that they were in the *potestas* and thus of a subjected status.

[73] *CAH* XIII, 94–101. [74] *CAH* XIII, 103. [75] CTh 13.11.2 (= CJ 11.48.10) + 3 (= CJ 11.58.3).
[76] A guarantee or surety exists only as long as the debt for which it is given exists.
[77] Schmidt-Hofner 2008a, 278. [78] As follows from Ammianus Marcellinus 31.5.5–10.

CTh 5.6.3 of 409 regulated the allocation of captive barbarians (Scyri and Chuni) as *coloni originales* on estates outside of Thrace (where they came from). These captives did not, apparently, become slaves, although we may doubt whether they thereby became Romans. It argues for the administrative nature of the colonate that the *civitas* or *natio* did not matter.

In 409 if a *colonus* wanted to become a cleric, his estate owner had to agree, and the *colonus* remained liable for *capitatio* and *obsequia* (CJ 11.64.3 jo. CJ 1.3.16). It means that, unlike before, entrance into the Church and the resulting loss of labour was now hesitatingly allowed and the estate owner would bear the loss. This allowance we do not see in the west, which is likely due to the great interest in theology in the east and the growth of the monastic movement.

56.3 Development after the Theodosian Code

The Theodosian Code fixated the legislation on the *coloni* for the entire Empire, for the western part and for the eastern part, and thus the situation as described. At that time, release by manumission or lifting the poll tax was the applied way of release from the colonate. After that, west and east went different ways. In the west, unwanted migration continued to cause problems, but at the same time the imperial administration gradually disintegrated while barbarian rulers took over. After 476, even Italy was ruled by a barbarian. The colonate existed still, but we no longer see the link with the fisc, that is, that it served to guarantee the payment of the poll tax. It seems that only the land tax remained. Only in the Visigothic kingdom was this unchanged in 506; yet even here there is a suggestion that in reality that link was a fiction. The colonate was now a *condicio* only, a personal status, defined by the descendance, but still connected to an estate. That makes it a different colonate, and so the Roman colonate as formed as an institution under Diocletian found its end here.

In the east, where the imperial administration continued unimpaired, the two kinds of colonate remained in existence. The Roman 'normal' colonate was, probably in 491, mitigated by Anastasius: after thirty years of service the *colonus adscripticius* became a 'free' *colonus*. Under Justinian, legislation improved their status again. The abolition of the *senatusconsultum Claudianum* in 531–534 lifted the restrictions on the consequences of a marriage of a *colonus* with a free woman, but Justinian allowed the *colonus*' master to recall him from his marriage. Nevertheless, his status remained that of *alieno iure subiecti*. As to the 'free' colonate, it continued to exist too.

Bibliography

Sources and Abbreviations

AARC	*Atti dell'Accademia Romanistica Costantiniana*
App	Appendices, in Nov.
B	Basilica
BIDR	*Bulletino dell'Istituto di Diritto Romano 'Vittorio Scialoja'*
Brev.	Breviarium Alarici
BS	*Basilicorum libri LX. Ser. B., Scholia*, edited by H. J. Scheltema, N. van der Wal, and D. Holwerda, Groningen 1953–1985
BT	*Basilicorum libri LX. Ser. A., Textus librorum*, edited by H. J. Scheltema and N. van der Wal, Groningen 1955–1988
c.	caput (i.e., chapter)
CAH	*Cambridge Ancient History*, 2nd edn (Cambridge 1970–2005)
CIL	*Corpus Inscriptionum Latinarum* (Berlin 1863–)
CJ	Codex Justinianus (*Corpus iuris civilis*, vol. 2, edited by P. Krüger, Berlin 1954 [repr.])
CTh	Codex Theodosianus (*Theodosiani libri XVI cum constitutionibus Sirmondianis*, vol. 1, edited by T. Mommsen and P. Krüger, Berlin 1905)
D	Digest (*Corpus iuris civilis*, vol. 1, edited by T. Mommsen and P. Krüger, Berlin 1954 [repr.])
EdTh	Edictum Theodorici
ep.	epistle
Gai	*Institutes* of Gaius
I	*Interpretationes*, see LRV; cited according to and in combination with the CTh edition
LB	Lex Burgundionum
LRB	Lex Romana Burgundionum
LRV	Lex Romana Visigothorum
Mansi	J. D. Mansi, *Sacrorum Conciliorum nova et amplissima collectio*, Florence 1759–1798

Nov.	Novels (*Corpus iuris civilis*, vol. 3, edited by R. Schoell and G. Kroll, Berlin 1954 [repr.])
Nov. [emperor]	Novels (*Leges novellae ad Theodosianum pertinentes*, edited by T. Mommsen and P. M. Meyer, Berlin 1905; *Jus Graecoromanum*, vol. 1, edited by D. Zepos and P. Zepos, Athens 1930)
OLD	*Oxford Latin Dictionary*, edited by P. G. W. Glare, Oxford 1982
OSS	*Das Corpus Juris Civilis, in's Deutsche übersetzt von einem Vereine Rechtsgelehrter*, edited by C. E. Otto, B. Schilling, and C. F. Sintenis, Leipzig 1830–1833
P	papyrus
P.Oxy	*Oxyrhynchus Papyri*, edited by B. P. Grenfell and A. S. Hunt, London 1898–
PS	*Pauli sententiae* (in *Fontes iuris Romani anteiustiniani*, vol. II. *Auctores*, edited by S. Riccobono, J. Baviera, C. Ferrini, J. Furlani, and V. Arangio-Ruiz, 2nd edn, Florence, 1940)
PSI	Pubblicazioni della Società italiana per la ricerca dei papyri greci et latini in Egitto
PW	*Paulys Real-Encyclopädie der Classischen Altertumswissenschaft*, edited by G. Wissowa, W. Kroll, and K. Ziegler, Stuttgart 1903–1978
RIDA	*Revue Internationale des Droits de l'Antiquité*
SB	Sammelbuch Griechischer Urkunden aus Ägypten
SCTh	Summaria antiqua codicis Theodosiani
ZSS-R	*Zeitschrift der Savigny-Stiftung, Romanistische Abteilung*

Periodicals are further referred to with the sigla as given in P. Rosumek, *Index des Périodiques ... et index de leur sigles, suppl. à l'Année Philologique*, 51, 1982.

Constitutiones are cited as text and as referenced according to their inclusion in the CTh or CJ. The dating of constitutions is primarily done on basis of the CTh and CJ, with eventually further precision as suggested by Seeck 1919. The *inscriptio* is only retained if needed for the text but not translated; the *subscriptio* is always left out.

Secondary Literature

Adams, B. *Paramonè und verwandte Texte, Studien zum Dienstvertrag im Rechte der Papyri*, Berlin 1964.

Aiello, V. Vittore di Vita e la legislazione vandale in Africa, *AARC* XV, 2005, 253–283.

Amarelli, F. *Colonatus*, *AARC* XXII, 2017, 75–61.

Arnold, J. J., Shane Bjornlie, M., Sessa, K. eds. *A companion to Ostrogothic Italy*, Leiden/Boston 2016.

Atzeri, L. *Gesta Senatus Romae de Theodosiano publicando*, Berlin 2008.
Aubert, J. J., Blanchard, Ph., eds. *Droit, religion et société dans le Code Théodosien*, Genève 2009.
Ausbüttel, F. M. Die Dedition der Westgothen von 382 und ihre historische Bedeutung, *Athenaeum* 66, 1988, 604–613.
Avotins, I. *On the Greek of the Novels of Justinian*, Hildesheim 1992.
Babusiaux, U. The *nova clausula* Iuliani – a change of paradigm in the praetorian law of succession?, in *Nova ratione: change of paradigms in Roman law*, ed. B. Sirks, Wiesbaden 2014, 9–31.
Bagnall, R. S. *Egypt in Late Antiquity*, Princeton 1993.
Banaji, J. Agrarian history and the labour organisation of Byzantine large estates, in *Agriculture in Egypt from Pharaonic to modern times*, Proceedings of the British Academy 96, ed. A. K. Bowman, E. Rogan, Oxford 1999, 193–216.
Banaji, J. *Agrarian change in Late Antiquity: gold, labour and aristocratic dominance*, Oxford 2001.
Banaji, J. Aristocracies, peasantries and the framing of the early Middle Ages, *Journal of Agrarian Change* 9, 2009, 59–91.
Barnish, S. J. B. Taxation, land and barbarian settlement in the western Empire, *Papers of the British School at Rome* 54, 1986, 170–195.
Bartusis, M. C. *Land and privilege in Byzantium: the institution of pronoia*, Cambridge 2012.
Bassanelli Sommariva, G. Il codice teodosiano ed il codice giustinianeo posti a confronto, *MEFRA* 125.2, 2013, https://doi.org/10.4000/mefra.1895.
Beaudouin, E. Les grands domaines dans l'empire romain d'après des travaux récents, *RHDFE* 21, 1897, 1, 543–599; 2, 623–720; 22, 1898, 3, 27–115; 4, 194–219; 5, 310–315; 6, 545–583; 7, 694–746.
Benaïssa, A. P.Oxy. LXXVII 5123 and the economic relations between the Apion estate and its *coloni adscripticii*, *JJP* L, 2020, 49–66.
Berger, A. *Encyclopedic Dictionary of Roman Law*, Philadelphia 1954.
Berneker, E. v. Παραμονή, *PW* 36, 1949, 1212–1214.
Besson, A. *Constitutio Antoniniana: l'universalité de la citoyenneté romaine au 3e siècle*, Basel 2020.
Bianchini, M. *Sul regime delle unione fra libere e adscripticii nella legislazione giustinianea*, Studi in onore di Cesare Sanfilippo, vol. V, Milano 1984.
Bingen, J. Les comptes dans les archives d'Heroninos, *Chronique d'Égypte* 26, 1951, 378–385.
Biondi, B. *Il diritto romano cristiano*, Milano 1952–1954.
Bobbink, R. *Antichresis en pandgebruik*, Deventer 2021.
Bondue, D. Esclavage et colonat dans le Bréviaire d'Alaric, in *Le Bréviaire d'Alaric: aux origines du Code civil*, ed. M. Rouche, B. Dumézil, Paris 2008, 91–101.
Bott, H. *Die Grundzüge der diokletianischen Steuerverfassung*, Darmstadt 1928.
Botta, F. De his qui suscipiunt alienos agricolas, Intorno a Edict. Praef. Praet. XXV, *BIDR* 111, 2017, 1–19.
Bowman, A. Diocletian and the first Tetrarchy, in *CAH XII*, 2nd edn, Cambridge 2005, 193–337.

Bradley, K. R. On the Roman slave supply and slavebreeding, *Slavery and Abolition* 8, 1987, 42–64.

Bransbourg, G. Capital in the sixth century: the dynamics of tax and estate in Roman Egypt, *Journal of Late Antiquity* 9.2, 2016, 305–412.

Brooks, E. W. *Historia ecclesiastica Zachariae Rhetori vulgo adscripta*, Louvain 1919–1924.

Brown, T. S. *Gentlemen and officers: imperial administration and aristocratic power in Byzantine Italy AD 500–800*, Rome 1984.

Brósz, R. Les changements sémantiques du mot 'Colonus' dans les sources du droit romain, *Ann. Univ. Scient. Budapestinensis de Rolando Eötvös nominatae, section iuridica*, I, 1959, 39–55.

Bueno, M. *El Breviario de Alarico*, *AARC* XIV, 2003, 629–637.

Burdeau, F. Le ius perpetuum et le régime fiscal des res privatae et des fonds patrimoniaux, *Iura* 23, 1972, 1–25.

Burdeau, F. L'administration des fonds patrimoniaux et emphytéotiques au bas-Empire romain, *RIDA* 20, 1973, 285–310.

Burgmann, L. Zwei Editionen, *Rechtshistorisches Journal* 1984.3, 1984, 19–23.

Cambridge Ancient History, Vol. XIII, ed. A. Cameron, P. Garnsey, Cambridge 1998.

Cambridge Ancient History, Vol. XIV, ed. A. Cameron, B. Ward-Perkins, M. Whitby, Cambridge 2001.

Cambridge Ancient History, Vol. XII, ed. A. K. Bowman, A. Cameron, P. Garnsey, 2nd edn, Cambridge 2005.

Carrié, J.-M. Le 'colonat' du Bas-Empire: un mythe historiographique? *Opus* 1.2, 1982, 351–370.

Carrié, J.-M. Un roman des origines: les généalogies du 'colonat du Bas-Empire', *Opus* 2.1, 1983, 205–251.

Carrié, J.-M. Figures du 'colonat' dans les papyrus d'Égypte, lexique, contexte, in *Actes du XVII Congr. Intern. Papirologia [Napoli 1983]*, Napoli 1984, 939–948.

Carrié, J.-M. Le reforme di Diocleziano, in *Storia di Roma, Vol. 3.1*, Torino 1993, 292–301.

Carrié, J.-M. Dioclétien et la fiscalité, *Antiquité Tardive* 2, 1994, 33–64.

Carrié, J.-M. 'Colonato del Basso Impero': la resistenza del mito, in *Terre, proprietari e contadini dell'impero romano: dall'affitto romano al colonato tardoantico*, ed. E. Lo Cascio, Roma 1997, 75–150.

Carrié, J.-M. Problèmes de la terre dans l'Antiquité Tardive: réalités archéologiques, structures agraires et normes juridiques, *AARC* XXII, 2017, 5–56.

Cerati, A. *Caractère annonaire et assiette de l'impôt foncier au Bas-Empire*, Paris 1975.

Clausing, R. *The Roman colonate: the theories of its origin*, New York 1925.

Codex of Justinian. *The Codex of Justinian: a new annotated translation, with parallel Latin and Greek text, based on a translation by Justice Fred H. Blume*, general ed. B. W. Frier, Cambridge 2016.

Conrat, M. *Breviarium Alaricianum*, Leipzig 1903, repr. Aalen 1963.

Conte, E. Declino e rilancio della servitù: tra teoria e pratica giuridica, *Mélanges de l'École française de Rome, Moyen-Age* 112.2, 2000, 663–685.
Corcoran, S. The donation and will of Vincent of Huesca: Latin text and English translation, *Antiquité Tardive* 11, 2004, 215–222.
Courtois, Ch., Leschi, L., Perrat, Ch., Saumagne, Ch. *Les Tablettes Albertini: Actes privés de l'époque vandale (fin du Ve siècle)*, Paris 1952.
Cracco Ruggini, L. 'Coloni' e 'inquilini': 'miseri et egeni homines'?, *AARC* VIII, 1990, 199–216.
Cramer, F. v. Lugdunum, *PW* 13, Stuttgart 1927, c. 1718–1724.
Cuiacius, J. *Iacobi Cuiacii praestantissimi operum priorum: commentarius in tres postremos Codicis Justiniani libros, Tomus II*, Napoli 1758.
Cuneo, P. O. *La legislazione di Costantino II, Costanzo II e Costante (337–361)*, Milano 1997.
Dalton, O. M. *The letters of Sidonius*, Oxford 1915.
de Blécourt, A. S., Fischer, H. F. W. D. *Kort begrip van het Oud-Vaderlands burgerlijk recht*, Groningen/Djakarta 1950.
de Jong, H. Using the *Basilica*, *ZSS-R* 133, 2016, 286–321.
De Martino, F. *Wirtschaftsgeschichte des alten Rom*, München 1985.
De Martino, F. Il colonato fra economia e diritto, in *Storia di Roma, Vol. 3.1*, Torino 1993, 798–822.
de Neeve, P. W. *Colonus*, Amsterdam 1985.
De Zulueta, F. *De patrociniis vicorum*, in *Oxford studies in social and legal history*, ed. P. Vinogradoff, Oxford 1909, 3–78.
Delmaire, R. *Largesses sacrées et res privata: l'aerarium impérial et son administration du IVe au VIe siècle*, Rome 1989.
Demandt, A. *Die Spätantike: Römische Geschichte von Diocletian bis Justinian 284–565 n.Chr.*, München 2007.
Demicheli, A. Inquilinato e unioni miste per condizione sociale tra IV e V secolo. Da una lettera (ep. 5,19) di Sidonio Apollinare, *AARC* XVIII, 2012, 275–304.
Di Cintio, L. *L''Interpretatio Visigothorum' al 'Codex Theodosianus', I. Il libro IX*, Milano 2013.
Di Cintio, L. *Nuove richerche sulla 'Interpretatio Visigothorum' al 'Codex Theodosianus', Libri I–II*, Milano 2018.
Díaz, P. C. El testamento de Vicente: propietarios y dependientes en la Hispania de s. VI, in *Romanización y Reconquista en la Península Ibérica: nuevas perspectivas*, ed. M. J. Hidalgo, D. Pérez, M. J. R. Gervás, Salamanca 1998, 257–270.
Dillon, J. N. Conjectures and criticism in Book 1 of the Codex Justinianus, *CQ* 65, 2015, 321–343.
Dolezalek, G. *Repertorium manuscriptorum veterum Codicis Iustiniani*, Frankfurt am Main 1985.
Dossey, L. *Peasant and empire in Christian North Africa*, Berkeley/Los Angeles, 2010.
Edmonson, J. T. Mining in the Later Roman Empire and beyond: continuity or disruption?, *JRS* 79, 1989, 84–102.

Eibach, D. *Untersuchungen zum spätantiken Kolonat in der kaiserlichen Gesetzgebung, unter besonderer Berücksichtigung der Terminologie*, Köln 1980.

Enßlin, W. s.v. *peraequatores*, *PW* 19, Stuttgart 1937, 564.

Esders, S. 'Öffentliche' Abgaben und Leistungen im Übergang von der Spätantike zum Frühmittelalter: Konzeptionen und Befunde, in *Von der Spätantike zum frühen Mittelalter: Kontinuitäten und Brüche, Konzeptionen und Befunde*, ed. Th. Kölzer, R. Schieffer, Ostfildern 2009, 189–244.

Faure, E. *Étude de la capitation de Dioclétien d'après le Panégyrique VII, [Varia IV]*, Paris 1961.

Feissel, D. Une inscription de Kos et une loi de Valens (Iscrizioni di Cos ED 90 et CTh 13, 10, 7), *Chiron* 39, 2009, 297–318.

Feltenius, L. *Intransitivization in Latin*, Stockholm 1977.

Fikhman, I. F. On the structure of Egyptian large estates in the sixth century, *Proc. of the XIIIth Intern. Congress of Papyrology*, München 1974, 127–132, repr. in Fikhman 2006, 42–47.

Fikhman, I. F. Les *patrocinia* dans les papyrus d'Oxyrhynchus, *Actes du XVe congrès international de papyrologie, Vol. IV*, Bruxelles 1978, 186–194, repr. in Fikhman 2006, 152–160.

Fikhman, I. F. Les cautionnements pour les *coloni adscripticii, Proc. XVIth Intern. Congr. Papyrology*, Chico 1981, 469–477, repr. in Fikhman 2006, 169–177.

Fikhman, I. F. Coloni adscripticii – ἐναπόγραφοι γεωργοί in den Papyri, *Problemy social'nykh otnos*enij I form zavisimosti na drevnem Vostoke*, Moskva 1984, 166–226, translation in Fikhman 2006, 190–250 (references are to this version).

Fikhman, I. F. De nouveau sur le colonat du Bas-Empire, in *Miscellanea papyrologica in occasione del bicentenario dell'edizione della Charta Borgiana*, ed. M. Capasso, G. Messeri Savorelli, R. Pintaudi, M. Gigante, Firenze 1990, 159–179, repr. in Fikhman 2006, 258–278.

Fikhman, I. F. *Wirtschaft und Gesellschaft im spätantiken Ägypten: Kleine Schriften Itzhak F. Fikhman*, ed. A. Jördens, Stuttgart 2006.

Fitting, H. H. Ueber einige Rechtsquellen der vorjustinianischen spätern Kaiserzeit, *ZSS-R* 10, 1872, 317–340.

Fitting, H. H. Die sog. westgothische Interpretation, *ZRG* 11, 1873, 222–249.

Fusco, S.-A. *Pecuniam commodare*, Perugia 1980.

Fustel de Coulanges, N. D. Le Colonat romain, in *N. D. Fustel de Coulanges. Recherches sur quelques problèmes d'histoire*, Paris 1885, 3rd edn, Paris 1913, 1–186.

Gamauf, R. Ch. 102 Klage aufgrund Sonderguts oder Zuwendung an den Gewalthaber Rn. 36 (ius deductionis), *Handbuch des Römischen Privatrechts*, ed. U. Babusiaux, Chr. Baldus, W. Ernst, F.-S. Meissel, J. Platschek, Th. Rüfner, Tübingen 2023.

García Moreno, L. A. From *coloni* to *servi*: a history of the peasantry in Visigothic Spain, *Klio* 83, 2001, 198–212.

Gascou, J. *Les grands domaines, la cité et l'état en Égypte byzantine*, Travaux et Mémoires 9, Paris 1985.

Gaudemet, J. L'Église dans l'empire Romain, Paris 1958.

Geary, P. J. *Aristocracy in Provence: the Rhône Basin at the dawn of the Carolingian Age*, Stuttgart 1985.

Georges, K. E. *Ausführliches lateinisch-deutsches Handwörterbuch*, Hannover/Leipzig 1918.

Giardina, A. Gli schiavi, I coloni e i problemi di una transizione, *Terre* 1997, 311–323.

Giardina, A. The transition to Late Antiquity, *Colonatus*, in *The Cambridge Economic History of the Greco-Roman World*, ed. W. Scheidel, I. Morris, R. P. Saller, Cambridge 2007, 749–753.

Giglio, S. *Patrocinio e diritto privato nel tardo impero romano*, Perugia 1995, 2nd edn, 2008.

Gil, J. *Miscellanea Wisigothica*, Sevilla 1972.

Giliberti, G. *Le comunità agricole nell'Egitto romano*, Napoli 1993.

Giliberti, G. Il colonato tardo-antico, in *Storia della società italiana, vol. 4: restaurazione e destrutturazione nella tarda antichità*, Milano 1998, 24–30.

Giliberti, G. Servi della terra: ricerche per una storia del colonato, Torino 1999.

Goetz, H.-W. Serfdom and the beginning of a 'seigneurial system' in the Carolingian period: a survey of the evidence, *Early Medieval Europe*, 2, 1993, 29–51.

Goffart, W. *Barbarians and Romans, AD 418–584: the techniques of accommodation*, Princeton 1980.

Gonis, N., Obbink, D. eds. *The Oxyrhynchus papyri: volume LXIX*. London 2005.

Gorecki, D. Land tenure in Byzantine property law: *iura in re aliena*, *Greek, Roman, and Byzantine Studies* 22, 1981, 191–210.

Grey, C. Contextualising *colonatus*: the *crigo* of the Late Roman Empire, *JRS* XCVII, 2007a, 155–175.

Grey, C. Revisiting the problem of the *agri deserti* in the Late Roman Empire, *JRA* 20, 2007b, 362–376.

Grey, C. Two young lovers: an abduction marriage and its consequences in fifth-century Gaul, *CQ* 58, 2008, 286–302.

Grey, C. *Constructing communities in the Late Roman countryside*, Cambridge 2011.

Grey, C. Concerning rural matters, in *The Oxford Handbook of Late Antiquity*, ed. S. F. Johnson, Oxford 2012, 625–666.

Haarer, F. K. *Anastasius I: politics and empire in the late Roman world*, Cambridge 2006.

Haenel, G. *Lex Romana Visigothorum*, Leipzig 1848, repr. Aalen 1962.

Hahn, I. Das bäuerliche Patrocinium in Ost und West, *Klio* 50, 1968, 261–276.

Hardie, E. R. *The large estates of Byzantine Egypt*, New York 1931.

Harmand, L. *Le patronat sur les collectivités publiques des origines au Bas-Empire*, Paris 1957.

Harper, K. The Greek census inscriptions of Late Antiquity, *JRS* 98, 2008, 83–119.

Harper, K. The *Senatusconsultum Claudianum* in the Codex Theodosianus: social history and legal texts, *CQ* 60, 2010, 610–638.

Harper, K. *Slavery in the Late Roman world AD 275–425*, Cambridge 2011.

Harries, J. *Sidonius Apollinaris and the fall of Rome*, Oxford 1994.

Heather, P. State, lordship and community in the west (c. AD 400–600), in *CAH XIV*, Cambridge 2000, 437–468.

Heisterbergk, B. *Die Entstehung des Colonats*, Heidelberg 1876.

Hengst, J. *Private Arbeitsverhältnisse freier Personen in den hellenistischen Papyri bis Diokletian*, Bonn 1972.

Heumann, H., Seckel, E. *Handlexikon zu den Quellen des römischen Rechts*, Jena 1907.

Hickey, T. *Wine, wealth, and the state in Late Antique Egypt*, Ann Arbor 2012.

Hildesheim, U., *Personalaspekte der frühbyzantinischen Steuerordnung. Die Personalveranlagung und ihre Einbindung in das System der capitatio – iugatio*, Pfaffenweiler 1988.

His, R. *Die Domänen der römischen Kaiserzeit*, Leipzig 1896.

Höbenreich, E. Betrachtung über Beziehung zwischen Freien, Kolonen und Sklaven, *RIDA* 54, 2007, 275–292.

Humbert, M. Enfants à louer ou à vendre: Augustin et l'autorité parentale (Ep. 10* et 24*), in *Les Lettres de Saint Augustin découvertes par Johannes Divjak*, Paris 1983, 189–204.

Jaillette, P. La structure agraire dans l'empire tardif au miroir du Code Théodosien: quelques observations, *Antiquité Tardive* 20, 2012, 123–135.

Johne, K.-P., Köhn, J., Weber, V. *Die Kolonen in Italen und den westlichen Provinzen des römischen Reiches*, Berlin 1983.

Johne, K.-P. *Kolonenwirtschaft und Kolonat: Proc. XVth conference Eirene, Thracia VII*, Sofia 1985, 66–71.

Johne, K.-P. Zum Begriff Kolonat in der Spätantike, in *From Late Antiquity to Early Byzantium: Proc. XVIth conference Eirene*, Praha 1986, 97–100.

Johne, K.-P. Römische Grundherren und Pächter, *Altertum* 33, 1987, 163–170.

Johne, K.-P. Von der Kolonenwirtschaft zum Kolonat, in *Gesellschaft und Wirtschaft des Römischen Reiches im 3. Jahrhundert*, ed. K.-P. Johne, Berlin 1993, 64–97.

Johnson, S. F. ed., *The Oxford Handbook of Late Antiquity*, Oxford 2012.

Jones, A. H. M. Census records of the Later Roman Empire, *JRS* 43, 1953, 49–64.

Jones, A. H. M. *The Later Roman Empire 284–602: a social, economic and administrative survey*, Oxford 1964.

Jones, A. H. M. The Roman colonate, in *The Roman Economy*, ed. P. A. Brunt, Oxford 1974, 293–307.

Jones, A. H. M., Grierson, P., Crook, J. A. The authenticity of the 'testamentum S. Remigii', *Revue Belge de Philologie et d'histoire* 35, 1957, 356–373.

Jördens, A., Bodl, P. I: Ein προχρεία-Vertrag, *ZPE* 116, 1997, 81–84.

Jurewicz Actor, A. R. *Colonus, conductor, procurator* in einem Brief des Kaisers Honorius, *Tijdschrift voor Rechtsgeschiedenis* 88, 2020, 94–121.

Kacprzak, A. 'Ratihabitio' nel diritto romano classico, Napoli 2002, 91–113.

Kaiser, W., Chronopoulos, S. Das Gesetz über Darlehen an Bauern (Nov. 32 und 34), *ZSS-R* 129, 2012, 475–500.

Kaplan, M. L'économie paysanne dans l'Empire byzantin du Ve au Xe siècle, *Klio* 68, 1986, 198–232.

Kaplan, M. *Les hommes et la terre à Byzance du VIe au XIe siècle*, Paris 1992.

Karayannopoulos, J. *Das Finanzwesen des frühbyzantinischen Staates*, München 1958.

Karayannopoulos, J. Die Jugatio-Capitatio-Frage und die Bindung der Agrarbevölkerung an die Scholle, in *Actes du VIIe congrès de la Fédération Internationale des Associations d'Études classiques*, Budapest 1984, 59–72.

Karayannopoulos, J. Die Bindung der Agrarbevölkerung an die Scholle und ihre Ursachen, in *From Late Antiquity to Early Byzantium, Proc. XVIth conference Eirene*, Praha 1986, 93–96.

Kaser, M. *Das römische Privatrecht, II. Teil*, München 1971.

Kaser, M. *Das römische Privatrecht, I. Teil*, München 1975.

Kaser, M., Hackl, K. *Das römische Zivilprozessrecht*, München 1996.

Keenan, J. G. On P.Oxy. XXVII.2479, *ZPE* 38, 1980, 246–248.

Kolendo, J. *Le colonat en Afrique sous le Haut-Empire romain*, Paris 1991.

Kolendo, J. La continuità delle strutture agrarie in Africa romana?, *Terre* 1997, 151–161.

Koptev, A. The raptor and the disgraced girl in Sidonius Apollinaris' Epistula V 19, *Ancient Society* 34, 2004, 275–304.

Koptev, A. The colonate in the Theodosian Code and its interpretation in the Breviary of Alaric, in *Droit, religion et société dans le Code Théodosien*, ed. J.-J. Aubert, Ph. Blanchard, Genève 2009, 261–285.

Koptev, A. The late Roman colonus as persona iuris alieni, *AARC* XVIII, 2012, 305–339.

Kramer, N. *From the tablets of Sumer: twenty-five firsts in man's recorded history*, Indian Hills, 1956.

Krause, J.-U. *Spätantike Patronatsformen im Westen des Römischen Reiches*, München 1987.

Krause, J.-U. s.v. *patrocinium*, *Der neue Pauly*, Stuttgart 2000.

Kränzlein, A. Rez. von M. Mirković: *The later Roman colonate and freedom*, Philadelphia 1997, *ZSS-R* 116, 1999, 363–368.

Krüger, P. *Codex Iustinianus*, Berlin 1877.

Krüger, P. *Codex Theodosianus*, Berlin 1923–1926.

Krusch, B. ed., *Vita Remigii episcopi Remensis auctore Hincmaro*, MGH Scriptores rerum Merovingicarum III, Hannoverae 1896.

Kubitschek, J. W. s.v. census, *PW* 5, Stuttgart 1897.

Lafferty, S. D. W. Law and society in Ostrogothic Italy: evidence from the Edictum Theoderici, *Journal of Late Antiquity* 3.2, 2010, 337–364.

Lafferty, S. D. W. *Law and society in the age of Theoderic the Great: a study of the Edictum Theoderici*, Cambridge 2013.

Lambertini, R. *La codificazione di Alarico II*, Torino 1991.

Laquerrière-Lacroix, A. La *vicinitas* à l'épreuve du droit: la mutation des *iura vicinitatis* dans l'Antiquité tardive, in *Droit, religion et société dans le Code Théodosien*, ed. J.-J. Aubert, Ph. Blanchard, Genève 2009, 303–325.

Lenski, N. Peasant and slave in late antique North Africa, c. 100–600 CE, in *Late Antiquity in contemporary debate*, ed. R. Lizzi Testa, Newcastle upon Tyne 2017, 113–155.

Lepelley, C. Liberté, colonat et esclavage d'après la Lettre 24*: la juridiction épiscopale 'de liberali causa', in *Les lettres de Saint Augustin découvertes par Johannes Divjak*, Paris 1983, 329–342.

Liddell, H. G., Scott, R. *A Greek-English lexicon, with a revised supplementum*, Oxford 1996.

Liebs, D. Die pseudopaulinischen Sentenzen, Versuch einer neuen Palingenesie, *ZSS-R* 112, 1995, 151–171.

Liebs, Die pseudopaulinischen Sentenzen II, Versuch einer neuen Palingenesie, *ZSS-R* 113, 1996, 132–242.

Liebs, D. *Römische Jurisprudenz in Gallien (2. bis 8. Jahrhundert)*, Freiburger rechtsgeschichtliche Abhandlungen 38, Berlin, 2002.

Liebs, D. *Römische Jurisprudenz in Africa, mit Studien zu den pseudopaulinischen Sentenzen*, Berlin 2005, 2nd edn.

Litewski, W. Die römische Appelation in Zivilsachen, *RIDA* 12–15, 1965–1968, 347–436, 231–323, 301–403, 143–351.

Lo Cascio, E. Forme dell'economia imperiale, in *Storia di Roma, Vol. 2.2*, Torino 1991, 313–365.

Lot, F. *La fin du monde antique et le début du moyen âge, Paris 1927, troisième partie*, Paris 1927, new edn, 1968.

MacCoull, L. S. B. Patronage and the social order in Coptic Egypt, in *Egitto e storia antica dall'ellenismo all'età araba: bilancio di un confronto atti del Colloquio internazionale Bologna, 31 agosto–2 settembre 1987*, ed. L. Criscuolo, G. Geraci, Bologna 1989, 497–502.

MacMullen, R. *Corruption and the decline of Rome*, New Haven 1988.

Marcone, A. Il colonato del tardo impero: un mito storiografico?, *Athenaeum* 63, 1985, 513–520.

Marcone, A. *Il colonato tardoantico nella storiografia moderna (da Fustel de Coulanges ai nostri giorni)*, Como 1988.

Marcone, A. Il lavoro nelle campagne, in *Storia di Roma, vol. 3.I*, Torino 1993, 823–843.

Marcone, A. Il colonato tardoantico: i problemi aperti, *Terre* 1997a, 225–251.

Marcone, A. Proprietà della terra e colonato nella storiografia italiana dell'Ottocento, *Quaderni di storia* 46, 1997b, 25–44.

Marquardt, J. *Das Privatleben der Römer*, 2nd edn, A. Mau, Leipzig 1886.

Marrou, H.-I. *L'Église de l'Antiquité tardive 303–604*, Paris 1963, 214–216.

Martini, R. *Penuria colonorum: raritas colonorum, IVRA* 37, 1986, 89–93.

Maas, M. ed. *A companion to the age of Justinian*, Cambridge 2005.

Mathisen, R. Concepts of citizenship, in *The Oxford Handbook of Late Antiquity*, ed. S. F. Johnson, Oxford 2012, 744–763.

Matthews, J. *Laying down the law*, Oxford 2000.

McLynn, N. Administrator: Augustine in his diocese, in *A companion to Augustine*, ed. M. Vessey, with the assistance of Shelley Reid, Chichester 2012, 310–322.

Meier, M. *Das andere Zeitalter Justinians, Kontingenzerfahrung und Kontingenzbewältigung im 6. Jahrhundert n. Chr.*, Göttingen 2004.

Meier, M. *Anastasios I., Die Entstehung des Byzantinischen Reiches*, Stuttgart 2009.

Meier, M. ed. *Justinian*, Darmstadt 2011.
Meier, M. *Geschichte der Völkerwanderung*, München 2019.
Meyer-Marthali, E. *Einflüsse des römischen Rechts in den Formeln und in der Praxis: Schweiz, IRMAEI, 2b, dd, δ*, Mediolani 1975.
Millar, F. *A Greek Roman empire: power and belief under Theodosius II (408–450)*, Oxford 2006.
Miller, D. J. D., Sarris, P. *The Novels of Justinian: a complete annotated English translation*, Cambridge 2018.
Mirković, M. Colonus iuris alieni and the taxation, *Opus* 5, 1986, 53–73.
Mirković, M. The Roman colonate, liberty and Justinian's 'humanity', *RIDA* 41, 1994, 287–300.
Mirković, M. *Autopragia* and the village Aphrodito, *ZSS-R* 113, 1996, 346–357.
Mirković, M. *The later Roman colonate and freedom*, Philadelphia 1997.
Moorhead, J. The Byzantines in the west in the sixth century, in *New Cambridge medieval history, vol. I*, ed. P. Fouracre, Cambridge 2005, 118–139.
Munier, C. ed. *Corpus Christianorum, Concilia Galliae a. 314–506*, Turnhout 1963.
Munzinger, M. *Vincula deterrimae condicionis. Die rechtliche Stellung der spätantiken Kolonen im Spannungsfeld zwischen Sklaverei und Freiheit*, München 1998.
Murga, J. L. Una extraña aplicación del senadoconsulto Claudiano en el Código de Teodosio, *Studi Sanfilippo* I, 1982, 417–442.
Nörr, D. Origo: Studien zur Orts-, Stadt- und Reichszugehörigkeit in der Antike, *Tijdschrift voor Rechtsgeschiedenis* 31, 1963, 525–600.
Nörr, D. s.v. *origo*, *PW* Supp. 10, Stuttgart 1965, 434–473.
Oehler, K. s.v. Anastasios, *PW* 1, 1899, c. 2065–2067.
Oikonomides, N. *Η 'ΠΕΙΡΑ' ΠΕΡΙ ΠΑΡΟΙΚΩΝ, in Byzantium from the ninth century to the fourth Crusade, studies, texts, monuments*, Aldershot 1992, XIII.
Ostrogorsky, G. *Geschichte des byzantinischen Staates*, München 1963, 3rd. ed.
Pallasse, M. Les 'Tablettes Albertini' intéressent-elles le colonat roman du Bas-Empire?, *RHDFE* 33, 1955, 267–281.
Palme, B. Gestellungsbürgschaften und Enthaftungsbürgschaften, unpublished.
Palme, B. Bauernsterben und Fiskalverwaltung im byzantinischen Aphrodite, review of Zuckerman 2004, *Chronique d'Égypte* LXXXII, 2007, 330–336.
Panitschek, P. Der spätantike Kolonat: ein Substitut für die 'Halbfreiheit' peregriner Rechtssetzungen?, *ZSS-R* 107, 1990, 135–154.
Papadatou, D. Antichresis in Byzantine law, *Revue des études byzantines* 66, 2008, 209–220.
Peachin, M. *Iudex vice Caesaris: deputy emperors and the administration of justice during the principate*, Stuttgart 1966.
Percival, J. Seigneurial aspects of late Roman estate management, *The English Historical Review* 1969, 449–473.
Perelman Fajardo, M. Estado y aristocracia en el Imperio romano: la cuestión del colonato, *Anuario del Centro de Estudios Históricos 'Prof. Carlos S.A. Sagreti'*, 19, 2019, 19–33.
Perezius, A., *Praelectiones in duodecim libros codicis Justiniani Imp.*, Amsterdam 1661.

Pergami, F. *La legislazione di Valentiniano e Valente (364–375)*, Milano 1993.

Pergami, F. Il regime del patrimonio immobiliare imperiale nella legislazione del tardo diritto romano, in *Altri Studi di diritto tardoantico*, Torino 2019, 195–215.

Petot, P. L'hérédité de la condition servile en France au Moyen Age, in *Mélanges Philippe Meylan, vol. II*, Lausanne 1963, 1–9.

Pharr, C., Sherrer Davidson, Th., Brown Pharr, M., eds. *The Theodosian Code and Novels, and the Sirmondian Constitutions: a translation*, Princeton 1952.

Piquer Marí, J. M. El colonato visigodo a través de las interpretaciones del Breviarium Alarici al Codex Theodosianus, in *Ravenna Capitale: Codice Teodosiano e tradizione giuridiche in Occidente*, Santarcangelo di Romagna 2016, 113–163.

Poethke, G. Metrocomiae und Autopragie in Ägypten, in *Graeco-Coptica. Griechen und Kopten im byzantinischen Ägypten*, ed. P. Nagel, Halle 1984, 41–43.

Polara, G. 'Inquilini qui praediis adhaerent', *BIDR* 72, 1969, 139–179.

Popescou, E. Quelques remarques sur le sens du terme μισθωτός dans les Basiliques, in *Beiträge zur byzantinischen Geschichte im 9.–11. Jahrhundert: Akten des Colloquium Byzanz auf dem Höhepunkt seiner Macht*, ed. V. Vavrinek, Praha 1978, 99–106.

Porena, P. *L'insediamento degli Ostrogoti in Italia*, Roma 2012.

Pothier, R. J. *The Pandectae Justinianeae in novum ordinem digestae*, Paris 1748–1752.

Preisigke, F. *Girowesen im griechischen Ägypten*, Straßburg i.E. 1910.

Puliatti, S. *Ricerche sulle novelle di Giustino II*, Milano 1984.

Puliatti, S. Disciplina del patronato e persistenza della piccola proprietà in età tardoantica, *AARC* XXII, 2017, 129–145.

Rathbone, D. *Economic rationalism and rural society in third-century AD Egypt: the Heroninos Archive and the Appianus Estate*, Cambridge 1991.

Rathbone, D. The ancient economy and Graeco-Roman Egypt, in *The ancient economy*, ed. W. Scheidel, S. von Reden, Edinburgh 2002, 155–169.

Rathbone, D. Economic rationalism and the Heroninos Archive, *Topoi*, 12.1, 2005, 261–269.

Riedlberger, P. *Prolegomena zu den antiken Konstitutionen. Nebst einer Analyse der erbrechtlichen und verwandten Sanktionen gegen Heterodoxe*, Stuttgart/Bad Cannstatt 2020.

Rio, A. Freedom and unfreedom in early medieval Francia: the evidence of the legal formulae, *Past and Present* 193, 2006, 7–40.

Rio, A. *Slavery after Rome, 500–1000*, Oxford 2017.

Rosafio, P. *Inquilinus*, *Opus* 3, 1984, 121–131.

Rosafio, P. *Studies in the Roman colonate*, diss. Cambridge 1991a.

Rosafio, P. Dalla locazione al colonato: per un tentativio di ricostruzione, *AION (archeol.)* 13, 1991, 237–281.

Rosafio, P. *Studi sul colonato*, Bari 2002.

Rosafio, P. Il peculio dei coloni nella tarda antichità, in *Droit, Religion et société dans le Code Théodosien*, ed. J.-J. Aubert, Ph. Blanchard, Genève 2009, 287–302.

Roth, U. Slavery and the Church in Visigothic Spain: the donation and will of Vincent of Huesca, *Antiquité Tardive* 24, 2016, 433–452.

Rouche, M., Dumézil B. eds. *Le Bréviaire d'Alaric: aux origines du Code civil*, Paris 2008.

Rowlandson, J. *Landowners and tenants in Roman Egypt*, Oxford 1996.

Santifaller, L. Die Urkunde des Königs Odovaker vom Jahre 489, *Mitteilungen des Instituts für österreichische Geschichtsforschung* LX, 1952, 1–30 plus reproductions.

Santilli, A. Appunti sull'origine del colonato, *Studi Senesi* 87, 1975, 139–194.

Santilli, A. *Quaedam servitus*, in *Societas-ius: munuscula di allievi a Feliciano Serrao*, Napoli 1999, 275–291.

Sarris, P. *Economy and Society in the Age of Justinian*, Cambridge 2006.

Sarris, P. Introduction: aristocrats, peasants and the transformation of rural society, c. 400–800, *Journal of Agrarian Change* 9.1, 2009, 1–22.

Sarris, P. Aristocrats, peasants, and the state in the Later Roman Empire, in *Der wiederkehrende Leviathan*, ed. P. Eich, S. Schmidt-Hofner, Ch. Wieland, Heidelberg 2011, 375–392.

Saumagne, Ch. Du rôle de l'origo' et du 'cens' dans la formation du colonat romain, *Byzantion* 12, 1937, 487–581.

von Savigny, F. C. Ueber den Römischen Colonat, Berlin 1822–1823, 1825, repr. *Vermischte Schriften, Bd.* 2, Berlin 1850, 1–66.

Scheidel, W. Sklaven und Freigelassene als Pächter und ihre ökonomische Funktion in der römischen Landwirtschaft (Colonus-Studien III), in *De agricultura: in memoriam Pieter Willem de Neeve (1945–1990)*, Amsterdam 1993, 182–196.

Scheidel, W. Slaves of the soil, *Journal of Roman Archaeology* 13, 2000, 727–732, review of Lo Cascio 1997 and Mirković 1997.

Scheidel, W., Morris, I., Saller, R. P. eds. *The Cambridge Economic History of the Greco-Roman World*, Cambridge 2007.

Schiavo, S. *Ricerche sugli editti dei prefetti del pretorio del Cod. Bodl. Roe 18, processo e documento*, Napoli 2018.

Schipp, O. *Der weströmische Kolonat von Konstantin bis zu den Karolingern (331 bis 861)*, Hamburg 2009.

Schmidt-Hofner, S. *Reagieren und Gestalten. Der Regierungsstil des spätrömischen Kaisers am Beispiel der Gesetzgebung Valentinians I*, München 2008a.

Schmidt-Hofner, S. Regesten der Kaiser Valentinian und Valens, *ZSS-R* 125, 2008b, 498–602.

Schmitz, W. Appendix 1 der justinianischen Novellen – Eine Wende der Politik Justinians gegenüber *adscripticii* und *coloni*?, *Historia* 35, 1986, 381–386.

Schmitz, W. s.v. *tamieion*, *Der neue Pauly*, Stuttgart 2002.

Schulten, A. *Die römischen Grundherrschaften: eine agrarhistorische Untersuchung*, Weimar 1896.

Seeck, O. s.v. *colonatus*, *PW* 4, Stuttgart 1901, 583–510.

Seeck, O. *Regesten der Kaiser und Päpste*, Stuttgart 1919.

Segrè, A. The Byzantine colonate, *Traditio* 5, 1947, 103–133.

Shelton, J. Ostraka from Elephantine in the Fitzwilliam Museum, *ZPE* 80, 1990, 221–238.

Shelton, J. C., Whitehorne, J. E. G., Austin, C. F. L. eds. *The Oxyrhynchus papyri: volume LXII*, London 1995.

Sijpesteijn, P. J., Worp, K. A. *Eine Steuerliste aus Pheretnuis (P.Pher)*, Amsterdam 1993.

Sirks, A. J. B. Sulpicius Severus' letter to Salvius, *Bulletino dell'Istituto di Diritto Romano* 85, 1982, 143–170.

Sirks, A. J. B. From the Theodosian to the Justinian Code, *AARC* VI, 1986, 265–302.

Sirks, *Food for Rome: the legal structure of the transportation and processing of supplies for the imperial distributions in Rome and Constantinople*, Amsterdam 1991.

Sirks, A. J. B. Reconsidering the Roman Colonate, *ZSS-R* 110, 1993a, 331–369.

Sirks, A. J. B. Did the Late Roman government try to tie people to their status or profession?, *TYCHE* 8, 1993b, 159–175.

Sirks, A. J. B. *Obnoxietas*, in *Questions de responsabilité: XLVème session de la SIHDA*, Miskolc 1993c, 325–332.

Sirks, A. J. B. The sources of the Code, in *The Theodosian Code*, ed. J. Harries, I. Wood, London 1993d, 45–67.

Sirks, A. J. B. The Summaria Antiqua Codicis Theodosiani in the ms. Vat. reg. Lat. 886, *ZSS-R* 113, 1996, 243–267.

Sirks, A. J. B. Continuità nel colonato?, in *Terre, proprietari e contadini dell'impero romano: dall'affitto romano al colonato tardoantico*, ed. E. Lo Cascio, Roma 1997, 163–184.

Sirks, A. J. B. Review of *Vincula deterrimae condiciones: Die rechtliche Stellung der spätantiken Kolonen im Spannungsfeld zwischen Sklaverei und Freiheit*, by M. Munzinger, *Gnomon* 75.1, 2003, 84–85.

Sirks, A. J. B. Der Zweck des Senatus Consultum Claudianum von 52 n.Chr., *ZSS-R.* 122, 2005, 138–149.

Sirks, A. J. B. *The Theodosian Code: a study*, Friedrichsdorf 2007.

Sirks, A. J. B. The Colonate in Justinian's reign, *JRS* 98, 2008, 120–143.

Sirks, A. J. B. Die Voraussetzungen und Methode von Seeck in seinen Regesten, *Tijdschrift voor Rechtsgeschiedenis* 78, 2010a, 395–430.

Sirks, A. J. B. Collective liability in fiscal matters in Late Antiquity?, *AARC* XVIII, 2010b, 587–595.

Sirks, A. J. B. The *Senatus Consultum Claudianum* in 438 and after in the west, in *Römische Jurisprudenz – Dogmatik, Überlieferung, Rezeption. Festschrift für Detlef Liebs zum 75. Geburtstag*, Berlin 2011, 623–635.

Sirks, A. J. B. Did poverty lie at the origin of the Colonate?, *Koinonia* 36, 2012, 133–143.

Sirks, A. J. B. Mommsen und der Theodosianus, in *Theodor Mommsen und die Bedeutung des römischen Rechts*, ed. I. Fargnoli, S. Rebenich, Berlin 2013, 121–140.

Sirks, A. J. B. The Theodosian project and the Lex Citandi, in *Interpretare il Digesto: storia e metodi*, ed. D. Mantovani, A. P. Schioppa, Pavia 2015, 76–104.

Sirks, A. J. B. Chirographs: negotiable instruments?, *ZSS-R* 133, 2016, 265–285.

Sirks, A. J. B. Die Bedeutung von in bonis in der *actio Serviana*, *ZSS-R* 136, 2019a, 84–110.

Sirks, A. J. B. Emanzipazione come rite de passage, *Ravenna Capitale* 2019b, 177–187.
Sirks, A. J. B. Traces of legal business in the letters of Gregory the Great, *Ravenna Capitale* 2019c, 113–127.
Sirks, A. J. B. Die Schriftheimat von Vat.Reg.Lat. 886 (Codex Theodosianus IX–XVI), *TvR* 88, 2020a, 42–49.
Sirks, A. J. B. Emanzipation als rite de passage, *ZSS-R* 137, 2020b, 331–341.
Sirks, A. J. B. Could after the division of administration in 364 an emperor issue a law for the entire empire? *Zeitschrift der Savigny-Stiftung* 138, 2021a, 555–567.
Sirks, A. J. B. Did the published Theodosian Code include obsolete constitutions?, *Tijdschrift voor Rechtsgeschiedenis* 89, 2021b, 70–92.
Sirks, A. J. B. The Summaria Antiqua, forthcoming in the research project Redhis 'Rediscovering the hidden structure. A new appreciation of Juristic texts and Patterns of thought in Late Antiquity'.
Sirmond, J. *Concilia Galliae*, Lutetia 1629.
Souter, A. *A glossary of Later Latin*, Oxford 1949.
Svoronos, N. Histoire des institutions de l'empire byzantin, *École pratique des hautes études, 4e section, Annuaire* 1976–1977, 407–434.
Teja, R. Economía y sociedad en el Bajo Imperio, in *Historia de España antigua, tomo II: Hispania romana*, Madrid 1988, 537–587.
Thomas, Y. *'Origine' et 'commune patrie': étude de droit public romain (89 av. J.-C. – 212 ap. J.-C.*, Roma 1996.
Thonemann, P. Estates and the land in Late Roman Asia Minor, *Chiron* 37, 2007, 435–478.
Triantaphyllopoulos, J. EYTHHNIA, *REG* 80, 1967, 355–360.
Turner, E. G. ed. *The Oxyrhynchus papyri: volume XXVII*, London 1962.
Vacca, L. La riforma di Giustiniano in materia di 'usucapio' e 'longi temporis praescriptio' fra concezioni dommatiche classiche e prassi postclassica, *BIDR* 35/36, 1993–1994, 147–186.
van der Wal, N., Lokin, J. H. A. *Historiae iuris graeco-romani delineatio*, Groningen 1985.
van Minnen, P. Patronage in fourth-century Egypt. A Note on P.Ross.Georg. III.8, *JJP* 27, 1997, 67–73.
Vandendriessche, S. *Possessio und Dominium im postklassischen römischen Recht*, Hamburg 2005.
Vera, D. Forme e funzioni della rendita fondiaria nella tarda antichità, in *Società romana e impero tardoantico*, vol. 1, ed. A. Giardina, Roma 1986, 369–447, repr. in Vera 2019, 60–114.
Vera, D. Enfiteusi, colonato e trasformazioni agrarie nell'Africa Proconsolare del tardo impero, *L'Africa romana* 4, 1987, 267–293, repr. in Vera 2019, 135–147.
Vera, D. Schiavitù rurale e colonato nell'Italia imperiale, *Scienze dell'Antichità* 6–7, 1992–1993, 291–339, repr. in Vera 2019, 177–205.
Vera, D. Padroni, contadini, contratti: *realia* del colonato tardoantico, in *Terre, proprietari e contadini dell'impero romano: dall'affitto romano al colonato tardoantico*, ed. E. Lo Cascio, Roma 1997, 185–224, repr. in Vera 2019, 253–270.

Vera, D. La legislazione sul colonato tardoantico: *cui prodest?*, in *Diritto enunciato e diritto applicato in Grecia e a Roma, Incontro tra storici e giuristi, Bologna 2 dicembre 2004*, Rivista Storica dell'Antichità 35, 2005, 327–343, repr. in Vera 2019, 317–325.

Vera, D. Essere 'schiavi della terra' nell'Italia tardoantica: le razionalità di una dipendenza, *Studia Historica, Historia Antigua* 25, 2007, 489–505, repr. in Vera 2019, 355–364.

Vera, D. 'Schiavi dell terra' nell'Italia tardo antica, in *La tarda antichità tra fonti scritte e archeologiche*, ed. P. Galetti, Bologna 2010, 15–33.

Vera, D. Questioni di storia agraria tardoromana: schiavi, coloni, *villae, Antiquité Tardive* 20, 2012, 115–122, repr. in Vera 2019, 365–372.

Vera, D. *I doni di Cerere: storie della terra nella tarda antichità (strutture, società, economia)*, Bibliothèque de l'Antiquité Tardive 36, Turnhout 2019.

Vial-Dumas, M. *Famiglia, diritto e proprietà: una lettura comparata del Mediterraneo cristiano occidentale e bizantino tra I e XII secolo*, Città del Vaticano 2020.

Vial-Dumas, M. The matrimonial family in Byzantine imperial law: an overview from Late Antiquity until the tenth century, *The Journal of Legal History* 42, 2021, 35–64.

Voss, W. E. Der Grundsatz der ärgeren Hand bei Sklaven, Kolonen und Hörigen, in *Römisches Recht in der europäischen Tradition: Symposion aus Anlaß des 75. Geburtstag von Franz Wieacker*, ed. O. Behrends, M. Diesselhorst, W. E. Voss, Ebelsbach 1985, 118–182.

Vössing, K. *Das Königreich der Vandalen: Geiserichs Herrschaft und Imperium Romanum*, Darmstadt 2014.

Vössing, K. *Die Vandalen*, München 2018.

Wacke, A. Die potentiores in den Rechtsquellen, in *ANRW II*, 13, Berlin/New York 1980, 562–607.

Walde, A., Hofmann, J. B. *Lateinisches etymologisches Wörterbuch*, Heidelberg 1982, 5th edn.

Waldstein, W. *Paramone und operae libertorum, in Festschrift für Arnold Kränzlein*, ed. G. Wesener, H. Stiegler, G. Klingenberg, M. Rainer, Graz 1986, 143–147.

Ward-Perkins, B. Land, labour and settlement, in *CAH XIV*, Cambridge 2000, 315–344.

Ward-Perkins, B. *The fall of Rome and the end of civilisation*, Oxford 2005.

Ward-Perkins, B. Jones and the Late Roman economy, in *A. H. M. Jones and the Later Roman Empire*, ed. D. M. Gwynn, Leiden 2008, 193–211.

Weaver, P. R. C. *Familia Caesaris*, Cambridge 1972.

Wenger, L. *Die Quellen des römischen Rechts*, Wien 1954.

Westbrook, R. The nature and origin of the XII Tables, *ZSS-R* 105, 1988, 74–121.

Weßel, H. *Das Recht der Tablettes Albertini*, Berlin 2003.

Whittaker, C. R. Circe's pigs: from slavery to serfdom in the later Roman world, *Slavery and Abolition* 8, 1987, 88–122.

Whittaker, C. R., Garnsey, P. Rural life in the later Roman empire, in *CAH XIII*, Cambridge 1998, 277–311.

Wiart, R. *Le régime des terres du fisc au Bas-Empire*, Paris 1894.
Wickham, Chr. *Framing the early Middle Ages: Europe and the Mediterranean 400–800*, Oxford 2005.
Wollentin, U. Ὁ κινδύνος in den Papyri, Inaug. Diss., Köln 1961.
Wood, I. *The Merovingian Kingdoms 450–751*, London/New York 1994.
Zachariae, C. E. *Anekdota Theodori scholastici breviarium novellarum, Edicta praefectiorum praetorio*, Lipsiae 1843.
Zachariae, E. *Geschichte des griechisch-römischen Rechts*, Berlin 1892.
Zepos, P. J. Servi e paroeci nel diritto bizantino e postbizantino, *RAL* 35, 1980, 419–435.
Zuckerman, A. Du village à l'Empire: autour du registre fiscal d'Aphroditô, Paris 2004.

Index Locorum

Page numbers in bold refer to a fuller treatment of the subject.

Legal Sources

Breviarium/ Lex Romana Visigothorum
- 2.30.1 270
- 2.30.2 270
- 2.31.1 270
- 2.32.1 270, 284
- 4.8.2 271n81
- 4.8.3 270
- 4.20.1 270
- 4.21.1 270
- 5.3.1 270
- 5.9.1 270
- 5.9.2 270
- 5.10.1 258, 270, 274
- 5.11.1 271
- 8.1.1 271
- 9.19.1 265n51

Byzantine Sources
- Αἱ Ῥοπαί 10 101, 105
- B 55.1.19 101n174
- BT 2533.1–5 101n174

Codex Justinianus
- c. Cordi 14n46
- c. Haec 14n46
- c. Haec 2 248n20
- 1.2.14pr 88, 243
- 1.2.14 34n13
- 1.2.14.1 88, 243
- 1.2.14.9 88, 243
- 1.2.24 34n16
- 1.3.7 111n200, 243n7
- 1.3.16 42, 59, 85, 98, 100, 110, 138, 139, 168n47, 171n54, 245, 261, 320
- 1.3.16pr 98
- 1.3.20 34n13, 168n47, 171
- 1.3.20.1 47, 307
- 1.3.27.2 307
- 1.3.28.4 53
- 1.3.36 34n13
- 1.3.36pr 100, 211n131, 245
- 1.3.36.1 211n131
- 1.3.36.2 245
- 1.3.53 81n129
- 1.4.24 34n13, 92n152, 99
- 1.5.8.6 53
- 1.12.5 53n64
- 1.12.6.9 34n13, 111, 243
- 1.13.1 264
- 1.13.2 265
- 1.27 247
- 1.27.1 249n1
- 1.27.1.16 34n13
- 1.27.2 249n1
- 1.27.2.11 34n13
- 1.34.1 34n16
- 1.55.4 126n245, 223n150
- 2.4.43 34n13, 41, 103n182, 104
- 2.7.21 41n34, 100, 103n182, 104
- 2.7.22 34n13
- 2.7.22.1 110, 246
- 2.7.22.3 110, 246
- 2.7.24 34n13
- 2.7.24.1 110, 246
- 2.7.24.3 110, 246
- 2.55.4.6 229
- 3.12.6 163n38
- 3.26.R 119n229
- 3.26.5 241
- 3.26.6 119
- 3.26.7 34n13, 119, 217, 222, 223, 314
- 3.26.8 34n13, 119, 119n229, 120, 126, 217, 222, 241, 314
- 3.26.11 119, 241
- 3.37.11 107n191
- 3.38.11 34n13, 34n15, 88, 213, 243, 247, 276
- 4.10.3 34n13, 135n259

4.10.11 34n13, 135n259, 178
4.21.19 34n13, 57
4.21.19pr 34n13, 135n259
4.24.1 297
4.26.R 168
4.26.10 169
4.26.13 34n13, 49n50, 108, 177, 178, 179
4.26.13pr 48
4.26.13.4 49
4.35.22 108, 108n192
4.35.23 245n15
4.44.65 34, 67, 135
4.47.2 200
4.47.3 200, 307
4.49.9 22
4.65.5 34n13, 135n259
4.65.9 34n13, 135n259
4.65.27 34n13, 135n259
4.65.35 34n13
4.65.35pr 34n13, **42**, 135n259
4.66.1 114n212
5.17.11 81n129
5.27.3.1 53
5.27.3.2 73, 77, 78
5.27.4 53
5.34.13 34n13, 123, 135n259, 220, 223
5.62.8 34n13, 135n259
5.70.7.6a 307
6.4.2 125, 222
6.6.1 45n43
6.7.3 45n43
6.23.18 307
6.23.23 307
6.25.9.1 53
6.30.22.14a 307
7.3.9 97n170
7.6.1 247
7.6.1.10 308
7.14.1 68
7.16.18 39, 39n30, 40
7.16.22 39
7.24.1 69, 81n129, 139, 247, 260
7.24.1pr **70**
7.24.1.1 34n13, 24n62, **70**, 73, 81, 82, 138
7.30.1 34n13, 34n15, 45n44, 135n259, 136
7.32.5 34n13
7.32.12 34n13, 126
7.33.1 211n133
7.37.12pr–1 45
7.38.1 34n13, 214, 221, 221n147
7.38.2 34n13, 126, 222
7.38.3 307
7.39.3 203, 206, 214
7.39.3.1 307
7.39.4 245
7.39.4.2 104
7.39.5 97n167, 103n182, 104, 104n184, 245
7.39.6 245
7.39.41 97
7.41.2 307
8.5.1 34n13, 111
8.5.1.1 111
8.15.8 34n13, 49, 49n51, 179
8.16.7.1 53
8.16.8 60, 317
8.17.11 80
8.47.7 68
8.51.1 34n13, 98, 107n191
8.51.3 34n13, 98, 99
8.51.3pr 92n152
8.51.3.1–2 99
8.53.7 307n51
8.53.8 307n51
9.13.1 81n129
9.24.1.5 34n13, 111, 135n259, 215
9.27.4 34n13, 112, 133, 215
9.27.5 34n13, 112, 121, 133, **136**, 137, 137n265, 222, 223, 233
9.27.6 137
9.30.2 111, 243
9.41.4 44n39
9.42.7 34n16
9.49.7.1 34n13, 34n16, 126n245, 204, 223n150
10.19.1 61
10.19.4 **117**
10.19.6 61
10.19.7 61
10.19.8 53, 226n164, 241
10.19.9 61
10.27.1 245
10.32.29 126, 198, 223, 293
10.32.36 68n105
10.36.1 54n69, 307
10.39.1 67, 68, 160
10.39.2 68
10.39.3 67, 160
10.39.4 68, 160, 258, 294
10.39.5 67, 68
10.40.7 67n103
10.71.3 34n13, 156, 177
10.71.3.1 109
11.7.7 26n71, 41, 308
11.8.1 80, 193
11.8.3 80
11.8.7 34n13, 80, 193
11.8.11 80
11.8.12 80
11.8.15 80, 190
11.23 247

Codex Justinianus (cont.)
11.24.6 60n80
11.26 247
11.26.1 34n13, 41, 138, 167, 235
11.28.1.1 126n245
11.28.22.2 38n26
11.39.4 130n253
11.46.1 18
11.48.R 127n249
11.48.1 **42**, 62, 168, 188, 219
11.48.1.1 70, 189
11.48.2 34n13, 85, 87, 88n143, **199**, 202, 205, 237, 243n8
11.48.2pr 248
11.48.2.1 88, 139
11.48.3 203
11.48.4 34n13, 52n61, 55, **58**, 144n273, 162n37, 219, 236
11.48.4pr 53, 59n77, 138
11.48.4.1 47, 55, **58**, 60, 105n189,139, 140
11.48.5 **42**, 141, 238
11.48.6 34n13, 42, 91, 93, 107n191, 139, 206, 217, 232, 238, 247, 316
11.48.7 88, 88n143, 91, 202, 204, 233n184, 238, 243n8, 258, 316
11.48.7pr–1 202
11.48.7pr–2 **86**, 202
11.48.7.2 202, 205, 209
11.48.7.2–3 203
11.48.7.3 203
11.48.8 27, 48, 50, 91, 94, 129, 175, 188, 188n91, 189, 239, 247, 316
11.48.8pr 54, 59n77, 94
11.48.8pr–1 54n68
11.48.8.1 178
11.48.8.2 49, 66n98, 95, 172, 210
11.48.9 60, 188
11.48.10 33, 52, 53, 54, 59, 59n76, 162, 181, 319n75
11.48.11 34n13, 42, 55n70, 91, 98, 100, 210, 239, 307
11.48.12 42, 93, 93n155, 156n24, **207n122**, 238, 239
11.48.12pr 34n13, 207
11.48.12.2 247
11.48.13 34n13, 197, 204, 285, 293
11.48.13pr 82, 82n132, 189, **195**, 205n117, 235
11.48.13.1 87, 88, 186, **203**, 237, 261, 285
11.48.13.1–2 34n16
11.48.14 34n13, 95, **208**
11.48.15 34n13, 42, 50, 60, 91, 139, 203n112, 206, 236, 317
11.48.16 93, 191, 196, 213, 238
11.48.17 34n13, 49, 49n51, 179
11.48.18 98, 100, 197, 210, 239, 286n125, 308, 318
11.48.19 34n13, 27, 30, 40, 42, 43n37, 47, 55n73, 100, **101**, 103, 103n182, 104, **105**, 107, 107n190, 108, 108n192, 110, 129, 130, 132, 133, 134, 139, 140, 144, 144n273, 145, 245
11.48.20 34n13, 55, 57, 60, 67, 135, 145, 146n281, 267
11.48.20pr 52, 67, 91, 162n40, 301
11.48.20.3 54, **55**, 59n76, 146
11.48.20.3a 54, **55**,
11.48.20–22 162n37
11.48.21 24n62, 42, 44, 71, **74**, 77n120, 78, 138, 139
11.48.21pr 73, **76**, 166, 191, 198
11.48.21.19n24 24n62, 42, 45, 71, 76, 76n119, 80, 99, 125, 139, 144, 286n125, 290
11.48.22 34n13, 36, **37**, 40, 43n37, 60, 104
11.48.22pr 26n71, 73, 138
11.48.22pr–1 138
11.48.22pr–2 40n33
11.48.22.2 308
11.48.22.3 77n121, 91, 97
11.48.22.3–4 129
11.48.22.3–5 97
11.48.22.4 97
11.48.23 34n13, 43n37, 103n180, 104, 129, 145
11.48.23pr 96
11.48.23pr–1 144n273
11.48.23.1 **43**, 53, 100, 101, 102, 103, 105, 106, 107n190, 108, 130, 133
11.48.23.2 102
11.48.23.3 41, 43n37
11.48.23.4–5 93, 103, 131
11.48.23.5 43n37, 54, 54n69, 91, 92
11.48.24 74, 80, 82n134, 82n135, 84, 260
11.48.24pr 70
11.48.24.1 73, 76, 80, 82, 83
11.48.24.1.1 70, 81
11.49.1 53, 59, 59n76, 181
11.50.1 34n13, 42, 44n39, 45n43, 66n98, 133, 139, 237, 238
11.50.2 34n13, 42, 43n17, 50, 139, 168, 168n48, 180, 215, 273n87
11.50.2pr 129, 139, 169, 237
11.50.2pr–1 **43**
11.50.2pr–2 73
11.50.2.1 45, 215, 237
11.50.2.3 **45**, 141n268, 180, **170**, 238, 319
11.50.2.4 44, 73, 238
11.51–53 232
11.51.1 34n13, 53, 92, 129, 130, 131, 139, 159, 188n90, 232, 319
11.52.1 34n13, 52, 53, 129, 130, 131, 134, 319

11.52.1pr 54, 99, 133
11.52.1.1 42, 103, 130, 132, 139, 156n24
11.52.1–2 134
11.52.1.2 132, 133, 134
11.52.2.3 139
11.53.1 34n13, 53, 73n116, 129, 130, 131, 188n90, 250, 319
11.53.1.1 42, 130, 156n24
11.53.1.2 131, 132
11.53.1.3 68, 103, 132, 133
11.54–57 135
11.54.1 109, 224n153, 241, 242
11.54.1pr 241
11.54.1.1 242
11.54.1.2 242
11.54.2 231, 242
11.55.1–2 135n259
11.56.1 226n164, 242
11.57.1 60n80, 244
11.57.2 229, 229n168
11.58.2 196
11.58.3 34n13, 135n259, 215, 319n75
11.59–71 152
11.59.13 317
11.59.16 182n80
11.60.3 114n213
11.61.3 34n13, 123, 126, 234
11.61.3.1 135n259
11.62.5 34n13, 135n259
11.62.12 234
11.62.14 104, 104n183, 104n184, 118
11.63.1–3 123
11.63.1 34n13, 218
11.63.1pr 123, 217
11.63.1.1–2 123, 217
11.63.2 114
11.63.3 34n13, **219**
11.63.4 123, 218, 314, 319
11.63.4pr–1 122, 218
11.64.R 123
11.64.1 34n13, 122, 122n233, 218, 314
11.64.2 34n13, 122, 219, 238
11.64.3 122, 123, **218**, 314, 320
11.65.1 117
11.65.3 117
11.66.R 123
11.66.1 34n13
11.66.6 34n13, 97, 126, 211, 213, 223
11.67.2 307
11.68.1 34n13, 22, 23, 116, **123**, 124, 216, 220, 220n144, 314
11.68.2 34n13, 119, 124, 220, 220n144, 293
11.68.3 34n13, 124, 125, 214, 221, 221n147, 314
11.68.4 34n13, **125**, 126, 198, 221, 222
11.68.5 34n13, 126, 223, 315
11.68.6 34n13, 127, 171, 221
11.69.R 115
11.69.1 34n13, 118, 243
11.69.1pr 127, 128
11.69.1.1 127, 128
11.69.2 115, 118, 244
11.70 114n207
11.71 114n207
11.73.1 115n218
11.74.1–3 118
11.75.1 34n13, 117, 126, 221
12.10.2 34n13, 110, 246
12.19.12 34n13
12.19.12pr 110, 246
12.19.12.3 110, 246
12.21.8 34n13
12.21.8pr 110, 244, 246
12.23.2 115n216
12.33.3 34n13, 210, 239
12.35.10 87, 201
12.43.1 34n13, 98, 210, 215, 308
12.49.3 158
12.50.17 97n168, 126n244
12.54.3 34n13, 98, 109, 308
12.60.4 179
12.62.14 245

Codex Theodosianus
1.4.2 282
1.10.3 207n122
2.1.1 220
2.14.R 224n156
2.14.1 224n156
2.25.1 88n143, 213, 243n8
2.30.1 280
2.30.2 179, 280
2.31.1 172n56, 177, 280, 305n47
2.32.1 **178**, 179, 180, 236, 280, 289n140
3.1.2 200, 281
3.3.1 275
4.8.4–5 157
4.8.7 157, 275
4.10.3 318
4.11.2 203
4.12.3 69, 128, 156, 198, 234, 247, 260, 281n116, 315
4.12.5 156, 156n22
4.14.1 203, 206, 214, 256, 318
4.22.1 156n23, 279
4.23.1 177, **208**, 209, 237, 238, 279, 317
5.3.1 156, 157, 168n47, **171**, 171n55, 180, 238, 279
5.6.3 36n19, 156, 160, 164, 164n43, 164n44, 167, 202, 235, 237, 238
5.6.3 272n85, 277n105, 320
5.12–16 151

Codex Theodosianus (cont.)
5.12.3 234
5.13.4 221n146
5.15 150
5.16.34 171, 221
5.17–19 151, 152
5.17.117 21, 22, 24, 156, 157, 159, **160**, 160n35, 167, 169, 174, 180,181, 185n88, 188, 188n91, 189, 196, 205, 219, 235, 236, 237, 238, 239, 247, **271**, 274, 281, 282, 293, 315
5.17.1pr 205
5.17.1.1 168, 205
5.17.2 93n155, 156, 218, 219, 238, 247, 277, 319
5.17.3 207n122, 239
5.18.1 156, 167, 191n95, **212n134**, 238, 256, 274, 276, 293, 318
5.18.1pr–1 167
5.18.1.1–2 191
5.18.1.2 **176**, 209, 214, 235, 238, 239, 251
5.18.1.3 79n124, 167, 191, 211, 238, 261
5.18.1.3–4 261
5.18.1.4 191, 198, 213, 238
5.18.2 178
5.18.3 257
5.18.3–4 191, 193, 196
5.19.1 47n46, 169, 170, 175, 180, 238, **272**, 273n90
6.23.3 17
6.23.4 17
6.35.14.1 27, 158
7.1.8 314
7.1.10 157
7.6.5 182
7.7.4 234
7.7.5 234
7.8.11 317
7.13.6 156, 156, 210, 215
7.13.7.3 210
7.13.20 318n71
7.14.1 97n168, 126n244
7.18.8 215
8.1.3 158, **181**
8.1.4 158
8.1.5 158
8.1.6 158
8.1.7 158, 181
8.1.8 158, 158n29
8.1.11 158
8.2.4 159
8.2.5 156, 197, 273, **277**, 317
8.4.22 167, 207, 210
8.4.23 318n71
8.5.58 97n168
8.8.10 179
8.10.4 318n71
8.21.3 207n122
9.5.1 95n161
9.11.1 169
9.21.2 215
9.24.1 265n51
9.27.1 315
9.27.6 215, 315
9.27.7 222, 223, 233,
9.42.7 157, 204
10.1.11 222, 286
10.1.15 307n50
10.4.3 222
10.12.2 156, 156n24, 157, 208, 272n86, 316
10.12.2.2 156b24, 234
10.12.3 234, 236
10.19 253
10.19.15.1 26n71
10.20.1 197, 293, 315
10.20.3 194
10.20.3 293
10.20.5 318
10.20.7 235
10.20.10 **80**, 156, **192**, 293
10.20.10pr 193, 198
10.20.10.1 193, 194, 198
10.20.10.3 198
10.20.15 198
10.20.16 194
10.20.17 160, **166**, 190, 194, 198, 318
11.1–19 150
11.1 253n13
11.1.7 161, 182
11.1.14 44n40, 81n131, 156, 160, **161**, 163n39, 164, 169n49, 171, 181, 186, 232, 233, 235, 236
11.1.14.1 210n129
11.1.15 274, 281
11.1.17 274, 281
11.1.26 107n190, 164, **186**, 188, 189, 202, 233, 236
11.1.31 318n71
11.1.32 318n71
11.1.33 221
11.3.1 200
11.3.3 182n78, 274, 281
11.3.5 201, 281
11.6.1 274, 281
11.7.1 154n15
11.7.2 17, 22, 156, 156n24, **182**, 234, 236, 293
11.7.4 274, 281
11.7.11 156n23, 221
11.7.12 154n15
11.7.19–21 318n71
11.7.20 274, 281
11.11.1 281
11.16.4 168

11.16.5 156n23, 221, 314
11.16.11 281
11.17.1 156n23, 234
11.23.2 156, 165
11.24.1 27n72, 225, 228, 230
11.24.2 225, 225n159, 226, 232
11.24.3 225n157, 225n159
11.24.4 225n159, 227n165
11.24.4–6 225
11.24.5 225, 225n158, 225n159
11.24.6 171, 225, **227**, 229n171
11.24.6pr 186, 226, 226n161, 229, 230, 232, 242n4
11.24.6.1 226, 227, 233, 242
11.24.6.2 227, 233
11.24.6.3 227, 228, 228n167, 237, 238
11.24.6.4 226n164
11.24.6.5 224n153
11.24.6.6 226
11.24.6.6–8 226n161
11.24.6.7 225, 232
11.24.6.8 226
11.28.7 318n71
11.28.8 318n71
11.30.6 207n122
11.36.30 207n122
12.1.6 262
12.1.33 220n144, 221, 247, 262
12.1.178 69
12.1.186 182, 182n80
12.6.14 222
12.6.21 234
12.6.31 318n71
12.19.R 159
12.19.1 195, 198, 213, 260, 264n43, 317
12.19.1–3 293
12.19.2 211, 213, 223, 316, 317
12.19.3 211, 223, 317
13.1.3 315
13.1.8 156n23, 221, 223
13.1.10 156n23, 221
13.1.13 281
13.3.2 201
13.3.3 201
13.3.4 201
13.7.1 224, 225n160
13.7.2 224, 224n156
13.10.1 253n13, 281
13.10.2 181
13.10.3 203n112, 237
13.10.4 188
13.10.5 274, 281
13.10.6 188
13.10.7 52n69, 154n16, **183**, 184n85, 185n88, 195, 236
13.10.8 188
13.10–11 150
13.11.2 162, 181, 186, 319n75
13.11.3 215
13.11.10 164n44
13.11.13 171, 171n53
14.7.1 77, 77n120, 78, 78n123, 82n133, 194, 195, 197, 198, 260
14.8.1 268
14.9.2 159
14.18.1 160, 167, 235
15.6.1 18
15.14.13 318n71
16.5.52 178, 318n71
16.5.54 178, 178n72, 318n71
16.6.2 18
16.6.4 156

Collatio
1.11.2 26n68

Digest
1.5.5.1 283n121, 304n45
2.4.4.1 45n43, 141
6.1.1.2 92, 92n150, 92n152, 205, 205n119
9.4.32–35 288n136
14.6.1.3 46
14.6.2 46n45, 139
16.3.27 69n108
24.3.22.13 69n108
28.3.6 283n121
28.3.6.5 304n45
41.2.1.5 45, 45n44
41.2.1.9 45n44
43.30.1–2 92
43.30.1pr 92
43.30.3.5 92
47.2.83pr 285
47.2.83.2 285
48.6.5.2 267n58
48.15.5 103
49.17.15.3 46n45, 139
50.1.20 68n104
50.4.3.15 303
50.15.4 41, 107n190
50.15.4.8 7n18, 35, 41, 59, 59n77, 307
50.15.4.9 195

Edicta Praefectorum Praetorio
25 34n13, 93, 103

Edictum Theodorici
17 265n51
21 265n51
22 266n52

Edictum Theodorici (cont.)
46 224n156
59 266n53
64 288n139
67 275
84 250
98 288, 288n138
128 288
142 289, 289n142

Fragmenta Vaticana
35 200

Gaius' Institutes
1.10 72
1.12 72n114
1.67 26n69
1.78 26n69
1.80 26n69
1.84 68n104
1.87 26n69
1.124–126 72, 76, 235n188
1.138 72n115, 142n272, 315n69

Interpretationes to the Codex Theodosianus
2.1.1 279
2.25.1 276
2.32.1 **280**
4.22.1 279
4.23.1 279
4.8.7 265, 275
5.17.1 **271**, 272, 272n86, 273, 274, 274n92, 279, 290
5.17.2 273, 274
5.18.1 274
5.19.1 **272**
5.3.1 280
8.2.5 **278**
13.10.1 281n115
14.7.1 290n146

Interpretationes to the Novels of Maiorian
7 262n39, 263

Interpretationes to the Novels of Valentinian III
27 257, 257n29, 275
31 260, 275, 276, 276n103, 277
35 205n119, 260n36, 261, 279
35.5 255n23

Justinian's Institutes
1.16.3 304n44, 308

Lex Romana Burgundionum
6.2 207n122, 239
6.4 250, 250n6, 274, 288, 288n135
14.6 131, **168**, 168n48, 170, 175, 294
37.5 271n8138.8, 155n18
43 224n156
46 264n42

Lex Ribuaria
10 271n81

Lex Romana Curiensis
5.9 274
18.11 279n112

Novels
4.1 58
7pr 34n16
14 247, 304n46
14pr 298n12
17.13 242n4
17.14 93
20 127n249
22.17pr 34n13
30 117, 117n222, 127n249
30.1.1 115n216
30.5.1 115n216
30.5pr 115n216
30.6pr 115n216
30.7pr 115n216
30.7.1 115n216
30.8pr 115n216
32–34 133n256
32 133n255
32.3 115n216
33 133n255
34 133n255
38.6 115, 128
52.1 244n10
54.1 34n13, 81
54pr 34n13, 81
120 34n16,
123.17.1 34n13
123.35 34n13, 103n180
126.2.1 81
128.14 59, 60
128.14.3 34n13
134.7 296n9
135.35 100
156.1 34n13,
156.2pr 34n13
162 82n135
162.2pr 34n13, 84
162.2 34n13, 84

162.2.1 34n13, 82, 83, 102, 105, 106, 130
162.3 34n13
162.4 34n13
162.4 34n13
167 34n13
App. 1 34n13, 82, 82n135
App. 1.1 82, 82n135
App. 6 34n13, 84, 93
App. 7 94
App. 7.11 85
App. 7.16 34n13
App. 9 34n13, 84

Post-Justinian Novels
Nov. Justini 6 82n135, 84
Nov. Tib. 13 82n135, 84

Post-Theodosian Novels
Nov. Theod. 1.5 17
Nov. Theod. 22 126n245, 223n150
Nov. Theod. 22.1.8 73, 77, 82n133
Nov. Theod. 7.4.2 241
Nov. Val. 23 254n20
Nov. Val. 23.3 256
Nov. Val. 26 249
Nov. Val. 26.8 172n59
Nov. Val. 27 97n170, 203, 254n20, 256, 257, 262, 276
Nov. Val. 27.3 279
Nov. Val. 31 203, 254n20, 257, 258, 260n35, 274, 276
Nov. Val. 31pr 257
Nov. Val. 31.1 105, 257, 274
Nov. Val. 31.1–4 260
Nov. Val. 31.2 205n119, 261
Nov. Val. 31.2–3 276
Nov. Val. 31.3 257, 258n31
Nov. Val. 31.5 256n28, 258, 259, 282
Nov. Val. 31.5–6 318
Nov. Val. 31.6 195n98, 199, **259**, 260, 262, 290n146
Nov. Val. 35 254n20, 257, 261, 276
Nov. Val. 35.2 318
Nov. Val. 35.3 261, 264n42, 279
Nov. Val. 35.5 261
Nov. Val. 35.6 261, 279
Nov. Val. 35.12 83n136
Nov. Val. 35.18 261
Nov. Maior. 7 254n20, 262
Nov. Maior. 7pr–1 262
Nov. Maior. 7.2 262
Nov. Maior. 7.3 262, 264n43
Nov. Maior. 7.4 262
Nov. Maior. 7.4–5 264n42
Nov. Maior. 7.5 262
Nov. Maior. 7.5–17 263
Nov. Maior. 7.5–6 263
Nov. Maior. 7.6 263
Nov. Maior. 7.7 255n23, 263
Nov. Marcian. 2.1 249n3
Nov. Sev. 1 255
Nov. Sev. 2 254n20
Nov. Sev. 2 264

Pauli Sententiae
2.18.1 **282**, 283n121, 306, 306n48
2.31.30 285, 285n123
3.6.47 **283**
3.6.48 **284**, 285

Summaria Antiqua
Summaria 248n20
10.1.11 286, 286n125
10.1.14 286
10.4.3 286
13.1.3 286
13.1.8 286
13.1.10 286
13.10.3 286
13.11.3 286
16.5.52 286

Epigraphical, Papyrological and other Sources

Church Councils
Orange 264, 264n45
Arles 264, 264n45

Epigraphica
CIL VIII 10570 7n10
CIL VIII 25902 7n10

Formulae
And. 19 273n88
And. 20 265
And. 23 265, 265n48
And. 38 **283**, 298n14
Visigothica 34 268

Papyri
BGU 560 229n174
BGU 618 229n174, 230n178
P. Alex. inv. 281 verso 298n13
P. Amherst II 149 64, 66
P. Brussels descr. 300, 301
P. Cairo Maspero I 67019 146
P. Erlangen 37 64
P. Florence 2 231
P. Florence 151 300
P. Fuad Univ. 25 298n13
P. Heidelberg III 248 95n161

Papyri (cont.)
P. Ital. 13 155n18
P. Ital. 3.II.1 155n18
P. London 2.254.137, 141 229n174
P. London III 778 63n90, 95n161
P. Merton II 98 95n161, 139, 140
P. Michigan V 355 299n17, 304n42
P.Oxy. I 133 96n164
P.Oxy. I 135 95n161, 96, 139
P.Oxy. I 137 65n95
P.Oxy. VI 996 95n161
P.Oxy. X 1254 231
P.Oxy. XV 1684 300, 300n25
P.Oxy. XVI 1979 64, 85n141, 95n161, 96n165
P.Oxy. XVI 1985 64
P.Oxy. XVII 2203 95n161
P.Oxy. XXVII 2478 **50**, 54, 54n67, 63n90, 64, 95n161, 96n164
P.Oxy. XXVII 2479 41, 61n81, **89**, 89n144, 301
P.Oxy. XLIV 3204 95n161
P.Oxy. XLVII 3364 7n18
P.Oxy. XLIX 3512 64
P.Oxy. LV 3804 96n164
P.Oxy. LXI 4118, 231P.Oxy. LXII 4350, 51, 62n83, **64**, 64n92, 85n141
P.Oxy. LXIII 4398 **49**, 54, 96n164
P.Oxy. LXVI 4535 **50**
P.Oxy. LXVII 4615 34n14, 38n26, 51, 65, 67, 135
P.Oxy. LXVII 4616 65n95
P.Oxy. LXVII 4697 65, 65n95
P.Oxy. LXIX 4755 65,65n95
P.Oxy. LXIX 4782 65, 65n95
P.Oxy. LXIX 4784 65, 65n95
P.Oxy. LXIX 4785 65
P.Oxy. LXIX 4788 65, 65n95
P.Oxy. LXIX 4789 64
P.Oxy. LXIX 4793 65, 65n95
P.Oxy. LXIX 4794 66
P.Oxy. LXIX 4797 **65**, 65n95
P.Oxy. LXIX 4799 66
P.Oxy. LXIX 4800 65
P.Oxy. LXIX 4801 65, 65n95
P.Oxy. LXX 4756 95n161
P.Oxy. LXX 4757 95n161
P.Oxy. LXX 4758 95n161
P.Oxy. LXX 4781 65, 65n95
P.Oxy. LXX 4787 95n161
P.Oxy. LXX 4788 49n50, 66n98
P.Oxy. LXX 4790 95n161
P.Oxy. LXX 4791 95n161
P.Oxy. LXX 4794 50n52, 62n83, 95n161
P.Oxy. LXX 4796 65n95
P.Oxy. LXX 4797 49n50, 65n96, 66n98, 79n127
P.Oxy. LXX 4798 65n95
P.Oxy. LXX 4799 65n95
P.Oxy. LXX 4801 79n127
P.Oxy. LXX 4802 95n161
P.Oxy. LXXVII 5123 51, 66n98
P.Oxy. LXXXII 5331 51, 65
P.Oxy. LXXXII 5332 51, 65
P.Oxy. LXXXIII 5375 50n54
P.Oxy. LXXXIII 5380 50n54
P.Oxy. LXXXIII 5382 50n54
P.Oxy. LXXXIII 5383 50n54
P.Oxy. LXXXIII 5384 63n90
P.Oxy. LXXXIII 5385 65n95, 85n141
P.Oxy. LXXXIII 5393 65n95
P.Oxy. LXXXIII 5394 65n95
P.Oxy. LXXXIII 5398 65n95
P. Pher. l. 301 201n107
P. Prague 108 299
P. Reinach 113 301n32, 304n43
P.Ross.-Georg. III.8 38n25
P. Rylands 209.40 229n174
PSI VIII 902 299n17, 304n42
PSI 52 65, 95n161
PSI 59 95n161
PSI 62 95n161, 96n164
P. Washington University I 25 65, 79n127
SB XVI 12484 95n161
SB XVIII 14006 95n161
SB 6.9429 300, 300n25
Wilcken Chrest. 63 229n174

Non-Documentary Sources

Amm. Marc. 28.5.15 164
Amm. Marc. 31.5.5–10 319n78
Aug. de civitate Dei 10.1.2 7n15, 176, 176n68
Aug. ennarr. in ps. 93 173n61, 175, 175n65
Aug. ep. 10* 173
Aug. ep. 20* 173
Aug. ep. 24* 173, 174n62, 235, 284
Aug. ep. 247 173
Frontinus I.4–6 200n105
Gregorii Magni ep. 1.53 275n99
Gregorii Magni ep. 4.21 269n67
Hist. Aug. Cl. 9.4 164n44
Lact. de mortibus 23.1–2 8n22
Libanios or. 11–12 226
Libanios or. 47.7–8 226n162
Libanios or. 47.11 224, 226n163, 233
Quint. Inst. Or. 5.10.60 44n42
S. Hieronymi vita Malchi monachi captivi II 227n165, 233
Sidonius Apollinaris ep. 5.19 **265**
Testamentum Remigii 267
Victor Vit. Hist. persec. 3.20 168n66
Vulg. 1 Cor. 15:22 44n39
Zach. Rhetor Hist. Eccl. VIII.6 246

General Index

Page numbers in bold refer to a fuller treatment of the subject.

adscripticius see *coloni*

capitatio humana poll tax see taxation
capitatio terrena land tax see taxation
census 24, 25–26, 34n16, 41, 43, 53, 54, 55, 59, 73, 83, 98, 118n226, 153, 164, 166, 195, 250, 253, 268, **306–308**, 311
  registration in the census 37–38, **41**, **43–44**, 48, 51, 53, 73, 81, 86f, 99, 138ff, 160, 163–164, 181f, 183–185, 185n88, 189, 190, 195f, 199, 202, 210, 212, 230, 235, 267
colonate
  and agricultural exploitation **3–6**, **62–67**, 89–90, 94, **112f**, 154–156, 204, 289, 309–310
  and servage, Hörigkeit 9, 133–135, 253
  theories **6–12**, 61, 105, 107, 313–314
coloni **27**, 32–35, 156–157
  coloni in the CJ 32–35
  coloni in the CTh 150–152, 156
  coloni and the Church 47, 88, 89, 110, 112, 171, 243, 245, 248, 254,261, 264f, 267, 279f, 292
  coloni liberi see 'free' *coloni*
  actors in private law 49, see occupations
  flight, migration, recall 83–84, **89–96**, 106, **161**, 204, 205, 206ff, 271
  harbouring *coloni* 54, 93, 95, 103, 182, 189, 207, 214, 219, 231, 239, 274, 281, 287
  homologi 227–232
  limitation of prescription 57, 84, 86–87, **96–97**, 101, 104, 107, 125, 126, 177, 203, 206, 208, 211, 214, 221, 223, **256–258**, 275, 293, 318
  occupations 61–62, 63–67, 85
  on state/imperial lands **216f**
  on patrimonial/emphyteuticarian land 122ff, 217, 218–220
  on lands of the *res privata* 123ff, 220f
  on lands of the Domus Augusta 126–127, 222–223
  on lands of the fisc (*tamieion*) 127–128, 243–244, 246
  social status 36–37, 73, 79, 99, 168, 196, 215, 260, 262, 279
  subjection see *potestas*, *condicio coloniaria* – status
  term and equivalent 24–25, 27
  transfer **85–88**, **199–204**, 201f, 202f, 284
  unions with slaves **78ff**, 262
  unions with *condicionales* 192–193, 195, 198, 214, 293
  unions with *coloni* see *condicio coloniaria* – transmission
condicio coloniaria **36–40**, 76, 95–96, **157f**
  agreement to enter 36ff, 164, 167, 282, 311
  division of offspring **211–214**, 257, 261, 276
  immunity **97f**, 100, 109, 117, 125, 158, 168, 210, 212n134, 221, 223, 225, 241, 245, 256, 261, 314, 315
  imposition 41, 105, 164–165 (Scyri), 167, 258, 259–260, 268 (Africa)
  nature 272, 279, 282–283, 287–289, 306ff
  obligations, public 42, 52, 55, 225, 231, 280f
  obligations, inherent 63, 44, 61, 101, 103, 104, 110, 122, 132, 134, **140–141**, 142, 146, 164, 168, 172, 176, 205, 214, 257, 268, 287f, 292, 297, 310, 319; see also *peculium* and *potestas*
  privileges 110–111, 112, 119–121, 123, 124, 126, 128–129, 167, 207, 210, 217, 221–222, 223, 239, 241, 247, 314–315
  proof 39, 40–41, 73, 129, 207, 209, 275
  release, individual **99–100**, 264, 265, 266
  release, institutional **100–103**, 104f, 106, 245
  (social) status 37–41, 65, 72–73, 141, 215, 256, 270, **271–272**, 282–283, 288f, **308**
  transmission 41, **67–68**, **79–80**, 125, 128, 160, 166, 167

condicio coloniaria (cont.)
restrictions, public 215, 240–241, 277–278
restrictions, private see *potestas, peculium*
condicionales 92, 135, 158–159, 166, 181, 194, 197, 198, 214, 293, 308
coniugium non aequale 24, 73, 74–78, 79f, 83, 125, 127, 138, 166, 194–197, 223, 236, 244, 260, 290, 293, 315–316, 318

dominium 28–29

enapographos see *coloni*
Exposition of children 98–99

Farmers who are not *coloni* 135–137, 233, 269
'Free' *coloni* 28, 44, 45, 48, 82–82, 101f, 129–131, 134, 232–233, 292, 319

ingenuitas, ingenuus 39, 69, 71f, 73, 76, 78, 103, 105, 128, 131, 134, 157f, 174, 193f, 236, 258, 259f, 265, 275, 276, 278, 311, 316
Imperial lands, status 116–118
isophorion 300

Liturgies 45, 54, 64, 67, 81, 92, 160, 162, 167, 171, 190, 225, 227, 228, 230, 231f, 295, 296, 299–300, 302, 303, 304, 308

metrèmatiaioi 296–301

oiketai 296, 301
originalis, originarius see *coloni, origo*
origo 25–27, 67–68, 73, 78, 81–82, 86, 88, 91, 98, 99, 102, 116, 122, 123, 125, 126, 130, 132, 142, 143, 160, 164, 167, 171, 191, 195f, 207, 212n134, 216, 218, 222, 235, 236, 258, 273, 289, 292, 294, 304, 308, 311

paramonè, paramonarios 296–298, 302, 305, 305n46, 310
patrocinium 224, 225, 241f
vicorum 223–232, 242
peculium 42, 45–51, 81, 99, 101f, 133, 141, 168–173, 177–180, 211, 236, 261, 272, 275, 279, 281, 283–284, 294, 311
possessio see *dominium*
potestas 42–45, 48, 51, 71–72, 73, 74, 76, 82, 92, 100, 102, 107, 109, 130ff, 133, 142, 157, 161, 167–169, 173–174, 175, 177, 194, 205, 232, 245, 250f, 265, 273, 282, 292, 294, 303, 304, 306, 319

Status see *coloniaria condicio* – status

Taxation
Diocletian's reforms 294–295, 312
land tax 54, 58, 153–154, 163, 182
paying tax 55–56, 181, 186–190
poll tax 23, 32, 52–57, 81, 94ff, 96n164, 100, 102, 118, 129f, 137, 142, 153–154, 161, 162–163, 166, 183, 189, 190, 195, 231–232, 236, 245, 253, 268, 273–274, 281, 285, 289, 295, 303, 304, 306, 309
guarantee for the poll tax 56, 58–59, 60, 103, 121, 142, 162, 164, 182, 186, 201, 282, 294, 304–305
tributarius see *coloni*
tributum see taxation
Senatusconsultum Claudianum 69–74, 80, 128, 143, 192–194, 196, 260, 263, 318, 320
its abolition 70, 81ff
its connection with the colonate 71
Sources
Codex Justinianus 14–16
background CJ 30–32
Codex Theodosianus 16–17, 147, 150, 152
background CTh 152–156
Post-Theodosian Novels 249–251
background Post-Theodosian Novels 251–254
Breviarium (Lex Romana Visigothorum) 269f

For EU product safety concerns, contact us at Calle de José Abascal, 56–1°,
28003 Madrid, Spain or eugpsr@cambridge.org.

www.ingramcontent.com/pod-product-compliance
Lightning Source LLC
LaVergne TN
LVHW011704200926
848484LV00004B/1061
* 9 7 8 1 0 0 9 1 7 2 6 0 8 *